ISBN 978-1-331-48674-9
PIBN 10196718

This book is a reproduction of an important historical work. Forgotten Books uses state-of-the-art technology to digitally reconstruct the work, preserving the original format whilst repairing imperfections present in the aged copy. In rare cases, an imperfection in the original, such as a blemish or missing page, may be replicated in our edition. We do, however, repair the vast majority of imperfections successfully; any imperfections that remain are intentionally left to preserve the state of such historical works.

1 MONTH OF
FREE
READING

at

www.ForgottenBooks.com

By purchasing this book you are eligible for one month membership to ForgottenBooks.com, giving you unlimited access to our entire collection of over 700,000 titles via our web site and mobile apps.

To claim your free month visit:

www.forgottenbooks.com/free196718

English
Français
Deutsche
Italiano
Español
Português

www.forgottenbooks.com

Mythology Photography **Fiction**
Fishing Christianity **Art** Cooking
Essays Buddhism Freemasonry
Medicine **Biology** Music **Ancient
Egypt** Evolution Carpentry Physics
Dance Geology **Mathematics** Fitness
Shakespeare **Folklore** Yoga Marketing
Confidence Immortality Biographies
Poetry **Psychology** Witchcraft
Electronics Chemistry History **Law**
Accounting **Philosophy** Anthropology
Alchemy Drama Quantum Mechanics
Atheism Sexual Health **Ancient History**
Entrepreneurship Languages Sport
Paleontology Needlework Islam
Metaphysics Investment Archaeology
Parenting Statistics Criminology
Motivational

BOHN'S ANTIQUARIAN LIBRARY.

THE WORKS

OF

SIR THOMAS BROWNE.

VOLUME III.

THE WORKS

OF

SIR THOMAS BROWNE.

EDITED BY

SIMON WILKIN, F.L.S.

VOLUME III.

CONTAINING

URN-BURIAL, CHRISTIAN MORALS, MISCELLANIES,
CORRESPONDENCE, ETC.

LONDON:

HENRY G. BOHN, YORK STREET, COVENT GARDEN.

MDCCCLII.

CONTENTS OF VOL. III.

REPERTORIUM.

MISCELLANIES.

DOMESTIC CORRESPONDENCE, JOURNALS, &c.

MISCELLANEOUS CORRESPONDENCE.

HYDRIOTAPHIA.

URN BURIAL ; OR, A DISCOURSE OF THE SEPULCHRAL URNS
LATELY FOUND IN NORFOLK.

NINTH EDITION.

––––––––

ORIGINALLY PUBLISHED IN

1658.

En sum quod digitis qui que levatur onus.—PROPERT.

THE EPISTLE DEDICATORY.

THOMAS LE GROS, of CROSTWICK, ESQUIRE.[1]

WHEN the funeral pyre was out, and the last valediction over, men took a lasting adieu of their interred friends, little expecting the curiosity of future ages should comment upon their ashes; and, having no old experience of the duration of their relicks, held no opinion of such after-considerations.

But who knows the fate of his bones, or how often he is to be buried ? Who hath the oracle of his ashes, or whither they are to be scattered ? The relicks of many lie like the ruins of Pompey's,* in all parts of the earth; and when they arrive at your hands these may seem to have wandered far, who, in a direct and meridian travel,† have but few miles of known earth between yourself and the pole.

That the bones of Theseus should be seen again in Athens‡ was not beyond conjecture and hopeful expectation : but that these should arise so opportunely to serve yourself was an hit of fate, and honour beyond prediction.

* *Pompeios juvenes Asia atque Europa, sed ipsum terrâ tegit Libyos.*
† Little directly but sea, between your house and Greenland.[2]
‡ Brought back by Cimon Plutarch.

[1] *Le Gros, &c.*] Descended from an ancient family of the name (Le Gross, or Groos), settled at Sloly, near Crostwick, so early as the reign of Stephen, and who became possessed of the manor and hall of Crostwick in the 38th of Henry VIII. His grandfather, Sir Thomas, was knighted by James I. at the Charter-house, in 1603. The property descended to his nephew, Charles Harman, who took the name of Le Gros, but sold the estate to the Walpole family in 1720.
[2] *Little directly, &c.*] Crostwick-hall is not twenty miles distant from the north coast of Norfolk.

We cannot but wish these urns might have the effect of theatrical vessels and great Hippodrome urns* in Rome, to resound the acclamations and honour due unto you. But these are sad and sepulchral pitchers, which have no joyful voices; silently expressing old mortality, the ruins of forgotten times, and can only speak with life, how long in this corruptible frame some parts may be uncorrupted; yet able to outlast bones long unborn, and noblest pile among us.†

We present not these as any strange sight or spectacle unknown to your eyes, who have beheld the best of urns and noblest variety of ashes; who are yourself no slender master of antiquities, and can daily command the view of so many imperial faces; which raiseth your thoughts unto old things and consideration of times before you, when even living men were antiquities; when the living might exceed the dead, and to depart this world could not be properly said to go unto the greater number.‡ And so run up your thoughts upon the ancient of days, the antiquary's truest object, unto whom the eldest parcels are young, and earth itself an infant, and without Egyptian§ account makes but small noise in thousands.

We were hinted by the occasion, not catched the opportunity to write of old things, or intrude upon the antiquary. We are coldly drawn unto discourses of antiquities, who have scarce time before us to comprehend new things, or make out learned novelties. But seeing they arose, as they lay almost in silence among us, at least in short account suddenly passed over, we were very unwilling they should die again, and be buried twice among us.

Beside, to preserve the living, and make the dead to live, to keep men out of their urns, and discourse of human fragments in them, is not impertinent unto our profession; whose study is life and death, who daily behold examples of mortality, and of all men least need artificial *mementos*, or coffins by our bedside, to mind us of our graves.

* The great urns in the Hippodrome at Rome, conceived to resound the voices of people at their shows.
† Worthily possessed by that true gentleman, Sir Horatio Townshend, my honoured friend.
‡ *Abiit ad plures.*
§ Which makes the world so many years old.

'Tis time to <u>observe occurrences, and let nothing remark-</u>
<u>able escape us</u> : the supinity of elder days hath left so much
in silence, or time hath so martyred the records, that the
most industrious heads* do find no easy work to erect a new
Britannia.

'Tis opportune to look back upon old times, and contem-
plate our forefathers. Great examples grow thin, and to be
fetched from the passed world. Simplicity flies away, and
iniquity comes at long strides upon us. We have enough to
do to make up ourselves from present and passed times, and
the whole stage of things scarce serveth for our instruction.
A complete piece of virtue must be made from the Centos
of all ages, as all the beauties of Greece could make but one
handsome Venus.

When the bones of King Arthur were digged up,† the old
race might think they beheld therein some originals of
themselves ; unto these of our urns none here can pretend
relation, and can only behold the relicks of those persons
who, in their life giving the laws unto their predecessors,
after long obscurity, now lie at their mercies. But, remem-
bering the early civility they brought upon these countries,
and forgetting long-passed mischiefs, we mercifully preserve
their bones, and piss not upon their ashes.

In the offer of these antiquities we drive not at ancient
families, so long outlasted by them. We are far from
erecting your worth upon the pillars of your forefathers,
whose merits you illustrate. We honour your old virtues,
conformable unto times before you, which are the noblest
armoury. And, having long experience of your friendly
conversation, void of empty formality, full of freedom,
constant and generous honesty, I look upon you as a gem
of the old rock,‡ and must profess myself even to urn
and ashes,

Your ever faithful Friend and Servant,

THOMAS BROWNE.

Norwich, May 1st.

* Wherein Mr. Dugdale hath excellently well endeavoured, and
worthy to be countenanced by ingenuous and noble persons.
    † In the time of Henry the second.—*Camden.*
    ‡ *Adamas de rupe veteri præstantissimus.*

HYDRIOTAPHIA.

—◆—

CHAPTER I.

I~ the deep discovery of the subterranean world, a shallow
part would satisfy some enquirers; who, if two or three
yards were open about the surface, would not care to rake
the bowels of Potosi,* and regions towards the centre.
Nature hath furnished one part of the earth, and man another.
The treasures of time lie high, in urns, coins, and monuments, scarce below the roots of some vegetables. Time
hath endless rarities, and shows of all varieties; which
reveals old things in heaven, makes new discoveries in earth,
and even earth itself a discovery. That great antiquity
America lay buried for thousands of years, and a large part
of the earth is still in the urn unto us.

Though if Adam were made out of an extract of the earth,
all parts might challenge a restitution, yet few have returned
their bones far lower than they might receive them; not
affecting the graves of giants, under hilly and heavy
coverings, but content with less than their own depth, have
wished their bones might lie soft, and the earth be light
upon them. Even such as hope to rise again, would not
be content with central interment, or so desperately to place
their relicks as to lie beyond discovery; and in no way to be
seen again; which happy contrivance hath made communication with our forefathers, and left unto our view some
parts, which they never beheld themselves.

* The rich mountain of Peru.

Though earth hath engrossed the name, yet water hath proved the smartest grave; which in forty days swallowed almost mankind, and the living creation; fishes not wholly escaping, except the salt ocean were handsomely contempered by a mixture of the fresh element.

Many have taken voluminous pains to determine the state of the soul upon disunion; but men have been most phantastical in the singular contrivances of their corporal dissolution: whilst the soberest nations have rested in two ways, of simple inhumation and burning.

That carnal interment or burying was of the elder date, the old examples of Abraham and the patriarchs are sufficient to illustrate; and were without competition, if it could be made out that Adam was buried near Damascus, or Mount Calvary, according to some tradition. God himself, that buried but one, was pleased to make choice of this way, collectible from Scripture expression, and the hot contest between Satan and the archangel, about discovering the body of Moses. But the practice of burning was also of great antiquity, and of no slender extent. For (not to derive the same from Hercules) noble descriptions there are hereof in the Grecian funerals of Homer, in the formal obsequies of Patroclus and Achilles; and somewhat elder in the Theban war, and solemn combustion of Meneceus, and Archemorus, contemporary unto Jair the eighth judge of Israel. Confirmable also among the Trojans, from the funeral pyre of Hector, burnt before the gates of Troy: and the burning of Penthesilea the Amazonian queen:* and long continuance of that practice, in the inward countries of Asia; while as low as the reign of Julian, we find that the king of Chionia† burnt the body of his son, and interred the ashes in a silver urn.

The same practice extended also far west;‡ and, besides Herulians, Getes, and Thracians, was in use with most of the Celtæ, Sarmatians, Germans, Gauls, Danes, Swedes, Norwegians; not to omit some use thereof among Carthaginians and Americans. Of greater antiquity among the

---

* Q. Calaber. lib. i.

† Gumbrates, king of Chionia, a country near Persia.—Ammianus Marcellinus.

‡ Arnold. Montan. not. in Cæs. Commentar. L. Gyraldus. Kirkmannus.

Romans than most opinion, or Pliny seems to allow: for (beside the old table laws of burning or burying within the city,* of making the funeral fire with planed wood, or quenching the fire with wine), Manlius the consul burnt the body of his son: Numa, by special clause of his will, was not burnt but buried; and Remus was solemnly burned, according to the description of Ovid.†

Cornelius Sylla was not the first whose body was burned in Rome, but the first of the Cornelian family; which, being indifferently, not frequently used before; from that time spread, and became the prevalent practice. Not totally pursued in the highest run of cremation; for when even crows were funerally burnt, Poppæa the wife of Nero found a peculiar grave interment. Now as all .customs were founded upon some bottom of reason, so there wanted not grounds for this; according to several apprehensions of the most rational dissolution. Some being of the opinion of Thales, that water was the original of all things, thought it most equal[1] to submit unto the principle of putrefaction, and conclude in a moist relentment.[2] Others conceived it most natural to end in fire, as due unto the master principle in the composition, according to the doctrine of Heraclitus; and therefore heaped up large piles, more actively to waft them toward that element, whereby they also declined a visible degeneration into worms, and left a lasting parcel of their composition.

Some apprehended a purifying virtue in fire, refining the grosser commixture, and firing out the æthereal particles so deeply immersed in it. And such as by tradition or rational conjecture held any hint of the final pyre of all things; or that this element at last must be too hard for all the rest; might conceive most naturally of the fiery dissolution. Others pretending no natural grounds, politickly declined

---

* 12 *Tabul.* part i. *de jure sacro.* *Hominem mortuum in urbe ne sepelito, neve urito,* tom. 2. *Rogum ascid ne polito,* tom. 4. *Item Vigeneri Annotat. in Livium, et Alex. cum Tiraquello.* *Roscinus cum Dempstero.*

† *Ultimo prolata subdita flamma rogo.* *De Fast.* lib. iv. *cum Car. Neapol. Anaptyxi.*

[1] *most equal.*] Most equitable.
[2] *relentment.*] Dissolution: not in Johnson.

the malice of enemies upon their buried bodies. Which
consideration led Sylla unto this practice; who having thus
served the body of Marius, could not but fear a retaliation
upon his own; entertained after in the civil wars, and
revengeful contentions of Rome.

But as many nations embraced, and many left it indifferent, so others too much affected, or strictly declined this
practice. The Indian Brachmans seemed too great friends
unto fire, who burnt themselves alive, and thought it the
noblest way to end their days in fire; according to the
expression of the Indian, burning himself at Athens,* in
his last words upon the pyre unto the amazed spectators,
thus I make myself immortal.

But the Chaldeans, the great idolaters of fire, abhorred
the burning of their carcases, as a pollution of that deity.
The Persian magi declined it upon the like scruple, and
being only solicitous about their bones, exposed their flesh
to the prey of birds and dogs. And the Persees now in
India, which expose their bodies unto vultures, and endure
not so much as *feretra* or biers of wood, the proper fuel of
fire, are led on with such niceties. But whether the ancient
Germans, who burned their dead, held any such fear to
pollute their deity of Herthus, or the earth, we have no
authentic conjecture.

The Egyptians were afraid of fire, not as a deity, but
a devouring element, mercilessly consuming their bodies,
and leaving too little of them; and therefore by precious
embalments, depositure in dry earths, or handsome inclosure
in glasses, contrived the notablest ways of integral conservation. And from such Egyptian scruples, imbibed by
Pythagoras, it may be conjectured that Numa and the
Pythagorical sect first waved the fiery solution.

The Scythians, who swore by wind and sword, that is, by
life and death, were so far from burning their bodies, that
they declined all interment, and made their graves in the
air: and the Ichthyophagi, or fish-eating nations about
Egypt, affected the sea for their grave; thereby declining
visible corruption, and restoring the debt of their bodies.

* And therefore the inscription of his tomb was made accordingly.—
Nic. Damasc.

Whereas the old heroes, in Homer, dreaded nothing more
than water or drowning; probably upon the old opinion of
the fiery substance of the soul, only extinguishable by that
element; and therefore the poet emphatically implieth the
total destruction in this kind of death, which happened to
Ajax Oileus.*

The old Balearians† had a peculiar mode, for they used
great urns and much wood, but no fire in their burials,
while they bruised the flesh and bones of the dead, crowded
them into urns, and laid heaps of wood upon them.
And the Chinese‡ without cremation or urnal interment of
their bodies, make use of trees and much burning, while
they plant a pine-tree by their grave, and burn great numbers of printed draughts of slaves and horses over it, civilly
content with their companies *in effigy*, which barbarous
nations exact unto reality.

Christians abhorred this way of obsequies, and though
they sticked not to give their bodies to be burnt in their
lives, detested that mode after death; affecting rather a
depositure than absumption, and properly submitting unto
the sentence of God, to return not unto ashes but unto dust
again, conformable unto the practice of the patriarchs, the
interment of our Saviour, of Peter, Paul, and the ancient
martyrs. And so far at last declining promiscuous interment with Pagans, that some have suffered ecclesiastical
censures,§ for making no scruple thereof.

The Musselman believers will never admit this fiery resolution. For they hold a present trial from their black and
white angels in the grave; which they must have made so
hollow, that they may rise upon their knees.

The Jewish nation, though they entertained the old way
of inhumation, yet sometimes admitted this practice.
For the men of Jabesh burnt the body of Saul; and by no
prohibited practice, to avoid contagion or pollution, in time
of pestilence, burnt the bodies of their friends.|| And when
they burnt not their dead bodies, yet sometimes used great
burnings near and about them, deducible from the expressions concerning Jehoram, Zedechias, and the sumptuous

---

* Which *Magius* reads ἐξαπόλωλε.   † *Diodorus Siculus.*
‡ *Ramusius* in *Navigat.*   § *Martialis* the Bishop. *Cyprian.*
|| Amos vi. 10.

pyre of Asa. And were so little averse from Pagan burning, that the Jews lamenting the death of Cæsar their friend, and revenger on Pompey, frequented the place where his body was burnt for many nights together.* And as they raised noble monuments and mausoleums for their own nation,† so they were not scrupulous in erecting some for others, according to the practice of Daniel, who left that lasting sepulchral pile in Ecbatana, for the Median and Persian kings.‡

But even in times of subjection and hottest use, they conformed not unto the Roman practice of burning; whereby the prophecy was secured concerning the body of Christ, that it should not see corruption, or a bone should not be broken; which we believe was also providentially prevented, from the soldier's spear and nails that passed by the little bones both in his hands and feet; not of ordinary contrivance, that it should not corrupt on the cross, according to the laws of Roman crucifixion, or an hair of his head perish, though observable in Jewish customs, to cut the hairs of malefactors.

Nor in their long cohabitation with Egyptians, crept into a custom of their exact embalming, wherein deeply slashing the muscles, and taking out the brains and entrails, they had broken the subject of so entire a resurrection, nor fully answered the types of Enoch, Elijah, or Jonah, which yet to prevent or restore, was of equal facility unto that rising power, able to break the fasciations and bands of death, to get clear out of the cerecloth, and an hundred pounds of ointment, and out of the sepulchre before the stone was rolled from it.

But though they embraced not this practice of burning, yet entertained they many ceremonies agreeable unto Greek and Roman obsequies. And he that observeth their funeral feasts, their lamentations at the grave, their music, and weeping mourners; how they closed the eyes of their friends, how they washed, anointed, and kissed the dead; may easily

* *Sueton. in vita Jul. Cæs.*

† As that magnificent sepulchral monument erected by *Simon*, 1 Macc. xiii.

‡ Κατασκεύασμα θαυμασίως πεποιημένον, whereof a *J*ewish priest had always the custody, unto *J*osephus his days.—*Jos. Antiq.* lib. x.

conclude these were not mere Pagan civilities. But whether that mournful burthen, and treble calling out after Absalom,* had any reference unto the last conclamation, and triple valediction, used by other nations, we hold but a wavering conjecture.

Civilians make sepulture but of the law of nations, others do naturally found it and discover it also in animals. They that are so thick-skinned as still to credit the story of the Phœnix, may say something for animal burning. More serious conjectures find some examples of sepulture in elephants, cranes, the sepulchral cells of pismires, and practice of bees,—which civil society carrieth out their dead, and hath exequies, if not interments.

CHAPTER II.

THE solemnities, ceremonies, rites of their cremation or interment, so solemnly delivered by authors, we shall not disparage our reader to repeat. Only the last and lasting part in their urns, collected bones and ashes, we cannot wholly omit or decline that subject, which occasion lately presented, in some discovered among us.

In a field of Old Walsingham, not many months past, were digged up between forty and fifty urns, deposited in a dry and sandy soil, not a yard deep, nor far from one another.—Not all strictly of one figure, but most answering these described: some containing two pounds of bones, distinguishable in skulls, ribs, jaws, thigh bones, and teeth, with fresh impressions of their combustion; besides the extraneous substances, like pieces of small boxes, or combs handsomely wrought, handles of small brass instruments, brazen nippers, and in one some kind of opal.†

Near the same plot of ground, for about six yards compass, were digged up coals and incinerated substances, which begat conjecture that this was the *ustrina* or place of

---

* 2 Sam. xviii. 33.

† In one sent me by my worthy friend, Dr. Thomas Witherly of Walsingham.

burning their bodies, or some sacrificing place unto the *manes*, which was properly below the surface of the ground, as the *æra* and altars unto the gods and heroes above it.

That these were the urns of Romans from the common custom and place where they were found, is no obscure conjecture, not far from a Roman garrison, and but five miles from Brancaster, set down by ancient record under the name of Branodunum. And where the adjoining town, containing seven parishes, in no very different sound, but Saxon termination, still retains the name of Burnham, which being an early station, it is not improbable the neighbour parts were filled with habitations, either of Romans themselves, or Britons Romanized, which observed the Roman customs.

Nor is it improbable, that the Romans early possessed this country. For though we meet not with such strict particulars of these parts before the new institution of Constantine and military charge of the count of the Saxon shore, and that about the Saxon invasions, the Dalmatian horsemen were in the garrison of Brancaster; yet in the time of Claudius, Vespasian, and Severus, we find no less than three legions dispersed through the province of Britain. And as high as the reign of Claudius a great overthrow was given unto the Iceni, by the Roman lieutenant Ostorius. Not long after, the country was so molested, that, in hope of a better state, Prasutagus bequeathed his kingdom unto Nero and his daughters; and Boadicea, his queen, fought the last decisive battle with Paulinus. After which time, and conquest of Agricola, the lieutenant of Vespasian, probable it is, they wholly possessed this country; ordering it into garrisons or habitations best suitable with their securities. And so some Roman habitations not improbable in these parts, as high as the time of Vespasian, where the Saxons after seated, in whose thin-filled maps we yet find the name of Walsingham. Now if the Iceni were but Gammadims, Anconians, or men that lived in an angle, wedge, or elbow of Britain, according to the original etymology, this country will challenge the emphatical appellation, as most properly making the elbow or *iken* of Icenia.[3]

---

[3] *Now if the, &c.*] That is to say, *if* `"iken` (as well αγκων) signified

That Britain was notably populous is undeniable, from
that expression of Cæsar.* That the Romans themselves
were early in no small numbers (seventy thousand, with
their associates), slain by Boadicea, affords a sure account.
And though many Roman habitations are now unknown, yet
some, by old works, rampiers, coins, and urns, do testify
their possessions. Some urns have been found at Castor,
some also about Southcreak, and, not many years past, no
less than ten in a field at Buxton, † not near any recorded
garrison. Nor is it strange to find Roman coins of copper
and silver among us; of Vespasian, Trajan, Adrian, Commodus, Antoninus, Severus, &c.; but the greater number
of Dioclesian, Constantine, Constans, Valens, with many of
Victorinus Posthumius, Tetricus, and the thirty tyrants in
the reign of Gallienus; and some as high as Adrianus have
been found about Thetford, or Sitomagus, mentioned in the
Itinerary of Antoninus, as the way from Venta or Castor unto
·London.‡ But the most frequent discovery is made at the
two Castors by Norwich and Yarmouth,§ at Burghcastle,
and Brancaster.‖

* *Hominum infinita multitudo est, creberrimaque ; ædificia ferè Gallicis
consimilia.*—*Cæs. de Bello Gal.* l. v.
† In the ground of my worthy friend Robert Jegon, Esq.; wherein
some things contained were preserved by the most worthy Sir William
Paston, Bart.
‡ From Castor to Thetford the Romans accounted thirty-two miles,
and from thence observed not our common road to London, but passed
by *Combretonium ad Ansam, Canonium, Cæsaromagus, &c.* by Bretenham,
Coggeshall, Chelmsford, Brentwood, &c.
§ Most at Castor by Yarmouth, found in a place called East-bloudy-
burgh Furlong, belonging to Mr. Thomas Wood, a person of civility,
industry, and knowledge in this way, who hath made observation of
remarkable things about him, and from whom we have received divers
silver and copper coins.
‖ Belonging to that noble gentleman, and true example of worth,
Sir Ralph Hare, Bart., my honoured friend.

an elbow—and thus, the Icenians were but "men that lived in an angle
or elbow," then would the inhabitants of Norfolk have the best claim
to the appellation, that county being most emphatically the *elbow* of
Icenia. But, unfortunately, *iken* does *not* signify an elbow; and it
appears that the Iceni derived their name from the river Ouse, on whose
banks they resided,—anciently called Iken, Yken, or Ycin. Whence,
also, Ikenild-street, Ikenthorpe, Ikenworth.

Besides the Norman, Saxon, and Danish pieces of Cuthred, Canutus, William, Matilda,* and others, some British coins of gold have been dispersedly found, and no small number of silver pieces near Norwich,† with a rude head upon the obverse, and an ill-formed horse on the reverse, with inscriptions *Ic. Duro. T.;* whether implying Iceni, Durotriges, Tascia, or Trinobantes, we leave to higher conjecture. Vulgar chronology will have Norwich Castle as old as Julius Cæsar; but his distance from these parts, and its gothick form of structure, abridgeth such antiquity. The British coins afford conjecture of early habitation in these parts, though the city of Norwich arose from the ruins of Venta; and though, perhaps, not without some habitation before, was enlarged, builded, and nominated by the Saxons. In what bulk or populosity it stood in the old East-Angle monarchy tradition and history are silent. Considerable it was in the Danish eruptions, when Sueno burnt Thetford and Norwich,‡ and Ulfketel, the governor thereof, was able to make some resistance, and after endeavoured to burn the Danish navy.

How the Romans left so many coins in countries of their conquests seems of hard resolution; except we consider how they buried them under ground when, upon barbarous invasions, they were fain to desert their habitations in most part of their empire, and the strictness of their laws forbidding to transfer them to any other uses: wherein the Spartans§ were singular, who, to make their copper money useless, contempered it with vinegar. That the Britons left any, some wonder, since their money was iron and iron rings before Cæsar; and those of after-stamp by permission, and but small in bulk and bigness. That so few of the Saxons remain, because, overcome by succeeding conquerors upon the place, their coins, by degrees, passed into other stamps and the marks of after-ages.

Than the time of these urns deposited, or precise antiquity of these relicks, nothing of more uncertainty; for since the lieutenant of Claudius seems to have made the first progress

---

* A piece of Maud, the empress, said to be found in Buckenham Castle, with this inscription,—*Elle n' a elle.*

† At Thorpe.   ‡ *Brampton Abbas Journallensis.*

§ *Plut. in vitâ Lycurg.*

into these parts, since Boadicea was overthrown by the forces of Nero, and Agricola put a full end to these conquests, it is not probable the country was fully garrisoned or planted before; and, therefore, however these urns might be of later date, not likely of higher antiquity.

And the succeeding emperors desisted not from their conquests in these and other parts, as testified by history and medal-inscription yet extant: the province of Britain, in so divided a distance from Rome, beholding the faces of many imperial persons, and in large account; no fewer than Cæsar, Claudius, Britannicus, Vespasian, Titus, Adrian, Severus, Commodus, Geta, and Caracalla.

A great obscurity herein, because no medal or emperor's coin enclosed, which might denote the date of their interments; observable in many urns, and found in those of Spitalfields, by London,* which contained the coins of Claudius, Vespasian, Commodus, Antoninus, attended with lacrymatories, lamps, bottles of liquor, and other appurtenances of affectionate superstition, which in these rural interments were wanting.

Some uncertainty there is from the period or term of burning, or the cessation of that practice. Macrobius affirmeth it was disused in his days; but most agree, though without authentic record, that it ceased with the Antonini,—most safely to be understood after the reign of those emperors which assumed the name of Antoninus, extending unto Heliogabalus. Not strictly after Marcus; for about fifty years later, we find the magnificent burning and consecration of Severus; and, if we so fix this period or cessation, these urns will challenge above thirteen hundred years.

But whether this practice was only then left by emperors and great persons, or generally about Rome, and not in other provinces, we hold no authentic account; for after Tertullian, in the days of Minucius, it was obviously objected upon Christians, that they condemned the practice of burning.† And we find a passage in Sidonius,‡ which asserteth that practice in France unto a lower account. And, perhaps,

* *Stowe's Survey of London.*
† *Execrantur rogos, et damnant ignium sepulturam.—Min. in Oct.*
‡ *Sidon. Apollinaris.*

not fully disused till Christianity fully established, which
gave the final extinction to these sepulchral bonfires.

Whether they were the bones of men, or women, or
children, no authentic decision from ancient custom in distinct places of burial. Although not improbably conjectured,
that the double sepulture, or burying-place of Abraham,*
had in it such intention. But from exility of bones, thin-
ness of skulls, smallness of teeth, ribs, and thigh bones, not
improbable that many thereof were persons of minor age,
or women. Confirmable also from things contained in them.
In most were found substances resembling combs, plates like
boxes, fastened with iron pins, and handsomely overwrought
like the necks or bridges of musical instruments ; long brass
plates overwrought like the handles of neat implements ;
brazen nippers, to pull away hair ; and in one a kind of opal,
yet maintaining a bluish colour.

Now that they accustomed to burn or bury with them,
things wherein they excelled, delighted, or which were dear
unto them, either as farewells unto all pleasure, or vain
apprehension that they might use them in the other world,
is testified by all antiquity, observable from the gem or beryl
ring upon the finger of Cynthia, the mistress of Propertius,
when after her funeral pyre her ghost appeared unto him ;
and notably illustrated from the contents of that Roman urn
preserved by Cardinal Farnese,† wherein besides great number of gems with heads of gods and goddesses, were found
an ape of agath, a grasshopper, an elephant of amber, a
crystal ball, three glasses, two spoons, and six nuts of crystal ;
and beyond the content of urns, in the monument of
Childerick the first,‡ and fourth king from Pharamond,
casually discovered three years past at Tournay, restoring
unto the world much gold richly adorning his sword, two
hundred rubies, many hundred imperial coins, three hundred
golden bees, the bones and horse-shoes of his horse interred
with him, according to the barbarous magnificence of those
days in their sepulchral obsequies. Although, if we steer
by the conjecture of many and septuagint expression, some
trace thereof may be found even with the ancient Hebrews,

* Gen. xxiii. 4.　　　　　　† Vigeneri Annot. in 4. Liv.
‡ Chifflet. in Anast. Childer.

not only from the sepulchral treasure of David, but the circumcision knives which Joshua also buried.

Some men, considering the contents of these urns, lasting pieces and toys included in them, and the custom of burning with many other nations, might somewhat doubt whether all urns found among us, were properly Roman relicks, or some not belonging unto our British, Saxon, or Danish forefathers.

In the form of burial among the ancient Britons, the large discourses of Cæsar, Tacitus, and Strabo are silent. For the discovery whereof, with other particulars, we much deplore the loss of that letter which Cicero expected or received from his brother Quintus, as a resolution of British customs; or the account which might have been made by Scribonius Largus, the physician, accompanying the Emperor Claudius, who might have also discovered that frugal bit of the old Britons,* which in the bigness of a bean could satisfy their thirst and hunger.

But that the Druids and ruling priests used to burn and bury, is expressed by Pomponius; that Bellinus, the brother of Brennus, and king of the Britons, was burnt, is acknowledged by Polydorus, as also by Amandus Zierexensis in *Historia*, and Pineda in his *Universa Historia* (Spanish). That they held that practice in Gallia, Cæsar expressly delivereth. Whether the Britons (probably descended from them, of like religion, language, and manners) did not sometimes make use of burning, or whether at least such as were after civilized unto the Roman life and manners, conformed not unto this practice, we have no historical assertion or denial. But since, from the account of Tacitus, the Romans early wrought so much civility upon the British stock, that they brought them to build temples, to wear the gown, and study the Roman laws and language, that they conformed also unto their religious rites and customs in burials, seems no improbable conjecture.

That burning the dead was used in Sarmatia is affirmed by Gaguinus; that the Sueons and Gothlanders used to burn their princes and great persons, is delivered by Saxo and Olaus; that this was the old German practice, is also

---

* *Dionis excerpta per Xiphilin. in Severo.*

asserted by Tacitus. And though we are bare in historical particulars of such obsequies in this island, or that the Saxons, Jutes, and Angles burnt their dead, yet came they from parts where 'twas of ancient practice ; the Germans using it, from whom they were descended. And even in Jutland and Sleswick in Anglia Cymbrica, urns with bones were found not many years before us.

But the Danish and northern nations have raised an era or point of compute from their custom of burning their dead : * some deriving it from Unguinus, some from Frotho the great, who ordained by law, that princes and chief commanders should be committed unto the fire, though the common sort had the common grave interment. So Stark-atterus, that old hero, was burnt, and Ringo royally burnt the body of Harold the king slain by him.

What time this custom generally expired in that nation, we discern no assured period ; whether it ceased before Christianity, or upon their conversion, by Ausgurius the Gaul, in the time of Ludovicus Pius the son of Charles the Great, according to good computes ; or whether it might not be used by some persons, while for an hundred and eighty years Paganism and Christianity were promiscuously embraced among them, there is no assured conclusion. About which times the Danes were busy in England, and particularly infested this county ; where many castles and strongholds were built by them, or against them, and great number of names and families still derived from them. But since this custom was probably disused before their invasion or conquest, and the Romans confessedly practised the same since their possession of this island, the most assured account will fall upon the Romans; or Britons Romanized.

However, certain it is, that urns conceived of no Roman original, are often digged up both in Norway and Denmark, handsomely described, and graphically represented by the learned physician Wormius.† And in some parts of Denmark in no ordinary number, as stands delivered by authors exactly describing those countries.‡ And they contained

* Roisold, Brendetyde. Ild tyde.
† Olai Wormii Monumenta et Antiquitat. Dan.
‡ Adolphus Cyprius in Annal. Sleswick. urnis adeo abundabat collis, &c.

not only bones, but many other substances in them, as knives, pieces of iron, brass, and wood, and one of Norway a brass gilded jew's-harp.

Nor were they confused or careless in disposing the noblest sort, while they placed large stones in circle about the urns or bodies which they interred: somewhat answerable unto the monument of Rollrich stones in England,* or sepulchral monument probably erected by Rollo, who after conquered Normandy; where 'tis not improbable somewhat might be discovered. Meanwhile to what nation or person belonged that large urn found at Ashbury,† containing mighty bones, and a buckler; what those large urns found at Little Massingham;‡ or why the Anglesea urns are placed with their mouths downward, remains yet undiscovered.

CHAPTER III.

PLAISTERED and whited sepulchres were anciently affected in cadaverous and corrupted burials; and the rigid Jews were wont to garnish the sepulchres of the righteous.§ Ulysses, in Hecuba, cared not how meanly he lived, so he might find a noble tomb after death.‖ Great princes affected great monuments; and the fair and larger urns contained no vulgar ashes, which makes that disparity in those which time discovereth among us. The present urns were not of one capacity, the largest containing above a gallon, some not much above half that measure; nor all of one figure, wherein there is no strict conformity in the same or different countries; observable from those represented by Casalius, Bosio, and others, though all found in Italy; while many have handles, ears, and long necks, but most imitate a circular figure, in a spherical and round composure; whether from any mystery, best duration or capacity, were but a conjecture. But the common form with

* In Oxfordshire, *Camden.*
† In Cheshire, *Twinus de rebus Albionicis.*
‡ In Norfolk, *Hollingshead.*　　§ Matt. xxiii.　　‖ *Euripides.*

necks was a proper figure, making our last bed like our
first ; nor much unlike the urns of our nativity while we
lay in the nether part of the earth,* and inward vault of
our microcosm.   Many urns are red, these but of a black
colour somewhat smooth, and dully sounding, which begat
some doubt, whether they were burnt, or only baked in oven
or sun, according to the ancient way, in many bricks, tiles,
pots, and testaceous works ; and, as the word *testa* is properly to be taken, when occurring without addition and
chiefly intended by Pliny, when he commendeth bricks and
tiles of two years old, and to make them in the spring.
Nor only these concealed pieces, but the open magnificence
of antiquity, ran much in the artifice of clay.   Hereof the
house of Mausolus was built, thus old Jupiter stood in the
Capitol, and the statua of Hercules, made in the reign of
Tarquinius Priscus, was extant in Pliny's days.   And such
as declined burning or funeral urns, affected coffins of clay,
according to the mode of Pythagoras, a way preferred by
Varro.   But the spirit of great ones was above these circumscriptions, affecting copper, silver, gold, and porphyry
urns, wherein Severus lay, after a serious view and sentence
on that which should contain him.†   Some of these urns
were thought to have been silvered over, from sparklings in
several pots, with small tinsel parcels ; uncertain whether
from the earth, or the first mixture in them.

Among these urns we could obtain no good account of
their coverings ; only one seemed arched over with some kind
of brick-work.   Of those found at Buxton, some were
covered with flints, some, in other parts, with tiles; those at
Yarmouth Caster were closed with Roman bricks, and some
have proper earthen covers adapted and fitted to them.
But in the Homerical urn of Patroclus, whatever was the
solid tegument, we find the immediate covering to be a
purple piece of silk : and such as had no covers might have
the earth closely pressed into them, after which disposure
were probably some of these, wherein we found the bones
and ashes half mortared unto the sand and sides of the urn,
and some long roots of quich, or dog's-grass, wreathed about
the bones.

* Psal. lxiii.

† Χωρήσεις τὸν ἄνθρωπον, ὃν ἡ οἰκουμένη οὐκ ἐχώρησεν.—*Dion.*

No lamps, included liquors, lacrymatories, or tear bottles, attended these rural urns, either as sacred unto the *manes*, or passionate expressions of their surviving friends. While with rich flames, and hired tears, they solemnized their obsequies, and in the most lamented monuments made one part of their inscriptions.* Some find sepulchral vessels containing liquors, which time hath incrassated into jellies. For, besides these lacrymatories, notable lamps, with vessels of oils, and aromatical liquors, attended noble ossuaries; and some yet retaining a vinosity† and spirit in them, which, if any have tasted, they have far exceeded the palates of antiquity. Liquors not to be computed by years of annual magistrates, but by great conjunctions and the fatal periods of kingdoms.‡ The draughts of consulary date were but crude unto these, and Opimian wine§ but in the must unto them.

In sundry graves and sepulchres we meet with rings, coins, and chalices. Ancient frugality was so severe, that they allowed no gold to attend the corpse, but only that which served to fasten their teeth.‖ Whether the Opaline stone in this were burnt upon the finger of the dead, or cast into the fire by some affectionate friend, it will consist with either custom. But other incinerable substances were found so fresh, that they could feel no singe from fire. These, upon view, were judged to be wood; but, sinking in water, and tried by the fire, we found them to be bone or ivory. In their hardness and yellow colour they most resembled box, which, in old expressions, found the epithet of eternal,¶ and perhaps in such conservatories might have passed uncorrupted.

That bay leaves were found green in the tomb of S. Humbert,** after an hundred and fifty years, was looked upon as miraculous. Remarkable it was unto old spectators, that the cypress of the temple of Diana lasted so many hundred

---

* *Cum lacrymis posuêre.*   † *Lazius.*
‡ About five hundred years.—*Plato.*
§ *Vinum Opiminianum annorum centum.*—*Petron.*
‖ 12 *Tabul.* l. xi. *De Jure Sacro. Neve aurum adito ast quoi aurc dentes vincti escunt im cum ilo sepelire urereve, se fraude esto.*
¶ *Plin.* l. xvi. *Inter* ξύλα ἀσαπῆ *numerat Theophrastus.*
** *Surius.*

years. The wood of the ark, and olive-rod of Aaron, were
older at the captivity ; but the cypress of the ark of Noah
was the greatest vegetable of antiquity, if Josephus were
not deceived by some fragments of it in his days : to omit
the moor logs and fir trees found under-ground in many
parts of England ; the undated ruins of winds, floods, or
earthquakes, and which in Flanders still show from what
quarter they fell, as generally lying in a north-east position.*
· But though we found not these pieces to be wood, according to first apprehensions, yet we missed not altogether
of some woody substance ; for the bones were not so clearly
picked but some coals were found amongst them ; a way to
make wood perpetual, and a fit associate for metal, whereon
was laid the foundation of the great Ephesian temple, and
which were made the lasting tests of old boundaries and
landmarks. Whilst we look on these, we admire not observations of coals found fresh after four hundred years.† In
a long-deserted habitation‡ even egg-shells have been found
fresh, not tending to corruption.

In the monument of King Childerick the iron relicks
were found all rusty and crumbling into pieces ; but our
little iron pins, which fastened the ivory works, held well
together, and lost not their magnetical quality, though
wanting a tenacious moisture for the firmer union of parts ;
although it be hardly drawn into fusion, yet that metal soon
submitteth unto rust and dissolution. In the brazen pieces
we admired not the duration, but the freedom from rust,
and ill savour, upon the hardest attrition ; but now exposed
unto the piercing atoms of air, in the space of a few months,
they begin to spot and betray their green entrails. We
conceive not these urns to have descended thus naked as
they appear, or to have entered their graves without the old
habit of flowers. The urn of Philopœmen was so laden with
flowers and ribbons, that it afforded no sight of itself. The
rigid Lycurgus allowed olive and myrtle. The Athenians
might fairly except against the practice of Democritus,
to be buried up in honey, as fearing to embezzle a great
commodity of their country, and the best of that kind in

* *Gorop. Becanus in Niloscopio.*
† Of *Beringuccio nella pyrotechnia.*   ‡ At Elmham.

Europe.   But Plato seemed too frugally politick, who
allowed no larger monument than would contain four heroick
verses, and designed the most barren ground for sepulture:
though we cannot commend the goodness of that sepulchral
ground which was set at no higher rate than the mean
salary of Judas.   Though the earth had confounded the
ashes of these ossuaries, yet the bones were so smartly
burnt, that some thin plates of brass were found half melted
among them.   Whereby we apprehend they were not of
the meanest carcases, perfunctorily fired, as sometimes in
military, and commonly in pestilence, burnings ; or after the
manner of abject corpses, huddled forth and carelessly
burnt, without the Esquiline Port at Rome; which was an
affront continued upon Tiberius, while they but half burnt
his body,* and in the amphitheatre, according to the custom
in notable malefactors ; whereas Nero seemed not so much
to fear his death as that his head should be cut off and his
body not burnt entire.

Some, finding many fragments of skulls in these urns,
suspected a mixture of bones; in none we searched was
there cause of such conjecture, though sometimes they declined not that practice.—The ashes of Domitian† were
mingled with those of Julia ; of Achilles with those of
Patroclus.   All urns contained not single ashes ; without
confused burnings they affectionately compounded their
bones ; passionately endeavouring to continue their living
unions.   And when distance of death denied such conjunctions, unsatisfied affections conceived some satisfaction
to be neighbours in the grave, to lie urn by urn, and touch
but in their manes.   And many were so curious to continue
their living relations, that they contrived large and family
urns, wherein the ashes of their nearest friends and kindred
might successively be received,‡ at least some parcels
thereof, while their collateral memorials lay in minor vessels
about them.

Antiquity held too light thoughts from objects of mor-

---

* *Sueton. in vitâ Tib.   Et in amphitheatro semiustulandum,* not.
Casaub.

† *Sueton. in vitâ Domitian.*

‡ See the most learned and worthy Mr. M. Casaubon upon Antoninus.

tality, while some drew provocatives of mirth from anatomies,* and jugglers showed tricks with skeletons.   When fiddlers made not so pleasant mirth as fencers, and men could sit with quiet stomachs, while 'hanging was played before them.†   Old considerations made few mementos by skulls and bones upon their monuments.   In the Egyptian obelisks and hieroglyphical figures it is not easy to meet with bones.   The sepulchral lamps speak nothing less than sepulture, and in their literal draughts prove often obscene and antick pieces.   Where we find _D. M._‡ it is obvious to meet with sacrificing _pateras_ and vessels of libation upon old sepulchral monuments.   In the Jewish hypogæum§ and subterranean cell at Rome, was little observable beside the variety of lamps and frequent draughts of the holy candlestick.   In authentick draughts of Anthony and Jerome we meet with thigh bones and death's-heads ; but the cemeterial cells of ancient Christians and martyrs were filled with draughts of Scripture stories; not declining the flourishes of cypress, palms, and olive, and the mystical figures of peacocks, doves, and cocks ; but iterately affecting the portraits of Enoch, Lazarus, Jonas, and the vision of Ezekiel, as hopeful draughts, and hinting imagery of the resurrection, which is the life of the grave, and sweetens our habitations in the land of moles and pismires.

Gentile inscriptions precisely delivered the extent of men's lives, seldom the manner of their deaths, which history itself so often leaves obscure in the records of memorable persons.   There is scarce any philosopher but dies twice or thrice in Laertius; nor almost any life without two or three deaths in Plutarch ; which makes the tragical ends of noble persons more favourably resented by compassionate readers who find some relief in the election of such differences.

The certainty of death is attended with uncertainties, in time, manner, places.   The variety of monuments hath often obscured true graves ; and cenotaphs confounded

---

* _Sic erimus cuncti, &c.   Ergo dum vivimus vivamus._

† Ἀγώνον παίζειν.   A barbarous pastime at feasts, when men stood upon a rolling globe, with their necks in a rope and a knife in their hands, ready to cut it when the stone was rolled away ; wherein if they failed, they lost their lives, to the laughter of their spectators.—_Athenæus._

‡ _Diis manibus._   § _Bosio._

sepulchres. For beside their real tombs, many have found honorary and empty sepulchres. The variety of Homer's monuments made him of various countries. Euripides* had his tomb in Africa, but his sepulture in Macedonia. And Severus† found his real sepulchre in Rome, but his empty grave in Gallia.

He that lay in a golden urn ‡ eminently above the earth, was not like to find the quiet of his bones. Many of these urns were broke by a vulgar discoverer in hope of enclosed treasure. The ashes of Marcellus§ were lost above ground, upon the like account. Where profit hath prompted, no age hath wanted such miners. For which the most barbarous expilators found the most civil rhetorick. Gold once out of the earth is no more due unto it; what was unreasonably committed to the ground, is reasonably resumed from it; let monuments and rich fabricks, not riches, adorn men's ashes. The commerce of the living is not to be transferred unto the dead; it is not injustice to take that which none complains to lose, and no man is wronged where no man is possessor.

What virtue yet sleeps in this *terra damnata* and aged cinders, were petty magic to experiment. These crumbling relicks and long fired particles superannuate such expectations; bones, hairs, nails, and teeth of the dead, were the treasures of old sorcerers. In vain we revive such practices; present superstition too visibly perpetuates the folly of our forefathers, wherein unto-old observation‖ this island was so complete, that it might have instructed Persia.

Plato's historian of the other world lies twelve days incorrupted, while his soul was viewing the large stations of the dead. How to keep the corpse seven days from corruption by anointing and washing, without exenteration, were an hazardable piece of art, in our choicest practice. How they made distinct separation of bones and ashes from fiery admixture, hath found no historical solution; though they

---

* *Pausan. in Atticis.* † *Lamprid. in vit. Alexand. Severi.*
‡ *Trajanus.—Dion.*
§ *Plut. in vit. Marcelli.* The commission of the Gothish King Theodoric for finding out sepulchral treasure.—*Cassiodor. var.* I. 4.
‖ *Britannia hodie eam attonitè celebrat tantis ceremoniis ut dedisse Persis videri possit.—Plin.* I. 29.

seemed to make a distinct collection, and overlooked not
Pyrrhus his toe which could not be burnt. Some provision they might make by fictile vessels, coverings, tiles, or
flat stones, upon and about the body (and in the same
field, not far from these urns, many stones were found under
ground), as also by careful separation of extraneous matter,
composing and raking up the burnt bones with forks,
observable in that notable lamp of [Joan.]· Galvanus.*
Martianus, who had the sight of the *vas ustrinum*† or vessel
wherein they burnt the dead, found in the Esquiline field at
Rome, might have afforded clearer solution. But their
insatisfaction herein begat that remarkable invention in the
funeral pyres of some princes, by incombustible sheets
made with a texture of asbestos, incremable flax, or sala-
mander's wool, which preserved their bones and ashes
incommixed.

How the bulk of a man should sink into so few pounds of
bones and ashes, may seem strange unto any who considers
not its constitution, and how slender a mass will remain
upon an open and urging fire of the carnal composition.
Even bones themselves, reduced into ashes, do abate a
notable proportion. And consisting much of a volatile salt,
when that is fired out, make a light kind of cinders. Although their bulk be disproportionable to their weight, when
the heavy principle of salt is fired out, and the earth almost
only remaineth; observable in sallow, which makes more
ashes than oak, and discovers the common fraud of selling
ashes by measure, and not by ponderation.

Some bones make best skeletons,‡ some bodies quick and
speediest ashes. Who would expect a quick flame from
hydropical Heraclitus? The poisoned soldier when his
belly brake, put out two pyres in Plutarch.§ But in the
plague of Athens,‖ one private pyre served two or three
intruders; and the Saracens burnt in large heaps, by the
king of Castile,¶ showed how little fuel sufficeth. Though

---

* To be seen *in Licet. de reconditis veterum lucernis* [p. 599, fol. 1653].

† *Typograph. Roma ex Martiano. Erat et vas ustrinum appellatum,
quod in eo cadavera comburerentur. Cap. de Campo Esquilino.*

‡ Old bones according to Lyserus. Those of young persons not tall
nor fat according to Columbus.

§ *In vitâ Gracc.* ‖ *Thucydides.* . ¶ *Laurent. Valla.*

the funeral pyre of Patroclus took up an hundred foot,* a piece of an old boat burnt Pompey; and if the burthen of Isaac were sufficient for an holocaust, a man may carry his own pyre.

From animals are drawn good burning lights, and good medicines against burning.† Though the seminal·humour seems of a contrary nature to fire, yet the body completed proves a combustible lump, wherein fire finds flame even from bones, and some fuel almost from all parts; though the metropolis of humidity‡ seems least disposed unto it, which might render the skulls of these urns less burned than other bones. But all flies or sinks before fire almost in all bodies: when the common ligament is dissolved, the attenuable parts ascend, the rest subside in coal, calx, or ashes.

To burn the bones of the king of Edom for lime,§ seems no irrational ferity; but to drink of the ashes of dead relations,‖ a passionate prodigality. He that hath the ashes of his friend, hath an everlasting treasure; where fire taketh leave, corruption slowly enters. In bones well burnt, fire makes a wall against itself; experimented in cupels,[5] and tests of metals, which consist of such ingredients. What the sun compoundeth, fire analyzeth, not transmuteth. That devouring agent leaves almost always a morsel for the earth, whereof all things are but a colony; and which, if time permits, the mother element will have in their primitive mass again.

He that looks for urns and old sepulchral relicks, must not seek them in the ruins of temples, where no religion anciently placed them. These were found in a field, according to ancient custom, in noble or private burial; the old practice of the Canaanites, the family of Abraham, and the burying-place of Joshua, in the borders of his possessions;

---

* Ἑκατόμπεδον ἔνθα ἢ ἔνθα.

† *Alb. Ovor.*   ‡ The brain. *Hippocrates.*

§ Amos ii. 1.   ‖ As Artemisia of her husband Mausolus.

[5] *cupels.*] "A chemical vessel, made of earth, ashes, or burnt bones, and in which assay-masters try metals. It suffers all baser ores, when fused and mixed with lead, to pass off, and retains only gold and silver."

and also agreeable unto Roman practice to bury by high-ways, whereby their monuments were under eye;—memorials of themselves, and mementos of mortality unto living passengers; whom the epitaphs of great ones were fain to beg to stay and look upon them,—a language though sometimes used, not so proper in church inscriptions.* The sensible rhetorick of the dead, to exemplarity of good life, first admitted the bones of pious men and martyrs within church walls, which in succeeding ages crept into promiscuous practice: while Constantine was peculiarly favoured to be admitted into the church porch, and the first thus buried in England, was in the days of Cuthred.

Christians dispute how their bodies should lie in the grave.† In urnal interment they clearly escaped this controversy. Though we decline the religious consideration, yet in cemeterial and narrower burying-places, to avoid confusion and cross-position, a certain posture were to be admitted: which even Pagan civility observed. The Persians lay north and south; the Megarians and Phœnicians placed their heads to the east; the Athenians, some think, towards the west, which Christians still retain. And Beda will have it to be the posture of our Saviour. That he was crucified with his face toward the west, we will not contend with tradition and probable account; but we applaud not the hand of the painter, in exalting his cross so high above those on either side: since hereof we find no authentic account in history, and even the crosses found by Helena, pretend no such distinction from longitude or dimension.

To be gnawed out of our graves, to have our skulls made drinking-bowls, and our bones turned into pipes, to delight and sport our enemies, are tragical abominations escaped in burning burials.

Urnal interments and burnt relicks lie not in fear of worms, or to be an heritage for serpents. In carnal sepulture, corruptions seem peculiar unto parts; and some speak of snakes out of the spinal marrow. But while we suppose common worms in graves, 'tis not easy to find any there; few in churchyards above a foot deep, fewer or none in churches though in fresh-decayed bodies. Teeth, bones,

---

* *Siste viator.*   † *Kirkmannus de funer.*

and hair, give the most lasting defiance to corruption.[6]   In
an hydropical body, ten years buried in the churchyard, we
met with a fat concretion, where the nitre of the earth, and
the salt and lixivious liquor. of the body, had coagulated
large lumps of fat into the consistence of the hardest Castile soap, whereof part remaineth with us.[7]   After a battle
with the Persians, the Roman corpses decayed in few days,
while the Persian bodies remained dry and uncorrupted.
Bodies in the same ground do not uniformly dissolve, nor
bones equally moulder; whereof in the opprobrious disease,
we expect no long duration.   The body of the Marquis of
Dorset seemed sound and handsomely cereclothed, that after
seventy-eight years was found uncorrupted.*   Common
tombs preserve not beyond powder: a firmer consistence
and compage of parts might be expected from arefaction,
deep burial, or charcoal.   The greatest antiquities of mortal
bodies may remain in putrefied bones, whereof, though we
take not in the pillar of Lot's wife, or metamorphosis of
Ortelius,† [8] some may be older than pyramids, in the putre-

---

* Of Thomas, Marquis of Dorset, whose body being buried 1530, was
1608, upon the cutting open of the cerecloth, found perfect and nothing
corrupted, the flesh not hardened, but in colour, proportion, and softness like an ordinary corpse newly to be interred.—*Burton's Descript.
of Leicestershire.*
   † In his map of Russia.

[6] *hair, &c.*]   This assertion of the durability of human hair has been
corroborated by modern experiment.   M. Pictet, of Geneva, instituted
a comparison between recent human hair and that from a mummy
brought from Teneriffe, with reference to the constancy of those proper-
ties which render hair important as a hygrometrick substance.   For
this purpose, hygrometers, constructed according to the principles of
Saussure were used ; one with a fresh hair, the other from the mummy.
The results of the experiments were, that the hygrometrick quality of
the Guanche hair is sensibly the same as that of recent hair.—*Edin.
Phil. Journal,* xiii. 196.
   [7] *In an hydropical body, &c.*]   This substance was afterwards found
in the cemetery of the Innocents at Paris, by Fourcroy, and became
known to the French chemists under the name of *adipo-cire.*   Sir
Thomas is admitted to have been the first discoverer of it.
   [8] *metamorphosis, &c.*]   His map of Russia (*Theatrum orbis Terrarum,*
fol. Lond. 1606) exhibits but one "metamorphosis,"—a vignette of
some figures kneeling before a figure seated in a tree, who is sprinkling
something upon his audience.   On other trees in the distance hang

fied relicks of the general inundation. When Alexander opened the tomb of Cyrus, the remaining bones discovered his proportion, whereof urnal fragments afford but a bad conjecture, and have this disadvantage of grave interments, that they leave us ignorant of most personal discoveries. For since bones afford not only rectitude and stability but figure unto the body, it is no impossible physiognomy to conjecture at fleshy appendencies, and after what shape the muscles and carnous parts might hang in their full consistencies. A full-spread *cariola** shows a well-shaped horse behind; handsome formed skulls give some analogy to fleshy resemblance. A critical view of bones makes a good distinction of sexes. Even colour is not beyond conjecture, since it is hard to be deceived in the distinction of Negroes' skulls.† Dante's ‡ characters are to be found in skulls as well as faces. Hercules is not only known by his foot. Other parts make out their comproportions and inferences upon whole or parts. And since the dimensions of the head measure the whole body, and the figure thereof gives

---

* That part in the skeleton of a horse, which is made by the haunch-bones.

† For their extraordinary thickness.[9]

‡ The poet Dante, in his view of Purgatory, found gluttons so meagre, and extenuated, that he conceited them to have been in the siege of Jerusalem, and that it was easy to have discovered *Homo* or *Omo* in their faces : M being made by the two lines of their cheeks, arching over the eye-brows to the nose, and their sunk eyes making O O which makes up *Omo*.

> *Parén l'occhiaje anella senza gemme :*
> *Chi, nel viso degli uomini legge* OMO,
> *Bene avria quivi conosciuto l'emme.—Purgat.* xxiii. 31.

---

several figures. This is the legend beneath :—"*Kergessi gens catervatim degit, id est in hordis : habetque ritum hujusmodi. Cum rem divinam ipsorum sacerdos peragit, sanguinem, lac et fimum jumentorum accipit, ac terræ miscet, inque vas quoddam infundit eoque arborem scandit, atque concione habita, in populum spargit, atque hæc aspersio pro Deo habetur et colitur. Cum quis diem inter illos obit, loco sepulturæ arboribus suspendit.*"

[9] The remark in the text is more correct than the explanation given of it in the note. The configuration of the skull (more particularly with reference to the *facial angle*) affords a criterion by which the various races of mankind may, with sufficient certainty, be discriminated.

conjecture of the principal faculties, physiognomy outlives ourselves, and ends not in our graves.

Severe contemplators, observing these lasting relicks, may think them good monuments of persons past, little advantage to future beings; and, considering that power which subdueth all things unto itself, that can resume the scattered atoms, or identify out of any thing, conceive it superfluous to expect a resurrection out of relicks: but the soul subsisting, other matter, clothed with due accidents, may solve the individuality. Yet the saints, we observe, arose from graves and monuments about the holy city. Some think the ancient patriarchs so earnestly desired to lay their bones in Canaan, as hoping to make a part of that resurrection; and, though thirty miles from Mount Calvary, at least to lie in that region which should produce the first fruits of the dead. And if, according to learned conjecture, the bodies of men shall rise where their greatest relicks remain, many are not like to err in the topography of their resurrection, though their bones or bodies be after translated by angels into the field of Ezekiel's vision, or as some will order it, into the valley of judgment, or Jehosaphat.*

CHAPTER IV.

CHRISTIANS have handsomely glossed the deformity of death by careful consideration of the body, and civil rites which take off brutal terminations: and though they conceived all reparable by a resurrection, cast not off all care of interment. And since the ashes of sacrifices burnt upon the altar of God were carefully carried out by the priests, and deposed in a clean field; since they acknowledged their bodies to be the lodging of Christ, and temples of the Holy Ghost, they devolved not all upon the sufficiency of soul-existence; and therefore with long services and full solemnities, concluded their last exequies, wherein to all distinctions the Greek devotion seems most pathetically ceremonious.†

Christian invention hath chiefly driven at rites, which

---

* *Tirin.* in Ezek.
† *Rituale Græcum, operâ J. Goar, in officio exequiarum.*

speak hopes of another life, and hints of a resurrection.
And if the ancient Gentiles held not the immortality of
their better part, and some subsistence after death, in several
rites, customs, actions, and expressions, they contradicted
their own opinions : wherein Democritus went high, even
to the thought of a resurrection, as scoffingly recorded by
Pliny.* What can be more express than the expression of
Phocylides ?† Or who would expect from Lucretius ‡ a
sentence of Ecclesiastes ? Before Plato could speak, the
soul had wings in Homer, which fell not, but flew out of
the body into the mansions of the dead ; who also observed
that handsome distinction of Demas and Soma, for the body
conjoined to the soul, and body separated from it.   Lucian
spoke much truth in jest, when he said that part of Hercules
which proceeded from Alcmena perished, that from Jupiter
remained immortal.   Thus Socrates§ was content that his
friends should bury his body, so they would not think they
buried Socrates ; and, regarding only his immortal part,
was indifferent to be burnt or buried. From such considerations, Diogenes might contemn sepulture, and, being satisfied that the soul could not perish, grow careless of corporal
interment.   The Stoicks, who thought the souls of wise
men had their habitation about the moon, might make slight
account of subterraneous deposition ; whereas the Pytha-
goreans and transcorporating philosophers, who were to be
often buried, held great care of their interment.   And the
Platonicks rejected not a due care of the grave, though
they put their ashes to unreasonable expectations, in their
tedious term of return and long set revolution.

Men have lost their reason in nothing so much as their
religion, wherein stones and clouts make martyrs ; and,
since the religion of one seems madness unto another, to
afford an account or rational of old rites requires no rigid
reader.   That they kindled the pyre aversely, or turning

---

* *Similis * * * * reviviscendi promissa Democrito vanitas, qui non
revixit ipse.   Quæ (malum) ista dementia est, iterari vitam morte ?*—Plin.
l. vii. c. 58.

† Καὶ τάχα δ' ἐκ γαίης ἐλπίζομεν ἐς φάος ἐλθεῖν λεῖψαν ἀποιχο-
μένων, *et deinceps.*

‡ *Cedit enim retro de terrâ quod fuit ante in terram, &c.*—*Lucret.*

§ *Plato in Phæd.*

their face from it, was an handsome symbol of unwilling ministration. That they washed their bones with wine and milk; that the mother wrapped them in linen, and dried them in her bosom, the first fostering part and place of their nourishment; that they opened their eyes towards heaven before they kindled the fire, as the place of their hopes or original, were no improper ceremonies. Their last valediction,* thrice uttered by the attendants, was also very·solemn, and somewhat answered by Christians, who thought it too little, if they threw not the earth thrice upon the interred body. That, in strewing their tombs, the Romans affected the rose; the Greeks amaranthus and myrtle: that the funeral pyre consisted of sweet fuel, cypress, fir, larix, yew, and trees perpetually verdant, lay silent expressions of their surviving hopes. Wherein Christians, who deck their coffins with bays, have found a more· elegant emblem; for that it, seeming dead, will restore itself from the root, and its dry and exsuccous leaves resume their verdure again; which, if we mistake not, we have also observed in furze. Whether the planting of yew in churchyards hold not its original from ancient funeral rites, or as an emblem of resurrection, from its perpetual verdure, may also admit conjecture.

They made use of musick to excite or quiet the affections of their friends, according to different harmonies. But the secret and symbolical hint was the harmonical nature of the soul; which, delivered from the body, went again to enjoy the primitive harmony of heaven, from whence it first descended; which, according to its progress traced by antiquity, came down by Cancer, and ascended by Capricornus.

They burnt not children before their teeth appeared, as apprehending their bodies too tender a morsel for fire, and that their gristly bones would scarce leave separable relicks after the pyral combustion. That they kindled not fire in their houses for some days after was a strict memorial of the late afflicting fire. And mourning without hope, they had an happy fraud against excessive lamentation, by a common opinion that deep sorrows disturb their ghosts.†

* *Vale, vale, nos te ordine quo natura permittet sequamur.*
† *Tu manes ne lædemeos.*

That they buried their dead on their backs, or in a supine position, seems agreeable unto profound sleep, and common posture of dying; contrary to the most natural way of birth; nor unlike our pendulous posture, in the doubtful state of the womb.   Diogenes was singular, who preferred a prone situation in the grave; and some Christians* like neither, who decline the figure of rest, and make choice of an erect posture.

That they carried them out of the world with their feet forward, not inconsonant unto reason, as contrary unto the native posture of man, and his production first into it; and also agreeable unto their opinions, while they bid adieu unto the world, not to look again upon it; whereas Mahometans who think to return to a delightful life again, are carried forth with their heads forward, and looking toward their houses.

They closed their eyes, as parts which first die, or first discover the sad effects of death.   But their iterated clamations to excitate their dying or dead friends, or revoke them unto life again, was a vanity of affection; as not presumably ignorant of the critical tests of death, by apposition of feathers, glasses, and reflection of figures, which dead eyes represent not: which, however not strictly verifiable in fresh and warm *cadavers,* could hardly elude the test, in corpses of four or five days.†

That they sucked in the last breath of their expiring friends, was surely a practice of no medical institution, but a loose opinion that the soul passed out that way, and a fondness of affection, from some Pythagorical foundation,‡ that the spirit of one body passed into another, which they wished might be their own.

That they poured oil upon the pyre, was a tolerable practice, while the intention rested in facilitating the accension. But to place good omens in the quick and speedy burning, to sacrifice unto the winds for a dispatch in this office, was a low form of superstition.

The archimime, or jester, attending the funeral train, and imitating the speeches, gesture, and manners of the deceased,

---

* Russians, &c.   † At least by some difference from living eyes.
‡ *Francesco Perucci, Pompe funebri.*

was too light for such solemnities, contradicting their funeral orations and doleful rites of the grave.

That they buried a piece of money with them as a fee of the Elysian ferryman, was a practice full of folly. But the ancient custom of placing coins in considerable urns, and the present practice of burying medals in the noble foundations of Europe, are laudable ways of historical discoveries, in actions, persons, chronologies; and posterity will applaud them.

We examine not the old laws of sepulture, exempting certain persons from burial or burning. But hereby we apprehend that these were not the bones of persons planet-struck or burnt with fire from heaven; no relicks of traitors to their country, self-killers, or sacrilegious malefactors; persons in old apprehension unworthy of the earth; condemned unto the Tartarus of hell, and bottomless pit of Pluto, from whence there was no redemption.

Nor were only many customs questionable in order to their obsequies, but also sundry practices, fictions, and conceptions, discordant or obscure, of their state and future beings. Whether unto eight or ten bodies of men to add one of a woman, as being more inflammable, and unctuously constituted for the better pyral combustion, were any rational practice; or whether the complaint of Periander's wife be tolerable, that wanting her funeral burning, she suffered intolerable cold in hell, according to the constitution of the infernal house of Pluto, wherein cold makes a great part of their tortures; it cannot pass without some question.

Why the female ghosts appear unto Ulysses, before the heroes and masculine spirits,—why the Psyche or soul of Tiresias is of the masculine gender,* who, being blind on earth, sees more than all the rest in hell; why the funeral suppers consisted of eggs, beans, smallage, and lettuce, since the dead are made to eat asphodels † about the Elysian meadows,—why, since there is no sacrifice acceptable, nor any propitiation for the covenant of the grave, men set up the deity of Morta, and fruitlessly adored divinities without ears, it cannot escape some doubt.

* In Homer :—Ψυχὴ Θηβαίου Τειρεσίαο σκῆπτρον ἔχων.
† In Lucian.

The dead seem all alive in the human Hades of Homer, yet cannot well speak, prophesy, or know the living, except they drink blood, wherein is the life of man. And therefore the souls of Penelope's paramours, conducted by Mercury, chirped like bats, and those which followed Hercules, made a noise but like a flock of birds.

The departed spirits know things past and to come; yet are ignorant of things present. Agamemnon foretells what should happen unto Ulysses; yet ignorantly enquires what is become of his own son. The ghosts are afraid of swords in Homer; yet Sibylla tells Æneas in Virgil, the thin habit of spirits was beyond the force of weapons. The spirits put off their malice with their bodies, and Cæsar and Pompey accord in Latin hell; yet Ajax, in Homer, endures not a conference with Ulysses : and Deiphobus appears all mangled in Virgil's ghosts, yet we meet with perfect shadows among the wounded ghosts of Homer.

Since Charon in Lucian applauds his condition among the dead, whether it be handsomely said of Achilles, that living contemner of death, that he had rather be a ploughman's servant, than emperor of the dead ? How Hercules his soul is in hell, and yet in heaven; and Julius his soul in a star, yet seen by Æneas in hell?—except the ghosts were but images and shadows of the soul, received in higher mansions, according to the ancient division of body, soul, and image, or *simulachrum* of them both. The particulars of future beings must needs be dark unto ancient theories, which Christian philosophy yet determines but in a cloud of opinions. A dialogue between two infants in the womb concerning the state of this world,[9] might handsomely illustrate our ignorance of the next, whereof methinks we yet discourse in Plato's den, and are but embryo philosophers.

Pythagoras escapes in the fabulous hell of Dante,* among

* *Del Inferno*, cant. 4.

[9] *A dialogue, &c.*] In one of Sir Thomas's Common-place Books occurs this sentence, apparently as a memorandum to write such a dialogue. And from "*A Catalogue of MSS. written by, and in the possession of, Sir Thomas Browne, M.D., late of Norwich, and of his son Dr. Edward Browne, late President of the College of Physicians, London,*" in the Bodleian Library (*MSS. Rawlinson*, 390, xi.), it appears that he actually did write such a Dialogue. I have searched, hitherto in vain, for it, as I have elsewhere lamented.

that swarm of philosophers, wherein, whilst we meet with Plato and Socrates, Cato is to be found in no lower place than purgatory.   Among all the set, Epicurus is most con-siderable, whom men make honest without an Elysium, who contemned life without encouragement of immortality, and making nothing after death, yet made nothing of the king of terrors.

Were the happiness of the next world as closely appre-hended as the felicities of this, it were a martyrdom to live ; and unto such as consider none hereafter, it must be more than death to die, which makes us amazed at those audacities that durst be nothing and return into their chaos again. Certainly such spirits as could contemn death, when they expected no better being after, would have scorned to live, had they known any.   And therefore we applaud not the judgment of Machiavel, that Christianity makes men cowards, or that with the confidence of but half-dying, the despised virtues of patience and humility have abased the spirits of men, which Pagan principles exalted; but rather regulated the wildness of audacities, in the attempts, grounds, and eternal sequels of death; wherein men of the boldest spirits are often prodigiously temerarious.   Nor can we extenuate the valour of ancient martyrs, who contemned death in the uncomfortable scene of their lives, and in their decrepit martyrdoms did probably lose not many months of their days, or parted with life when it was scarce worth the living.   For (beside that long time past holds no consideration unto a slender time to come) they had no small disadvantage from the constitution of old age, which naturally makes men fear-ful, and complexionally superannuated from the bold and courageous thoughts of youth and fervent years.   But the contempt of death from corporal animosity, promoteth not our felicity.   They may sit in the orchestra, and noblest seats of heaven, who have held up shaking hands in the fire, and humanly contended for glory.

Meanwhile Epicurus lies deep in Dante's hell, wherein we meet with tombs enclosing souls which denied their immortalities.   But whether the virtuous heathen, who lived better than he spake, or erring in the principles of himself, yet lived above philosophers of more specious maxims, lie so deep as he is placed, at least so low as not to rise against Christians, who believing or knowing that truth, have lastingly denied it in their practice and conversation—were a query too sad to insist on.

But all or most apprehensions rested in opinions of some future being, which, ignorantly or coldly believed, begat those perverted conceptions, ceremonies, sayings, which Christians pity or laugh at. Happy are they which live not in that disadvantage of time, when men could say little for futurity, but from reason: whereby the noblest minds fell often upon doubtful deaths, and melancholy dissolutions. With these hopes, Socrates warmed his doubtful spirits against that cold potion; and Cato, before he durst give the fatal stroke, spent part of the night in reading the Immortality of Plato, thereby confirming his wavering hand unto the animosity of that attempt.

It is the heaviest stone that melancholy can throw at a man, to tell him he is at the end of his nature; or that there is no further state to come, unto which this seems progressional, and otherwise made in vain. Without this accomplishment, the natural expectation and desire of such a state, were but a fallacy in nature; unsatisfied considerators would quarrel the justice of their constitutions, and rest content that Adam had fallen lower; whereby, by knowing no other original, and deeper ignorance of themselves, they might have enjoyed the happiness of inferior creatures, who in tranquillity possess their constitutions, as having not the apprehension to deplore their own natures, and, being framed below the circumference of these hopes, or cognition of better being, the wisdom of God hath necessitated their contentment: but the superior ingredient and obscured part of ourselves, whereto all present felicities afford no resting contentment, will be able at last to tell us, we are more than our present selves, and evacuate such hopes in the fruition of their own accomplishments.

CHAPTER V.

Now since these dead bones have already out-lasted the living ones of Methuselah, and in a yard under ground, and thin walls of clay, out-worn all the strong and specious buildings above it; and quietly rested under the drums and tramplings of three conquests: what prince can promise such diuturnity unto his relicks, or might not gladly say,

Sic ego componi versus in ossa velim ? *

Time, which antiquates antiquities, and hath an art to make dust of all things, hath yet spared these minor monuments.

In vain we hope to be known by open and visible conservatories, when to be unknown was the means of their continuation, and obscurity their protection. If they died by violent hands, and were thrust into their urns, these bones become considerable, and some old philosophers would honour them,† whose souls they conceived most pure, which were thus snatched from their bodies, and to retain a stronger propension unto them; whereas they weariedly left a languishing corpse, and with faint desires of re-union. If they fell by long and aged decay, yet wrapt up in the bundle of time, they fall into indistinction, and make but one blot with infants. If we begin to die when we live, and long life be but a prolongation of death, our life is a sad composition; we live with death, and die not in a moment. How many pulses made up the life of Methuselah, were work for Archimedes: common counters sum up the life of Moses his man.‡ Our days become considerable, like petty sums, by minute accumulations; where numerous fractions make up but small round numbers; and our days of a span long, make not one little finger.§

If the nearness of our last necessity brought a nearer conformity into it, there were a happiness in hoary hairs, and no calamity in half-senses. But the long habit of living indisposeth us for dying; when avarice makes us the sport of death, when even David grew politickly cruel, and

---

* *Tibullus.*

† *Oracula Chaldaica cum scholiis Pselli et Phethonis.* Βίη λιπόντων σῶμα ψυχαὶ καθαρώταται. *Vi corpus relinquentium animæ purissimæ.*

‡ In the Psalm of Moses.

§ According to the ancient arithmetick of the hand, wherein the little finger of the right hand contracted, signified an hundred.—*Pierius in Hieroglyph.*

Solomon could hardly be said to be the wisest of men.
But many are too early old, and before the date of age.
Adversity stretcheth our days, misery makes Alcmena's
nights,* and time hath no wings unto it. But the most
tedious being is that which can unwish itself, content to be
nothing, or never to have been, which was beyond the mal-
content of Job, who cursed not the day of his life, but his
nativity; content to have so far been, as to have a title to
future being, although he had lived here but in an hidden
state of life, and as it were an abortion.

What song the Syrens sang, or what name Achilles
assumed when he hid himself among women, though puzzling questions,† are not beyond all conjecture. What time
the persons of these ossuaries entered the famous nations
of the dead,‡ and slept with princes and counsellors, might
admit a wide solution. But who were the proprietaries of
these bones, or what bodies these ashes made up, were a
question above antiquarism; not to be resolved by man, nor
easily perhaps by spirits, except we consult the provincial
guardians, or tutelary observators. Had they made as good
provision for their names, as they have done for their
relicks, they had not so grossly erred in the art of perpe-
tuation. But to subsist in bones, and be but pyramidally
extant, is a fallacy in duration. Vain ashes which in the
oblivion of names, persons, times, and sexes, have found
unto themselves a fruitless continuation, and only arise
unto late posterity, as emblems of mortal vanities, antidotes
against pride, vain-glory, and madding vices. Pagan vain-
glories which thought the world might last for ever, had
encouragement for ambition; and, finding no *atropos* unto
the immortality of their names, were never dampt with the
necessity of oblivion. Even old ambitions had the advantage of ours, in the attempts of their vain-glories, who
acting early, and before the probable meridian of time, have
by this time found great accomplishment of their designs,
whereby the ancient heroes have already out-lasted their

* One night as long as three.
† The puzzling questions of Tiberius unto grammarians.—*Marcel.
Donatus in Suet.*
‡ Κλυτὰ ἔθνεα νεκρῶν.—*Hom. Job.*

monuments, and mechanical preservations. But in this latter scene of time, we cannot expect such mummies unto our memories, when ambition may fear the prophecy of Elias,* and Charles the Fifth can never hope to live within two Methuselahs of Hector.†

And therefore, restless inquietude for the diuturnity of our memories unto present considerations seems a vanity almost out of date, and superannuated piece of folly. We cannot hope to live so long in our names, as some have done in their persons. One face of Janus holds no proportion unto the other. 'Tis too late to be ambitious. The great mutations of the world are acted, or time may b too short for our designs. To extend our memories by monuments, whose death we daily pray for, and whose duration we cannot hope, without injury to our expectations in the advent of the last day, were a contradiction to our beliefs. We whose generations are ordained in this setting part of time, are providentially taken off from such imaginations; and, being necessitated to eye the remaining particle of futurity, are naturally constituted unto thoughts of the next world, and cannot excusably decline the consideration of that duration, which maketh pyramids pillars of snow, and all that's past a moment.

Circles and right lines limit and close all bodies, and the mortal right-lined circle ‡ must conclude and shut up all. There is no antidote against the opium of time, which temporally considereth all things : our fathers find their graves in our short memories, and sadly tell us how we may be buried in our survivors. Grave-stones tell truth scarce forty years.§ Generations pass while some trees stand, and old families last not three oaks. To be read by bare inscriptions like many in Gruter,‖ to hope for eternity by enigmatical epithets or first letters of our names, to be studied by antiquaries, who we were, and have new names given us like

---

* That the world may last but six thousand years.

† Hector's fame lasting above two lives of Methuselah, before that famous prince was extant.

‡ The character of death.

§ Old ones being taken up, and other bodies laid under them.

‖ *Gruteri Inscriptiones Antiquæ.*

many of the mummies,* are cold consolations unto the students of perpetuity, even by everlasting languages.

To be content that times to come should only know there was such a man, not caring whether they knew more of him, was a frigid ambition in Cardan ;† disparaging his horoscopal inclination and judgment of himself. Who cares to subsist like Hippocrates's patients, or Achilles's horses in Homer, under naked nominations, without deserts and noble acts, which are the balsam of our memories, the *entelechia* and soul of our subsistences ? To be nameless in worthy deeds, exceeds an infamous history. The Canaanitish woman lives more happily without a name, than Herodias with one. And who had not rather have been the good thief, than Pilate ?

But the iniquity of oblivion blindly scattereth her poppy, and deals with the memory of men without distinction to merit of perpetuity. Who can but pity the founder of the pyramids ? Herostratus lives that burnt the temple of Diana, he is almost lost that built it. Time hath spared the epitaph of Adrian's horse, confounded that of himself. In vain we compute our felicities by the advantage of our good names, since bad have equal durations, and Thersites is like to live as long as Agamemnon. Who knows whether the best of men be known, or whether there be not more remarkable persons forgot, than any that stand remembered in the known account of time ? Without the favour of the everlasting register, the first man had been as unknown as the last, and Methuselah's long life had been his only chronicle.

Oblivion is not to be hired. The greater part must be content to be as though they had not been, to be found in the register of God, not in the record of man. Twenty-seven names make up the first story before the flood, and the recorded names ever since contain not one living century. The number of the dead long exceedeth all that shall live. The night of time far surpasseth the day, and who knows when was the equinox ? Every hour adds unto that current arithmetick, which scarce stands one moment. And since

* Which men show in several countries, giving them what names they please ; and unto some the names of the old Egyptian kings, out of Herodotus.

† *Cuperem notum esse quod sim, non opto ut sciatur qualis sim.—Card. in vita propria.*

death must be the _Lucina_ of life, and even Pagans* could
doubt, whether thus to live were to die; since our longest
sun sets at right descensions, and makes but winter arches,
and therefore it cannot be long before we lie down in darkness, and have our light in ashes;† since the brother of
death¹ daily haunts us with dying mementos, and time that
grows old in itself, bids us hope no long duration;—diuturnity is a dream and folly of expectation.²

. Darkness and light divide the course of time, and oblivion
shares with memory a great part even of our living beings;
we slightly remember our felicities, and the smartest strokes
of affliction leave but short smart upon us. Sense endureth
no extremities, and sorrows destroy us or themselves. To
weep into stones are fables. Afflictions induce callosities;
miseries are slippery, or fall like snow upon us, which notwithstanding is no unhappy stupidity. To be ignorant of
evils to come, and forgetful of evils past, is a merciful provision in nature, whereby we digest the mixture of our few
and evil days, and, our delivered senses not relapsing into
cutting remembrances, our sorrows are not kept raw by the
edge of repetitions. A great part of antiquity contented

* Euripides.
† According to the custom of the _Jews_, who place a lighted wax-
candle in a pot of ashes by the corpse.—_Leo._

¹ _the brother of death._] That is, _sleep._ See a Fragment _On Dreams,_
post.
² _Diuturnity, &c._] Here may properly be noticed a similar passage
which I find in _MS. Sloan._ 1848, fol. 194.
"Large are the treasures of oblivion, and heaps of things in a state
next to nothing almost numberless; much more is buried in silence
than recorded, and the largest volumes are but epitomes of what hath
been. The account of time began with night, and darkness still attendeth
it. Some things never come to light; many have been delivered; but
more hath been swallowed in obscurity and the caverns of oblivion.
How much is as it were _in vacuo,_ and will never be cleared up, of those
long living times when men could scarce remember themselves young;
and men seem to us not ancient but antiquities, when they [lived] longer
in their lives than we can now hope to do in our memories; when men
feared not apoplexies and palsies after seven or eight hundred years; when
living was so lasting that homicide might admit of distinctive qualifications from the age of the person, and it might seem a lesser injury to
kill a man at eight hundred than at forty, and when life was so well worth
the living that few or none would kill themselves."

their hopes of subsistency with a transmigration of their souls,—a good way to continue their memories, while having the advantage of plural successions, they could not but act something remarkable in such variety of beings, and enjoying the fame of their passed selves, make accumulation of glory unto their last durations. Others, rather than be lost in the uncomfortable night of nothing, were content to recede into the common being, and make one particle of the public soul of all things, which was no more than to return into their unknown and divine original again. Egyptian ingenuity was more unsatisfied, contriving their bodies in sweet consistencies, to attend the return of their souls. But all was vanity,* feeding the wind, and folly. The Egyptian mummies, which Cambyses or time hath spared, avarice now consumeth. Mummy is become merchandise, Mizraim cures wounds, and Pharaoh is sold for balsams.

In vain do individuals hope for immortality, or any patent from oblivion, in preservations below the moon; men have been deceived even in their flatteries, above the sun, and studied conceits to perpetuate their names in heaven. The various cosmography of that part hath already varied the names of contrived constellations; Nimrod is lost in Orion, and Osyris in the Dog-star. While we look for incorruption in the heavens, we find they are but like the earth;—durable in their main bodies, alterable in their parts; whereof, beside comets and new stars, perspectives begin to tell tales, and the spots that wander about the sun, with Phaeton's favour, would make clear conviction.

There is nothing strictly immortal, but immortality. Whatever hath no beginning, may be confident of no end;—which is the peculiar of that necessary essence that cannot destroy itself;—and the highest strain of omnipotency, to be so powerfully constituted as not to suffer even from the power of itself: all others have a dependent being and within the reach of destruction. But the sufficiency of Christian immortality frustrates all earthly glory, and the quality of either state after death, makes a folly of posthumous memory. God who can only destroy our souls, and hath assured our

---

* Omnia vanitas et pastio venti, νομὴ ἀνέμου καὶ βόσκησις, ut olim Aquila et Symmachus. v. Drus. Eccles.

resurrection, either of our bodies or names hath directly promised no duration. Wherein there is so much of chance,
that the boldest expectants have found unhappy frustration;
and to hold long subsistence, seems but a scape in oblivion.
But man is a noble animal, splendid in ashes, and pompous
in the grave, solemnizing nativities and deaths with equal
lustre, nor omitting ceremonies of bravery in the infamy of
his nature.[3]

Life is a pure flame, and we live by an invisible sun within
us. A small fire sufficeth for life, great flames seemed too
little after death, while men vainly affected precious pyres,
and to burn like Sardanapalus; but the wisdom of funeral
laws found the folly of prodigal blazes, and reduced undoing
fires unto the rule of sober obsequies, wherein few could
be so mean as not to provide wood, pitch, a mourner, and
an urn.*

Five languages secured not the epitaph of Gordianus.†
The man of God lives longer without a tomb than any by
one, invisibly interred by angels, and adjudged to obscurity,
though not without some marks directing human discovery.
Enoch and Elias, without either tomb or burial, in an
anomalous state of being, are the great examples of perpetuity, in their long and living memory, in strict account
being still on this side death, and having a late part yet to
act upon this stage of earth. If in the decretory term of
the world we shall not all die but be changed, according to
received translation, the last day will make but few graves;
at least quick resurrections will anticipate lasting sepultures.
Some graves will be opened before they be quite closed, and

---

* According to the epitaph of Rufus and Beronica, in Gruterus.

nec ex
Eorum bonis plus inventum est, quam
Quod sufficeret ad emendam pyram
Et picem quibus corpora cremarentur,
Et præfica conducta, et olla empta.

† In Greek, Latin, Hebrew, Egyptian, Arabic; defaced by Lici-
nius the emperor.

[3] *Man is a noble animal, &c.*] Southey quotes this striking passage
in the opening of his *Colloquies,*—but in a note he conjectures that
Browne wrote *infimy* instead of *infamy.*

Lazarus be no wonder. When many that feared to die, shall groan that they can die but once, the dismal state is the second and living death, when life puts despair on the damned; when men shall wish the coverings of mountains, not of monuments, and annihilations shall be courted.

While some have studied monuments, others have studiously declined them,[4] and some have been so vainly boisterous, that they durst not acknowledge their graves; wherein Alaricus* seems most subtle, who had a river turned to hide his bones at the bottom. Even Sylla, that thought himself safe in his urn, could not prevent revenging tongues, and stones thrown at his monument. Happy are they whom privacy makes innocent, who deal so with men in this world, that they are not afraid to meet them in the next; who, when they die, make no commotion among the dead, and are not touched with that poetical taunt of Isaiah.†

Pyramids, arches, obelisks, were but the irregularities of vain-glory, and wild enormities of ancient magnanimity. But the most magnanimous resolution rests in the Christian religion, which trampleth upon pride, and sits on the neck of ambition, humbly pursuing that infallible perpetuity, unto which all others must diminish their diameters, and be poorly seen in angles of contingency.‡

Pious spirits who passe their days in raptures of futurity, made little more of thisdworld, than the world that was before it, while they lay obscure in the chaos of pre-ordination, and night of their fore-beings. And if any have been so happy as truly to understand Christian annihilation, ecstasies, exolution, liquefaction, transformation, the kiss of the spouse, gustation of God, and ingression into the divine shadow, they have already had an handsome anticipation of

---

* *Jornandes de rebus Geticis.*
† Isa. xiv. 16, &c.   ‡ *Angulus contingentiæ,* the least of angles.

[4] *others have studiously declined them.*] In a work entitled ΠΕΡΙΑΜΜΑ ΕΝΔΗΜΙΟΝ, or *Vulgar Errours in Practice censured,* is a chapter on Decent Sepulture, the greater part of which is devoted to a censure against "the affectation of epitaphs," which, the author observes, are of Pagan origin, and are not even once mentioned in the whole book of God.

heaven; the glory of the world is surely over, and the earth in ashes unto them.

To subsist in lasting monuments, to live in their productions, to exist in their names and predicament of chimeras, was large satisfaction unto old expectations, and made one part of their Elysiums. But all this is nothing in the metaphysicks of true belief. To live indeed, is to be again ourselves, which being not only an hope, but an evidence in noble believers, 'tis all one to lie in St. Innocent's* churchyard, as in the sands of Egypt. Ready to be anything, in the ecstasy of being ever, and as content with six foot as the *moles* of Adrianus.†

> *tabésne cadavera solvat,*
> *An rogus, haud refert.*—LUCAN.

---

* In Paris, where bodies soon consume.

† A stately mausoleum or sepulchral pile, built by Adrianus in Rome, where now standeth the castle of St. Angelo.

END OF HYDRIOTAPHIA.

BRAMPTON URNS.

PARTICULARS

OF SOME URNS FOUND IN BRAMPTON FIELD, FEBRUARY 1667-8.

THIRD EDITION.

CORRECTED FROM THREE MS. COPIES IN THE BRITISH MUSEUM AND
THE BODLEIAN LIBRARY.

ORIGINALLY PUBLISHED IN

1712.

"*A Roman Urn drawn with a coal taken out of it, and found
among the burnt bones, and is now in the possession of Dr. Hans Sloane,
to whom this plate is most humbly inscribed.*"—FIRST EDITION.

BRAMPTON URNS.

I THOUGHT I had taken leave of urns, when I had some years past given a short account of those found at Walsingham;* but a new discovery being made, I readily obey your commands in a brief description thereof.

In a large arable field, lying between Buxton and Brampton, but belonging to Brampton, and not much more than a furlong from Oxnead-park, divers urns were found. A part of the field being designed to be inclosed, the workmen digged a ditch from north to south, and another from east to west, in both which they fell upon divers urns; but earnestly and carelessly digging, they broke all they met with, and finding nothing but ashes and burnt bones, they scattered what they found. Upon notice given unto me, I went myself to observe the same, and to have obtained a whole one; and though I met with two in the side of the ditch, and used all care I could with the workmen, yet they were broken. Some advantage there was from the wet season alone that day, the earth not readily falling from about them, as in the summer. When some were digging the north and south ditch, and others at a good distance the east and west one, those at this latter upon every stroke which was made at the other ditch, heard a hollow sound near to them, as though the ground had been arched, vaulted, or hollow, about them. It is very probable there are very many urns about this place, for they were found in both ditches, which were one hundred yards from each other; and this very sounding of the earth, which might be

* See *Hydriotaphia, Urn Burial: or, a Discourse of the Sepulchral Urns lately found in Norfolk.* 8vo. London, printed 1658.

caused by hollow vessels in the earth, might make the same
probable. There was nothing in them but fragments of
burnt bones; not any such implements and extraneous substances as I found in the Walsingham urns: some pieces of
skulls and teeth were easily discernible. Some were very
large, some small, some had coverings, most none.

Of these pots none were found above three-quarters of
a yard in the ground; whereby it appeareth, that in all this
time the earth hath little varied its surface, though this
ground hath been ploughed to the utmost memory of man.
Whereby it may be also conjectured, that this hath never
been a wood-land, as some conceive all this open part to
have been; for in such places they made no common burying-places in old time, except for some special persons in
groves: and likewise that there hath been an ancient habitation about these parts; for at Buxton also, not a mile off,
urns have been found in my memory; but in their magnitude, figure, colour, posture, &c., there was no small variety;
some were large and capacious, able to contain above two
gallons, some of a middle, others of a smaller size.
The great ones probably belonging to greater persons, or
might be family urns, fit to receive the ashes successively
of their kindred and relations, and therefore, of these, some
had coverings of the same matter, either fitted to them, or
a thin flat stone, like a grey slate, laid over them; and
therefore also great ones were but thinly found, but others
in good number. Some were of large wide mouths, and
bellies proportionable, with short necks, and bottoms of
three inches diameter, and near an inch thick; some small,
with necks like jugs, and about that bigness; the mouths
of some few were not round, but after the figure of a circle
compressed, not ordinarily to be imitated; though some had
small, yet none had pointed bottoms, according to the figures
of those which are to be seen in Roma Sotterranea, Viginerus,
or Mascardus.

In the colours also there was great variety; some were
whitish, some blackish, and inclining to a blue, others yellowish, or dark red, arguing the variety of their materials.[1]

---

[1] *arguing the variety of their materials.*] More probably, perhaps,
their being more or less thoroughly burned.

'Some fragments, and especially bottoms of vessels, which seemed to be handsome neat pans, were also found of a fine coral-like red,' somewhat like Portugal vessels, as though they had been made out of some fine Bolary earth, and very smooth; but the like had been found in divers places, as Dr. Casaubon hath observed about the pots found at Newington, in Kent, and as other pieces do yet testify, which are to be found at Burrow Castle, an old Roman station, not far from Yarmouth.

Of the urns, those of the larger sort, such as had coverings, were found with their mouths placed upwards; but great numbers of the others were, as they informed me (and one I saw myself), placed with their mouths downward, which were probably such as were not to be opened again, or receive the ashes of any other person. Though some wondered at this position, yet I saw no inconveniency in it; for the earth being closely pressed, and especially in minor-mouthed pots, they stand in a posture as like to continue as the other, as being less subject to have the earth fall in, or the rain to soak into them. And the same posture has been observed in some found in other places, as Holingshead delivers of divers found in Anglesea.

Some had inscriptions, the greatest part none; those with inscriptions, were of the largest sort, which were upon the reverted verges thereof. The greatest part of those which I could obtain were somewhat obliterated : yet some of the letters to be made out : the letters were between lines, either single or double, and the letters of some few, after a fair Roman stroke, others more rudely and illegibly drawn, wherein there seemed no great variety; " NUON " being upon very many of them; only upon the inside of the bottom of a small red pan-like vessel, with a glaze, or varnish, like pots which come from Portugal, but finer, were legibly set down in embossed letters, *CRACUNA F.;* which might imply *Cracuna figulus*, or *Cracuna fecit*, the name of the manufactor; for inscriptions commonly signified the name of the person interred, the names of servants official to such provisions, or the name of the artificer, or manufactor of such vessels; all which are particularly exemplified by the learned Licetus,* where the same in-

* Vid. *Licet. de Lucernis.*

scription is often found, it is probably of the artificer, or where the name also is in the genitive case, as he also observeth.

Out of one was brought unto me a silver denarius, with the head of Diva Faustina on the obverse side, and with this inscription, *Diva Augusta Faustina*, and on the reverse the figures of the emperor and empress joining their right hands, with this inscription, *Concordia*; the same is to be seen in Augustino, and must be coined after the death of Faustina (who lived three years wife unto Antoninus Pius), from the title of Diva, which was not given them before their deification. I also received from some men and women then present, coins of Posthumus and Tetricus, two of the thirty tyrants in the reign of Galienus, which being of much later date, begat an inference that burning of the dead and urn-burial lasted longer, at least in this country, than is commonly supposed. Good authors conceive that this custom ended with the reign of the Antonini, whereof the last was Antoninus Heliogabalus, yet these coins extend about fourscore years lower; and since the head of Tetricus is made with a radiated crown, it must be conceived to have been made after his death, and not before his consecration, which, as the learned Tristan conjectures, was most probably in the reign of the emperor Tacitus, and the coin not made, or at least not issued abroad, before the time of the emperor Probus, for Tacitus reigned but six months and a half, his brother Florianus but two months, unto whom Probus succeeding, reigned five years.

In the digging they brake divers glasses and finer vessels, which might contain such liquors as they often buried, in or by the urns; the pieces of glass were fine and clear, though thick; and a piece of one was finely streaked with smooth white streaks upon it. There were also found divers pieces of brass, of several figures; and one piece which seemed to be of bell-metal. And in one urn was found a nail two inches long; whether to declare the trade or occupation of the person is uncertain. But upon the monuments of smiths, in Gruter, we meet with the figures of hammers, pincers, and the like; and we find the figure of a cobler's awl on the tomb of one of that trade, which was in the custody of Berini, as Argulus hath set it down in his notes upon *Onuphrius, of the antiquities of Verona.*

Now, though urns have been often discovered in former ages, many think it strange there should be many still found, yet assuredly there may be great numbers still concealed. For,—though we should not reckon upon any who were thus buried before the time of the Romans (although that the Druids were thus buried it may be probable, and we read of the urn of Chindonactes, a Druid, found near Dijon in Burgundy, largely discoursed by Licetus), and though I say, we take not in any infant which was *minor igne rogi*, before seven months, or appearance of teeth, nor should account this practice of burning among the Britons higher than Vespasian, when it is said by Tacitus, that they conformed unto the manners and customs of the Romans, and so both nations might have one way of burial;—yet from his days, to the dates of these urns, were about two hundred years. And therefore if we fall so low as to conceive there were buried in this nation yearly but twenty thousand persons, the account of the buried persons would amount unto four millions, and consequently so great a number of urns dispersed through the land, as may still satisfy the curiosity of succeeding times, and arise unto all ages.

The bodies whose reliques these urns contained seemed thoroughly burned; for beside pieces of teeth, there were found few fragments of bones, but rather ashes in hard lumps and pieces of coals, which were often so fresh, that one sufficed to make a good draught of its urn, which still remaineth with me.

Some persons digging at a little distance from the urn places, in hopes to find something of value, after they had digged about three-quarters of a yard deep, fell upon an observable piece of work, whose description [hereupon followeth]. The work was square, about two yards and a quarter on each side. The wall, or outward part, a foot thick, in colour red, and looked like brick; but it was solid, without any mortar, or cement, or figured brick in it, but of an whole piece, so that it seemed to be framed and burnt in the same place where it was found. In this kind of brickwork were thirty-two holes, of about two inches and a half diameter, and two above a quarter of a circle in the east and west sides. Upon two of these holes on the east side, were placed two pots, with their mouths downward; putting in their arms they found the work hollow below, and the earth being cleared off, much water was found below them, to the quantity of a barrel, which was conceived to have been the rain-water which soaked in through the earth above them.

The upper part of the work being broke, and opened, they found a floor about two foot below, and then digging onward, three floors successively under one another, at the distance of a foot and half, the floors being of a slaty, not bricky substance; in these partitions some pots were found, but broke by the workmen, being necessitated to use hard blows for the breaking of the floors; and in the last partition but one, a large pot was found of a very narrow mouth, short ears, of the capacity of fourteen pints, which lay in an inclining posture, close by, and somewhat under a kind of arch in the solid wall, and by the great care of my worthy friend, Mr. William Marsham, who employed the workmen, was taken up whole, almost full of water, clean, and without smell, and insipid, which being poured out, there still remains in the pot a great lump of an heavy crusty substance. What work this was we must as yet reserve unto better conjecture. Meanwhile we find in Gruter that some monuments of the dead had divers holes successively to let in the ashes of their relations; but holes in such a great number to that intent, we have not anywhere met with.

About three months after, my noble and honoured friend, Sir Robert Paston, had the curiosity to open a piece of ground in his park at Oxnead, which adjoined unto the former field, where fragments of pots were found, and upon one the figure of a well-made face; and there was also found an unusual coin of the emperor Volusianus, having on the obverse the head of the emperor, with a radiated crown, and this inscription, *Imp. Cæs. C. Vib. Volusiano Aug.;* that is, *Imperatori Cæsari Caio Vibio Volusiano Augusto.* On the reverse an human figure, with the arms somewhat extended, and at the right foot an altar, with the inscription *Pietas.* This emperor was son unto Caius Vibius Tribonianus

Gallus, with whom he jointly reigned after the Decii, about the year 254; both he himself, and his father, were slain by the emperor Æmilianus. By the radiated crown this piece should be coined after his death and consecration, but in whose time it is not clear in history. But probably this ground had been opened and digged before, though out of the memory of man, for we found divers small pieces of pots, sheep's bones, sometimes an oyster-shell a yard deep in the earth.

END OF BRAMPTON URNS.

LETTER TO A FRIEND,

UPON OCCASION OF THE DEATH OF HIS INTIMATE FRIEND.

FIFTH EDITION.

———————

ORIGINALLY PUBLISHED IN

1690.

EDITOR'S PREFACE.

THE LETTER TO A FRIEND was printed, after the author's death, by his son, as a folio pamphlet, in 1690. The only copy I ever saw is in the library of the British Museum. It was reprinted, in the Posthumous Works, in 1712; and the latter portion of it (from page 48, *Posthumous Works*) was included in the Christian Morals, and for that reason is not here reprinted.

From a collation with a MS. copy in the British Museum, (MS. Sloan. 1862), several additional passages are given.

EDITOR'S PREFACE

LETTER TO A FRIEND.

GIVE me leave to wonder that news of this nature should have such heavy wings that you should hear so little concerning your dearest friend, and that I must make that unwilling repetition to tell you, *ad portam rigidos calces extendit*, that he is dead and buried, and by this time no puny among the mighty nations of the dead; for though he left this world not very many days past, yet every hour you know largely addeth unto that dark society; and considering the incessant mortality of mankind, you cannot conceive there dieth in the whole earth so few as a thousand an hour.

Although at this distance you had no early account or particular of his death, yet your affection may cease to wonder that you had not some secret sense or intimation thereof by dreams, thoughtful whisperings, mercurisms, airy nuncios or sympathetical insinuations, which many seem to have had at the death of their dearest friends: for since we find in that famous story, that spirits themselves were fain to tell their fellows at a distance that the great Antonio was dead, we have a sufficient excuse for our ignorance in such particulars, and must rest content with the common road, and Appian way of knowledge by information. Though the uncertainty of the end of this world hath confounded all human predictions; yet they who shall live to see the sun and moon darkened and the stars to fall from heaven, will hardly be deceived in the advent of the last day; and therefore strange it is, that the common fallacy of consumptive persons who feel not themselves dying, and therefore still hope to live, should also reach their friends in perfect health and judgment;—that you should be so little acquainted with Plautus's sick complexion, or that almost an Hippocratical face should not alarum you to higher fears, or rather despair, of his continuation in such an emaciated state, wherein medical predictions fail not, as sometimes in acute diseases, and wherein 'tis as dangerous to be sentenced by a physician as a judge.

Upon my first visit I was bold to tell them who had not let fall all hopes of his recovery, that in my sad opinion he was not like to behold a grasshopper, much less to pluck another fig; and in no long time after seemed to discover that odd mortal symptom in him not mentioned by Hippocrates, that is, to lose his own face, and look like some of his near relations; for he maintained not his proper countenance, but looked like his uncle, the lines of whose face lay deep and invisible in his healthful visage before: for as from our beginning we run through variety of looks, before we come to consistent and settled faces; so before our end, by sick and languishing alterations, we put on new visages: and in our retreat to earth, may fall upon such looks which from community of seminal originals were before latent in us.

He was fruitlessly put in hope of advantage by change of air, and imbibing the pure aerial nitre of these parts; and therefore, being so far spent, he quickly found Sardinia in Tivoli,[1] and the most healthful air of little effect, where death had set his broad arrow;[2] for he lived not unto the middle of May, and confirmed the observation of Hippocrates[3] of that mortal time of the year when the leaves of the fig-tree resemble a daw's claw. He is happily seated who lives in places whose air, earth, and water, promote not the infirmities of his weaker parts, or is early removed into regions that correct them. He that is tabidly inclined, were unwise to pass his days in Portugal: cholical persons will find little comfort in Austria or Vienna: he that is weak-legged must not be in love with Rome, nor an infirm

---

[1] *Tivoli.*] Cum mors venerit, in medio Tibure Sardinia est.

[2] *where death, &c.*] In the king's forests they set the figure of a broad arrow upon trees that are to be cut down.

[3] *observation of, &c.*] See *Hip. Epidem.*

head with Venice or Paris. Death hath not only particular
stars in heaven, but malevolent places on earth, which single
out our infirmities, and strike at our weaker parts ; in which
concern, passager and migrant birds have the great advantages ; who are naturally constituted for distant habitations,
whom no seas nor places limit, but in their appointed seasons
will visit us from Greenland and Mount Atlas, and as some
think, even from the Antipodes.[4]

Though we could not have his life, yet we missed not our
desires in his soft departure, which was scarce an expira-
tion ; and his end not unlike his beginning, when the salient
point scarce affords a sensible motion, and his departure so
like unto sleep, that he scarce needed the civil ceremony of
closing his eyes; contrary unto the common way, wherein
death draws up, sleep lets fall the eye-lids. With what
strife and pains we came into the world we know not; but
'tis commonly no easy matter to get out of it: yet if it
could be made out, that such who have easy nativities have
commonly hard deaths, and contrarily; his departure was
so easy, that we might justly suspect his birth was of
another nature, and that some Juno sat cross-legged at his
nativity.

Besides his soft death, the incurable state of his disease
might somewhat extenuate your sorrow, who know that
monsters but seldom happen, miracles more rarely in physic.[5]
Angelus Victorius gives a serious account of a consumptive,
hectical, phthisical woman, who was suddenly cured by the
intercession of Ignatius.[6] We read not of any in scripture
who in this case applied unto our Saviour, though some may
be contained in that large expression, that he went about
Galilee healing all manner of sickness and all manner of
diseases.[7] Amulets, spells, sigils, and incantations, practised
in other diseases, are seldom pretended in this; and we find
no sigil in the Archidoxis of Paracelsus to cure an extreme
consumption or marasmus, which, if other diseases fail, will

[4] *Antipodes.*] *Bellonius de Avibus.*
[5] *who know that monsters but seldom happen, miracles, &c.*] Monstra
contingunt in medicina. *Hippoc.*—"Strange and rare escapes there
happen sometimes in physick."
[6] *Angeli Victorii Consultationes.*
[7] Matt. iv. 25.

F 2

put a period unto long livers, and at last makes dust of all. And therefore the stoics could not but think that the fiery principle would wear out all the rest, and at last make an end of the world, which notwithstanding without such a lingering period the Creator may effect at his pleasure: and to make an end of all things on earth, and our planetical system of the world, he need but put out the sun.

I was not so curious to entitle the stars unto any concern of his death, yet could not but take notice that he died when the moon was in motion from the meridian; at which time an old Italian long ago would persuade me that the greatest part of men died: but herein I confess I could never satisfy my curiosity; although from the time of tides in places upon or near the sea, there may be considerable deductions; and Pliny[8] hath an odd and remarkable passage concerning the death of men and animals upon the recess or ebb of the sea. However, certain it is, he died in the dead and deep part of the night, when Nox might be most apprehensibly said to be the daughter of Chaos, the mother of sleep and death, according to old genealogy; and so went out of this world about that hour when our blessed Saviour entered it, and about what time many conceive he will return again unto it. Cardan hath a peculiar and no hard observation from a man's hand to know whether he was born in the day or night, which I confess holdeth in my own. And Scaliger to that purpose hath another from the tip of the ear:[9] most men are begotten in the night, animals in the day; but whether more persons have been born in the night or the day, were a curiosity undecidable, though more have perished by violent deaths in the day; yet in natural dissolutions both times may hold an indifferency, àt least but contingent inequality. The whole course of time runs out in the nativity and death of things; which whether they happen by succession or coincidence, are best computed by the natural not artificial day.

---

[8] *Pliny.*] Aristoteles nullum animal nisi æstu recedente expirare affirmat; observatum id multum in Gallico Oceano et duntaxat in homine compertum, lib. 2, cap. 101.

[9] *Scaliger, &c.*] Auris pars pendula lobus dicitur, non omnibus ea pars est auribus; non enim iis qui noctu nati sunt, sed qui interdiu, maxima ex parte.—*Com. in Aristot. de Animal.* lib. 1.

That Charles the Fifth was crowned upon the day of his nativity, it being in his own power so to order it, makes no singular animadversion; but that he should also take King Francis prisoner upon that day, was an unexpected coincidence, which made the same remarkable. Antipater, who had an anniversary feast every year upon his birth-day, needed no astrological revolution to know what day he should die on. When the fixed stars have made a revolution unto the points from whence they first set out, some of the ancients thought the world would have an end; which was a kind of dying upon the day of his nativity. Now the disease prevailing and swiftly advancing about the time of his nativity, some were of opinion that he would leave the world on the day he entered into it: but this being a lingering disease, and creeping softly on, nothing critical was found or expected, and he died not before fifteen days after. Nothing is more common with infants than to die on the day of their nativity, to behold the worldly hours, and but the fractions thereof; and even to perish before their nativity in the hidden world of the womb, and before their good angel is conceived to undertake them. But in persons who out-live many years, and when there are no less than three hundred and sixty-five days to determine their lives in every year; that the first day should make the last, that the tail of the snake should return into its mouth precisely at that time, and they should wind up upon the day of their nativity,[1] is indeed a remarkable coincidence, which, though astrology hath taken witty pains to salve, yet hath it been very wary in making predictions of it.

In this consumptive condition and remarkable extenuation, he came to be almost half himself, and left a great part behind him, which he carried not to the grave. And though that story of Duke John Ernestus Mansfield[2] be not so easily swallowed, that at his death his hart was found not to be so big as a nut; yet if the bones of a good skeleton weigh little more than twenty pounds, his nwards and flesh remaining could make no bouffage,[3] but a ight bit for the grave. I never more lively beheld the starved characters of

---

[1] *nativity.*] According to the Egyptian hieroglyphic.

[2] *John Ernestus Mansfield.*] Turkish history.

[3] *bouffage.*] Probably from *bouffée*, inflation.

Dante[4] in any living face; an *aruspex* might have read a lecture upon him without exenteration, his flesh being so consumed, that he might, in a manner, have discerned his bowels without opening of him: so that to be carried, *sextâ cervice*,[5] to the grave, was but a civil unnecessity; and the complements of the coffin might outweigh the subject of it.

Omnibonus Ferrarius[6] in mortal dysenteries of children looks for a spot behind the ear: in consumptive diseases some eye the complexion of moles; Cardan eagerly views the nails, some the lines of the hand, the thenar or muscle of the thumb; some are so curious as to observe the depth of the throat-pit, how the proportion varieth of the small of the legs unto the calf, or the compass of the neck unto the circumference of the head: but all these, with many more, were so drowned in a mortal visage, and last face of Hippocrates, that a weak physiognomist might say at first eye, this was a face of earth, and that *Morta*[7] had set her hard seal upon his temples, easily perceiving what *caricatura*[8] draughts death makes upon pined faces, and unto what an unknown degree a man may live backward.

Though the beard be only made a distinction of sex, and sign of masculine heat by *Ulmus*,[9] yet the precocity and early growth thereof in him, was not to be liked in reference unto long life. Lewis, that virtuous but unfortunate king of Hungary, who lost his life at the battle of Mohacz, was said to be born without a skin, to have bearded at fifteen, and to have shown some grey hairs about twenty; from whence the diviners conjectured that he would be spoiled of his kingdom, and have but a short life: but hairs make fallible predictions, and many temples early grey have outlived the psalmist's period.[1] Hairs which have most amused me have not been in the face or head, but on the back, and not in men but children, as I long ago observed in that endemial distemper of little children in Languedoc, called the

---

[4] *Dante.*] In the poet Dante's description.
[5] *sextâ cervice.*] i.e. "by six persons."
[6] *Omnibonus Ferrarius.*] *De Morbis Puerorum.*
[7] *Morta.*] Morta, the deity of death or fate.
[8] *caricatura.*] When men's faces are drawn with resemblance to some other anim s, the Italians call it, to be drawn *in caricatura.*
[9] *Ulmus.*] U nus de usu barbæ humanæ.
[1] *period.*] T life of a man is three-score and ten.

morgellons,[2] wherein they critically break out with harsh hairs on their backs, which takes off the unquiet symptoms of the disease, and delivers them from coughs and convulsions.[3]

The Egyptian mummies that I have seen, have had their mouths open, and somewhat gaping, which affordeth a good opportunity to view and observe their teeth, wherein 'tis not easy to find any wanting or decayed; and therefore in Egypt, where one man practised but one operation, or the diseases but of single parts, it must needs be a barren profession to confine unto that of drawing of teeth, and little better than to have been tooth-drawer unto King Pyrrhus,[4] who had but two in his head. How the banyans of India maintain the integrity of those parts, I find not particularly observed; who notwithstanding have an advantage of their preservation by abstaining from all flesh, and employing their teeth in such food unto which they may seem at first framed, from their figure and conformation: but sharp and corroding rheums had so early mouldered those rocks and hardest parts of his fabric, that a man might well conceive that his years were never like to double or twice tell over his teeth.[5] Corruption had dealt more severely with them than sepulchral fires and smart flames with those of burnt bodies of old; for in the burnt fragments of urns which I have enquired into, although I seem to find few incisors or shearers, yet the dog teeth and grinders do notably resist those fires.[6]

[2] *morgellons*.] See *Picotus de Rheumatismo*.

[3] *convulsions*.] The following occurs in *MS. Sloan*. 1862 :—"Though hairs afford but fallible conjectures, yet we cannot but take notice of them. They grow not equally on bodies after death: women's skulls afford moss as well as men's, and the best I have seen was upon a woman's skull, taken up and laid in a room after twenty-five years' burial. Though the skin be made the place of hairs, yet sometimes they are found on the heart and inward parts. The plica or gluey locks happen unto both sexes, and being cut off will come again: but they are wary of cutting off the same, for fear of head-ache and other diseases." —*MS. Sloan*, 1862.

[4] *King Pyrrhus*.] His upper and lower jaw being solid, and without distinct rows of teeth.

[5] *teeth*.] Twice tell over his teeth, never live to threescore years.

[6] *fires*.] In the *MS. Sloan*. 1862, occurs the following paragraph :— "Affection had so blinded some of his nearest relations, as to retain

In the years of his childhood he had languished under
the disease of his country, the rickets; after which, notwithstanding, many have become strong and active men;
but whether any have attained unto very great years, the
disease is scarce so old as to afford good observation.
Whether the children of the English plantations be subject
unto the same infirmity, may be worth the observing.
Whether lameness and halting do still increase among the
inhabitants of Rovigno in Istria, I know not; yet scarce
twenty years ago Monsieur du Loyr observed that a third part
of that people halted: but too certain it is, that the rickets
encreaseth among us; the small-pox grows more pernicious
than the great:·the king's purse knows that the king's evil
grows more common.   Quartan agues are become no strangers in Ireland; more common and mortal in England: and
though the ancients gave that disease[7] very good words, yet
now that bell makes no strange sound which rings out for
the effects thereof.[8]

some hope of a postliminious life, and that he might come to life again,
and therefore would not have him coffined before the third day.   Some
such virbiasses [so in M.S.], I confess, we find in story, and one or two
I remember myself, but they lived not long after.   Some contingent
reanimations are to be hoped in diseases wherein the lamp of life is
but puffed out and seemingly choaked, and not where the oil is quite
spent and exhausted.   Though Nonnus will have it a fever, yet of what
diseases Lazarus first died, is uncertain from the text, as his second
death from good authentic history ; but since some persons conceived to
be dead do sometimes return again unto evidence of life, that miracle
was wisely managed by our Saviour ; for had he not been dead four
days and under corruption, there had not wanted enough who would
have cavilled [at] the same, which the scripture now puts out of doubt :
and tradition also confirmeth, that he lived thirty years after, and being
pursued by the Jews, came by sea into Provence, by Marseilles, with
Mary Magdalen, Maximinus, and others ; where. remarkable places
carry their names unto this day.   But to arise from the grave to return
again into it, is but an uncomfortable reviction.   Few men would be
content to cradle it once again ; except a man can lead his second life
better than the first, a man may be doubly condemned for living evilly
twice, which were but to make the second death in scripture the third,
and to accumulate in the punishment of two bad livers at the last day.
To have performed the duty of corruption in the grave, to live again as
far from sin as death, and arise like our Saviour for ever, are the only
satisfactions of well-weighed expectations."

    [7] *disease.*]   Ἀσφαλέστατος καὶ ῥήϊστος, securissima et facillima.—
Hippoc.
    [8] *that bell, &c.*]   Pro febre quartana raro sonat campana.   The fol-
lowing paragraph occurs here in *MS. Sloan.* 1862 :—

Some think there were few consumptions in the old world, when men lived much upon milk; and that the ancient inhabitants of this island were less troubled with coughs when they went naked and slept in caves and woods, than men now in chambers and featherbeds. Plato will tell us, that there was no such disease as a catarrh in Homer's time, and that it was but new in Greece in his age. Polydore Virgil delivereth that pleurisies were rare in England, who lived but in the days of Henry the Eighth. Some will allow no diseases to be new, others think that many old ones are ceased: and that such which are esteemed new, will have but their time: however, the mercy of God hath scattered the great heap of diseases, and not loaded any one country with all: some may be new in one country which have been old in another. New discoveries of the earth discover new diseases: for besides the common swarm, there are endemial and local infirmities proper unto certain regions, which in the whole earth make no small number: and if Asia, Africa, and America, should bring in their list, Pandora's box would swell, and there must be a strange pathology.

Most men expected to find a consumed kell,[9] empty and bladder-like guts, livid and marbled lungs, and a withered pericardium in this exsuccous corpse: but some seemed too much to wonder that two lobes of his lungs adhered unto his side; for the like I have often found in bodies of no suspected consumptions or difficulty of respiration. And the same more often happeneth in men than other animals: and some think in women than in men: but the most remarkable I have met with, was in a man, after a cough of almost fifty years, in whom all the lobes adhered unto the pleura,[1] and each lobe unto another; who having also been

---

"Some I observed to wonder how, in his consumptive state, his hair held on so well, without that considerable defluvium which is one of the last symptoms in such diseases; but they took not notice of a mark in his face, which if he had lived was a probable security against baldness (if the observation of Aristotle will hold, that persons are less apt to be bald who are double-chinned), nor of the various and knotted veins in his legs, which they that have, in the same author's assertions, are less disposed to baldness. (According as Theodorus Gaza renders it: though Scaliger renders the text otherwise.)"

[9] *kell.*] The caul, or *omentum.*
[1] *pleura.*] So A. F.

much troubled with the gout, brake the rule of Cardan,[2] and died of the stone in the bladder. Aristotle makes a query, why some animals cough, as man; some not, as oxen. If coughing be taken as it consisteth of a natural and voluntary motion, including expectoration and spitting out, it may be as proper unto man as bleeding at the nose; otherwise we find that Vegetius and rural writers have not left so many medicines in vain against the coughs of cattle; and men who perish by coughs die the death of sheep, cats, and lions: and though birds have no midriff, yet we meet with divers remedies in Arrianus against the coughs of hawks. And though it might be thought that all animals who have lungs do cough; yet in cetaceous fishes, who have large and strong lungs, the same is not observed; nor yet in oviparous quadrupeds: and in the greatest thereof, the crocodile, although we read much of their tears, we find nothing of that motion.

From the thoughts of sleep, when the soul was conceived nearest unto divinity, the ancients erected an art of divination, wherein while they too widely expatiated in loose and inconsequent conjectures, Hippocrates[3] wisely considered dreams as they presaged alterations in the body, and so afforded hints toward the preservation of health, and prevention of diseases; and therein was so serious as to advise alteration of diet, exercise, sweating, bathing, and vomiting; and also so religious as to order prayers and supplications unto respective deities, in good dreams unto Sol, Jupiter cœlestis, Jupiter opulentus, Minerva, Mercurius, and Apollo; in bad unto Tellus and the heroes.

And therefore I could not but take notice how his female friends were irrationally curious so strictly to examine his dreams, and in this low state to hope for the phantasms of health. He was now past the healthful dreams of the sun, moon, and stars, in their clarity and proper courses. 'Twas too late to dream of flying, of limpid fountains, smooth waters, white vestments, and fruitful green trees,

---

[2] *Cardan.*] Cardan in his *Encomium Podagræ* reckoneth this among the *Dona Podagræ*, that they are delivered thereby from the phthisis and stone in the bladder.

[3] *Hippocrates.*] Hippoc. *de Insomniis.*

which are the visions of healthful sleeps, and at good distance from the grave.

And they were also too deeply dejected that he should dream of his dead friends, inconsequently divining, that he would not be long from them; for strange it was not that he should sometimes dream of the dead, whose thoughts run always upon death; beside, to dream of the dead, so they appear not in dark habits, and take nothing away from us, in Hippocrates' sense was of good signification: for we live by the dead, and every thing is or must be so before it becomes our nourishment. And Cardan, who dreamed that he discoursed with his dead father in the moon, made thereof no mortal interpretation: and even to dream that we are dead, was no condemnable phantasm in old oneiro-criticism, as having a signification of liberty, vacuity from cares, exemption and freedom from troubles unknown unto the dead.

Some dreams I confess may admit of easy and feminine exposition; he who dreamed that he could not see his right shoulder, might easily fear to lose the sight of his right eye; he that before a journey dreamed that his feet were cut off, had a plain warning not to undertake his intended journey. But why to dream of lettuce should presage some ensuing disease, why to eat figs should signify foolish talk, why to eat eggs great trouble, and to dream of blindness should be so highly commended, according to the oneirocritical verses of Astrampsychus and Nicephorus, I shall leave unto your divination.

He was willing to quit the world alone and altogether, leaving no earnest behind him for corruption or after-grave, having small content in that common satisfaction to survive or live in another, but amply satisfied that his disease should die with himself, nor revive in a posterity to puzzle physic, and make sad mementos of their parent hereditary. Leprosy awakes not sometimes before forty, the gout and stone often later; but consumptive and tabid[4] roots sprout more early, and at the fairest make seventeen years of our life doubtful before that age. They that enter the world with original

---

[4] *tabid.*] Tabes maxime contingunt ab anno decimo octavo ad trigesimum quintum.—*Hippoc.*

diseases as well as sin, have not only common mortality but
sick traductions to destroy them, make commonly short
courses, and live not at length but in figures ; so that a
sound Cæsarean nativity[5] may out-last a natural birth, and
a knife may sometimes make way for a more lasting fruit
than a midwife ; which makes so few infants now able to
endure the old test of the river,[6] and many to have feeble
children who could scarce have been married at Sparta, and
those provident states who studied strong and healthful
generations ; which happen but contingently in mere pecu-
niary matches or marriages made by the candle, wherein
notwithstanding there is little redress to be hoped from
an astrologer or a lawyer, and a good discerning physician
were like to prove the most successful counsellor.

Julius Scaliger, who in a sleepless fit of the gout could
make two hundred verses in a night, would have but five[7]
plain words upon his tomb. And this serious person,
though no minor wit, left the poetry of his epitaph unto
others : either unwilling to commend himself or to be
judged by a distich, and perhaps considering how unhappy
great poets have been in versifying their own epitaphs :
wherein Petrarca, Dante, and Ariosto, have so unhappily
failed, that if their tombs should out-last their works, posterity would find so little of Apollo on them, as to mistake
them for Ciceronian poets.

In this deliberate and creeping progress unto the grave,
he was somewhat too young and of too noble a mind, to fall
upon that stupid symptom observable in divers persons near
their journey's end, and which may be reckoned among the
mortal symptoms of their last disease ; that is, to become
more narrow-minded, miserable, and tenacious, unready to
part with anything, when they are ready to part with all,
and afraid to want when they have no time to spend ;
meanwhile physicians, who know that many are mad but in
a single depraved imagination, and one prevalent decipiency ;

---

[5] *a sound Cæsarean nativity.*] A sound child cut out of the body of
the mother.

[6] *river.*] Natos ad flumina primum deferimus sævoque gelu duramus
et undis.

[7] *but five.*] Julii Cæsaris Scaligeri quod fuit.—*Joseph. Scaliger in
vita patris.*

and that beside and out of such single deliriums a man may meet with sober actions and good sense in bedlam ; cannot but smile to see the heirs and concerned relations gratulating themselves on the sober departure of their friends ; and though they behold such mad covetous passages, content to think they die in good understanding, and in their sober senses.

Avarice, which is not only infidelity but idolatry, either from covetous progeny or questuary education, had no root in his breast, who made good works the expression of his faith, and was big with desires unto public and lasting charities ; and surely where good wishes and charitable intentions exceed abilities, theorical beneficency may be more than a dream. They build not castles in the air who would build churches on earth : and though they leave no such structures here, may lay good foundations in heaven. In brief, his life and death were such, that I could not blame them who wished the like, and almost to have been himself; almost, I say ; for though we may wish the prosperous appurtenances of others, or to be another in his happy accidents, yet so intrinsical is every man unto himself, that some doubt may be made, whether any would exchange his being, or substantially become another man.

He had wisely seen the world at home and abroad, and thereby observed under what variety men are deluded in the pursuit of that which is not here to be found. And although he had no opinion of reputed felicities below, and apprehended men widely out in the estimate of such happiness yet his sober contempt of the world wrought no Democritism or Cynicism, no laughing or snarling at it, as well understanding there are not felicities in this world to satisfy a serious mind ; and therefore, to soften the stream of our lives, we are fain to take in the reputed contentions of this world, to unite with the crowd in their beatitudes, and to make ourselves happy by consortion, opinion, or co-existimation : for strictly to separate from received and customary felicities, and to confine unto the rigour of realities, were to contract the consolation of our beings unto too uncomfortable circumscriptions.

Not to fear death,[8] nor desire it, was short of his reso-

[8] *death.*] Summum nec metuas diem nec optes.

lution: to be dissolved, and be with Christ, was his dying ditty. He conceived his thread long, in no long course of years, and when he had scarce out-lived the second life of Lazarus;[9] esteeming it enough to approach the years of his Saviour, who so ordered his own human state, as not to be old upon earth.

But to be content with death may be better than to desire it; a miserable life may make us wish for death, but a virtuous one to rest in it; which is the advantage of those resolved Christians, who looking on death not only as the sting, but the period and end of sin, the horizon and isthmus between this life and a better, and the death of this world but as a nativity of another, do contentedly submit unto the common necessity, and envy not Enoch or Elias.

Not to be content with life is the unsatisfactory state of those who destroy themselves;[1] who being afraid to live, run blindly upon their own death, which no man fears by experience: and the stoics had a notable doctrine to take away the fear thereof; that is, in such extremities, to desire that which is not to be avoided, and wish what might be feared; and so made evils voluntary, and to suit with their own desires, which took off the terror of them.

But the ancient martyrs were not encouraged by such fallacies; who, though they feared not death, were afraid to be their own executioners; and therefore thought it more wisdom to crucify their lusts than their bodies, to circumcise than stab their hearts, and to mortify than kill themselves.

His willingness to leave this world about that age, when most men think they may best enjoy it, though paradoxical unto worldly ears, was not strange unto mine, who have so often observed, that many, though old, oft stick fast unto the world, and seem to be drawn like Cacus's oxen, backward, with great struggling and reluctancy unto the grave. The long habit of living makes mere men more hardly to part

[9] *Lazarus.*] Who upon some accounts, and tradition, is said to have lived thirty years after he was raised by our Saviour.—*Baronius.*

[1] *themselves.*] In the speech of Vulteius in Lucan, animating his soldiers in a great struggle to kill one another.—"Decernite lethum, et metus omnis abest, cupias quodcunque necesse est." "All fear is over, do but resolve to die, and make your desires meet necessity."

with life, and all to be nothing, but what is to come.   To
live at the rate of the old world, when some could scarce
remember themselves young, may afford no better digested
death than a more moderate period.   Many would have
thought it an happiness to have had their lot of life in some
notable conjunctures of ages past; but the uncertainty of
future times hath tempted few to make a part in ages to
come.   And surely, he that hath taken the true altitude of
things, and rightly calculated the degenerate state of this
age, is not like to envy those that shall live in the next,
much less three or four hundred years hence, when no man
can comfortably imagine what face this world will carry:
and therefore since every age makes a step unto the end of
all things, and the scripture affords so hard a character of
the last times; quiet minds will be content with their
generations, and rather bless ages past, than be ambitious of
those to come.

Though age had set no seal upon his face, yet a dim eye
might clearly discover fifty in his actions; and therefore,
since wisdom is the grey hair, and an unspotted life old age;
although his years came short, he might have been said to
have held up with longer livers, and to have been Solomon's[2]
old man.   And surely if we deduct all those days of our
life which we might wish unlived, and which abate the
comfort of those we now live; if we reckon up only those
days which God hath accepted of our lives, a life of good
years will hardly be a span long: the son in this sense may
out-live the father, and none be climacterically old.   He
that early arriveth unto the parts and prudence of age, is
happily old without the uncomfortable attendants of it;
and 'tis superfluous to live unto grey hairs, when in a precocious temper we anticipate the virtues of them.   In brief,
he cannot be accounted young who out-liveth the old man.
He that hath early arrived unto the measure of a perfect
stature in Christ, hath already fulfilled the prime and
longest intention of his being: and one day lived after the
perfect rule of piety, is to be preferred before sinning
immortality.

Although he attained not unto the years of his prede-

[2] *Solomon's.*] Wisdom, cap. iv.

cessors, yet he wanted not those preserving virtues which
confirm the thread of weaker constitutions. *Cautelous*
chastity and *crafty* sobriety were far from him; those jewels
were *paragon*, without flaw, hair, ice, or cloud in him:
which affords me a hint to proceed in these good wishes,
and few mementos unto you.

₊ The rest of this letter served as the basis for his larger work, the
Christian Morals, in which having, with some few alterations, been included, it is here omitted.

END OF LETTER TO A FRIEND.

CHRISTIAN MORALS.

PUBLISHED FROM THE ORIGINAL AND CORRECT MANUSCRIPT OF THE
AUTHOR,

BY J.OHN JEFFERY, D.D.

ARCHDEACON OF NORWICH.

WITH NOTES ADDED TO THE SECOND EDITION,

BY DR. JOHNSON.

FOURTH EDITION.

ORIGINALLY PUBLISHED IN

1716.

EDITOR'S PREFACE.

The original edition of the CHRISTIAN MORALS, by Archdeacon Jeffery, was printed at Cambridge, in 1716; and is one of the rarer of Sir Thomas's detached works. Dodsley, in 1756, brought out a new edition, with additional notes, and a life by Dr. Johnson. It has been said that Dr. Johnson inserted in the *Literary Magazine* a review of the work, but I have not been able to find it. The sixth volume of *Memoirs of Literature* contains a meagre account of the Posthumous Works, but no notice of the Christian Morals.

The latter portion of the Letter to a Friend is incorporated in various parts of the Christian Morals; except some passages, which are given in notes to the present edition; together with some various readings from MSS. in the British Museum.

DAVID, EARL OF BUCHAN,

MY LORD,—The honour you have done our family obligeth us to make all just acknowledgments of it: and there is no form of acknowledgment in our power, more worthy of your lordship's acceptance, than this dedication of the last work of our honoured and learned father. Encouraged hereunto by the knowledge we have of your lordship's judicious relish of universal learning, and sublime virtue, we beg the favour of your acceptance of it, which will very much oblige our family in general, and her in particular, who is,

My Lord,

Your lordship's most humble Servant,

ELIZABETH LITTLETON.

THE PREFACE.

IF any one, after he has read Religio Medici, and the
ensuing discourse, can make doubt whether the same person,
was the author of them both, he may be assured, by the
testimony of Mrs. Littleton, Sir Thomas Browne's daughter,
who lived with her father when it was composed by him;
and who, at the time, read it written by his own hand; and
also by the testimony of others (of whom I am one) who
read the manuscript of the author, immediately after his
death, and who have since read the same; from which it hath
been faithfully and exactly transcribed for the press. The
reason why it was not printed sooner is, because it was un-
happily lost, by being mislaid among other manuscripts, for
which search was lately made in the presence of the Lord
Archbishop of Canterbury, of which his Grace, by letter,
informed Mrs. Littleton, when he sent the manuscript to
her. There is nothing printed in the discourse, or in the
short notes, but what is found in the original manuscript of
the author, except only where an oversight had made the
addition or transposition of some words necessary.

JOHN JEFFERY,
Archdeacon of Norwich.

CHRISTIAN MORALS.

PART THE FIRST.

TREAD softly and circumspectly in this funambulatory track[1] and narrow path of goodness : pursue virtue virtuously :[2] leaven not good actions, nor render virtue disputable. Stain not fair acts with foul intentions ; maim not uprightness by halting concomitances, nor circumstantially deprave substantial goodness.

Consider[3] whereabout thou art in Cebes's[4] table, or that old philosophical pinax[5] of the life of man : whether thou art yet in the road of uncertainties ; whether thou hast yet entered the narrow gate, got up the hill and asperous way, which leadeth unto the house of sanity ; or taken that purifying potion from the hand of sincere erudition, which may send thee clear and pure away unto a virtuous and happy life.

In this virtuous voyage of thy life hull not about like the ark, without the use of rudder, mast, or sail, and bound for no port. Let not disappointment cause despondency, nor difficulty despair. Think not that you are sailing from Lima

---

[1] *funambulatory track.*] Narrow, like the walk of a rope-dancer.—*Dr. J.*

[2] *Tread, &c.*] This sentence begins the closing reflections to the *Letter to a Friend*, which were afterwards amplified into the *Christian Morals*, and therefore have been omitted as duplicate in the present edition.

[3] *Consider, &c.*] The remainder of this section comprises the second and third paragraphs of the closing reflections to the *Letter to a Friend.*

[4] *Cebes's table.*] The table or picture of Cebes, an allegorical representation of the characters and conditions of mankind ; which is translated by Mr. Collier, and added to the *Meditations of Antoninus.—Dr. J.*

[5] *pinax.*] Picture.—*Dr. J.*

to Manilla,[6] when you may fasten up the rudder, and sleep before the wind; but expect rough seas, flaws,[7] and contrary blasts: and 'tis well, if by many cross tacks and veerings, you arrive at the port; for we sleep in lions' skins[8] in our progress unto virtue, and we slide not but climb unto it.

Sit not down in the popular forms and common level of virtues. Offer not only peace-offerings but holocausts unto God: where all is due make no reserve, and cut not a cummin-seed with the Almighty: to serve Him singly to serve ourselves, were too partial a piece of piety, not like[9] to place us in the illustrious mansions of glory.

SECT. II.[1]—Rest not in an ovation* but a triumph over thy passions. Let anger walk hanging down the head; let malice go manacled, and envy fettered after thee. Behold within thee the long train of thy trophies, not without thee. Make the quarrelling Lapithytes sleep, and Centaurs within lie quiet.[2] Chain up the unruly legion of thy breast.

* Ovation, a petty and minor kind of triumph.

[6] *Lima to Manilla.*] Over the Pacific Ocean, in the course of the ship which now sails from Acapulco to Manilla, perhaps formerly from Lima, or more properly from Callao, Lima not being a sea-port.—*Dr.J.*

[7] *flaws.*] Sudden gusts or violent attacks of bad weather.—*Dr. J.*

[8] *lion's skins, &c.*] That is, in armour, in a state of military vigilance. One of the Grecian chiefs used to represent open force by the lion's skin, and policy by the fox's tail.—*Dr. J.*

[9] *like.*] Likely.

[1] SECT. II.] The first and last two sentences compose par. 17th of closing reflections to the *Letter to a Friend.* The succeeding par. (18) is given here, having been omitted in the *Christian Morals:*—"Give no quarter unto those vices which are of thine inward family, and, having a root in thy temper, plead a right and property in thee. Examine well thy complexional inclinations. Raise early batteries against those strongholds built upon the rock of nature, and make this a great part of the militia of thy life. The politic nature of vice must be opposed by policy, and therefore wiser honesties project and plot against sin; wherein notwithstanding we are not to rest in generals, or the trite stratagems of art: that may succeed with one temper which may prove successless with another. There is no community or commonwealth of virtue; every man must study his own economy, and erect these rules unto the figure of himself."

[2] *Make the quarrelling, &c.*] That is, thy turbulent and irascible passions. For the Lapithytes and Centaurs, see Ovid.—*Dr. J.*

Lead thine own captivity captive, and be Cæsar within thyself.[3]

SECT. III.[4]—He that is chaste and continent not to impair his strength, or honest for fear of contagion, will hardly be heroically virtuous. Adjourn not this virtue until that temper when Cato[5] could lend out his wife, and impotent satyrs write satires upon lust; but be chaste in thy flaming days, when Alexander dared not trust his eyes upon the fair sisters of Darius, and when so many think there is no other way but Origen's.*

SECT. IV.[6]—Show thy art in honesty, and lose not thy virtue by the bad managery of it. Be temperate and sober; not to preserve your body in an ability for wanton ends; not to avoid the infamy of common transgressors that way, and thereby to hope to expiate or palliate obscure and closer vices; not to spare your purse, nor simply to enjoy health; but, in one word, that thereby you may truly serve God, which every sickness will tell you you cannot well do without health. The sick man's sacrifice is but a lame oblation. Pious treasures, laid up in healthful days, plead for sick non-performances; without which we must needs look back with anxiety upon the lost opportunities of health; and may

---

* Who is said to have castrated himself.

[3] *thyself.*] In *MS. Sloan.* 1848, I met with the following passage, which may be fitly introduced as a continuation to this section :—" To restrain the rise of extravagances, and timely to ostracise the most overgrowing enormities makes a calm and quiet state in the dominion of ourselves, for vices have their ambitions, and will be above one another; but though many may possess us, yet is there commonly one that hath the dominion over us; one that lordeth over all, and the rest remain slaves unto the humour of it. Such towering vices are not to be temporally exostracised, but perpetually exiled, or rather to be served like the rank poppies in Tarquin's garden, and made shorter by the head; for the sharpest arrows are to be let fly against all such imperious vices, which, neither enduring priority or equality, Cæsarean or Pompeian primity, must be absolute over all; for these opprobriously denominate us here, and chiefly condemn us hereafter, and will stand in capital letters over our heads as the titles of our sufferings."

[4] SECT. III.] The 4th paragraph of closing reflections to the *Letter to a Friend*.

[5] *Cato.*] The censor, who is frequently confounded, and by Pope, amongst others, with Cato of Utica.—*Dr. J.*

[6] SECT. IV.] Except the first sentence, this section concludes the first paragraph of the concluding reflections of *Letter to a Friend*.

have cause rather to envy than pity the ends of penitent public sufferers, who go with healthful prayers unto the last scene of their lives, and in the integrity of their faculties[7] return their spirit unto God that gave it.

SECT. V.—Be charitable before wealth make thee covetous, and lose not the glory of the mite. If riches increase, let, thy mind hold pace with them; and think it not enough to be liberal, but munificent. Though a cup of cold water from some hand may not be without its reward, yet stick not thou for wine and oil for the wounds of the distressed; and treat the poor, as our Saviour did the multitude, to the reliques of some baskets.[8] Diffuse thy beneficence early, and while thy treasures call thee master; there may be an atropos[9] of thy fortunes before that of thy life, and thy wealth cut off before that hour, when all men shall be poor; for the justice of death looks equally upon the dead, and Charon expects no more from Alexander than from Irus.

. SECT. VI.—Give not only unto seven, but also unto eight, that is, unto more than many.* Though to give unto every one that asketh may seem severe advice,† yet give thou also before asking; that is, where want is silently clamorous, and men's necessities not their tongues do loudly call for thy mercies. For though sometimes necessitousness be dumb, or misery speak not out, yet true charity is sagacious, and will find out hints for beneficence. Acquaint thyself with the physiognomy of want, and let the dead colours and first lines of necessity suffice to tell thee there is an object for thy bounty. Spare not where thou canst not easily be prodigal, and fear not to be undone by mercy; for since he who hath pity on the poor lendeth unto the Almighty rewarder, who observes no ides[1] but every day for his payments,

* Ecclesiasticus.   † Luke.

[7] *and in the integrity, &c.*] With their faculties unimpaired.—*Dr. J.*

[8] *Be charitable, &c.*] The preceding part of this section constitutes the 5th paragraph of the closing reflections of *Letter to a Friend.*

[9] *atropos.*] Atropos is the lady of destiny that cuts the thread of life.—*Dr. J.*

[1] *ides, &c.*] The ides was the time when money lent out at interest was commonly repaid.

Fœnerator Alphius
Suam relegit Idibus pecuniam,
Quærit calendis ponere.—HOR.—*Dr. J.*

charity becomes pious usury, Christian liberality the most thriving industry; and what we adventure in a cockboat may return in a carrack unto us. He who thus casts his bread upon the water shall surely find it again; for though it falleth to the bottom, it sinks but like the axe of the prophet, to rise again unto him.

SECT. VII.[2]—If avarice be thy vice, yet make it not thy punishment. Miserable men commiserate not themselves, bowelless unto others, and merciless unto their own bowels. Let the fruition of things bless the possession of them, and think it more satisfaction to live richly than die rich. For since thy good works, not thy goods, will follow thee; since wealth is an appurtenance of life, and no dead man is rich; to famish in plenty, and live poorly to die rich, were a multiplying improvement in madness, and use upon use in folly.

SECT. VIII.[3]—Trust not to the omnipotency of gold, and say not unto it, thou art my confidence. Kiss not thy hand to that terrestrial sun, nor bore thy ear unto its servitude. A slave unto mammon makes no servant unto God. Covetousness cracks the sinews of faith; numbs the apprehension of anything above sense; and, only affected with the certainty of things present, makes a peradventure of things to come; lives but unto one world, nor hopes but fears another; makes their own death sweet unto others, bitter unto themselves; brings formal sadness, scenical mourning, and no wet eyes at the grave.

SECT. IX.[4]—Persons lightly dipt, not grained in generous honesty,[5] are but pale in goodness, and faint hued in integrity. But be thou what thou virtuously art, and let not the ocean wash away thy tincture. Stand magnetically upon that axis,[6] when prudent simplicity hath fixt there; and let

[2] SECT. VII.] Paragraph 7th of closing reflections of *Letter to a Friend.*

[3] SECT. VIII.] Paragraph 6th of closing reflections to the *Letter to a Friend.*

[4] SECT. IX.] Paragraph 8th of closing reflections to the *Letter to a Friend.*

[5] *not grained in generous, &c.*] Not deeply tinged, not dyed in grain. —*Dr. J.*

[6] *that axis.*] That is, "with a position as immutable as that of the magnetical axis," which is popularly supposed to be invariably parallel to the meridian, or to stand exactly north and south.—*Dr. J.*

no attraction invert the poles of thy honesty.   That vice
may be uneasy and even monstrous unto thee, let iterated
good acts and long-confirmed habits make virtue almost
natural, or a second nature in thee.   Since virtuous super-
structions have commonly generous foundations, dive into
thy inclinations, and early discover what nature bids thee to
be or tells thee thou mayest be.   They who thus timely
descend into themselves, and cultivate the good seeds which
nature hath set in them, prove not shrubs but cedars in their
generation.   And to be in the form of the best of the bad*
or the worst of the good, will be no satisfaction unto them.

SECT. x.[7]—Make not the consequence of virtue the ends
thereof.   Be not beneficent for a name or cymbal of applause ; nor exact and just in commerce for the advantages
of trust and credit, which attend the reputation of true and
punctual dealing: for these rewards, though unsought for,
plain virtue will bring with her.   To have other by-ends in
good actions sours laudable performances, which must have
deeper roots, motives, and instigations, to give them the
stamp of virtues.[8]

SECT. xi.[9]—Let not the law of thy country be the non
ultra of thy honesty ; nor think that always good enough
which the law will make good.   Narrow not the law of
charity, equity, mercy.   Join gospel righteousness with legal
right.   Be not a mere Gamaliel in the faith, but let the sermon in the mount be thy targum unto the law of Sinai.[1]

SECT. xii.—Live by old ethicks and the classical rules of

---

* Optimi malorum pessimi bonorum.

[7] SECT. x.]   Paragraph 10th of closing reflections to the *Letter to a
Friend.*
[8] *virtues.*]   The following (11th par. of closing reflections to the
Letter, &c.) seems to have been omitted in the *Christian Morals :*—
"Though human infirmity may betray thy heedless days into the popular ways of extravagancy, yet let not thine own depravity, or the torrent
of vicious times, carry thee into desperate enormities in opinions, manners, or actions : if thou hast dipped thy foot in the river, yet venture
not over *Rubicon ;* run not into extremities from whence there is no
regression, nor be ever so closely shut up within the holds of vice and
iniquity, as not to find some escape by a postern of recipiscency.'
[9] SECT. xi.]   Paragraph 9th of closing reflections to the *Letter to a
Friend.*
[1] *targum, &c.*]   A paraphrase or amplification.

honesty. Put no new names or notions upon authentic virtues and vices.[2] Think not that morality is ambulatory; that vices in one age are not vices in another; or that virtues, which are under the everlasting seal of right reason, may be stamped by opinion. And therefore, though vicious times invert the opinions of things, and set up new ethicks against virtue, yet hold thou unto old morality; and rather than follow a multitude to do evil, stand like Pompey's pillar conspicuous by thyself, and single in integrity. And since the worst of times afford imitable examples of virtue; since no deluge of vice is like to be so general but more than eight will escape;[3] eye well those heroes who have held their heads above water, who have touched pitch and not been defiled, and in the common contagion have remained uncorrupted.

SECT. XIII.[4]—Let age, not envy, draw wrinkles on thy cheeks; be content to be envied, but envy not. Emulation may be plausible and indignation allowable, but admit no treaty with that passion which no circumstance can make good. A displacency at the good of others because they enjoy it, though not unworthy of it, is an absurd depravity, sticking fast unto corrupted nature, and often too hard for humility and charity, the great suppressors of envy. This surely is a lion not to be strangled but by Hercules himself, or the highest stress of our minds, and an atom of that power which subdueth all things unto itself.

SECT. XIV.[5]—Owe not thy humility unto humiliation from adversity, but look humbly down in that state when others look upwards upon thee. Think not thy own shadow longer than that of others, nor delight to take the altitude of thyself. Be patient in the age of pride, when men live by short intervals of reason under the dominion of humour and passion, when it's in the power of every one to transform thee

---

[2] vices.] From MS. Sloan. 1847, the following clause is added:— "Think not modesty will never gild its like; fortitude will not be degraded into audacity and foolhardiness; liberality will not be put off with the name of prodigality, nor frugality exchange its name with avarice and solid parsimony, and so our vices be exalted into virtues."

[3] eight will escape.] Alluding to the flood of Noah.

[4] SECT. XIII.] Paragraph 13th of closing reflections to the Letter to a Friend.

SECT. XIV.] Paragraph 12th of closing reflections to the Letter to a Friend.

out of thyself, and run thee into the short madness. If you cannot imitate Job, yet come not short of Socrates,[6] and those patient pagans who tired the tongues of their enemies, while they perceived they spit their malice at brazen walls and statues.

SECT. XV.[7]—Let not the sun in Capricorn* go down upon thy wrath, but write thy wrongs in ashes. Draw the curtain of night upon injuries, shut them up in the tower of oblivion,† and let them be as though they had not been. To forgive our enemies, yet hope that God will punish them, is not to forgive enough. To forgive them ourselves, and not to pray God to forgive them, is a partial piece of charity. Forgive thine enemies totally, and without any reserve that however God will revenge thee.

SECT. XVI.[8]—While thou so hotly disclaimest the devil, be not guilty of diabolism. Fall not into one name with that unclean spirit, nor act his nature whom thou so much abhorrest; that is, to accuse, calumniate, backbite, whisper, detract, or sinistrously interpret others. Degenerous depravities, and narrow-minded vices! not only below St. Paul's noble Christian but Aristotle's true gentleman.‡ Trust not with some that the epistle of St. James is apocryphal, and so read with less fear that stabbing truth, that in company with this vice "thy religion is in vain." Moses broke the

* Even when the days are shortest.
† Alluding unto the tower of oblivion mentioned by Procopios, which was the name of a tower of imprisonment among the Persians: whoever was put therein was as it were buried alive, and it was death for any but to name him.
‡ See Aristotle's Ethics, chapter of Magnanimity.

[6] *Socrates.*]

> Dulcique senex vicinus Hymetto,
> Qui partem acceptæ sæva inter vincla cicutæ
> Accusatori nollet dare.—JUV.

Not so mild Thales, nor Chrysippus thought ;
Nor the good man who drank the pois'nous draught
With mind serene, and could not wish to see
His vile accuser drink as deep as he :
Exalted Socrates !—CREECH.—*Dr. J.*

[7] SECT. XV.] Paragraph 15th of closing reflections to the *Letter to a Friend.*

[8] SECT. XVI.] Paragraph 14th of closing reflections to the *Letter to a Friend.*

tables without breaking of the law; but where charity is broke, the law itself is shattered, which cannot be whole without love, which is "the fulfilling of it." Look humbly upon thy virtues; and though thou art rich in some, yet think thyself poor and naked without that crowning grace, which "thinketh no evil, which envieth not, which beareth, hopeth, believeth, endureth all things." With these sure graces, while busy tongues are crying out for a drop of cold water, mutes may be in happiness, and sing the *trisagion** in heaven.

SECT. XVII.—However thy understanding may waver in the theories of true and false, yet fasten the rudder of thy will, steer straight unto good and fall not foul on evil. Imagination is apt to rove, and conjecture to keep no bounds. Some have run out so far, as to fancy the stars might be but the light of the crystalline heaven shot through perforations on the bodies of the orbs. Others more ingeniously doubt whether there hath not been a vast tract of land in the Atlantic ocean, which earthquakes and violent causes have long ago devoured.[9] Speculative misapprehensions may be innocuous, but immorality pernicious; theoretical mistakes and physical deviations may condemn our judgments, not lead us into judgment. But perversity of will, immoral and sinful enormities walk with Adraste and Nemesis[1] at their backs, pursue us unto judgment, and leave us viciously miserable.

SECT. XVIII..—Bid early defiance unto those vices which are of thine inward family, and having a root in thy temper plead a right and propriety in thee. Raise timely batteries against those strongholds built upon the rock of nature, and make this a great part of the militia of thy life. Delude not thyself into iniquities from participation or community, which abate the sense but not the obliquity of them. To conceive sins less or less of sins, because others also transgress, were morally to commit that natural fallacy of man,

* Holy, holy, holy.

[9] *devoured.*] Add from *MS.* CIX. *Rawl.*—"Whether there hath not been a passage from the Mediterranean into the Red Sea, and whether the ocean at first had a passage into the Mediterranean by the straits of Hercules."

[1] *Adraste and Nemesis.*] The powers of vengeance.—*Dr. J.*

to take comfort from society, and think adversities less because others also suffer them. The politic nature of vice must be opposed by policy; and, therefore, wiser honesties project and plot against it : wherein, notwithstanding, we are not to rest in generals, or the trite stratagems of art. That may succeed with one, which may prove successless with another: there is no community or commonweal of virtue : every man must study his own economy, and adapt such rules unto the figure of himself.

SECT. XIX.[2]—Be substantially great in thyself, and more than thou appearest unto others; and let the world be deceived in thee, as they are in the lights of heaven. Hang early plummets upon the heels of pride, and let ambition have but an epicycle[3] and narrow circuit in thee. Measure not thyself by thy morning shadow, but by the extent of thy grave : and reckon thyself above the earth, by the line thou must be contented with under it. Spread not into boundless expansions either of designs or desires. Think not that mankind liveth but for a few ; and that the rest are born but to serve those ambitions, which make but flies of men and wildernesses of whole nations. Swell not into vehement actions which imbroil and confound the earth ; but be one of those violent ones which force the kingdom of heaven.* If thou must needs rule, be Zeno's king,[4] and enjoy that empire which every man gives himself. He who is thus his own monarch contentedly sways the sceptre of himself, not envying the glory of crowned heads and *elohims* of the earth. Could the world unite in the practice of that despised train of virtues, which the divine ethics of our Saviour hath so inculcated upon us, the furious face of things must disappear ; Eden would be yet to be found,

* Matthew xi.

[2] SECT. XIX.] Paragraph 16th of closing reflections to the *Letter to a Friend.*

[3] *epicycle.*] An epicycle is a small revolution made by one planet in the wider orbit of another planet. The meaning is, " Let not ambition form thy circle of action, but move upon other principles ; and let ambition only operate as something extrinsic and adventitious."—*Dr. J.*

[4] *Zeno's king.*] That is, "the king of the stoics," whose founder was Zeno, and who held, that the wise man alone had power and royalty.— *Dr. J.*

and the angels might look down, not with pity, but joy upon us.

SECT. xx.[5]—Though the quickness of thine ear were able to reach the noise of the moon, which some think it maketh in its rapid revolution; though the number of thy ears should equal Argus's eyes; yet stop them all with the wise man's wax,[6] and be deaf unto the suggestions of tale-bearers, calumniators, pickthank or malevolent delators, who, while quiet men sleep, sowing the tares of discord and division, distract the tranquillity of charity and all friendly society. These are the tongues that set the world on fire, cankers of reputation, and like that of Jonas's gourd, wither a good name in a night. Evil spirits may sit still, while these spirits walk about and perform the business of hell. To speak more strictly, our corrupted hearts are the factories of the devil, which may be at work without his presence: for when that circumventing spirit hath drawn malice, envy, and all unrighteousness unto well-rooted habits in his disciples, iniquity then goes on upon its own legs; and if the gate of hell were shut up for a time, vice would still be fertile and produce the fruits of hell. Thus when God forsakes us, Satan also leaves us: for such offenders he looks upon as sure and sealed up, and his temptations then needless unto them.

SECT. xxi.—Annihilate not the mercies of God by the oblivion of ingratitude; for oblivion is a kind of annihilation; and for things to be as though they had not been, is like unto never being. Make not thy head a grave, but a repository of God's mercies. Though thou hadst the memory of Seneca or Simonides, and conscience the punctual memorist within us, yet trust not to thy remembrance in things which need phylacteries.[7] Register not only strange,

---

[5] SECT. xx.] The first part of this section, varying slightly, is preserved in MSS. in the Rawlinson collection at Oxford, No. cix. It is immediately followed, without break, by the whole of the 17th section, with slight variations, and with the addition which is now added to that section, in a note at page 95.

[6] *wise man's wax.*] Alluding to the story of Ulysses, who stopped the ears of his companions with wax when they passed by the Sirens. —Dr. J.

[7] *phylacteries.*] A phylactery is a writing bound upon the forehead

but merciful occurrences. Let Ephemerides not Olympiads[8] give thee account of his mercies : let thy diaries stand thick with dutiful mementos and asterisks of acknowledgment. And to be complete and forget nothing, date not his mercy from thy nativity; look beyond the world, and before the era of Adam.

SECT. XXII.—Paint not the sepulchre of thyself, and strive not to beautify thy corruption. Be not an advocate for thy vices, nor call for many hour-glasses[9] to justify thy imperfections. Think not that always good which thou thinkest thou canst always make good, nor that concealed which the sun doth not behold: that which the sun doth not now see, will be visible when the sun is out, and the stars are fallen from heaven. Meanwhile there is no darkness unto conscience; which can see without light, and in the deepest obscurity give a clear draught of things, which the cloud of dissimulation hath concealed from all eyes. There is a natural standing court within us, examining, acquitting, and condemning at the tribunal of ourselves; wherein iniquities have their natural thetas[1] and no nocent[2] is absolved by the verdict of himself. And therefore, although our transgressions shall be tried at the last bar, the process need not be long: for the judge of all knoweth all, and every man will nakedly know himself; and when so few are like to plead not guilty, the assize must soon have an end.

SECT. XXIII.—Comply with some humours, bear with others, but serve none. Civil complacency consists with decent honesty; flattery is a juggler, and no kin unto sincerity. But while thou maintainest the plain path, and scornest to flatter others, fall not into self-adulation, and

containing something to be kept constantly in mind. This was practised by the Jewish doctors with regard to the Mosaic law.—*Dr. J.*

[8] *Olympiads, &c.*] Particular journals of every day, not abstracts comprehending several years under one notation. An Ephemeris is a diary, an Olympiad is the space of four years.—*Dr. J.*

[9] *hour-glasses, &c.*] That is, "do not speak much or long in justification of thy faults." The ancient pleaders talked by a clepsydra, or measurer of time.—*Dr. J.*

[1] *thetas.*] Θ a theta inscribed upon the judge's tessera or ballot was a mark for death or capital condemnation.—*Dr. J.*

[2] *nocent.*]   Se

Judice nemo nocens absolvitur.—JUV.—*Dr. J.*

become not thine own parasite. Be deaf unto thyself, and be not betrayed at home. Self-credulity, pride, and levity lead unto self-idolatry. There is no Damocles[3] like unto self-opinion, nor any syren to our own fawning conceptions. To magnify our minor things, or hug ourselves in our apparitions;[4] to afford a credulous ear unto the clawing suggestions[5] of fancy; to pass our days in painted mistakes of ourselves; and though we behold our own blood,[6] to think ourselves the sons of Jupiter;* are blandishments of self-love, worse than outward delusion. By this imposture, wise men sometimes are mistaken in their elevation, and look above themselves. And fools, which are antipodes[7] unto the wise, conceive themselves to be but their periœci,[8] and in the same parallel with them.

SECT. XXIV.—Be not a Hercules furens abroad, and a poltroon within thyself. To chase our enemies out of the field, and be led captive by our vices; to beat down our foes, and fall down to our concupiscences; are solecisms in moral schools, and no laurel attends them. To well manage our affections, and wild horses of Plato, are the highest *circenses*:[9] and the noblest digladiation[1] is in the theatre of ourselves; for therein our inward antagonists, not only like common gladiators, with ordinary weapons and downright blows make at us, but also, like retiary and laqueary[2] combatants, with nets, frauds, and entanglements fall upon us. Weapons for such combats, are not to be forged at Lipara :[3]

* As Alexander the Great did.

[3] *Damocles.*] Damocles was a flatterer of Dionysius.—*Dr. J.*
[4] *apparitions.*] Appearances without realities.—*Dr. J.*
[5] *clawing suggestions, &c.*] Tickling, flattering. A clawback is an old word for a flatterer. Jewel calls some writers for popery "the pope's clawbacks."—*Dr. J.*
[6] *our own blood.*] That is, "though we bleed when we are wounded, though we find in ourselves the imperfections of humanity."—*Dr. J.*
[7] *antipodes.*] Opposites.—*Dr. J.*
[8] *periœci.*] Only placed at a distance in the same line.—*Dr. J.*
[9] *circenses.*] Circenses were Roman horse races.—*Dr. J.*
[1] *digladiation.*] Fencing match.—*Dr. J.*
[2] *retiary and laqueary.*] The *retiarius* or *laquearius* was a prize-fighter, who entangled his opponent in a net, which by some dexterous management he threw upon him.—*Dr. J.*
[3] *Lipara.*] The Liparæan islands, near Italy, being volcanoes, were fabled to contain the forges of the Cyclops.—*Dr. J.*

Vulcan's art doth nothing in this internal militia; wherein not the armour of Achilles, but the armature of St. Paul, gives the glorious day, and triumphs not leading up into capitols, but up into the highest heavens. And, therefore, while so many think it the only valour to command and master others, study thou the dominion of thyself, and quiet thine own commotions. Let right reason be thy Lycurgus,[4] and lift up thy hand unto the law of it: move by the intelligences of the superior faculties, not by the rapt of passion, nor merely by that of temper and constitution. They who are merely carried on by the wheel of such incli-nations, without the hand and guidance of sovereign reason, are but the automatous[5] part of mankind, rather lived than living, or at least underliving themselves.

SECT. XXV.—Let not fortune, which hath no name in scripture, have any in thy divinity. Let providence, not chance, have the honour of thy acknowledgments, and be thy Œdipus in contingencies. Mark well the paths and winding ways thereof; but be not too wise in the construc-tion, or sudden in the application. The hand of providence writes often by abbreviatures, hieroglyphics or short charac-ters, which, like the laconism on the wall,[6] are not to be made out but by a hint or key from that spirit which indicted them. Leave future occurrences to their uncertainties, think that which is present thy own; and, since 'tis easier to foretel an eclipse than a foul day at some distance, look for little regular below. Attend with patience the uucer-tainty of things, and what lieth yet unexerted in the chaos of futurity. The uncertainty and ignorance of things to come, makes the world new unto us by unexpected emer-gencies; whereby we pass not our days in the trite road of affairs affording no novity; for the novelizing spirit of man lives by variety, and the new faces of things.

SECT. XXVI.—Though a contented mind enlargeth the di-mension of little things; and unto some it is wealth enough not to be poor; and others are well content, if they be but

---

[4] *Lycurgus.*] Thy lawgiver.

[5] *automatous.*] Moved not by choice, but by some mechanical im-pulse.—*Dr. J.*

[6] *laconism on the wall.*] The short sentence written on the wall of Belshazzar. See *Daniel.—Dr. J.*

rich enough to be honest, and to give every man his due: yet fall not into that obsolete affectation of bravery, to throw away thy money, and to reject all honours or honourable stations in this courtly and splendid world. Old generosity is superannuated, and such contempt of the world out of date. No man is now like to refuse the favour of great ones, or be content to say unto princes, "Stand out of my sun."[7] And if any there be of such antiquated resolutions, they are not like to be tempted out of them by great ones; and 'tis fair if they escape the name of hypochondriacks from the genius of latter times, unto whom contempt of the world is the most contemptible opinion; and to be able, like Bias, to carry all they have about them were to be the eighth wise man. However, the old tetrick[8] philosophers looked always with indignation upon such a face of things; and observing the unnatural current of riches, power, and honour in the world, and withal the imperfection and demerit of persons often advanced unto them, were tempted unto angry opinions, that affairs were ordered more by stars than reason, and that things went on rather by lottery than election.

SECT. XXVII.—If thy vessel be but small in the ocean of this world, if meanness of possessions be thy allotment upon earth, forget not those virtues which the great disposer of all bids thee to entertain from thy quality and condition; that is, submission, humility, content of mind, and industry. Content may dwell in all stations. To be low, but above contempt, may be high enough to be happy. But many of low degree may be higher than computed, and some cubits above the common commensuration; for in all states virtue gives qualifications and allowances, which make out defects. Rough diamonds are sometimes mistaken for pebbles; and meanness may be rich in accomplishments, which riches in vain desire. If our merits be above our stations, if our intrinsical value be greater than what we go for, or our value than our valuation, and if we stand higher in God's, than in the censor's book;[9] it may make some equitable

[7] *stand out of my sun.*] The answer made by Diogenes to Alexander, who asked him what he had to request.—*Dr. J.*

[8] *tetrick.*] Sour, morose.—*Dr. J.*

[9] *censor's book.*] The book in which the census, or account of every man's estate was registered among the Romans.—*Dr. J.*

balance in the inequalities of this world, and there may be
no such vast chasm or gulf between disparities as common
measures determine. The divine eye looks upon high and
low differently from that of man. They who seem to
stand upon Olympus, and high mounted unto our eyes, may
be but in the valleys, and low ground unto his; for he looks
upon those as highest who nearest approach his divinity,
and upon those as lowest who are farthest from it.

SECT. XXVIII.—When thou lookest upon the imperfections
of others, allow one eye for what is laudable in them, and
the balance they have from some excellency, which may
render them considerable. While we look with fear or
hatred upon the teeth of the viper, we may behold his eye
with love. In venomous natures something may be amiable:
poisons afford antipoisons: nothing is totally, or altogether
uselessly bad. Notable virtues are sometimes dashed with
notorious vices, and in some vicious tempers have been found
illustrious acts of virtue; which makes such observable
worth in some actions of king Demetrius, Antonius, and
Ahab, as are not to be found in the same kind in Aristides,
Numa, or David. Constancy, generosity, clemency, and
liberality have been highly conspicuous in some persons not
marked out in other concerns for example or imitation. But
since goodness is exemplary in all, if others have not our
virtues, let us not be wanting in theirs; nor scorning them
for their vices whereof we are free, be condemned by their
virtues wherein we are deficient. There is dross, alloy, and
embasement in all human tempers; and he flieth without
wings, who thinks to find ophir or pure metal in any. For
perfection is not, like light, centered in any one body; but,
like the dispersed seminalities of vegetables at the creation,
scattered through the whole mass of the earth, no place
producing all and almost all some. So that 'tis well, if a
perfect man can be made out of many men, and, to the perfect eye of God, even out of mankind. Time, which perfects
some things, imperfects also others. Could we intimately apprehend the ideated man, and as he stood in the intellect of
God upon the first exertion by creation, we might more
narrowly comprehend our present degeneration, and how
widely we are fallen from the pure exemplar and idea of our
nature: for after this corruptive elongation from a primitive

and pure creation, we are almost lost in degeneration; and Adam hath not only fallen from his Creator, but we ourselves from Adam, our tycho [1] and primary generator.[2]

SECT. XXIX.—Quarrel not rashly with adversities not yet understood; and overlook not the mercies often bound up in them: for we consider not sufficiently the good of evils, nor fairly compute the mercies of providence in things afflictive at first hand. The famous Andreas Doria being invited to a feast by Aloysio Fieschi, with design to kill him, just the night before fell mercifully into a fit of the gout, and so escaped that mischief. When Cato intended to kill himself, from a blow which he gave his servant, who would not reach his sword unto him, his hand so swelled that he had much ado to effect his design. Hereby any one but a resolved stoic might have taken a fair hint of consideration, and that some merciful genius would have contrived his preservation. To be sagacious in such intercurrences is not superstition, but wary and pious discretion; and to contemn such hints were to be deaf unto the speaking hand of God, wherein Socrates and Cardan[3] would hardly have been mistaken.

SECT. XXX.—Break not open the gate of destruction, and make no haste or bustle unto ruin. Post not heedlessly

[1] *tycho*] 'Ο τύχων qui facit, 'Οτύχων qui adeptus est; he that makes, or he that possesses; as Adam might be said to contain within him the race of mankind.—*Dr. J.*

[2] *generator.*] Add from *MS. Sloan.* 1885, the following passage:— "But at this distance and elongation we dearly know that depravity hath overspread us, corruption entered like oil into our bones. Imperfections upbraid us on all hands, and ignorance stands pointing at us in every corner in nature. We are unknowing in things which fall under cognition, yet drive at that which is above our comprehension. We have a slender knowledge of ourselves, and much less of God, wherein we are like to rest until the advantage of another being; and therefore in vain we seek to satisfy our souls in close apprehensions and piercing theories of the divinity even from the divine word. Meanwhile we have a happy sufficiency in our own natures, to apprehend his good will and pleasure; it being not of our concern or capacity from thence to apprehend or reach his nature, the divine revelation in such points being not framed unto intellectuals of earth. Even the angels and spirits have enough to admire in their sublimer created natures; admiration being the act of the creature and not of God, who doth not admire himself."

[3] *Socrates and Cardan.*] Socrates and Cardan, perhaps in imitation of him, talked of an attendant spirit or genius, that hinted from time to time how they should act.—*Dr. J.*

on unto the *non ultra* of folly, or precipice of perdition. Let vicious ways have their tropics[4] and deflections, and swim in the waters of sin but as in the Asphaltick lake,[5] though smeared and defiled, not to sink to the bottom. If thou hast dipped thy foot in the brink, yet venture not over Rubicon.[6] Run not into extremities from whence there is no regression. In the vicious ways of the world it mercifully falleth out that we become not extempore wicked, but it taketh some time and pains to undo ourselves. We fall not from virtue, like Vulcan from heaven, in a day. Bad dispositions require some time to grow into bad habits; bad habits must undermine good, and often-repeated acts make us habitually evil: so that by gradual depravations, and while we are but staggeringly evil, we are not left without parenthesis of considerations, thoughtful rebukes, and merciful interventions, to recall us unto ourselves. For the wisdom of God hath methodized the course of things unto the best advantage of goodness, and thinking considerators overlook not the tract thereof.

SECT. XXXI.—Since men and women have their proper virtues and vices; and even twins of different sexes have not only distinct coverings in the womb, but differing qualities and virtuous habits after; transplace not 'their proprieties, and confound not their distinctions. Let masculine and feminine accomplishments shine in their proper orbs, and adorn their respective subjects. However, unite not the vices of both sexes in one; be not monstrous in iniquity, nor hermaphroditically vicious.

SECT. XXXII.—If generous honesty, valour, and plain dealing be the cognisance of thy family, or characteristic of thy country, hold fast such inclinations sucked in with thy first breath, and which lay in the cradle with thee. Fall not into transforming degenerations, which under the old name create a new nation. Be not an alien in thine own nation;

---

[4] *tropics.*] The tropic is the point where the sun turns back.—*Dr. J.*

[5] *Asphaltick lake.*] The lake of Sodom; the waters of which being very salt, and therefore heavy, will scarcely suffer an animal to sink.— *Dr. J.*

[6] *Rubicon.*] The river, by crossing which Cæsar declared war against the senate.—*Dr. J.*

bring not Orontes into Tiber:[7] learn the virtues not the vices of thy foreign neighbours, and make thy imitation by discretion not contagion. Feel something of thyself in the noble acts of thy ancestors, and find in thine own genius that of thy predecessors. Rest not under the expired merits of others, shine by those of thy own. Flame not like the central fire which enlighteneth no eyes, which no man seeth, and most men think there's no such thing to be seen. Add one ray unto the common lustre; add not only to the number but the note of thy generation; and prove not a cloud but an asterisk[8] in thy region.

SECT. XXXIII.—Since thou hast an alarum[9] in thy breast, which tells thee thou hast a living spirit in thee above two thousand times in an hour; dull not away thy days in slothful supinity and the tediousness of doing nothing. To strenuous minds there is an inquietude in over quietness, and no laboriousness in labour; and to tread a mile after the slow pace of a snail, or the heavy measures of the lazy of Brazilia,[1] were a most tiring penance, and worse than a race of some furlongs at the Olympics.[2] The rapid courses of the heavenly bodies are rather imitable by our thoughts, than our corporeal motions; yet the solemn motions of our lives amount unto a greater measure than is commonly apprehended. Some few men have surrounded the globe of the earth; yet many in the set locomotions and movements of their days have measured the circuit of it, and twenty thousand miles have been exceeded by them. Move circumspectly not meticulously,[3] and rather carefully solicitous than anxiously solicitudinous. Think not there is a lion in the way, nor walk with leaden sandals in the

---

[7] *Orontes into Tiber.*] In Tiberim defluxit Orontes : "Orontes has mingled her stream with the Tiber," says Juvenal, speaking of the confluence of foreigners to Rome.—*Dr. J.*

[8] *asterisk.*] A small star.—*Dr. J.*

[9] *alarum.*] The motion of the heart, which beats about sixty times in a minute ; or, perhaps, the motion of respiration, which is nearer to the number mentioned.—*Dr. J.*

[1] *lazy of Brazilia.*] An animal called more commonly the sloth, which is said to be several days in climbing a tree.—*Dr. J.*

[2] *Olympics.*] The Olympic Games, of which the race was one of the chief.—*Dr. J.*

[3] *meticulously.*] Timidly.—*Dr. J.*

paths of goodness; but in all virtuous motions let prudence determine thy measures. Strive not to run, like Hercules, a furlong in a breath: festination may prove precipitation; deliberating delay may be wise cunctation, and slowness no slothfulness.

SECT. XXXIV.—Since virtuous actions have their own trumpets, and, without any noise from thyself, will have their resound abroad; busy not thy best member in the encomium of thyself. Praise is a debt we owe unto the virtues of others, and due unto our own from all, whom malice hath not made mutes, or envy struck dumb. Fall not, however, into the common prevaricating way of self-commendation and boasting, by denoting the imperfections of others. He who discommendeth others obliquely, commendeth himself. He who whispers their infirmities, proclaims his own exemptions from them; and, consequently, says, I am not as this publican, or *hic niger*,* whom I talk of. Open ostentation and loud vain-glory is more tolerable than this obliquity, as but containing some froth, no ink; as but consisting of a personal piece of folly, nor complicated with uncharitableness.[4] Superfluously we seek a precarious applause abroad; every good man hath his plaudit[5] within

* Hic niger est, hunc tu Romane caveto.—*Hor.*
　　This man is vile; here, Roman, fix your mark;
　　His soul is black, as his complexion's dark.—*Francis.*

[4] *uncharitableness.*] Add from *MS. Sloan.* 1847:—" They who thus closely and whisperingly calumniate the absent living, will be apt to strayn their voyce and be apt to be loud enough in infamy of the dead; wherein there should be a civil amnesty and an oblivion concerning those who are in a state where all things are forgotten; but Solon will make us ashamed to speak evil of the dead, a crime not actionable in Christian governments, yet hath been prohibited by Pagan laws and the old sanctions of Athens. Many persons are like many rivers, whose mouths are at a vast distance from their heads, for their words are as far from their thoughts as Canopus from the head of Nilus. These are of the former of those men, whose punishment in Dante's hell is to look everlastingly backward: if you have a mind to laugh at a man, or disparage the judgment of any one, set him a talking of things to come or events of hereafter contingency: which elude the cognition of such an arrogate, the knowledge of them whereto the ignorant pretend not, and the learned imprudently faill; wherein men seem to talk but as babes would do in the womb of their mother, of the things of the world which they are entering into."

[5] *plaudit.*] *Plaudite* was the term by which the ancient theatrical performers solicited a clap.—*Dr. J.*

himself; and though his tongue be silent, is not without loud cymbals in his breast. Conscience will become his panegyrist, and never forget to crown and extol him unto himself.

Sect. xxxv.—Bless not thyself only that thou wert born in Athens;* but, among thy multiplied acknowledgments, lift up one hand unto heaven, that thou wert born of honest parents; that modesty, humility, patience, and veracity, lay in the same egg, and came into the world with thee. From such foundations thou mayst be happy in a virtuous precocity,[6] and make an early and long walk in goodness; so mayst thou more naturally feel the contrariety of vice unto nature, and resist some by the antidote of thy temper. As charity covers, so modesty preventeth a multitude of sins; withholding from noon-day vices and brazen-browed iniquities, from sinning on the house-top, and painting our follies with the rays of the sun. Where this virtue reigneth, though vice may show its head, it cannot be in its glory. Where shame of sin sets, look not for virtue to arise; for when modesty taketh wing, Astrea† goes soon after.

Sect. xxxvi.—The heroical vein of mankind runs much in the soldiery, and courageous part of the world; and in that form we oftenest find men above men. History is full of the gallantry of that tribe; and when we read their notable acts, we easily find what a difference there is between a life in Plutarch[7] and in Laertius.[8] Where true fortitude dwells, loyalty, bounty, friendship, and fidelity may be found. A man may confide in persons constituted for noble ends, who dare do and suffer, and who have a hand to burn for their country and their friend.[9] Small and creeping things are the product of petty souls. He is like to be mistaken, who makes choice of a covetous man for a friend, or relieth upon the reed of narrow and poltroon

* As Socrates did. Athens a place of learning and civility.
† Astrea, goddess of justice and consequently of all virtue.

[6] precocity.] A ripeness preceding the usual time.—Dr. J.
[7] Plutarch.] Who wrote the lives, for the most part, of warriors.—Dr. J.
[8] Laertius.] Who wrote the lives of philosophers.—Dr. J.
[9] and their friend.] Like Mutius Scævola.—Dr. J.

friendship. Pitiful things are only to be found in the cottages of such breasts; but bright thoughts, clear deeds, constancy, fidelity, bounty, and generous honesty are the gems of noble minds; wherein, to derogate from none, the true heroic English gentleman hath no peer.

PART THE SECOND.

SECT. I.—Punish not thyself with pleasure; glut not thy sense with palative delights; nor revenge the contempt of temperance by the penalty of satiety. Were there an age of delight or any pleasure durable, who would not honour Volupia? but the race of delight is short, and pleasures have mutable faces. The pleasures of one age are not pleasures in another, and their lives fall short of our own. Even in our sensual days, the strength of delight is in its seldomness or rarity,[1] and sting in its satiety: mediocrity is its life, and immoderacy its confusion. The luxurious emperors of old inconsiderately satiated themselves with the dainties of sea and land, till wearied through all varieties, their refections became a study unto them, and they were fain to feed by invention: novices in true epicurism! which, by mediocrity, paucity, quick and healthful appetite, makes delights smartly acceptable; whereby Epicurus himself found Jupiter's brain in a piece of Cytheridian cheese,* and the tongues of nightingales in a dish of onions.[2] Hereby healthful and temperate poverty hath the start of nauseating luxury; unto whose clear and naked appetite every meal is a feast, and in one single dish the first course of Metellus;[3]† who are cheaply hungry, and never lose

* Cerebrum Jovis, for a delicious bit.
† His riotous pontifical supper, the great variety whereat is to be seen in Macrobius.

[1] the strength, &c.] Voluptates commendat rarior usus.—Dr. J.
[2] tongues of nightingales, &c.] A dish used among the luxurious of antiquity.—Dr. J.
[3] Metellus.] The supper was not given by Metellus, but by Lentulus when he was made priest of Mars, and recorded by Metellus.—Dr. J.

.their hunger, or advantage of a craving appetite, because obvious food contents it; while Nero,* half famished, could not feed upon a piece of bread, and, lingering after his snowed water, hardly got down an ordinary cup of Calda.[4]† By such circumscriptions of pleasure the contemned philosophers reserved unto themselves the secret of delight, which the helluos[5] of those days lost in their exorbitances. In vain we study delight; it is at the command of every sober mind, and in every sense born with us: but nature, who teacheth us the rule of pleasure, instructeth also in the bounds thereof, and where its line expireth. And, therefore, temperate minds, not pressing their pleasures until the sting appeareth, enjoy their contentations contentedly, and without regret, and so escape the folly of excess, to be pleased unto displacency.

SECT. II.—Bring candid eyes unto the perusal of men's works, and let not Zoilism[6] or detraction blast well-intended labours. He that endureth no faults in men's writings must only read his own, wherein, for the most part, all appeareth white. Quotation mistakes, inadvertency, expedition, and human lapses, may make not only moles but warts in learned authors; who, notwithstanding, being judged by the capital matter, admit not of disparagement. I should unwillingly affirm that Cicero was but slightly versed in Homer, because in his work, *De Gloria*, he ascribed those verses unto Ajax, which were delivered by Hector. What if Plautus, in the account of Hercules, mistaketh nativity for conception? Who would have mean thoughts of Apollinaris Sidonius, who seems to mistake the river Tigris for Euphrates? and, though a good historian and learned bishop of Avergne had the misfortune to be out in the story of David, making mention of him when the ark was sent back by the Philistines upon a cart; which was before his time. Though I have no great opinion of Machiavel's learning, yet I shall not presently say that he was but a novice in Roman history, because he was

---

* Nero, in his flight.   † Caldæ gelidæque minister.

[4] *Calda.*] Warm water.—*Dr. J.*
[5] *helluos.*] Gluttons.—*Dr. J.*
[6] *Zoilism, &c.*] From Zoilus, the calumniator of Homer.—*Dr. J.*

mistaken in placing Commodus after the Emperor Severus. Capital truths are to be narrowly eyed; collateral lapses and circumstantial deliveries not to be too strictly sifted. And if the substantial subject be well forged out, we need not examine the sparks which irregularly fly from it.

SECT. III.—Let well-weighed considerations, not stiff and peremptory assumptions, guide thy discourses, pen, and actions. To begin or continue our works like Trismegistus of old, "*verum certe verum atque verissimum est*,"[7]* would sound arrogantly unto present ears in this strict enquiring age; wherein, for the most part, 'probably' and 'perhaps' will hardly serve to mollify the spirit of captious contradictors. If Cardan saith that a parrot is a beautiful bird, Scaliger will set his wits to work to prove it a deformed animal. The compage of all physical truths is not so closely jointed, but opposition may find intrusion; nor always so closely maintained, as not to suffer attrition. Many positions seem quodlibetically[8] constituted, and, like a Delphian blade, will cut on both sides.[9] Some truths seem almost falsehoods, and some falsehoods almost truths; wherein falsehood and truth seem almost æquilibriously stated, and but a few grains of distinction to bear down the balance. Some have digged deep, yet glanced by the royal vein;[1] and a man may come unto the pericardium,[2] but not the heart of truth. Besides, many things are known, as some are seen, that is by parallaxis,[3] or at some distance from their true and proper beings, the superficial regard of things having a different aspect from their true and central natures. And this moves sober pens unto suspensory and timorous assertions, nor presently to obtrude them as

* In Tabula Smaragdina.

[7] *verum certe, &c.*] It is true, certainly true, true in the highest degree.—*Dr. J.*

[8] *quodlibetically.*] Determinable on either side.—*Dr. J.*

[9] *like a Delphian blade, &c.*] The Delphian sword became proverbial, not because it cut on both sides, but because it was used to different purposes.—*Dr. J.*

[1] *royal vein.*] I suppose the main vein of a mine.—*Dr. J.*

[2] *pericardium.*] The integument of the heart.—*Dr. J.*

[3] *parallaxis.*] The parallax of a star is the difference between its real and apparent place.—*Dr. J.*

Sybil's leaves,[4] which after considerations may find to be but folious appearances, and not the central and vital interiors of truth.

SECT. IV.—Value the judicious, and let not mere acquests in minor parts of learning gain thy pre-existimation. 'Tis an unjust way of compute, to magnify a weak head for some Latin abilities ; and to undervalue a solid judgment, because he knows not the genealogy of Hector. When that notable king of France* would have his son to know but one sentence in Latin ; had it been a good one, perhaps it had been enough. Natural parts and good judgments rule the world. States are not governed by ergotisms.[5] Many have ruled well, who could not, perhaps, define a commonwealth ; and they who understand not the globe of the earth, command a great part of it. Where natural logic prevails not, artificial too often faileth. Where nature fills the sails, the vessel goes smoothly on ; and when judgment is the pilot, the insurance need not be high. When industry builds upon nature, we may expect pyramids : where that foundation is wanting, the structure must be low. They do most by books, who could do much without them ; and he that chiefly owes himself unto himself, is the substantial man.

SECT. V.—Let thy studies be free as thy thoughts and contemplations : but fly not only upon the wings of imagination ; join sense unto reason, and experiment unto speculation, and so give life unto embryon truths, and verities yet in their chaos. There is nothing more acceptable unto the ingenious world, than this noble eluctation[6] of truth ; wherein, against the tenacity of prejudice and prescription, this century now prevaileth. What libraries of new volumes after times will behold, and in what a new world of knowledge the eyes of our posterity may be happy, a few ages may joyfully declare ; and is but a cold thought unto those who cannot hope to behold this exantlation of truth, or that

* Louis the Eleventh. Qui nescit dissimulare nescit regnare.

[4] *Sybil's leaves.*] On which the Sybil wrote her oraculous answers.— *Virgil.*

[5] *ergotisms.*] Conclusions deduced according to the forms of logic.— *Dr. J.*

[6] *eluctation.*] Forcible eruption.—*Dr. J.*

obscured virgin half out of the pit: which might make some content with a commutation of the time of their lives, and to commend the fancy of the Pythagorean metempsychosis ;[7] whereby they might hope to enjoy this happiness in their third or fourth selves, and behold that in Pythagoras, which they now but foresee in Euphorbus.* The world, which took but six days to make, is like to take six thousand to make out: meanwhile, old truths voted down begin to resume their places, and new ones arise upon us; wherein there is no comfort in the happiness of Tully's Elysium,† or any satisfaction from the ghosts of the ancients, who knew so little of what is now well known. Men disparage not antiquity, who prudently exalt new enquiries; and make not them the judges of truth, who were but fellow enquirers of it. Who can but magnify the endeavours of Aristotle, and the noble start which learning had under him; or less than pity the slender progression made upon such advantages? while many centuries were lost in repetitions and transcriptions, sealing up the book of knowledge. And, therefore, rather than to swell the leaves of learning by fruitless repetitions, to sing the same song in all ages, nor adventure at essays beyond the attempt of others, many would be content that some would write like Helmont or Paracelsus ;[8] and be willing to endure the monstrosity of some opinions, for divers singular notions requiting such aberrations.

SECT. VI.—Despise not the obliquities of younger ways, nor despair of better things whereof there is yet no prospect. Who would imagine that Diogenes, who in his younger days was a falsifier of money, should in the after-course of his life be so great a contemner of metal? Some negroes who believe the resurrection, think that they shall rise white.‡ Even in this life, regeneration may imitate resurrection;

* Ipse ego, nam memini, Trojani tempore belli,
   Panthoides Euphorbus eram.—OVID.

† Who comforted himself that he should there converse with the old philosophers.

‡ Mandelslo's travels.

[7] *Pythagorean metempsychosis.*] Transmigration of the soul from body to body.—*Dr. J.*

[8] *Helmont or Paracelsus.*] Wild and enthusiastic authors of romantic chemistry.—*Dr. J.*

our black and vicious tinctures may wear of, and goodness clothe us with candour. Good admonitions knock not always in vain. There will be signal examples of God's mercy, and the angels must not want their charitable rejoices for the conversion of lost sinners. Figures of most angles do nearest approach unto circles which have no angles at all. Some may be near unto goodness, who are conceived far from it; and many things happen, not likely to ensue from any promises of antecedences. Culpable beginnings have found commendable conclusions, and infamous courses pious retractations. Detestable sinners have proved exemplary converts on earth, and may be glorious in the apartment of Mary Magdalen in heaven. Men are not the same through all divisions of their ages: time, experience, self-reflections, and God's mercies, make in some well-tempered minds a kind of translation before death, and men to differ from themselves as well as from other persons. Hereof the old world afforded many examples, to the infamy of latter ages, wherein men too often live by the rule of their inclinations; so that, without any astral prediction, the first day gives the last:* men are commonly as they were: or rather, as bad dispositions run into worser habits, the evening doth not crown, but sourly conclude the day.

SECT. VII.—If the Almighty will not spare us according to his merciful capitulation at Sodom; if his goodness please not to pass over a great deal of bad for a small pittance of good, or to look upon us in a lump; there is slender hope for mercy, or sound presumption of fulfilling half his will, either in persons or nations: they who excel in some virtues being so often defective in others; few men driving at the extent and amplitude of goodness, but computing themselves by their best parts, and others by their worst, are content to rest in those virtues which others commonly want. Which makes this speckled face of honesty in the world; and which was the imperfection[9] of the old philosophers and great pre-

---

* Primusque dies dedit extremum.

[9] *few men, &c.*] Instead of this passage, I find the following in *MS. Sloan.* 1874 :—"Persons, sects, and nations, mainly settling upon some Christian particulars, which they conceive most acceptable unto God, and promoting the interest of their inclinations, parties, and divisions;

tenders unto virtue, who well declining the gaping vices of intemperance, incontinency, violence, and oppression, were yet blindly peccant in iniquities of closer faces, were envious, malicious, contemners, scoffers, censurers, and stuffed with vizard vices, no less depraving the ethereal particle and diviner portion of man. For envy, malice, hatred, are the qualities of Satan, close and dark like himself; and where such brands smoke, the soul cannot be white. Vice may be had at all prices; expensive and costly iniquities, which make the noise, cannot be every man's sins: but the soul may be foully inquinated[1] at a very low rate; and a man may be cheaply vicious, to the perdition of himself.

SECT. VIII.—Opinion rides upon the neck of reason; and men are happy, wise, or learned, according as that empress shall set them down in the register of reputation. However, weigh not thyself in the scales of thy own opinion, but let the judgment of the judicious be the standard of thy merit. Self-estimation is a flatterer too readily entitling us unto knowledge and abilities, which others solicitously labour after, and doubtfully think they attain. Surely such confident tempers do pass their days in best tranquillity, who resting in the opinion of their own abilities, are happily gulled by such contentation; wherein pride, self-conceit, confidence, and opiniatrity, will hardly suffer any to complain of imperfection. To think themselves in the right, or all that right, or only that, which they do or think, is a fallacy of high content; though others laugh in their sleeves, and look upon them as in a deluded state of judgment: wherein, notwithstanding, 'twere but a civil piece of complacency to suffer them to sleep who would not wake, to let them rest in their securities, nor by dissent or opposition to stagger their contentments.

every one reckoning and preferring himself by the particulars wherein he excelleth, and decrying all others, though highly eminent in other Christian virtues. Which makes this speckled face of honesty in the world; whereas, if men would not seek themselves abroad; if every one would judge and reckon himself by his worst, and others by their best parts, this deception must needs vanish; humility would gain ground; charity would overspread the face of the church, and the fruits of the spirit not be so thinly found among us.

"This was the imperfection," &c.

[1] *inquinated.*] Defiled.—*Dr. J.*

SECT. IX.[2]—Since the brow speaks often truth, since eyes and noses have tongues, and the countenance proclaims the heart and inclinations; let observation so far instruct thee in physiognomical lines, as to be some rule for thy distinction, and guide for thy affection unto such as look most like men. Mankind, methinks, is comprehended in a few faces, if we exclude all visages which any way participate of symmetries and schemes of look common unto other animals. For as though man were the extract of the world, in whom all were " in coagulato,"[3] which in their forms were " in soluto"[4] and at extension; we often observe that men do most act those creatures, whose constitution, parts, and complexion, do most predominate in their mixtures. This is a corner stone in physiognomy, and holds some truth not only in particular persons but also in whole nations. There are, therefore, provincial faces, national lips and noses, which testify not only the natures of those countries, but of those which have them elsewhere. Thus we may make England the whole earth, dividing it not only into Europe, Asia, Africa, but the particular regions thereof; and may in some latitude affirm, that there are Egyptians, Scythians, Indians among us, who, though born in England, yet carry the faces and air of those countries, and are also agreeable and correspondent unto their natures. Faces look uniformly unto our eyes: how they appear unto some animals of a more piercing or differing sight, who are able to discover the inequalities, rubs, and hairiness of the skin, is not without good doubt: and, therefore, in reference unto man, Cupid is said to be blind. Affection should not be too sharp-eyed, and love is not to be made by magnifying glasses. If things were seen as they truly are, the beauty of bodies would be much abridged. And, therefore, the wise contriver hath drawn the pictures and outsides of things softly and amiably unto the natural edge of our eyes, not leaving them able to discover those uncomely asperities, which make oyster-shells in good faces, and hedgehogs even in Venus's moles.

SECT. X.—Court not felicity too far, and weary not the

[2] SECT. IX.] This is a very fanciful and indefensible section.—*Dr. J.*
[3] *were " in coagulato."*] i.é. "In a congealed or compressed mass."—*Dr. J.*
[4] *in soluto.*] "In a state of expansion and separation."—*Dr. J.*

favourable hand of fortune. Glorious actions have their times, extent, and non ultras. To put no end unto attempts were to make prescription of successes, and to bespeak unhappiness at the last: for the line of our lives is drawn with white and black vicissitudes, wherein the extremes hold seldom one complexion. That Pompey should obtain the surname of Great at twenty-five years, that men in their young and active days should be fortunate and perform notable things, is no observation of deep wonder; they having the strength of their fates before them, nor yet acted their parts in the world for which they were brought into it; whereas men of years, matured for counsels and designs, seem to be beyond the vigour of their active fortunes, and high exploits of life, providentially ordained unto ages best agreeable unto them. And, therefore, many brave men finding their fortune grow faint, and feeling its declination, have timely withdrawn themselves from great attempts, and so escaped the ends of mighty men, disproportionable to their beginnings.[5] But magnanimous thoughts have so dimmed the eyes of many, that forgetting the very essence of fortune, and the vicissitude of good and evil, they apprehend no bottom in felicity; and so have been still tempted on unto mighty actions, reserved for their destructions. For fortune lays the plot of our adversities in the foundation of our felicities, blessing us in the first quadrate,[6] to blast us more sharply in the last. And since in the highest felicities there lieth a capacity of the lowest miseries, she hath this advantage from our happiness to make us truly miserable: for to become acutely miserable we are to be first happy. Affliction smarts most in the most happy state, as having somewhat in it of Belisarius at beggar's bush, or Bajazet in the grate.[7]

---

[5] *beginnings.*] *MS. Sloan.* 1874, proceeds thus;—"Wisely stopping about the meridian of their felicities, and unwilling to hazard the favours of the descending wheel, or to fight downward in the setting arch of fortune. 'Sic longius ævium destruit ingentes animos, et vita superstes fortunæ, nisi summa dies cum fine bonorum affluit, et celeri prævertit tristia letho dedecori est fortuna prior quisquam ne secundis tradere se fatis audet nisi morte parcitâ.'—*Lucan 7.*"

[6] *quadrate, &c.*] That is, "in the first part of our time," alluding to the four quadratures of the moon.—*Dr. J.*

[7] *Belisarius, &c.*] Belisarius, after he had gained many victories, is said to have been reduced, by the displeasure of the emperor, to actual

And this the fallen angels severely understand; who have
acted their first part in heaven, are made sharply miserable by
transition, and more afflictively feel the contrary state of hell.[8]

SECT. XI.—Carry no careless eye upon the unexpected
scenes of things; but ponder the acts of Providence in the
public ends of great and notable men, set out unto the view
of all for no common memorandums.[9] The tragical exits
and unexpected periods of some eminent persons, cannot

beggary : Bajazet, made captive by Tamerlane, is reported to have been
shut up in a cage. It may somewhat gratify those who deserve to be
gratified, to inform them that both these stories are false.—*Dr. J.*

Lord Mahon, in his recent life of Belisarius, has related the mendicity
and loss of sight of this great man, and says in his preface that those
facts, " which every writer for the last century and a half has treated as
a fable, may be established on firm historical grounds."

[8] *And this the fallen angels, &c.*] Instead of this passage, I find the
following in *MS. Sloan.* 1874 :—"And this is the observable course ;
not only in this visible stage of things, but may be feared in our
second beings and everlasting selves ; wherein the good things past are
seconded by the bad to come : and many to whom the embraces of fortune are open here, may find Abraham's arms shut unto him hereafter ;
which wakes serious consideration, not so much to pity as envy some
men's infelicities, wherein, considering the circle of both our beings, and
the succession of good unto evil, tyranny may sometimes prove courteous,
and malice mercifully cruel. Wherein, notwithstanding, if swelling
beginnings have found uncomfortable conclusions, it is by the method
and justice of providence equalizing one with the other, and reducing
the sum of the whole unto a mediocrity by the balance of extremities :
that in the sum the felicities of great ones hold truth and parity with
most that are below them : whereby the minor favourites of fortune
which incur not such sharp transitions, have no cause to whine, nor men
of middle fates to murmur at their indifferences.

" By this method of providence the devil himself is deluded ; who
maligning us at all points, and bearing felicity from us even in this earthly
being, he becomes assistant unto our future happiness, and blessed vicissitude of the next. And this is also the unhappiness of himself, who
having acted his first part in heaven, is made sharply miserable by
transition, and more afflictively feels the contrary state of hell."

[9] *memorandums.*] This sentence is thus continued in *MS. Sloan.*
1874 :—" Whereof I, that have not seen the sixtieth part of time, have
beheld great examples. Than the incomparable Montrose, no man
acted a more fortunate part in the first scene of his adventures; but
courageous loyalty continuing his attempts, he quickly felt that fortune's favours were out ; and fell upon miseries smartly answering his
felicities, which was the only accomplishment wanting before to make
him fit for Plutarch's pen, and to parallel the lives of his heroic
captains."

but amaze considerate observators ; wherein, notwithstanding, most men seem to see by extramission,[1] without reception
or self-reflection, and conceive themselves unconcerned by
the fallacy of their own exemption: whereas, the mercy of
God hath singled out but few to be the signals of his justice,
leaving the generality of mankind to the pedagogy of example.   But the inadvertency of our natures not. well
apprehending this favourable method and merciful decima-
tion,[2] and that he showeth in some what others also deserve ;
they entertain no sense of his hand beyond the stroke of
themselves.   Whereupon the whole becomes necessarily
punished, and the contracted hand of God extended. unto
universal judgments: from whence, nevertheless, the stupidity of our tempers receives but faint impressions, and in.
the most tragical state of times holds but starts of good
motions.   So that to continue us in goodness there must be
iterated returns of misery, and a circulation in afflictions is
necessary.[3] And since we cannot be wise by warnings ; since
plagues are insignificant, except we be personally plagued ;
since also we cannot be punished unto amendment by proxy
or commutation, nor by vicinity, but contraction ; there is an
unhappy necessity that we must smart in our own skins, and
the provoked arm of the Almighty must fall upon ourselves.
The capital sufferings of others are rather our monitions

[1] *extramission.*] By the passage of sight from the eye to the object.--*Dr. J.*
[2] *dicimation.*] The selection of every tenth man for punishment, a
practice sometimes used in general mutinies.—*Dr. J.*
[3] *necessary.*] The following passage occurs here in *MS. Sloan.* 1874 :
"Which is the amazing part of that incomprehensible patience, to con-
descend to act over these vicissitudes even in the despair of our better-
ments : and how that omnipotent spirit that would not be exasperated
by our forefathers above 1600 years, should thus lastingly endure our
successive transgressions, and still contend with flesh ; or how he can
forgive those sins which will be committed again, and accept of repentances, which must have after-penitences, is the riddle of his mercies.
"If God had not determined a settled period unto the world, and
ordered the duration thereof unto his merciful intentions, it seems a
kind of impossibility that he should have thus long continued it.   Some
think there will be another world after this.   Surely God, who
hath beheld the iniquity of this, will hardly make another of the same
nature ; and some wonder why he ever made any at all since he was
so happy in himself without it, and self-sufficiently free from all pro-
vocation, wrath, and indignation, arising from this world, which sets
his justice and his mercy at perpetual contention."

than acquitments. There is but one who died salvifically[4] for us, and able to say unto death, hitherto shalt thou go and no farther; only one enlivening death, which makes gardens of graves, and that which was sowed in corruption to arise and flourish in glory; when death itself shall die, and living shall have no period; when the damned shall mourn at the funeral of death; when life not death shall be the wages of sin: when the second death shall prove a miserable life, and destruction shall be courted.

SECT. XII.—Although their thoughts may seem too severe, who think that few ill-natured men go to heaven; yet it may be acknowledged that good-natured persons are best founded for that place; who enter the world with good dispositions and natural graces, more ready to be advanced by impressions from above, and christianized unto pieties; who carry about them plain and downright dealing minds, humility, mercy, charity, and virtues acceptable unto God and man. But whatever success they may have as to heaven, they are the acceptable men on earth, and happy is he who hath his quiver full of them for his friends. These are not the dens wherein falsehood lurks, and hypocrisy hides its head; wherein frowardness makes its nest; or where malice, hard-heartedness, and oppression love to dwell; nor those by whom the poor get little, and the rich sometime lose all; men not of retracted looks, but who carry their hearts in their faces, and need not to be looked upon with perspectives; not sordidly or mischievously ingrateful; who cannot learn to ride upon the neck of the afflicted, nor load the heavy laden, but who keep the temple of Janus[5] shut by peaceable and quiet tempers; who make not only the best friends, but the best enemies, as easier to forgive than offend, and ready to pass by the second offence before they avenge the first; who make natural royalists, obedient subjects, kind and merciful princes, verified in our own, one of the best-natured kings of this throne. Of the old Roman emperors the best were the best-natured; though they made but a small number, and might be writ in a ring. Many of the rest were as bad men as princes; humorists rather than of

---

[4] *salvifically.*] "So as to procure salvation."—*Dr. J.*

[5] *Janus.*] The temple of *J*anus among the Romans was shut in time of peace, and opened at a declaration of war.—*Dr. J.*

good humours ; and of good natural parts rather than of good natures, which did but arm their bad inclinations, and make them wittily wicked.

SECT. XIII.—With what shift and pains we come into the world, we remember not : but 'tis commonly found no easy matter to get out of it.   Many have studied to exasperate the ways of death, but fewer hours have been spent to soften that necessity.   That the smoothest way unto the grave is made by bleeding, as common opinion presumeth, beside the sick and fainting languors, which accompany that effusion, the experiment in Lucan and Seneca[6] will make us doubt ; under which the noble stoic so deeply laboured, that to conceal his affliction, he was fain to retire from the sight of his wife, and not ashamed to implore the merciful hand of his physician to shorten his misery therein.   Ovid,* the old heroes, and the stoics, who were so afraid of drowning, as dreading thereby the extinction of their soul, which they conceived to be a fire, stood probably in fear of an easier way of death; wherein the water, entering the possessions of air, makes a temperate suffocation, and kills as it were without a fever.   Surely many, who have had the spirit to destroy themselves, have not been ingenious in the contrivance thereof.   'Twas a dull way practised by Themistocles, to overwhelm himself with bull's blood,† who, being an Athenian, might have held an easier theory of death from the state potion of his country ; from which Socrates in Plato seemed not to suffer much more than from the fit of an ague. Cato is much to be pitied, who mangled himself with poniards; and Hannibal seems more subtle, who carried his delivery, not in the point but the pummel of his sword.‡

* Demito naufragium, mors mihi munus erit.   † Plutarch's lives.

‡ Pummel, wherein he is said to have carried something whereby, upon a struggle or despair, he might deliver himself from all misfortunes.   Juvenal says, it was carried in a ring :

    Cannarum vindex, et tanti sanguinis ultor,
    Annulus.

Nor swords at hand, nor hissing darts afar,
Are doom'd t' avenge the tedious bloody war,
But poison drawn thro' a ring's hollow plate.—DRYDEN.

[6] *that the smoothest way unto the grave, &c.*]   Seneca, having opened his veins, found the blood flow so slowly, and death linger so long, that he was forced to quicken it by going into a warm bath.—*Dr. J.*

The Egyptians were merciful contrivers, who destroyed their malefactors by asps, charming their senses into an invincible sleep, and killing as it were with Hermes's rod.[7] The Turkish emperor,* odious for other cruelty, was herein a remarkable master of mercy, killing his favourite in his sleep, and sending him from the shade into the house of darkness. He who had been thus destroyed would hardly have bled at the presence of his destroyer: when men are already dead by metaphor, and pass but from one sleep unto another, wanting herein the eminent part of severity, to feel themselves to die; and escaping the sharpest attendant of death, the lively apprehension thereof. But to learn to die, is better than to study the ways of dying. Death will find some ways to untie or cut the most gordian knots of life, and make men's miseries as mortal as themselves; whereas evil spirits, as undying substances, are inseparable from their calamities; and, therefore, they everlastingly struggle under their *angustias*,[8] and bound up with immortality can never get out of themselves.

PART THE THIRD.

SECT. I.—'Tis hard to find a whole age to imitate, or what century to propose for example. Some have been far more approvable than others; but virtue and vice, panegyrics and satires, scatteringly to be found in all. History sets down not only things laudable, but abominable: things which should never have been, or never have been known; so that noble patterns must be fetched here and there from single persons, rather than whole nations; and from all nations, rather than any one. The world was early bad, and the first sin the most deplorable of any. The younger world afforded the oldest men, and perhaps the best and the worst, when

* Solyman.

[7] *rod.*] Which procured sleep by a touch.—*Dr. J.*
[8] *angustias.*] Agonies.—*Dr. J.*

length of days made virtuous habits heroical and immovable, vicious, inveterate, and irreclaimable. And since 'tis said that the imaginations of their hearts were evil, only evil, and continually evil; it may be feared that their sins held pace with their lives; and their longevity swelling their impieties, the longanimity of God would no longer endure such vivacious abominations. Their impieties were surely of a deep dye, which required the whole element of water to wash them away, and overwhelmed their memories with themselves; and so shut up the first windows of time, leaving no histories of those longevous generations, when men might have been properly historians, when Adam might have read long lectures unto Methuselah, and Methuselah unto Noah. For had we been happy in just historical accounts of that unparalleled world, we might have been acquainted with wonders; and have understood not a little of the acts and undertakings of Moses's mighty men, and men of renown of old; which might have enlarged our thoughts, and made the world older unto us. [For the unknown part of time shortens the estimation, if not the compute of it. What hath escaped our knowledge, falls not under our consideration; and what is and will be latent, is little better than non-existent.[9]

SECT. II.—Some things are dictated for our instruction, some acted for our imitation; wherein 'tis best to ascend unto the highest conformity, and to the honour of the exemplar. He honours God, who imitates him; for what we virtuously imitate we approve and admire: and since we delight not to imitate inferiors, we aggrandize and magnify those we imitate; since also we are most apt to imitate those we love, we testify our affection in our imitation of the inimitable. To affect to be like, may be no imitation: to act, and not to be what we pretend to imitate, is but a mimical conformation, and carrieth no virtue in it. Lucifer imitated not God, when he said he would be like the highest: and he[1] imitated not Jupiter, who counterfeited thunder. Where

---

[9] *non-existent.*] This sentence concludes thus :—"The world is not half itself, nor the moiety known of its occurrences, of what hath been acted."—*MS. Sloan.* 1848.

[1] *he.*] Salmoneus.—*Dr. J.*

imitation can go no farther, let admiration step on, whereof there is no end in the wisest form of men. Even angels and spirits have enough to admire in their sublimer natures; admiration being the act of the creature, and not of God, who doth not admire himself. Created natures allow of swelling hyperboles: nothing can be said hyperbolically of God, nor will his attributes admit of expressions above their own exuperances.[2] Trismegistus's cïrcle, whose centre is everywhere, and circumference nowhere, was no hyperbole. Words cannot exceed where they cannot express enough. Even the most winged thoughts fall at the setting out, and reach not the portal of divinity.

SECT. III.—In bivious theorems,[3] and Janus-faced doctrines, let virtuous considerations state the determination. Look upon opinions as thou dost upon the moon, and choose not the dark hemisphere for thy contemplation. Embrace not the opacous and blind side of opinions, but that which looks most luciferously or influentially unto goodness. 'Tis better to think that there are guardian spirits, than that there are no spirits to guard us; that vicious persons are slaves, than that there is any servitude in virtue; that times past have been better than times present, than that times were always bad; and that to be men it sufficeth to be no better than men in all ages, and so promiscuously to swim down the turbid stream, and make up the grand confusion. Sow not thy understanding with opinions, which make nothing of iniquities, and fallaciously extenuate transgressions. Look upon vices and vicious objects with hyperbolical eyes; and rather enlarge their dimensions, that their unseen deformities may not escape thy sense, and their poisonous parts and stings may appear massy and monstrous unto thee: for the undiscerned particles and atoms of evil deceive us, and we are undone by the invisibles of seeming goodness. We are only deceived in what is not discerned, and to err is but to be blind or dimsighted as to some perceptions.

[2] *exuperances.*] Exaggerations.—*Dr. J.*
[3] *bivious theorems.*] Speculations which open different tracks to the mind; which lead *two ways.*—*Dr. J.*

SECT. IV.—To be honest in a right line,* and virtuous by epitome, be firm unto such principles of goodness, as carry in them volumes of instruction and may abridge thy labour. And since instructions are many, hold close unto those whereon the rest depend: so may we have all in a few, and the law and the prophets in sacred writ in stenography,[4] and the Scripture in a nut-shell. To pursue the osseous and solid part of goodness, which gives stability and rectitude to all the rest; to settle on fundamental virtues, and bid early defiance unto mother-vices, which carry in their bowels the seminals of other iniquities; makes a short cut in goodness, and strikes not off an head, but the whole neck of Hydra. For we are carried into the dark lake, like the Egyptian river into the sea, by seven principal ostiaries: the mother-sins[5] of that number are the deadly engines of evil spirits that undo us, and even evil spirits themselves; and he who is under the chains thereof is not without a possession. Mary Magdalen had more than seven devils, if these with their imps were in her; and he who is thus possessed, may literally be named "Legion." Where such plants grow and prosper, look for no champain or region void of thorns; but productions like the tree of Goa,† and forests of abomination.

SECT. V.—Guide not the hand of God, nor order the finger of the Almighty unto thy will and pleasure; but sit quiet in the soft showers of providence, and favourable distributions in this world, either to thyself or others. And since not only judgments have their errands, but mercies their commissions; snatch not at every favour, nor think thyself passed by if they fall upon thy neighbour. Rake not up envious displacencies at things successful unto others, which the wise disposer of all thinks not fit for thyself. Reconcile the events of things unto both beings, that is, of this world and the next: so will there not seem so many

* Linea recta brevissima.

† Arbor Goa de Ruyz, or Ficus Indica, whose branches send down shoots which root in the ground, from whence there successively rise others, till one tree becomes a wood.

[4] *stenography.*] In short hand.—*Dr. J.*

[5] *mother-sins.*] Pride, covetousness, lust, envy, gluttony, anger, sloth.—*Dr. J.*

riddles in Providence, nor various inequalities in the dispensation of things below.[6] If thou dost not anoint thy face, yet put not on sackcloth at the felicities of others. Repining at the good, draws on rejoicing at the evils of others: and so falls into that inhuman vice,* for which so few languages have a name. The blessed spirits above rejoice at our happiness below: but to be glad at the evils of one another, is beyond the malignity of hell; and falls not on evil spirits, who, though they rejoice at our unhappiness, take no pleasure at the afflictions of their own society or of their fellow natures. Degenerous heads! who must be fain to learn from such examples, and to be taught from the school of hell.

SECT. VI.—Grain not thy vicious stains;[7] nor deepen those swart tinctures, which temper, infirmity, or ill habits have set upon thee; and fix not, by iterated depravations, what time might efface, or virtuous washes expunge. He, who thus still advanceth in iniquity, deepeneth his deformed hue; turns a shadow into night, and makes himself a negro in the black jaundice; and so becomes one of those lost ones, the disproportionate pores of whose brains afford no entrance unto good motions, but reflect and frustrate all counsels, deaf unto the thunder of the laws, and rocks unto the cries of charitable commiserators. He who hath had the patience of Diogenes, to make orations unto statues, may more sensibly apprehend how all words fall to the ground, spent upon such a surd and earless generation of men, stupid unto all instruction, and rather requiring an exorcist than an orator for their conversion!

SECT. VII.—Burden not the back of Aries, Leo, or Taurus,[8] with thy faults; nor make Saturn, Mars, or

* Ἐπικαιρεκακία.

[6] *below.*] The following passage occurs here from *MS. Sloan.* 1847:— "So mayst thou carry a smooth face, and sit down in contentation, without those cancerous commotions which take up every suffering, displeasing at things successful unto others; which the arch-disposer of all thinks not fit for ourselves. To rejoice only in thine [own] good, exclusively to that of others, is a stiff piece of self-love, wanting the supplying oil of benevolence and charity."

[7] *vicious stains.*] See note [5], p. 91.

[8] *Aries, &c.*] The Ram, Lion, or Bull, signs in the Zodiack.—*Dr. J.*

Venus, guilty of thy follies. Think not to fasten thy imperfections on the stars, and so despairingly conceive thyself under a fatality of being evil. Calculate thyself within; seek not thyself in the moon, but in thine own orb or microcosmical circumference.[9] Let celestial aspects admonish and advertise, not conclude and determine thy ways. For since good and bad stars moralize not our actions, and neither excuse or commend, acquit or condemn our good or bad deeds at the present or last bar; since some are astrologically well disposed, who are morally highly vicious; not celestial figures, but virtuous schemes, must denominate and state our actions. If we rightly understood the names whereby God calleth the stars; if we knew his name for the dog-star, or by what appellation Jupiter, Mars, and Saturn obey his will; it might be a welcome accession unto astrology, which speaks great things, and is fain to make use of appellations from Greek and barbarick systems. Whatever influences, impulsions, or inclinations there be from the lights above, it were a piece of wisdom to make one of those wise men who overrule their stars,* and with their own militia contend with the host of heaven. Unto which attempt there want not auxiliaries from the whole strength of morality, supplies from Christian ethics, influences also and illuminations from above, more powerful than the lights of heaven.

SECT. VIII.—Confound not the distinctions of thy life which nature hath divided; that is, youth, adolescence, manhood, and old age: nor in these divided periods, wherein thou art in a manner four, conceive thyself but one. Let every division be happy in its proper virtues, nor one vice run through all. Let each distinction have its salutary transition, and critically deliver thee from the imperfections of the former; so ordering the whole, that prudence and virtue may have the largest section. Do as a child but when thou art a child, and ride not on a reed at twenty. He who hath not taken leave of the follies of his youth, and in his maturer state scarce got out of that division, dispro-

---

* Sapiens dominabitur astris.

[9] *microcosmical circumference.*] In the compass of thy own little world.—*Dr. J.*

portionately divideth his days, crowds up the latter part of his life, and leaves too narrow a corner for the age of wisdom; and so hath room to be a man scarce longer than he hath been a youth. Rather than to make this confusion, anticipate the virtues of age, and live long without the infirmities of it. So mayst thou count up thy days as some do Adam's;* that is, by anticipation; so mayst thou be coetaneous unto thy elders, and a father unto thy contemporaries.

SECT. IX.—While others are curious in the choice of good air, and chiefly solicitous for healthful habitations, study thou conversation, and be critical in thy consortion. The aspects, conjunctions, and configurations of the stars, which mutually diversify, intend, or qualify their influences, are but the varieties of their nearer or farther conversation with one another, and like the consortion of men, whereby they become better or worse, and even exchange their natures. Since men live by examples, and will be imitating something, order thy imitation to thy improvement, not thy ruin. Look not for roses in Attalus's garden,† or wholesome flowers in a venomous plantation. And since there is scarce any one bad, but some others are the worse for him; tempt not contagion by proximity, and hazard not thyself in the shadow of corruption. He who hath not early suffered this shipwreck, and in his younger days escaped this Charybdis, may make a happy voyage, and not come in with black sails into the port.[1] Self-conversation, or to be alone, is better than such consortion. Some school-men tell us, that he is properly alone, with whom in the same place there is no other of the same species. Nebuchadnezzar was alone, though among the beasts of the field; and a wise man may be tolerably said to be alone, though with a rabble of people little better than beasts about him. Unthinking heads, who have not learned to be alone, are in a prison to themselves, if they be not also with others: whereas, on the

* Adam, thought to be created in the state of man, about thirty years old.

† Attalus made a garden which contained only venomous plants.

[1] *black sails, &c.*] Alluding to the story of Theseus, who had black sails when he went to engage the Minotaur in Crete.—*Dr. J.*

contrary, they whose thoughts are in a fair, and hurry within, are sometimes fain to retire into company, to be out of the crowd of themselves. He who must needs have company, must needs have sometimes bad company. Be able to be alone. Lose not the advantage of solitude, and the society of thyself; nor be only content, but delight to be alone and single with Omnipresency. He who is thus prepared, the day is not uneasy nor the night black unto him. Darkness may bound his eyes, not his imagination. In his bed he may lie, like Pompey and his sons,* in all quarters of the earth; may speculate the universe, and enjoy the whole world in the hermitage of himself. Thus the old ascetick Christians found a paradise in a desert, and with little converse on earth held a conversation in heaven; thus they astronomized in caves, and, though they beheld not the stars, had the glory of heaven before them.

SECT. X.—Let the characters of good things stand indelibly in thy mind, and thy thoughts be active on them. Trust not too much unto suggestions from reminiscential amulets,[2] or artificial memorandums. Let the mortifying Janus of Covarrubias† be in thy daily thoughts, not only on thy hand and signets. Rely not alone upon silent and dumb remembrances. Behold not death's heads till thou dost not see them, nor look upon mortifying objects till thou overlookest them. Forget not how assuefaction unto anything minorates the passion from it; how constant objects lose their hints, and steal an inadvertisement upon us. There is no excuse to forget what everything prompts unto us. To thoughtful observators, the whole world is a phylactery;[3]

---

* Pompeios Juvenes Asia atque Europa, sed ipsum Terra tegit Libyes.

† Don Sebastian de Covarrubias writ three centuries of moral emblems in Spanish. In the 88th of the second century he sets down two faces averse, and conjoined Janus-like; the one, a gallant beautiful face, the other, a death's head face, with this motto out of Ovid's Metamorphoses :—

Quid fuerim, quid simque, vide.
You discern
What now I am, and what I was shall learn.—ADDIS.

[2] *reminiscential amulets.*] Any thing worn on the hand or body, by way of monition or remembrance.—*Dr. J.*

[3] *phylactery.*] See page 97, note [7].—*Dr. J.*

and everything we see an item of the wisdom, power, or goodness of God. Happy are they who verify their amulets, and make their phylacteries speak in their lives and actions. To run on in despite of the revulsions and pull-backs of such remoras aggravates our transgressions. When death's heads on our hands have no influence upon our heads, and fleshless cadavers abate not the exorbitances of the flesh; when crucifixes upon men's hearts suppress not their bad commotions, and his image who was murdered for us withholds not from blood and murder; phylacteries prove but formalities, and their despised hints sharpen our condemnation.

SECT. XI.—Look not for whales in the Euxine sea, or expect great matters where they are not to be found. Seek not for profundity in shallowness, or fertility in a wilderness. Place not the expectations of great happiness here below, or think to find heaven on earth; wherein we must be content with embryon felicities, and fruitions of doubtful faces: for the circle of our felicities makes but short arches. In every clime we are in a periscian state; [4] and with our light, our shadow and darkness walk about us. Our contentments stand upon the tops of pyramids ready to fall off, and the insecurity of their enjoyments abrupteth our tranquillities. What we magnify is magnificent; but, like to the Colossus, noble without, stuft with rubbage and coarse metal within. Even the sun, whose glorious outside we behold, may have dark and smoky entrails. In vain we admire the lustre of anything seen: that which is truly glorious is invisible. Paradise was but a part of the earth, lost not only to our fruition but our knowledge. And if, according to old dictates, no man can be said to be happy before death, the happiness of this life goes for nothing before it be over, and while we think ourselves happy we do but usurp that name. Certainly, true beatitude groweth not on earth, nor hath this world in it the expectations we have of it. He swims in oil, [5] and can hardly avoid sinking, who hath such light

---

[4] *periscian state.*] "With shadows all around us." The Periscii are those who, living within the polar circle, see the sun move round them, and, consequently, project their shadows in all directions.—*Dr. J.*

[5] *He swims in oil.*] Which being a light fluid, cannot support any heavy body.—*Dr. J.*

foundations to support him: 'tis, therefore, happy that we have two worlds to hold on. To enjoy true happiness, we must travel into a very far country, and even out of ourselves; for the pearl we seek for is not to be found in the Indian but in the Empyrean ocean.[6]

SECT. XII.—Answer not the spur of fury, and be not prodigal or prodigious in revenge. Make not one in the *Historia Horribilis;** flay not thy servant for a broken glass,[7] nor pound him in a mortar who offendeth thee;[8] supererogate not in the worst sense, and overdo not the necessities of evil; humour not the injustice of revenge. Be not stoically mistaken in the equality of sins, nor commutatively iniquitous in the valuation of transgressions; but weigh them in the scales of heaven, and by the weights of righteous reason. Think that revenge too high, which is but level with the offence. Let thy arrows of revenge fly short; or be aimed like those of Jonathan, to fall beside the mark. Too many there be to whom a dead enemy smells well, and who find musk and amber in revenge. The ferity of such minds holds no rule in retaliations, requiring too often a head for a tooth, and the supreme revenge for trespasses which a night's rest should obliterate. But patient meekness takes injuries like pills, not chewing but swallowing them down, laconically suffering, and silently passing them over; while angered pride makes a noise, like Homerican Mars,† at every scratch of offences. Since women

* A book so intitled, wherein are sundry horrid accounts.

† Tu miser exclamas, ut Stentora vincere possis
  Vel potius quantum Gradivus Homericus.—JUV.

Thus translated by Creech :—
        You rage and storm, and, blasphemously loud,
        As Stentor bellowing to the Grecian crowd,
        Or Homer's Mars.

[6] *Empyrean ocean.*] In the expanses of the highest heaven.—*Dr. J.*
[7] *flay not thy servant, &c.*] When Augustus supped with one of the Roman senators, a slave happened to break a glass, for which his master ordered him to be thrown into his pond to feed his lampreys. Augustus, to punish his cruelty, ordered all the glasses in the house to be broken.—*Dr. J.*
[8] *nor pound him in a mortar, &c.*] Anaxarchus, an ancient philosopher, was beaten in a mortar by a tyrant.—*Dr. J.*

do most delight in revenge,[9] it may seem but feminine manhood to be vindictive. If thou must needs have thy revenge of thine enemy, with a soft tongue break his bones,* heap coals of fire on his head, forgive him and enjoy it. To forgive our enemies is a charming way of revenge, and a short Cæsarian conquest overcoming without a blow; laying our enemies at our feet, under sorrow, shame and repentance; leaving our foes our friends, and solicitously inclined to grateful retaliations. Thus to return upon our adversaries, is a healing way of revenge; and to do good for evil a soft and melting ultion, a method taught from heaven,[1] to keep all smooth on earth. Common forcible ways make not, an end of evil, but leave hatred and malice behind them.[2] An enemy thus reconciled is little to be trusted, as wanting the foundation of love and charity, and but for a time restrained by disadvantage or inability. If thou hast not mercy for others, yet be not cruel unto thyself. To ruminate upon evils, to make critical notes upon injuries, and be too acute in their apprehensions, is to add unto our own tortures, to feather the arrows of our enemies, to lash ourselves with the scorpions of our foes, and to resolve to sleep no more; for injuries long dreamt on, take away at last all rest; and he sleeps but like Regulus, who busieth his head about them.

SECT. XIII.—Amuse not thyself about the riddles of future things. Study prophecies when they are become histories, and past hovering in their causes. Eye well things past and present, and let conjectural sagacity suffice for things to come. There is a sober latitude for prescience in contin-

---

* A soft tongue breaketh the bones.—PROV. xxv. 15.

[9] *Since women, &c.*]

               Minuti
Semper et infirmi est animi exiguique voluptas
Ultio————Sic collige, quod vindictâ
Nemo magis gaudet, quam fœmina.—JUV.

       Revenge! which still we find
The weakest frailty of a feeble mind.
Degenerous passion, and for man too base,
It seats its empire in the female race.—CREECH.

[1] *from heaven.*] "Not to be learned elsewhere."—*MS. Sloan.* 1847.
[2] *behind them.*] "Quiet one party, but leave unquietness in the other,—of a seeming friend making but a close adversary."—*MS. Sloan.* 1847.

gencies of discoverable tempers, whereby discerning heads
see sometimes beyond their eyes, and wise men become
prophetical.   Leave cloudy predictions to their periods, and
let appointed seasons have the lot of their accomplishments.
'Tis too early to study such prophecies before they have
been long made, before some train of their causes have
already taken fire, lay open in part what lay obscure and
before buried unto us.   For the voice of prophecies is like
that of whispering-places : they who are near, or at a little
distance, hear nothing ; those at the farthest extremity will
understand all.   But a retrograde cognition of times past,
and things which have already been, is more satisfactory
than a suspended knowledge of what is yet unexistent. And
the greatest part of time being already wrapt up in things
behind us ; it's now somewhat late to bait after things before
us ; for futurity still shortens, and time present sucks in
time to come.   What is prophetical in one age proves historical in another, and so must hold on unto the last of
time ; when there will be no room for prediction, when
Janus shall lose one face, and the long beard of time shall
look like those of David's servants, shorn away upon one
side ; and when, if the expected Elias should appear, he
might say much of what is past, not much of what's to
come.

· SECT. XIV.—Live unto the dignity of thy nature, and leave
it not disputable at last, whether thou hast been a man ;
or, since thou art a composition of man and beast, how
thou hast predominantly passed thy days, to state the denomination.   Unman not, therefore, thyself by a bestial
transformation, nor realize old fables.   Expose not thyself by
four-footed manners unto monstrous draughts, and cari-
cature representations.   Think not after the old Pythagorean conceit, what beast thou mayst be after death.   Be
not under any brutal metempsychosis,[3] while thou livest
and walkest about erectly under the scheme of man.   In
thine own circumference, as in that of the earth, let the
rational horizon be larger than the sensible, and the circle
of reason than of sense : let the divine part be upward, and
the region of beast below ; otherwise, 'tis but to live in-

---

[3] metempsychosis, &c.]   See page 112, note[7].—Dr. J.

vertedly, and with thy head unto the heels of thy antipodes. Desert not thy title to a divine particle and union with invisibles. Let true knowledge and virtue tell the lower world thou art a part of the higher. Let thy thoughts be of things which have not entered into the hearts of beasts: think of things long past, and long to come: acquaint thyself with the choragium[4] of the stars, and consider the vast expansion beyond them. Let intellectual tubes give thee a glance of things which visive organs reach not. Have a glimpse of incomprehensibles; and thoughts of things, which thoughts but tenderly touch. Lodge immaterials in thy head; ascend unto invisibles; fill thy spirit with spirituals, with the mysteries of faith, the magnalities of religion, and thy life with the honour of God; without which, though giants in wealth and dignity, we are but dwarfs and pygmies in humanity, and may hold a pitiful rank in that triple division of mankind into heroes, men, and beasts. For though human souls are said to be equal, yet is there no small inequality in their operations; some maintain the allowable station of men; many are far below it; and some have been so divine, as to approach the apogeum[5] of their natures, and to be in the confinium of spirits.

SECT. XV.—Behold thyself by inward opticks and the crystalline of thy soul.[6] Strange it is, that in the most perfect sense there should be so many fallacies, that we are fain to make a doctrine, and often to see by art. But the greatest imperfection is in our inward sight, that is, to be ghosts unto our own eyes; and while we are so sharp-sighted as to look through others, to be invisible unto ourselves; for the inward eyes are more fallacious than the outward. The vices we scoff at in others, laugh at us within ourselves. Avarice, pride, falsehood lie undiscerned and blindly in us, even to the age of blindness; and, therefore, to see ourselves interiorly, we are fain to borrow other men's eyes; wherein true friends are good informers,

---

[4] *choragium.*] Dance.—*Dr. J.*

[5] *apogeum, &c.*] To the utmost point of distance from earth and earthly things.—*Dr. J.*

[6] *crystalline, &c.*] Alluding to the crystalline humour of the eye.—*Dr. J.*

and censurers no bad friends. Conscience only, that can see without light, sits in the areopagy[7] and dark tribunal of our hearts, surveying our thoughts and condemning their obliquities. Happy is that state of vision that can see without light, though all should look as before the creation, when there was not an eye to see, or light to actuate a vision : wherein, notwithstanding, obscurity is only imaginable respectively unto eyes ; for unto God there was none : eternal light was ever; created light was for the creation, not himself; and, as he saw before the sun, may still also see without it. In the city of the new Jerusalem there is neither sun nor moon; where glorified eyes must see by the archetypal sun,[8] or the light of God, able to illuminate intellectual eyes, and make unknown visions. Intuitive perceptions in spiritual beings may, perhaps, hold some analogy unto vision : but yet how they see us, or one another, what eye, what light, or what perception is required unto their intuition, is yet dark unto our apprehension ; and even how they see God, or how unto our glorified eyes the beatifical vision will be celebrated, another world must tell us, when perceptions will be new, and we may hope to behold invisibles.

SECT. XVI.—When all looks fair about, and thou seest not a cloud so big as a hand to threaten thee, forget not the wheel of things : think of sullen vicissitudes, but beat not thy brains to foreknow them. Be armed against such obscurities, rather by submission than fore-knowledge. The knowledge of future evils mortifies present felicities, and there is more content in the uncertainty or ignorance of them. This favour our Saviour vouchsafed unto Peter, when he foretold not his death in plain terms, and so by an ambiguous and cloudy delivery damped not the spirit of his disciples. But in the assured fore-knowledge of the deluge, Noah lived many years under the affliction of a flood ; and Jerusalem was taken unto Jeremy, before it was besieged. And, therefore, the wisdom of astrologers, who speak of future things, hath wisely softened the severity of their doctrines ; and even in their sad predictions, while they tell us of inclina-

[7] *areopagy.*] The great court, like the Areopagus of Athens.—*Dr. J.*
[8] *archetypal sun.*] Original.—*Dr. J.*

tion not coaction from the stars, they kill us not with Stygian oaths and merciless necessity, but leave us hopes of evasion.

SECT. XVII.—If thou hast the brow to endure the name of traitor, perjured, or oppressor, yet cover thy face when ingratitude is thrown at thee. If that degenerous vice possess thee, hide thyself in the shadow of thy shame, and pollute not noble society. Grateful ingenuities are content to be obliged within some compass of retribution; and being depressed by the weight of iterated favours, may so labour under their inabilities of requital, as to abate the content from kindnesses. But narrow self-ended souls make prescription of good offices, and obliged by often favours think others still due unto them: whereas, if they but once fail, they prove so perversely ungrateful, as to make nothing of former courtesies, and to bury all that's past. Such tempers pervert the generous course of things; for they discourage the inclinations of noble minds, and make beneficency cool unto acts of obligation, whereby the grateful world should subsist, and have their consolation. Common gratitude must be kept alive by the additionary fuel of new courtesies: but generous gratitudes, though but once well obliged, without quickening repetitions or expectation of new favours, have thankful minds for ever; for they write not their obligations in sandy but marble memories, which wear not out but with themselves.

SECT. XVIII.—Think not silence the wisdom of fools; but, if rightly timed, the honour of wise men, who have not the infirmity, but the virtue of taciturnity; and speak not out of the abundance, but the well-weighed thoughts of their hearts. Such silence may be eloquence, and speak thy worth above the power of words. Make such a one thy friend, in whom princes may be happy, and great counsels successful. Let him have the key of thy heart, who hath the lock of his own, which no temptation can open; where thy secrets may lastingly lie, like the lamp in Olybius's urn,* alive, and light, but close and invisible.

SECT. XIX.—Let thy oaths be sacred, and promises be

---

* Which after many hundred years was found burning under ground, and went out as soon as the air came to it.

made upon the altar of thy heart.   Call not Jove * to witness·
with a stone in one hand, and a straw in another; and so
make chaff and stubble of thy vows.   Worldly spirits, whose
interest is their belief, make cobwebs of obligations; and, if
they can find ways to elude the urn of the Prætor,[9] will
trust the thunderbolt of Jupiter: and, therefore, if they
should as deeply swear as Osman to Bethlem Gabor;† yet
whether they would be bound by those chains, and not find
ways to cut such Gordian knots, we could have no just
assurance.   But honest men's words are Stygian oaths, and
promises inviolable.   These are not the men for whom the
fetters of law were first forged; they needed not the solemn-
ness of oaths; by keeping their faith they swear, and
evacuate such confirmations.‡

SECT. XX.—Though the world be histrionical, and most
men live ironically, yet be thou what thou singly art, and
personate only thyself.   Swim smoothly in the stream of thy
nature, and live but one man.   To single hearts doubling is
discruciating: such tempers must sweat to dissemble, and
prove but hypocritical hypocrites.   Simulation must be short:
men do not easily continue a counterfeiting life, or dissemble
unto death.   He who counterfeiteth, acts a part; and is, as
it were, out of himself: which, if long, proves so irksome,
that men are glad to pull off their vizards, and resume
themselves again; no practice being able to naturalize such
unnaturals, or make a man rest content not to be himself.
And, therefore, since sincerity is thy temper, let veracity be
thy virtue, in words, manners, and actions.   To offer at
iniquities, which have so little foundations in thee, were to
be vicious up-hill, and strain for thy condemnation.   Persons
viciously inclined, want no wheels to make them actively
vicious; as having the elater and spring of their own natures
to facilitate their iniquities.   And, therefore, so many, who
are sinistrous unto good actions, are ambi-dexterous unto

* *J*ovem lapidem jurare.
† See the oath of Sultan Osman, in his life, in the addition to Knoll's
Turkish history.
‡ Colendo fidem jurant.—CURTIUS.

[9] *to elude the urn of the Prætor.*]   The vessel, into which the ticket of
condemnation or acquittal was cast.—*Dr. J.*

bad; and Vulcans in virtuous paths, Achilleses in vicious motions.

SECT. XXI.—Rest not in the high-strained paradoxes of old philosophy, supported by naked reason, and the reward of mortal felicity; but labour in the ethics of faith, built upon heavenly assistance, and the happiness of both beings. Understand the rules, but swear not unto the doctrines of Zeno or Epicurus.[1] Look beyond Antoninus, and terminate not thy morals in Seneca or Epictetus.[2] Let not the twelve but the two tables be thy law: let Pythagoras be thy remembrancer, not thy textuary and final instructor: and learn the vanity of the world, rather from Solomon than Phocylides.[3] Sleep not in the dogmas of the Peripatus, Academy, or Porticus.[4] Be a moralist of the mount,[5] an Epictetus in the faith, and christianize thy notions.

SECT. XXII.—In seventy or eighty years, a man may have a deep gust of the world; know what it is, what it can afford, and what 'tis to have been a man. Such a latitude of years may hold a considerable corner in the general map of time; and a man may have a curt epitome of the whole course thereof in the days of his own life; may clearly see he hath but acted over his forefathers; what it was to live in ages past, and what living will be in all ages to come.

He is like to be the best judge of time, who hath lived to see about the sixtieth part thereof. Persons of short times may know what 'tis to live, but not the life of man, who, having little behind them, are but Januses of one face, and know not singularities enough to raise axioms of this world: but such a compass of years will show new examples of old things, parallelisms of occurrences through the whole course of time, and nothing be monstrous unto him; who may in that time understand not only the varieties of men, but the variation of himself, and how many men he hath been in that extent of time.

He may have a close apprehension what is to be forgotten,

---

[1] *Epicurus.*] The authors of the Stoical and Epicurean philosophy.—*Dr. J.*

[2] *Antoninus, &c.*] Stoical philosophers.—*Dr. J.*

[3] *Phocylides.*] A writer of moral sentences in verse.—*Dr. J.*

[4] *Peripatus, &c.*] Three schools of philosophy.—*Dr. J.*

[5] *mount.*] That is, according to the rules laid down in our Saviour's sermon on the mount.—*Dr. J.*

while he hath lived to find none who could remember his father, or scarce the friends of his youth; and may sensibly see with what a face in no long time oblivion will look upon himself. His progeny may never be his posterity; he may go out of the world less related than he came into it; and considering the frequent mortality in friends and relations, in such a term of time, he may pass away divers years in sorrow and black habits, and leave none to mourn for himself; orbity may be his inheritance, and riches his repentance.

In such a thread of time, and long observation of men, he may acquire a physiognomical intuitive knowledge; judge the interiors by the outside, and raise conjectures at first sight; and knowing what men have been, what they are, what children probably will be, may in the present age behold a good part and the temper of the next; and since so many live by the rules of constitution, and so few overcome their temperamental inclinations, make no improbable predictions.

Such a portion of time will afford a large prospect backward, and authentic reflections how far he hath performed the great intention of his being, in the honour of his Maker: whether he hath made good the principles of his nature, and what he was made to be; what characteristic and special mark he hath left, to be observable in his generation; whether he hath lived to purpose or in vain; and what he hath added, acted, or performed, that might considerably speak him a man.

In such an age, delights will be undelightful, and pleasures grow stale unto him; antiquated theorems will revive, and Solomon's maxims[6] be demonstrations unto him; hopes or presumptions be over, and despair grow up of any satisfaction below. And having been long tossed in the ocean of this world, he will by that time feel the in-draught of another, unto which this seems but preparatory, and without it of no high value. He will experimentally find the emptiness of all things, and the nothing of what is past; and wisely grounding upon true Christian expectations, finding so much past, will wholly fix upon what is to come.

---

[6] *Solomon's maxims.*] That all is vanity.—*Dr. J.*

He will long for perpetuity, and live as though he made haste to be happy. The last may prove the prime part of his life, and those his best days which he lived nearest heaven.

SECT. XXIII.—Live happy in the Elysium of a virtuously composed mind, and let intellectual contents exceed the delights wherein mere pleasurists place their paradise. Bear not too slack reins upon pleasure, nor let complexion or contagion betray thee unto the exorbitancy of delight. Make pleasure thy recreation or intermissive relaxation, not thy Diana, life, and profession. Voluptuousness is as insatiable as covetousness. Tranquillity is better than jollity, and to appease pain than to invent pleasure. Our hard entrance into the world, our miserable going out of it; our sicknesses, disturbances, and sad rencounters in it, do clamorously tell us we come not into the world to run a race of delight, but to perform the sober acts and serious purposes of man; which to omit were foully to miscarry in the advantage of humanity, to play away an uniterable life, and to have lived in vain. Forget not the capital end, and frustrate not the opportunity of once living. Dream not of any kind of metempsychosis[7] or transanimation, but into thine own body, and that after a long time; and then also unto wail or bliss, according to thy first and fundamental life. Upon a curricle in this world depends a long course of the next, and upon a narrow scene here an endless expansion hereafter. In vain some think to have an end of their beings with their lives. Things cannot get out of their natures, or be or not be in despite of their constitutions. Rational existences in heaven perish not at all, and but partially on earth: that which is thus once, will in some way be always: the first living human soul is still alive, and all Adam hath found no period.

SECT. XXIV.—Since the stars of heaven do differ in glory; since it hath pleased the Almighty hand to honour the north pole with lights above the south; since there are some stars so bright that they can hardly be looked on, some so dim that they can scarce be seen, and vast numbers not to be seen at all, even by artificial eyes; read thou the

[7] *metempsychosis.*] See note [7], page 112.—*Dr. J.*

earth in heaven, and things below from above. Look contentedly upon the scattered difference of things, and expect not equality in lustre, dignity, or perfection, in regions or persons below; where numerous numbers must be content to stand like lacteous or nebulous stars, little taken notice of, or dim in their generations. All which may be contentedly allowable in the affairs and ends of this world, and in suspension unto what will be in the order of things hereafter, and the new system of mankind which will be in the world to come; when the last may be the first, and the first the last; when Lazarus may sit above Cæsar, and the just obscure on earth, shall shine like the sun in heaven; when personations shall cease, and histrionism of happiness be over; when reality shall rule, and all shall be as they shall be for ever.

SECT. XXV.—When the stoic said that life* would not be accepted, if it were offered unto such as knew it, he spoke too meanly of that state of being which placeth us in the form of men. It more depreciates the value of this life, that men would not live it over again; for although they would still live on, yet few or none can endure to think of being twice the same men upon earth, and some had rather never have lived than to tread over their days once more. Cicero in a prosperous state had not the patience to think of beginning in a cradle again.[8] Job would not only curse the day of his nativity, but also of his renascency, if he were to act over his disasters and the miseries of the dunghill. But the greatest underweening of this life is to undervalue that, unto which this is but exordial or a passage leading unto it. The great advantage of this mean life is thereby to stand in a capacity of a better; for the colonies of heaven must be drawn from earth, and the sons of the first Adam are only heirs unto the second. Thus Adam came into this world with the power also of another; not only to replenish the earth, but the everlasting mansions of heaven. Where we were when the foundations of the earth were laid, when the morning stars

---

* Vitam nemo acciperet, si daretur scientibus.—*Seneca.*

[8] *Cicero, &c.*] Si quis Deus mihi largiatur, ut repuerascam et in cunis vagiam, valde recusem.—*Cic. de Senectute.*—*Dr. J.*

sang together, and all the sons of God shouted for joy,* He must answer who asked it; who understands entities of preordination, and beings yet unbeing; who hath in his intellect the ideal existences of things, and entities before their extances. Though it looks but like an imaginary kind of existency, to be before we are; yet since we are under the decree or prescience of a sure and omnipotent power, it may be somewhat more than a non-entity, to be in that mind, unto which all things are present.

SECT. XXVI.—If the end of the world shall have the same foregoing signs, as the period of empires, states, and dominions in it, that is, corruption of manners, inhuman degenerations, and deluge of iniquities; it may be doubted, whether that final time be so far off, of whose day and hour there can be no prescience. But while all men doubt, and none can determine how long the world shall last, some may wonder that it hath spun out so long and unto our days. For if the Almighty had not determined a fixed duration unto it, according to his mighty and merciful designments in it; if he had not said unto it, as he did unto a part of it, hitherto shalt thou go and no farther; if we consider the incessant and cutting provocations from the earth; it is not without amazement, how his patience hath permitted so long a continuance unto it; how he, who cursed the earth in the first days of the first man, and drowned it in the tenth generation after, should thus lastingly contend with flesh, and yet defer the last flames. For since he is sharply provoked every moment, yet punisheth to pardon, and forgives to forgive again; what patience could be content to act over such vicissitudes, or accept of repentances which must have after-penitences, his goodness can only tell us. And surely if the patience of heaven were not proportionable unto the provocations from earth, there needed an intercessor not only for the sins, but the duration of this world, and to lead it up unto the present computation. Without such a merciful longanimity, the heavens would never be so aged as to grow old like a garment. It were in vain to infer from the doctrine of the sphere, that the time might come, when Capella, a noble northern star, would have its motion in the equator; that

* Job xxxviii.

the northern zodiacal signs would at length be the southern, the southern the northern, and Capricorn become our Cancer. However, therefore, the wisdom of the Creator hath ordered the duration of the world, yet since the end thereof brings the accomplishment of our happiness, since some would be content that 'it should have no end, since evil men and spirits do fear it may be too short, since good men hope it may not be too long; the prayer of the saints under the altar will be the supplication of the righteous world, that his mercy would abridge their languishing expectation, and hasten the accomplishment of their happy state to come.

SECT. XXVII.—Though good men are often taken away from the evil to come; though some in evil days have been glad that they were old, nor long to behold the iniquities of a wicked world, or judgments threatened by them; yet is it no small satisfaction unto honest minds, to leave the world in virtuous well-tempered times, under a prospect of good to come, and continuation of worthy ways acceptable unto God and man. Men who die in deplorable days, which they regretfully behold, have not their eyes closed with the like content; while they cannot avoid the thoughts of proceeding or growing enormities, displeasing unto that spirit unto whom they are then going, whose honour they desire in all times and throughout all generations. If Lucifer could be freed from his dismal place, he would little care though the rest were left behind. Too many there may be of Nero's mind,[9] who, if their own turn were served, would not regard what became of others; and when they die themselves, care not if all perish. But good men's wishes extend beyond their lives, for the happiness of times to come, and never to be known unto them. And, therefore, while so many question prayers for the dead, they charitably pray for those who are not yet alive; they are not so enviously ambitious to go to heaven by themselves; they cannot but humbly wish, that the little flock might be greater, the narrow gate wider, and that, as many are called, so not a few might be chosen.

SECT. XXVIII.—That a greater number of angels remained

---

[9] *Nero's mind.*] Nero often had this saying in his mouth, 'Εμοῦ θάνοντος γαῖα μιχθήτω πυρί: "when I am once dead, let the earth and fire be jumbled together."—*Dr. J.*

in heaven, than fell from it, the schoolmen will tell us; that the number of blessed souls will not come short of that vast number of fallen spirits, we have the favourable calculation of others. What age or century hath sent most souls unto heaven, he can tell who vouchsafeth that honour unto them. Though the number of the blessed must be complete before the world can pass away; yet since the world itself seems in the wane, and we have no such comfortable prognosticks of latter times; since a greater part of time is spun than is to come, and the blessed roll already much replenished; happy are those pieties, which solicitously look about, and hasten to make one of that already much filled and abbreviated list to come.

SECT. xxix.—Think not thy time short in this world, since the world itself is not long. The created world is but a small parenthesis in eternity, and a short interposition, for a time, between such a state of duration as was before it and may be after it., And if we should allow of the old tradition, that the world should last six thousand years, it could scarce have the name of old, since the first man lived near a sixth part thereof, and seven Methuselahs would exceed its whole duration. However, to palliate the shortness of our lives, and somewhat to compensate our brief term in this world, it's good to know as much as we can of it; and also, so far as possibly in us lieth, to hold such a theory of times past, as though we had seen the same. He who hath thus considered the world, as also how therein things long past have been answered by things present; how matters in one age have been acted over in another; and how there is nothing new under the sun; may conceive himself in some manner to have lived from the beginning, and be as old as the world; and if he should still live on, 'twould be but the same thing.

SECT. xxx.[1]—Lastly;[2] if length of days be thy portion,

---

[1] SECT. XXX.] This section terminating at the words "and close apprehension of it," concludes the *Letter to a Friend.—Dr. J.*
[2] *Lastly.*]

> Omnem crede diem tibi diluxisse supremum,
> Grata superveniet quæ non sperabitur hora.—HORACE.
>> Believe, that ev'ry morning's ray
>> Hath lighted up thy latest day;
>> Then, if to-morrow's sun be thine,
>> With double lustre shall it shine.
>>> FRANCIS.—*Dr. J.*

make it not thy expectation. Reckon not upon long life : think every day the last, and live always beyond thy account. He that so often surviveth his expectation lives many lives, and will scarce complain of the shortness of his days. Time past is gone like a shadow; make time to come present. Approximate thy latter times by present apprehensions of them : be like a neighbour unto the grave, and think there is but little to come. And since there is something of us that will still live on, join both lives together, and live in one but for the other. He who thus ordereth the purposes of this life, will never be far from the next; and is in some manner already in it, by a happy conformity, and close apprehension of it. And if, as we have elsewhere declared,[3] any have been so happy, as personally to understand Christian annihilation, ecstasy, exolution, transformation, the kiss of the spouse, and ingression into the divine shadow, according to mystical theology, they have already had an handsome anticipation of heaven ; the world is in a manner over, and the earth in ashes unto them.

[3] *declared.*] In his treatise of *Urn-burial.* Some other parts of these essays are printed in a letter among Browne's Posthumous Works. Those references to his own books prove these essays to be genuine.— *Dr. J.*

In the present edition, the " other parts " here mentioned are pointed out, and some passages from the *Letter to a Friend* are given, which were not included in *Christian Morals.*

END OF CHRISTIAN MORALS.

CERTAIN

MISCELLANY TRACTS.

ORIGINALLY PUBLISHED IN

1684.

———————

ALSO

MISCELLANIES.

ORIGINALLY PUBLISHED WITH HIS POSTHUMOUS WORKS IN

1712.

VOL. III.   L

EDITOR'S PREFACE.

Most of these Tracts were (as Archbishop Tenison remarks in his preface), Letters in reply to enquiries addressed
to the author, by various, and some very eminent correspondents. The second, " *Of Garlands, &c.*," was written to
Evelyn, as I find from his own handwriting, in the margin
of his copy of the original edition. On the same authority
(probably from the information of Sir Thomas himself), we
learn that the greater number were addressed to Sir Nicholas
Bacon. *See MS. Note in first page.* The ninth, " *Of Artificial Hills,*" was in reply to Sir William Dugdale.

Such enquiries he delighted to satisfy; and the immense
stores of information amassed during a long life of curious
reading, and inquisitive research, eminently qualified him for
resolving questions on subjects the most dissimilar. Scarcely
any could be brought before him, upon which he could not
bring to bear the results of reiterated experiments, or of an
extensive acquaintance with the most singular and recondite
literature; and, where these treasures failed him, there remained the inexhaustible resources of his own matchless
fancy.

The first and second Tracts have been collated with MS.
Sloan. No. 1841; the eighth, tenth, and eleventh, with Nos.
1827 and 1839 : the thirteenth with No. 1874; the twelfth
with MS. Rawlinson, No. 58, in the Bodleian—and all the
others with MS. Sloan. No. 1827. Whatever discrepancies
seemed of sufficient importance have been preserved in
notes.

The second edition were published with the folio edition of
his works, in 1686; and none have since been reprinted;

except *Museum Clausum*, which, with *Hydriotaphia*, and the *Letter to a Friend*, were published in a neat 18mo. volume, by Mr. Crossley, of Manchester.

For the sake of keeping distinct the whole of the unpublished works, I have added to the Miscellany Tracts, his remarks on *Iceland*, together with some miscellaneous observations, which made their appearance in that ill-assorted collection, the *Posthumous Works*, in 1712.

THE PUBLISHER TO THE READER.

THE papers from which these Tracts were printed, were a while since, delivered to me by those worthy persons, the lady and son of the excellent author. He himself gave no charge concerning his manuscripts, either for the suppressing or the publishing of them. Yet, seeing he had procured transcripts of them, and had kept those copies by him, it seemeth probable, that he designed them for public use.

Thus much of his intention being presumed, and many who had tasted of the fruits of his former studies being covetous of more of the like kind; also these Tracts having been perused and much approved of by some judicious and learned men; I was not unwilling to be instrumental in fitting them for the press.

To this end, I selected them out of many disordered papers, and disposed them into such a method as they seemed capable of; beginning first with plants, going on to animals, proceeding farther to things relating to men, and concluding with matters of a various nature.

Concerning the plants, I did, on purpose, forbear to range them (as some advised) according to their tribes and families; because, by so doing, I should have represented that as a studied and formal work, which is but a collection of occasional essays. And, indeed, both this Tract, and those which follow, were rather the diversions than the labours of his pen : and, because he did, as it were, drop down his thoughts of a sudden, in those little spaces of vacancy which he snatched from those very many occasions which gave him hourly interruption. If there appears, here and there, any incorrectness in the style, a small degree of candour sufficeth to excuse it.

If there be any such errors in the words, I am sure the

press has not made them fewer: but I do not hold myself obliged to answer for that which I could not perfectly govern. However, the matter is not of any great moment: such errors will not mislead a learned reader ; and he who is not such in some competent degree, is not a fit peruser of these letters. Such these Tracts are ; but, for the persons to whom they were written, I cannot well learn their names from those few obscure marks which the author has set at the beginning of them. And these essays being letters, as many as take offence at some few familiar things which the author hath mixed with them, find fault with decency. Men are not wont to set down oracles in every line they write to their acquaintance.

There still remain other brief discourses written by this most learned and ingenious author. Those, also, may come forth, when some of his friends shall have sufficient leisure ; and at such due distance from these Tracts, that they may follow rather than stifle them.

Amongst these manuscripts there is one which gives a brief account of all the monuments of the cathedral of Norwich. It was written merely for private use : and the relations of the author expect such justice from those into whose hands some imperfect copies of it are fallen, that, without their consent first obtained, they forbear the publishing of it.

The truth is, matter equal to the skill of the antiquary, was not there afforded: had a fit subject of that nature offered itself, he would scarce have been guilty of an oversight like to that of Ausonius, who, in the description of his native city of Bourdeaux, omitted the two famous antiquities of it, Palais de Tutele, and Palais de Galien.

Concerning the author himself, I choose to be silent, though I have had the happiness to have been, for some years, known to him. There is on foot a design of writing his life ; and there are already some memorials collected by one of his ancient friends. Till that work be perfected, the reader may content himself with these present Tracts; all which commending themselves by their learning, curiosity, and brevity, if he be not pleased with them, he seemeth to me to be distempered with such a niceness of imagination, as no wise man is concerned to humour.

THOMAS TENISON.

MISCELLANY TRACTS.

TRACT 1.[1]

Sir,—Though many ordinary heads run smoothly over the Scripture, yet I must acknowledge it is one of the hardest books I have met with; and therefore well deserveth those numerous comments, expositions, and annotations, which make up a good part of our libraries.

However, so affected I am therewith, that I wish there had been more of it, and a larger volume of that divine piece, which leaveth such welcome impressions, and somewhat more, in the readers, than the words and sense after it. At least, who would not be glad that many things barely hinted were at large delivered in it ? The particulars of the dispute between the doctors and our Saviour could not but be welcome to those who have every word in honour which proceedeth from his mouth, or was otherwise delivered by him ; and so would be glad to be assured, what he wrote with his finger on the ground : but especially to have a particular of that instructing narration or discourse which he made unto the disciples after his resurrection, where 'tis said : " And beginning at Moses, and all the prophets, he

---

[1] TRACT I.]   "Most of these letters were written to Sir Nicholas Bacon."—*MS. Note, written in pencil, by Evelyn, in a copy formerly belonging to him, now in the Editor's possession.*

expounded unto them, in all the Scriptures, the things concerning himself."

But, to omit theological obscurities, you must needs observe that most sciences do seem to have something more nearly to consider in the expressions of the Scripture.

Astronomers find herein the names but of few stars, scarce so many as in Achilles's buckler in Homer, and almost the very same. But in some passages of the Old Testament they think they discover the zodiacal course of the sun; and they, also, conceive an astronomical sense ·in that elegant expression of St. James "concerning the father of lights, with whom there is no variableness, neither shadow of turning:" and therein an allowable allusion unto the tropical conversion of the sun, whereby ensueth a variation of heat, light, and also of shadows from it. But whether the *stellæ erraticæ* or wandering stars, in St. Jude, may be referred to the celestial planets or some meteorological wandering stars, *ignes fatui, stellæ cadentes et erraticæ*, or had any allusion unto the impostor Barchochebas[2] or Stellæ Filius, who afterward appeared, and wandered about in the time of Adrianus, they leave unto conjecture.

Chirurgeons may find their whole art in that one passage, concerning the rib which God took out of Adam; that is, their διαίρεσις in opening the flesh; ἐξαίρεσις in taking out the rib; and σύνθεσις in closing and healing the part again.

Rhetoricians and orators take singular notice of very many excellent passages, stately metaphors, noble tropes and elegant expressions, not to be found or paralleled in any other author.

Mineralists look earnestly into the twenty-eighth of Job; take special notice of the early artifice in brass and iron, under Tubal Cain: and find also mention of gold, silver,

---

[2] *Barchochebas.*] One of the impostors who assumed the character of Messias; he changed his true name, *Bar-Coziba*, son of a lie, to that of *Barchochebas*, son of a star! He excited a revolt against the Romans, which led to a very sanguinary contest, terminating with his death, at the storming of Bither, by the Romans, under Julius Severus. Bossuet supposes him to be the star mentioned in the eighth chap. of Revelation.

The apostle Jude more probably alluded to the term "star," by which the Jews often designated their teachers, and applied it here to some of the Christian teachers, whose unholy motives, erroneous doctrines, or wandering and unsettled habits exposed them to his rebuke.

brass, tin, lead, iron: beside refining, soldering, dross,[3] nitre, salt-pits, and in some manner also of antimony.[*]

Gemmary naturalists read diligently the precious stones in the holy city of the Apocalypse; examine the breast-plate of Aaron, and various gems upon it; and think the second row[4] the nobler of the four. They wonder to find the art of engravery so ancient upon precious stones and signets; together with the ancient use of ear-rings and bracelets. And are pleased to find pearl, coral, amber, and crystal, in those sacred leaves, according to our translation. And when they often meet with flints and marbles, cannot but take notice that there is no mention of the magnet or loadstone, which in so many similitudes, comparisons, and allusions, could hardly have been omitted in the works of Solomon: if it were true that he knew either the attractive or directive power thereof, as some have believed.

Navigators consider the ark, which was pitched without and within, and could endure the ocean without mast or sails: they take special notice of the twenty-seventh of Ezekiel; the mighty traffic and great navigation of Tyre, with particular mention of their sails, their masts of cedar, oars of oak, their skilful pilots, mariners, and caulkers; as also of the long voyages of the fleets of Solomon; of Jehosaphat's ships broken at Ezion-Geber; of the notable voyage and shipwreck of St. Paul so accurately delivered in the Acts.

Oneirocritical diviners apprehend some hints of their knowledge, even from divine dreams; while they take notice of the dreams of Joseph, Pharaoh, Nebuchadnezzar, and the angels on Jacob's ladder; and find, in Artemidorus and Achmetes, that ladders signify travels, and the scales thereof preferment; and that oxen lean and fat naturally denote scarcity or plenty, and the successes of agriculture.

Physiognomists will largely put in from very many passages of Scripture. And when they find in Aristotle, *quibus frons quadrangula commensurata, fortes, referuntur ad leones*, cannot but take special notice of that expression concerning the Gadites; mighty men of war, fit for battle, whose faces were as the faces of lions.

---

[*] *Depinxit oculos stibio.*—2 Kings ix. 30; Jeremiah iv. 30; Ezekiel xxiii. 40.

[3] *dross.*] *MS. Sloan.* 1841, adds, "sulphur."

[4] *second row.*] The emerald, sapphire, and diamond.

Geometrical and architectonical artists look narrowly upon the description of the ark, the fabric of the temple, and the holy city in the Apocalypse.

But the botanical artist meets everywhere with vegetables, and from the fig leaf in Genesis to the star wormwood in the Apocalypse, are variously interspersed expressions from plants, elegantly advantaging the significancy of the text: whereof many being delivered in a language proper unto Judæa and neighbour countries, are imperfectly apprehended by the common reader, and now doubtfully made out, even by the Jewish expositor.

And even in those which are confessedly known, the elegancy is often lost in the apprehension of the reader, unacquainted with such vegetables, or but nakedly knowing their natures: whereof holding a pertinent apprehension, you cannot pass over such expressions without some doubt or want of satisfaction[5] in your judgment. Hereof we shall only hint or discourse some few which I could not but take notice of in the reading of holy Scripture.

Many plants are mentioned in Scripture which are not distinctly known in our countries, or under such names in the original, as they are fain to be rendered by analogy, or by the name of vegetables of good affinity unto them, and so maintain the textual sense, though in some variation from identity.

1. That plant which afforded a shade unto Jonah,* mentioned by the name of *kikaion*, and still retained, at least marginally, in some translations, to avoid obscurity Jerome rendered *hedera* or ivy ;[6] which notwithstanding (except in its scandent nature) agreed not fully with the other, that is, to grow up in a night, or be consumed with a worm ; ivy being of no swift growth, little subject unto worms, and a scarce plant about Babylon.

* *J*onah iv. 6. a gourd.

[5] *want of satisfaction.*] "Insatisfaction."—*MS. Sloan.* 1841.
[6] *Jerome rendereth ivy.*] Augustine called it a gourd, and accused Jerome of heresy for the opinion he held. Yet they both seem to have been wrong. It was in all probability the *kiki* of the Egyptians, a plant of the same family as the *ricinus ;* and according to Dioscorides, of rapid growth ; bearing a berry from which an oil is expressed ; rising to the height of ten or twelve feet, and furnished with very large leaves, like those of the plane-tree ; so that the people of the East plant it before their shops for the sake of its shade.

2. That hyssop[7] is taken for that plant which cleansed the leper, being a well-scented and very abstersive simple, may well be admitted; so we be not too confident, that it is strictly the same with our common hyssop: the hyssop of those parts differing from that of ours; as Bellonius hath observed in the hyssop which grows in Judæa, and the hyssop of the wall mentioned in the works of Solomon, no kind of our hyssop; and may tolerably be taken for some kind of minor capillary, which best makes out the antithesis with the cedar. Nor when we meet with *libanotis*, is it to be conceived our common rosemary, which is rather the first kind thereof amongst several others, used by the ancients.

3. That it must be taken for hemlock, which is twice so rendered in our translation,* will hardly be made out, otherwise than in the intended sense, and implying some plant, wherein bitterness or a poisonous quality is considerable.

4. What Tremellius rendereth *spina*, and the vulgar translation *paliurus*, and others make some kind of *rhamnus*, is allowable in the sense; and we contend not about the species, since they are known thorns in those countries, and in our fields or gardens among us: and so common in Judæa, that men conclude the thorny crown[8] of our Saviour was made either of *paliurus* or *rhamnus*.

5. Whether the bush which burnt and consumed not, were properly a *rubus* or bramble, was somewhat doubtful from the original and some translations, had not the Evangelist, and St. Paul expressed the same by the Greek word βάτος, which, from the description of Dioscorides, herbalists accept for *rubus* : although the same word βάτος expresseth not only the *rubus* or kinds of bramble, but other thorny bushes, and the hip-brier is also named κυνόσβατος, or the dog-brier or bramble.

6. That *myrica* is rendered heath,[9]† sounds instructively

* Hosea x. 4; Amos vi. 2.   † *Myrica*, Cant. i. 14.

---

[7] *hyssop*.] A diminutive herb of a very bitter taste, which Hasselquist mentions as growing on the mountains near Jerusalem, as well as on the walls of the city. Pliny mentions it in connection with the *vinegar* and the *sponge. Nat. Hist.* lib. xxiii. c. 1.

[8] *thorny crown*.] Our Lord's crown was supposed by Bodæus and Theophylact to have been made of some species of *acacia*. Hasselquist considers it to have been the *rhamnus*, or *nubca paliurus Athenei*.

[9] *heath*.] "Be as the heath in the wilderness."—*MS. Sl.* 1847. The

enough to our ears, who behold that plant so common in
barren plains among us: but you cannot but take notice
that *erica*, or our heath, is not the same plant with *myrica*
or tamarice, described by Theophrastus and Dioscorides, and
which Bellonius declareth to grow so plentifully in the
deserts of Judæa and Arabia.

7. That the βότρυς τῆς κύπρου, *botrus cypri*, or clusters of
cypress,[1]* should have any reference to the cypress tree,
according to the original, *copher*, or clusters of the noble
vine of Cyprus, which might be planted into Judæa, may
seem to others allowable in some latitude. But there seeming some noble odour to be implied in this place, you may
probably conceive that the expression drives at the κύπρος of
Dioscorides, some oriental kind of *ligustrum* or *alcharma*,
which Dioscorides and Pliny mention under the name of
κύπρος and *cyprus*, and to grow about Egypt and Ascalon,
producing a sweet and odorate bush of flowers, and out of
which was made the famous *oleum cyprinum*.

But why it should be rendered camphor your judgment
cannot but doubt, who know that our camphor was unknown
unto the ancients, and no ingredient into any composition of
great antiquity: that learned men long conceived it a bituminous and fossil body, and our latest experience discovereth
it to be the resinous substance of a tree, in Borneo and
China ; and that the camphor that we use is a neat preparation of the same.

8. When 'tis said in Isaiah xli. " I will plant in the wilderness the cedar, the shittah tree, and the myrtle, and the oil
tree, I will set in the desert, the fir tree, and the pine, and
the box tree: though some doubt may be made of the
shittah tree,[2] yet all these trees here mentioned being such

* Cant. i. 14.

LXX. in *Jer.* xlviii. 6, instead of *orur*, evidently read *orud*, "a
wild ass ;" which suits that passage (as well as *Jer.* xvii. 6) better than
"heath !"

[1] *cypress*.] Aquila, the LXX., Theodotion, and others, consider the tree
thus called in Isa. xliv. 14, to be rather the wild oak, or *ilex ;* Bishop
Lowth and Parkhurst think the pine is intended.   But the wood of the
cypress was more adopted to the purpose specified.

[2] *shittah-tree*.]   According to Dr. Shaw and others, it was the *acacia
vera* or *spina Egyptiaca*, which grows to about the the size of the mulberry, and produces yellow flowers and pods like lupines.

as are ever green, you will more emphatically apprehend the
merciful meaning of God in this mention of no fading, but
always verdant trees in dry and desert places.

9. "And · they cut down a branch with one cluster of
grapes,[3] and they·bare it between two upon a staff, and they
brought pomegranates and figs." This cluster of grapes
brought upon a staff by the spies was an incredible sight, in
Philo Judæus, seemed notable in the eyes of the Israelites,
but more wonderful in our own, who look only upon northern vines. But herein you are like to consider, that the
cluster was thus carefully carried to represent it entire,
without bruising or breaking ; that this was not one bunch,
but an extraordinary cluster, made up of many depending
upon one gross stalk. And, however, might be paralleled
with the eastern clusters of Margiana and Caramania, if we
allow but half the expressions of Pliny and Strabo, whereof
one would lade a curry or small cart; and may be made out
by the clusters of the grapes of Rhodes presented unto
Duke Radzivil,* each containing three parts of an ell in
compass, and the grapes as big as prunes.

10. Some things may be doubted in the species of the
holy ointment [4] and perfume.† With amber, musk, and civet
we meet not in the Scripture, nor any odours from animals ;
except we take the *onycha* of that perfume, for the covercle
of a shell-fish, called *unguis odoratus*, or *blatta byzantina*,
which Dioscorides affirmeth to be taken from a shell-fish of
the Indian lakes, which feedeth upon the aromatical plants,
is gathered when the lakes are dry. But whether that which
we now call *blatta byzantina* or *unguis odoratus*, be the same
with that odorate one of antiquity, great doubt may be made ;
since Dioscorides saith it smelled like *castoreum*, and that
which we now have is of an ungrateful odour.

---

* Radzivil, in his Travels.   † Exod. xxx. 34, 35.

[3] *cluster of grapes.*] Doubdan (*Voyage de la Terre Sainte*, ch. xxi.)
speaks of bunches weighing ten or twelve pounds. Forster, on the
authority of a religious, who had long resided in Palestine, says, that
there grew in the valley of Hebron bunches so large that two men could
scarcely carry one.

[4] *holy ointment.*] Frankincense was one of the ingredients therein ;
an aromatic gum produced by a tree not certainly known, called by the
ancients *thurifera.*

No little doubt may be also made of *galbanum*[5] prescribed in the same perfume, if we take it for *galbanum*, which is of common use among us, approaching the evil scent of *assafœtida*; and not rather for *galbanum* of good odour, as the adjoining words declare, and the original *chelbena* will bear; which implieth a fat or resinous substance; that which is commonly known among us being properly a gummous body and dissoluble also in water.

The holy ointment of stacte or pure myrrh,[6] distilling from the plant without expression· or firing, of cinnamon, cassia, and *calamus*, containeth less questionable species, if the cinnamon of the ancients were the same with ours, or managed after the same manner. For thereof Dioscorides made his noble unguent. And cinnamon was so highly valued by princes, that Cleopatra carried it unto her sepulchre with her jewels; which was also kept in wooden boxes among the rarities of kings; and was of such a lasting nature, that at his composing of treacle for the Emperor Severus, Galen made use of some which had been laid up by Adrianus.

11. That the prodigal son desired to eat of husks given unto swine, will hardly pass in your apprehension for the husks of pease, beans,' or such edulious pulses; as well understanding that the textual word κεράτιον, or *ceration*, properly intendeth the fruit of the *siliqua* tree, so common in Syria, and fed upon by men and beasts; called also by some the fruit of the locust tree, and *panis sancti Johannis*, as conceiving it to have been part of the diet of the Baptist in the desert. The tree and fruit is not only common in Syria and the eastern parts, but also well known in Apuleia and the kingdom of Naples; growing along the Via Appia, from Fundi unto Mola; the hard cods or husks making a rattling noise in windy weather, by beating against one another : called by the Italians, *caróba* or *caróbala*, and by the French, *carouges*. With the sweet pulp hereof some conceive that the Indians preserve ginger, mirabolans, and ·

[5] *galbanum*.] A gum issuing from an umbelliferous plant, growing in Persia and Africa;—when first drawn, white and soft;—afterwards reddish ; of a strong smell, bitter and acid, inflammable, and soluble in water.

[6] *myrrh*.] The gum of a tree growing in Egypt, Arabia, and Abyssinia :—believed to possess the power of resisting putrefaction, and therefore used by the Jews and Egyptians in embalming.

nutmegs. Of the same (as Pliny delivers) the ancients made
one kind of wine, strongly expressing the juice thereof; and
so they might after give the expressed and less useful part of
the cods and remaining pulp unto their swine : which, being
no gustless or unsatisfying offal, might be well desired by
the prodigal in his hunger.

12. No marvel it is that the Israelites, having lived long
in a well-watered country, and been acquainted with the
noble water of Nilus, should complain for water in the dry
and barren wilderness. More remarkable it seems that they
should extol and linger after the cucumbers[7] and leeks,
onions and garlick of Egypt; wherein, notwithstanding, lies
a pertinent expression of the diet of that country in ancient
times, even as high as the building of the pyramids, when
Herodotus delivereth, that so many talents were spent in
onions and garlick, for the food of labourers and artificers ;
and is also answerable unto their present plentiful diet in
cucumbers, and the great varieties thereof, as testified by
Prosper Alpinus, who spent many years in Egypt.

13. What fruit that was which our first parents tasted in
Paradise, from the disputes of learned men, seems yet indeterminable.[8] More clear it is that they covered their naked-
ness or secret parts with fig leaves ;[9] which, when I read, I
cannot but call to mind the several considerations which
antiquity had of the fig tree, in reference unto those parts,
particularly how fig leaves, by sundry authors, are described
to have some resemblance unto the genitals, and so were
aptly formed for such contection of those parts; how also,
in that famous statua of Praxiteles, concerning Alexander

[7] *cucumbers.*] Hasselquist thus describes the *cucumis chate*, or queen
of cucumbers. "It grows in the fertile earth round Cairo, after the
inundation of the Nile, and not in any other place in Egypt, nor in any
other soil. It ripens with water melons : its flesh is almost of the same
substance, but is not near so cool. The grandees eat it as the most
pleasant food they find, and that from which they have least to apprehend. It is the most excellent of this tribe of any yet known."—*Hasselquist's Trav.* p. 258.

[8] *yet indeterminable.*] Jewish tradition considers it to have been
the *citron*, which, in all probability, was the fruit spoken of in Cant. ii.
13, rather than the *apple*, as it is translated.

[9] *fig-leaves.*] The fig-tree is called *taneh*, or the "grief tree," from its
rough leaves. Hence the Rabbins and others represent Adam to have
selected it as a natural sackcloth, to express his contrition.

and Bucephalus, the secret parts are veiled with fig leaves; how this tree was sacred unto Priapus, and how the diseases of the secret parts have derived their name from figs.

14. That the good Samaritan, coming from Jericho, used any of the Judean balsam [1] upon the wounded traveller, is not to be made out, and we are unwilling to disparage his charitable surgery in pouring oil into a green wound; and, therefore, when "tis said he used oil and wine, may rather conceive that he made an *oinelæum*, or medicine of oil and wine beaten up and mixed together, which was no improper medicine, and is an art now lately studied by some so to incorporate wine and oil, that they may lastingly hold together, which some pretend to have, and call it *oleum Samaritanum*, or Samaritan's oil.

15. When Daniel would not pollute himself with the diet of the Babylonians, he probably declined pagan commensation, or to eat of meats forbidden to the Jews, though common at their tables, or so much as to taste of their Gentile immolations, and sacrifices abominable unto his palate.

But when 'tis said that he made choice of the diet of pulse [2] and water, whether he strictly confined unto a leguminous food, according to the vulgar translation, some doubt may be raised from the original word *zeragnim*, which signifies *seminalia*, and is so set down in the margin of Arias Montanus; and the Greek word *spermata*, generally expressing seeds, may signify any edulious or cerealious grains besides ὄσπρια or leguminous seeds.

Yet, if he strictly made choice of a leguminous food, and water, instead of his portion from the king's table, he handsomely declined the diet which might have been put

---

[1] *balsam.*] An evergreen, rising to about fourteen feet high, indigenous in Azab and all along the coast of Babelmandel; bearing but few leaves, and small white flowers, like those of the acacia. Three kinds of balsam were extracted from this tree :—1. The *opobalsamum*, the most valuable sort, which flowed, on incision, from the trunk or branches. 2. *Carpobalsamum*, from pressure of the ripe fruit. 3. *Hylobalsamum*, made by a decoction of the buds and young twigs. The tree has entirely disappeared from Palestine.

[2] *pulse.*] Parched peas or corn; both of which make part of the food of the Eastern people. "On the road from Acra to Seide," says Hasselquist, "we saw a herdsman eating his dinner, consisting of half-ripe ears of wheat, which he toasted, and ate with as good an appetite as a Turk does his pillans."

upon him, and particularly that which was called the *poti-basis* of the king, which, as Athenæus informeth, implied the bread of the king, made of barley and wheat, and the wine of Cyprus, which he drank in an oval cup. And, therefore, distinctly from that he chose plain fare of water, and the gross diet of pulse, and that, perhaps, not made into bread, but parched and tempered with water.

Now that herein (beside the special benediction of God) he made choice of no improper diet to keep himself fair and plump, and so to excuse the eunuch his keeper, physicians will not deny, who acknowledge a very nutritive and impinguating faculty in pulses, in leguminous food, and in several sorts of grains and corns, is not like to be doubted by such who consider that this was probably a great part of the food of our forefathers before the flood, the diet also of Jacob; and that the Romans (called therefore *pultifagi*) fed much on pulse for six hundred years; that they had no bakers for that time: and their pistours were such as, before the use of mills, beat out and cleansed their corn. As also that the athletic diet was of pulse, *alphiton, maza,* barley and water; whereby they were advantaged sometimes to an exquisite state of health, and such as was not without danger. And, therefore, though Daniel were no eunuch, and of a more fattening and thriving temper, as some have fancied, yet was he by this kind of diet sufficiently maintained in a fair and carnous state of body; and, accordingly, his picture not improperly drawn, that is, not meagre and lean, like Jeremy's, but plump and fair, answerable to the most authentic draught of the Vatican, and the late German Luther's bible.

The cynicks in Athenæus make iterated courses of lentils, and prefer that diet before the luxury of Seleucus. The present Egyptians, who are observed by Alpinus to be the fattest nation, and men to have breasts like women, owe much, as he conceiveth, unto the water of Nile, and their diet of rice, pease, lentils, and white cicers. The pulse-eating cynicks and stoicks are all very long livers in Laertius. And Daniel must not be accounted of few years, who, being carried away captive in the reign of Joachim, by King Nebuchadnezzar, lived, by Scripture account, unto the first year of Cyrus.

16. "And Jacob took rods of green poplar, and of the
hazel, and the chesnut tree, and pilled white streaks in them,
and made the white appear which was in the rods, &c."
Men multiply the philosophy of Jacob, who beside the
benediction of God, and the powerful effects of imagination,
raised in the goats and sheep from pilled and party-coloured
objects, conceive that he chose out these particular plants
above any other, because he understood they had a particular
virtue unto the intended effects, according unto the conception of Georgius Venetus.*

Whereto you will hardly assent, at least till you be better
satisfied and assured concerning the true species of the
plants intended in the text, or find a clearer consent and
uniformity in the translation: for what we render poplar,
hazel, and chesnut, the Greek translateth *virgam styracinam,
nucinam, plantaninam*, which some also render a pomegranate; and so observing this variety of interpretations concerning common and known plants among us, you may more
reasonably doubt, with what propriety or assurance others
less known be sometimes rendered unto us.

17. Whether in the sermon of the mount, the lilies of
the field did point at the proper lilies,[3] or whether those
flowers grew wild in the place where our Saviour preached,
some doubt may be made; because κρίνον, the word in that
place, is accounted of the same signification with λείριον,
and that in Homer is taken for all manner of specious
flowers; so received by Eustachius, Hesychius, and the
scholiast upon Apollonius, Καθόλου τὰ ἄνθη λείρια λέγεται.
And κρίνον is also received in the same latitude, not signify-

* *G. Venetus, Problem.* 200.

[3] *lilies.*] "At a few miles from Adowa, we discovered a new and
beautiful species of amaryllis, which bore from ten to twelve spikes of
bloom on each stem, as large as those of the belladonna, springing from
one common receptacle. The general colour of the corolla was white,
and every petal was marked with a single streak of bright purple down
the middle. The flower was sweet scented, and its smell, though much
more powerful, resembled that of the lily of the valley. This superb
plant excited the admiration of the whole party; and it brought immediately to my recollection the beautiful comparison used on a particular
occasion by our Saviour, ' I say unto you, that Solomon in all his glory
was not arrayed like one of these.' "—*Salt's Voyage to Abyssinia*, p. 419.

ing only lilies, but applied unto daffodils, hyacinths, irises, and the flowers of colocynthis.

Under the like latitude of acception, are many expressions in the Canticles to be received.   And when it is said "he feedeth among the lilies," therein may be also implied other specious flowers, not excluding the proper lilies. But in that expression, "the lilies drop forth myrrh," neither proper lilies nor proper myrrh can be apprehended, the one not proceeding from the other, but may be received in a metaphorical sense: and in some latitude may be made out from the roscid and honey drops observable in the flowers of martagon, and inverted flowered lilies, and, 'tis like, is the standing sweet dew on the white eyes of the crown imperial, now common among us.

And the proper lily may be intended in that expression of 1 Kings vii., that the brazen sea was of the thickness of a hand breadth, and the brim like a lily.   For the figure of that flower being round at the bottom, and somewhat repandous, or inverted at the top, doth handsomely illustrate the comparison.

But that the lily of the valley, mentioned in the Canticles, " I am the rose of Sharon, and the lily of the valley," is that vegetable which passeth under the same name with us, that is, *lilium convallium,* or the May lily, you will more hardly believe, who know with what insatisfaction the most learned botanists reduce that plant unto any described by the ancients; that Anguillara will have it to be the *œnanthe* of Athenæus, Cordus, the *pothos* of Theophrastus, and Lobelius, that the Greeks had not described it; who find not six leaves in the flower, agreeably to all lilies, but only six small divisions in the flower, who find it also to have a single, and no bulbous root, nor leaves shooting about the bottom, nor the stalk round, but angular.   And that the learned Bauhinus hath not placed it in the classis of lilies, but nervifolious plants.

18. "Doth he not cast abroad the fitches,[4] and scatter the cummin seed, and cast in the principal wheat, and the

---

[4] *fitches.*] There are two Hebrew words rendered *fitches* by our translators, *ketzach* and *kesmet;* the latter probably *rye,* the former is considered by Jerom, Maimonides, and the Rabbins to be *gith,* in Greek μελανθων, in Latin *nigella.* Parkhurst supposes it to have been *fennel.*

appointed barley, and the rye in their place?" Herein though the sense may hold under the names assigned, yet is it not ' so easy to determine the particular seeds and grains, where the obscure original causeth such differing translations. For in the vulgar we meet with *milium* and *gith*, which our translation declineth, placing fitches for *gith*, and rye for *milium* or millet, which, notwithstanding, is retained by the Dutch.

That it might be *melanthium*, *nigella*, or *gith*, may be allowably apprehended, from the frequent use of the seed thereof among the Jews and other nations, as also from the translation of Tremellius; and the original implying a black seed, which is less than cummin, as, out of Aben Ezra, Buxtorfius hath expounded it.

But whereas *milium* or κέγχρος of the Septuagint is by ours rendered rye, there is little similitude or affinity between those grains; for *milium* is more agreeable unto *spelta* or *espaut*, as the Dutch and others still render it.

That we meet so often with cummin[5] seed in many parts of Scripture in reference unto Judæa, a seed so abominable at present unto our palates and nostrils, will not seem strange unto any who consider the frequent use thereof among the ancients, not only in medical but dietetical use and practice : for their dishes were filled therewith, and the noblest festival preparations in Apicius were not without it; and even in the *polenta*, and parched corn, the old diet of the Romans (as Pliny recordeth), unto every measure they mixed a small proportion of linseed and cummin seed.

And so cummin is justly set down among things of vulgar and common use, when it is said in Matthew xxiii. 23, " You pay tithe of mint, anise, and cummin."   But how to make out the translation of anise we are still to seek, there being no word in that text which properly signifieth anise : the original being ἄνηθον, which the Latins call *anethum*, and is properly Englished dill.

That among many expressions, allusions, and illustrations made in Scripture from corns, there is no mention made of oats, so useful a grain among us, will not seem very strange

---

[5] *cummin.*] An umbelliferous plant resembling fennel ; producing a bitterish, warm, aromatic seed,

unto you, till you can clearly discover that it was a grain
of ordinary use in those parts; who may also find that
Theophrastus, who is large about other grains, delivers very
little of it. That Dioscorides is also very short therein.
And Galen delivers that it was of some use in Asia Minor,
especially in Mysia, and that rather for beasts than men:
and Pliny affirmeth that the *pulticula* thereof was most in
use among the Germans. Yet that the Jews were not
without all use of this grain seems confirmable from the
Rabbinical account, who reckon five grains liable unto their
offerings, whereof the cake presented might be made; that
is, wheat, oats, rye, and two sorts of barley.

19. Why the disciples being hungry plucked the ears of
corn, it seems strange to us, who observe that men half-
starved betake not themselves to such supply; except we
consider the ancient diet of *alphiton* and *polenta*, the meal
of dried and parched corn, or that which was ὠμήλυσις,
or meal of crude and unparched corn, wherewith they
being well acquainted, might hope for some satisfaction from
the corn yet in the husks; that is, from the nourishing pulp
or mealy part within it.

20. The inhuman oppression of the Egyptian task-mas-
ters, who, not content with the common tale of brick, took
also from the children of Israel their allowance of straw,
and forced them to gather stubble where they could find it,
will be more nearly apprehended, if we consider how hard
it was to acquire any quantity of stubble in Egypt, where the
stalk of corn was so short, that to acquire an ordinary
measure it required more than ordinary labour; as is discoverable from that account which Pliny hath happily left
unto us.* In the corn gathered in Egypt the straw is
never a cubit long: because the seed lieth very shallow, and
hath no other nourishment than from the mud and slime
left by the river; for under it is nothing but sand and gravel.
So that the expression of Scripture is more emphatical
than is commonly apprehended, when 'tis said, "The people
were scattered abroad through all the land of Egypt to
gather stubble instead of straw." For the stubble being
very short, the acquist was difficult; a few fields afforded it

* Lib. 18. *Nat. Hist.*

not, and they were fain to wander far to obtain a sufficient quantity of it.

21. It is said in the *Song of Solomon*, that "The vines with the tender grape give a good smell." That the flowers of the vine should be emphatically noted to give a pleasant smell seems hard unto our northern nostrils, which discover not such odours, and smell them not in full vineyards; whereas in hot regions, and more spread and digested flowers, a sweet savour may be allowed, denotable from several human expressions, and the practice of the ancients, in putting the dried flowers of the vine into new wine to give it a pure and flosculous race or spirit, which wine was therefore called οἰνάνθινον, allowing unto every *cadus* two pounds of dried flowers.

And therefore, the vine flowering but in the spring, it cannot but seem an impertinent objection of the Jews, that the apostles were " full of new wine at Pentecost," when it was not to be found. Wherefore we may rather conceive that the word γλεύκυ in that place implied not new wine or must, but some generous strong and sweet wine, wherein more especially lay the power of inebriation.

But if it be to be taken for some kind of must, it might be some kind of αἰείγλευκος, or long lasting must, which might be had at any time of the year, and which, as Pliny delivereth, they made by hindering and keeping the must from fermentation or working, and so it kept soft and sweet for no small time after.

22. When the dove, sent out of the ark, returned with a green olive leaf, according to the original: how the leaf, after ten months, and under water, should still maintain a verdure or greenness, need not much amuse the reader, if we consider that the olive tree is αἰείφυλλον, or continually green; that the leaves are of a bitter taste, and of a fast and lasting substance. Since we also find fresh and green leaves among the olives which we receive from remote countries; and since the plants at the bottom of the sea, and on the sides of rocks, maintain a deep and fresh verdure.

How the tree should stand so long in the deluge under water, may partly be allowed from the uncertain determination of the flows and currents of that time, and the qualification of the saltness of the sea, by the admixture of fresh water, when the whole watery element was together.

And it may be signally illustrated from the like examples in Theophrastus* and Pliny† in words to this effect: even the sea affordeth shrubs and trees; in the Red Sea whole woods do live, namely of bays and olives bearing fruit. The soldiers of Alexander, who sailed into India, made report, that the tides were so high in some islands, that they overflowed, and covered the woods, as high as plane and poplar trees. The lower sort wholly, the greater all but the tops, whereto the mariners fastened their vessels at high water, and at the root in the ebb; that the leaves of these sea-trees while under water looked green, but taken out presently dried with the heat of the sun. The like is delivered by Theophrastus, that some oaks do grow and bear acorns under the sea.

23. "The kingdom of heaven is like to a grain of mustard-seed, which a man took and sowed in his field, which indeed is the least of all seeds; but when 'tis grown is the greatest among herbs, and becometh a tree, so that the birds of the air come and lodge in the branches thereof."

Luke xiii. 19. "It is like a grain of mustard-seed, which a man took and cast it into his garden, and it waxed a great tree, and the fowls of the air lodged in the branches thereof."

This expression by a grain of mustard-seed, will not seem so strange unto you, who well consider it. That it is simply the least of seeds, you cannot apprehend, if you have beheld the seeds of *rapunculus*, marjorane, tobacco, and the smallest seed of *lunaria*.

But you may well understand it to be the smallest seed among herbs which produce so big a plant, or the least of herbal plants, which arise unto such a proportion, implied in the expression; the smallest of seeds, and becometh the greatest of herbs.

And you may also grant that it is the smallest of seeds of plants apt to δενδρίζειν, *arborescere, fruticescere,* or to grow unto a ligneous substance, and from an herby and oleraceous vegetable, to become a kind of tree, and to be

---

* *Theophrast. Hist.* lib. iv. cap. 7, 8.   † *Pliny,* lib. xiii. cap. ultimo.

accounted among the *dendrolachana* or *arboroleracea*: as upon strong seed, culture, and good ground, is observable in some cabbages, mallows, and many more, and therefore expressed by γίνεται τὸ δένδρον and γίνεται εἰς τὸ δένδρον, it becometh a tree, or *arborescit*, as Beza rendereth it.

Nor if warily considered doth the expression contain such difficulty. For the parable may not ground itself upon generals, or imply any or every grain of mustard, but point at such a grain as, from its fertile spirit, and other concurrent advantages, hath the success to become arboreous, shoot into such a magnitude, and acquire the like tallness. And unto such a grain the kingdom of heaven is likened, which from such slender beginnings shall find such increase and grandeur.

The expression also that it might grow into such dimensions that birds might lodge in the branches thereof, may be literally conceived; if we allow the luxuriancy of plants in Judæa, above our northern regions; if we accept of but half the story taken notice of by Tremellius, from the Jerusalem Talmud, of a mustard tree that was to be climbed like a fig tree; and of another, under whose shade a potter daily wrought; and it may somewhat abate our doubts, if we take in the advertisement of Herodotus concerning lesser plants of *milium* and *sesamum*, in the Babylonian soil: *milium ac sesamum in proceritatem instar arborum crescere, etsi mihi compertum, tamen memorare supersedeo, probè sciens eis qui nunquam Babyloniam regionem adierunt perquam incredibile visum iri.* We may likewise consider that the word κατασκηνῶσαι doth not necessarily signify making a nest, but rather sitting, roosting, cowering, and resting in the boughs, according as the same word is used by the Septuagint in other places,* as the vulgate rendereth it in this, *inhabitant*, as our translation, "lodgeth," and the Rhemish, "resteth in the branches."

24. "And it came to pass that on the morrow Moses went into the tabernacle of witness, and behold the rod of Aaron for the house of Levi was budded, and brought forth buds, and bloomed blossoms, and yielded almonds."†

In the contention of the tribes and decision of priority

---

* Dan. iv. 9.   Psalm i. 14, 12.
† The Rod of Aaron, Numb. xvii. 8.

and primogeniture of Aaron, declared by the rod, which in a night budded, flowered, and brought forth almonds, you cannot but apprehend a propriety in the miracle from that species of tree which leadeth in the vernal germination of the year, unto all the classes of trees; and so apprehend how properly in a night and short space of time the miracle arose, and somewhat answerable unto its nature the flowers and fruit appeared in this precocious tree, and whose original name* implieth such speedy efflorescence, as in its proper nature flowering in February, and showing its fruit in March.

This consideration of that tree maketh the expression in Jeremy more emphatical, when 'tis said, "What seest thou? and he said, a rod of an almond tree. Then said the Lord unto me, thou hast well seen, for I will hasten the word to perform it."† I will be quick and forward like the almond tree, to produce the effects of my word, and hasten to display my judgments upon them.

And we may hereby more easily apprehend the expression in Ecclesiastes; "when the almond tree shall flourish,"‡ that is, when the head, which is the prime part, and first showeth itself in the world, shall grow white, like the flowers of the almond tree, whose fruit, as Athenæus delivereth, was first called κάρηνον, or the head, from some resemblance and covering parts of it.

How properly the priority was comfirmed by a rod or staff, and why the rods and staffs of the princes were chosen for this decision, philologists will consider. For these were the badges, signs, and cognisances of their places, and were a kind of sceptre in their hands, denoting their supereminencies. The staff of divinity is ordinarily described in the hands of gods and goddesses in old draughts. Trojan and Grecian princes were not without the like, whereof the shoulders of Thersites felt from the hands of Ulysses. Achilles in Homer, as by a desperate oath, swears by his wooden sceptre, which should never bud nor bear leaves again; which seeming the greatest impossibility to him, advanceth the miracle of Aaron's rod. And if it could be

---

* Shacher, from Shachar festinus fuit or maturuit.   † Jer. i. 11.
‡ Eccles. xii. 5.

well made out that Homer had seen the books of Moses, in that expression of Achilles, he might allude unto this miracle.

That power which proposed the experiment by blossoms in the rod, added also the fruit of almonds; the text not strictly making out the leaves, and so omitting the middle germination; the leaves properly coming after the flowers, and before the almonds. And therefore if you have well perused medals, you cannot but observe how in the impress of many shekels, which pass among us by the name of the Jerusalem shekels, the rod of Aaron is improperly laden with many leaves, whereas that which is shown under the name of the Samaritan shekel, seems most conformable unto the text, which describeth the fruit without leaves.

25. "Binding[6] his foal unto the vine, and his ass's colt unto the choice vine."

That vines, which are commonly supported, should grow so large and bulky, as to be fit to fasten their juments, and beasts of labour unto them, may seem a hard expression unto many: which notwithstanding may easily be admitted, if we consider the account of Pliny, that in many places out of Italy vines do grow without any stay or support: nor will it be otherwise conceived of lusty vines, if we call to mind how the same author* delivereth, that the statua of Jupiter was made out of a vine; and that out of one single Cyprian vine a scale or ladder was made that reached unto the roof of the temple of Diana at Ephesus.

26. "I was exalted as a palm tree in Engaddi, and as a rose plant[7] in Jericho." That the rose of Jericho, or

* *Plin.* lib. xiv.

[6] *Binding, &c.*] In some parts of Persia, it was formerly the custom to turn their cattle into the vineyards after the vintage, to browse on the vines, some of which are so large that a man can scarcely compass their trunks in his arms.

[7] *rose plant in Jericho.*] Sir R. K. Porter gives the following description of the oriental rose trees probably here intended:—"On first entering this bower of fairy land, I was struck with the appearance of two rose trees; full *fourteen feet high,* laden with thousands of flowers, in every degree of expansion, and of a bloom and delicacy of scent, that imbued the whole atmosphere with the most exquisite perfume; indeed, I believe that in no country of the world does the rose grow in such

that plant which passeth among us under that denomination, was signified in this text, you are not like to apprehend with some, who also .name it the rose of St. Mary, and deliver, that it openeth the branches, and flowers upon the eve of our Saviour's nativity : but rather conceive it some proper kind of rose, which thrived and prospered in Jericho more than in the neighbour countries. For our rose of Jericho is a very low and hard plant, a few inches above the ground ; one whereof brought from Judæa I have kept by me many years, nothing resembling a rose tree, either in flowers, branches, leaves, or growth ; and so improper to answer the emphatical word of exaltation in the text : growing not only about Jericho, but other parts of Judæa and Arabia, as Bellonius hath observed : which being a dry and ligneous plant, is preserved many years, and though crumpled and furled up, yet, if infused in water, will swell and display its parts.

27. *Quasi Terebinthus extendi ramos*, when it is said in the same chapter, " as a turpentine tree[8] have I stretched out my branches." It will not seem strange unto such as have either seen that tree or examined its description : for it is a plant that widely displayeth its branches : and though in some European countries it be but of a low and fruticeous growth, yet Pliny observeth that it is great in Syria* and so allowably, or at least not improperly mentioned in the expression of Hosea† according to the vulgar translation, *Super capita montium sacrificant, &c., sub quercu, populo, et terebintho, quoniam bona est umbra ejus.* And this diffusion and spreading of its branches hath afforded the proverb of *terebintho stultior*, applicble unto arrogant or boasting

---

* Terebinthus in Macedonia fruticat, in Syria, magna est, lib. xiii. *Plin.*
† Hos. iv. 13.

perfection as in Persia, in no country is it so cultivated, and prized by the natives. Their gardens and courts are crowded with its plants, their rooms ornamented with vases filled with its gathered bunches, and every bath strewed with the full-blown flowers, plucked from the ever-replenished stems."

[8] *turpentine tree.*] An evergreen of moderate size, with a top and branches large in proportion ; leaves like the olive, but green, mixed with red and purple ; the flowers purple, growing in branches, like the vine ; fruit like that of the juniper, and of a ruddy purple.

persons, who spread and display their own acts, as Erasmus
hath observed.

28. It is said in our translation, " Saul tarried in the
uppermost parts of Gibeah, under a pomegranate tree which
is in Migron: and the people which were with him were
about six hundred men." And when it is said in some
Latin translations, *Saul morabatur fixo tentorio sub malo-
granato,* you will not be ready to take it in the common
literal sense, who know that a pomegranate tree is but low
of growth, and very unfit to pitch a tent under it: and
may rather apprehend it as the name of a place, or the
rock of Rimmon, or Pomegranate; so named from pomegranates which grew there, and which many think to have
been the same place mentioned in Judges.*

29. It is said in the book of Wisdom, " Where water
stood before, dry land appeared, and out of the Red Sea
a way appeared without impediment, and out of the violent
streams a green field;" or as the Latin renders it, *campus
germinans de profundo:* whereby it seems implied that the
Israelites passed over a green field at the bottom of the
sea: and though most would have this but a metaphorical
expression, yet may it be literally tolerable; and so may be
safely apprehended by those that sensibly know what great
number of vegetables (as the several varieties of *algæ*, sea
lettuce, *phasganium, conferva, caulis marina, abies, erica,*
tamarice, divers sorts of *muscus, fucus, quercus marina,* and
corallines), are found at the bottom of the sea. Since it is
also now well known, that the western ocean, for many
degrees, is covered with *sargasso* or *lenticula marina,* and
found to arise from the bottom of that sea ; since, upon the
coast of Provence by the isles of Eres, there is a part of
the Mediterranean Sea, called *la Prairie,* or the meadowy
sea, from the bottom thereof so plentifully covered with
plants : since vast heaps of weeds are found in the bellies of
some whales taken in the northern ocean, and at a great distance from the shore : and since the providence of nature hath
provided this shelter for minor fishes ; both for their spawn,
and safety of their young ones. And this might be more
peculiarly allowed to be spoken of the Red Sea, since the

* Judges xx. 45, 47 ; xxi. 13.

Hebrews named it *suph* or the weedy sea: and, also, seeing
Theophrastus and Pliny, observing the growth of vegetables
under water, have made their chief illustrations from those
in the Red Sea.

. 30. You will readily discover how widely they are mistaken, who accept the sycamore mentioned in several parts
of Scripture for the sycamore or tree of that denomination
with us; which is properly but one kind or difference of
acer, and bears no fruit with any resemblance unto a fig.

.But you will rather, thereby, apprehend. the. true and
genuine sycamore or *sycaminus*, which is a stranger in our
parts.   A tree (according to the description of .Theo-
phrastus, Dioscorides, and Galen), resembling a mulberry
tree in the leaf, but in the fruit a fig;[9] which it produceth
not in the twigs but in the trunk or greater branches,
answerable to the sycamore of Egypt, the Egyptian fig or
giamez of the Arabians, described by Prosper Alpinus, with
a leaf somewhat broader than a mulberry, and in its fruit
like a fig.   Insomuch that some have fancied it to have had
its first production from a fig tree grafted on a mulberry.
It is a tree common in Judæa, whereof they made frequent
use in buildings; and so understood, it explaineth that
expression in Isaiah:* "*Sycamori excisi sunt, cedros sub-
stituemus.*   The bricks are fallen down, but we will build
with hewn stones : the sycamores are cut down, but we will
change them into cedars."

It is a broad spreading tree, not only fit for walks, groves,
and shade, but also affording profit. And therefore it is
said that King David† appointed Baalhanan to be over his
olive trees and sycamores, which were in great plenty ; and
it is accordingly delivered, that "Solomon made cedars to
be as the sycamore trees that are in the vale for abundance."‡   That is, he planted many, though they did not
come to perfection in his days.

And as it grew plentifully about the plains, so was the
fruit good for food; and, as Bellonius and late accounts

---

* Isaiah ix. 10.   † 1 Chron. xxvii. 28.   ‡ 1 Kings x. 27.

[9] *resembling in fruit a fig.*]   In smell and figure, but not in the mode
of growth ; they grow in clusters at the end of a fruit stalk, not singly
like figs.

deliver, very refreshing unto travellers in those hot and dry countries:' whereby the expression of Amos* becomes more intelligible, when he said he was an herdsman, and a gatherer of sycamore fruit. And the expression of David† also becomes more emphatical; "He destroyed their vines with hail, and their sycamore trees with frost." That is, their *sicmoth* in the original, a word in the sound not far from the sycamore.

Thus, when it is said, "If ye had faith as a grain of mustard seed, ye might say unto this sycamine tree, be thou plucked up by the roots, and be thou placed in the sea, and it should obey you :"‡ it might be more significantly spoken of this sycamore; this being described to be *arbor vasta*, a large and well-rooted tree, whose removal was more difficult than many others. And so the instance in that text, is very properly made in the sycamore tree, one of the largest and less removable trees among them. A tree so lasting and well-rooted, that the sycamore which Zaccheus ascended is still shown in Judæa unto travellers; as also the hollow sycamore at Maturæa in Egypt, where the blessed virgin is said to have remained: which though it relisheth of the legend, yet it plainly declareth what opinion they had of the lasting condition of that tree, to countenance the tradition; for which they might not be without some experience, since the learned describer of the pyramids§ observeth, that the old Egyptians made coffins of this wood, which he found yet fresh and undecayed among divers of their mummies.

And thus, also, when Zaccheus climbed up into a sycamore above any other tree, this being a large and fair one, it cannot be denied that he made choice of a proper and advantageous tree to look down upon our Saviour.

31. Whether the expression of our Saviour in the parable of the sower, and the increase of the seed unto thirty, sixty, and a hundred fold, had any reference unto the ages of believers, and measure of their faith, as children, young and old persons, as to beginners, well advanced and strongly confirmed Christians, as learned men have hinted; or whether in this progressional ascent there were any latent

---

* Amos vii. 14.   † Psalm lxxviii. 47.
‡ Luke xvii. 6.   § D. Greaves.

mystery, as the mystical interpreters of numbers may apprehend, I pretend not to determine.

But, how this multiplication may well be conceived, and
in what way apprehended, and that this centesimal increase
is not naturally strange, you that are no stranger in agriculture, old and new, are not like to make great doubt.

That every grain should produce an ear affording an hundred grains, is not like to be their conjecture who behold
the growth of corn in our fields, wherein a common grain
doth produce far less in number. For barley, consisting
but of two *versus* or rows, seldom exceedeth twenty grains,
that is, ten upon each στοῖχος, or row; rye, of a square
figure, is very fruitful at forty: wheat, besides the frit and
uruncus, or imperfect grains of the small husks at the top
and bottom of the ear, is fruitful at ten treble *glumi* or
husks in a row, each containing but three grains in breadth,
if the middle grain arriveth at all to perfection; and so
maketh up threescore grains in both sides.

Yet even this centesimal fructification may be admitted in
some sorts of *cerealia*, and grains from one ear: if we take
in *triticum centigranum*, or *fertilissimum Plinii*, Indian
wheat, and *panicum;* which, in every ear, containeth hun-
dreds of grains.

But this increase may easily be conceived of grains in
their total multiplication, in good and fertile grounds, since,
if every grain of wheat produceth but three ears, the increase will arise above that number. Nor are we without
examples of some grounds which have produced many more
ears, and above this centesimal increase: as Pliny hath left
recorded of the Byzacian field in Africa.* *Misit ex eo loco
procurator ex uno grano quadraginta paucis minus germina.
Misit et Neroni similiter tercentum quadraginta stipulas ex
uno grano. Cum centesimos quidem Leontini Siciliæ campi
fundunt, aliique, et tota Bætica, et imprimis Ægyptus.*
And even in our own country, from one grain of wheat
sowed in a garden, I have numbered many more than an
hundred.[1]

* *Plin. Hist. Nat.* lib. xviii. cap. 21.

[1] *many more than an hundred.*]   The manuscript in the British
Museum reads, "no less than three hundred stalks and ears."—*MS.
Sloan.* 1841.

And though many grains are commonly lost which come not to sprouting or earing, yet the same is also verified in measure; as that one bushel should produce a hundred, as is exemplified by the corn in Gerar: "Then Isaac sowed in that land, and received in the same year an hundred fold."* That is, as the Chaldee explaineth it, a hundred for one, when he measured it. And this Pliny seems to intend, when he saith of the fertile Byzacian territory before mentioned, *ex uno centeni quinquaginta modii redduntur.* And may be favourably apprehended of the fertility of some grounds in Poland; wherein, after the accounts of Gaguinus, from rye sowed in August, come thirty or forty ears, and a man on horseback can scarce look over it.

In the sabbatical crop of Judæa, there must be admitted a large increase, and probably not short of this centesimal multiplication: for it supplied part of the sixth year, the whole seventh, and eighth, until the harvest of that year.

The seven years of plenty in Egypt must be of high increase; when, by storing up but the fifth part, they supplied the whole land, and many of their neighbours after: for it is said, "the famine was in all the land about them."† And therefore though the causes of the dearth in Egypt be made out from the defect of the overflow of Nilus, according to the dream of Pharaoh; yet was that no cause of the scarcity in the land of Canaan, which may rather be ascribed to the want of the former and latter rains, for some succeeding years, if their famine held time and duration with that of Egypt; as may be probably gathered from that expression of Joseph, "come down unto me (into Egypt) and tarry not, and there will I nourish thee: for yet there are five years of famine, lest thou and thy household, and all that thou hast, come to poverty."‡

How they preserved their corn so long in Egypt may seem hard unto northern and moist climates, except we consider the many ways of preservation practised by antiquity, and also take in that handsome account of Pliny; what corn soever is laid up in the ear, it taketh no harm keep it as long as you will, although the best and most assured way

---

* Gen. xxvi. 12.

† Gen. xli. 56.   ‡ Gen. xlv. 9, 11.

to keep corn is in caves and vaults under ground, according to the practice of Cappadocia and Thracia.

In Egypt and Mauritania above all things they look to this, that their granaries stand on high ground; and how dry soever their floor be, they lay a course of chaff betwixt it and the ground. Besides, they put up their corn in granaries and bins together with the ear. And Varro delivereth that wheat laid up in that manner will last fifty years; millet an hundred; and beans so conserved, in a cave of Ambracia, were known to live an hundred and twenty years; that is, from the time of King Pyrrhus, unto the Pyratick war under the conduct of Pompey.

More strange it may seem how, after seven years, the grains conserved should be fruitful for a new production. For it is said that Joseph delivered seed unto the Egyptians, to sow their land for the eighth year: and corn after seven years is like to afford little or no production, according to Theophrastus; " *ad sementem semen anniculum optimum putatur, binum deterius et trinum; ultra sterile fermè est, quanquam ad usum cibarium idoneum.*"*

Yet since, from former exemplifications, corn may be made to last so long, the fructifying power may well be conceived to last in some good proportion, according to the region and place of its conservation, as the same Theophrastus hath observed, and left a notable example from Cappadocia, where corn might be kept sixty years, and remain fertile at forty ; according to his expression thus translated; *in Cappadociæ loco quodam Petra dicto, triticum ad quadraginta annos fæcundum est, et ad sementem percommodum durare proditum est, sexagenos aut septuagenos ad usum cibarium servari posse idoneum.* The situation of that conservatory was, as he delivereth, ὑψηλὸν, εὔπνουν, εὔαυρον, high, airy, and exposed to favourable winds. And upon such consideration of winds and ventilation, some conceived the Egyptian granaries were made open, the country being free from rain. However it was, that contrivance could not be without some hazard: for the great mists and dews of that country might dispose the corn unto corruption.†

---

* *Theoph. Hist.* lib. viii.

† Egypt ὀμιχλῶδης, καὶ δρόσερος.   Vide *Theophrastum.*

More plainly may they mistake, who, from some analogy of name (as if pyramid were derived from πῦρον, *triticum*), conceive the Egyptian pyramids to have been built for granaries, or look for any settled monuments about the deserts erected for that intention; since their store-houses were made in the great towns, according to Scripture expression, "He gathered up all the food for seven years, which was in the land of Egypt, and laid up the food in the cities: the food of the field which was round about every city, laid he up in the same."*

32. "For if thou wert cut out of the olive tree, which is wild by nature, and wert grafted, contrary to nature, into a good olive tree, how much more shall these which be the natural branches, be grafted into their own olive tree?" In which place, how answerable[2] to the doctrine of husbandry this expression of St. Paul is, you will readily apprehend who understand the rules of insition or grafting, and that way of vegetable propagation; wherein it is contrary to nature, or natural rules which art observeth: viz. to make use of scions more ignoble than the stock, or to graft wild upon domestic and good plants, according as Theophrastus hath anciently observed,† and, making instance in the olive, hath left this doctrine unto us: *urbanum sylvestribus ut satis oleastris inserere. Nam si è contrario sylvestrem in urbanos severis, etsi differentia quædam erit, tamen bonæ frugis arbor nunquam profecto reddetur:*‡ which is also agreeable unto our present practice, who graft pears on thorns, and apples upon crab-stocks, not using the contrary insition. And when it is said, "how much more shall these, which are the natural branches, be grafted into their own natural olive tree?" this is also agreeable unto the rule of the same author; ἔστι δὲ βελτίων ἐγκεντορισμός ὁμοίων εἰς ὅμοια, *insitio melior est similium in similibus:* for the nearer consanguinity there is between the scions and the stock, the readier comprehension is made, and the nobler fructification. According also unto

---

* Gen. xli. 48.   † *De Causis Plant.* lib. i. cap. 7.
          ‡ καλλικαρπεῖν οὐκ ἕξει.

[2] *how answerable.*] "How geographically answerable." — *MS. Sloan.* 1841.

the later caution of Laurenbergius ;* *arbores domesticæ insitioni destinatæ, semper anteponendæ sylvestribus.* And though the success be good, and may suffice upon stocks of the same denomination; yet, to be grafted upon their own and mother stock, is the nearest insition : which way, though less practised of old, is now much embraced, and found a notable way for melioration of the fruit, and much the rather, if the tree to be grafted on be a good and generous plant, a good and fair olive, as the apostle seems to imply by a peculiar word,† scarce to be found elsewhere.

It must be also considered, that the *oleaster*, or wild olive, by cutting, transplanting, and the best managery of art, can be made but to produce such olives as Theophrastus saith were particularly named *phaulia*, that is, but bad olives ; and that it was among prodigies for the *oleaster* to become an olive tree.

And when insition and grafting, in the text, is applied unto the olive tree, it hath an emphatical sense, very agreeable unto that tree which is best propagated this way; not at all by surculation, as Theophrastus observeth,‡ nor well by seed, as hath been observed. *Omne semen simile genus perficit, præter oleam, oleastrum enim generat, hoc est sylvestrem oleam, et non oleam veram.*

" If, therefore, thou Roman and Gentile branch, which wert cut from the wild olive, art now, by the signal mercy of God, beyond the ordinary and commonly expected way, grafted into the true olive, the church of God; if thou, which neither naturally nor by human art canst be made to produce any good fruit, and, next to a miracle, to be made a true olive, art now by the benignity of God grafted into the proper olive; how much more shall the Jew, and natural branch, be grafted into its genuine and mother tree, wherein propinquity of nature is like, so readily and prosperously, to effect a coalition ? And this more especially by the expressed way of insition or implantation, the olive being not successfully propagable by seed, nor at all by surculation."

---

* *De horticultura.*   † καλλιέλαιον, Rom. xi. 24.
‡ *Geoponic.* lib. x.

33. " As for the stork, the fir trees are her house."*
This expression, in our translation, which keeps close to the
original *chasideh*, is somewhat different from the Greek and
Latin translation ; nor agreeable unto common observation,
whereby they are known commonly to build upon chimneys,
or the tops of houses and high buildings, which notwithstanding, the common translation may clearly consist with
observation, if we consider that this is commonly affirmed of
the black stork, and take notice of the description of *Orni-
thologus* in Aldrovandus, that such storks are often found in
divers parts, and that they do *in arboribus nidulari, præsertim
in abietibus ;* make their nests on trees,[3] especially upon
fir trees. Nor wholly disagreeing unto the practice of the
common white stork, according unto Varro, *nidulantur in
agris :* and the concession of Aldrovandus that sometimes
they build on trees : and the assertion of Bellonius,† that
men dress them nests, and place cradles upon high trees, in
marish regions, that storks may breed upon them : which
course some observe for herons and cormorants with us.
And this building of storks upon trees, may be also answerable unto the original and natural way of building of storks
before the political habitations of men, and the raising of
houses and high buildings ; before they were invited by
such conveniences and prepared nests, to relinquish their
natural places of nidulation. I say, before or where such
advantages are not ready ; when swallows found other places
than chimneys, and daws found other places than holes in
high fabricks to build in.

34. " And therefore, Israel said, carry down the man a
present, a little balm, a little honey, and myrrh, nuts, and
almonds."‡ Now whether this, which Jacob sent, were the
proper balsam extolled by human writers, you cannot but
make some doubt, who find the Greek translation to be
ρησίνη, that is, *resina*, and so may have some suspicion that
it might be some pure distillation from the turpentine tree ;
which grows prosperously and plentifully in Judæa, and

* Psalm civ. 17.   † *Bellonius de Avibus.*   ‡ Gen. xliii. 11.

[3] *make their nests on trees.*] Doubdan saw immense numbers of these
birds in Galilee resting in the evening on trees. *Harmer's Observations*,
vol. iii. p. 323.

seems so understood by the Arabic; and was indeed esteemed by Theophrastus and Dioscorides the chiefest of resinous bodies, and the word *resina* emphatically used for it.

That the balsam plant hath grown and prospered in Judæa we believe without dispute. For the same is attested by Theophrastus, Pliny, Justinus, and many more. From the commendation that Galen affordeth of the balsam of Syria, and the story of Cleopatra, that she obtained some plants of balsam from Herod the Great to transplant into Egypt. But whether it was so anciently in Judæa as the time of Jacob; nay, whether this plant was here before the time of Solomon, that great collector of vegetable rarities, some doubt may be made from the account of Josephus, that the queen of Sheba, a part of Arabia, among presents unto Solomon brought some plants of the balsam tree, as one of the peculiar estimables of her country.

Whether this ever had its natural growth, or were an original native plant in Judæa, much more that it was peculiar unto that country, a greater doubt may arise: while we read in Pausanias, Strabo, and Diodorus, that it grows also in Arabia, and find in Theophrastus,* that it grew in two gardens about Jericho in Judæa. And more especially while we seriously consider that notable discourse between Abdella, Abdachim, and Alpinus, concluding the natural and original place of this singular plant to be in Arabia, about Mecha and Medina, where it still plentifully groweth, and mountains abound therein;† from whence it hath been carefully transplanted by the bashas of Grand Cairo, into the garden of Matarea: where, when it dies, it is repaired again from those parts of Arabia, from whence the Grand Signior yearly receiveth a present of balsam from the xeriff of Mecha, still called by the Arabians *balessan;* whence they believe arose the Greek appellation balsam. And since these balsam plants are not now to be found in Judæa, and though purposely cultivated, are often lost in Judæa, but everlastingly live, and naturally renew in Arabia, they probably concluded, that those of Judæa were foreign and transplanted from these parts.

---

* *Theophrast.* lib. ix. cap. 6.   † *Prosper Alpinus, de Balsamo.*

All which notwithstanding, since the same plant may grow naturally and spontaneously in several countries, and either from inward or outward causes be lost in one region, while it continueth and subsisteth in another, the balsam tree might possibly be a native of Judæa as well as of Arabia; which because *de facto* it cannot be clearly made out, the ancient expressions of Scripture become doubtful in this point. But since this plant hath not for a long time grown in Judæa, and still plentifully prospers in Arabia, that which now comes in precious parcels to us, and still is called the balsam of Judæa, may now surrender its name, and more properly be called the balsam of Arabia[4].

35. "And the flax and the barley was smitten; for the barley was in the ear, and the flax was bolled, but the wheat and the rye were not smitten, for they were not grown up."* How the barley and the flax should be smitten in the plague of hail in Egypt, and the wheat and rye escape, because they were not yet grown up, may seem strange unto English observers, who call barley summer corn, sown so many months after wheat, and [who] beside (*hordeum polystichon*, or big barley), sow not barley in the winter to anticipate the growth of wheat.

And the same may also seem a preposterous expression unto all who do not consider the various agriculture, and different husbandry of nations, and such as was practised in Egypt, and fairly proved to have been also used in Judæa, wherein their barley harvest was before that of wheat; as is confirmable from that expression in Ruth, that she came into Bethlehem at the beginning of barley harvest, and staid unto the end of wheat harvest; from the death of Manasses, the father of Judith, emphatically expressed to have happened in the wheat harvest, and more advanced heat of the sun; and from the custom of the Jews, to offer the barley sheaf of the first fruits in March, and a cake of wheat flour but at the end of Pentecost, consonant unto the practice of the Egyptians, who (as Theophrastus delivereth) sowed their barley early in reference to their first-fruits; and also

* Exod. ix. 31.

[4] *Arabia.*] See note on the balsam, or Balm of Gilead, at page 160.

the common rural practice, recorded by the same author, *mature seritur triticum, hordeum, quod etiam maturius seritur;* wheat and barley are sowed early, but barley earlier of the two.

Flax was also an early plant, as may be illustrated from the neighbour country of Canaan. For the Israelites kept the passover in Gilgal, in the fourteenth day of the first month, answering unto part of our March, having newly passed Jordan : and the spies which were sent from Shittim unto Jericho, not many days before, were hid by Rahab under the stalks of flax, which lay drying on the top of her house : which showeth that the flax was already and newly gathered. For this was the first preparation of flax, and before fluviation or rotting, which, after Pliny's account, was after wheat harvest.

" But the wheat and the rye were not smitten, for they were not grown up." The original signifies that it was hidden, or dark, the vulgar and septuagint that it was *serotinous* or *late*, and our old translation that it was late sown. And so the expression and interposition of Moses, who well understood the husbandry of Egypt, might emphatically declare the state of wheat and rye in that particular year; and if so, the same is solvable from the time of the flood of Nilus, and the measure of its inundation. For if it were very high, and over-drenching the ground, they were forced to later seedtime; and so the wheat and the rye escaped; for they were more slowly growing grains, and, by reason of the greater inundation of the river, were sown later than ordinary that year, especially in the plains near the river, where the ground drieth latest.

Some think the plagues of Egypt were acted in one month, others but in the compass of twelve. In the delivery of Scripture there is no account of what time of the year or particular month they fell out; but the account of these grains, which were either smitten or escaped, makes the plague of hail to have probably happened in February. This may be collected from the new and old account of the seedtime and harvest in Egypt. For, according to the account of Radzivil,* the river rising in June, and the banks

* *Radzivil's Travels.*

being cut in September, they sow about St. Andrew's, when the flood is retired, and the moderate dryness of the ground permitteth. So that the barley, anticipating the wheat, either in time of sowing or growing, might be in ear in February.

The account of Pliny* is little different. They cast their seed upon the slime and mud when the river is down, which commonly happeneth in the beginning of November. They begin to reap and cut down a little before the calends of April, or about the middle of March, and in the month of May their harvest is in. So that barley, anticipating wheat, it might be in ear in February, and wheat not yet grown up, at least to the spindle or ear, to be destroyed by the hail. For they cut down about the middle of March, at least their forward corns, and in the month of May all sorts of corn were in.

The "turning of the river into blood" shows in what month this happened not. That is, not when the river had overflown ; for it is said, " the Egyptians digged round about the river for water to drink," which they could not have done if the river had been out and the fields under water.

In the same text you cannot, without some hesitation, pass over the translation of rye, which the original nameth *cassu-meth*, the Greek rendereth *olyra*, the French and Dutch *spelta*, the Latin *zea*, and not *secale*, the known word for rye. But this common rye, so well understood at present, was not distinctly described, or not well known from early antiquity. And, therefore, in this uncertainty, some have thought it to have been the *typha* of the ancients. Cordus will have it to be *olyra*, and Ruellius some kind of *oryza*. But having no vulgar and well-known name for those grains, we warily embrace an appellation of near affinity, and tolerably render it rye.

While flax, barley, wheat, and rye are named, some may wonder why no mention is made of rice, wherewith, at present, Egypt so much aboundeth. But whether that plant grew so early in that country, some doubt may be made ; for rice is originally a grain of India, and might not then be transplanted into Egypt.

---

* *Plin.* lib. xviii. cap. 18.

36. " Let them become as the grass growing upon the house top, which withereth before it be plucked up, wherewith the mower filleth not his hand, nor he that bindeth sheaves his bosom."* Though the "filling of the hand," and mention of "sheaves of hay" may seem strange unto us, who use neither handful or sheaves in that kind of husbandry, yet may it be properly taken, and you are not like to doubt thereof, who may find the like expressions in the authors *De Re Rustica*, concerning the old way of this husbandry.

Columella,† delivering what works were not to be permitted upon the Roman *feriæ*, or festivals, among others, sets down that upon such days it was not lawful to carry or bind up hay, *Nec fœnum vincire nec vehere per religiones pontificum licet.*

Marco Varro‡ is more particular; *Primum de pratis herbarum cum crescere desiit, subsecari falcibus debet, et quoad peracescat furcillis versari, cum peracuit, de his manipulos fieri et vehi in villam.*

And their course of mowing seems somewhat different from ours. For they cut not down clear at once, but used an after section, which they peculiarly called *sicilitium*, according as the word is expounded by Georgius Alexandrinus and Beroaldus, after Pliny: *Sicilire est falcibus consectari quæ fœnisecæ præterierunt, aut ea secare quæ fœnisecæ præterierunt.*

37. When 'tis said that Elias lay and slept under a juniper tree, some may wonder how that tree, which in our parts groweth but low and shrubby, should afford him shade and covering.[5] But others know that there is a lesser and a larger kind of that vegetable; that it makes a tree in its proper soil and region. And may find in Pliny that in the temple of Diana Saguntina, in Spain, the rafters were made of juniper.

In that expression of David,§ "Sharp arrows of the mighty, with coals of juniper." Though juniper be left out in the last translation, yet may there be an emphatical sense

* Psalm cxxix. 7.   † *Columella*, lib. ii. cap. 22.
‡ *Varro*, lib. i. cap. 49.   § Psalm cxx. 4.

[5] *When 'tis said, &c.*] Parkhurst suggests that the prophet took up with this humble shelter *for want of a better.*

from that word; since juniper abounds with a piercing oil, and makes a smart fire. And the rather, if that quality be half true, which Pliny affirmeth, that the coals of juniper raked up will keep a glowing fire for the space of a year. For so the expression will emphatically imply, not only the " smart burning but the lasting fire of their malice."

That passage of Job,* wherein he complains that poor and half-famished fellows despised him, is of greater difficulty; " For want and famine they were solitary, they cut up mallows by the bushes, and juniper roots for meat." Wherein we might at first doubt the translation, not only from the Greek text, but the assertion of Dioscorides, who affirmeth that the roots of juniper are of a venomous quality. But Scaliger hath disproved the same from the practice of the African physicians, who use the decoction of juniper roots against the venereal disease. The Chaldee reads it *genista*, or some kind of broom, which will be also unusual and hard diet, except thereby we understand the *orobanche*, or broom rape, which groweth from the roots of broom; and which, according to Dioscorides, men used to eat raw or boiled, in the manner of asparagus.

And, therefore, this expression doth highly declare the misery, poverty, and extremity, of the persons who were now mockers of him; they being so contemptible and necessitous, that they were fain to be content, not with a mean diet, but such as was no diet at all, the roots of trees, the roots of juniper, which none would make use of for food, but in the lowest necessity, and some degree of famishing.

38. While some have disputed whether Theophrastus knew the scarlet berry, others may doubt whether that noble tincture were known unto the Hebrews, which, notwithstanding, seems clear from the early and iterated expressions of Scripture concerning the scarlet tincture, and is the less to be doubted, because the scarlet berry grew plentifully in the land of Canaan, and so they were furnished with the materials of that colour. For though Dioscorides saith it groweth in Armenia and Cappadocia; yet that it also grew in Judæa seems more than probable from the account of Bellonius, who observed it to be so plentiful in that

---

* Job xxx. 3, 4.

country, that it afforded a profitable commodity, and great quantity thereof was transported by the Venetian merchants.

How this should be fitly expressed by the word *tolagnoth*, *vermis*, or worm, may be made out from Pliny, who calls it *coccus scolecius*, or the wormy berry; as also from the name of that colour called vermilion, or the worm colour: and which is also answerable unto the true nature of it. For this is no proper berry containing the fructifying part, but a kind of vesicular excrescence, adhering commonly to the leaf of the *ilex coccigera*, or dwarf and small kind of oak, whose leaves are always green, and its proper seminal parts acorns. This little bag containeth a red pulp, which, if not timely gathered, or left to itself, produceth small red flies, and partly a red powder, both serviceable under the tincture. And, therefore, to prevent the generation of flies, when it is first gathered, they sprinkle it over with vinegar, especially such as make use of the fresh pulp for the confection of *alkermes;* which still retaineth the Arabic name, from the *kermes-berry;* which is agreeable unto the description of Bellonius and Quinqueranus. And the same we have beheld in Provence and Languedoc, where it is plentifully gathered, and called *manna rusticorum*, from the considerable profit which the peasants make by gathering of it.

39. Mention is made of oaks in divers parts of Scripture, which though the Latin sometimes renders a turpentine tree, yet surely some kind of oak may be understood thereby; but whether our common oak, as is commonly apprehended, you may well doubt; for the common oak, which prospereth so well with us, delighteth not in hot regions. And that diligent botanist, Bellonius, who took such particular notice of the plants of Syria and Judæa, observed not the vulgar oak in those parts. But he found the *ilex, chesne vert,* or evergreen oak, in many places; as also that kind of oak which is properly named *esculus:* and he makes mention thereof in places about Jerusalem, and in his journey from thence unto Damascus, where he found *montes ilice, et esculo virentes;* which in his discourse of Lemnos, he saith are always green. And therefore when it is said of Absalom, that "his mule went under the thick boughs of a great oak, and his head caught hold of the oak,

and he was taken up between the heaven and the earth,"* that oak might be some *ilex* or rather *esculus*. For that is a thick and bushy kind, in *orbem comosa*, as Dalechampius; *ramis in orbem dispositis comans*, as Renealmus describeth it. And when it is said that "Ezechias broke down the images, and cut down the groves,"† they might much consist of oaks, which were sacred unto Pagan deities, as this more particularly, according to that of Virgil,

> Nemorumque *J*ovi quæ maxima frondet
> Esculus.

And, in Judæa, where no hogs were eaten by the Jews, and few kept by others, 'tis not unlikely that they most cherished the *esculus*, which might serve for food for men. For the acorns thereof are the sweetest of any oak, and taste like chesnuts; and so, producing an edulious or esculent fruit, is properly named *esculus*.

They which know the *ilex* or evergreen oak, with somewhat prickled leaves, named πρίνος, will better understand the irreconcileable answer of the two elders, when the one accused Susanna of incontinency under a πρίνος or evergreen oak, the other under a σχῖνος, *lentiscus*, or mastic tree, which are so different in bigness, boughs, leaves, and fruit, the one bearing acorns, the other berries : and without the knowledge, will not emphatically or distinctly understand that of the poet,

> Flavaque de viridi stillabant ilice mella.

40. When we often meet with the cedars of Libanus, that expression may be used, not only because they grew in a known and neighbour country, but also because they were of the noblest and largest kind of that vegetable : and we find the Phœnician cedar magnified by the ancients. The cedar of Libanus is a *coniferous* tree, bearing *cones* or clogs (not berries) of such a vastness, that Melchior Lussy, a great traveller, found one upon Libanus, as big as seven men could compass. Some are now so curious as to keep the branches and *cones* thereof among their rare collections. And, though

---

* 2 Sɛm. xviii. 9, 14.   † 2 Kings xviii. 4.

much cedar wood be now brought from America, yet 'tis time to take notice of the true cedar of Libanus, employed in the temple of Solomon: for they have been much destroyed and neglected, and become at last but thin. Bellonius could reckon but twenty-eight, Rowolfius and Radzivil but twenty-four, and Bidulphus the same number. And a later account of some English travellers* saith, that they are now but in one place, and in a small compass, in Libanus.[6]

Quando ingressi fueritis terram, et plantaveritis in illa ligna pomifera, auferetis præputia eorum. Poma quæ germinant, immunda erunt vobis, nec edetis ex eis. Quarto autem anno, omnis fructus eorum sanctificabitur, laudabilis domino. Quinto autem anno comedetis fructus. By this law they were enjoined not to eat of the fruits of the trees which they planted for the first three years: and, as the vulgar expresseth it, to take away the *prepuces*, from such trees, during that time: the fruits of the fourth year being holy unto the Lord, and those of the fifth allowable unto others. Now if *auferre præputia* be taken, as many learned men have thought, to pluck away the bearing buds, before they proceed unto flowers or fruit, you will readily apprehend the metaphor, from the analogy and similitude of those sprouts and buds, which, shutting up the fruitful particle, resembleth the preputial part.

And you may also find herein a piece of husbandry not mentioned in Theophrastus or Columella. For by taking away of the buds and hindering fructification, the trees be-

---

* *A Journey to Jerusalem*, 1672.

[6] *in a small compass, &c.*] Burckhardt thus describes the cedars of Libanus:—"They stand on uneven ground, and form a small wood. Of the oldest and best-looking trees, I counted eleven or twelve; twenty-five very large ones: about fifty of middling size; and more than three hundred smaller and younger ones. The oldest trees are distinguished, by having the foliage and small branches at the top only, and by four, five, or even seven trunks springing from one base; the branches and foliage of the others were lower, but I saw none whose leaves touched the ground, like those in Kew Gardens. The trunks of the old trees are covered with the names of travellers and other persons who have visited them; I saw a date of the seventeenth century. The trunks of the oldest trees seem to be quite dead; the wood is of a grey tint."— *Travels in Syria*, 19, 20.

come more vigorous, both in growth and future production. By such a way king Pyrrhus got into a lusty race of beeves, and such as were desired over all Greece, by keeping them from generation until the ninth year.

And you may also discover a physical advantage in the goodness of the fruit, which becometh less crude and more wholesome, upon the fourth or fifth year's production.

41. While you read in Theophrastus or modern herbalists, a strict division of plants, into *arbor, frutex, suffrutex et herba,* you cannot but take notice of the Scriptural division at the creation, into tree and herb ; and this may seem too narrow to comprehend the class of vegetables; which, notwithstanding, may be sufficient, and a plain and intelligible division thereof. And therefore, in this difficulty concerning the division of plants, the learned botanist, Cæsalpinus, thus concludeth, *clarius agemus si alterâ divisione neglectâ, duo tantum plantarum genera substituamus, arborem scilicet, et herbam, conjungentes cum arboribus fructices, et cum herba suffrutices; frutices* being the lesser trees, and *suffrutices* the larger, harder, and more solid herbs.

And this division into herb and tree may also suffice, if we take in that natural ground of the division of perfect plants, and such as grow from seeds. For plants, in their first production, do send forth two leaves adjoining to the seed; and then afterwards, do either produce two other leaves, and so successively before any stalk ; and such go under the name of πόα, βοτάνη or herb; or else, after the two first leaves succeeded to the seed leaves, they send forth a stalk or rudiment of a stalk, before any other leaves, and such fall under the classes of δένδρον or tree. So that, in this natural division, there are but two grand differences, that is, tree and herb. The *frutex* and *suffrutex* have the way of production from the seed, and in other respects the *suffrutices* or *cremia,* have a middle and participating nature, and referable unto herbs.

42. " I have seen the ungodly in great power, and flourishing like a green bay tree."[7] Both Scripture and human

---

[7] *flourishing, &c.*]   " Spreading himself (is the English version) like a green bay tree :"—more accurately " like a *native* tree"—a tree grow-

writers draw frequent illustrations from plants. Scribonius Largus illustrates the old cymbals from the *cotyledon palustris* or *umbilicus veneris*. Who would expect to find Aaron's mitre in any plant? Yet Josephus hath taken some pains to make out the same in the seminal knop of *hyoscyamus* or henbane. The Scripture compares the figure of manna unto the seed of coriander. In Jeremy * we find the expression, "straight as a palm tree." And here the wicked in their flourishing state are likened unto a bay tree." Which, sufficiently answering the sense of the text, we are unwilling to exclude that noble plant from the honour of having its name in Scripture. Yet we cannot but observe, that the septuagint renders it cedars, and the vulgar accordingly, *vidi impium superexaltatum, et elevatum sicut cedros Libani;* and the translation of Tremellius mentions neither bay nor cedar; *sese explicantem tanquam arbor indigena virens;* which seems to have been followed by the last low Dutch translation. A private translation renders it like a green self-growing laurel.† The high Dutch of Luther's Bible retains the word laurel; and so doth the old Saxon and Iceland translation; so also the French, Spanish, and Italian of Diodati: yet his notes acknowledge that some think it rather a cedar, and others any large tree in a prospering and natural soil.

But however these translations differ, the sense is allowable and obvious unto apprehension : when no particular plant is named, any proper to the sense may be supposed; where either cedar or laurel is mentioned, if the preceding words (exalted and elevated) be used, they are more appliable unto the cedar; where the word (flourishing) is used, it is more agreeable unto the laurel, which, in its prosperity, abounds with pleasant flowers, whereas those of the cedar are very little, and scarce perceptible, answerable to the fir, pine, and other coniferous trees.

43. "And in the morning, when they were come from Bethany, he was hungry; and seeing a fig tree afar off having leaves, he came, if haply he might find anything

* Jer. x. 5.　　　　　† *Ainsworth.*

ing in its native soil, not having suffered by transplantation, and therefore spreading itself luxuriantly. Psalm xxxvii. 35.

thereon; and when he came to it, he found nothing but leaves: for the time of figs was not yet." Singular conceptions have passed from learned men to make out this passage of St. Mark which St. Matthew* so plainly delivereth; most men doubting why our Saviour should curse the tree for bearing no fruit, when the time of fruit was not yet come; or why it is said that the time of figs was not yet,[8] when, notwithstanding, figs might be found at that season.

Heinsius,† who thinks that Elias must salve the doubt, according to the received reading of the text, undertaketh to vary the same, reading οὐ γὰρ ἦν, καιρὸς σύκων, that is, for where he was, it was the season or time for figs.

A learned interpreter‡ of our own, without alteration of accents or words, endeavours to salve all, by another interpretation of the same, οὐ γὰρ καιρὸς σύκων, for it was not a good or seasonable year for figs.

But, because men part not easily with old beliefs or the received construction of words, we shall briefly set down what may be alleged for it.

And, first, for the better comprehension of all deductions hereupon, we may consider the several differences and distinctions both of fig trees and their fruits. Suidas upon the word ἰσχάς makes four divisions of figs, ὄλυνθος, φήληξ, σῦκον and ἰσχάς. But because φήληξ makes no considerable distinction, learned men do chiefly insist upon the three others; that is, ὄλυνθος, or *grossus*, which are the buttons, or small sorts of figs, either not ripe, or not ordinarily proceeding to

---

* Mark xi. 13 ; Matt. xxi. 19.   † *Heinsius in Nonnum.*
‡ Dr. Hammond.

[8] *for the time of figs, &c.*] The difficulty of this passage is simply and adequately solved, by reading, *though the fig harvest was not yet.* When it is considered that the fig tree produces its fruit before its leaves, our Saviour was justified in looking for fruit on a fig tree which was in leaf, and before the time *for gathering figs* had arrived. To find a tree which was, at that time, *without figs*, was, in fact, to find *a barren fig tree.*

In reference to the mode in which the fig tree vegetates, Jortin has the following beautiful remark :—" A good man may be said to resemble the fig tree ; which, without producing blossoms and flowers, like some other trees, and raising expectations which are often deceitful, seldom fails to produce fruit in its season."—*Jortin's Tracts,* vol. ii. p. 537.

ripeness, but fall away at least in the greatest part, and especially in sharp winters, which are. also named σνκάδες, and distinguished from the fruit of the wild fig, or *caprificus*, which is named ἐρινεὸς, and never cometh unto ripeness. The second is called σῦκον or *ficus*, which commonly proceedeth unto ripeness in its due season. A third, the ripe fig dried, which maketh the ἰσχάδες or *carrier*.

Of fig trees there are also many divisions: for some are *prodromi* or precocious, which bear fruit very early, whether they bear once or oftener in the year; some are *protericæ*, which are the most early of the precocious trees, and bear soonest of any; some are *æstivæ*, which bear in the common season of the summer, and some *serotinæ* which bear very late.

Some are *biferous* and *triferous*, which bear twice or thrice in the year, and some are of the ordinary standing course, which make up the expected season of figs.

Again, some fig trees, either in their proper kind, or fertility in some single ones, do bear fruit or rudiments of fruit all the year long; as is annually observable in some kind of fig trees in hot and proper regions; and may also be observed in some fig trees of more temperate countries, in years of no great disadvantage, wherein, when the summer ripe fig is past, others begin to appear, and so standing in buttons all the winter, do either fall away before the spring, or else proceed to ripeness.

Now according to these distinctions, we may measure the intent of the text, and endeavour to make out the expression. For, considering the diversity of these trees and their several fructifications, probable or possible it is that some thereof were implied, and may literally afford a solution.

And first, though it was not the season for figs, yet some fruit might have been expected, even in ordinary bearing trees. For the *grossi* or buttons appear before the leaves, especially before the leaves are well grown. Some might have stood during the winter, and by this time been of some growth: though many fall off, yet some might remain on, and proceed towards maturity. And we find that good husbands had an art to make them hold on, as is delivered by Theophrastus.

The σῦκον, or common summer fig, was not expected; for

that is placed by Galen among the *fructus horarii* or *horæi*, which ripen in that part of summer, called ὥρα, and stands commended by him above other fruits of that season. And of this kind might be the figs which were brought unto Cleopatra in a basket together with an asp, according to the time of her death, on the nineteenth of August. And that our Saviour expected not such figs, but some other kind, seems to be implied in the indefinite expression, " if haply he might find anything thereon ;" which in that country, and the variety of such trees, might not be despaired of, at this season, and very probably hoped for in the first precocious and early bearing trees. And that there were precocious and early bearing trees in Judæa, may be illustrated from some expressions in Scripture concerning precocious figs ; *calathus unus habebat ficus bonas nimis, sicut solent esse ficus primi temporis ;* " one basket had very good figs, even like the figs that are first ripe."* And the like might be more especially expected in this place, if this remarkable tree be rightly placed in some maps of Jerusalem ; for it is placed, by Adrichomius, in or near Bethphage, which some con-jecturers will have to be the house of figs : and at this place fig trees are still to be found, if we consult the travels of Bidulphus.

Again, in this great variety of fig trees, as precocious, proterical, biferous, triferous, and always-bearing trees, some-thing might have been expected, though the time of common figs was not yet. For some trees bear in a manner all the year ; as may be illustrated from the epistle of the empe-ror Julian, concerning his present of Damascus figs, which he commendeth from their successive and continued growing and bearing, after the manner of the fruits which Homer describeth in the garden of Alcinous. And though it were then but about the eleventh of March, yet, in the latitude of Jerusalem, the sun at that time hath a good power in the day, and might advance the maturity of precocious often-bearing or ever-bearing figs. And therefore when it is said that St. Peter † stood and warmed himself by the fire in the judgment-hall, and the reason is added ("for it was cold"‡),

---

* Jer. xxiv. 2.   † St. Mark xiv. 67; St. Luke xxii. 55, 56.
‡ St. John xviii. 18.

that expression might be interposed either to denote the coolness in the morning, according to hot countries, or some extraordinary and unusual coldness, which happened at that time. For the same Bidulphus, who was at that time of the year at Jerusalem, saith, that it was then as hot as at mid-summer in England : and we find in Scripture that the first sheaf of barley was offered in March.

Our Saviour, therefore, seeing a fig tree with leaves well spread, and so as to be distinguished afar off, went unto it, and when he came, found nothing but leaves ; he found it to be no precocious or always-bearing tree : and though it were not the time for summer figs, yet he found no rudiments thereof ; and though he expected not common figs, yet something might haply have been expected of some other kind, according to different fertility and variety of production ; but, discovering nothing, he found a tree answering the state of the Jewish rulers, barren unto all expectation.

And this is consonant unto the mystery of the story, wherein the fig tree denoteth the synagogue and rulers of the Jews, whom God having peculiarly cultivated, singularly blessed and cherished, he expected from them no ordinary, slow, or customary fructification, but an earliness in good works, a precocious or continued fructification, and was not content with common after-bearing ; and might justly have expostulated with the Jews, as God by the prophet Micah did with their forefathers ; * *præcoquas ficus desideravit anima mea,* "my soul longed for (or desired) early ripe fruits, but ye are become as a vine already gathered, and there is no cluster upon you."

Lastly, in this account of the fig tree, the mystery and symbolical sense is chiefly to be looked upon. Our Saviour, therefore, taking a hint from his hunger to go unto this specious tree, and intending, by this tree, to declare a judgment upon the synagogue and people of the Jews, he came unto the tree, and, after the usual manner, inquired and looked about for some kind of fruit, as he had done before in the Jews, but found nothing but leaves and specious outsides, as he had also found in them ; and when it bore no fruit like them, when he expected it, and came to look for it,

* Micah vii. 1.
o 2

though it were not the time of ordinary fruit, yet failing
when he required it, in the mysterious sense, 'twas fruitless
longer to expect it.   For he had come unto them, and they
were nothing fructified by it, his departure approached, and
his time of preaching was now at an end.

Now, in this account, besides the miracle, some things are
naturally considerable.   For it may be questioned how the
fig tree, naturally a fruitful plant, became barren, for it had
no show or so much as rudiment of fruit: and it was in old
time, a signal judgment of God, that "the fig tree should
bear no fruit:" and therefore this tree may naturally be
conceived to have been under some disease indisposing it to
such fructification.   And this, in the pathology of plants,
may be the disease of φυλλομανία, ἐμφυλλισμὸς, or super-
foliation mentioned by Theophrastus; whereby the fructifying juice is starved by the excess of leaves; which in this
tree were already so full spread, that it might be known and
distinguished afar off.   And this was, also, a sharp resemblance of the hypocrisy of the rulers, made up of specious
outsides, and fruitless ostentation, contrary to the fruit of
the fig tree, which, filled with a sweet and pleasant pulp,
makes no show without, not so much as of any flower.

Some naturals are also considerable from the propriety of
this punishment settled upon a fig tree: for infertility and
barrenness seems more intolerable in this tree than any, as
being a vegetable singularly constituted for production; so
far from bearing no fruit that it may be made to bear almost
any.   And therefore the ancients singled out this as the
fittest tree whereon to graft and propagate other fruits, as
containing a plentiful and lively sap, whereby other scions
would prosper: and, therefore, this tree was also sacred unto
the deity of fertility; and the statua of Priapus was made
of the fig tree;

> Olim truncus eram ficulneus inutile lignum.

It hath also a peculiar advantage to produce and maintain
its fruit above all other plants, as not subject to miscarry in
flowers and blossoms, from accidents of wind and weather.
For it beareth no flowers outwardly, and such as it hath, are
within the coat, as the later examination of naturalists hath
discovered.

Lastly, it was a tree wholly constituted for fruit, wherein if it faileth, it is in a manner useless, the wood therof being of so little use, that it affordeth proverbial expressions, *homo ficulneus, argumentum ficulneum,* or things of no validity.

44. "I said I will go up into the palm tree, and take hold of the boughs thereof."* This expression is more agreeable unto the palm than is commonly apprehended, for that it is a tall bare tree, bearing its boughs but at the top and upper part; so that it must be ascended before its boughs or fruit can be attained; and the going, getting, or climbing up, may be emphatical in this tree; for the trunk or body thereof is naturally contrived for ascension, and made with advantage for getting up, as having many welts and eminences, and so, as it were a natural ladder, and staves by which it may be climbed, as Pliny observeth *palmæ teretes atque proceres, densis quadratisque pollicibus faciles se ad scandendum præbent,*† by this way men are able to get up into it. And the figures of Indians thus climbing the same are graphically described in the travels of Linschoten. This tree is often mentioned in Scripture, and was so remarkable in Judæa, that in after-times it became the emblem of that country, as may be seen in that medal of the emperor Titus, with a captive woman sitting under a palm, and the inscription of *Judæa capta.* And Pliny confirmeth the same when he saith *Judæa palmis inclyta.*

45. Many things are mentioned in Scripture, which have an emphasis from this or the neighbour countries: for besides the cedars, the Syrian lilies are taken notice of by writers. That expression in the Canticles, "thou art fair, thou art fair, thou hast dove's eyes,"‡ receives a particular character, if we look, not upon our common pigeons, but the beauteous and fine-eyed doves of Syria.

When the rump is so strictly taken notice of in the sacrifice of the peace offering, in these words, "the whole rump, it shall be taken off hard by the back-bone,"§ it becomes the more considerable in reference to this country where sheep had so large tails; which, according to Aristotle,|| were a

* Cant. vii. 8.   † *Plin.* xiii. cap. 4.   ‡ Cant. iv. 1.
§ Levit. iii. 9. || *Arist. Hist. Animal.* lib. viii.

cubit broad; and so they are still, as Bellonius hath delivered.

When 'tis said in the Canticles, " thy teeth are as a flock of sheep which go up from the washing, whereof every one beareth twins, and there is not one barren among them ;" * it may seem hard unto us of these parts to find whole flocks bearing twins, and not one barren among them ; yet may this be better conceived in the fertile flocks of those countries, where sheep have so often two, sometimes three, and sometimes four, and which is so frequently observed by writers of the neighbour country of Egypt. And this fe-cundity, and fruitfulness of their flocks, is answerable unto the expression of the Psalmist, " that our sheep may bring forth thousands and ten thousands in our streets." † And hereby, besides what was spent at their tables, a good supply was made for the great consumption of sheep in their several kinds of sacrifices ; and of so many thousand male unblemished yearling lambs, which were required at their passovers.

Nor need we wonder to find so frequent mention both of garden and field plants; since Syria was notable of old for this curiosity and variety, according to Pliny, *Syria hortis operosissima ;* and since Bellonius hath so lately observed of Jerusalem, that its hilly parts did so abound with plants, that they might be compared unto mount Ida in Crete or Candia; which is the most noted place for noble simples yet known.

46. Though so many plants have their express names in Scripture, yet others are implied in some texts which are not explicitly mentioned. In the feast of tabernacles or booths, the law was this, " thou shalt take unto thee boughs of goodly trees, branches of the palm, and the boughs of thick trees, and willows of the brook." Now though the text de-scendeth not unto particulars of the goodly trees and thick trees ; yet Maimonides will tell us that for a goodly tree they made use of the citron tree, which is fair and goodly to the eye, and well prospering in that country : and that for the thick trees they used the myrtle, which was no rare or infre-quent plant among them. And though it groweth but low in our gardens, was not a little tree in those parts ; in which

* Cant. iv. 2.   † Psalm cxliv. 13.

plant also the leaves grew thick, and almost covered the stalk. And Curtius Symphorianus * in his description of the exotic myrtle, makes it *folio densissimo senis in ordinem versibus.* The paschal lamb was to be eaten with bitterness or bitter herbs, not particularly set down in Scripture : but the Jewish writers declare, that they. made use of succory, and wild lettuce, which herbs while some conceive they could not get down, as being very bitter, rough, and prickly, they may consider that the time of the passover was in the spring, when these herbs are young and tender, and consequently less unpleasant: besides, according to the Jewish custom, these herbs were dipped in the *charoseth*, or sauce made of raisins stamped with vinegar, and were also eaten with bread; and they had four cups of wine allowed unto them; and it was sufficient to take but a pittance of herbs, or the·quantity of an olive.

47. Though the famous paper reed of Egypt be only particularly named in Scripture ; yet when reeds are so often mentioned without special name or. distinction, we may conceive their differences may be comprehended, and that they were not all of one kind, or that the common reed was only implied.   For mention is made in Ezekiel † of " a measuring reed of six cubits;" we find that they smote our Saviour on the head with a reed,‡ and put a sponge with vinegar on a reed, which was long enough to reach to his mouth,[9] while he was upon the cross.   And with such differences of reeds, *vallatory, sagittary, scriptory,* and others, they might be furnished in Judæa. For we find in the portion of Ephraim,§ *vallis arundineti ;* and so set down in the maps of Adricomius; and in our translation the river Kana, or brook of Canes. And Bellonius tells us that the river Jordan affordeth plenty and variety of reeds ; out of some whereof the Arabs make darts and light lances, and out of others, arrows; and withal that there plentifully groweth the fine *calamus, arundo scriptoria,* or writing reed, which they gather with the greatest care, as being of singular use and commodity

* *Curtius de Hortis.*   † Ezek. xl. 5.
‡ St. Matt. xxvii. 30, 48.   § *J*osh. xvi. 17.

[9] *A reed which was long enough to reach to his mouth.*] In the neighbourhood of Suez some reeds grow to the height of twelve yards.

at home and abroad; a hard reed about the compass of a goose or swan's quill, whereof I have seen some polished and cut with a web [neb? or nib?]; which is in common use for writing throughout the Turkish dominions, they using not the quills of birds.

And whereas the same author, with other describers of these parts, affirmeth, that the river Jordan, not far from Jericho, is but such a stream as a youth may throw a stone over it, or about eight fathoms broad, it doth not diminish the account and solemnity of the miraculous passage of the Israelites under Joshua. For it must be considered that they passed it in the time of harvest, when the river was high, and the grounds about it under water, according to that pertinent parenthesis:—"As the feet of the priests, which carried the ark, were dipped in the brim of the water, for Jordan overfloweth all its banks at the time of harvest."* In this consideration it was well joined with the great river Euphrates, in that expression in Ecclesiasticus, " God maketh the understanding to abound like Euphrates, and as Jordan in the time of harvest."†

48. The kingdom of heaven is likened unto a man which sowed good seed in his field, but while men slept, his enemy came and sowed "tares," or as the Greek, *zizania,* "among the wheat."

Now, how to render *zizania,* and to what species of plants to confine it, there is no slender doubt; for the word is not mentioned in other parts of Scripture, nor in any ancient Greek writer: it is not to be found in Aristotle, Theophrastus, or Dioscorides. Some Greek and Latin fathers have made use of the same, as also Suidas and Phavorinus; but probably they have all derived it from this text.

And, therefore, this obscurity might easily occasion such variety in translations and expositions. For some retain the word *zizania,* as the vulgar, that of Beza, of Junius, and also the Italian and Spanish. The low Dutch renders it *oncruidt,* the German *oncraut,* or *herba mala,* the French *yvroye* or *lolium,* and the English *tares.*

Besides, this being conceived to be a Syriac word, it may still add unto the uncertainty of the sense. For though this

* *Josh.* iii. 15.   † Eccles. xxiv. 26.

gospel were first written in Hebrew or Syriac, yet it is not unquestionable whether the true original be any where extant. And that Syriac copy which we now have, is conceived to be of far later time than St. Matthew.

Expositors and annotators are also various. Hugo Grotius hath passed the word *zizania* without a note. Diodati, retaining the word *zizania*, conceives that it was some peculiar herb growing among the corn of those countries, and not known in our fields. But Emanuel de Sa interprets it *plantas semini noxias*, and so accordingly some others.

Buxtorfius, in his *Rabbinical Lexicon*, gives divers interpretations, sometimes for degenerated corn, sometimes for the black seeds in wheat, but withal concludes, *an hæc sit eadem vox aut species cum zizaniâ apud evangelistam, quærant alii.* But lexicons and dictionaries by *zizania* do almost generally understand *lolium*, which we call darnel, and commonly confine the signification to that plant. Notwithstanding, since *lolium* had a known and received name in Greek, some may be apt to doubt why, if that plant were particularly intended, the proper Greek word was not used in the text. For Theophrastus[*] named *lolium* αἶρα, and hath often mentioned that plant; and in one place saith, that corn doth sometimes *loliescere* or degenerate into darnel. Dioscorides, who travelled over Judæa, gives it the same name, which is also to be found in Galen, Ætius, and Ægineta; and Pliny hath sometimes Latinized that word into *æra*.

Besides, *lolium* or darnel shows itself in the winter, growing up with the wheat; and Theophrastus observed, that it was no vernal plant, but came up in the winter; which will not well answer the expression of the text, "And when the blade came up, and brought forth fruit," or gave evidence of its fruit, the *zizania* appeared. And if the husbandry of the ancients were agreeable unto ours, they would not have been so earnest to weed away the darnel; for our husbandmen do not commonly weed it in the field, but separate the seed after thrashing. And, therefore, Galen delivereth, that in an unseasonable year, and great scarcity of corn, when they neglected to

---

[*] οὐ ξαίρησθαι. *Theophrast. Hist. Plant.* lib. 8.

separate the darnel, the bread proved generally unwholesome, and had evil effects on the head.

Our old and later translators render *zizania* tares, which name our English botanists give unto *aracus, cracca; vicia sylvestris,* calling them tares and strangling tares. And our husbandmen by tares understand some sorts of wild fitches, which grow amongst corn, and clasp unto it, according to the Latin etymology, *vicia à vinciendo.* Now in this uncertainty of the original, tares, as well as some others, may make out the sense, and be also more agreeable unto the circumstances of the parable. For they come up and appear what they are, when the blade of the corn is come up, and also the stalk and fruit discoverable. They have likewise little spreading roots, which may entangle or rob the good roots, and they have also tendrils and claspers, which lay hold of what grows near them, and so can hardly be weeded without endangering the neighbouring corn.

However, if by *zizania* we understand *herbas segeti noxias,* or *vitia segetum,* as some expositors have done, and take the word in a more general sense, comprehending several weeds and vegetables offensive unto corn, according as the Greek word in the plural number may imply, and as the learned Laurenbergius* hath expressed, *runcare, quod apud nostrates weden dicitur, zizanias inutiles est evellere.* If, I say, it be thus taken, we shall not need to be definite, or confine unto one particular plant, from a word which may comprehend divers. And this may also prove a safer sense,[1] in such obscurity of the original.

And, therefore, since in this parable the sower of the *zizania* is the devil, and the *zizania* wicked persons; if **any** from this larger acception will take in thistles, darnel, cockle, wild straggling fitches, bindweed, *tribulus,* restharrow, and other *vitia segetum;* he may, both from the natural and symbolical qualities of those vegetables, have plenty of matter to illustrate the variety of his mischiefs, and of the wicked of this world.

* *De Horti Cultura.*

[1] *This may also prove a safer sense.*] But the later commentators seem rather disposed, with Forskäl, to consider it to have been the darnel.

49. When 'tis said in Job, " Let thistles grow up instead of wheat, and cockle[1] instead of barley," the words are intelligible, the sense allowable and significant to this purpose : but whether the word cockle doth strictly conform unto the original, some doubt may be made from the different translations of it; for the vulgar renders it *spina*, Tremellius *vitia frugum*, and the Geneva *yvroye*, or darnel. Besides, whether cockle were common in the ancient agriculture of those parts, or what word they used for it, is of great uncertainty. For the elder botanical writers have made no mention thereof, and the moderns have given it the name of *pseudomelanthium nigellastrum, lychnoides segetum*, names not known unto antiquity. And, therefore, our translation hath warily set down " noisome weeds" in the margin.

TRACT II.

OF GARLANDS AND CORONARY OR GARLAND PLANTS.[2]

SIR,—The use of flowery crowns and garlands is of no slender antiquity, and higher than I conceive you apprehend it. For, besides the old Greeks and Romans, the

---

[1] *cockle.*] Celsius, and after him Michaelis, supposes this to have been the aconite.

[2] In the margin of Evelyn's copy is this manuscript note :—"*This letter was written to me from Dr. Browne; more at large in the Coronaric Plants.*"

In order to preserve unaltered, as far as possible, the order of Sir Thomas Browne's published works, I have thought proper not to transplant into the "*Correspondence*" the present and several other Tracts, though they were, in fact, epistolary, and it has been ascertained to whom they were addressed. In the preface to Evelyn's *Acetaria* (reprinted by Mr. Upcott, in his *Collection of Evelyn's Miscellaneous Writings*), we find his "Plan of a Royal Garden, in three Books." It was in reference to this projected work (of which however *Acetaria* was the only part ever published), that Browne's assistance was asked and given. Among the subjects named in that plan the following are

Egyptians made use hereof; who, besides the bravery of their garlands, had little birds upon them to peck their heads and brows, and so to keep them [from] sleeping at their festival compotations. This practice also extended as far as India: for at the feast of the Indian king, it is peculiarly observed by Philostratus, that their custom was to wear garlands, and come crowned with them unto their feast.

The crowns and garlands of the ancients were either gestatory, such as they wore about their heads or necks; portatory, such as they carried at solemn festivals; pensile or suspensory, such as they hanged about the posts of their houses in honour of their gods, as Jupiter Thyræus or Limeneus; or else they were depository, such as they laid upon the graves and monuments of the dead. And these were made up after all ways of art, compactile, sutile, plectile; for which work there were σεφανοπλόκοι, or expert persons to contrive them after the best grace and propriety.

Though we yield not unto them in the beauty of flowery garlands, yet some of those of antiquity were larger than any we lately met with; for we find in Athenæus, that a myrtle crown, of one and twenty feet in compass, was solemnly carried about at the Hellotian feast in Corinth, together with the bones of Europa.

And garlands were surely of frequent use among them; for we read in Galen,* that when Hippocrates cured the great plague of Athens by fires kindled in and about the city: the fuel thereof consisted much of their garlands. And they must needs be very frequent and of common use, the ends thereof being many. For they were convivial,

---

* *De Theriaca ad Pisonem.*

referred to in the present Tract, and in other of Browne's Letters to Evelyn :—

Book ii. chap. 6. Of a seminary; nurseries; and of propagating trees, plants, and flowers; planting and transplanting, &c.

Chap. 16. Of the coronary garden.

Chap. 18. Of stupendous and wonderful plants.

Book iii. chap. 9. Of garden burial.

Chap. 10. Of paradise, and of the most famous gardens in the world, ancient and modern.

festival, sacrificial, nuptial, honorary, funebrial. We who propose unto ourselves the pleasures of two senses, and only single out such as are of beauty and good odour, cannot strictly confine ourselves unto imitation of them.

For, in their convivial garlands, they had respect unto plants preventing drunkenness, or discussing[1] the exhalations from wine; wherein, beside roses, taking in ivy, vervain, melilote, &c., they made use of divers of small beauty or good odour. The solemn festival garlands were made properly unto their gods, and accordingly contrived from plants sacred unto such deities; and their sacrificial ones were selected under such considerations. Their honorary crowns triumphal, ovary, civical, obsidional, had little of flowers in them : and their funebrial garlands had little of beauty in them besides roses, while they made them of myrtle, rosemary, *apium*, &c., under symbolical intimations; but our florid and purely ornamental garlands, delightful unto sight and smell, nor framed according to any mystical and symbolical considerations, are of more free election, and so may be made to excel those of the ancients: we having China, India, and a new world to supply us, beside the great distinction of flowers unknown unto antiquity, and the varieties thereof arising from art and nature.

But, beside vernal, æstival and autumnal, made of flowers, the ancients had also the hyemal garlands; contenting themselves at first with such as were made of horn dyed into several colours, and shaped into the figure of flowers, and also of *æs coronarium* or *clincquant*, or brass thinly wrought out into leaves commonly known among us. But the curiosity of some emperors for such intents had roses brought from Egypt until they had found the art to produce late roses in Rome, and to make them grow in winter, as is delivered in that handsome epigram of Martial—

> At tu Romanæ jussus jam cedere brumæ
> Mitte tuas messes, accipe, Nile, rosas.

Some American nations, who do much excel in garlands, content not themselves only with flowers, but make elegant

---

[1] *discussing.*] Dr. Johnson quotes this passage as his example of the use of the word *discuss* in the sense of *disperse.*

crowns of feathers, whereof they have some of greater radiancy and lustre than their flowers: and since there is an art to set into shapes, and curiously to work in choicest feathers, there could nothing answer the crowns made of the choicest feathers of some *tomineios* and sun birds.

The catalogue of coronary plants is not large in Theophrastus, Pliny, Pollux, or Athenæus: but we may find a good enlargement in the accounts of modern botanists; and additions may still be made by successive acquists of fair and specious plants, not yet translated from foreign regions, or little known unto our gardens; he that would be complete may take notice of these following :—

Flos Tigridis.
Flos Lyncis.
Pinea Indica Recchi, Talama Ouiedi.
Herba Paradisea.
Volubilis Mexicanus.
Narcissus Indicus Serpentarius.
Helichrysum Mexicanum.
Xicama.
Aquilegia novæ Hispaniæ Cacoxochitli Recchi.
Aristochæa Mexicana.
Camaratinga sive Caragunta quarta Pisonis.
Maracuia Granadilla.
Cambay sive Myrtus Americana.
Flos Auriculæ Flor de la Oreia.
Floripendio novæ Hispaniæ.
Rosa Indica.
Zilium Indicum.
Fula Magori Garciæ.
Champe Garciæ Champacca Bontii.
*Daullontas frutex odoratus seu Chamæmelum arborescens
    Bontii.*
Beidelsar Alpini.
Sambuc.
Amberboi Turcarum.
Nuphar Ægyptium.
Lilionarcissus Indicus.
Bamma Ægyptiacum.
Hiucca Canadensis horti Furnesiani.
Bupthalmum novæ Hispaniæ Alepocapath.

Valeriana seu Chrysanthemum Americanum Acocotlis.
Flos Corvinus Coronarius Americanus.
Capolin Cerasus dulcis Indicus Floribus racemosis.
Asphodelus Americanus.
Syringa Lutea Americana.
Bulbus unifolius.
Moly latifolium Flore luteo.[2]
Conyza Americana purpurea.
Salvia Cretica pomifera Bellonii.
Lausus Serrata Odora.
Ornithogalus Promontorii Bonæ Spei.
Fritillaria crassa Soldanica Promontorii Bonæ Spei.
Sigillum Solomonis Indicum.
Tulipa Promontorii Bonæ Spei.
Iris Uvaria.
Nopolxock sedum elegans novæ Hispaniæ.

More might be added unto this list;[3] and I have only taken the pains to give you a short specimen of those, many more which you may find in respective authors, and which time and future industry may make no great strangers in England. The inhabitants of *nova Hispania,* and a great part of America, Mahometans, Indians, Chinese, are eminent promoters of these coronary and specious plants; and the annual tribute of the king of Bisnaguer in India, arising out of odours and flowers, amounts unto many thousands of crowns.

Thus, in brief, of this matter. I am, &c.

---

[2] *Moly latifolium Flore luteo.*] Sir Thomas, in a subsequent letter (see *Correspondence*), corrects this name;—"for *Moly Flore luteo,*" he says, "you may please to put in *Moly Hondianum novum.*"

[3] *More might be added unto this list.*] Which Sir Thomas sent me a catalogue of from Norwich.—*MS. note of Evelyn's.*

This list has not been found.

TRACT III.

OF THE FISHES EATEN BY OUR SAVIOUR WITH HIS DIS-CIPLES AFTER HIS RESURRECTION FROM THE DEAD.

SIR,—I have thought a little upon the question proposed by you [viz. what kind of fishes those were,[1] of which our Saviour ate with his disciples after his resurrection ?*] and I return you such an answer, as, in so short a time for study, and in the midst of my occasions, occurs to me.

The books of Scripture (as also those which are apocryphal) are often silent or very sparing, in the particular names of fishes; or in setting them down in such manner as to leave the kinds of them without all doubt and reason for further inquiry. For, when it declareth what fishes were allowed the Israelites for their food, they are only set down in general which have fins and scales: whereas, in the account of quadrupeds and birds, there is particular mention made of divers of them. In the book of Tobit that fish which he took out of the river is only named a great fish, and so there remains much uncertainty to determine the species thereof. And even the fish which swallowed Jonah, and is called a great fish, and commonly thought to be a great whale, is not received without all doubt; while some learned men conceive it to have been none of our whales, but a large kind of *lamia*.

And, in this narration of St. John, the fishes are only expressed by their bigness and number, not their names, and therefore it may seem undeterminable what they were: notwithstanding, these fishes being taken in the great lake or sea of Tiberias, something may be probably stated therein. For since Bellonius, that diligent and learned traveller, informeth us, that the fishes of this lake were trouts, pikes, chevins, and tenches; it may well be conceived that either

---

* St. John xxi. 9, 10, 11—13.

---

[1] *what kind, &c.*] *MS. Sloan.* 1827, reads, "of what kind those little fish were, which fed the multitude in the wilderness, or, &c."

all or some thereof are to be understood in this Scripture. And these kind of fishes become large and of great growth, answerable unto the expression of Scripture, " one hundred fifty and three great fishes;" that is, large in their own kinds, and the largest kinds in this lake and fresh water, wherein no great variety, and of the larger sort of fishes, could be expected. For the river Jordan, running through this lake, falls into the lake of Asphaltus, and hath no mouth into the sea, which might admit of great fishes or greater variety to come up into it.

And out of the mouth of some of these fore-mentioned fishes might the tribute money be taken, when our Saviour, at Capernaum, seated upon the same lake, said unto Peter, " Go thou to the sea, and cast an hook, and take up the fish that first cometh; and when thou hast opened his mouth thou shalt find a piece of money ; that take and give them for thee and me."

And this makes void that common conceit and tradition of the fish called *faber marinus*, by some, a peter or penny fish; which having two remarkable round spots upon either side, these are conceived to be the marks of St. Peter's fingers or signatures of the money : for though it hath these marks, yet is there no probability that such a kind of fish was to be found in the lake of Tiberias, Gennesareth, or Galilee, which is but sixteen miles long and six broad, and hath no communication with the sea ; for this is a mere fish of the sea and salt water, and (though we meet with some thereof on our coast) is not to be found in many seas.

Thus having returned no improbable answer unto your question, I shall crave leave to ask another of yourself concerning that fish mentioned by Procopius,* which brought the famous king Theodorick to his end: his words are to this effect : " The manner of his death was this ; Symmachus and his son-in-law Boëthius, just men and great relievers of the poor, senators, and consuls, had many enemies, by whose false accusations Theodorick being persuaded that they plotted against him, put them to death, and confiscated their estates. Not long after his waiters set before him at supper a great head of a fish, which seemed to him to be the

---

* *De Bello Gothico*, lib. i.

head of Symmachus lately murdered : and with his teeth sticking out, and fierce glaring eyes to threaten him : being frighted, he grew chill, went to bed, lamenting what he had done to Symmachus and Boëthius; and soon after died." What fish do you apprehend this to have been ?   I would learn of you ; give me your thoughts about it.

I am, &c.

TRACT IV.

AN ANSWER TO CERTAIN QUERIES RELATING TO FISHES, BIRDS, AND INSECTS.

SIR,—I return the following answers to your queries, which were these :—

1. What fishes are meant by the names, *halec* and *mugil ?*

2. What is the bird which you will receive from the bearer, and what birds are meant by the names *halcyon, nysus, ciris, nycticorax ?*

3. What insect is meant by the word *cicada ?*

ANSWER 1. The word *halec* we are taught to render an herring, which, being an ancient word, is not strictly appropriable unto a fish not known or not described by the ancients; and which the modern naturalists are fain to name *harengus :* the word *halecula* being applied unto such little fish out of which they are fain to make pickle; and *halec* or *alec*, taken for the *liquamen* or liquor itself, according to that of the poet,

Ego fæcem primus et alec
Primus et inveni album.

And was a conditure and sauce much affected by antiquity, as was also *muria* and *garum*.

In common constructions *mugil* is rendered a mullet, which, notwithstanding, is a different fish from the *mugil*

described by authors;[1] wherein, if we mistake, we cannot
so closely apprehend the expression of Juvenal,

Quosdam ventres et mugilis intrat.

And misconceive the fish whereby fornicators were so opprobriously and irksomely punished; for the *mugil*, being
somewhat rough and hard-skinned, did more exasperate the
guts of such offenders: whereas the mullet was a smooth
fish, and of too high esteem to be employed in such offices.

ANSWER 2. I cannot but wonder that this bird you sent
should be a stranger unto you, and unto those who had a
sight thereof; for, though it be not seen every day, yet we
often meet with it in this country. It is an elegant bird,
which he that once beholdeth can hardly mistake any other
for it. From the proper note it is called an hoopebird with
us: in Greek *epops*, in Latin *upupa*. We are little obliged
unto our school instruction, wherein we are taught to render
upupa a lapwing, which bird our natural writers name *van-
nellus;* for thereby we mistake this remarkable bird, and
apprehend not rightly what is delivered of it.

We apprehend not the hieroglyphical considerations which
the old Egyptians made of this observable bird; who, considering therein the order and variety of colours, the twenty-
six or twenty-eight feathers in its crest, his latitancy, and
mewing this handsome outside in the winter: they made it
an emblem of the varieties of the world, the succession of
times and seasons, and signal mutations in them. And,
therefore, Orus, the hieroglyphic of the world, had the head
of an hoopebird upon the top of his staff.

Hereby we may also mistake the *duchiphath*, or bird forbidden for food in Leviticus;* and, not knowing the bird,
may the less apprehend some reasons of that prohibition;
that is, the magical virtues ascribed unto it by the Egyptians, and the superstitious apprehensions which the nation
held of it, whilst they precisely numbered the feathers and
colours thereof, while they placed it on the heads of their

* Levit. xi. 19.

[1] *authors.*] *MS. Sloan.* proceeds thus: "for which I know not,
perhaps, whether we have any proper name in English; and other
nations nearly imitate the Latin, wherein," &c.—*MS. Sloan.* 1827.

P 2

gods, and near their Mercurial crosses, and so highly magnified this bird in their sacred symbols.

Again, not knowing or mistaking this bird, we may misapprehend, or not closely apprehend, that handsome expression of Ovid, when Tereus was turned into an *upupa*, or hoopebird :—

> Vertitur in volucrem cui sunt pro vertice cristæ,
> Protinus immodicum surgit pro cuspide rostrum
> Nomen epops volucri, facies armata videtur.

For, in this military shape, he is aptly fancied even still revengefully to pursue his hated wife, Progne : in the propriety of his note crying out, *pou, pou, ubi, ubi* : or, Where are you ?

Nor are we singly deceived in the nominal translation of this bird : in many other animals we commit the like mistake. So *gracculus* is rendered a jay, which bird, notwithstanding, must be of a dark colour according to that of Martial,

> Sed quandam volo nocte nigriorem
> Formica, pice, gracculo, cicada.

Halcyon is rendered a kingfisher,* a bird commonly known among us, and by zoographers and naturals the same is named· *ispida*, a well coloured bird, frequenting streams and rivers, building in holes of pits, like some martins, about the end of the spring; in whose nests we have found little else than innumerable small fish bones, and white round eggs of a smooth and polished surface, whereas the true *halcyon* is a sea bird, makes an handsome nest floating upon the water, and breedeth in the winter.

That *nysus* should be rendered either an hobby or a sparrow-hawk in the fable of Nysus and Scylla in Ovid, because we are much to seek in the distinction of hawks according to their old denominations, we shall not much contend, and may allow a favourable latitude therein: but that the *ciris* or bird into which Scylla was turned should be translated a lark, it can hardly be made out agreeable unto the description of Virgil, in his poem of that name,

> Inde alias volucres mimoque infecta rubenti crura——.

But seems more agreeable unto some kind of *hæmantopus* or

---

* See *Vulg. Err.* b. iii. c. 10.

redshank: and so the *nysus* to have been some kind of hawk, which delighteth about the sea and marshes, where such prey most aboundeth, which sort of hawk, while Scaliger determineth to be a merlin, the French translator warily expoundeth it to be some kind of hawk.

Nycticorax we may leave unto the common and verbal translation of a night-raven, but we know no proper kind of raven unto which to confine the same, and, therefore, some take the liberty to ascribe it unto some sort of owls, and others unto the bittern; which bird, in its common note, which he useth out of the time of coupling and upon the wing, so well resembleth the croaking of a raven, that I have been deceived by it.[2]

ANSWER 3. While *cicada* is rendered a grasshopper, we commonly think that which is so called among us to be the true *cicada;* wherein, as we have elsewhere declared,[*] there is a great mistake: for we have not the *cicada* in England,[3] and, indeed, no proper word for that animal, which the French name *cigale.* That which we commonly call a grasshopper, and the French *saulterelle,* being one kind of locust, so rendered in the plague of Egypt, and, in old Saxon, named *gersthop.*[4]

I have been the less accurate in these answers, because the queries are not of difficult resolution, or of great moment : however, I would not wholly neglect them or your satisfaction, as being, Sir,   Yours, &c.

* *Vulg. Err.* b. v. c. 3.

[2] *Nycticorax, &c.*]   Very possibly the night-raven, *ardea nycticorax,* Lin.

[3] *we have not the* cicada *in England.*] Of the true Linnæan *cicadæ* (*Tettigonia Fabr.*), the first British species was discovered in the New Forest, by Mr. Bydder, a collector whom I employed there for a considerable period, nearly twenty years since. It has been named *C. Anglica,* and is figured by Samouelle, *Comp.* pl. 5, fig. 2, and by Curtis, *British Entomology,* Feb. 1st, 1832, No. 392.

[4] *gersthop.*] "Gerstrappa," in *MS. Sloan.* 1827.

TRACT V.

OF HAWKS AND FALCONRY, ANCIENT AND MODERN.

SIR,—In vain you expect much information, *de re accipi-traria*, of falconry, hawks, or hawking, from very ancient Greek or Latin authors; that art being either unknown or so little advanced among them, that it seems to have proceeded no higher than the daring of birds: which makes so little thereof to be found in Aristotle, who only mentions some rude practice thereof in Thracia; as also in Ælian, who speaks something of hawks and crows among the Indians; little or nothing of true falconry being mentioned before Julius Firmicus, in the days of Constantius, son to Constantine the Great.

Yet, if you consult the accounts of later antiquity left by Demetrius the Greek, by Symmachus and Theodotius, and by Albertus Magnus, about five hundred years ago, you, who have been so long acquainted with this noble recreation, may better compare the ancient and modern practice, and rightly observe how many things in that art are added, varied, disused, or retained, in the practice of these days.

In the diet of hawks, they allowed of divers meats which we should hardly commend. For beside the flesh of beef,[1] they admitted of goat, hog, deer, whelp, and bear. And how you will approve the quantity and measure thereof, I make some doubt; while by weight they allowed half a pound of beef, seven ounces of swine's flesh, five of hare, eight ounces of whelp, as much of deer, and ten ounces of he-goats' flesh.

In the time of Demetrius they were not without the practice of phlebotomy or bleeding, which they used in the thigh and pounces;[2] they plucked away the feathers on the thigh, and rubbed the part; but if the vein appeared not in that part, they open the vein of the fore talon.

In the days of Albertus, they made use of cauteries in

---

[1] *beef.*] Lamb, mutton, beef.—*MS. Sloan.* 1827.
[2] *pounces.*] The pounce is the talon or claw of a bird of prey.

divers places : to advantage their sight they seared them under the inward angle of the eye ; above the eye in distillations and diseases of the head ; in upward pains they seared above the joint of the wing, and in the bottom of the foot, against the gout ; and the chief time for these cauteries they made to be the month of March.

In great coldness of hawks they made use of fomentations, some of the steam or vapour of artificial and natural baths, some wrapt them up in hot blankets, giving them nettle seeds and butter.

No clysters are mentioned, nor can they be so profitably used; but they made use of many purging medicines   They purged with aloe, which, unto larger hawks, they gave in the bigness of a Greek bean ; unto lesser, in the quantity of a *cicer*,[3] which notwithstanding I should rather give washed, and with a few drops of oil of almonds : for the guts of flying fowls are tender and easily scratched by it ; and upon the use of aloe both in hens and cormorants I have sometimes observed bloody excretions.

In phlegmatic cases they seldom omitted stavesaker,[4] but they purged sometimes with a mouse, and the food of boiled chickens, sometimes with good oil and honey.

They used also the ink of cuttle fishes, with smallage, betony, wine, and honey.   They made use of stronger medicines than present practice doth allow.   For they were not afraid to give *coccus baphhicus;*[5] beating up eleven of its grains into a *lentor*,[6] which they made up into five pills wrapt up with honey and pepper: and, in some of their old medicines, we meet with scammony and *euphorbium*.   Whether, in the tender bowels of birds, infusions of rhubarb, agaric and *mechoachan*, be not of safer use, as to take of agaric two drachms, of cinnamon half a drachm, of liquorice a scruple, and, infusing them in wine, to express a part into the mouth of the hawk, may be considered by present practice.

Few mineral medicines were of inward use among them : yet sometimes we observe they gave filings of iron in the

---

[3] *cicer*.]   The seed of a vetch.
[4] *stavesaker*.]   Or *stave's-acre*, a plant ; *Delphinium staphisagria,* Lin.
[5] *coccus baphicus*.]   Or mezerion.—*MS. Sloan.* 1827.
[6] *lentor*.]   A stiff paste.

straitness of the chest, as also lime in some of their pectoral medicines.

But they commend unguents of quicksilver against the scab : and I have safely given six or eight grains of *mercurius dulcis* unto kestrils and owls, as also crude and current quicksilver, giving the next day small pellets of silver or lead till they came away uncoloured : and this, if any [way], may probably destroy that obstinate disease of the filander or back-worm.

A peculiar remedy they had against the consumption of hawks. For, filling a chicken with vinegar, they closed up the bill, and hanging it up until the flesh grew tender, they fed the hawk therewith : and to restore and well flesh them, they commonly gave them hog's flesh, with oil, butter, and honey ; and a decoction of cumfory to bouze.[3]

They disallowed of salt meats and fat ; but highly esteemed of mice in most indispositions ; and in the falling sickness had great esteem of boiled bats : and in many diseases, of the flesh of owls which feed upon those animals. In epilepsies they also gave the brain of a kid drawn through a gold ring ; and, in convulsions, made use of a mixture of musk and *stercus humanum aridum.*

For the better preservation of their health they strewed mint and sage about them ; and for the speedier mewing of their feathers, they gave them the slough of a snake, or a tortoise out of the shell, or a green lizard cut in pieces.

If a hawk were unquiet, they hooded him, and placed him in a smith's shop for some time, where, accustomed to the continual noise of hammering, he became more gentle and tractable.

They used few terms of art, plainly and intelligibly expressing the parts affected, their diseases and remedies. This heap of artificial terms first entering with the French artists : who seem to have been the first and noblest falconers in the western part of Europe : although, in their language, they have no word which in general expresseth an hawk.

They carried their hawks in the left hand, and let them

---

[3] *bouze.*] *MS. Sloan.* 1827, reads "drink ; and had a notable medicine against the inflammation of the eyes, by juice of purslain, opium, and saffron."

fly from the right. They uséd a bell, and took great care that their jesses should not be red, lest eagles should fly at them. Though they used hoods, we have no clear description of them, and little account of their lures.

The ancient writers left no account of the swiftness of hawks or measure of their flight: but Heresbachius* delivers, that William Duke of Cleve had an hawk, which in one day made a flight out of Westphalia into Prussia. And upon good account, an hawk in this county of Norfolk made a flight at a woodcock near thirty miles in one hour. How far the hawks, merlins, and wild fowl which come unto us with a north-west wind in the autumn, fly in a day, there is no clear account: but coming over sea their flight hath been long or very speedy. For I have known them to light so weary on the coast, that many have been taken with dogs, and some knocked down with staves and stones.

Their perches seemed not so large as ours: for they made them of such a bigness that their talons might almost meet: and they chose to make them of sallow, poplar, or lime tree.

They used great clamours and hallowing in their flight, which they made by these words, *ou loi, la, la, la;* and to raise the fowls, made use of the sound of a cymbal.

Their recreation seem more sober and solemn than ours at present, so improperly attended with oaths and imprecations. For they called on God at their setting out, according to the account of Demetrius, τὸν Θεὸν ἐπικαλέσαντες, in the first place calling upon God.

The learned Rigaltius thinketh, that if the Romans had well known this airy chase, they would have left or less regarded their Circensial recreations. The Greeks understood hunting early, but little or nothing of our falconry. If Alexander had known it, we might have found something of it and more of hawks in Aristotle; who was so unacquainted with that way, that he thought that hawks would not feed upon the heart of birds. Though he hath mentioned divers hawks, yet Julius Scaliger, an expert falconer, despaired to reconcile them unto ours. And 'tis well if among them, you can clearly make out a lanner, a sparrow-hawk, and a

---

* *De Re Rustica.*

kestril, but must not hope to find your gier falcon there, which is the noble hawk; and I wish you one no worse than that of Henry king of Navarre; which, Scaliger saith, he saw strike down a buzzard, two wild geese, divers kites, a crane, and a swan.

Nor must you expect from high antiquity the distinctions of eyes and ramage hawks, of stores and entermewers, of hawks of the lure and the fist; nor that material distinction into short and long winged hawks: from whence arise such differences in their taking down of stones; in their flight, their striking down or seizing of their prey, in the strength of their talons, either in the heel and fore talon, or the middle and the heel: nor yet what eggs produce the different hawks, or when they lay three eggs, that the first produceth a female and large hawk, the second of a middler sort, and the third a smaller bird, tercellene, or tassel, of the male sex; which hawks being only observed abroad by the ancients, were looked upon as hawks of different kinds, and not of the same eyrie or nest. As for what Aristotle affirmeth, that hawks and birds of prey drink not; although you know that it will not strictly hold, yet I kept an eagle two years, which fed upon cats, kitlings, whelps, and rats, without one drop of water.

If anything may add unto your knowledge in this noble art, you must pick it out of later writers than those you enquire of. You may peruse the two books of falconry writ by that renowed emperor, Frederick the Second; as also the works of the noble Duke Belisarius, of Tardiffe, Francherius, of Francisco Sforzino of Vicensa; and may not a little inform or recreate yourself with that elegant poem of Thuanus.* I leave you to divert yourself by the perusal of it, having, at present, no more to say but that I am, &c.

* *De Re Accipitraria*, in 3 books.†

† Or more of late by P. Rapinus in verse.—*MS. note of Evelyn's.*

TRACT VI.

OF CYMBALS, ETC.

SIR,—With what difficulty, if possibility, you may expect satisfaction concerning the music, or musical instruments, of the Hebrews, you will easily discover if you consult the attempts of learned men upon that subject: but for the cymbals, of whose figure you enquire, you may find some described in Bayfius, in the comment of Rhodius upon Scribonius Largus, and others.

As for κύμβαλον ἀλαλάζον mentioned by St. Paul,* and rendered a tinkling cymbal, whether the translation be not too soft and diminutive, some question may be made: for the word ἀλαλάζον implieth no small sound, but a strained and lofty vociferation, or some kind of hallowing sound, according to the exposition of Hesychius, ἀλαλάξατε ἐνυψώσατε τὴν φωνήν. A word drawn from the lusty shout of soldiers, crying ἀλαλὰ at the first charge upon their enemies, according to the custom of the eastern nations, and used by the Trojans in Homer; and is also the note of the chorus in Aristophanes ἀλαλαὶ ἢ παιών. In other parts of Scripture we read of loud and high-sounding cymbals; and in Clemens Alexandrinus, that the Arabians made use of cymbals in their wars instead of other military music; and Polyænus in his *Stratagems* affirmeth that Bacchus gave the signal of battle unto his numerous army, not with trumpets but with tympans and cymbals.

And now I take the opportunity to thank you for the new book sent me, containing the anthems sung in our cathedral and collegiate churches: 'tis probable there will be additions, the masters of music being now active in that affair. Beside my naked thanks I have yet nothing to return you but this enclosed, which may be somewhat rare unto you, and that is a Turkish hymn, translated into French out of the Turkish metre, which I thus render unto you.

* 1 Cor. xiii. 1.

" O what praise doth he deserve, and how great is that Lord, all whose slaves are as so many kings!

" Whosoever shall rub his eyes with the dust of his feet, shall behold such admirable things that he shall fall into an ecstasy.

" He that shall drink one drop of his beverage, shall have his bosom like the ocean, filled with gems and precious liquors.

" Let not loose the reins unto thy passions in this world: he that represseth them shall become a true Solomon in the faith.

" Amuse not thyself to adore riches, nor to build great houses and palaces.

" The end of what thou shalt build is but ruin.

" Pamper not thy body with delicacies and dainties; it may come to pass one day that this body may be in hell.

" Imagine not that he who findeth riches, findeth happiness. He that findeth happiness is he that findeth God.

" All who prostrating themselves in humility shall this day believe in Vele,* if they were poor, shall be rich; and if rich, shall become kings."

After the sermon ended, which was made upon a verse in the Alcoran containing much morality, the Dervises in a gallery apart sung this hymn, accompanied with instrumental music, which so affected the ears of Monsieur du Loir, that he would not omit to set it down, together with the musical notes, to be found in his first letter unto Monsieur Bouliau, prior of Magny.

Excuse my brevity: I can say but little where I understand but little.

I am, &c.

* Vele, the founder of the convent.

TRACT VII.

OF ROPALIC OR GRADUAL VERSES, ETC.

Mens mea sublimes rationes præmeditatur.

SIR,—Though I may justly allow a good intention in this poem presented unto you, yet I must needs confess, I have no affection for it; as being utterly averse from all affectation in poetry, which either restrains the fancy, or fetters the invention to any strict disposure of words. A poem of this nature is to be found in *Ausonius*, beginning thus,

Spes Deus æternæ stationis conciliator.

These are verses *ropalici* or *clavales*, arising gradually like the knots in a ῥοπάλη or club; named also *fistulares* by Priscianus, as Elias Vinetus* hath noted. They consist properly of five words, each thereof increasing by one syllable. They admit not of a *spondee* in the fifth place, nor can a golden or silver verse be made this way. They run smoothly both in Latin and Greek, and some are scatteringly to be found in Homer,

Ω μάκαρ 'Ατρείδη μοιρηγενὲς ὀλβιοδαίμον,

Libere dicam sed in aurem, ego versibus hujusmodi ropalicis, longo syrmate protractis, Ceraunium affigo.

He that affecteth such restrained poetry, may peruse the long poem of Hugbaldus the monk, wherein every word beginneth with a C, penned in the praise of *calvities* or baldness, to the honour of Carolus Calvus, king of France,

Carmina clarisonæ calvis cantate Camænæ.

The rest may be seen at large in the *Adversaria* of Barthius: or if he delighteth in odd contrived fancies, may he please himself with antistrophes, counterpetories, retrogrades, rebuses, leonine verses, &c., to be found in *Sieur des Accords*. But these and the like are to be looked upon, not pursued.

* *El Vinet. in Auson.*

Odd work might be made by such ways; and for your recreation I propose these few lines unto you.[1]

Arcu paratur quod arcui sufficit.
Misellorum clamoribus accurrere non tam humanum quam sulphureum est.
Asino teratur quæ asino teritur.
Ne asphodelos comedas, phœnices manduca.
Cœlum aliquid potest, sed quæ mira præstat papilio est.

Not to put you unto endless amusement, the key hereof is the homonomy of the Greek made use of in the Latin words, which rendereth all plain.   More enigmatical and dark expressions might be made if any one would speak or compose them out of the numerical characters or characteristical numbers set down by Robertus de Fluctibus.[2]*

As for your question concerning the contrary expressions of the Italians and Spaniards in their common affirmative answers, the Spaniard answering *cy Sennor*, the Italian *Signior cy*, you must be content with this distich,

Why saith the Italian *Signior cy*, the Spaniard *Sy Sennor?*
Because the one puts that behind, the other puts before.

And because you are so happy in some translations, I pray return me these two verses in English,

Occidit heu tandem multos quæ occidit amantes,
Et cinis est hodiè quæ fuit ignis heri.[3]

My occasions make me to take off my pen.   I am, &c.

* *Tract 2, part* lib. i.

[1] *and, &c.*] *MS. Sloan.* reads thus, "And I remember I once pleased a young hopeful person with a dialogue between two travellers, beginning in this manner : well drunk, my old friend, the famous king of Macedon ; that is, well overtaken, my old friend Alexander, your friend may proceed.   With another way I shall not omit to acquaint you, and for your recreation I present these few lines."

[2] *More enigmatical, &c.*] These are more largely noticed in *MS. Sloan.* 1837 : thus, "One way more I shall mention, though scarce worth your notice :—Two pestels and a book come short of a retort, as much as a spear and an ass exceed a dog's tail. This is to be expounded by the numerical characters, or characteristical numbers set down by Robertus de Fluctibus, and speaks only this text :—two and four come short of six, as much as ten exceed six ; the figure of an ass standing for a cipher."

[3] *Occidit heu tandem, &c.*] In *MS. Sloan.* 1827, is the following translation—

"She is dead at last, who many made expire,
Is dust to-day which yesterday was fire."

TRACT VIII.

OF LANGUAGES, AND PARTICULARLY OF THE SAXON TONGUE.

SIR,—The last discourse we had of the Saxon tongue recalled to my mind some forgotten considerations.[1] Though the earth were widely peopled before the flood (as many learned men conceive), yet whether, after a large dispersion, and the space of sixteen hundred years, men maintained so uniform a language in all parts, as to be strictly of one tongue, and readily to understand each other, may very well be doubted. For though the world preserved in the family of Noah before the confusion of tongues might be said to be of one lip, yet even permitted to themselves their humours, inventions, necessities, and new objects (without the miracle of confusion at first), in so long a tract of time, there had probably been a Babel. For whether America were first peopled by one or several nations, yet cannot that number of different planting nations answer the multiplicity of their present different languages, of no affinity unto each other, and even in their northern nations and incommunicating angles,[2] their languages are widely differing. A native interpreter brought from California proved of no use[3] unto the Spaniards upon the neighbour shore. From Chiapa to Guatemala, S. Salvador, Honduras, there are at least eighteen several languages; and so numerous are they both in the Peruvian and Mexican regions, that the great princes are fain to have one common language, which, besides their vernaculous and mother tongues, may serve for commerce between them.

And since the confusion of tongues at first fell only upon those which were present in Sinaar at the work of Babel, whether the primitive language from Noah were only pre-

---

[1] *forgotten considerations.*] "Both of that and other languages."—*MS. Sloan.*

[2] *angles.*] "Where they may be best conceived to have most single originals."

[3] *of no use.*] "Of little use."—*MS. Sloan.*

served in the family of Heber, and not also in divers others, which might be absent at the same, whether all came away, and many might not be left behind in their first plantations about the foot of the hills, whereabout the ark rested, and Noah became an husbandman,[4] is not absurdly doubted.

For so the primitive tongue might in time branch out into several parts of Europe and Asia, and thereby the first or Hebrew tongue, which seems to be ingredient into so many languages, might have larger originals and grounds of its communication and traduction than from the family of Abraham, the country of Canaan, and words contained in the Bible, which come short of the full of that language. And this would become more probable from the septuagint or Greek chronology strenuously asserted by Vossius; for making five hundred years between the deluge and the days of Peleg, there ariseth a large latitude of multiplication and dispersion of people into several parts, before the descent of that body which followed Nimrod unto Sinaar from the east.

They who derive the bulk of European tongues from the Scythian and the Greek, though they may speak probably in many points, yet must needs allow vast difference or corruptions from so few originals, which, however, might be tolerably made out in the old Saxon, yet hath time much confounded the clearer derivations. And as the knowledge thereof now stands in reference unto ourselves, I find many words totally lost, divers of harsh sound disused or refined in the pronunciation, and many words we have also in common use not to be found in that tongue, or venially derivable from any other from whence we have largely borrowed, and yet so much still remaineth with us that it maketh the gross of our language.

The religious obligation unto the Hebrew language hath so notably continued the same, that it might still be understood by Abraham, whereas by the Mazorite points and

---

[4] *husbandman, &c.*]   *MS. Sloan.* 1827, adds here the following clause: "whether in that space of 150 years, according to common compute, before the conduct of Nimrod, many might not expatriate northward, eastward, or southward, and many of the posterity of Noah might not disperse themselves before the great migration unto Sinaar, and many also afterwards ; is not," &c.

Chaldee character the old letters stand so transformed, that if Moses were alive again, he must be taught to read his own law.[5]

The Chinese, who live at the bounds of the earth, who have admitted little communication, and suffered successive incursions from one nation, may possibly give account of a very ancient language: but, consisting of many nations and tongues, confusion, admixtion, and corruption in length of time might probably so have crept in, as, without the virtue of a common character and lasting letter of things, they could never probably make out those strange memorials which they pretend, while they still make use of the works of their great Confucius many hundred years before Christ, and in a series ascend as high as Poncuus, who is conceived our Noah.

The present Welsh, and remnant of the old Britons, hold so much of that ancient language, that they make a shift to understand the poems of Merlin, Enerin, Telesin, a thousand years ago, whereas the Herulian *Pater Noster*, set down by Wolfgangus Lazius, is not without much criticism made out, and but in some words; and the present Parisians can hardly hack out those few lines of the league between Charles and Lewis, the sons of Ludovicus Pius, yet remaining in old French.

The Spaniards in their corruptive traduction and romance, have so happily retained the terminations from the Latin, that, notwithstanding the Gothic and Moorish intrusion of words, they are able[6] to make a discourse completely consisting of

---

[5] *law.*] In *MS. Sloan.* 1827, the following additional paragraph occurs:—"Though this language be duly magnified, and always of high esteem, yet if, with Geropius Becanus, we admit that tongue to be most perfect which is most copious or expressive, most delucid and clear unto the understanding, most short, or soon delivered, and best pronounced with most ease unto the organs of speech, the Hebrew now known unto us will hardly obtain the place; since it consisteth of fewer words than many others, and its words begin not with vowels, since it is so full of homonymies, and words which signify many things, and so ambiguous, that translations so little agree; and since, though the radices consist but of three letters, yet they make two syllables in speaking; and since the pronunciation is such, as St. Jerome, who was born in a barbarous country, thought the words anhelent, strident, and of very harsh sound.

[6] *they are able.*]　"This will appear very unlikely to a man that con-

grammatical Latin and Spanish, wherein the Italians and French will be very much to seek.[7]

The learned Casaubon conceiveth that a dialogue might be composed in Saxon, only of such words as are derivable from the Greek, which surely might be effected, and so as the learned might not uneasily find it out. Verstegan made no doubt that he could contrive a letter which might be understood by the English, Dutch, and East Frislander, which, as the present confusion standeth, might have proved no very clear piece, and hardly to be hammered out: yet so much of the Saxon still remaineth in our English, as may admit an orderly discourse and series of good sense, such as not only the present English, but Ælfric, Bede, and Alfred might understand after so many hundred years.

Nations that live promiscuously under the power and laws of conquest, do seldom escape the loss of their language with their liberties ; wherein the Romans were so strict, that the Grecians were fain to conform in their judicial processes ;[8] which made the Jews lose more in seventy years' dispersion

---

siders the Spanish terminations ; and Howel, who was eminently skilful in the three provincial languages, declares, that after many essays he never could effect it."—*Dr. Johnson.*

[7] *seek.*] The following paragraphs occur here, in *MS. Sloan.* 1827.

"The many mother tongues spoke in divers corners of Europe, and quite different from one another, are not reconcileable to any one common original ; whereas the great languages of Spain, France, and Italy, are derivative from the Latin ; that of Greece and its islands from the old Greek ; the rest of the family of the Dutch or Schlavonian. As for the *lingua Fullana,* spoken in part of Friuli, and the *lingua Curvallea* in Rhætia, they are corruptions of the Italian, as that of Sardinia is also of the Spanish.

"Even the Latin itself, which hath embroiled so many languages of Europe, if it had been the speech of one country, and not continued by writers, and the consent and study of all ages since, it had found the same fate, and been swallowed like other languages ; since, in its ancient state, one age could scarce understand another, and that of some generations before must be read by a dictionary by a few successions after ; as, beside the famous pillar of Quillius, may be illustrated in these few lines, ' Eundo omnibus honestitudo præterbitunda nemo escit. Quianam itaque istuc effexis hauscio, temperi et toppertutemet tam hibus insegne, quod ningribus potestur aut ruspare nevolt. Sapsam saperdæ seneciones sardare nequinunt cuoi siemps et socienum quissis sperit ? ' "

[8] *to conform in their, &c.*] "To conform, and make use of Latin in their," &c.—*MS. Sloan.*

in the provinces of Babylon, than in many hundred in their distinct habitation in Egypt; and the English which dwelt dispersedly to lose their language in Ireland, whereas more tolerable reliques there are thereof in Fingall, where they were closely and almost solely planted; and the Moors which were most huddled together and united about Granada have yet left their *Arvirage* among the Granadian Spaniards.

But shut up in angles and inaccessible corners, divided by laws and manners, they often continue long with little mixture, which hath afforded that lasting life unto the Cantabrian and British tongues, wherein the Britons are remarkable, who having lived four hundred years together with the Romans, retained so much of the British as it may be esteemed a language; which either they resolutely maintained in their cohabitation with them in Britain, or retiring after in the time of the Saxons into countries and parts[9] less civilized and conversant with the Romans, they found the people distinct, the language more entire, and so fell into it again.

But surely no languages have been so straitly locked up as not to admit of commixture. The Irish, although they retain a kind of a Saxon character,[1] yet have admitted many words of Latin and English. In the Welsh are found many words from Latin, some from Greek and Saxon. In what parity and incommixture the language of that people stood, which were casually discovered in the heart of Spain, between the mountains of Castile, no longer ago than in the time of Duke d'Alva, we have not met with a good account; any farther than that their words were Basquish or Cantabrian; but the present Basquensa, one of the minor mother tongues of Europe, is not without commixture of Latin and Castilian, while we meet with *santifica, tentationeten, gloria, puissanea,* and four more [words] in the short form of the Lord's prayer, set down by Paulus Merula: but although in this brief form we may find such commixture, yet the bulk of their language seems more distinct, consisting of words of no affinity unto

---

[9] *into countries, &c.*] "Into Wales, and countries," &c.—*MS. Sloan.*
[1] *The Irish, although they, &c.*] The Irish using the same characters with the Anglo-Saxons, does not prove any affinity of language, nor does it exist. They both took their alphabet from the Roman.—*G.*

others, of numerals totally different, of differing grammatical rules, as may be observed in the Dictionary and short Basquensa · Grammar, composed by Raphael Nicoleta, a priest of Bilboa.

· And if they use the auxiliary verbs of *equin* and *ysan*, answerable unto *hazer* and *ser*, to have and be, in the Spanish, which forms came in with the northern nations into the Italian, Spanish, and French, and if that form were used by them before, and crept not in from imitation of their neighbours, it may show some ancienter traduction from northern nations,[2] or else must seem very strange : since the southern nations had it not of old, and I know not whether any such mode be found in the languages of any part of America.

The Romans, who made the great commixture and alteration of languages in the world, effected the same, not only by their proper language, but those also of their military forces, employed in several provinces, as holding a standing militia in all countries, and commonly of strange nations ; so while the cohorts and forces of the Britons were quartered in Egypt, Armenia, Spain, Illyria, &c., the Stablæsians and Dalmatians here, the Gauls, Spaniards, and Germans, in other countries, and other nations in theirs, they could not but leave many words behind them, and carry away many with them, which might make, that, in many words of very distinct nations, some may still remain of very unknown and doubtful genealogy.

And if, as the learned Buxhornius contendeth,[3] the Scythian language as the mother tongue runs through the nations of Europe, and even as far as Persia, the community in many words, between so many nations, hath a more reasonable original traduction, and were rather derivable from the common tongue diffused through them all, than from any particular nation, which hath also borrowed and holdeth but at second hand.

---

[2] *traduction from northern nations.*] Adelung considers the Basque to be *radically* different from any European *tribe* of languages—though many words are Teutonic borrowed from the Visigoths.

The great Danish philologist, Rask, also classes it by itself.—*G.*

[3] *And if, &c.*] Dr. Jamieson has discussed this subject in his Hermes Scythicus, the object of which work is to connect the Goths and Greeks, through the Pelasgi and Scythians.—*G.*

The Saxons, settling over all England, maintained an uniform language, only diversified in dialects, idioms, and minor
differences, according to their different nations which came
in unto the common conquest, which may yet be a cause of
the variation in the speech and words of several parts of
England, where different nations most abode or settled, and
having expelled the Britons, their wars were chiefly among
themselves, with little action with foreign nations until the
union of the heptarchy under Egbert: after which time,
although the Danes infested this land, and scarce left any
part free, yet their incursions made more havoc in buildings,
churches and cities, than [in] the language of the country,[4]
because their language was in effect the same, and such as
whereby they might easily understand one another.

And if the Normans, which came into Neustria or Normandy with Rollo the Dane, had preserved their language
in their new acquists, the succeeding conquest of England,
by Duke William of his race, had not begot among us such
notable alterations; but having lost their language in their
abode in Normandy, before they adventured upon England,
they confounded the English with their French, and made the
grand mutation, which was successively increased by our
possessions in Normandy, Guien, and Acquitain, by our long
wars in France, by frequent resort of the French, who, to
the number of some thousands, came over with Isabel, queen
to Edward the Second, and the several matches of England
with the daughters of France before and since that time.

But this commixture, though sufficient to confuse, proved
not of ability to abolish the Saxon words, for from the French
we have borrowed many substantives, adjectives, and some
verbs, but the great body of numerals, auxiliary verbs,
articles, pronouns, adverbs, conjunctions, and prepositions,
which are the distinguishing and lasting part of a language,
remain with us from the Saxon, which, having suffered no
great alteration for many hundred years, may probably still

---

[4] *yet their incursions, &c.*] Yet the Danes had a great effect upon the
Saxon language. The portion of the Saxon Chronicle written during
their sway in England, is quite in a different dialect from the former
part, and it is called the Dano-Saxon—it is not, however, so marked a
departure from the early Anglo-Saxon, as the next dialect—the Norman-
Saxon.—*G.*

remain, though the English swell with the inmates of Italian, French, and Latin. An example whereof may be observed in this following :—

ENGLISH I.—The first and foremost step to all good works is the dread and fear of the Lord of heaven and earth, which through the Holy Ghost enlighteneth the blindness of our sinful hearts to tread the ways of wisdom, and leads our feet into the land of blessing.

SAXON I.—The erst and fyrmost stæp to eal gode weorka is the dræd and feurt of the Lauord of heofan and eorth, whilc thurh the Heilig Gast onlihtneth the blindnesse of ure sinfull heorte to træd the wæg of wisdome, and thone læd ure fet into the land of blessung.

ENGLISH II.—For to forget his law is the door, the gate, and key to let in all unrighteousness, making our eyes, ears, and mouths to answer the lust of sin, our brains dull to good thoughts, our lips dumb to his praise, our ears deaf to his gospel, and our eyes dim to behold his wonders, which witness against us that we have not well learned the word of God, that we are the children of wrath, unworthy of the love and manifold gifts of God, greedily following after the ways of the devil and witchcraft of the world, doing nothing to free and keep ourselves from the burning fire of hell, till we be buried in sin and swallowed in death, not to arise again in any hope of Christ's kingdom.

SAXON II.—For to fuorgytan his laga is the dure, the gat, and cæg to let in eal unrightwisnysse, makend ure eyge, eore, and muth to answare the lust of sin, ure brægan dole to gode theoht, ure lippau dumb to his preys, ure earen deaf to his gospel, and ure eyge dim to behealden his wundra, whilc ge witnysse ongen us that wee œf noht wel gelæred the weord of God, that wee are the cilda of ured, unwyrthe of the lufe and mænigfeald gift of God, grediglice felygend æfter the wægen of the deoful and wiccraft of the weorld, doend nothing to fry and cæp ure saula from the byrnend fyr of hell, till we be geburied in synne and swolgen in death, not to arise agen in ænig hope of Christes kynedome.

ENGLISH III.—Which draw from above the bitter doom of the Almighty of hunger, sword, sickness, and brings more sad plagues than those of hail, storms, thunder, blood, frogs, swarms of gnats and grasshoppers, which ate the corn, grass, and leaves of the trees in Egypt.

SAXON III.—Whilc drag from buf the bitter dome of the Almagan of hunger, sweorde, seoknesse, and bring mere sad plag, thone they of hagal, storme, thunner, blode, frog, swearme of gnæt and gærsupper, whilc eaten the corn, gærs, and leaf of the treowen in Ægypt.

ENGLISH IV.—If we read his book and holy writ, these among many others, we shall find to be the tokens of his hate, which gathered together might mind us of his will, and teach us when his wrath beginneth, which sometimes comes in open strength and full sail, oft steals like a thief in the night, like shafts shot from a bow at midnight, before we think upon them.

SAXON IV.—Gyf we ræd his boc and heilig gewrit, these gemong mænig othern, we sceall findan the tacna of his hatung, whilc gegatherod together miht gemind us of his willan, and teac us whone his ured onginneth, whilc sometima come in open strength and fill seyle, oft stæl gelyc a theof in the niht, gelyc sceaft scoten fram a boge at midneoht, befor an we thinck uppen them.

ENGLISH V.—And though they were a deal less, and rather short than beyond our sins, yet do we not a whit withstand or forbear them, we are wedded to, not weary of our misdeeds, we seldom look upward, and are not ashamed under sin ; we cleanse not ourselves from the blackness and deep hue of our guilt ; we want tears and sorrow, we weep not, fast not, we crave not forgiveness from the mildness, sweetness, and goodness of God, and with all livelihood and steadfastness to our uttermost will hunt after the evil of guile, pride, cursing, swearing, drunkenness, over-eating, uncleanness, all idle lust of the flesh, yes many uncouth and nameless sins, hid in our inmost breast and bosoms, which stand betwixt our forgiveness, and keep God and man asunder.

SAXON V.—And theow they wære a dæl lesse, and reither scort thone begond oure sinnan, get do we naht a whit withstand and forbeare them, we care bewudded to, noht werig of ure agen misdeed, we seldon loc upweard, and ear not ofschæmod under sinne, we cleans noht ure selvan from the blacnesse and dæp hue of ure guilt; we wan teare and sara, we weope noht, fæst noht, we craft noht foregyfnesse fram the mildnesse, sweetnesse, and goodnesse of God, and mit eal lifelyhood and stedfastnesse to ure uttermost will hunt

æfter the ufel of guile, pride, cursung, swearung, druncen-
nesse, overeat, uncleannesse and eal idle lust of the flæsc, yis
mænig uncuth and nameleas sinnan, hid in ure inmæst brist
and bosome, while stand betwixt ure foregyfnesse, and cæp
God and man asynder.

ENGLISH VI.—Thus are we far beneath and also worse
than the rest of God's works ; for the sun and moon, the
king and queen of stars, snow, ice, rain, frost, dew, mist,
wind, fourfooted and creeping things, fishes and feathered
birds, and fowls either of sea or land, do all hold the laws of
his will.

SAXON VI.—Thus care we far beneoth and ealso wyrse
thone the rest of Gods weorka ; for the sun and mone, the
cyng and cquen of stearran, snaw, ise, ren, frost, deaw, miste,
wind, feower fet and crypend dinga, fix yefetherod brid, and
fælan auther in sæ or land do eal heold the lag of his willan.

Thus have you seen in few words how near the Saxon and
English meet.[5]

Now of this account the French will be able to make nothing ; the modern Danes and Germans, though from several
words they may conjecture at the meaning, yet will they be
much to seek in the orderly sense and continued construction thereof. Whether the Danes can continue such a
series of sense out of their present language and the old
Runick, as to be intelligible unto present and ancient times,
some doubt may well be made ; and if the present French
would attempt a discourse in words common unto their
present tongue and the old *Romana Rustica* spoken in elder
times, or in the old language of the Francks, which came to
be in use some successions after Pharamond, it might prove
a work of some trouble to effect.

---

[5] *how near the Saxon, &c.*] Johnson observes, "the words are, indeed, Saxon, but the phraseology is English ; and, I think, would not
have been understood by Bede or Ælfric, notwithstanding the confidence of our author. He has, however, sufficiently proved his position,
that the English resembles its parental language more than any modern
European dialect." This opinion exactly coincides with that of a still
higher authority, Miss Gurney, of Northrepps Cottage, the translator
of the Saxon Chronicle ; on whose recommendation I have preferred to
reprint the Saxon passages as they stand, rather than to adopt any
additions or variations from partial transcripts of them in the British
Museum and Bodleian.

It were not impossible to make an original reduction of
many words of no general reception in England, but of common use in Norfolk, or peculiar to the East Angle countries ;
as bawnd, bunny, thurck, enemmis, sammodithee, mawther,
kedge, seele, straft, clever, matchly, dere, nicked, stingy,
noneare, feft, thepes, gosgood, kamp, sibrit, fangast, sap,
cothish, thokish, bide owe, paxwax :[6] of these and some

---

[6] *Bawnd, &c.*] Some time before the appearance of "*The Vocabulary
of East Anglia, by the Rev. W. Forby,*" I had been favoured with valuable
illustrations of this curious list of words in common use in Norfolk
during Sir Thomas's life, by Miss Gurney, and Mr. Black, of the British
Museum, of which I have availed myself in the following notes.

Bawnd ;—swollen. Not in present use ; at least, not known to be so.
Isl. *bon,* tumidus.—*Forby.*

Bunny ;—a common word for a rabbit, especially among children.—
Blk.——A small swelling caused by a fall or blow. Perhaps a diminutive *bump.* One would be glad to derive it from the Greek βουνος, a
hillock. It may be so through the Gothic.—*Forby.*

Thurck ;—appears to mean dark, if it be the same as in the *Promp-
torium Parvulorum Clericorum.*—*MS. Harl.* 221. "Therke or dyrk,
tenebrosus, caliginosus ; terknesse or derknesse."—*Blk.*——Dark. So
say Hickes and Ray ; may have been for ought we can say to the contrary.—*Forby.*

Enemmis ;—Qu. *et neanmoins ?—G.*—I will not say that this is the old
word *anempst* for *anenst* (*anent* in modern Scottish), about, concerning ;
because I know not its proper collocation.—*Blk.*——Of very obscure
and doubtful meaning, like most of Sir Thomas Browne's words. Hickes
says it means *lest* (ne forte), and he derives it from Isl. *einema,* an adv.
of exclusion, as he says. It may mean, notwithstanding, N. Fr. *nemis.*
Or it may be an adjective, signifying variable, as *emmis* is in L. sc. which
JAM. derives from Isl. *ymiss,* varius. But as the word is quite extinct,
it is impossible to decide upon its meaning, when it was in use.—*Forby.*
——The word is not extinct, but still used in Norfolk in the sense of
lest : though its usual sound would rather lead us to spell it *enammons.*

Sammodithee ;—Samod o'thi ; the like of that.—*G.*——*Sammodithee*
is an old oath or asseveration, *sá mót I thé,* so may I thrive. "*Als mote
I the*" is common in ancient English, and "*So the ik*" in Chaucer. See
Tyrwhitt's and other Glossaries, in v. *The,* which is the A. S. *dean,* to
thrive.—*Blk.*——This uncouth cluster of little words (for such it is)
is recorded by Sir Thomas Browne as current in his time. It is now
totally extinct. It stands thus in the eighth tract "On Languages."
Dr. Hickes has taken the liberty of changing it to *sammoditha,* and
interprets it, "Say me how dost thou ;" in pure Saxon "*sæg me hu dest
thu.*" "Say me," for "tell me," is in use to this day in some counties.
It is in the dialect of Sedgmoor. Ray adduces, as a sort of parallel to
this jumble of words, one which he says was common in his time ;
muchgooditte, "much good do it thee."—*F.*

others of no easy originals, when time will permit, the resolution may be attempted; which to effect, the Danish language‑

Mawther ;—the same as the vulgar *mawkes*, a wench.—*Blk.*——A girl. Tusser uses it.   So does B. *J*onson :— "You talk like a foolish *mauther*," says Restive to Dame Pliant, in the Alchemist.   It seems peculiarly an East Anglian word.   So at least it was considered by Sir Henry Spelman.   It is highly amusing to find so grave an antiquary endeavouring earnestly, and at no inconsiderable length, to vindicate the honour of his mother-tongue ; and to rescue this important word from the contempt with which some, as it seems, through their ignorance, were disposed to treat it.   "Quod rident cæteri Angli," says he, "vocis nescientes probitatem."   He assures us that it was applied by our very early ancestors, even to the noble virgins who were selected to sing the praises of heroes.   They were called *scald-moers*, q. d. *singing mauthers !*   "En quantum in spretâ jam voce antiquæ gloriæ !"   He complains that the old word *moer* had been corrupted to *mother*, and so confounded with a very different word.   We distinguish them very effectually by pronunciation, and, what is more, we actually come very near to the original word in the abbreviated form we use in addressing a *mauther.*   We commonly call her *mau'r.*   Dan. *moer.*   Belg. *modde,* innupta puella.—*Forby.*

Kedge ;—I should rather think is the "*Kygge* or *J*oly, Jocundus, Hillaris," of *Prompt.* than "*cadge,* to carry, of *Wilbr. Appendix.*"— *Blk.*——Brisk, active.   This is Sir Thomas Browne's spelling.   We pronounce it *kidge,* and apply it exclusively, or nearly so, to hale and cheerful old persons.   In Ray, the word CADGE has the same meaning. It is by mere change of vowels *cadge, kedge, kidge.*   Dan. *kaud,* lascivus. Lowland Scotch *kedgie* and *caigie.*—*Forby.*

Seele ;—is this our sell, haysell, or seel time ?—*G.*——Take these from *Prompt.* "*sele,* horsys harneys, arquillus.   "*Selle,* stoddyng howse cella."   "*Sylle* of an howse.   Silla Solma."   I cannot offer anything else.—*Blk.*——Seal, time, season.   Hay-*seal,* wheat-*seal,* barley-*seal,* are the respective seasons of mowing or sowing those products of the earth.   But it goes as low as hours.   Of an idle and dissipated fellow, we say that he "keeps bad *seals,*" of poachers, that they are out at all *seals* of the night ; of a sober, regular, and industrious man, that "he attends to his business at all *seals,*" or that "he keeps good *seals* and meals."   Sir Thomas Browne spells it seele ; but we seem to come nearer to the Saxon *sœl,* opportunitas.—*Forby.*

Straft ;—Iratus, irâ exclamans, vox in agro Norf. usitata.   Hickes derivat ab Is. *straffa,* objurgere, corripere, increpare.   *L. Junius Etymol.* I cannot find the passage on a cursory examination of Hickes in his little *Dict. Islandicum.*   In the 2nd vol. of the Thesaur. p. 89, Hickes gives "Straff, gannitus," but the usual meaning is punishment, and this is the meaning given by Biorn Halderson.—*G.*——I will adduce a word from *Wachter's German Glossary.*   "*Straff,* rigidus, durus, astrictus, severus."—*Blk.*——A scolding bout; an angry strife of tongues.   Isl. *straffa,* iratus.—*Forby.*

new and more ancient may prove of good advantage : which
nation remained here fifty years upon agreement, and have

Clever ;—perhaps some unusual meaning of our present adj. unless
the first vowel should be pronounced long.—*Blk.*——Dextrous, adroit ;
Ray says, neat, elegant : in either sense it is so very common and general,
and appears so to have been for so many years, that it seems difficult to
conceive how Sir Thomas Browne should have been struck with it as a
provincialism, and still more, how Ray, long afterwards, should have
let it pass as such without any remark.   If not when Sir Thomas wrote
his tract, certainly long before the second edition of Ray, S. E. C., published by the author, it had been used by Butler, L'Estrange, and South.
In L'Estrange, indeed, it might be positively provincial ; in Butler,
low, ludicrous, or even burlesque ; in South too familiar and undignified
for the pulpit ; but in neither provincial.   But what shall we say of
Addison, who had also used it ?   In Todd's *Johnson* it is said to be low,
and scarcely ever used but in burlesque, and in conversation.   A col-
loquial and familiar term it certainly is ; but assuredly not provincial,
nor even low.   Sir Thomas Browne is the only guarantee of its insertion
here.   And if it must be ours, let it by all means be taken with our
own rustic pronunciation, *claver.—Forby.*——My friend Mr. Black's
suggestion,—that there is some unusual meaning attached in Norfolk to
this word, which justifies its insertion among provincialisms,—is correct.
The poor in this county, speaking of any one who is kind and liberal
towards them, say very commonly, "He is a *claver* gentleman ! "
" 'Twas a *claver* thing he did for us ! "   "He always behave very *claver*
to the poor."——Moor says that it means handsome, good-looking ;—
e. g. a *clever* horse, a *clever* gal (girl).
    Matchly ;—perhaps may mean proportionately, or corresponding.—
Blk.——Exactly alike, fitting nicely.   Another of Sir Thomas Browne's
words, happily explained by modern pronunciation, *mackly.*   A. S.
maka, par.—*Forby.*
    Dere ;—dire, sad.   But it is Old English.   Chaucer has it, and
Shakspeare, in "Love's Labour Lost :"—"Deaf'd with the clamour of
their own *dear* groans."   Dr. Johnson observes that *dear* is for *dere.*
And yet the words "own *dear*" may seem to come very nearly to the
sense of the adjective φίλος in Homer ; φίλον ἦτορ, φίλον ὄμμα, φίλα
γούνατα.   It is a sense of close and particular endearment, in which
certainly we often use those two words, in speaking of anything we
particularly cherish, as our beloved kindred or friends, or, as in Homer,
the limbs or organs of our bodies.—*Forby.*
    Nicked ;—cheated, as yet among the vulgar.   I think to have seen (in
Wachter) *nicken,* obstinate.—*Blk.*——Exactly hit ; in the very nick ;
at the precise point.   Another of Sir Thomas Browne's words, at which
one cannot but marvel.   The very same authorities are produced by
Johnson, for the verb *nick* in this sense, as for the adjective CLEVER ;—
those of Butler, L'Estrange, and South.   It is not possible to conceive
that the word had at that time any other sense in which it might be
considered as a provincial word. Ray explains it thus : *Nickled,* beaten

left many families in it, and the language of these parts had
surely been more commixed and perplext, if the fleet of

down and intricately entangled, as growing corn or grass by rain and
wind.   Might not this be the word meant by Sir Thomas Browne, and
imperfectly heard ?—*Forby.*——Both these are wrong ; the following is
the correct explanation :—To *nick* is to notch the under part of a horse's
tail, to make it stand out or erect.   An instance occurs in the Monthly
Mag. for 1812, part i. p. 28, in the memoir of *J*ohn Fransham ; who,
when at Norwich, could not bear "the cruel practices there carried on
of cropping, *nicking*, and docking horses."   I transcribe this from a
more recent communication from Mr. Black.   But that a Norfolk man
(Mr. Forby) should have been ignorant of the meaning of so common a
provincialism, seems singular.

Stingy ;—with a soft *g*, commonly means parsimonious.—*Blk.*——
This is its commonly received sense.   Its provincial acceptation is given
by Forby :—1. Cross, ill-humoured ; 2. churlish, biting ; as applied to the
state of the air.   It was most probably in one or in both these senses in
which Sir Thomas Browne remarked it as provincial.   He must surely
have been acquainted with it in its commonly current sense.   That,
indeed, seems to be perverted from another word, of very different
origin.   This of ours, in both its senses, is very clearly from A.S. *stinge*,
aculeus.—*Forby.*——Moor remarks that, "in bees the propensity to •
hoard and *resent* is proverbial ;" here the two principal meanings of the
word *stingy* equally apply.

Noneare ;—Lye thus explains this word between brackets, marking
it as an addition of his own to *J*unius's Etymol. Angl. [Modò—vox
Norf. etiamnum in usu, ab Isl. *nunœr* idem significante, ut monet
Hickesius. L.]   I cannot find it in Hickes.   Nor is the compound word
nunœr in Biorn Halderson's Ice. Dict. but it is, in fact, *now-near*,
anon.—*G.*——Not till now.   So says Ray.   But we know nothing of
the word whatever.   Sir Thomas Browne might.   Isl. *nunœr*, modo.—
Forby.

Feft ;—Prompt. feffyd, feofatus ; but not likely to be the right word.—
Blk.——To persuade, or endeavour to persuade, says Ray in pref. to
N. C. W.   Yet he adds that in his own county, Essex, it meant, to
"put off wares ;" but that he was to seek for an etymon.   So are we.
But it is of no importance.   It is one of Sir Thomas Browne's words
become obsolete.—*Forby.*

Thepes ;—or rather *thapes*.   *Gooseberries.*   I cannot find any word
resembling this as a fruit ; but *Tap* in Danish is the *uvula* of the throat.
V. FAPES.—*Forby*, p. 110.

Gosgood ;—A vulgar London word for a gooseberry is goosegog.—
Blk.——Yeast.   Ray says, that in his time, it was in use also in Kent.
But he does not say, nor is it possible to conceive, how it is entitled to
so exalted an interpretation as he bestows upon it,—*God's Good !* A
meaning much more suitable and seemly, and surely not improbable,
may be conjectured.   It may have had its origin from A. S. *gos*, anser.
In Norfolk, if not in every part of East Anglia, yeast dumplings have

Hugo de Bones had not been cast away, wherein threescore thousand soldiers out of Britany and Flanders were to be

been immemorially associated with a roasted goose ; and when properly soaked in the natural gravy of the fowl, are of a very delicious savour to a true East Anglian palate. In this sense yeast may be said to be *good. with goose,* and called *goose-good,* or in the most ancient form, *gos-good.* But the word is now utterly extinct. The taste remains.—*Forby.*

Kamp;—May, perhaps, be the game of foot-ball, from these words in *Prompt.* "*Camper,* or player at foot-ball," also "*camping.*" I suppose so named by reason of the space required for this game.—*Blk.*

Sibrit ;—or *Sibberet,* means the bands of marrage ; "sibberidge" in *Wilb.* and "sybrede banna" in *Prompt.*—*Blk*——It is one of Sir Thomas. Browne's words, and in full use at this day. It is explained by Hickes, A. S. *syb,* cognatio, and *byrht,* manifestus, q. d. a public announcing or proclamation of an intended affinity. This is unquestionably preferable to the unfounded notion, that the word is corrupted from "*Si quis sciverit,*" the supposed first words of the publication of banns in the Roman Latin service.—*Forby.*——This word has been derived from *sib,* said to mean akin ; and to imply, that by banns the parties have a. *right* to become akin, that is, *sib-right.* Some say it is *rib-right,* the right to take a rib. Ray has this proverb : As much *sibb'd* as sieve and riddle that grew in the same wood, p. 225. And he says that. "*sibb'd* means akin, and that in Suffolk the banns of matrimony are called sibberidge," which is correct ; though *sibrit* be most common. Both are in extensive use. *Sib* is also Scottish. It occurs twice in the sense of relationship in Scottish colloquialism in Guy Mannering, ii. 183, 219. It occurs also in the Antiquary, iii. 75 ;—"By the religion of our holy church they are ower sibb thegither." Again, "They may be brought to think themselves sae sibb as on Christian law will permit. them wedlock." I do not find, however, that *sibrit* or *sibridge* is. Scottish.—*Moor.*

Fangast;—A marriageable maid. The word is not now known, and is, therefore, given with Ray's interpretation and etymon. A. S. *fangan,, capere,* and *gast,* amor.—*Forby.*

Sap ;—*sapy, foolish ;* perhaps only *sappy,* ill pronounced.—*G.*—— Mr. Forby was unacquainted with the meaning suggested by Miss Gurney, and in which I have often heard the word used :—a silly fellow is called a *sap ;* he is also termed *sapy* or *sappy.* The comparison in. tended is possibly to the sap in timber, which is of little value, and soon becomes unsound and useless.

Cothish ;—is likely to be an adj. from this noun in *Prompt.* "*cothe,* or swowning, sincopa.*"—*Blk.*——*Cothish, cothy,* adj. faint, sickly, ailing. There can surely be no doubt of the identity of these words ; the former is Sir Thomas Browne's, the latter the modern form. Yet in the pref. to R. N. C. it is interpreted *morose,* without a word of explanation or proof. It never could have been used in that sense. Its derivation is so very obvious, that it is wonderful it escaped Ray. It is amply justi- fied by modern and very frequent use. A dog is said to be *cothy* when he is meek and delicate. A. S. *cothe,* morbus.

wafted over, and were by king John's appointment to have a settled habitation in the counties of Norfolk and Suffolk.[7]

Thokish ;—thoke, as on-sadde (*sad* meant firm) fysh, humorosus, ·insolidus, *Prompt.* applied to boggy land.—*Blk.*——Slothful : sluggish. This is Ray's interpretation, and may be right for ought we know.—*Forby.*——The sense suggested by Mr. Black I believe to be the true one.

*Bide-owe ;—*interpreted by Ray (Pr. to N. C.) "*poenas dare.*" It may be so. It is impossible to assent or gainsay, as it is totally extinct. It is one of Sir Thomas Browne's words.—*Forby.*——Let us, in such failure of authorities, hazard a conjecture ; that it means " wait a while,"—*bide a wee.*

" *Paxwax ;—*synewe," *Prompt.* It is still used dialectically for our *pathwax* or *packwax.*—*Blk.*——The strong tendon in the neck of animals. It is a word which has no proper claim to admission here, for it is quite general ; yet must be admitted, because it is on Sir Thomas Browne's list. It must certainly have been in use in his time. And it is very strange he should not have heard it till he came into Norfolk. Ray, in the preface to N. C., makes no remark to this effect, but takes this as he finds it with the other words. Yet he had himself used it in his great work on the Creation, and to all appearance as a word well known. He spells it *pack-wax,* indeed, but that can surely make no difference. He not only gives no derivation, but declines giving one, at the same time declaring his own knowledge of the very extensive, if not general, use of the word. The fact is, that it is not even confined to the English language. It is used by Linnæus, somewhere in the Upsal Amœnitates Academicæ. A friend, who undertook the search, has not been able to find the passage ; but it is not likely that anything explanatory would be found. Indeed, it is a sort of *crux etymologorum.* They, very reasonably, do not care to come near it. And they might all frankly avow, as Ray does, that they " have nothing to say to it." BR. has *fix-fax.*—*Forby.*

[7] *the Danish language, &c.*] I do not see the Danish original of most of the Norfolk words here given ; but there are several which can be traced to no other, and I have found several which are, I suspect, peculiar to the coast :—

*Hefty ;—*stormy. Dan. *heftig,* angry.

*Swale ;—*shade. Dan. or Ice. *svala,* cold.

*Willock ;—*a guillemot, or any sea bird of the awk or diver kind.

*Roke ;—*fog or sea haze.——*Rak,* wet, Ice. " With cloudy gum and rak ouerquhelmst the are."—*Gawin Douglas.*

*To shrepe ;—*used by the fishermen in the sense of " to clear." " The fog begins to *shrepe* yonder." Ice. *skreppa.* Dilabi, se subducere.

*Lum ;—*the handle of an oar. Ice. *hlummr.* In other parts of England, however, it is called the *loom* of an oar.

*Rooms ;—*the spaces between the thwarts of a boat. Ice. *rum,* used only in this sense.

*To go driving ;—*to go fishing : chiefly applied to the herring fishers, I think.—*G.*

But beside your laudable endeavours in the Saxon, you are not like to repent you of your studies in the other European and western languages, for therein are delivered many excellent historical, moral, and philosophical discourses, wherein men merely versed in the learned languages are often at a loss : but although you are so well accomplished in the French, you will not surely conceive that you are master of all the languages in France, for to omit the Briton, Britonant or old British, yet retained in some part of Britany, I shall only propose this unto your construction.

Chavalisco d'aquestes Boemes chems an freitado lou cap cun taules Jargonades, ero necy chi voluiget bouta sin tens embè aquelles. Anin à lous occells, che dizen tat prou ben en ein voz L' ome nosłp comochodochi yen ay jes de plazer, d'ausir la mitat de paraulles, en el mon.

This is a part of that language which Scaliger nameth Idiotismus Tectofagicus or Langue d'oc, counterdistinguishing it unto the Idiotismus Francicus or Langue d'ouy, not understood in a petty corner or between a few mountains, but in parts of early civility in Languedoc, Provence, and Catalonia, which put together will make little less than England.

Without some knowledge herein you cannot exactly understand the works of Rabelais : by this the French themselves

---

I have added, from a list of *Norfolk words* furnished me by the same correspondent, the following, which are either new to Forby, or with different derivations :—

" *Wips and strays,*" not *waifs and strays,* but "wipper and straae." Dan. "heads and straws of corn," odds and ends. I found this expression in a list of provincialisms of the Danish island of Zealand.

To lope ;—to stride along. Ger. *hlaupen,* to run.

Unstowly ;—applied to children ; unruly.

Car ;—a low marshy grove. Alder car, osier car. *Kior,* Ice. marsh.

Skep or skip ;—a basket ; toad's skep (not *cap,* I think.) *Skieppe* is a Danish half-bushel measure.

Pottens ;—crutches.

Hobby ;—small horse. Dan. *hoppe,* a mare.

Wunt ;—to sit as a hen. Sax. *wunian,* to abide.

Shacking ;—In German *yechen* is to club—and "zur yeche gehen," literally, "to go to shack," is an expression in use, meaning to take a common share. The essence of our shacking is that the pigs and geese run in common over the fields to pick up the remains of the harvest.—*G.*

are fain to make out that preserved relique of old French:
containing the league between Charles and Lewis, the sons of
Ludovicus Pius.   Hereby may tolerably be understood the
several tracts, written in the Catalonian tongue; and in this
is published the Tract of Falconry written by Theodosius and
Symmachus ; in this is yet conserved the poem Vilhuardine
concerning the French expedition in the holy war, and the
taking of Constantinople, among the works of Marius Æqui-
cola, an Italian poet.   You may find in this language, a
pleasant dialogue of love ; this, about an hundred years ago,
was in high esteem, when many Italian wits flocked into
Provence; and the famous Petrarcha wrote many of his
poems in Vaucluse in that country.[8]

[8] *country.*] In the *MS. Sloan.* 1827, I find the following very odd
passage ; respecting which, most certainly, the author's assertion is
incontrovertible, that "the sense may afford *some trouble.*" I insert it,
not expecting that many readers will take that trouble—but it appeared
too characteristic to be omitted.

    "Now having wearied you with old languages or little understood,
I shall put an end unto your trouble in modern French, by a short
letter composed by me for your sake, though not concerning yourself;
wherein, though the words be plain and genuine, yet the sense may
afford some trouble.

    "MONSIEUR,—Ne vous laisses plus manger la laine sur le dors.
Regardes bien ce gros magot, lequel vous voyez de si bon œil. Assurement il fait le mitou.   Monsieur, vous chausses les lunettes de travers,
ne voyant point comme il pratique vos dependants.   Il s'est desïa queri
de mal St. Francois, et bride sa mule a vostre despens.   Croyez moi, il
ne s'amusera pas a la moutarde ; mais, vous ayant miné et massacré vos
affaires, au dernier coup il vous rendra Monsieur sans queue.

    "Mais pour l'autre goulafie et benueur a tire la rigau, qui vous a si
rognement fait la barbe, l'envoyes vous a Pampelune. Mais auparavant,
a mon advis, il auroit a miserere jusques a vitulos, et je le ferois un
moutton de Berry.   En le traittant bellement et de bon conseil, vous
assuyes de rompre un anguille sur les genoux.   Ne lui fies poynt : il ne
rabbaissera le menton, et mourra dans sa peau.   Il scait bien que les
belles paroles n'escorchent pas la guele, les quelles il payera a sepmaine
de deux Jeudies.   Chasses le de chez vous a bonne heure, car il a estè
a Naples sans passer les monts ; et ancore que parle en maistre, est
patient de St. Cosme.

    "Soucies vous aussi de la garcïonaire, chez vous, qu'elle n'ayst le
mal de neuf mois.   Assurement elle a le nez tourné a la friandise, et
les talons bien courts.   Elle jouera voluntiers a l'Home ; et si le hault
ne defend le bas, avant la venue des cicoignes, lui s'enlevera la juppe.

    "Mais, pour le petit Gymnosophiste chez vous, caresses le vous aux
bras ouverts.   Voyez vous pas comme a toutes les menaces de Fortune

For the word (Dread) in the royal title (Dread sovereign) of which you desire to know the meaning, I return answer unto your question briefly thus.

Most men do vulgarly understand this word dread after the common and English acceptation, as implying fear, awe, or dread.

Others may think to expound it from the French word *droit* or *droyt*. For, whereas, in elder times, the presidents and supremes of courts were termed sovereigns, men might conceive this a distinctive title and proper unto the king as eminently and by right the sovereign.

A third exposition may be made from some Saxon original, particularly from *Driht, Domine*, or *Drihten, Dominus*, in the Saxon language, the word for *Dominus*, throughout the Saxon Psalms, and used in the expression of the year of our Lord in the Decretal Epistle of Pope Agatho unto Athelred king of the Mercians, *anno* 680.

Verstegan would have this term *Drihten* appropriate unto God. Yet, in the constitutions of Withred king of Kent,* we find the same word used for a lord or master, *si in vesperâ præcedente solem servus ex mandato Domini aliquod opus servile egerit, Dominus (Drihten)* 80 *solidis luito*. However, therefore, though *Driht Domine*, might be most eminently applied unto the Lord of heaven, yet might it be also transferred unto potentates and gods on earth, unto whom fealty is given or due, according unto the feudist term *ligeus*,[9] *à ligando*, unto whom they were bound in fealty.

* *V. Cl. Spelmanni Concil.*

il branle comme la Bastille? Vrayment il est Stoic a vingt-quatre carrats, et de mesme calibre avec les vieux Ascetiques. Alloran[1] lui vault autant que l'isle de France, et la tour de Cordan[2] lui vault le mesme avec la Louvre.

"Serviteur très-humble,
THOMAS BROUNE."

[9] *ligeus.*] "Or liege lord."—*MS. Sloan.* 1827.

---

[1] *Note;*—"Alloran, Allusama, or Insula Erroris; a small desolate barren island, whereon nothing liveth but coneys, in the Mediterranean sea, between Carthagena and Calo-de-tres-furcus, in Barbary."

[2] *Note;*—"A small island or rock, in the mouth of the river Garonne, with one tower in it, where a man liveth, to take care of lights for such as go to, or come from, Bordeaux."

And therefore from *Driht, Domine,* dread sovereign, may, probably, owe its original.

I have not time to enlarge upon this subject : pray let this pass, as it is, for a letter and not for a treatise.

I am, yours, &c.

TRACT IX.

OF ARTIFICIAL HILLS, MOUNTS, OR BURROWS, IN MANY PARTS OF ENGLAND : WHAT THEY ARE, TO WHAT END RAISED, AND BY WHAT NATIONS.

My Honoured Friend Mr. W. D.'s[1] Query.

IN my last journey through Marshland, Holland, and a great part of the Fens, I observed divers artificial heaps of earth of a very large magnitude, and I hear of many others which are in other parts of those countries, some of them are at least twenty feet in direct height from the level whereon they stand. I would gladly know your opinion of them, and whether you think not that they were raised by the Romans or Saxons, to cover the bones or ashes of some eminent persons ?

My Answer.

WORTHY SIR,—Concerning artificial mounts and hills, raised without fortifications attending them, in most parts

---

[1] *Mr. W. D.*] The initials, in both the preceding editions, are " E. D. :" but it has been clearly ascertained that this is an error. The query was Sir William Dugdale's ; and his reply to the present discourse will be found elsewhere. A reference to Dugdale's History of Embanking and Draining, will show that he availed himself of the reply he obtained to his enquiry : for he has transcribed the quotations from Leland and Wormius in illustration of the Saxon and Danish mode of sepulture ; and has given almost *verbatim* the passage referring to Germanicus.

of England, the most considerable thereof I conceive to be of two kinds; that is, either signal boundaries and land-marks, or else sepulchral monuments or hills of interment for remarkable and eminent persons, especially such as died in the wars.

As for such which are sepulchral monuments, upon bare and naked view, they are not appropriable unto any of the three nations of the Romans, Saxons, or Danes, who, after the Britons, have possessed this land; because upon strict account, they may be appliable unto them all.[2]

For that the Romans used such hilly sepultures, beside many other testimonies, seems confirmable from the practice of Germanicus, who thus interred the unburied bones of the slain soldiers of Varus; and that expression of Virgil of high antiquity among the Latins,

facit ingens monte sub alio
Regis Dercenni terreno ex aggere bustum.

That the Saxons made use of this way is collectible from several records, and that pertinent expression of Lelandus,*
Saxones, gens Christi ignara, in hortis amœnis, si domi forte ægroti moriebantur; sin foris et bello occisi, in egestis per campos terræ tumulis (quos burgos appellabant) sepulti sunt.

That the Danes observed this practice, their own antiqui-ties do frequently confirm, and it stands precisely delivered by Adolphus Cyprius, as the learned Wormius † hath ob-

* *Leland in Assertione Regis Arthuri.*
† *Wormius in Monumentis Danicis.*

[2] *appliable unto them all.*] Mr. Pegge, in a paper published in the Archæologia, on the Arbour Lows, in Derbyshire, expresses the same opinion; ascribing these burrows or *tumuli* to Britons, Romans, Saxons, and Danes,—and not to any one of those people exclusively. Some he supposes to be British, from their being dispersed over moors, and usually on eminences; not placed with any regard to roads, as the Roman *tumuli* generally are. The Danish lows would frequently ex-hibit a circle of stones round their base. But the contents would furnish the best and perhaps the only sure criterion to judge by; kistvaens and stone coffins, rings, beads, and other articles, peculiar to 'the Britons, being found in some; Roman coins, urns, and implements in others, and the arms and utensils of the Saxons or Danes in others.—*Archæologia,* vii. 131, &c.

served. *Dani olim in memoriam regum et heroum, ex terra coacervata ingentes moles, montium instar eminentes, erexisse, credibile omnino ac probabile est, atque illis in locis ut plurimum, quo sæpe homines commearent, atque iter haberent, ut in viis publicis posteritati memoriam consecrarent, et quodammodo immortalitati mandarent.* And the like monuments are yet to be observed in Norway and Denmark in no small numbers.

So that upon a single view and outward observation they may be the monuments of any of these three nations: although the greatest number, not improbably, of the Saxons; who fought many battles with the Britons and Danes, and also between their own nations, and left the proper name of burrows for these hills still retained in many of them, as the seven burrows upon Salisbury plain, and in many other parts of England.

But of these and the like hills there can be no clear and assured decision without an ocular exploration, and subterraneous enquiry by cutting through one of them either directly or cross-wise. For so with lesser charge discovery may be made what is under them, and consequently the intention of their erection. For if they were raised for remarkable and eminent boundaries, then about their bottom will be found the lasting substances of burnt bones of beasts, of ashes, bricks, lime, or coals.

If urns be found, they might be erected by the Romans before the term of urn burying or custom of burning the dead expired: but if raised by the Romans after that period, inscriptions, swords, shields, and arms, after the Roman mode, may afford a good distinction.

But if these hills were made by Saxons or Danes, discovery may be made from the fashion of their arms, bones of their horses, and other distinguishing substances buried with them.

And for such an attempt there wanteth not encouragement. For a like mount or burrow was opened in the days of King Henry the Eighth upon Barham Down in Kent, by the care of Mr. Thomas Digges, and charge of Sir Christopher Hales; and a large urn with ashes was found under it, as is delivered by Thomas Twinus, *de Rebus Albionicis,* a learned man of that country, *sub incredibili terræ acervo, urna cinere ossium magnorum fragmentis plena, cum galeis, clypeis æneis et ferreis rubigine fere consumptis, inusitatæ magnitudinis, eruta est: sed nulla inscriptio nomen, nullum testimonium tempus, aut fortunam exponebant:* and not very long ago, as Camden delivereth,* in one of the mounts of Barklow hills, in Essex, being levelled, there were found three troughs, containing broken bones, conceived to have been of Danes: and in later time we find, that a burrow was opened in the Isle of Man, wherein fourteen urns were found with burnt bones in them; and one more neat than the rest, placed in a bed of fine white sand, containing nothing but a few brittle bones, as having passed the fire; according to the particular account thereof in the description of the Isle of Man.† Surely many noble bones and ashes have been contented with such hilly tombs; which neither admitting ornament, epitaph, or inscription, may, if earthquakes spare them, out-last all other monuments. *Suæ sunt metis metæ.* Obelisks have their term, and pyramids will tumble, but these mountainous monuments may stand, and are like to have the same period with the earth.

More might be said, but my business of another nature, makes me take off my hand.

I am, yours, &c.

---

* *Camd. Brit.* p. 326.
† *Published* 1656, *by Dan. King.*

TRACT X.

OF TROAS, WHAT PLACE IS MEANT BY THAT NAME.
ALSO, OF THE SITUATIONS OF SODOM, GOMORRAH, ADMAH,
ZEBOIM, IN THE DEAD SEA.

SIR,—To your geographical queries, I answer as follows :—
In sundry passages of the New Testament, in the Acts of
the Apostles, and Epistles of St. Paul, we meet with the
word Troas ;[1] how he went from Troas to Philippi, in Macedonia, from thence unto Troas again: how he remained
seven days in that place : from thence on foot to Assos,
whither the disciples had sailed from Troas, and, there
taking him in, made their voyage unto Cæsarea.

Now, whether this Troas be the name of a city or a certain
region of Phrygia seems no groundless doubt of yours : for
that it was sometimes taken in the signification of some
country, is acknowledged by Ortellius, Stephanus, and Grotius ; and it is plainly set down by Strabo, that a region of
Phrygia in Asia Minor, was so taken in ancient times; and
that at the Trojan war, all the territory which comprehended
the nine principalities subject unto the king of Ilium Τροίη
λεγουμένη, was called by the name of Troja.   And this might
seem sufficiently to solve the intention of the description,
when he came or went from Troas, that is some part of that
region ; and will otherwise seem strange unto many how he
should be said to go or come from that city which all writers
had laid in the ashes about a thousand years before.

---

[1] *Troas.*]   Troas was a small country lying to the west of Mysia,
upon the sea.   It took this name from its principal city, Troas, a sea-
port, and built, as is said, about some four miles from the situation of
old Troy, by Lysimachus, one of Alexander the Great's captains, who
peopled it from neighbouring cities, and called it Alexandria, or Troas
Alexandri, in honour of his master Alexander ; who began the work,
but lived not to bring it to any perfection.   But in following times it
came to be called simply Troas.   The name may be understood as
taken by the sacred writers to denote the country as well as city so
called, but chiefly the latter.

All which notwithstanding,—since we read in the text a particular abode of seven days, and such particulars as leaving of his cloak, books, and parchments at Troas, and that St. Luke seems to have been taken in to the travels of St. Paul at this place, where he begins in the Acts to write in the first person—this may rather seem to have been some city or special habitation, than any province or region without such limitation.

Now, that such a city there was, and that of no mean note, is easily verified from historical observation. For though old Ilium was anciently destroyed, yet was there another raised by the relicts of that people, not in the same place, but about thirty furlongs westward, as is to be learned from Strabo.

Of this place Alexander, in his expedition against Darius, took especial notice, endowing it with sundry immunities, with promise of greater matters, at his return from Persia; inclined hereunto from the honour he bore unto Homer, whose earnest reader he was, and upon whose poems, by the help of Anaxarchus and Callisthenes, he made some observations: as also much moved hereto upon the account of his cognation with the Æacides, and kings of Molossus, whereof Andromache, the wife of Hector, was queen. After the death of Alexander, Lysimachus surrounded it with a wall, and brought the inhabitants of the neighbour towns unto it; and so it bore the name of Alexandria; which, from Antigonus, was also called Antigonia, according to the inscription of that famous medal in Goltsius, *Colonia Troas Antigonia Alexandrea, legio vicesima prima.*

When the Romans first went into Asia against Antiochus, it was but a κωμόπολις, and no great city; but, upon the peace concluded, the Romans much advanced the same. Fimbria, the rebellious Roman, spoiled it in the Mithridatick wars, boasting that he had subdued Troy in eleven days, which the Grecians could not take in almost as many years. But it was again rebuilt and countenanced by the Romans, and became a Roman colony, with great immunities conferred on it; and accordingly it is so set down by Ptolemy. For the Romans, deriving themselves from the Trojans, thought no favour too great for it; especially Julius Cæsar, who, both in imitation of Alexander, and for his own descent

from Julus, of the posterity of Æneas, with much passion
affected it, and in a discontented humour,* was once in mind
to translate the Roman wealth unto it; so that it became a
very remarkable place, and was, in Strabo's time,† one of
the noble cities of Asia.

And, if they understood the prediction of Homer in reference unto the Romans, as some expound it in Strabo, it
might much promote their affection unto that place; which
being a remarkable prophecy, and scarce to be paralleled in
Pagan story, made before Rome was built, and concerning
the lasting reign of the progeny of Æneas, they could not
but take especial notice of it. For thus is Neptune made
to speak, when he saved Æneas from the fury of Achilles.

> Verum agite hunc subito præsenti à morte trahamus
> Ne Cronides ira flammet si fortis Achilles
> Hunc mactet, fati quem lex evadere jussit.
> Ne genus intereat de læto semine totum
> Dardani ab excelso præ cunctis prolibus olim,
> Dilecti quos è mortali stirpe creavit,
> Nunc etiam Priami stirpem Saturnius odit,
> Trojugenum post hæc Æneas sceptra tenebit
> Et nati natorum et qui nascentur ab illis.

The Roman favours were also continued unto St. Paul's
days; for Claudius,‡ producing an ancient letter of the
Romans unto King Seleucus concerning the Trojan privileges,
made a release of their tributes; and Nero elegantly pleaded
for their immunities, and remitted all tributes unto them.§ ·

And, therefore, there being so remarkable a city in this
territory, it may seem too hard to lose the same in the general name of the country; and since it was so eminently
favoured by emperors, enjoying so many immunities, and
full of Roman privileges, it was probably very populous, and
a fit abode for St. Paul, who, being a Roman citizen, might
live more quietly himself, and have no small number of
faithful well-wishers in it.

Yet must we not conceive that this was the old Troy, or
re-built in the same place with it: for Troas was placed
about thirty furlongs west, and upon the sea shore: so that,
to hold a clearer apprehension hereof than is commonly

---

* *Sueton.*   † ἐλλογίμων πόλεων.   ‡ *Sueton.*
§ *Tacit. Ann.* 1. 13.

delivered in the discourses of Troy, we may consider one inland Troy, or old Ilium, which was built farther within the land, and so was removed from the port where the Grecian fleet lay in Homer; and another maritime Troy, which was upon the sea coast, placed in the maps of Ptolemy, between Lectum and Sigæum or Port Janizam southwest from the old city, which was this of St. Paul, and whereunto are appliable the particular accounts of Bellonius, when, not an hundred years ago, he described the ruins of Troy with their baths, aqueducts, walls, and towers, to be seen from the sea as he sailed between it and Tenedos; and where, upon nearer view, he observed some signs and impressions of his conversion in the ruins of churches, crosses, and inscriptions upon stones.

Nor was this only a famous city in the days of St. Paul, but considerable long after. For, upon the letter of Adrianus, Herodes, Atticus,* at a great charge, repaired their baths, contrived aqueducts and noble water courses in it. As is also collectible from the medals of Caracalla, of Severus, and Crispina; with inscriptions, *Colonia Alexandria Troas,* bearing on the reverse either an horse, a temple, or a woman; denoting their destruction by an horse, their prayers for the emperor's safety, and as some conjecture, the memory of Sibylla Phrygia, or Hellespontica.

Nor wanted this city the favour of Christian princes, but was made a bishop's see under the archbishop of Cyzicum; but in succeeding discords was destroyed and ruined, and the nobler stones translated to Constantinople by the Turks to beautify their mosques and other buildings.

Concerning the Dead Sea, accept of these few remarks.

In the map of the Dead Sea we meet with the figure of the cities which were destroyed: of Sodom, Gomorrah, Admah, and Zeboim; but with no uniformity; men placing them variously, and from the uncertainty of their situation, taking a fair liberty to set them where they please.

For Admah, Zeboim, and Gomorrah, there is no light from the text to define their situation. But, that Sodom could not be far from Segor, which was seated under the mountains near the lake, seems inferrible from the sudden arrival of

---

* *Philostrat. in Vita Herodis Attici.*

Lot, who coming from Sodom at day-break, attained to Segor at sun-rising; and therefore Sodom is to be placed not many miles from it, not in the middle of the lake, which against that place is about eighteen miles over, and so will leave nine miles to be gone in so small a space of time.

The valley being large, the lake now in length about seventy English miles, the river Jordan and divers others running over the plain, 'tis probable the best cities were seated upon those streams; but how the Jordan passed or winded, or where it took in the other streams, is a point too old for geography to determine.

For, that the river gave the fruitfulness unto this valley by over-watering that low region, seems plain from that expression in the text,* that it was watered, *sicut Paradisus et Ægyptus,* like Eden and the plains of Mesopotamia, where Euphrates yearly overfloweth; or like Egypt where Nilus doth the like; and seems probable also from the same course of the river not far above this valley where the Israelites passed Jordan, where 'tis said that "Jordan overfloweth its banks in the time of harvest."

That it must have had some passage under ground in the compass of this valley before the creation of this lake, seems necessary from the great current of Jordan, and from the rivers Arnon, Cedron, Zaeth, which empty into this valley; but where to place that concurrence of waters or place of its absorbition, there is no authentic decision.

The probablest place may be set somewhat southward, below the rivers that run into it on the east or western shore; and somewhat agreeable unto the account which Brocardus received from the Saracens which lived near it, *Jordanem ingredi mare mortuum et rursum egredi, sed post exiguum intervallum a terra absorberi.*

Strabo speaks naturally of this lake, that it was first caused by earthquakes, by sulphureous and bituminous eruptions, arising from the earth. But the Scripture makes it plain to have been from a miraculous hand, and by a remarkable expression, *pluit dominus ignem et sulphur à domino.*[2] See also Deut. xxix. *in ardore salis :* burning the

---

* Gen. xiii. 10.

[2] *But the Scripture, &c.*] Dr. Wells supports this opinion at con-

cities and destroying all things about the plain, destroying the vegetable nature of plants and all living things, salting and making barren the whole soil, and, by these fiery showers, kindling and setting loose the body of the bituminous mines, which showed their lower veins before but in some few pits and openings, swallowing up the foundation of their cities; opening the bituminous treasures below, and making a smoke like a furnace able to be discerned by Abraham at a good distance from it.

If this little may give you satisfaction, I shall be glad, as being, Sir,   Yours, &c.

———◆———

TRACT XI.

OF THE ANSWERS OF THE ORACLE OF APOLLO AT DELPHOS TO CRŒSUS, KING OF LYDIA.

SIR,[1]—Among the oracles of Apollo* there are none more celebrated than those which he delivered unto Crœsus king of Lydia;† who seems of all princes to have held the greatest dependence on them. But most considerable are

---

* See *Vul. Err.* l. vii. c. 12.   † *Herod.* l. i. *46, 47, &c. 90, 91.*

siderable length and by a series of very satisfactory arguments.—See *Geography of the Old and New Testament,* i. 153.

[1] *Sir.*] The copy of this tract in *MS. Sloan.* is thrown more into the form of an essay, by the following introductory passage :—" Men looked upon ancient oracles as natural, artificial, demoniacal, or all. They conceived something natural of them, as being in places affording exhalations, which were found to operate upon the brains of persons unto raptures, strange utterances, and divinations ; which being observed and admired by the people, an advantage was taken thereof; an artificial contrivance made by subtle crafty persons confederating to carry on a practice of divination ; pretending some power of divinity therein ; but because they sometimes made very strange predictions, and above the power of human reason, men were inclined to believe some demoniacal co-operation, and that some evil spirit ruled the whole scene ; having so fair an opportunity to delude mankind, and to advance his own worship ; and were thought to proceed from the spirit of Apollo or other heathen deities ; so that these oracles were not only appre-

his plain and intelligible replies which he made unto the same king, when he sent his chains of captivity unto Delphos, after his overthrow by Cyrus, with sad expostulations why he encouraged him unto that fatal war by his oracle, saying, προλέγουσαι Κροίσῳ, ἢν στρατεύηται ἐπὶ Πέρσας, μεγάλην ἀρκήν μιν καταλύσειν, Crœsus, if he wars against the Persians, shall dissolve a great empire.* Why, at least, he prevented not that sad infelicity of his devoted and bountiful servant, and whether it were fair or honourable for the gods of Greece to be ungrateful: which being a plain and open delivery of Delphos, and scarce to be paralleled in any ancient story, it may well deserve your farther consideration.

1. His first reply[2] was, that Crœsus suffered not for himself; but paid the transgression of his fifth predecessor, who killed his master, and usurped the dignity unto which he had no title.

Now whether Crœsus suffered upon this account or not, hereby he plainly betrayed his insufficiency to protect him; and also obliquely discovered he had a knowledge of his misfortune; for knowing that wicked act lay yet unpunished, he might well divine some of his successors might smart for it: and also understanding he was like to be the last of that race, he might justly fear and conclude this infelicity upon him.

Hereby he also acknowledged the inevitable justice of God; that though revenge lay dormant, it would not always sleep; and consequently confessed the just hand of God

* *Herod.* l. i. 54.

hended to be natural, human, or artificial, but also demoniacal, according to common opinion, and also of learned men; as Vossius hath declared:—'Constitere quidem oracula fraudibus vatum, sed non solis; solertia humana, sed sæpe etiam diabolica. Cum multa predixerint, ad quæ nulla ratione humana mentis acumen perlegisset in natura humana non est subsistendum, sed assurgendum ad causas superioris naturæ, quales sunt dæmones.' According to which sense and opinion we shall enlarge upon this following oracle of Delphos."

[2] *His first reply.*] This is a mistake; the oracle began his answer by alleging the impossibility of avoiding the determination of fate. It was the second observation, that Crœsus was expiating the crimes of Gyges, his ancestor in the fifth descent. (Ardys, Sadyattes, and Atyattes, were the intervening descendants.)

punishing unto the third and fourth generation, nor suffering such iniquities to pass for ever unrevenged.[3]

Hereby he flatteringly encouraged him in the opinion of his own merits, and that he only suffered for other men's transgressions: meanwhile he concealed Crœsus his pride, elation of mind and secure conceit of his own unparalleled felicity, together with the vanity, pride, and height of luxury of the Lydian nation, which the spirit of Delphos knew well to be ripe and ready for destruction.

2. A second excuse was, that it is not in the power of God to hinder the decree of fate. A general evasion for any falsified prediction founded upon the common opinion of fate, which impiously subjecteth the power of heaven unto it; widely discovering the folly of such as repair unto him concerning future events: which, according unto this rule, must go on as the fates have ordered, beyond his power to prevent or theirs to avoid; and consequently teaching that his oracles had only this use to render men more miserable by foreknowing their misfortunes; whereof Crœsus himself had sensible experience in that demoniacal dream concerning his eldest son, that he should be killed by a spear, which, after all care and caution, he found inevitably to befal him.

3. In his third apology he assured him that he endeavoured to transfer the evil fate and to pass it upon his children; and did, however, procrastinate his infecility, and deferred the destruction of Sardis and his own captivity three years longer than was fatally decreed upon it.

Wherein while he wipes off the stain of ingratitude, he leaves no small doubt whether, it being out of his power to contradict or transfer the fates of his servants, it be not also beyond it to defer such signal events, and whereon the fates of whole nations do depend.

As also, whether he intended or endeavoured to bring to pass what he pretended, some question might be made. For that he should attempt or think he could translate his

[3] *unrevenged.*]   In *MS. Sloan.* occurs here this passage:— "The devil, who sees how things of this nature go on in kingdoms, nations, and families, is able to say much on this point; whereas, we, that understand not the reserved judgments of God, or the due time of their executions, are fain to be doubtfully silent."

254 ANSWERS OF THE DELPHIAN ORACLE [TRACT XI.

infelicity upon his sons, it could not consist with his judgment, which attempts not impossibles or things beyond his power; nor with his knowledge of future things, and the fates of succeeding generations : for he understood that monarchy was to expire in himself, and could particularly foretell the infelicity of his sons, and hath also made remote predictions unto others concerning the fortunes of many succeeding descents, as appears in that answer unto Attalus,

> Be of good courage, Attalus, thou shalt reign,
> And thy sons' sons, but not their sons again.

As also unto Cypselus, king of Corinth.

> Happy is the man who at my altar stands,
> Great Cypselus, who Corinth now commands.
> Happy is he ; his sons shall happy be ;
> But for their sons, unhappy days they'll see.

Now, being able to have so large a prospect of future things, and of the fate of many generations, it might well be granted he was not ignorant of the fate of Crœsus's sons, and well understood it was in vain to think to translate his misery upon them.

4. In the fourth part of his reply, he clears himself of ingratitude, which hell itself cannot hear of; alleging that he had saved his life when he was ready to be burnt, by sending a mighty shower, in a fair and cloudless day, to quench the fire already kindled, which all the servants of Cyrus could not do. Though this shower might well be granted, as much concerning his honour, and not beyond his power;[4] yet whether this merciful shower fell not out contingently, or were not contrived by an higher power,[5]

[4] *not beyond his power.*] *MS. Sloan.* adds, "when countenanced by divine permission or decree."

[5] *or were not contrived by an higher power.*] That is, "that of the devil." The whole course of these observations on the Delphian oracle reminds us of what in his former works Sir Thomas had declared to be his opinion—viz. that it was a Satanic agency. And several passages of *Religio Medici* betray this sentiment—(see §§ 13 and 46) : and in his larger work, *Pseud. Epid.* he devotes a chapter (the 13th of book vii.) to the subject of the "cessation of oracles ;" in which he takes no pains to *prove* them to have existed in any other way than by the mere juggle of the priests, imposing on the ignorance and superstition of the people ; but, *assuming* the fact that a real divination, through the agency of Satan, was permitted to exist in Pagan antiquity, he only discusses the

which hath often pity upon Pagans, and rewardeth their
virtues sometimes with extraordinary temporal favours;
also, in no unlike case, who was the author of those few
fair minutes, which, in a showery day, gave only time enough
for the burning of Sylla's body, some question might be
made.

5. The last excuse devolveth the error and miscarriage of
the business upon Crœsus, and that he deceived himself by
an inconsiderate misconstruction of his oracle; that if he
had doubted, he should not have passed it over in silence,
but consulted again for an exposition of it. Besides, he
had neither discussed, nor well perpended his oracle concerning Cyrus, whereby he might. have understood not to
engage against him.

Wherein, to speak indifferently, the deception and miscarriage seems chiefly to lie at Crœsus's door, who, if not
infatuated with confidence and security, might justly have
doubted the construction; besides, he had received two
oracles before, which clearly hinted an unhappy time unto
him : the first concerning Cyrus.

> Whenever a mule shall o'er the Medians reign,
> Stay not, but unto Hermus fly amain.

Herein, though he understood not the Median mule, or
Cyrus, that is, of his mixed descent from Assyrian and
Median parents, yet he could not but apprehend some mis-
fortune from that quarter.

Though this prediction seemed a notable piece of divination, yet did it not so highly magnify his natural sagacity or
knowledge of future events as was by many esteemed; he
having no small assistance herein from the prophecy of
Daniel concerning the Persian monarchy, and the prophecies
of Jeremiah and Isaiah, wherein he might read the name of
Cyrus, who should restore the captivity of the Jews, and

question how and when such permission was withdrawn and oracles
ceased to exist.

Since the preceding remarks were written, I turned to Dr. Johnson's
brief account of these *Miscellany Tracts*, in his life of the author, and find
the following observation : " In this tract nothing deserves notice, more
than that Browne considers the oracles as evidently and indubitably
supernatural, and founds all his disquisition upon that postulate."

must, therefore, be the great monarch and lord of all those nations.

The same misfortune was also foretold when he demanded of Apollo if ever he should hear his dumb son speak.

> O foolish Crœsus! who hast made this choice,
> To know when thou shalt hear thy dumb son's voice
> Better he still were mute, would nothing say ;—
> When he first speaks, look for a dismal day!

This, if he contrived not the time and the means of his recovery, was no ordinary divination : yet how to make out the verity of the story, some doubts may yet remain. For, though the causes of deafness and dumbness were removed, yet since words are attained by hearing, and men speak not without instruction, how he should be able immediately to utter such apt and significant words, as ῎Ανθρωπε, μὴ κτεῖνε Κροῖσον, " O man! slay not Crœsus,"* it cannot escape some doubt: since the story also delivers, that he was deaf and dumb, that he then first began to speak, and spake all his life after.

Now, if Crœsus[6] had consulted again for a clearer exposition of what was doubtfully delivered, whether the oracle would have spake out the second time, or afforded a clearer answer, some question might be made from the examples of his practice upon the like demands.

So, when the Spartans had often fought with ill success against the Tegeates, they consulted the oracle, what God they should appease, to become victorious over them.   The answer was, "That they should remove the bones of Orestes." Though the words were plain, yet the thing was obscure, and like finding out the body of Moses. And, therefore, they once more demanded in what place they should find the same ; unto whom he returned this answer,

> When in the Tegean plains a place thou find'st
> Where blasts are made by two impetuous winds,
> Where that that strikes is struck, blows follow blows,
> There doth the earth Orestes' bones enclose.

Which obscure reply the wisest of Sparta could not make

* *Herod.* l. i. 85.

6 *Now, if Crœsus.*]   *MS. Sloan.* reads, " Now, notwithstanding this plausible apology and evasion, if Crœsus."

out, and was casually unriddled by one talking with a smith, who had found large bones of a man buried about his house; the oracle implying no more than a smith's forge, expressed by a double bellows, the hammer and anvil therein.

Now, why the oracle should place such consideration upon the bones of Orestes, the son of Agamemnon, a madman and a murderer, if not to promote the idolatry of the heathens, and maintain a superstitious veneration of things of no activity, it may leave no small obscurity.

Or why, in a business so clear in his knowledge, he should affect so obscure expressions it may also be wondered; if it were not to maintain .the wary and evasive method in his answers : for, speaking obscurely in things beyond doubt within his knowledge, he might be more tolerably dark in matters beyond his prescience.

Though EI were inscribed over the gate of Delphos, yet was there no uniformity in his deliveries. Sometimes with that obscurity as argued a fearful prophecy; sometimes so plainly as might confirm a spirit of divinity; sometimes morally, deterring from vice and villany; another time viciously, and in the spirit of blood and cruelty; observably modest in his civil enigma and periphrasis of that part which old Numa would plainly name,* and Medea would not understand, when he advised Ægeus not to draw out his foot before, until he arrived upon the Athenian ground; whereas another time he seemed too literal in that unseemly epithet unto Cyanus, king of Cyprus,† and put a beastly trouble upon all Egypt to find out the urine of a true virgin.

Sometimes, more beholding unto memory than invention, he delighted to express himself in the bare verses of Homer. But that he principally affected poetry, and that the priest not only nor always composed his prosal raptures into verse, seems plain from his necromantical prophecies, whilst the dead head in Phlegon delivers a long prediction in verse.; and at the rising of the ghost of Commodus unto Caracalla, when none of his ancestors would speak, the divining spirit versified his infelicities; corresponding herein

---

* *Plut. in Thes.*   † *V. Herod.*

unto the apprehensions of elder times, who conceived not only a majesty but something of divinity in poetry, and, as in ancient times, the old theologians delivered their inventions.

Some critical readers might expect in his oraculous poems a more than ordinary strain and true spirit of Apollo; not contented to find that spirits make verses like men, beating upon the filling epithet, and taking the licence of dialects and lower helps, common to human poetry; wherein, since Scaliger, who hath spared none of the Greeks, hath thought it wisdom to be silent, we shall make no excursion.

Others may wonder how the curiosity of elder times, having this opportunity of his answers, omitted natural questions; or how the old magicians discovered no more philosophy; and if they had the assistance of spirits, could rest content with the bare assertions of things, without the knowledge of their causes: whereby they had made their acts iterable by sober hands, and a standing part of philosophy. Many wise divines hold a reality in the wonders of the Egyptian magicians, and that those *magnalia* which they performed before Pharaoh were not mere delusions of sense. Rightly to understand how they made serpents out of rods: frogs, and blood of water, were worth half Porta's magic.

Hermolaus Barbarus was scarce in his wits, when, upon conference with a spirit, he would demand no other question than an explication of Aristotle's *Entelecheia.* Appion, the grammarian, that would raise the ghost of Homer to decide the controversy of his country, made a frivolous and pedantic use of necromancy, and Philostratus did as little, that called up the ghost of Achilles for a particular of the story of Troy. Smarter curiosities would have been at the great elixir, the flux and reflux of the sea, with other noble obscurities in nature; but, probably, all in vain: in matters cognoscible and framed for our disquisition, our industry must be our oracle and reason our Apollo.

Not to know things without the arch of our intellectuals, or what spirits apprehend, is the imperfection of our nature, not our knowledge, and rather inscience than ignorance in man. Revelation might render a great part of the creation easy, which now seems beyond the stretch of human indagation; and welcome no doubt from good hands might be a true almagest, and great celestial construction; a clear system of the planetical bodies of the invisible and seeming useless stars unto us; of the many suns in the eighth sphere; what they. are; what they contain; and to what more immediately those stupendous bodies are serviceable. But being not hinted in the authentic revelation of God, nor known how far their discoveries are stinted; if they should come unto us from the mouth of evil spirits, the belief thereof might be as unsafe as the enquiry.[7]

This is a copious subject; but having exceeded the bounds of a letter, I will not now pursue it further.

I am, yours, &c.

TRACT XII.[1]

A PROPHECY CONCERNING THE FUTURE STATE OF SEVERAL NATIONS, IN A LETTER WRITTEN UPON OCCASION OF AN OLD PROPHECY SENT TO THE AUTHOR FROM A FRIEND, WITH A REQUEST THAT HE WOULD CONSIDER IT.

SIR,—I take no pleasure in prophecies, so hardly intelligible, and pointing at future things from a pretended spirit of divination; of which sort this seems to be which came unto your hand, and you were pleased to send unto me. And therefore, for your easier apprehension, divertisement,

---

[7] *enquiry.*] *MS. Sloan.* adds this sentence, " and how far to credit the father of darkness and great obscurer of truth, might yet be obscure unto us." Here the *MS.* terminates.

[1] TRACT XII.] Dr. Johnson remarks, that in this tract the author plainly discovers his expectation to be the same with that entertained lately with more confidence by Dr. Berkley, "that America will be the seat of the fifth empire."

If this alludes to Berkley's favourite "Scheme for Converting the Savage Americans to Christianity," no just comparison can be drawn between it and Browne's speculations on the possible advancement of the New World in political consequence. I can, however, find nothing in

and consideration, I present you with a very different kind
of prediction: not positively or peremptorily telling you

Berkley about "America becoming the seat of the fifth *empire*," unless
it be in his "Verses on the prospect of planting arts and learning"
there ;—which he closes, after an allusion to the four *ages* (viz. of gold,
silver, brass, and iron), by anticipating the arrival of a second age of
gold, which he terms the "fifth,act in the course of empire."

Many of the more important speculations of our author, respecting the
New World, remain, after a lapse of nearly two centuries, matter of
speculation still ;—though, perhaps, to judge from the course of events
since Sir Thomas wrote, we may not unreasonably look forward to their
more complete fulfilment.

A very spirited writer in our own days has indulged himself (in the
specimen number of *The Argus* newspaper), with a similar anticipation
of events yet (if ever) to come.—By the provisions of that abomination—
in a land of liberty and literature—the STAMP ACT, it was forbidden to
relate real incidents, unless on stamped paper.—He therefore filled his
paper with imaginary events.   Some of his paragraphs relating to
"Foreign Affairs" may afford an amusing parallel to the present tract.

"Despatches have been this morning received at the Foreign Office,
from the allied Greek and Polish army before Moscow, announcing a
truce between the allies and the besieged, under the mediation of the
federative republic of France.   Negotiations for a final pacification are
to be immediately entered on, under the joint mediation of Great
Britain, France, and Austria; and it is confidently hoped that the
united efforts of these powers to put an end to the destructive five years'
war, will be finally successful, and will end in the acknowledgment, by
the Emperor Nicholas, of the independence of the crown of Warsaw, in
the person of Constantine."

"As we gather these facts from what may be considered official
sources, we give them this prominent place out of the general order of
our foreign news, on which we now enter, however, in detail, having
carefully examined all the letters of this morning's mail from our established and exclusive correspondents ; not doubting but that many will
be a little surprised at the extent and variety, to say nothing of the
novelty and interest, of the facts thus for the first time made public."

"*United Empire of America.*—Since the last census of the United
Empire of North and South America, it has been found that the popula-
tion now amounts to 180,620,000 inhabitants, including the whole
country, from Cape Horn to the Frozen Sea ; Upper and Lower Canada,
as well as Peru and Patagonia, being now incorporated in the Union.
The General Senate still holds its Parliament in the magnificent city of
Columbus, which reaches quite across the Isthmus of Darien, and has
its fortifications washed 'by the Atlantic on one side, and the Pacific on
the other, while the two provincial senates are held at Washington for
the north, and at Bolivar for the south, thus preserving the memory of
the first great discoverer, and the two greatest patriots, of this magnificent quarter of the globe."

"*Turkey.*—Since the elevation of Count Capo d'Istria to the throne what shall come to pass, yet pointing at things not without all reason or probability of their events; not built upon fatal decrees or inevitable designations, but upon conjectural foundations, whereby things wished may be promoted, and such as are feared may more probably be prevented.

The Prophecy.

WHEN New England shall trouble [2] New Spain;
When Jamaica shall be lady of the isles and the main;
When Spain shall be in America hid,
And Mexico shall prove a Madrid;
When Mahomet's ships on the Baltic shall ride,
And Turks shall labour to have ports on that side; [3]
When Africa shall no more sell out their blacks,
To make slaves and drudges to the American tracts; [4]
When Batavia the Old shall be contemn'd by the New;
When a new drove of Tartars shall China subdue;
When America shall cease to send out [5] its treasure,

of the New Greek Kingdom of the East, tranquillity reigns at Constantinople, and that city promises again to be the centre of commerce and the arts."

" *China.*—Letters from the capital of China state, that there are now not less than fifty commission-houses of Liverpool merchants established at Pekin alone, besides several agents from London establishments, and a few depôts for Birmingham and Manchester goods. The English nankeens are much preferred by the Chinese over their own, and Staffordshire porcelain is sold at nearly twice the price of the original china manufacture, in the bazaars."

" *Syria.*—Lady Hester Stanhope had left her beautiful residence between Tyre and Sidon, as well as her summer retreat amid the snows and cedars of Lebanon, and taken up her new abode in the valley of Jehoshaphat, between the Mount of Olives and Mount Zion, at Jerusalem. Her ladyship, though growing old, still retained all her benevolence and vivacity; and her house was the chief resort of all the intelligent visitors to the Jewish capital, which was increasing in splendour every day."

[2] *trouble.*]   "Terrify."—*MS. Rawl.* 58.

[3] *And Turks, &c.*]   "When we shall have ports on the Pacific side."—*MS. Rawl.* 58.

[4] *To make slaves, &c.*]   "But slaves must be had from *incognita* tracts."—*MS. Rawl.* 58.

[5] *out.*]   "Forth."—*MS. Rawl.* 58.

But employ it at home in [6] American pleasure ;
When the new world shall the old invade,
Nor count them their lords but their fellows in trade ;
When men shall almost pass to Venice by land,
Not in deep water but from sand to sand ;
When Nova Zembla shall be no stay
Unto those who pass to or from Cathay ;—
Then think strange things are come to light,
Whereof but few [7] have had a foresight.

The Exposition of the Prophecy.

When New England shall trouble New Spain ;

THAT is, when that thriving colony, which hath so much
increased in our days, and in the space of about fifty years,
that they can, as they report, raise between twenty and
thirty thousand men upon an exigency, shall in process of
time be so advanced, as to be able to send forth ships and
fleets, and to infest [8] the American Spanish ports and maritime dominions by depredations or assaults ; for which
attempts they are not like to be unprovided, as abounding
in the materials for shipping, oak and fir. And when length
of time shall so far increase that industrious people, that the
neighbouring country will not contain them, they will range
still farther, and be able, in time, to set forth great armies,
seek for new possessions, or make considerable and conjoined
migrations, according to the custom of swarming northern
nations ; wherein it is not likely that they will move northward, but toward the southern and richer countries, which
are either in the dominions or frontiers of the Spaniards :
and may not improbably erect new dominions in places not
yet thought of, and yet, for some centuries, beyond their
power or ambition.

When Jamaica shall be lady of the isles and the main ;

That is, when that advantageous island shall be well peo-

---

[6] *in.*]   "For."—*MS. Rawl.* 58.
[7] *few.*]   "Few eyes."—*MS. Rawl.* 58.
[8] *infest.*]   "Be a terror to."—*MS. Rawl.* 58.

pled, it may become so strong and potent as to overpower the neighbouring isles, and also a part of the mainland, especially the maritime parts. And already in their infancy they have given testimony of their power and courage in their bold attempts upon Campeche and Santa Martha; and in that notable attempt upon Panama on the western side of America: especially considering this island is sufficiently large to contain a numerous people, of a northern and war-like descent, addicted to martial affairs both by sea and land, and advantageously seated to infest their neighbours both of the isles and the continent, and like to be a receptacle for colonies of the same originals from Barbadoes and the neighbour isles.

> When Spain shall be in America hid,
> And Mexico shall prove a Madrid;

That is, when Spain, either by unexpected disasters or continued emissions of people into America, which have already thinned the country, shall be farther exhausted at home; or when, in process of time, their colonies shall grow by many accessions more than their originals, then Mexico may become a Madrid, and as considerable in people, wealth, and splendour: wherein that place is already so well advanced, that accounts scarce credible are given of it. And it is so advantageously seated, that, by Acapulco and other ports on the South Sea, they may maintain a communication and commerce with the Indian isles and territories, and with China and Japan, and on this side, by Porto Bello and others, hold correspondence with Europe and Africa.

> When Mahomet's ships in the Baltic shall ride,

Of this we cannot be out of all fear; for if the Turk should master Poland, he would be soon at this sea. And from the odd constitution of the Polish government, the divisions among themselves, jealousies between their kingdom and republic; vicinity of the Tartars, treachery of the Cossacks, and the method of Turkish policy, to be at peace with the emperor of Germany when he is at war with the Poles, there may be cause to fear that this may come to pass. And then he would soon endeavour to have ports upon that sea, as not wanting materials for shipping. And, having a new acquist of stout and warlike men, may be a terror unto the confiners on that sea, and to nations which now conceive themselves safe from such an enemy.[9]

When Africa shall no more sell out their blacks,[1]

That is, when African countries shall no longer make it a common trade to sell away their people to serve in the drudgery of American plantations. And that may come to pass whenever they shall be well civilized, and acquainted with arts and affairs sufficient to employ people in their countries: if also they should be converted to Christianity, but especially unto Mahometism; for then they would never sell those of their religion to be slaves unto Christians.[2]

When Batavia the Old shall be contemn'd by the New;

When the plantations of the Hollander at Batavia in the East Indies, and other places in the East Indies, shall, by their conquests and advancements, become so powerful in the Indian territories; then their original countries and states of Holland are like to be contemned by them, and obeyed only as they please. And they seem to be in a way unto it at present by their several plantations, new acquists, and enlargements: and they have lately discovered a part of the southern continent, and several places which may be serviceable unto them, whenever time shall enlarge them unto such necessities.

[9] *enemy.*] *MS. Rawl.* 58, proceeds thus;—"When we shall have ships, &c. on the Pacific side, or west side of America, which may come to pass hereafter, upon enlargement of trade or industrious navigation, when the Straits of Magellan, or more southerly passages be well known, and frequently navigated."

[1] *When Africa, &c.*] The abolition of the slave trade, and the American efforts to colonize and evangelize Africa, may be regarded as two important steps towards the fulfilment of this prophecy. One measure remains to be adopted,—the emancipation of the slaves in the West Indies:—a measure of equity—which, if not carried by legislation, will, ere long, be effected by means far less desirable.—Dec. 1832.

[2] *Christians.*] *MS. Rawl.* adds this sentence;—"then slaves must be sought for in other tracts, not yet well known, or perhaps from some parts of *terra incognita,* whenever hereafter they shall be discovered and conquered, or else when that trade shall be left, and slaves be made from captives, and from malefactors of the respective countries.

And a new drove of Tartars shall China subdue;

Which is no strange thing if we consult the histories of
China, and successive inundations made by Tartarian nations.
For when the invaders, in process of time, have degenerated
into the effeminacy and softness of the Chinese, then they
themselves have suffered a new Tartarian conquest and inundation.　And this hath happened from time beyond our
histories: for, according to their account, the famous wall
of China, built against the irruptions of the Tartars, was
begun above a hundred years before the incarnation.

When America shall cease to send forth its treasure,
But employ it at home in American pleasure;

That is, when America shall be better civilized, new poli-
cied and divided between great princes, it may come to pass
that they will no longer suffer their treasure of gold and
silver to be sent out to maintain the luxury of Europe and
other parts: but rather employ it to their own advantages,
in great exploits and undertakings, magnificent structures,
wars, or expeditions of their own.

When the new world shall the old invade,

That is, when America shall be so well peopled, civilized,
and divided into kingdoms, they are like to have so little
regard of their originals, as to acknowledge no subjection unto
them: they may also have a distinct commerce between themselves, or but independently with those of Europe,[3] and may
hostilely and piratically assault them, even as the Greek and
Roman colonies after a long time dealt with their original
countries.

When men shall almost pass to Venice by land,
Not in deep water but from sand to sand;

That is, when, in long process of time, the silt and
sands shall so choke and shallow the sea in and about it.
And this hath considerably come to pass within these fourscore years: and is like to increase from several causes,

---

[3] *Europe.*]　Here ends the *MS. Rawl.* 58.

especially by the turning of the river Brenta, as the learned
Castelli hath declared.

> When Nova Zembla shall be no stay
> Unto those who pass to or from Cathay;

That is, whenever that often sought for north-east passage[4] unto China and Japan shall be discovered; the
hinderance whereof was imputed to Nova Zembla; for this
was conceived to be an excursion of land shooting out
directly, and so far northward into the sea, that it discouraged from all navigation about it. And therefore adventurers took in at the southern part at a strait by Waygatz
next the Tartarian shore: and sailing forward they found
that sea frozen and full of ice, and so gave over the attempt.
But of late years, by the diligent enquiry of some Muscovites, a better discovery is made of these parts, and a map
or chart made of them. Thereby Nova Zembla is found to
be no island extending very far northward, but, winding
eastward, it joineth to the Tartarian continent, and so makes
a peninsula: and the sea between it which they entered at
Waygatz, is found to be but a large bay, apt to be frozen by
reason of the great river of Oby, and other fresh waters,
entering into it; whereas the main sea doth not freeze upon
the north of Zembla except near unto shores; so that if the
Muscovites were skilful navigators, they might, with less
difficulty, discover this passage unto China; but, however,
the English, Dutch, and Danes, are now like to attempt it
again.

But this is conjecture, and not prophecy; and so (I know)
you will take it. I am, Sir, &c.

[4] *north-east passage.*] These speculations may well be contrasted
with some observations of Mr. Barrow on the same subject, in his
Chronological History of Voyages into the Arctic Regions, p. 370. "Of
the three directions in which a passage has been sought for from the
Atlantic to the Pacific, that by the north-east holds out the least
encouraging hope; indeed the various unsuccessful attempts by the
English and the Dutch on the one side, and by the Russians on the
other, go far to prove the utter impracticability of a navigable passage
round the northern extremity of Asia; though the whole of this coast,
with the exception perhaps of a single point, has been navigated in
several detached parts, and at different times."

TRACT XIII.[1]

MUSÆUM CLAUSUM, OR, BIBLIOTHECA ABSCONDITA: CON-
TAINING SOME REMARKABLE BOOKS, ANTIQUITIES,
PICTURES, AND RARITIES OF SEVERAL KINDS, SCARCE
OR NEVER SEEN BY ANY MAN NOW LIVING.

SIR,—With many thanks I return that noble catalogue of books, rarities, and singularities of art and nature, which you were pleased to communicate unto me. There are many collections of this kind in Europe. And, besides the printed accounts of the Museum Aldrovandi,. Calceola-rianum, Moscardi, Wormianum; the Casa Abbellita at Loretto, and Tresor of St. Dennis, the Repository of the duke of Tuscany, that of the duke of Saxony, and that noble one of the emperor at Vienna, and many more, are of singular note. Of what in this kind I have by me I shall make no repetition, and you having already had a view thereof, I am bold to present you with the list of a collection, which I may justly say you have not seen before.

The title is as above:—*Musæum Clausum,* or *Bibliotheca Abscondita;* containing some remarkable books, antiquities, pictures, and rarities of several kinds, scarce or never seen by any man now living.

---

[1] TRACT XIII.] This curious Tract is well characterised by Mr. Crossley, as "the sport of a singular scholar. Warburton, in one of his notes on Pope, is inclined to believe that this list was imitated from Rabelais's Catalogue of the Books in the library of St. Victor; but the design of the two pieces appears so different, that this suggestion seems entitled to little regard."—*Preface to Tracts,* 18mo. Edin. 1822.

Bishop Warburton's opinion seems to me, nevertheless, highly probable. It had been suggested to me by a passage in *Religio Medici* (Part i. § 21); and seems to be in perfect consonance with Sir Thomas's character as a writer. He delighted, perhaps from the very originality of his own mind, to emulate the singularities of others. The preceding Tract was occasioned by some similar production which had been submitted to his criticism. His *Christian Morals* appears to have been written on the model of the *Book of Proverbs;* see an allusion, in his 21st section.

1. *Rare and generally unknown Books.*[2]

1. A Poem of Ovidius Naso,[3] written in the Getick language,* during his exile at Tomos; found wrapt up in wax,
at Sabaria, on the frontiers of Hungary, where there remains
a tradition that he died in his return towards Rome from
Tomos, either after his pardon or the death of Augustus.

2. The Letter of Quintus Cicero, which he wrote in
answer to that of his brother, Marcus Tullius, desiring of
him an account of Britany, wherein are described the country, state, and manners of the Britans of that age.

3. An ancient British Herbal, or description of divers
plants of this island, observed by that famous physician
Scribonius Largus, when he attended the Emperor Claudius
in his expedition into Britany.

4. An exact account of the Life and Death of Avicenna,
confirming the account of his death by taking nine clysters
together in a fit of the cholic, and not as Marius, the Italian
poet, delivereth, by being broken upon the wheel: left with
other pieces, by Benjamin Tudelensis, as he travelled from
Saragossa to Jerusalem, in the hands of Abraham Jarchi,
a famous rabbi of Lunet, near Montpellier, and found in a
vault when the walls of that city were demolished by Louis
the Thirteenth.

5. A punctual relation of Hannibal's march out of Spain
into Italy, and far more particular than that of Livy: whereabout he passed the river Rhodanus, or Rhone; at what
place he crossed the Isura, or L'Isere; when he marched
up towards the confluence of the Soane and the Rhone, or
the place where the city of Lyons was afterward built:
how wisely he decided the difference between King Brancus
and his brother; at what place he passed the Alps; what

---

* Ah pudet et scripsi Getico sermone libellum.

[2] *Books.*] The Irish antiquaries mention *public libraries* that were
before the flood: and Paul Christian Ilsker, with profounder erudition,
has given an exact catalogue of Adam's!—*D'Israeli's Cur. of Lit. 7th
edit. vol.* ii. 250.

[3] *A Poem of Ovidius, &c.*] Mr. Taylor, in his *Historic Survey of
German Poetry,* has a curious section on this poem of Ovid, whom he
considers as the earliest German poet on record.—See vol. i. § 2.

vinegar he used; and where he obtained such a quantity as to break and calcine the rocks made hot with fire.

6. A learned comment upon the Periplus of Hanno the Carthaginian; or his navigation upon the western coast of Africa, with the several places he landed at; what colonies he settled; what ships were scattered from his fleet near the equinoctial line, which were not afterward heard of, and which probably fell into the trade winds, and were carried over into the coast of America.

7. A particular Narration of that famous Expedition of the English into Barbary, in the ninety-fourth year of the Hegira, so shortly touched by Leo Africanus, whither called by the Goths, they besieged, took and burnt the city of Arzilla possessed by the Mahometans, and lately the seat of Guyland; with many other exploits, delivered at large in Arabic, lost in the ship of books and rarities which the king of Spain took from Siddy Hamet, king of Fez, whereof a great part were carried into the Escurial, and conceived to be gathered out of the relations of Hibuu Nachu, the best historian of the African affairs.

8. A Fragment of Pythæas, that ancient traveller of Marseilles; which we suspect not to be spurious; because, in the description of the northern countries, we find that passage of Pythæas mentioned by Strabo; that all the air beyond Thule is thick, condensed and gellied, looking just like sea lungs.

9. A Submarine Herbal, describing the several vegetables found on the rocks, hills, valleys, meadows, at the bottom of the sea, with many sorts of *alga, fucus, quercus, polygonum, gramen*, and others not yet described.

10. Some Manuscripts and Rarities brought from the libraries of Æthiopia, by Zaga Zaba, and afterwards transported to Rome, and scattered by the soldiers of the duke of Bourbon, when they barbarously sacked that city.

11. Some Pieces of Julius Scaliger, which he complains to have been stolen from him, sold to the bishop of Mende, in Languedoc, and afterward taken away and sold in the civil wars under the duke of Rohan.

12. A Comment of Dioscorides upon Hippocrates, procured from Constantinople by Amatus Lusitanus, and left in the hands of a Jew of Ragusa.

13. Marcus Tullius Cicero his Geography; as also a part of that magnified piece of his, *De Republica*, very little answering the great expectation of it, and short of pieces under the same name by Bodinus and Tholosanus.

14. King Mithridates his *Oneirocritica*.

Aristotle, *De Precationibus*.

Democritus, *de his quæ fiunt apud orcum, et oceani circumnavigatio.*[4]

Epicurus *De Pietate*.

A Tragedy of Thyestes, and another of Medea, writ by Diogenes the Cynick.

King Alfred, upon Aristotle *de Plantis*.

Seneca's Epistles to St. Paul.

King Solomon, *de Umbris Idæarum*, which Chicus Asculanus, in his comment upon Johannes de Sacrobosco, would make us believe he saw in the library of the duke of Bavaria.

15. *Artemidori Oneirocritici Geographia.*

Pythagoras, *de Mare Rubro*.

The works of Confucius, the famous philosopher of China, translated into Spanish.

16. Josephus, in Hebrew, written by himself.

17. The Commentaries of Sylla the Dictator.

18. A Commentary of Galen upon the Plague of Athens, described by Thucydides.

19. *Duo Cæsaris Anti-Catones*, or the two notable books writ by Julius Cæsar against Cato; mentioned by Livy, Sallustius, and Juvenal; which the cardinal of Liege told Ludovicus Vives were in an old library of that city.

Mazhapha Einok, or the prophecy of Enoch, which Ægidius Lochiensis, a learned eastern traveller, told Peireschius that he had found in an old library at Alexandria containing eight thousand volumes.

20. A collection of Hebrew Epistles, which passed between the two learned women of our age, Maria Molinea of Sedan, and Maria Schurman of Utrecht.

A wondrous collection of some writings of Ludovica Saracenica, daughter of Philibertus Saracenicus, a physician

[4] *Democritus, &c.*] *MS. Sloan.* 1847, adds the following article :— A defence of Arnoldus de Villa Nova, whom the learned Postellus conceived to be the author of *De Tribus Impostoribus.*

of Lyons, who, at eight years of age, had made a good progress in the Hebrew, Greek, and Latin tongues.

2. *Rarities in Pictures.*

1. A picture of the three remarkable steeples or towers in Europe, built purposely awry, and so as they seem falling. Torre Pisana at Pisa, Torre Garisenda in Bononia, and that other in the city of Colein.

2. A draught of all sorts of sistrums, crotaloes, cymbals, tympans, &c. in use among the ancients.

3. Large submarine pieces, well delineating the bottom of the Mediterranean Sea; the prairie or large sea-meadow upon the coast of Provence; the coral fishing; the gathering of sponges; the mountains, valleys, and deserts; the subterraneous vents and passages at the bottom of that sea.[5] Together with a lively draught of Cola Pesce, or the famous Sicilian swimmer, diving into the Voragos and broken rocks by Charybdis, to fetch up the golden cup, which Frederick, king of Sicily, had purposely thrown into that sea.

4. A moon piece, describing that notable battle between Axalla, general of Tamerlane, and Camares the Persian, fought by the light of the moon.

5. Another remarkable fight of Inghimmi, the Florentine, with the Turkish galleys, by moonlight; who being for three hours grappled with the Basha galley, concluded with a signal victory.

6. A delineation of the great fair of Almachara in Arabia, which, to avoid the great heat of the sun, is kept in the night, and by the light of the moon.

7. A snow piece, of land and trees covered with snow and ice, and mountains of ice floating in the sea, with bears, seals, foxes, and variety of rare fowls upon them.

8. An ice piece, describing the notable battle between the Jaziges and the Romans, fought upon the frozen Danubius; the Romans settling one foot upon their targets to hinder them from slipping; their fighting with the Jaziges when

---

[5] *passages, &c.*] *MS. Sloan.* 1874, reads—"the passage of Kircherus in his *Iter Submarinus* when he went down about Egypt, and rose again in the Red Sea."

they were fallen; and their advantages therein, by their art in volutation and rolling contention or wrestling, according to the description of Dion.

9. Socia, or a draught of three persons notably resembling each other. Of king Henry the Fourth of France and a miller of Languedoc; of Sforza, duke of Milan, and a soldier; of Malatesta, duke of Rimini, and Marchesinus the jester.[6]

10. A picture of the great fire which happened at Constantinople in the reign of Sultan Achmet. The janizaries in the mean time plundering the best houses, Nassa Bassa, the vizier, riding about with a cimeter in one hand and a janizary's head in the other to deter them; and the priests attempting to quench the fire, by pieces of Mahomet's shirt dipped in holy water and thrown into it.

11. A night piece of the dismal supper and strange entertain of the senators by Domitian, according to the description of Dion.

12. A vestal sinner in the cave, with a table and a candle.

13. An elephant dancing upon the ropes, with a negro dwarf upon his back.

14. Another describing the mighty stone falling from the clouds into Ægospotamos or the goats' river in Greece; which antiquity could believe that Anaxagoras was able to foretel half a year before.

15. Three noble pieces; of Vercingetorix, the Gaul, submitting his person unto Julius Cæsar; of Tigranes, king of Armenia, humbly presenting himself unto Pompey; and of Tamerlane ascending his horse from the neck of Bajazet.

16. Draughts of three passionate looks; of Thyestes when he was told at the table that he had eaten a piece of his own son; of Bajazet when he went into the iron cage; of Œdipus when he first came to know that he had killed his father and married his own mother.

17. Of the Cymbrian mother in Plutarch, who, after the overthrow by Marius hanged herself and her two children at her feet.

18. Some pieces delineating singular inhumanities in

---

[6] *jester.*] "Of Charles the First, and one Osburn, an hedger, whom I often employ."—*MS. note by Evelyn.*

tortures. The Scaphismus of the Persians. The living truncation of the Turks. The hanging sport at the feast of the Thracians. The exact method of flaying men alive, beginning between the shoulders, according to the description of Thomas Minadoi, in his Persian war. Together with the studied tortures of the French traitors at Pappa, in Hungaria: as also the wild and enormous torment invented by Tiberius, designed according unto the description of Suetonius. *Excogitaverunt inter genera cruciatûs, ut largâ meri potione per fallaciam oneratos repentè veretris deligatis fidicularum simul urinæque tormento distenderet.*

19. A picture describing how Hannibal forced his passage over the river Rhone with his elephants, baggage, and mixed army; with the army of the Gauls opposing him on the contrary shore, and Hanno passing over with his horse much above, to fall upon the rear of the Gauls.

20. A neat piece describing the sack of Fundi by the fleet and soldiers of Barbarossa, the Turkish admiral, the confusion of the people, and their flying up to the mountains, and Julia Gonzaga, the beauty of Italy, flying away with her ladies half naked on horseback over the hills.

21. A noble head of Franciscus Gonzaga, who, being imprisoned for treason, grew grey in one night, with this inscription,

O nox quam longa est quæ facit una senem.

22. A large picture describing the siege of Vienna by Solyman the Magnificent, and at the same time the siege of Florence, by the Emperor Charles the Fifth and Pope Clement the Seventh, with this subscription,

Tum vacui capitis populum Phæaca putares?

23. An exquisite piece properly delineating the first course of Metellus's pontificial supper, according to the description of Macrobius; together with a dish of *Pisces Fossiles*, garnished about with the little eels taken out of the backs of cods and perches; as also with the shell fishes found in stones about Ancona.

24. A picture of the noble entertain and feast of the duke of Chausue at the treaty of Collen, 1673, when in a very large room, with all the windows open, and at a very

large table, he sat himself, with many great persons and
ladies; next about the table stood a row of waiters, then a
row of musicians, then a row of musketeers.

25. Miltiades, who overthrew the Persians at the battle
of Marathon, and delivered Greece, looking out of a prison
grate in Athens, wherein he died, with this inscription,

> Non hoc terribiles Cymbri non Britones unquam,
> Sauromatæve truces aut immanes Agathyrsi.

26. A fair English lady drawn *Al Negro*, or in the
Ethiopian hue excelling the original white and red beauty,
with this subscription,

> Sed quandam volo nocte nigriorem.

27. Pieces and draughts in *caricatura*, of princes, car-
dinals, and famous men; wherein, among others, the painter
hath singularly hit the signatures of a lion and a fox in the
face of Pope Leo the Tenth.

28. Some pieces *a la ventura*, or rare chance pieces, either
drawn at random, and happening to be like some person, or
drawn for some, and happening to be more like another;
while the face, mistaken by the painter, proves a tolerable
picture of one he never saw.

29. A draught of famous dwarfs with this inscription,

> Nos facimus Bruti puerum nos Lagona vivum.

30. An exact and proper delineation of all sorts of dogs
upon occasion of the practice of Sultan Achmet; who in
a great plague at Constantinople, transported all the dogs
therein unto Pera, and from thence into a little island,
where they perished at last by famine: as also the manner
of the priests curing of mad dogs by burning them in the
forehead with St. Bellin's key.

31. A noble picture of Thorismund, king of the Goths,
as he was killed in his palace at Tholouse, who being let
blood by a surgeon, while he was bleeding, a stander-by took
the advantage to stab him.

32. A picture of rare fruits with this inscription,

> Credere quæ possis surrepta sororibus Afris.

33. An handsome piece of deformity expressed in a notable hard face, with this inscription,

Ora
Julius in Satyris qualia Rufus habet.

34. A noble picture of the famous duel between Paul Manessi and Caragusa the Turk, in the time of Amurath the Second; the Turkish army and that of Scanderbeg looking on; wherein Manessi slew the Turk, cut off his head, and carried away the spoils of his body.

3. *Antiquities and Rarities of several sorts.*

1. Certain ancient medals with Greek and Roman inscriptions, found about Crim Tartary : conceived to be left in those parts by the soldiers of Mithridates, when overcome by Pompey, he marched round about the north of the Euxine to come about into Thracia.

2. Some ancient ivory and copper crosses found with many others in China; conceived to have been brought and left there by the Greek soldiers who served under Tamerlane in his expedition and conquest of that country.

3. Stones of strange and illegible inscriptions, found about the great ruins which Vincent le Blanc describeth about Cephala in Africa, where he opinioned that the Hebrews raised some buildings of old, and that Solomon brought from thereabout a good part of his gold.

4. Some handsome engraveries and medals of Justinus and Justinianus, found in the custody of a Banyan in the remote parts of India, conjectured to have been left there by the friars mentioned in Procopius, who travelled those parts in the reign of Justinianus, and brought back into Europe the discovery of silk and silk worms.

5. An original medal of Petrus Aretinus, who was called *flagellum principum,* wherein he made his own figure on the obverse part with this inscription,

Il Divino Aretino.

On the reverse sitting on a throne, and at his feet ambassadors of kings and princes bringing presents unto him, with this inscription,

I Principi tributati dai Popoli tributano il Servitor loro.

6. *Mummia Tholosana ;* or the complete head and body of father Crispin, buried long ago in the vault of the Cordeliers at Tholouse, where the skins of the dead so dry and parch up without corrupting, that their persons may be known very long after, with this inscription,

Ecce iterum Crispinus.

7. A noble *quandros* or stone taken out of a vulture's head.

8. A large ostrich's egg, whereon is neatly and fully wrought that famous battle of Alcazar, in which three kings lost their lives.

9. An *Etiudros Alberti* or stone that is apt to be always moist : useful unto dry tempers, and to be held in the hand in fevers instead of crystal, eggs, lemons, cucumbers.

10. A small vial of water taken out of the stones therefore called *Enhydri,* which naturally include a little water in them, in like manner as the Ætites or Eagle stone doth another stone.

11. A neat painted and gilded cup made out of the *confiti di Tivoli,* and formed up with powdered egg-shells ; as Nero is conceived to have made his *piscina admirabilis,* singular against fluxes to drink often therein.

12. The skin of a snake bred out of the spinal marrow of a man.

13. Vegetable horns mentioned by Linschoten, which set in the ground grow up like plants about Goa.

14. An extract of the ink of cuttle fishes, reviving the old remedy of Hippocrates in hysterical passions.

15. Spirits and salt of Sargasso, made in the western ocean covered with that vegetable ; excellent against the scurvy.

16. An extract of *Cachunde* or *Liberans,* that famous and highly magnified composition in the East Indies against melancholy.

17. *Diarrhizon mirificum;* or an unparalleled composition of the most effectual and wonderful roots in nature.

R Rad. Butuæ Cuamensis.
Rad. Moniche Cuamensis.
Rad. Mongus Bazainensis.
Rad. Casei Bazainensis.
Rad. Columbæ Mozambiguensis.
Gim. Sem. Sinicæ.
Fo. Lim. lac. Tigridis dictæ.
Fo. seu Cort. Rad. Soldæ.
Rad. Ligni Solorani.
Rad. Malacensis madrededios dictæ an. ʒij.

M. fiat pulvis, qui cum gelatina Cornu Cervi Moschati Chinensis formetur in massas oviformes.

18. A transcendant perfume made of the richest odorates of both the Indies, kept in a book made of the Muschie stone of Niarienburg, with this inscription,

Deos rogato,
Totum ut te faciant, Fabulle, Nasum.

19. A *Clepselæa*, or oil hour-glass, as the ancients used those of water.

20. A ring found in a fish's belly taken about Gorro; conceived to be the same wherewith the duke of Venice had wedded the sea.

21. A neat crucifix made out of the cross bone of a frog's head.

22. A large agath, containing a various and careless figure, which looked upon by a cylinder representeth a perfect centaur. By some such advantages King Pyrrhus might find out Apollo and the nine Muses in those agaths of his whereof Pliny maketh mention.

23. *Batrachomyomachia,* or the Homerican battle between frogs and mice, neatly described upon the chisel bone of a large pike's jaw.

24. *Pyxis Pandoræ* or a box which held the *unguentum pestiferum,* which by anointing the garments of several persons begat the great and horrible plague of Milan.

25. A glass of spirits made of æthereal salt, hermetically

sealed up, kept continually in quicksilver; of so volatile a nature that it will scarce endure the light, and therefore only to be shown in winter, or by the light of a carbuncle, or bononian stone.

He who knows where all this treasure now is, is a great Apollo. I'm sure I am not he. However, I am,

Sir, yours, &c.

REPERTORIUM:

OR SOME ACCOUNT
OF THE TOMBS AND MONUMENTS IN THE CATHEDRAL CHURCH OF NORWICH.

[THE REPERTORIUM was one of the very last of Sir Thomas's productions; his especial object in drawing it up, was to preserve from oblivion, as far as possible, the monuments in the Cathedral of Norwich, many of which had been defaced during the civil wars. It pretends not to the character of a history of the antiquities of the church, and therefore neither deserves the sneer bestowed by Bagford (in his MS. collections in the British Museum, No. 8858), that "it rather feared than deserved publication;" nor justified the anxiety of the author's friends to prevent its publication, on the ground alleged by Archbishop Tenison (*Preface to Miscellany Tracts*), that "matter equal to the skill of the antiquary was not afforded." The volume containing it has afforded a favourite subject of illustration for topographers: the list of monuments was continued to the date of publication by the editor (said to have been John Hase, Esq., Richmond Herald), and very many copies exist with numerous manuscript additional continuations and notes, some of which I have availed myself of. The most valuable is that of the late Mr. John Kirkpatrick, now in the hands of Dr. Sutton, to whom I beg to offer my thanks for his kindness in affording me the use of it.]

IN the time of the late civil wars, there were about an hundred brass inscriptions stolen and taken away from grave-stones and tombs, in the cathedral church of Norwich; as I was informed by John Wright, one of the clerks, above eighty years old, and Mr. John Sandlin, one of the choir, who lived eighty-nine years; and, as I remember, told me that he was a chorister in the reign of Queen Elizabeth.

Hereby the distinct places of the burials of many noble and considerable persons become unknown; and, lest they should be quite buried in oblivion, I shall, of so many, set down only these following that are most noted to passengers, with some that have been erected since those unhappy times.

First,[1] in the body of the church, between the pillars of
the south aisle, stands a tomb, covered with a kind of touchstone; which is the monument of Miles Spencer, LL.D.,
and chancellor of Norwich, who lived unto ninety years.
The top stone was entire, but now quite broken, split, and
depressed by blows. There was more special notice taken
of this stone, because men used to try their money upon it;
and that the chapter demanded certain rents to be paid on it.
He was lord of the manor of Bowthorp and Colney, which
came unto the Yaxleys from him; also owner of Chapel in
the Field.

The next monument is that of Bishop Richard Nicks,
alias Nix, or the Blind Bishop, being quite dark many years
before he died. He sat in this see thirty-six years, in the
reigns of King Henry VII. and Henry VIII. The arches
are beautified above and beside it, where are to be seen
the arms of the see of Norwich, impaling his own, viz.,
a chevron, between three leopards' heads. The same coat
of arms is on the roof of the north and south cross aisle;
which roofs he either rebuilt or repaired. The tomb is low
and broad,[2] and 'tis said there was an altar at the bottom
of the eastern pillar. The iron-work, whereon the bell
hung, is yet visible on the side of the western pillar.

Then the tomb of Bishop John Parkhurst, with a legible
inscription on the pillar, set up by Dean Gardiner, running
thus:

> Johannes Parkhurst, Theol. Professor, Guilfordiæ natus,
> Oxoniæ educatus, temporibus Mariæ Reginæ pro
> Nitida conscientia tuenda Tigurinæ vixit exul
> Voluntarius : Postea presul factus, sanctissime
> Hanc rexit Ecclesiam per 16 an.   Obiit secundo die
> Febr. 1574.

A person he was of great esteem and veneration in the
reign of Queen Elizabeth. His coat of arms is on the
pillars, visible at the going out of the bishop's hall.[3]

---

[1] *First.*] Beginning from the west end.—*Kirkpatrick.*

[2] *broad.*] It fills up all the space between the two pillars, and on
the two sides there was a rail of iron, the going up (on the platform of
the monument) was at the west end of the south side.—*Kirkp.*

[3] *bishop's hall.*] Bishop Parkhurst " having lived much at his palace,
at Norwich, which he beautified and repaired, placing arms on the

Between the two uppermost pillars, on the same side, stood a handsome monument of Bishop Edmund Scamler, thus :

Natus apud Gressingham, in Com. Lanc. SS. Theol. Prof. apud Cantabrigienses. Obiit Ætat. 85. an. 1594 nonis Maii.

He was household chaplain to the archbishop of Canterbury, and died 1594. The monument was above a yard and a half high, with his effigies in alabaster, and all enclosed with a high iron grate. In the late times the grate was taken away, the statue broken, and the free-stone pulled down as far as the inward brick-work; which being unsightly, was afterwards taken away, and the space between the pillars left void, as it now remaineth.

In the south side of this aisle, according as the inscription denoteth, was buried George Gardiner, sometime dean.

Georgius Gardiner Barvici natus, Cantabrigiæ educatus, Primo minor Canonicus, secundo Præbendarius, tertio Archbidiaconus Nordovici, et demum 28 Nov. an. 1573, factus est Sacellanus Dominæ Reginæ, et Decanus hujus Ecclesiæ, in quo loco per 16 Annos rexit.

Somewhat higher is a monument for Dr. Edmund Porter, a learned prebendary sometime of this church.

Between two pillars of the north aisle in the body of the church, stands the monument of Sir James Hobart, attorney-general to King Henry VII. and VIII. He built Loddon church, St. Olave's bridge, and made the causeway adjoining upon the south side. On the upper part is the achievement of the Hobarts, and below are their arms; as also of the Nantons (viz. three martlets), his second lady being of that family. It is a close monument, made up of handsome stone-work: and this enclosure might have been

pillars going out of the hall, which lately were visible there, he died February 2nd, 1574, and was buried in the nave of the cathedral, on the south side, between the eighth and ninth pillars. Against the west part of the latter is a monument erected to his memory, engraved by Hulsberg, in Browne's posthumous works; but his figure in a gown and square cap, with his hands in a praying posture, and the following inscription (that in the text) was taken away in the civil war."—*Gents. Mag.* 1807. vol. 77, p. 510.

employed as an oratory.[4]   Some of the family of the Hobarts have been buried near this monument ; as Mr. James Hobart of Holt.   On the south side, two young sons and a daughter· of dean Herbert Astley, who married Barbara, daughter of John, only son of Sir John Hobart of Hales.

In the middle aisle, under a very large stone, almost over which a branch for lights hangeth,[5] was buried Sir Francis Southwell, descended from those of great name and estate in Norfolk, who formerly possessed Woodrising.

Under a fair stone, by Bishop Parkhurst's tomb, was buried Dr. Masters, chancellor.

> Gul. Maister, LL. Doctor Curiæ Cons. Epatus Norwicen.
> Officialis principalis.   Obiit 2 Feb. 1589.

At the upper end of the middle aisle, under a large stone, was buried Bishop Walter de Hart, *alias* le Hart,[6] or Lyghard.   He was bishop twenty-six years, in the times of Henry VI. and Edward IV.   He built the transverse stone partition or rood loft, on which the great crucifix was placed, beautified the roof of the body of the church, and paved it. Towards the north side of the partition wall are his arms, the bull, and towards the south side, a hart in water, as a rebus of his name, Walter Hart.   Upon the door, under the rood loft, was a plate of brass, containing those verses :

> Hic jacet absconsus sub marmore presul honestus.
> Anno milleno C quater cum septuageno
> Annexis binis instabat ei prope finis.
> Septima cum decima lux Maij sit numerata
> Ipsius est anima de corpore tunc separata.

---

[4] *oratory.*]   The enclosure to this monument was of stone-work, in the form of windows, having an entrance on the north side, the south side was surmounted by the arms which are now placed against the inside the pillar opposite the monument ; the tomb was also visible on this side, having an arch or canopy over, the upright wall of which was covered with stars, on the top the arms of Hobart, *sab.* a star of eight points, *or* between two flaunches, *erm.*, in the star a crescent for difference, and on the dexter side of the shield a bull (the crest of Hobart) as one supporter, and on the sinister, a martlet from the Nanton's coat as the other supporter.

[5] *hangeth.*]   This branch must have hung opposite Bishop Nix's monument, and directly in front of the ancient stone pulpit, the remains of which are still visible against the pillar, at the east end of the said monument.

[6] *le Hart.*]   Spelt Hert, or de Hert, in *MS. Sloan.* 1885.

Between this partition[7] and the choir on the north side, is the monument of Dame Elizabeth Calthorpe, wife of Sir Francis Calthorpe, and afterwards wife of John Cole-pepper,[8] Esq.

In the same partition, behind the dean's stall, was buried John Crofts, lately dean, son of Sir Henry Crofts, of Suffolk, and brother to the Lord William Crofts. He was some time fellow of All-Souls College, in Oxford, and the first dean after the restoration of his majesty King Charles II., whose predecessor, Dr. John Hassal, who was dean many years, was not buried in this church, but in that of Creek. He was of New College, in Oxford, and chaplain to the Lady Elizabeth, queen of Bohemia, who obtained this deanery for him.

On the south side of the choir, between two pillars, stands the monument of Bishop James Goldwell, dean of Salisbury, and secretary to King Edward IV., who sat in this see twenty-five years. His effigies is in stone, with a lion at his feet, which was his arms, as appears on his coat above the tomb, on the choir side. His arms are also to be seen in the sixth escutcheon, in the west side over the choir; as also in St. Andrew's church, at the deanery, in a window; at Trowse, Newton Hall, and at Charta-magna, in Kent, the place of his nativity; where he also built or repaired the chapel. He is said to have much repaired the east end of this church; did many good works, lived in great esteem, and died ann. 1498 or 1499.

Next above Bishop Goldwell, where the iron grates yet stand, Bishop John Wakering is said to have been buried. He was bishop in the reign of King Henry V., and was sent to the council of Constance: he is said also to have built the cloister in the bishop's palace, which led into it from the church door, which was covered with a handsome roof, before the late civil war. Also reported to have built the chapter-house, which being ruinous is now demolished, and the decayed parts above and about it handsomely repaired or new built. The arms of the see impaling his

[7] *partition.*] This partition was taken away in 1806 (when the interior of the church was repaired), and the monument removed to the north aisle of the choir near the confessional.

[8] *Colepepper.*] Cullpeper on the monument.

own coat, the three *Fleur des Lys*, are yet visible upon the wall by the door.[9] He lived in great reputation, and died 1426, and is said to have been buried before St. George's altar.

On the north side of the choir, between the two arches, next to Queen Elizabeth's seat, were buried[1] Sir Thomas Erpingham, and his wives the Lady Joan, &c., whose pictures were in the painted glass windows, next unto this place, with the arms of the Erpinghams. The insides of both the pillars were painted in red colours, with divers figures and inscriptions, from the top almost to the bottom, which are now washed out by the late whiting of the pillars. He was a knight of the garter in the time of Henry IV. and some part of Henry V., and I find his name in the list of the lord wardens of the Cinque Ports. He is said to have built the Black Friars church, or steeple, or both, now called New Hall Steeple. His arms are often on the steeple, which are an escutcheon within an *orle of martlets*, and also upon the outside of the gate,[2] next the school-house. There was a long brass inscription about the tomb-stone, which was torn away in the late times, and the name of Erpingham only remaining, *Johannes Dominus de Erpingham, Miles*, was buried in the parish church of Erpingham, as the inscription still declareth.

In the north aisle, near to the door, leading towards Jesus' chapel, was buried Sir William Denny, recorder of Norwich, and one of the counsellors at law to King Charles I.

In Jesus' chapel stands a large tomb (which is said to have been translated from our Lady's chapel, when that grew

[9] *The arms, &c.*] By him within the rayles under two great marble stones, lye two of the family of the Bulleyns, of which family Queen Elizabeth was.—*MS. note in Bodleian copy.*

[1] *were buried.*] In removing the pavement of the north aisle (near this place) to make a vault for the remains of Dr. Goodall, in 1781, a tombstone, thought to be that of Sir Thomas Erpingham, was found, with its face downward; it is of purbeck marble, ridge formed, and having a Calvary cross on the ridge; the rivets of a brass inscription on the edge of the stone are still visible: it remains near the place where it was found.

[2] *gate.*] In a niche of the wall above the gates is an armed knight on his knees.—*MS. note in a copy in Bib. Bodl.*

ruinous, and was taken down), whereof the brass inscription about it is taken away; but old Mr. Spendlow, who was a prebendary fifty years, and Mr. Sandlin, used to say, that it was the tombstone of the Windhams; and, in all probability, might have belonged to Sir Thomas Windham, one of King Henry VIII.'s counsellors, of his guard, and vice-admiral; for I find that there hath been such an inscription upon the tomb of a Windham in this church.[3]

> Orate pro anima Thome Windham, militis, Elianore, et Domine Elizabethe, uxorum ejus, &c. qui quidem Thomas fuit unus consilia-riorum
> Regis Henrici VIII. et unus militum pro corpore, ejusdem Domini, nec non Vice Admirallus.

And according to the number of the three persons in the inscription,[4] there are three figures upon the tomb.

On the north wall of Jesus' chapel there is a legible brass inscription[5] in Latin verses; and at the last line *Pater Noster*. This was the monument of *Randulfus Pulvertoft, custos caronelle.* Above the inscription was his coat of arms, viz. six ears of wheat with a border of cinque-foils; but now washed out, since the wall was whitened.

At the entrance of St. Luke's chapel, on the left hand, is

---

[3] *In Jesus' chapel, &c.*] " That Sir Thomas Windham, knight, by his will, dated 22nd October, 13 H. 8. 1521, willed that his body be buried in the middle of the chapel of the blessed virgin, within the scite of the monastery of the holy Trinity of the city of Norwich ; where he would have a tomb for him, with his arms and badges, and his two wives, if his wife Elizabeth will be there buried, &c.—*See his will among my papers of Felbryge.*"—*MS. Note in Bodl. copy.*

[4] *inscription.*] Weever saith that this (in his time maimed) inscription was upon a goodly tomb in the Chapter-house.—*Kirkp. MS.*

[5] *brass inscription.*] Inserted from Burton's Account of the Free-school, p. 22.

> En morior, prodest michi quid prius hoc quod habebam,
> Preterit omne quod est, eo nudus, sic veniebam,
> Sola michi requies manet, hic non sunt mea plura,
> Antea nulla quies, modo pro nichilo michi cura,
> Sed fleo, dum fueram modicum vel nil bene gessi,
> Crimina multa feram fuerant mea quando recessi,
> Pulvertoft Radulphus eram Custos Caronelle,
> Christe Deus pro me passus mea crimina pelle,
> Sic exoro petas qui mea scripta legas, Pater noster

an arched monument, said to belong to one of the family of the Bosviles or Boswill, sometime prior of the convent. At the east end of the monument are the arms of the church (the cross) and on the west end another (three bolt arrows), which is supposed to be his paternal coat. The same coat is to be seen in the sixth escutcheon of the south side, under the belfry. Some inscriptions upon this monument were washed out when the church was lately whitened; as among the rest, *O morieris! O morieris! O morieris!* The three bolts are the known arms of the Bosomes,[6] an ancient family in Norfolk; but whether of the Bosviles, or no, I am uncertain.

Next unto it is the monument of Richard Brome, Esq. whose arms thereon are ermines; and for the crest, a bunch or branch of broom with golden flowers. This might be Richard Brome, Esq. whose daughter married the heir of the Yaxleys of Yaxley, in the time of Henry VII. And one of the same name founded a chapel in the field in Norwich.

There are also in St. Luke's chapel, amongst the seats on the south side, two substantial marble and crossed tombs, very ancient, said to be two priors of this convent.[7]

At the entrance into the cloister, by the upper door on the right hand, next the stairs, was a handsome monument on the wall, which was pulled down in the late times, and a void place still remaineth. Upon this stone were the figures of two persons in a praying posture, on their knees. I was told by Mr. Sandlin, that it was said to be the monument for one of the Bigots, who built or beautified that arch by it, which leadeth into the church.

In the choir towards the high altar, and below the ascents, there is an old tomb, which hath been generally said to have been the monument of Bishop William Herbert, founder of the church, and commonly known by the name of the founder's tomb. This was above an ell high; but when the pulpit, in the late confusion, was placed at the pillar, where Bishop Overall's monument now is, and the aldermen's seats were at the east end, and the mayor's seat in the middle at

---

[6] *Bosomes.*] Bozouns.—*MS. note in Bodl. copy.*

[7] *There are also, &c.*] Taken away about 1738 to make room for seats. —*MS. note in Bodl. copy.*

the high altar, the height of the tomb being a hinderance unto the people, it was taken down to such a lowness as it now remains in.[8]   He was born at Oxford,[9] in good favour with King William Rufus, and King Henry I. removed the episcopal see from Thetford to Norwich, built the priory for sixty monks, the cathedral church, the bishop's palace, the church of St. Leonard, whose ruins still remain upon the brow of Mousehold hill; the church of St. Nicholas at Yarmouth, of St. Margaret at Lynn, of St. Mary at Elham, and instituted the Cluniack monks at Thetford.   Malmsbury saith he was *vir pecuniosus*, which his great works declare, and had always this good saying of St. Hierom in his mouth, *erravimus juvenes, emendemus senes.*

Many bishops of old might be buried about, or not far from the founder, as William Turbus, a Norman, the third bishop of Norwich, and John of Oxford the fourth, accounted among the learned man of his time, who built Trinity church in Ipswich, and died in the reign of King John ; and it is delivered, that these two bishops were buried near to Bishop Herbert, the founder.

In the same row, not far off, was buried Bishop Henry le Spencer, as lost brass inscriptions have declared.   And Mr. Sandlin told me, that he had seen an inscription on a gravestone thereabouts, with the name of Henricus de, or le Spencer :[1] he came young unto the see, and sat longer in it than any before or after him : but his time might have been shorter, if he had not escaped in the fray at Lennam[2] (a town of which he was lord), where forcing the magistrate's

---

[8] *as it now remains in.*]   The present tomb was built by the dean and prebendaries in 1682, and the Latin inscription thereon is said to have been composed by the learned Dr. Prideaux, who was at that time one of the prebendaries.—See *Blomefield's History of Norwich,* part i. p. 471.

[9] *Oxford.*]   The present inscription says, " qui *Oximi* in *Normania* natus ;" this is understood to allude to Hiems near Caen.

[1] *Spencer.*]   The stoute and warlike Henry Spencer, Bishop of Norwich, who supprest by his courriage and valour, that dangerous rebellion ; and about North Walsham, overthrew Litster the captaine, hath (as it is to be seene upon his monument in the body of the quire of Christchurch, in Norwich) over his proper coate of Spencer, upon an helmet, his episcopall miter, and upon that Michael, the archangell, with a drawn sword.—*Peachem's Compleat Gent.* p. 164.   Ed. 1634.

[2] *Lennam.*]   Lynn.—See *Blomefield's Norwich,* part i. p. 516.

tipstaff to be carried before him, the people with staves, stones, and arrows, wounded and put his servants to flight. He was also wounded, and left alone, as John Fox hath set it down out of the chronicle of St. Albans.

In the same row, of late times, was buried Bishop Richard Montague, as the inscription, *Depostum Montacutii Episcopi,* doth declare.

For his eminent knowledge in the Greek language, he was much countenanced by Sir Henry Savile, provost of Eaton college, and settled in a fellowship thereof: afterwards made bishop of Chichester; thence translated unto Norwich, where he lived about three years. He came unto Norwich with the evil effects of a quartan ague, which he had about a year before, and which accompanied him to his grave; yet he studied and wrote very much, had an excellent library of books, and heaps of papers, fairly written with his own hand, concerning the ecclesiastical history. His books were sent to London; and, as it was said, his papers against Baronius and others transmitted to Rome; from whence they were never returned.

On the other side was buried Bishop John Overall, fellow of Trinity College in Cambridge, master of Catherine Hall, regius professor, and dean of St. Paul's: and had the honour to be nominated one of the first governors of Sutton hospital, by the founder himself, a person highly reverenced and beloved; who being buried without any inscription, had a monument lately erected for him by Dr. Cosin, Lord Bishop of Durham, upon the next pillar.

Under the large sandy-coloured stone was buried Bishop Richard Corbet, a person of singular wit, and an eloquent preacher, who lived bishop of this see but three years, being before dean of Christ-church, then bishop of Oxford. The inscription is as follows :—

> Richardus Corbet Theologiæ Doctor,
> Ecclesiæ Cathedralis Christi Oxoniensis
> Primum alumnus, inde Decanus, exinde
> Episcopus, illinc huc translatus, et
> Hinc in cœlum, Jul. 28, Ann. 1635.

The arms on it, are the see of Norwich, impaling, *or,* a raven *sab.* Corbet.

Towards the upper end of the choir, and on the south side, under a fair large stone, was interred Sir William Boleyn, or Bullen, great grandfather to Queen Elizabeth. The inscription hath been long lost, which was this:—

Hic jacet corpus Willelmi Boleyn, militis,
Qui obiit x Octobris, Ann. Dom. MCCCCCV.

And I find in a good manuscript of the ancient gentry of Norfolk and Suffolk these words. Sir William Boleyn, heir unto Sir Thomas Boleyn, who married Margaret, daughter and heir of Thomas Butler, Earl of Ormond, died in the year 1505, and was buried on the south side of the chancel of Christ-church in Norwich. And surely the arms of few families have been more often found in any church, than those of the Boleyns, on the walls, and in the windows of the east part of this church. Many others of this noble family were buried in Blickling church.

Many other bishops might be buried in this church, as we find it so asserted by some historical accounts; but no history or tradition remaining of the place of their interment, in vain we endeavour to design and point out the same.

As of Bishop Johannes de Gray, who, as it is delivered, was interred in this church, was a favourite of King John, and sent by him to the pope: he was also lord deputy of Ireland, and a person of great reputation, and built Gaywood Hall, by Lynn.

As also of Bishop Roger Skerewyng [or de Skerning], in whose time happened that bloody contention between the monks and citizens, begun at a fair kept[3] before the gate; when the church was fired: to compose which, King Henry III. came to Norwich, and William de Brunham, prior, was much to blame.—See *Holingshed, &c.*

Or of Bishop William Middleton, who succeeded him, and was buried in this church; in whose time the church that was burnt while Skerewyng sat was repaired and consecrated, in the presence of King Edward I.

Or of Bishop John Salmon, sometime lord chancellor of England, who died 1325, and was here interred; his works

___

[3] *fair kept.*] This occurred on the 9th of August, 1272.—See *Blomefield's Norwich*, part i. p. 53.

were noble. He built the great hall in the bishop's palace ; the bishop's long chapel on the east side of the palace, which was no ordinary fabric ; and a strong handsome chapel at the west end of the church,[4] and appointed four priests for the daily service therein. Unto which great works he was the better enabled by obtaining a grant of the first fruits from Pope Clement.

Or of Bishop Thomas Percy, brother to the earl of Northumberland, in the reign of Richard II. who gave unto a chantry the lands about Carlton, Kimberly, and Wicklewood ; in whose time the steeple and belfry were blown down, and rebuilt by him and a contribution from the clergy.

Or of Bishop Anthony de Beck, a person of an unquiet spirit, very much hated, and poisoned by his servants.

Or likewise of Bishop Thomas Browne, who, being bishop of Rochester, was chosen bishop of Norwich, while he was at the council of Basil, in the reign of King Henry VI., was a strenuous assertor of the rights of the church against the citizens.

Or of Bishop William Rugge,[5] in whose last year happened Kett's rebellion, in the reign of Edward VI. I find his name Guil. Norwicensis among the bishops who subscribed unto a declaration against the pope's supremacy, in the time of Henry VIII.

Or of Bishop John Hopton, who was bishop in the time of Queen Mary, and died the same year with her. He is mentioned, together with his chancellor, Dunning, by John Fox, in his *Martyrology.*

Or lastly, of Bishop William Redman, of Trinity College, in Cambridge, who was archdeacon of Canterbury. His arms are upon a board on the north side of the choir, near to the pulpit.

Of the four bishops in Queen Elizabeth's reign, Parkhurst, Freake, Scamler, and Redman, Sir John Harrington, in his *History of the Bishops in her Time,* writeth thus :—For the four bishops in the queen's days, they liv'd as bishops should do, and were not warriours, like Bishop Spencer, their predecessor.

[4] *a strong handsome chapel at the west end of the church.*] St. John's chapel, now the Free-school.

[5] *Rugge.*] He lies in the midst of the choir.—*MS. in Bodl. copy.*

Some bishops were buried neither in the body of the church nor in the choir,￼but in our Lady's chapel, at the east end of the church, built by Bishop Walter de Suthfield,[6] (in the reign of Henry III.) wherein he was buried, and miracles said to be wrought at his tomb, he being a person of great charity and piety.

Wherein also was buried Bishop Simeon de Wanton, vel Walton, and Bishop Alexander, who had been prior of the convent; and also, as some think, Bishop Roger Skerewyng, and probably other bishops and persons of quality, whose tombs and monuments we now in vain enquire after in the church.

This was a handsome chapel; and there was a fair entrance into it out of the church, of a considerable height also, as may be seen by the outside, where it adjoined unto the wall of the church. But, being ruinous, it was, as I have heard, demolished in the time of Dean Gardiner; but what became of the tombs, monuments, and grave-stones, we have no account. In this chapel the bishop's consistory, or court, might be kept in old time: for we find in Fox's *Martyrology*, that divers persons accused of heresy were examined by the bishop, or his chancellor, in St. Mary's chapel. This famous bishop, Walter de Suthfield, who built this chapel, is also said to have built the hospital[7] not far off.

Again, divers bishops sat in this see, who left not their bones in this church; for some died not here, but at distant places; some were translated to other bishopricks; and some, though they lived and died here, were not buried in this church.

Some died at distant places, as Bishop Richard Courtney, chancellor of Oxford, and in great favour with King Henry V. by whom he was sent unto the king of France, to challenge his right unto that crown; but he dying in France, his body was brought into England, and interred in Westminster-abbey, among the kings.

Bishop William Bateman, LL.D., born in Norwich, who founded Trinity-hall, in Cambridge, and persuaded Gonvil to

---

[6] *Suthfield.*] Or Suffield.—*S. Wd.* He built the hospital of St. Giles in Norwich. P.L.N.—*MS. note by Le Neve, in Bodl. copy.*

[7] *hospital.*] Saint Giles's Hospital, Bishopsgate-street.

build Gonvil-college, died at Avignon, in France, being sent by the king to Rome,[8] and was buried in that city.

Bishop William Ayermin died near London.

Bishop Thomas Thirlby, doctor of law, died in Archbishop Matthew Parker's house, and was buried at Lambeth, with this inscription:—Hic jacet Thomas Thirlby, olim Episcopus Eliensis, qui obüt 26 die Augusti, Anno Domini 1570.

Bishop Thomas Jann, who was prior of Ely, died at Folkston-abbey, near Dover, in Kent.[9]

Some were translated unto other bishopricks; as Bishop William Ralegh was removed unto Winchester, by King Henry III.

Bishop Ralph de Walpole was translated to Ely, in the time of Edward I.; he is said to have begun the building of the cloister, which is esteemed the fairest in England.

Bishop William Alnwick built the church gates at the west end of the church, and the great window, and was translated to Lincoln, in the reign of Henry VI.

And of later time, Bishop Edmund Freake, who succeeded Bishop Parkhurst, was removed unto Worcester, and there lieth entombed.

Bishop Samuel Harsnet, master of Pembroke-hall, in Cambridge, and bishop of Chichester, was thence translated to York.

Bishop Francis White, almoner unto the king, formerly bishop of Carlisle, translated unto Ely.

Bishop Matthew Wren, dean of the chapel, translated also to Ely, and was not buried here.

Bishop John Jegon, who died 1617, was buried at Aylsham, near Norwich. He was master of Bennet-college, and dean of Norwich, whose arms, two chevrons with an eagle on a canton, are yet to be seen on the west side of the bishop's throne. ·

My honoured friend, Bishop Joseph Hall, dean of Worcester, and bishop of Exon, translated to Norwich, was buried

[8] *to Rome.*] Kirkpatrick, in his copy, has struck out these words, and substituted "thither," adding the following explanatory observation, "viz. to Pope Clement VI., who lived at Avignon."

[9] *Kent.*] In *Blomefield's Norwich*, part i. p. 543, it is stated, that what is here said of his having been prior of Ely, and in *Le Neve's Fasti* of his dying at Folkston-abbey, is a mistake.

at Heigham, near Norwich, where he hath a monument. When the revenues of the church were alienated, he retired unto that suburban parish, and there ended his days, being above eighty years of age. A person of singular humility, patience, and piety: his own works are the best monument and character of himself, which was also very lively drawn in his excellent funeral sermon, preached by my learned and faithful old friend, John Whitefoot, rector of Heigham, a very deserving clerk of the convocation of Norfolk. His arms, in the Register Office of Norwich, are sable, three talbots' heads erased, argent.

My honoured friend also, Bishop Edward Reynolds, was not buried in the church, but in the bishop's chapel; which was built by himself. He was born at Southampton, brought up at Merton-college, in Oxford, and the first bishop of Norwich after the king's restoration: a person much of the temper of his predecessor, Dr. Joseph Hall, of singular affability, meekness, and humility; of great learning; a frequent preacher, and constant resident. He sat in this see about seventeen years; and, though buried in his private chapel, yet his funeral sermon was preached in the cathedral, by Mr. Benedict Rively, now minister of St. Andrew's. He was succeeded by Dr. Anthony Sparrow, our worthy and honoured diocesan.

It is thought that some bishops were buried in the old bishop's chapel, said to be built by Bishop John Salmon [demolished in the time of the late war], for therein were many grave-stones, and some plain monuments. This old chapel was higher, broader, and much larger than the said new chapel built by Bishop Reynolds; but being covered with lead, the lead was sold, and taken away in the late rebellious times; and, the fabric growing ruinous and useless, it was taken down, and some of the stones made use of in the building of the new chapel.

Now, whereas there have been so many noble and ancient families in these parts, yet we find not more of them to have been buried in this, the mother church. It may be considered, that no small numbers of them were interred in the churches and chapels of the monasteries and religious houses of this city, especially in three thereof; the Austin-friars, the Black-friars, the Carmelite, or White-friars; for therein were

buried many persons of both sexes, of great and good fami-
lies, whereof there are few or no memorials in the cathedral.
And in the best preserved registers of such interments of
old, from monuments and inscriptions, we find the names of
men and women of many ancient families; as of Ufford,
Hastings, Radcliffe, Morley, Windham, Geney, Clifton,
Pigot, Hengrave, Garney, Howell, Ferris, Bacon, Boys,
Wichingham, Soterley; of Falstolph, Ingham, Felbrigge,
Talbot, Harsick, Pagrave, Berney, Woodhouse, Howldich; of
Argenton, Somerton, Gros, Benhall, Banyard, Paston, Crun-
thorpe, Withe, Colet, Gerbrigge, Berry, Calthorpe, Everard,
Hetherset, Wachesham. All lords, knights, and esquires,
with divers others. Beside the great and noble families of
the Bigots, Mowbrays, Howards, were the most part interred
at Thetford, in the religious houses of which they were
founders or benefactors. The Mortimers were buried at
Attleburgh; the Aubeneys at Wymondham, in the priory
or abbey founded by them. And Camden says, that a
great part of the nobility and gentry of those parts were
buried at Pentney abbey. Many others were buried dispersedly in churches or religious houses, founded or endowed
by themselves; and, therefore, it is the less to be wondered
at, that so many great and considerable persons of this
country were not interred in this church.

There are twenty-four escutcheons, viz., six on a side on
the inside of the steeple over the choir, with several coats of
arms, most whereof are memorials of things, persons, and
families, well-wishers, patrons, benefactors, or such as were
in special veneration, honour, and respect, from the church.
As particularly the arms of England, of Edward the Con-
fessor; an hieroglyphical escutcheon of the Trinity, unto
which this church was dedicated. Three cups within a
wreath of thorns, the arms of Ely, the arms of the see of
Canterbury impaling the coat of the famous and magnified
John Morton, archbishop of Canterbury, who was bishop of
Ely before; of Bishop James Goldwell, that honoured bishop
of Norwich. The three lions of England, St. George's
cross, the arms of the church impaled with Prior Bosvile's
coat, the arms of the church impaled with the private coats
of three priors, the arms of the city of Norwich.

There are here likewise the coats of some great and worthy families; as of Vere, Stanley, De la Pole, Wingfield,.
Heydon, Townshend, Bedingfield, Bruce, Clere; which being
little taken notice of, and time being still like to obscure,
and make them past knowledge, I would not omit to have a
draught thereof set down, which I keep by me.

There are also many coats of arms on the walls, and in
the windows of the east end of the church; but none so:
often as those of the Boleyns, viz. in a field argent, a chevron,
gules, between three bulls' heads couped, sable, armed, or;
whereof some are quartered with the arms of noble families.
As also about the church, the arms of Hastings, De la Pole,
Heydon, Stapleton, Windham, Wichingham, Clifton, Heveningham, Bokenham, Inglos.

In the north window of Jesus' chapel are the arms of
Radcliff and Cecil; and in the east window of the same ·
chapel the coats of Branch and of Beale.

There are several escutcheon boards fastened to the upper
seats of the choir; upon the three lowest on the south side
are the arms of Bishop Jegon, of the Pastous, and of the ·
Hobarts; and in one above the arms of the Howards. On
the board on the north side are the arms of Bishop Redmayn;
and of the Howards.

Upon the outside of the gate, next to the school, are the
escutcheons and arms of Erpingham, who built the gates
[also the coats of Clopton and Walton], being an orle of
martlets; or such families who married with the Erpinghams.
The word *pœna* [2] often upon the gates, shows it to have
been built upon penance.

. At the west end of the church are chiefly observable the
figure of King William Rufus, or King Henry I., and a
bishop on his knees receiving the charter from him: or else
of King Henry VI., in whose reign this gate and fair window
were built. Also the maimed statues of bishops, whose
copes are garnished and charged with a cross moline: and at

. [2] *pœna*.] This word is not pœna but **peñk**. the old way of writing·
think (this was first suggested by the late Dr. Sayers), it appears to have
been intended for his motto ;. as was also the word **Bewar** on a brass
label at the corner of his tombstone.—See *Blomefield's Norwich*, part ii. ·
p. 39, and *Britton's Norwich. Cathedral.*

their feet; escutcheons, with the arms of the church: and also escutcheons with crosses molines. That these, or some of them, were the statues of Bishop William Alnwick, seems more than probable; for he built the three gates, and the great window[3] at the west end of the church; and where the arms of the see are in a roundele, are these words— *Orate pro anima Domini Willelmi Alnwyk.*——Also in another escutcheon, charged with a cross moline, there is the same motto round about it.

Upon the wooden door on the outside, there are also the three mitres, which are the arms of the see upon one leaf, and a cross moline on the other.

Upon the outside of the end of the north cross aisle, there is a statue of an old person; which, being formerly covered and obscured by plaster and mortar over it, was discovered upon the late reparation or whitening of that end of the aisle. This may probably be the statue of Bishop Richard Nicks,[4] or the Blind Bishop; for he built the aisle, or that part thereof, and also the roof, where his arms are to be seen, a chevron between three leopards' heads, gules.

The roof of the church is noble and adorned with figures. In the roof of the body of the church there are no coats of arms, but representations from scripture story, as the story of Pharaoh; of Sampson towards the east end; figures of the last supper, and of our Saviour on the cross, towards the west end;[5] besides others of foliage and the like ornamental figures.

The north wall of the cloister was handsomely beautified, with the arms of some of the nobility in their proper colours,

[3] *the great window.*] The great west window has been found on a late survey to have been put in like a frame into the west front, and being ready to fall out was fastened with irons; Dean Bullock, about 1748, chipt off all the outer ornament of the west front and new cased it.— *MS. note probably by Ives.*

[4] *Nicks.*] Bishop Nix only re-built the roof, the effigy is of Herbert, the founder, it being exactly in the same manner as that on his seal.— *Blomefield's History of Norwich*, part i. p. 546.

[5] *end.*] This part was done in the time of, if not by Bishop Lyhert, as appears by his arms and his rebus alternately upon the pillars on each side, where the foundations of the vaulted roof begin upon the old work.—*Kirkpatrick's MS. notes.*

with their crests, mantlings, supporters, and the whole achievement quartered with the several coats of their matches, drawn very large from the upper part of the wall, and took up about half of the wall. They are eleven in number, particularly these: 1. An empty escutcheon. 2. The achievement of Howard, duke of Norfolk. 3. Of Clinton. 4. Russel. 5. Cheyney. 6. The queen's achievement. 7. Hastings. 8. Dudley. 9. Cecil. 10. Carey. 11. Hatton.

They were made soon after Queen Elizabeth came to Norwich, ann. 1758, where she remained a week, and lodged at the bishop's palace, in the time of Bishop Freake, attended by many of the nobility, and particularly by those whose arms are here set down.

They made a very handsome show, especially at that time, when the cloister windows were painted unto the cross bars. The figures of those coats, in their distinguishable and discernable colours, are not beyond my remembrance. But in the late times, when the lead was faulty and the stone work decayed, the rain falling upon the wall washed them away.

The pavement also of the cloister on the same side was broken and the stones taken away, a floor of dust remaining: but that side is now handsomely paved by the beneficence of my worthy friend William Burleigh, Esq.

At the stone cistern[6] in the cloister, there is yet perceivable a lion rampant, argent, in a field sable, which coat is now quartered in the arms of the Howards.

In the painted glass in the cloister, which hath been above the cross bars, there are several coats. And I find by an account taken thereof and set down in their proper colours, that here were these following, viz. the arms of Morley, Shelton, Scales, Erpingham, Gournay, Mowbray, Savage, now Rivers, three coats of Thorpes and one of a lion rampant, gules in a field or, not well known to what family it belongeth.

Between the lately demolished chapter-house and St. Luke's chapel, there is an handsome chapel, wherein the consistory or bishop's court is kept, with a noble gilded roof. This goeth under no name, but may well be called Beauchampe's

---

[6] cistern.] The lavatories at the south-west angle.

chapel or the chapel of our Lady and All Saints,. as being
built by William Beauchampe, according to this inscription[7]
—*In honore Beate Marie Virginis, et omnium sanctorum*
Willelmus Beauchampe *capellam hanc ordinavit, et ex propriis*
sumptibus construxit. This inscription is in old letters on
the outside of the wall, at the south side of the chapel, and
almost obliterated. He was buried under an arch in the
wall which was richly gilded ; and some part of the gilding
is yet to be perceived, though obscured and blinded by the
bench on the inside. I have heard there is a vault below
gilded like the roof of the chapel. The founder of this
chapel, William Beauchampe or de Bello Campo, might be
one of the Beauchampes who were lords of Abergavenny ;
for William lord Abergavenny had lands and manors in
this country. And in the register of institutions it is to be
seen, that William Beauchampe, lord of Abergavenny, was
lord patron of Berg-cum-Apton, five miles distant from
Norwich, and presented clerks to that living, 1406, and
afterward : so that if he lived a few years after, he might be
buried in the latter end of Henry IV., or in the reign of
Henry V., or in the beginning of Henry VI. Where to
find Heydon's chapel[8] is more obscure, if not altogether
unknown ; for such a place there was, and known by the
name of Heydon's chapel, as I find in a manuscript concerning some ancient families of Norfolk, in these words :—
John Heydon of Baconsthorpe, Esq., died in the reign of
Edward IV., ann. 1479. *He built a chapel on the south side*
of the cathedral church of Norwich, where he was buried.
He was in great favour with King Henry VI.; and took part
with the house of Lancaster against that of York.
     Henry Heydon, Knight, his heir, built the church of
Salthouse, and made the causey between Thursford and

[7] *inscription.*] Kirkpatrick, in his MS. notes to his copy of the
Posthumous Works (now in the possession of Dr. Sutton), says, "that
it was certainly William Bauchun who was the founder of this chapel
and gaue lands to it, in the latter end of King Edward the Second's
time, as out of the records of the church may be collected. The said
William Bauchun being often mentioned therein, but Beauchamp never.",
It also appears, from Kirkpatrick's sketch of the inscription, that there
was not sufficient space on the stone for more than "Bauchun."
     [8] *Heydon's chapel.*] This chapel is placed on the west side of Beau-
champe's or Bauchun's chapel.—See plan in *Blomefield's Norwich.*

Walsingham, at his own charge. He died in the time of Henry VII., and was buried in Heydon's chapel, joining to the cathedral aforesaid. The arms of the Heydons are argent, and gules a cross engrailed counter-changed, make the third escutcheon in the north-row over the choir, and are in several places in the glass windows, especially on the south side, and once in the deanery.

There was a chapel[9] to the south side of the gaol or prison, into which there is one door out of the entry of the cloister; and there was another out of the cloister itself, which is now made up of brick work: the stone work which remaineth on the inside is strong and handsome. This seems to have been a much-frequented chapel of the priory by the wearing of the steppings unto it, which are on the cloister side.

Many other chapels there were within the walls and circuit of the priory, as of St. Mary of the Marsh, of St. Ethelbert, and others.[1] But a strong and handsome fabric of one is still remaining, which is the chapel of St. John the Evangelist, said to have been founded by Bishop John Salmon, who died ann. 1325, and four priests were entertained for the daily service therein: that which was properly the chapel, is now the free-school: the adjoining buildings made up the refectory, chambers, and offices of the society.

Under the chapel, there was a charnel-house, which was a remarkable one in former times, and the name is still retained. In an old manuscript of a sacrist of the church, communicated to me by my worthy friend, Mr. John Burton,

---

[9] *There was, &c.*] There can be little doubt but that this was the original chapter-house; its octangular east end and its situation corresponding with those of the cathedrals of Durham, Hereford, Worcester, Gloucester, Lincoln, &c.

[1] *and others.*] The chapel of St. Edmund has been placed by Blomefield on the site of the chapter-house. In the late repairs, part of the old gaol has been appropriated to the dean's vestry, in the centre of which, in the intersecting groins is a *boss*, containing the representation of the head of a king, which I think can be no other than that of St. Edmund, and that we may with propriety consider this place as the chapel dedicated [to St. Edmund. Adjoining this, north, was another chapel, with a semicircular east end; corresponding with that on the east side of the north transept. This was probably the Priors' chapel.

the learned and very deserving master of the free-school, I find that the priests had a provisional allowance from the rectory of Westhall, in Suffolk. And of the charnel-house it is delivered, that with the leave of the sacrist, the bones of such as were buried in Norwich, might be brought into it. *In carnario subtus dictam capellam sancti Johannis constituto, ossa humana in civitate Norwici humata, de licentia sacristæ, qui dicti carnarii clavem et custodiam habebit specialem ut usque ad resurrectionem generalem honeste conserventur a carnibus integre denudata reponi volumus et obsignari.* Probably the bones were piled in good order, the skulls, arms, and leg bones, in their distinct rows and courses, as in many charnel-houses. How these bones were afterwards disposed of we have no account; or whether they had not the like removal with those in the charnel-house of St. Paul, kept under a chapel, on the north side of St. Paul's churchyard: for when the chapel was demolished, the bones which lay in the vault, amounting to more than a thousand cart loads, were conveyed into Finsbury Fields, and there laid in a moorish place, with so much soil to cover them as raised the ground for three windmills to stand on, which have since been built there, according as John Stow hath delivered in his survey of London.

There was formerly a fair and large but plain organ in the church, and in the same place with this at present. (It was agreed, in a chapter by the dean and prebends, that a new organ be made, and timber fitted to make a loft for it, June 6, ann. 1607, repaired 1626, and £10 which Abel Colls gave to the church, was bestowed upon it.) That in the late tumultuous time was pulled down, broken, sold, and made away. But since his majesty's restoration, another fair, well-tuned, plain organ, was set up by Dean Crofts and the chapter,[2] and afterwards painted, and beautifully adorned by the care and cost of my honoured friend Dr. Herbert Astley, the present worthy dean. There were also five or six copes belonging to the church; which, though they looked somewhat old, were richly embroidered. These were formerly carried into the market-place;[3] some blowing the

[2] *another organ, &c.*] Finished in 1664.—*MS. Kirkp.*
[3] *market-place.*] This occurred on the 9th of March, 1644; of which

organ pipes before them, and were cast into a fire provided for that purpose, with shouting and rejoicing: so that, at present, there is but one cope belonging to the church, which was presented thereunto by Philip Harbord, Esq., the present high sheriff of Norfolk, my honoured friend.

Before the late times, the combination[4] sermons were preached in the summer time at the cross in the green-yard, where there was a good accommodation for the auditors. The mayor, aldermen, with their wives and officers, had a well-contrived place built against the wall of the bishop's palace, covered with lead; so that they were not offended by rain. Upon the north side of the church, places were built gallery-wise, one above another; where the dean, prebends, and their wives, gentlemen, and the better sort, very well heard the sermon: the rest either stood, or sat in the green, upon long forms provided for them, paying a penny, or halfpenny apiece, as they did at St. Paul's-cross in London. The bishop and chancellor heard the sermons at the windows of the bishop's palace: the pulpit had a large

the following curious account is given in Bishop Hall's *Hard Measure*, p. 63.

"It is tragical to relate the furious sacrilege committed under the authority of Linsey, Tofts the sheriff, and Greenwood; what clattering of glasses, what beating down of walls, what tearing down of monuments, what pulling down of seats, and wresting out of irons and brass from the windows and graves; what defacing of arms, what demolishing of curious stone-work, that had not any representation in the world, but of the cost of the founder and skill of the mason; what piping on the destroyed organ pipes; vestments, both copes and surplices, together with the leaden cross, which had been newly sawed down from over the greenyard pulpit, and the singing books and service books were carried to the fire in the public market-place; a lewd wretch walking before the train in his cope trailing in the dirt, with a service book in his hand, imitating, in an impious scorn, the tune, and usurping the words of the litany, the ordnance being discharged on the Guild-day, the cathedral was filled with musketeers, drinking and tobacconing as freely as if it had turned alehouse."

[4] *combination.*] Dr. Littleton thus defines the word; "A combination, or circle of preachers in a cathedral or university church."— Vide *Lat. Dict.*

The combination preachers were appointed by the bishops from the clergy of the diocese; to come and preach a sermon in the cathedral, or its preaching yard, at their own charges: the Suffolk preachers in the summer half-year and the Norfolk in the winter; which is still continued.

covering of lead over it, and a cross upon it ; and there were
eight or ten stairs of stone about it, upon which the hospital
boys and others stood. The preacher had his face to the
. south, and there was a painted board, of a foot and a half
broad, and about a yard and a half long, hanging over his
head before, upon which were painted the arms of the benefactors[5] towards the combination sermon, • which he particularly commemorated in his prayer, and they were these ;
Sir John Suckling, Sir John Pettus, Edward Nuttel, Henry
Fasset, John Myngay.   But when the church was se-
questered, and the service put down, this pulpit was taken
down, and placed in New Hall-green, which had been the
artillery-yard, and the public sermon was there preached.
But the heirs of the benefactors denying to pay the wonted
beneficence for any sermon out of Christ-church (the
cathedral being now commonly so called), some other ways
were found to provide a minister, at a yearly salary, to
preach every Sunday, either in that pulpit in the summer,
or elsewhere in the winter.

I must not omit to say something of the shaft or spire of
this church, commonly called the pinnacle, as being a handsome and well-proportioned fabric, and one of the highest
in England, higher than the noted spires of Lichfield,
Chichester, or Grantham, but lower than that of Salisbury
(at a general chapter, holden June 4, 1633, it was agreed
that the steeple should be mended[6]), for that spire being
raised upon a very high tower, becomes higher from the
ground ; but this spire, considered by itself, seems, at least,
to equal that. It is an hundred and five yards and two feet
from the top of the pinnacle unto the pavement of the choir
under it. The spire is very strongly built, though the inside
be of brick. The upper aperture, or window, is the highest
ascent inwardly ; out of which, sometimes a long streamer
hath been hanged, upon the guild, or mayor's day. But at
his majesty's restoration, when the top was to be mended,

---

[5] *benefactors.*] These gentlemen, in consideration of the expense
necessarily incurred by the preachers in coming to Norwich, devised
certain estates, &c. to the corporation in trust, out of which each
preacher is paid one guinea towards his expenses.

[6] *at a general chapter, &c.*] Christ-church pinnacle was re-edified
1636.—*MS. Starling. Kirkp.*

.and a new gilded weathercock was to be placed upon it, there were stayings made at the upper window, and divers persons went up to the top of the pinnacle. They first went up into the belfry, and then by eight ladders, on the inside of the spire, till they came to the upper hole, or window; then went out unto the outside, where a staying was set, and so ascended up unto the top stone, on which the weathercock standeth.

The cock is three-quarters of a yard high, and one yard and two inches long; as is also the cross bar, and top stone of the spire, which is not flat, but consists of a half globe and channel about it; and from thence are eight leaves of stone spreading outward, under which begin the eight rows of crockets, which go down the spire at five feet distance.

From the top there is a prospect all about the country. Mousehold-hill seems low, and flat ground. The Castle hill, and high buildings, do very much diminish. The river looks like a ditch. The city, with the streets, make a pleasant show, like a garden with several walks in it.[7]

Though this church, for its spire, may compare, in a manner, with any in England, yet in its tombs and monuments it is exceeded by many.

No kings have honoured the same with their ashes, and but few with their presence.[8] And it is not without some

---

[7] *walks in it.*] The sea is also to be seen from the north-west towards Wells, to the south-east off the Suffolk coast; and with the aid of a telescope, vessels are to be seen sailing along the coast between Happisburgh and Lowestoft.

[8] *presence.*] This is certainly an error:—
Henry I. spent his Christmas at Norwich.—*Sax. Chron.* 1122.
Richard I. visited Norwich.—*Kirkpatrick's MS. notes.*
King John was at his castle in Norwich on the 12th and 13th of October, 1205.—*Archæologia*, vol. xxii. p. 142.
Henry III. visited Norwich, 1256 and 1272.—See *Blomefield.*
Edward I. kept his Easter at Norwich, 1277.—*Stowe.*
Edward II. was at Norwich in January 1327.—*Blomefield.*
Edward III. held a tournament at Norwich 1341, and was there again in 1342 and 1344.
Richard II. visited Norwich in 1383, according to *Hollingshed.*
Henry IV. visited the city in 1406, as appears by the Norwich Assembly Book.—*Blomefield.*
Henry V. visited Norwich.—*Kirkpatrick's MS. notes.*
Henry VI. visited Norwich in 1448 and 1449.—*Blomefield.*

wonder, that Norwich having been for a long time so considerable a place, so few kings have visited it; of which
number, among so many monarchs since the conquest, we
find but four, viz. King Henry III., Edward I., Queen
Elizabeth, and our gracious sovereign now reigning, King
Charles II., of which I had particular reason to take notice.[9]

The castle was taken by the forces of King William the
Conqueror; but we find not that he was here. King
Henry VII. by the way of Cambridge, made a pilgrimage
unto Walsingham; but records tell us not that he was at
Norwich.[1] King James I. came sometimes to Thetford for
his hunting recreation, but never vouchsafed to advance
twenty miles farther.

Not long after the writing of these papers, Dean Herbert
Astley died, a civil, generous, and public-minded person,
who had travelled in France, Italy, and Turkey, and was interred near the monument of Sir James Hobart: unto whom
succeeded my honoured friend Dr. John Sharpe, a prebend
of this church, and rector of St. Giles's in the fields,
London; a person of singular worth, and deserved estimation, the honour and love of all men; in the first year
of whose deanery, 1681, the prebends were these:

Mr. *J*oseph Loveland,	Dr. William Smith,
Dr. Hezekiah Burton,	Mr. Nathaniel Hodges,
Dr. William Hawkins,	Mr. Humphrey Prideaux.

(But Dr. Burton dying in that year, Mr. Richard Kidder
succeeded), worthy persons, learned men, and very good
preachers.

Edward IV. was in Norwich in 1469.—*Blomefield.*
Richard III. was in Norwich in 1483.—*Ibid.*
Henry VII. kept his Christmas at Norwich in 1486.—*Ibid.*
Elizabeth came on her progress to Norwich in 1578.—*Ibid.*
Charles II. visited Norwich in 1671, and is the last sovereign who visited
that city.
[9] Sir Thomas being then knighted.
[1] *but records, &c.*] From the authorities cited by Blomefield (*Norwich,*
part i. p. 174) there can be no doubt but that this sovereign visited
Norwich in his way to Walsingham.

ADDENDA.

I HAVE by me the picture of Chancellor Spencer, drawn when he was ninety years old, as the inscription doth declare, which was sent unto me from Colney.

Though Bishop Nix sat long in the see of Norwich, yet is not there much delivered of him: Fox in his Martyrology hath said something of him in the story of Thomas Bilney, who was burnt in Lollard's pit, without Bishopsgate, in his time.

Bishop Spencer lived in the reign of Richard II. and Henry IV., sat in the see of Norwich thirty-seven years: of a soldier made a bishop, and sometimes exercising the life of a soldier in his episcopacy; for he led an army into Flanders on the behalf of Pope Urban VI. in opposition to Clement the anti-pope; and also overcame the rebellious forces of Litster, the dyer, in Norfolk, by North Walsham, in the reign of King Richard II.

Those that would know the names of the citizens who were chief actors in the tumult in Bishop Skerewyng's time, may find them set down in the bull of Pope Gregory X.

Some bishops, though they lived and died here, might not be buried in this church, as some bishops probably of old, more certainly of later time.

Here concludes Sir Thomas Browne's MS.

MISCELLANIES.

CONCERNING THE TOO NICE CURIOSITY OF CENSURING THE PRESENT, OR JUDGING INTO FUTURE DISPENSATIONS.[1]

[POSTHUMOUS WORKS, p. 23. MS. SLOAN. 1885 & 1869.]

WE have enough to do rightly to apprehend and consider things as they are, or have been, without amusing ourselves how they might have been otherwise, or what variations, consequences, and differences might have otherwise arisen upon a different face of things, if they had otherwise fallen out in the state or actions of the world.

The learned King Alphonso would have had the calf of a man's leg placed before rather than behind: and thinks he could find many commodities from that position.

If, in the terraqueous globe, all that now is land had been sea, and all that is sea were land, what wide difference there would be in all things, as to constitution of climes, tides, disparity of navigation, and many other concerns, were a long consideration.

If Sertorius had pursued his designs to pass his days in the Fortunate Islands, who can tell but we might have had many noble discoveries of the neighbouring coasts of Africa; and perhaps America had not been so long unknown to us.

---

[1] *Concerning, &c.*] This most incorrect title I strongly incline to suspect is not genuine.

This piece and the following are mere extracts from Sir Thomas's Common Place Book.—Different copies of the first occur in two volumes of MSS. in the Sloanian Collection, from which I have inserted several additional passages.

If Nearchus, admiral to Alexander the Great, setting out from Persia, had sailed about Africa, and come into the Mediterranean, by the straits of Hercules, as was intended, we might have heard of strange things, and had probably a better account of the coast of Africa than was lost by Hanno.

If King Perseus had entertained the barbarous nations but stout warriors, which in so great numbers offered their service unto him, some conjecture it might be, that Paulus Emilius had not conquered Macedon.

If [Antiochus?] had followed the counsel of Hannibal, and come about by Gallia upon the Romans, who knows what success he might have had against them?

If Scanderbeg had joined his forces with Hunniades, as might have been expected before the battle in the plains of Cossoan, in good probability they might have ruined Mahomet, if not the Turkish empire.

If Alexander had marched westward, and warred with the Romans, whether he had been able to subdue that little but valiant people, is an uncertainty: we are sure he overcame Persia; histories attest and prophecies foretell the same. It was decreed that the Persians should be conquered by Alexander, and his successors by the Romans, in whom Providence had determined to settle the fourth monarchy, which neither Pyrrhus nor Hannibal must prevent; though Hannibal came so near it, that he seemed to miss it by fatal infatuation: which if he had effected, there had been such a traverse and confusion of affairs, as no oracle could have predicted. But the Romans must reign, and the course of things was then moving towards the advent of Christ, and blessed discovery of the Gospel: our Saviour must suffer at Jerusalem, and be sentenced by a Roman judge; St. Paul, a Roman citizen, must preach in the Roman provinces, and St. Peter be bishop of Rome, and not of Carthage.

UPON READING HUDIBRAS.

[POSTHUMOUS WORKS, p. 24.]

THE way of burlesque poems is very ancient, for there was a ludicrous mock way of transferring verses of famous poets into a jocose sense and argument, and they were called Ὠδέαι, or *Parodiæ;* divers examples of which are to be found in Athenæus.

The first inventor hereof was Hipponactes, but Hegemon, Sopater, and many more pursued the same vein ; so that the parodies of Ovid's Buffoon, Metamorphoses, Burlesques, Le Eneiade Travastito, are no new inventions, but old fancies revived.

An excellent parody there is of both the Scaligers upon an epigram of Catullus, which Stephens hath set down in his Discourse of Parodies : a remarkable one among the Greeks is that of Matron, in the words and epithets of Homer, describing the feast of Xenocles, the Athenian rhetorician, to be found in the fourth book of Athenæus, page 134, edit. Casaub.

AN ACCOUNT OF ISLAND, *alias* ICELAND, IN THE YEAR MDCLXII.[1]

[POSTHUMOUS WORKS, p. 1.]

GREAT [store of drift-wood, or float-wood, is every year cast up on their shores, brought down by the northern winds, which serveth them for fuel and other uses, the greatest part whereof is fir.

[1] *An account, &c.*] The following brief notices respecting Iceland were collected at the request of the Royal Society. They were partly obtained through correspondence with Theodore Jonas, a Lutheran minister, resident in the island ;—three of whose letters have been preserved in the British Museum. These letters I have preferred to place immediately after the paper to which they relate, rather than in the Correspondence.

Of bears there are none in the country, but sometimes they are brought down from the north upon ice, while they follow seals, and so are carried away. Two in this manner came over and landed in the north of Island, this last year, 1662.

No conies or hares, but of foxes great plenty, whose white skins are much desired, and brought over into this country.

The last winter, 1662, so cold and lasting with us in England, was the mildest they have had for many years in Island.

Two new eruptions, with slime and smoke, were observed the last year in some mountains about Mount Hecla.

Some hot mineral springs they have, and very effectual, but they make but rude use thereof.

The rivers are large, swift, and rapid, but have many falls, which render them less commodious; they chiefly abound with salmons.

They sow no corn, but receive it from abroad.

They have a kind of large lichen, which dried, becometh hard and sticky, growing very plentifully in many places; whereof they make use for food, either in decoction or powder, some whereof I have by me, different from any with us.

In one part of the country, and not near the sea, there is a large black rock, which, polished, resembleth touchstone, as I have seen in pieces thereof, of various figures.

There is also a rock, whereof I received one fragment, which seems to make it one kind of *pisolithes* or rather *orobites*, as made up of small pebbles, in the bigness and shape of the seeds of *ervum* or *orobus*.

They have some large well-grained white pebbles, and some kind of white cornelian or agath pebbles, on the shore, which polish well. Old Sir Edmund Bacon, of these parts, made use thereof in his peculiar art of tinging and colouring of stones.

For shells found on the sea shore, such as have been brought unto me are but coarse, nor of many kinds, as ordinary turbines, chamas, aspers, læves, &c.

I have received divers kinds of teeth and bones of cetaceous fishes, unto which they could assign no name.

An exceeding fine russet down is sometimes brought unto

us, which their great number of fowls afford, and sometimes store of feathers, consisting of the feathers of small birds.

Beside shocks and little hairy dogs, they bring another sort over, headed like a fox, which they say are bred betwixt dogs and foxes; these are desired by the shepherds of this country.

Green plovers, which are plentiful here in the winter, are found to. breed there in the beginning of summer.

Some sheep have been brought over, but of coarse wool, and some horses of mean stature, but strong and hardy; one whereof, kept in the pastures by Yarmouth, in the summer, would often take the sea, swimming a great way, a mile or two, and return the same : when its provision failed in the ship wherein it was brought, for many days fed upon hoops and cask; nor at the land would, for many months, be brought to feed upon oats.

These accounts I received from a native of Island, who comes yearly into England; and by reason of my long acquaintance and directions I send unto some of his friends against the *elephantiasis* (leprosy), constantly visits me before his return ; and is ready to perform for me what I shall desire in his country; wherein, as in other ways, I shall be very ambitious to serve the noble society, whose most honouring servant I am.

THOMAS BROWNE.

Norwich, January 15, 1663.

AN ACCOUNT OF BIRDS FOUND IN NORFOLK.

[MS. SLOAN. 1830, fol. 5—22; and 31.]

I WILLINGLY obey your command; in setting down such birds, fishes, and other animals, which for many years I have observed in Norfolk.

Besides the ordinary birds, which keep constantly in the country, many are discoverable, both in winter and summer, which are of a migrant nature, and exchange their seats according to the season. Those which come in the spring, coming for the most part from the southward; those which come in the autumn or winter, from the northward; so that they are observed to come in great flocks, with a north-east wind, and to depart with a south-west: nor to come only in flocks of one kind, but teal, woodcocks, fieldfares, thrushes, and small birds, to come and light together; for the most part some hawks and birds of prey attending them.

The great and noble kind of eagle, called *aquila Gesneri*,[1] I have not seen in this country; but one I met with in this country, brought from Ireland, which I kept two years, feeding with whelps, cats, rats, and the like; in all that while not giving it any water; which I afterward presented unto my worthy friend Dr. Scarburgh.

Of other sorts of eagles, there are several kinds, especially of the *halyætus* or fen eagles; some of three yards and a quarter from the extremity of the wings;[2] whereof one being taken alive, grew so tame, that it went about the yard feeding on fish, red herrings, flesh, and any offals, without the least trouble.

There is also a lesser sort of eagle, called an osprey,[3] which hovers about the fens and broads, and will dip his claw, and take up a fish, ofttimes; for which his foot is made of an extraordinary roughness, for the better fastening and holding of it; and the like they will do unto coots.

Aldrovandus takes particular notice of the great number of kites[4] about London and about the Thames. We are not without them here, though not in such numbers. Here are also the grey[5] and bald[6] buzzard; of all which the great

[1] *aquila Gesneri.*] *Falco chrysætos*, the golden eagle; the largest of the genus, known to breed in the mountainous parts of Ireland.

[2] *some, &c.*] *Haliætus nisus,—falco ossifragus*, Lin. The sea eagle. Few specimens, however, measure more than seven or eight feet from the extremities of the wings.

A specimen of F. *fulvus*, the ring-tailed eagle, has been caught at Cromer.— *G.*

[3] *osprey.*] *Falco haliætus*, Lin. The osprey. Sometimes met with near Cromer.—*G.*

[4] *kites.*] F. *milvus*, L.

[5] *grey.*] Probably F. *buteo*.

[6] *bald.*] The bald buzzard is a name usually given to the osprey. Dr. Browne, however, having just spoken of the osprey, must here refer to some other species—perhaps F. *æruginosus*.

number of broad waters and warrens make no small number, and more than in woodland counties.

Cranes are often seen here in hard winters, especially about the champian and fieldy part. It seems they have been more plentiful; for, in a bill of fare, when the mayor entertained the duke of Norfolk, I met with cranes in a dish.[7]

In hard winters, elks,[8] a kind of wild swan, are seen in no small number; in whom, and not in common swans, is remarkable that strange recurvation of the wind pipe through the sternon—and the same is also observable in cranes.[9] It is probable they come very far; for all the northern discoverers have observed them in the remotest parts; and like divers and other northern birds, if the winter be mild, they commonly come no farther southward than Scotland; if very hard, they go lower, and seek more southern places; which is the cause that, sometimes, we see them not before Christmas or the hardest time of winter.

A white large and strong-billed fowl, called a ganet, which seems to be the greater sort of *larus;* whereof I met with one killed by a greyhound, near Swaffham; another in Marshland, while it fought, and would not be forced to take wing: another entangled in a herring-net, which, taken alive, was fed with herrings for a while. It may be named *larus major, leucophæopterus;* as being white and the top of the wings brown.

In hard winters I have also met with that large and strong-billed fowl, which Clusius describeth by the name of *skua Hoyeri,*[2] sent him from the Faro Islands, by Hoierus, a physician; one whereof was shot at Hickling, while two thereof were feeding upon a dead horse.

As also that large and strong-billed fowl, spotted like a starling, which Clusius nameth *mergus major Farrensis,*[3]

---

[7] *dish.*] Cranes are no longer met with in this country.

[8] *elks.*] Elk; one of the popular names given to the wild swan, *A. cygnus.*

[9] *cranes.*] Willoughby.

[1] *ganet.*] *Pelecanus bassanus,* L.

[2] *skua Hoyeri.*] *Larus catarractes,* L. *Lestris catarractes,* Temm. *Skua gull,* Latham, Pennant, and Bewick.

[3] *mergus major Farrensis.*] Dr. Browne's description leaves little doubt that he refers to *colymbus glacialis,* L. the great northern diver;

as frequenting the Faro Islands, seated above Shetland ; one whereof I sent unto my worthy friend Dr. Scarburgh.

Here is also the *pica marina*,[4] or sea-pie.

Many sorts of *lari*, sea-mews, and cobs. The *larus major*,[5] in great abundance, in herring time, about Yarmouth.

Larus alba[6] or pewits, in such plenty, about Horsey, that they sometimes bring them in carts to Norwich, and sell them at small rates ; and the country people make use of their eggs in puddings, and otherwise ; great plenty thereof have bred about Scoulton Meers, and from thence sent to London.

Larus cinereus,[7] greater and smaller, but a coarse meat,. commonly called sterns.

Hirundo marina[8] or sea-swallow, a neat white and forked-tail bird ; but much longer than a swallow.

The *ciconia* or stork, I have seen in the fens ; and some have been shot in the marshes between this and Yarmouth.

The *platea* or shovelard,[9] which build upon the tops of high trees. They have formerly built in the Hernery, at Claxton and Reedham ; now at Trimley, in Suffolk. They come in March, and are shot by fowlers, not for their meat, but the handsomeness of the same ; remarkable in their white colour, copped crown, and spoon or spatule-like bill.

Corvus marinus,[1] cormorants ; building at Reedham, upon trees from whence King Charles the First was wont to be

though his synonym is not correctly given. It is called by Clusius, *colymbus maximus ferroensis, seu arcticus ;*—by Willoughby, *mergus maximus faroensis.*

[4] *pica marina.*] *Hæmatopus ostralegus*, L. The oyster-catcher.

[5] *larus major.*] This name was given long after, by Catesby, to *L. atricilla*, L. Dr. Browne, quoting from memory, may probably refer to *L. fuscus*, L. *L. cinereus maximus*, Will. The wagel gull.

[6] *larus alba.*] *Larus ridibundus*, L. The pewit gull.

[7] *larus cinereus.*] It seems not very easy to determine the species here referred to :—certainly not the "greater and lesser" stern, *sterna hirundo* and *minuta*, the former of which is certainly the bird next mentioned ; and neither of which is called the stern, which is *sterna fissipes.* He may refer to *S. minuta* and *fissipes ;* or possibly, but not so probably, to *L. cinerarius* and *canus*, L. the red-legged and common gulls, L. *cinereus major* and *minor* of Aldrovandus.

[8] *hirundo marina.*] *Sterna hirundo*, L.

[9] *shovelard.*] *Platalea leucorodia*, L. Spoonbill.

[1] *corvus marinus.*] *Pelecanus carbo*, L. The cormorant.

supplied. Beside the rock cormorant,[2] which breedeth in the rocks, in northern countries, and cometh to us in the winter, somewhat differing from the other in largeness and whiteness under the wings.

A sea-fowl called a sherewater,[3] somewhat billed like a cormorant, but much lesser ; a strong and fierce fowl, hovering about ships when they cleanse their fish. Two were kept six weeks, cramming them with fish which they would not feed on of themselves. The seamen told me they had kept them three weeks without meat; and I, giving over to feed them, found they lived sixteen days without taking anything.

Bernacles, brants, (*branta*)[4] are common.

Sheldrakes. *Sheledracus Jonstoni.*

Barganders, a noble-coloured fowl (*vulpanser*)[5] which herd in coney-burrows about Norrold and other places.

Wild geese. *Anser ferus.*[6]

Scotch goose. *Anser scoticus.*

Goosander. *Merganser.*[7]

Mergus acutirostris speciosus or loon, a handsome and specious fowl, cristated,[8] and with divided fin feet placed very backward, and after the manner of all such which the Dutch call *arsvoote.* They have a peculiar formation in the leg bone, which hath a long and sharp process extending above the thigh bone. They come about April, and breed in the broad waters ; so making their nest on the water, that their eggs are seldom dry while they are set on.

Mergus acutirostris cinereus,[9] which seemeth to be a difference of the former.

Mergus minor,[1] the smaller divers or dab-chicks, in rivers and broad waters.

[2] *rock cormorant.*] Probably the crested cormorant, thought to be but a variety of the preceding.

[3] *sherewater.*] *Procellaria puffinus,* L. The shearwater.

[4] *branta.*] *Anas erythropus* and *bernicla,* L. The bernacle and brent goose.

[5] *vulpanser.*] *Anas tadorna,* L. *Vulpanser,* Gesner and Aldrov. Sheldrake or burrow duck. "Barganders," the name given this species by Dr. Browne, may possibly be a corruption of *burrow-ganders.*

[6] *anser ferus.*] *Anas anser ferus,* L. The grey lag or grey leg.

[7] *merganser.*] *Mergus merganser,* L.

[8] *cristated.*] *Podiceps cristatus,* Lath. *Colymbus,* L.

[9] *mergus acutirostris cinereus.*] *Podiceps urinator,* Lath.

[1] *mergus minor.*] *Podiceps minor,* Ib.

Mergus serratus,[2] the saw-billed diver, bigger and longer
than a duck, distinguished from other divers by a notable
saw-bill, to retain its slippery prey, as living much upon
eels, whereof we have seldom failed to find some in their
bellies.

Divers other sorts of dive-fowl; more remarkable the
mustela fusca,[3] and *mustela variegata,*[4] the grey dun, and the
variegated or party-coloured weazel, so called from the resemblance it beareth unto a weasel in the head.

Many sorts of wild ducks which pass under names well
known unto fowlers, though of no great signification, as
smee, widgeon, arts, ankers, noblets:—

The most remarkable are, *anas platyrhinchos,*[5] a remarkably
broad-billed duck.

And the sea-pheasant,[6] holding some resemblance unto
that bird in some feathers in the tail.

Teals, *querquedula,*[7] wherein scarce any place more abounding. The condition of the country, and the very many
decoys, especially between Norwich and the sea, making this
place very much to abound in wild fowl.

Fulicæ cottæ,[8] coots, in very great flocks upon the broad
waters. Upon the appearance of a kite or buzzard, I have
seen them unite from all parts of the shore, in strange numbers; when, if the kite stoops near them, they will fling up,
and spread such a flash of water with their wings, that they
will endanger the kite, and so keep him off again and again
in open opposition; and a handsome provision they make
about their nest against the same bird of prey, by bending
and twining the rushes and reeds so about them, that they
cannot stoop at their young ones, or the dam while she
sitteth.

[2] *mergus serratus.*] Probably *mergus serrator,* L.
[3] *mustela fusca.*] *Mergus castor,* L. The dun diver?
[4] *mustela variegata.*] Probably *mergus albellus,* L. The smew; which
Gesner calls *M. mustelaris.*
[5] *platyrhinchos.*] *A. clypeata,* L. The shoveller.
[6] *sea-pheasant.*] *A. acuta,* L. The pintail duck. Sometimes taken
in the Hempstead decoy.—*G.*
[7] *querquedula.*] *A. crecca,* L. *Querquedula* of Gesner. Aldrovandus
and Ray scarcely distinguished the *teal* from the *gargany, A. querquedula,* L.
[8] *fulicæ cottæ.*] F. *atra,* L. The coot.

Gallinula aquatica,[9] moor hen, and a kind of *ralla aquatica,*[1] or water rail.

An *onocrotalus,* or pelican, shot upon Horsey Fen, May 22, 1663, which, stuffed and cleansed, I yet retain. It was three yards and a half between the extremities of the wings; the chowle and beak answering the usual description; the extremities of the wings for a span deep brown; the rest of the body white; a fowl which none could remember upon this coast. About the same time I heard one of the king's pelicans was lost at St. James's;[2] perhaps this might be the same.

Anas arctica Clusii,[3] which though he placeth about the Faro Islands, is the same we call a puffin, common about Anglesea, in Wales, and sometimes taken upon our seas, not sufficiently described by the name of *puffinus;* the bill being so remarkably differing from other ducks, and not horizontally, but meridionally, formed, to feed in the clefts of the rocks, of insects, shell-fish, and others.

The great number of rivers, rivulets, and plashes of water makes herns and herneries to abound in these parts; young herns being esteemed a festival dish, and much desired by some palates.

The *ardea stellaris, botaurus,* or bitour, is also common, and esteemed the better dish. In the belly of one I found a frog in a hard frost at Christmas. Another, kept in a garden two years, feeding it with fish, mice, and frogs; in defect whereof, making a scrape[4] for sparrows and small birds, the bitour made shift to maintain herself upon them.

Bistardæ, or bustards, are not unfrequent in the champian and fieldy part of this country. A large bird, accounted a dainty dish, observable in the strength of the breast-bone and short heel. Lays an egg much larger than a turkey.

[9] *gallinula aquatica.*] The moor hen is *gallinula chloropus,* Lath. (*fulica,* L.)

[1] *ralla aquatica.*] *Rallus aquaticus,* L. *G. aquatica,* of some authors.

[2] *St. James's.*] But for this information, the pelican might probably have been added to our *Fauna* on the authority of Dr. Browne.—See *Bray's Evelyn,* i. 373.

[3] *anas arctica Clusii.*] *Alca arctica,* L.

[4] *scrape.*] A scrape, or *scrap,* is a term used in Norfolk, for a quantity of chaff, mixed with grain, frequently laid as a decoy to attract small birds, for the purpose of shooting or netting them.

Morinellus,[5] or dotterell, about Thetford and the champian, which comes unto us in September and March, staying not long, and is an excellent dish.

There is also a sea dotterell, somewhat less but better coloured than the former.

Godwyts ; taken chiefly in Marshland ; though other parts are not without them ; accounted the daintiest dish in England ; and, I think, for the bigness, of the biggest price.

Gnats, or knots,[6] a small bird, which, taken with nets, grow excessively fat, being mewed and fed with corn. A candle lighted in the room, they feed day and night ; and when they are at their height of fatness, they begin to grow lame, and are then killed, as at their prime, and apt to decline.

Erythropus, or redshank ;[7] a bird common in the marshes, and of common food, but no dainty dish.

A may chit,[8] a small dark grey bird, little bigger than a stint, of fatness beyond any. It comes in May into Marshland and other parts, and abides not above a month or six weeks.

Stints[9] in great number about the sea shore and marshes, about Stiff key, Burnham, and other parts.

Another small bird, somewhat larger than a stint, called a *churr,*[1] and is commonly taken among them.

Pluvialis, or plover,[2] green and grey, in great plenty about Thetford, and many other heaths. They breed not with us, but in some parts of Scotland, and plentifully in Iceland.

The lapwing or *vanellus,*[3] common over all the heaths.

Cuckoos of two sorts ; the one far exceeding the other in bigness.[4] Some have attempted to keep them in warm rooms all the winter, but it hath not succeeded. In their migration they range very far northward ; for in the summer they are to be found as high as Iceland.

---

[5] *morinellus.*] *Charadrius morinellus,* L.

[6] *knots.*] *Tringa canutus,* L.

[7] *red-shank.*] *Scolopax calidris,* L.

[8] *a may chit.*] Probably one of the genus *tringa.*

[9] *stints.*] *Tringa cinclus.*

[1] *churr.*] Or *purre ?*

[2] *plover.*] *Charadrius pluvialis,* L.

[3] *vanellus.*] *Tringa vanellus,* L.

[4] *bigness.*] Differing only in age or sex.

Avis pugnans ;[5] ruffe ; a marsh bird of the greatest variety of colours, every one therein somewhat varying from other. The female is called a reeve, without any ruff about the neck, lesser than the other, and hardly to be got. They are almost all cocks, and, put together, fight and destroy each other; and prepare themselves to fight like cocks, though they seem to have no other offensive part but the bill. They lose their ruffs about the autumn, or beginning of winter, as we have observed, keeping them in a garden from May till the next spring. They most abound in Marshland, but are also in good number in the marshes between Norwich and Yarmouth.

Of *picus martius*,[6] or woodspeck, many kinds. The green, the red,[7] the *leucomelanus*,[8] or neatly marked black and white, and the *cinereus*[9] or dun-coloured little bird, called a nuthack. Remarkable, in the larger, are the hardness of the bill and skull, and the long nerves which tend unto the tongue, whereby it shooteth out the tongue above an inch out of the mouth, and so licks up insects. They make the holes in trees without any consideration of the winds or quarters of heaven; but as the rottenness thereof best affordeth convenience.

Black heron.[1] Black on the sides, the bottom of the neck, with white grey on the outside, spotted all along with black on the inside. A black coppe of small feathers, some a span long; bill pointed and yellow, three inches long; back, heron-coloured, intermixed with long white feathers; the strong feathers black; the breast black and white, most black; the legs and feet not green, but an ordinary dark cock colour.

The number of rivulets, becks, and streams, whose banks are beset with willows and alders, which give occasion of easier fishing and stooping to the water, makes that handsome-coloured bird abound, which is called *alcedo ispida*, or

---

[5] *avis pugnans.*] *Tringa pugnax*, L.

[6] *picus martius.*] The black woodpecker, extremely rare in this country. "*Habitat vix in Anglia,*" says Linnæus.

[7] *red.*] Probably *P. major*, L.

[8] *leucomelanus.*] *P. minor*, L.

[9] *cinereus.*] *Sitta Europea*, Lin. Nuthatch.

[1] *black heron.*] No British species appears to correspond so nearly with Dr. Browne's description as *Ardea Purpurea*.

the kingfisher. They build in holes about gravel-pits, wherein is to be found a great quantity of small fish-bones; and lay very handsome round and, as it were, polished eggs.

An hobby-bird:[2] so called because it comes either with, or a little before, the hobbies, in the spring. Of the bigness of a thrush, coloured and paned like a hawk; marvellously subject to the vertigo, and are sometimes taken in those fits.

Upupa, or hoopebird, so named from its note; a gallant marked bird, which I have often seen, and it is not hard to shoot them.

Ringlestones,[3] a small white and black bird, like a wagtail, and seems to be some kind of *motacilla marina*, common about Yarmouth sands. They lay their eggs in the sand and shingle, about June, and, as the Eringo diggers tell me, not set them flat, but upright, like eggs in salt.

The *arcuata*[4] or curlew, frequent about the sea-coast.

There is also a handsome tall bird, remarkably eyed, and with a bill not above two inches long, commonly called a stone curlew;[5] but the note thereof more resembleth that of a green plover, and breeds about Thetford, about the stone and shingle of the rivers.

Avoseta, called [a] shoeing-horn, a tall black and white bird, with a bill semicircularly reclining or bowed upward; so that it is not easy to conceive how it can feed; answerable unto the *avoseta Ibalorum*, in Aldrovandus, a summer marshbird, and not unfrequent in Marshland.

A yarwhelp,[6] so thought to be named from its note, a grey bird intermingled with some whitish yellowish feathers, somewhat long-legged, and the bill about an inch and a half; esteemed a dainty dish.

---

[2] *hobby-bird*.] Surely this may be *yunx torquilla*, L. the wryneck; the singular motion of its head and neck was probably attributed to vertigo.

[3] *ringlestones*.] *Charadrius hiaticula*, L. The ring dotterel. Plentiful near Blakeney.—*G.*

[4] *arcuata*.] *Scolopax arquata*, L.

[5] *curlew*.] *Charadrius œdicnemus*, L. The great or Norfolk plover, or thick-kneed bustard.

[6] *yarwhelp*.] *Scolopax Ægocephala*, L. is called the yarwhelp:—but the bill is four inches long.

Loxias[7] or *curvirostra*, a bird a little bigger than a thrush, of fine colours, and pretty note, differently from other birds, the upper and lower bill crossing each other; of a very tame nature; comes about the beginning of summer. I have known them kept in cages; but not to outlive the winter.

A kind of *coccothraustes*,[8] called a coble-bird, bigger than a thrush, finely coloured and shaped like a bunting. It is chiefly seen in summer, about cherry-time.

A small bird of prey, called a birdcatcher, about the bigness of a thrush, and linnet-coloured, with a longish white bill, and sharp; of a very fierce and wild nature, though kept in a cage, and fed with flesh;—a kind of *lanius.*

A dorhawk[9] or kind of *accipiter muscarius*, conceived to have its name from feeding upon flies and beetles; of a woodcock colour, but paned like a hawk; a very little pointed bill: large throat; breedeth with us; and lays a marvellous handsome spotted egg. Though I have opened many, I could never find anything considerable in their maws. *Caprimulgus.*

Avis trogloditica[1] or chock, a small bird, mixed of black and white, and breeding in coney-burrows; whereof the warrens are full from April to September; at which time they leave the country. They are taken with an hobby and a net; and are a very good dish.

Spermalegous rooks, which, by reason of the great quantity of corn-fields and rook groves, are in great plenty. The young ones are commonly eaten; sometimes sold in Norwich market, and many are killed for their livers, in order to the cure of the rickets.

Crows, as everywhere; and also the *corvus variegatus*,[2] or pied crow, with dun and black interchangeable. They come in the winter, and depart in the summer; and seem to be the same which Clusius describeth in the Faro Islands, from whence perhaps these come. I have seen them very

[7] *loxias*.] The crossbill. *Loxia curvirostra*, L.
[8] *coccothraustes*.] *Loxia coccothraustes*, L. The grossbeak.
[9] *dorhawk*.] *Caprimulgus Europæus*, L. The goat-sucker.
[1] *avis trogloditica*.} By the term *avis trogloditica*, Dr. Browne probably intended a kind of wren. He refers very possibly to the wheatear, *Motacilla œnanthe*, L.
[2] *corvus variegatus*.] *Corvus cornix*, L. The hooded crow.

common in Ireland; but not known in many parts of England.

Corvus major; ravens; in good plenty about the city;. which makes so few kites to be seen hereabout. They build in woods very early, and lay eggs in February.

Among the many *monedulas* or jackdaws, I could never in these parts observe the *pyrrhocorax* or Cornish chough, with red legs and bill, to be commonly seen in Cornwall; and,. though there be here very great store of partridges, yet the French red-legged partridge is not to be met with.[3] The *ralla* or rail, we have counted a dainty dish; as also no small number of quails. The heathpoult,[4] common in the north, is unknown here, as also the grouse; though I have heard some have been seen about Lynn. The calandrier or great-crested lark (*galerita*), I have not met with here,[5] though with three other sorts of larks;—the ground-lark, wood-lark, and tit-lark.

Stares or starlings, in great numbers. Most remarkable in their numerous flocks, which I have observed about the autumn, when they roost at night in the marshes, in safe places, upon reeds and alders; which to observe, I went to the marshes about sunset; where standing by their usual place of resort, I observed very many flocks flying from all quarters, which, in less than an hour's space, came all in, and settled in innumerable numbers in a small compass.

Great variety of finches and other small birds, whereof one very small, called a whin-bird, marked with fine yellow spots, and lesser than a wren. There is also a small bird, called a chipper, somewhat resembling the former, which comes in the spring, and feeds upon the first buddings of birches and other early trees.

A kind of *anthus*, goldfinch, or fool's coat, commonly called a draw-water, finely marked with red and yellow, and a white bill, which they take with trap-cages, in Norwich gardens, and, fastening a chain about them, tied to a box of water, it makes a shift, with bill and leg, to draw up the water in to

---

[3] *French, &c.*] Our Norfolk sportsmen can bear witness that this species is now to be found in various parts of the county.

[4] *heathpoult.*] Or black grouse.

[5] *here.*] Nor any one else, in England, if he refers to *alauda cristata,* which is the *A. sylvestris galerita* of Frisch.

it from the little pot, hanging by the chain about a foot below.

On the 14th of May, 1664, a very rare bird was sent me, killed about Crostwick, which seemed to be some kind of jay. The bill was black, strong, and bigger than a jay's; somewhat yellow claws, tipped black; three before and one claw behind. The whole bird not so big as a jay.

The head, neck, and throat, of a violet colour; the back and upper parts of the wing, of a russet yellow; the fore part of the wing, azure; succeeded downward by a greenish blue; then on the flying feathers, bright blue; the lower parts of the wing outwardly, of a brown; inwardly, of a merry blue; the belly, a light faint blue; the back, toward the tail, of a purple blue; the tail, eleven feathers of a greenish colour; the extremities of the outward feathers thereof, white with an eye of green.—*Garrulus argentoratensis.*[6]

[AN ACCOUNT OF FISHES, &c. FOUND IN NORFOLK AND ON THE COAST.]

[MS. SLOAN. 1830, fol. 23—30, & 32—38; & 1882,[1] fol. 145, 6.]

IT may well seem no easy matter to give any considerable account of fishes and animals of the sea; wherein, 'tis said, that there are things creeping innumerable, both small and great beasts, because they live in an element wherein they are not so easily discoverable. Notwithstanding, probable it is that after this long navigation, search of the ocean, bays, creeks, estuaries, and rivers, that there is scarce any fish but

---

[6] *garrulus argentoratensis.*] *Coracias garrula,* L. The roller.

[1] 1882] The first paragraph of this paper I met with in 1882 *MS. Sloan.* preceded by the words "*I willingly obey your co . . . . .*" which were left unfinished, and struck through with the pen. The author probably at one time intended the account of fishes, &c., to be distinct from that of birds, and wrote this as an introductory paragraph. I have therefore so preserved it; though both subjects are mentioned in the first paragraph of the tract on birds.

hath been seen by some man; for the large and breathing
sort thereof do sometimes discover themselves above water,
and the other are in such numbers that at one time or other
they are discovered and taken, even the most barbarous
nations being much addicted to fishing : and in America and
the new discovered world the people were well acquainted
with fishes of sea and rivers, and the fishes thereof have
been since described by industrious writers. Pliny seems
too short in the estimate of their number in the ocean, who
reckons up but one hundred and seventy-six species : but
the seas being now farther known and searched, Bellonius
much enlargeth; and in his book of birds thus delivereth
himself:—"Although I think it impossible to reduce the
same unto a certain number, yet I may freely say, that 'tis
beyond the power of man to find out more than five hundred
species of fishes, three hundred sorts of birds, more than
three hundred sorts of four-footed animals, and forty diversities of serpents."[2]

Of fishes sometimes the larger sort are taken or come
ashore. A spermaceti whale, of sixty-two feet long, near
Wells; another of the same kind, twenty years before, at
Hunstanton ; and, not far off, eight or nine came ashore, and
two had young ones after they were forsaken by the water.[3]

---

[2] *serpents.*] Naturalists now enumerate 800 species of beasts ; and at
least 50,000 of insects.—*Gray.*

[3] *sometimes, &c.*] A whale, 58 feet long, was cast ashore at Overstrand,
in the spring of 1822 (I think) ; and another went spouting past Cromer,
in the autumn of the same year.

Towards the end of 1829, a whale, only 24 feet long, was cast ashore
and killed at Runton. He was of the *Balæna* division, with a whale-
bone mouth, and no teeth ; and as far as I could make out, I think it
was one of the *boops balæna* species—as the man who made the capture
told me, the nose was very sharp pointed—but it was much hacked
before I saw it. I found the extreme width of the tail was 3 feet 11
inches. It was dark, nearly black on the back, and white below in
folds. There were two spout-holes close together in the middle of the
head. Almost an inch and half thickness of blubber ; and the oil
which has been made from it is remarkably fine. The *Whale-bone fringe*
in its mouth was nearly white : the length of the jaw-bones, 3 feet
7 inches. It did not look tempting enough to make me bring any of
the meat away ; but at Northrepps hall, a steak was cooked, and tasted
like tender beef.—*G.*

A grampus, above sixteen feet long, taken at Yarmouth, four years ago.[4]

The *tursio*, or porpoise,[5] is common. The dolphin[6] more rare, though sometimes taken, which many confound with the porpoise; but it hath a more waved line along the skin; sharper toward the tail; the head longer, and nose more extended; which maketh good the figure of Rondeletius; the flesh more red, and well cooked, of very good taste to most palates, and exceedeth that of porpoise.

The *vitulus marinus*,[7] sea-calf, or seal, which is often taken sleeping on the shore. Five years ago, one was shot in the river of Norwich, about Surlingham ferry, having continued in the river for divers months before. Being an amphibious animal, it may be carried about alive, and kept long if it can be brought to feed. Some have been kept for many months in ponds. The pizzell, the bladder, the *cartilago ensiformis*, the figure of the throttle, the clustered and racemose form of the kidneys, the flat and compressed heart, are remarkable in it. In stomachs of all that I have opened, I have found many worms.

I have also observed a *scolopendra cetacea* of about ten [inches] long, answering the figure in Rondeletius, which the mariners told me was taken in these seas.

A *pristis serra*,[8] or saw-fish, taken about Lynn, commonly mistaken for a sword-fish, and answers the figure in Rondeletius.

A sword-fish (*iphias*, or *gladius*[9]), entangled in the herring-nets at Yarmouth, agreeable unto the *icon* in Johnstonus, with a smooth sword, not unlike the *gladius* of Rondeletius, about a yard and a half long; no teeth; eyes very remarkable; enclosed in a hard cartilaginous covercle, about the bigness of a good apple; the vitreous humour plentiful; the crystalline larger than a nutmeg, remaining clear, sweet,

---

[4] *grampus, &c.*] Oct. 1827, the fishermen saw a fish which they called a grampus.—*G.*

[5] *tursio or porpoise.*] *Delphinus phocœna*, L.

[6] *dolphin.*] *D. Delphis*, L.

[7] *vitulus marinus.*] *Phoca vitulina*, L.

[8] *pristis serra.*] *Squalus pristis*, L.

[9] *iphias or gladius.*] *Xiphias gladius*, L.

and untainted, when the rest of the eye was under a deep corruption, which we kept clear and limpid many months, until an hard frost split it, and manifested the foliations thereof.

It is not unusual to take several sorts of *canis*, or dog-fish, great and small, which pursue the shoal of herrings and other fish; but this year [1662] one was taken entangled in the herring-nets, about nine feet in length, answering the last figure of Johnstonus, lib. vii. under the name of *canis carcharias alter;* and was, by the teeth and five gills, one kind of shark, particularly remarkable in the vastness of the optic nerves and three conical hard pillars, which supported the extraordinary elevated nose, which we have reserved with the skull. The seamen called this kind, a scrape.

Sturio, or sturgeon, so common on the other side of the sea, about the mouth of the Elbe, come seldom into our creeks, though some have been taken at Yarmouth, and more in the great Ouse, by Lynn; but their heads not so sharp as represented in the *icons* of Rondeletius and Johnstonus.

Sometimes we meet with a *mola*, or moon-fish,[1] so called from some resemblance it hath of a crescent in the extreme part of the body from one fin unto another. One being taken near the shore at Yarmouth, before break of day, seemed to shiver and grunt like a hog, as authors deliver of it. The flesh being hard and nervous, it is not like to afford a good dish; but from the liver, which is large, white, and tender, somewhat may be expected. The gills of these fish we found thick beset with a kind of sea-louse. In the year 1667, a *mola* was taken at Monsley, which weighed 200 pounds.

The *rana piscatrix*, or frog-fish,[2] is sometimes found in a very large magnitude, and we have taken the care to have them cleaned and stuffed, wherein we observed all the appendices whereby they catch fishes, but much larger than are described in the *icons* of Johnstonus, lib. xi. fig. 8.

The sea-wolf,[3] or *lupus nostras*, of Schoneveldus, remarkable for its spotted skin and notable teeth,—*incisores*, dog-teeth and grinders. The dog-teeth, both in the jaws and

---

[1] *mola or moon-fish*] *Tetraodon mola*, L.   Sun-fish.
[2] *frog-fish.*] *Lophius piscatorius*, L.
[3] *sea-wolf.*] *Anarhicas lupus*, L.

palates, scarce answerable by any fish of that bulk, for the
like disposure, strength, and solidity.

Mustela marina;[4] called by some a weazel ling, which,
salted and dried, becomes a good Lenten dish.

A lump, or *lumpus anglorum;*[5] so named by Aldrovandus,
by some esteemed a festival-fish, though it affordeth but a
glutinous jelly, and the skin is beset with stony knobs, after
no certain order. Ours most answereth the first figure in
the 13th table of Johnstonus, but seems more round and
arcuated than that figure makes it.

Before the herrings, there commonly cometh a fish, about
a foot long, by fishermen called a horse, resembling, in all
points, the *trachurus*[6] of Rondeletius, of a mixed shape,
between a mackerel and a herring; observable from its green
eyes, rarely sky-coloured back, after it is kept a day, and an
oblique bony line running on the outside from the gills unto
the tail; a dry and hard dish, but makes a handsome picture.

The *rubelliones*, or rochets, but thinly met with on this
coast. The *gornart cuculus*, or *lycæ species*,[7] more often;
which they seldom eat, but bending the back and spreading
the fins into a large posture, do hang them up in their
houses.

Beside the common *mullus*, or mullet,[8] there is another
not unfrequent, which some call a cunny-fish, but rather a
red mullet,[9] of a flosculous red, and somewhat rough on
the scales, answering the description and *icon* of Rondeletius,
under the name of *mullus, ruber asper;* but not the taste of
the usually-known mullet, as affording but a dry and lean
bit.

Several sorts of fishes there are which do or may bear the
names of sea-woodcocks; as the *acus major scolopax,* and

[4] *mustela marini.*] Perhaps *gadus mustela*, L. or *petromyzon marinus*,
L. The lamprey.
[5] *lumpus anglorum.*] *Cyclopterus lumpus*, L. The lump-fish or lump-
sucker.
[6] *trachurus.*] *Scomber Trachurus, L.* The scad or horse-mackerel:
caught with the mackerel.—*G.*
[7] *lycæ species.*] *Trigla cuculus*, L. The red-gurnard.
[8] *mullet.*] *Mugil cephalus*, L.
[9] *red mullet.*] *Mullus barbatus*, L. Sur-mullet. Sometimes caught
at Cromer.—*G.*

saurus.[1] The *saurus* we sometimes meet with young. Rondeletius confesseth it a very rare fish, somewhat resembling the *acus* or needle-fish before, and mackerel behind. We have kept one dried many years ago.

The *acus major,*[2] called by some a garfish, and greenback, answering the figure of Rondeletius, under the name of *acus prima species*, remarkable for its quadrangular figure, and verdigrease-green backbone.

A *scolopax*[3] or sea-woodcock, of Rondeletius, was given me by a seaman of these seas. About three inches long, and seems to be one kind of *acus* or needle-fish, answering the description of Rondeletius.

The *acus* of Aristotle,[4] lesser, thinner, corticated, and sex-angular; by divers called an addercock, and somewhat resembling a snake; ours more plainly finned than Rondeletius describeth it.

A little corticated fish, about three or four inches long, answering that which is named *piscis octangularis*, by Wormius; *cataphractus*, by Schoneveldeus. *Octagonius versus caput ; versus caudam hexagonius.*[5]

The *faber marinus,*[6] sometimes found very large, answering the figure of Rondeletius, which though he mentioneth as a rare fish, and to be found in the Atlantic and Gaditane ocean, yet we often meet with it in these seas, commonly called a peter-fish, having one black spot on either side the body ; conceived the perpetual signature, from the impression of St. Peter's fingers, or to resemble the two pieces of money which St. Peter took out of this fish ; remarkable also from its disproportionable mouth, and many hard prickles about other parts.

A kind of *scorpius marinus ;*[7] a rough, prickly, and monstrous headed fish, six, eight, or twelve inches long, answerable unto the figure of Schoneveldeus.

---

[1] *saurus.*] *Esox saurus*, L. ?
[2] *acus major.*] *Syngathus acus*, L. Needle-fish.
[3] *scolopax.*] *Centriscus scolopax*, L.
[4] *acus of Aristotle.*] *Syngathus typhle*, L. ?
[5] *hexagonius.*] Possibly a gurnard, *trigla cataphracta*, L.
[6] *faber marinus.*] *Zeus faber*, L. John Doree or Dory.
[7] *scorpius marinus.*] *Cottus scorpio*, L. Father Lasher

A sting-fish, wiver, or kind of opthidion,[8] or araneus; slender; narrow-headed; about four inches long, with a sharp, small, prickly fin along the back, which often venomously pricketh the hands of fishermen.

Aphia cebites marina, or a sea-loche.

Belennus : a sea miller's thumb.

Funduli marini ; sea gudgeons.

Alosæ, or chads ;[9] to be met with about Lynn.

Spirinches, or smelt,[1] in great plenty about Lynn; but where they have also a small fish, called a priame, answering in taste and shape a smelt, and perhaps are but the younger sort thereof.

Aselli, or cod, of several sorts.—*Asellus albus,* or whitings,[2] in great plenty.—*Asellus niger, carbonarius,* or coal-fish.[3]—*Asellus minor Schoneveldei (callarias Plinii),* or haddocks ;[4] with many more. Also a weed-fish, somewhat like a haddock, but larger, and drier meat. A basse,[5] also much resembling a flatter kind of cod.

Scombri, or mackerel; in great plenty. A dish much desired: but if, as Rondeletius affirmeth, they feed upon sea-stars and squalders, there may be some doubt whether their flesh be without some ill quality. Sometimes they are of a very large size; and one was taken this year, 1668, which was by measure an ell long; and of the length of a good salmon, at Lowestoft.

Herrings departed, sprats, or *sardæ,* not long after succeed in great plenty, which are taken with smaller nets, and smoked and dried like herrings, become a sapid bit, and vendible abroad.

Among these are found bleak, or *blicæ,*[6] a thin herring-like fish, which some will also take to be young herrings.

---

[8] *opthidion.*] Probably *trachinus draco,* L. The sting-bull or common weaver.
[9] *chads.*] *Clupea alosa,* L. Shad.
[1] *smelt.*] *Salmo eperianus,* L. Smelt.
[2] *whitings.*] *Gadus merlangus,* L.
[3] *coal-fish.*] *G. carbonarius,* L.
[4] *haddocks.*] *G. æglesinus,* L.
[5] *basse.*] *Perca labrax,* L.
[6] *blicæ.*] *Cyprinus alburnus,* L. Bleak.

And though this sea aboundeth not with pilchards, yet they are commonly taken among herrings ; but few esteem thereof, or eat them.

Congers are not so common on these coasts as in many seas about England ; but are often found upon the north coast of Norfolk, and in frosty weather left in pulks and plashes upon the ebb of the sea.

The sand eels (*Anglones* of Aldrovandus, or *Tobianus* of Schoneveldeus) commonly called smoulds,[7] taken out of the sea-sands with forks and rakes about Blakeney and Burnham : a small round slender fish, about three or four inches long, as big as a small tobacco-pipe ; a very dainty dish.

Pungilius marinus, or sea-bansticle, having a prickle on each side. The smallest fish of the sea, about an inch long, sometimes drawn ashore with nets, together with weeds and fragments of the sea.

Many sorts of flat fishes. The *pastinaca oxyrinchus*, with a long and strong aculeus in the tail, conceived of special venom and virtues.

Several sorts of *raias* (skates), and thornbacks. The *raia clavata oxyrinchus ; raia oculata, aspera, spinosa, fallonica*.

The great rhombus, or turbot,[8] *aculeatus et levis*.

The *passer*, or plaice.

Butts, of various kinds.

The *passer squamosus ;* bret, bretcock, and skulls ; comparable in taste and delicacy unto the sole.

The *buglossus solea*, or sole, *plana et oculata ;* as also the *lingula*, or small sole ; all in very great plenty.

Sometimes a fish about half a yard long, like a but or sole, called *asprage*, which I have known taken about Cromer.

[7] *smoulds*.] *Ammodytes tobianus*, L. Sand launce.

[8] *turbot*.] In *MS. Sloan.* 1784, I find this distich, with the subsequent explanatory notes attached :—

> Of wry-mouthed fish ! give me the left side black,*
> Except the sole,† which hath the noblest smack.

---

* *As turbot, bret, bretcock, skulls.*

† *Which is black on the right side ; as also butts, sandaps, and flounders.*

Sepia, or cuttle-fish, and great plenty of the bone or shelly substance, which sustaineth the whole bulk of that soft fish found commonly on the shore.

The *loligo sleve,* or *calamar,*[9] found often upon the shore, from head to tail sometimes about an ell long, remarkable for its parrot-like bill; the *gladiolus* or *celanus* along the back, and the notable crystalline of the eye, which equalleth, if not exceedeth, the lustre of oriental pearl.

A polypus, another kind of the mollia, sometimes we have met with.

Lobsters in great number, about Sherringham and Cromer, from whence all the country is supplied.

Astacus marinus pediculi marini facie, found also in that place. With the advantage of the long fore claws about four inches long.

Crabs, large and well-tasted; found also on the same coast.

Another kind of crab, taken for *canis fluvialis;* little, slender, and of a very quick motion, found in the river running through Yarmouth, and in Bliburgh river.

Oysters exceeding large about Burnham and Hunstanton, like those of Pool, St. Mallows, or Civita Vecchia, whereof many are eaten raw; the shells being broken with cleavers; the greater part pickled, and sent weekly to London and other parts.

Mituli, or muscles, in great quantity, as also chams or cockles, about Stiffkay and the north-west coast.

Pectines pectunculi varii, or scallops of the lesser sort.

Turbines, or smaller wilks, *leves, striati,* as also *trochi, trochili,* or sea tops, finely variegated and pearly. Likewise *purpuræ minores, nerites, cochleæ, tellinæ.*

Lepades, patellæ: limpits, of an univalve shell, wherein an animal like a snail cleaving fast unto the rocks.

Solenes, "cappe lunge" *Venetorum;* commonly a razor-fish; the shell thereof *dentalia,* by some called pin-patches, because the pin-meat thereof is taken out with a pin or needle.

---

[9] *loligo, &c.*] In digging for soles and shrimps, I have taken numbers of little *sepiæ,* an inch or two in length, in July and August, and have seen others (I believe of the species *loligo*), about twelve or eighteen inches long in the *sleeve* or *trunk,* in the autumn; *Cromer.—G.*

Cancellus turbinum et neritis. Bernard the hermit of Rondeletius. A kind of crab, or *astacus;* living in a forsaken wilk or *nerites.*

Echinus Echinometrites, sea hedgehog, whose neat shells are common on the shore. The fish alive often taken by the drags among the oysters.

Balani, a smaller sort of univalve growing commonly in clusters. The smaller kinds thereof to be found ofttimes upon oysters, wilks, and lobsters.

Concha anatifera, or *ansifera,* or barnacle-shell, whereof about four years past were found upon the shore no small number by Yarmouth, hanging by slender strings of a kind of *alga* unto several splinters or cleavings of fir-boards, unto which they were severally fastened, and hanged like ropes of onions : their shell flat, and of a peculiar form, differing from other shells; this being of four divisions ; containing a small imperfect animal, at the lower part divided into many shoots or streams, which prepossessed spectators' fancy to be the rudiment of the tail of some goose or duck to be produced from it. Some whereof in the shell, and some taken out and spread upon paper, we still keep by us.

Stellæ marinæ, or sea-stars, in great plenty, especially about Yarmouth. Whether they be bred out of the urticus, squalders, or sea-jellies, as many report, we cannot confirm; but the squalders in the middle seem to have some lines or first draughts not unlike. Our stars exceed not five points, though I have heard that some with more have been found about Hunstanton and Burnham ; where are also found *stellæ marinæ testaceæ,* or handsome crusted and brittle sea-stars, much less.

The *pediculus* and *culex marinus,* the sea louse and fly, are also no strangers.

Physsalus Rondeletii, or *eruca marina physsaloides,* according to the *icon* of Rondeletius, of very orient green and purple bristles.

Urtica marina of divers kinds ; some whereof called squalders. Of a burning and stinging quality, if rubbed in the hand. The water thereof may afford a good cosmetic.

Another very elegant sort there is often found cast up by shore in great numbers, about the bigness of a button, clear and welted, and may be called *fibula marina crystallina.*

Hirudines marini, or sea-leeches.

Vermes marini, very large worms, digged a yard deep out of the sands at ebb, for bait. It is known where they are to be found by a little flat over them, on the surface of the sand. As also *vermes in tubulis testacei*. Also *tethya*, or sea-dogs; some whereof resemble fritters. The *vesicaria marina* also, and *fanago*, sometimes very large; conceived to proceed from some testaceous animals, and particularly from the *purpura*; but ours more probably from other testaceous, we have not met with any large *purpura* upon this coast.

Many river fishes also and animals. Salmon no common fish in our rivers, though many are taken in the Ouse; in the Bure or North river; in the Waveney or South river; in the Norwich river but seldom, and in the winter. But four years ago fifteen were taken at Trowse mill, at Christmas, whose mouths were stuck with small worms or horse leeches, no bigger than fine threads. Some of these I kept in water three months. If a few drops of blood were put to the water, they would in a little time look red. They sensibly grew bigger than I first found them, and were killed by a hard frost freezing the water. Most of our salmon have a recurved piece of flesh in the end of the lower jaw, which, when they shut their mouths, deeply enters the upper, as Scaliger hath noted in some.

The rivers, lakes, and broads, abound in the *lucius* or pikes of a very large size, where also is found the *brama* or bream, large and well tasted. The *tinca* or tench; the *aulecula*, roach; as also rowds and dare or dace; *perca* or perch, great and small; whereof such as are taken in Breydon, on this side Yarmouth, in the mixed water, make a dish very dainty; and, I think, scarce to be bettered in England. But the blea, the chubbe, the barble, to be found in divers other rivers in England I have not observed in these. As also fewer minnows than in many other rivers.

The *trutta* or trout; the *gammarus* or crawfish; but scarce in our rivers; but frequently taken in the Bure or North river, and in the several branches thereof. And very remarkable large crawfishes to be found in the river which runs by Castleacre and Nerford.

The *aspredo perca minor*, and probably the *cernua* of Cardan, commonly called a ruff; in great plenty in Norwich

river, and even in the stream of the city; which though
Camden appropriates unto this city, yet they are also found
in the rivers of Oxford and Cambridge.

Lampetra, lampreys, great and small, found plentifully in
Norwich river, and even in the city, about May; whereof
some are very large; and, well cooked, are counted a dainty
bit collared up, but especially in pies.

Mustela fluviatilis or eel-pout, to be had in Norwich river,
and between it and Yarmouth, as also in the rivers of
Marshland; resembling an eel and a cod; a very good dish;
and the liver whereof well answers the commendations of
the ancients.

Gudgeons or *funduli fluviatiles;* many whereof may be.
taken within the river in the city.

Capitones fluviatiles or miller's thumb; *pungitias fluviatilis*
or stanticles. *Aphia cobites fluviatilis* or loches. In Norwich river, in the runs about Heveningham Heath, in the
North river and streams thereof.

Of eels, the common eel, and the glot, which hath somewhat a different shape in the bigness of the head and is
affirmed to have young ones often found within it; and we
have found an *uterus* in the same, somewhat answering the
icon thereof in Senesinus.

Carpiones, carp; plentiful in ponds, and sometimes large
ones in broads. Two of the largest I ever beheld were taken
in Norwich river.

Though the woods and drylands abound with adders and
vipers, yet are there few snakes about our rivers or meadows;
more to be found in Marshland. But ponds and plashes
abound in lizards or swifts.

The *gryllotalpa* or fen cricket, common in fenny places;
but we have met with them also in dry places, dunghills, and
churchyards, of this city.

Besides horseleeches and periwinkles, in plashes and
standing waters, we have met with *vermes setacei* or hard
worms: but could never convert horsehairs into them by
laying them in water. As also the great *hydrocantharus* or
black shining water-beetle, the *forficula, squilla, corculum,*
and *notonecton*, that swimmeth on its back.

Camden reports that in former time there have been
beavers in the river of Cardigan in Wales. This we are too.

sure of, that the rivers, great broads, and carrs, afford great store of otters with us; a great destroyer of fish, as feeding but from the vent downwards; not free from being a prey itself; for their young ones have been found in buzzards' nests. They are accounted no bad dish by many; are to be made very tame; and in some houses have served for turnspits.

ON THE OSTRICH.[1]

[MS. SLOAN. 1830, fol. 10, 11 ; 1847.]

THE ostrich hath a compounded name in Greek and Latin —*Struthio-Camelus*, borrowed from a bird and a beast, as being a feathered and biped animal, yet in some ways like a camel; somewhat in the long neck; somewhat in the foot; and, as some imagine, from a camel-like position in the part of generation.

It is accounted the largest and tallest of any winged and feathered fowl; taller than the gruen or cassowary. This ostrich, though a female, was about seven feet high, and some of the males were higher, either exceeding or answerable unto the stature of the great porter unto king Charles the First. The weight was a[2]   in grocer's scales.

Whosoever shall compare or consider together the ostrich and the tomineio, or humbird, not weighing twelve grains, may easily discover under what compass or latitude the creation of birds hath been ordained.

The head is not large, but little in proportion to the whole body. And, therefore, Julius Scaliger, when he mentioned birds of large heads (comparatively unto their bodies),

---

[1] *On the ostrich.*] This was drawn up for his son Edward, to be delivered in the course of his lectures. It occurs in the middle of the paper on Birds; but evidently was inserted by mistake in the binding; it is written on larger paper.

[2] *a . . . . .*] Utterly undecypherable in the original.

named the sparrow, the owl, and the woodpecker; and, reckoning up birds of small heads, instanceth in the hen, the peacock, and the ostrich.*

The head is looked upon by discerning spectators to resemble that of a goose rather than any kind of στροῦθος, or *passer :* and so may be more properly called *cheno-camelus,* or *ansero-camelus.*

There is a handsome figure of an ostrich in Mr. Willoughby's and Ray's *Ornithologia :* another in Aldrovandus and Jonstonus, and [Bellonius; but the heads not exactly ageeing. "Rostrum habet exiguum, sed acutum," saith Jonstoun; "un long bec et poinctu," saith Bellonius; men describing such as they have an opportunity to see, and perhaps some the ostriches of very different countries, wherein, as in some other birds, there may be some variety.

In Africa, where some eat elephants, it is no wonder that some also feed upon ostriches. They flay them with their feathers on, which they sell, and eat the flesh. But Galen and physicians have condemned that flesh, as hard and indigestible.[3] The emperor Heliogabalus had a fancy for the brains, when he brought six hundred ostriches' heads to one supper, only for the brains' sake; yet Leo Africanus saith that he ate of young ostriches among the Numidians with a good gust; and, perhaps, boiled, and well cooked, after the art of Apicius, with pepperm n , dates, and other good things, they might go down with some stomachs.

I do not find that the strongest eagles, or best-spirited hawks, will offer at these birds; yet, if there were such gyrfalcons as Julius Scaliger saith the duke of Savoy and Henry, king of Navarre, had, it is like they would strike at them, and, making at the head, would spoil them, or so disable them, that they might be taken.†

If these had been brought over in June, it is, perhaps,

---

* See Scaliger's *Exercitations.*

† See Scaliger's *Exercitations,* and in his *Comment.* on *Arist. De Historia Animal.*

[3] *as hard and indigestible.*] "And, therefore, when, according to Lampridius, the emperor Heliogabalus forced the Jews to eat ostriches, it was a meat not only hard of digestion to their stomachs, but also to their consciences, as being a forbidden meat food."—*Addition from MS. Sloan.* 1847.

likely we might have met with eggs in some of their bellies, whereof they lay very many : but they are the worst of eggs for food, yet serviceable unto many other uses in their country; for, being cut transversely, they serve for drinking cups and skull-caps; and, as I have seen, there are large circles of them, and some painted and gilded, which hang up in Turkish mosques, and also in Greek churches. They are preserved with us for rarities; and, as they come to be common, some use will be found of them in physic, even as of other eggshells and other such substances.

When it first came into my garden, it soon ate up all the gilliflowers, tulip-leaves, and fed greedily upon what was green, as lettuce, endive, sorrell; it would feed on oats, barley, peas, beans; swallow onions; eat sheep's lights and livers.—Then you mention what you know more.[4]

When it took down a large onion, it stuck awhile in the gullet, and did not descend directly, but wound backward behind the neck; whereby I might perceive that the gullet turned much; but this is not peculiar unto the ostrich; but the same hath been observed in the stork, when it swallows down frogs and pretty big bits.

It made sometimes a strange noise; had a very odd note, especially in the morning, and, perhaps, when hungry.

According to Aldrovandus, some hold that there is an antipathy between it and a horse, which an ostrich will not endure to see or be near; but, while I kept it, I could not confirm this opinion; which might, perhaps, be raised because a common way of hunting and taking them is by swift horses.

It is much that Cardanus should be mistaken with a great part of men, that the coloured and dyed feathers of ostriches were natural; as red, blue, yellow, and green; whereas, the natural colours in this bird were white and greyish. Of [the] fashion of wearing feathers in battles or wars by men, and women, see Scaliger, *Contra Cardan. Exercitat.* 220.

If wearing of feather-fans should come up again, it might much increase the trade of plumage from Barbary. Bellonius saith he saw two hundred skins with the feathers on in one shop of Alexandria.

[4] *Then you mention, &c.*] This must be considered as spoken "aside" to his son.

BOULIMIA CENTENARIA.[1]

[MS. SLOAN. 1833, and MS. RAWL. LVIII.]

THERE is a woman now living in Yarmouth, named Elizabeth Michell, an hundred and two years old; a person of four feet and half high, very lean, very poor, and living in a mean room with pitiful accommodation. She had a son after she was past fifty.[2]   Though she answers well enough unto ordinary questions, yet she apprehends her eldest daughter to be her mother; but what is most remarkable concerning her is a kind of *boulimia* or dog-appetite; she greedily eating day and night what her allowance, friends, or charitable persons afford her, drinking beer or water, and making little distinction or refusal of any food, either of broths, flesh, fish, apples, pears, and any coarse food, which she eateth in no small quantity, insomuch that the overseers for the poor have of late been fain to augment her weekly allowance. She sleeps indifferently well, till hunger awakes her ; then she must have no ordinary supply whether in the day or night. She vomits not, nor is very laxative. This is the oldest example of the *sal esurinum chymicorum*, which I have taken notice of; though I am ready to afford my charity unto her, yet I should be loth to spend a piece of ambergris I have upon her, and to allow six grains to every dose till I found some effect in moderating her appetite : though that be esteemed a great specific in her condition.

---

[1] *Boulimia.*] Brutus was attacked with this disease on his march to Durachium.—*Plutarch.*

[2] *She had a son, &c.*] A duplicate copy of this paper in the Bodleian (*MS. Rawl.* lviii.) reads "her youngest son is forty-five years old."

UPON THE DARK THICK MIST HAPPENING ON THE 27th OF NOVEMBER, 1674.

[MS. SLOAN. 1833, fol. 136.]

THOUGH it be not strange to see frequent mists, clouds, and rains, in England, as many ancient describers of this country have noted, yet I could not [but] take notice of a very great mist which happened upon the 27th of the last November, and from thence have taken this occasion to propose something of mists, clouds, and rains, unto your candid considerations.

Herein mists may well deserve the first place, as being, if not the first in nature, yet the first meteor mentioned in Scripture, and soon after the creation, for it is said, Gen. ii. thàt " God had not yet caused it to rain upon the earth, but a mist went up from the earth, and watered the whole face of the ground," for it might take a longer time for the elevation of vapours sufficient to make a congregation of clouds able to afford any store of showers and rain in so early days of the world.

Thick vapours, not ascending high but hanging about the earth and covering the surface of it, are commonly called mists; if they ascend high they are termed clouds. They remain upon the earth till they either fall down or are attenuated, rarified, and scattered.

The great mist was not only observable about London, but in remote parts of England, and as we hear, in Holland, so that it was of larger extent than mists are commonly apprehended to be; most men conceiving that they reach not much beyond the places where they behold them. Mists make an obscure air, but they beget not darkness, for the atoms and particles thereof admit the light, but if the matter thereof be very thick, close, and condensed, the mist grows considerably obscure and like a cloud, so the miraculous and palpable darkness of Egypt is conceived to have been effected by an extraordinary dense and dark mist or a kind of cloud spread over the land of Egypt, and also miraculously restrained from the neighbour land of Goshen.

z 2

Mists and fogs, containing commonly vegetable spirits, when they dissolve and return upon the earth, may fecundate and add some fertility unto it, but they may be more unwholesome in great cities than in country habitations: for they consist of vapours not only elevated from simple watery and humid places, but also the exhalations of draughts, common sewers, and fœtid places, and decoctions used by unwholesome and sordid manufactures: and also hindering the sea-coal smoke from ascending and passing away, it is conjoined with the mist and drawn in by the breath, all which may produce bad effects, inquinate the blood, and produce catarrhs and coughs. Sereins, well known in hot countries, cause headache, toothache, and swelled faces; but they seem to have their original from subtle, invisible, nitrous, and piercing exhalations, caused by a strong heat of the sun, which falling after sunset produce the effects mentioned.

There may be also subterraneous mists, when heat in the bowels of the earth, working upon humid parts, makes an attenuation thereof and consequently nebulous bodies in the cavities of it.

There is a kind of a continued mist in the bodies of animals, especially in the cavous parts, as may be observed in bodies opened presently after death, and some think that in sleep there is a kind of mist in the brain; and upon exceeding motion some animals cast out a mist about them.

When the cuttle fish, polypus, or loligo, make themselves invisible by obscuring the water about them; they do it not by any vaporous emission, but by a black humour ejected, which makes the water black and dark near them: but upon excessive motion some animals are able to afford a mist about them, when the air is cool and fit to condense it, as horses after a race, so that they become scarce visible.

[ACCOUNT OF A THUNDER STORM AT NOR-
WICH, 1665.]

[MS. SLOAN. 1866, fol. 96.]

June 28, 1665.

AFTER seven o'clock in the evening there was almost a
continued thunder until eight, wherein the *tonitru* and *fulgur*,
the noise and lightning, were so terrible, that they put the
whole city into an amazement, and most unto their prayers.
The clouds went low, and the cracks seemed near over our
heads during the most part of the thunder. About eight
o'clock, an *ignis fulmineus, pila ignea fulminans, telum ig-
neum fulmineum,* or fire-ball, hit against the little wooden
pinnacle of the high leucome window of my house, toward
the market-place, broke the flue boards, and carried pieces
thereof a stone's cast off; whereupon many of the tiles fell
into the street, and the windows in adjoining houses were
broken. At the same time either a part of that close-bound
fire, or another of the same nature, fell into the court-yard,
and whereof no notice was taken till we began to examine
the house, and then we found a freestone on the outside of
the wall of the entry leading to the kitchen, half a foot from
the ground, fallen from the wall; a hole as big as a foot-ball
bored through the wall, which is about a foot thick, and a
chest which stood against it, on the inside, split and carried
about a foot from the wall. The wall also, behind the leaden
cistern, at five yards distance from it, broken on the inside
and outside; the middle seeming entire. The lead on the
edges of the cistern turned a little up; and a great washing-
bowl, that stood by it, to recover the rain, turned upside
down, and split quite through. Some chimneys and tiles
were struck down in other parts of the city. A fire-ball also
struck down the walk in the market-place. And all this, God
be thanked! without mischief unto any person. The greatest
terror was from the noise, answerable unto two or three
cannon. The smell it left was ·strong, like that after the
discharge of a cannon. The balls· that flew were not like

fire in the flame, but the coal; and the people said it was like the sun. It was *discutiens, terebrans,* but not *urens.* It burnt nothing, nor any thing it touched smelt of fire; nor melted any lead of window or cistern, as I found it do in the great storm, about nine years ago, at Melton-hall, four miles off, at that time when the hail broke three thousand pounds worth of glass in Norwich, in half-a-quarter of an hour. About four days after, the like fulminous fire killed a man in Erpingham church, by Aylsham, upon whom it broke, and beat down divers which were within the wind of it. One also went off in Sir John Hobart's gallery, at Blickling. He was so near that his arm and thigh were numbed about an hour after. Two or three days after, a woman and horse were killed near Bungay; her hat so shivered that no piece remained bigger than a groat, whereof I had some pieces sent unto me. Granades, crackers, and squibs, do much resemble the discharge, and *aurum fulminans* the fury thereof. Of other thunderbolts or *lapides fulminei,* I have little opinion. Some I have by me under that name, but they are *è genere fossilium.*

THOMAS BROWNE.

Norwich, 1665.

[ON DREAMS.]

[MS. SLOAN. 1874, fol. 112, 120.]

HALF our days we pass in the shadow of the earth; and the brother of death exacteth a third part of our lives. A good part of our sleep is peered out with visions and fantastical objects, wherein we are confessedly deceived. The day supplieth us with truths; the night with fictions and falsehoods, which uncomfortably divide the natural account of our beings. And, therefore, having passed the day in sober labours and rational enquiries of truth, we are fain to betake ourselves unto such a state of being, wherein the soberest heads have acted all the monstrosities of melancholy, and which unto open eyes are no better than folly and madness.

Happy are they that go to bed with grand music, like Pythagoras, or have ways to compose the fantastical spirit, whose unruly wanderings take off inward sleep, filling our heads with St. Anthony's visions, and the dreams of Lipara in the sober chambers of rest.

Virtuous thoughts of the day lay up good treasures for the night; whereby the impressions of imaginary forms arise into sober similitudes, acceptable unto our slumbering selves and preparatory unto divine impressions.[1] Hereby Solomon's sleep was happy. Thus prepared, Jacob might well dream of angels upon a pillow of stone. And the best sleep of Adam might be the best of any after.[2]

That there should be divine dreams seems unreasonably doubted by Aristotle. That there are demoniacal dreams we have little reason to doubt. Why may there not be angelical? If there be guardian spirits, they may not be inactively about us in sleep; but may sometimes order our dreams : and many strange hints, instigations, or discourses, which are so amazing unto us, may arise from such foundations.

But the phantasms of sleep do commonly walk in the great road of natural and animal dreams, wherein the thoughts or actions of the day are acted over and echoed in the night. Who can therefore wonder that Chrysostom should dream of St. Paul, who daily read his epistles ; or that Cardan, whose head was so taken up about the stars, should dream that his soul was in the moon ! Pious persons, whose thoughts are daily busied about heaven, and the blessed state thereof, can hardly escape the nightly phantasms of it, which though sometimes taken for illuminations, or divine dreams, yet rightly perpended may prove but animal visions, and natural night-scenes of their awaking contemplations. *Modern*

Many dreams are made out by sagacious exposition, and from the signature of their subjects ; carrying their interpretation in their fundamental sense and mystery of similitude, whereby, he that understands upon what natural fundamental every notion dependeth, may, by symbolical adaptation, hold

---

[1] *Virtuous thoughts, &c.*] See an exquisite passage in *Religio Medici*, pp. 446, 447.

[2] *the best sleep of Adam, &c.*] The only sleep of Adam recorded, is that which God caused to fall upon him, and which resulted in the creation of woman. It does not very clearly appear whether Sir Thomas calls it the *best* sleep of Adam, in allusion to its origin, or its result.

a ready way to read the characters of Morpheus. In dreams
of such a nature, Artemidorus, Achmet, and Astrampsichus,
from Greek, Egyptian, and Arabian oneiro-criticism, may
hint some interpretation: who, while we read of a ladder in
Jacob's dream, will tell us that ladders and scalary ascents
signify preferment; and while we consider the dream of
Pharaoh, do teach us that rivers overflowing speak plenty,
lean oxen, famine and scarcity; and therefore it was but
reasonable in Pharaoh to demand the interpretation from
his magicians, who, being Egyptians, should have been well
versed in symbols and the hieroglyphical notions of things.
The greatest tyrant in such divinations was Nabuchodonosor,
while, besides the interpretation, he demanded the dream
itself; which being probably determined by divine immission,
might escape the common road of phantasms, that might
have been traced by Satan.

When Alexander, going to besiege Tyre, dreamt of a
Satyr, it was no hard exposition for a Grecian to say, "Tyre
will be thine." He that dreamed that he saw his father
washed by Jupiter and anointed by the sun, had cause to
fear that he might be crucified, whereby his body would be
washed by the rain, and drop by the heat of the sun. The
dream of Vespasian was of harder exposition; as also that
of the emperor Mauritius, concerning his successor Phocas.
And a man might have been hard put to it, to interpret the
language of Æsculapius, when to a consumptive person he
held forth his fingers; implying thereby that his cure lay in
dates, from the homonomy of the Greek, which signifies
dates and fingers.

We owe unto dreams that Galen was a physician, Dion
an historian, and that the world hath seen some notable
pieces of Cardan; yet, he that should order his affairs by
dreams, or make the night a rule unto the day, might be
ridiculously deluded; wherein Cicero is much to be pitied,
who having excellently discoursed of the vanity of dreams,
was yet undone by the flattery of his own, which urged him
to apply himself unto Augustus.

However dreams may be fallacious concerning outward
events, yet may they be truly significant at home; and whereby we may more sensibly understand ourselves. Men act
in sleep with some conformity unto their awaked senses;

and consolations or discouragements may be drawn from dreams which intimately tell us ourselves. Luther was not like to fear a spirit in the night, when such an apparition would not terrify him in the day. Alexander would hardly have run away in the sharpest combats of sleep, nor Demosthenes have stood stoutly to it, who was scarce able to do it in his prepared senses. Persons of radical integrity, will not easily be perverted in their dreams, nor noble minds do pitiful things in sleep. Crassus would have hardly been bountiful in a dream, whose fist was so close awake. But a man m. ht have lived all his life upon the sleeping hand of Autonius.[3]

. There is an art to make dreams, as well as their interpretations ; and physicians will tell us that some food makes turbulent, some gives quiet, dreams. Cato, who doated upon cabbage, might find the crude effects thereof in his sleep ; wherein the Egyptians might find some advantage by their superstitious abstinence from onions. Pythagoras might have [had] calmer sleeps, if he [had] totally abstained from beans. Even Daniel, the great interpreter of dreams, in his leguminous diet, seems to have chosen no advantageous food for quiet sleeps, according to Grecian physic.

To add unto the delusion of dreams, the fantastical objects seem greater than they are ; and being beheld in the vaporous state of sleep, enlarge their diameters unto us ; whereby it may prove more easy to dream of giants than pigmies. Democritus might seldom dream of atoms, who so often thought of them. He almost might dream himself a bubble extending unto the eighth sphere. A little water makes a sea ; a small puff of wind a tempest. A grain of sulphur kindled in the blood may make a flame like Ætna ; and a small spark in the bowels of Olympias a lightning over all the chamber. *Neurosis*

But, beside these innocent delusions, there is a sinful state of dreams. Death alone, not sleep, is able to put an end unto sin ; and there may be a night-book of our iniquities ; for beside the transgressions of the day, casuists will tell

---

[3] *sleeping hand of Antonius.*] Who awake was *open-handed* and liberal, in contrast with the *close-fistedness* of Crassus, and therefore would have been munificent in his dreams.

us of mortal sins in dreams, arising from evil precogitations ; meanwhile human law regards not noctambulos ; and if a night-walker should break his neck, or kill a man, takes no notice of it.

Dionysius was absurdly tyrannical to kill a man for dreaming that he had killed him ; and really to take away his life, who had but fantastically taken away his. Lamia was ridiculously unjust to sue a young man for a reward, who had confessed that pleasure from her in a dream which she had denied unto his awaking senses : conceiving that she had merited somewhat from his fantastical fruition and shadow of herself. If there be such debts, we owe deeply unto sympathics ; but the common spirit of the world must be ready in such arrearages.

If some have swooned, they may have also died in dreams, since death is but a confirmed swooning. Whether Plato died in a dream, as some deliver, he must rise again to inform us. That some have never dreamed, is as improbable as that some have never laughed. That children dream not the first half-year ; that men dream not in some countries, with many more, are unto me sick men's dreams ; dreams out of the ivory gate,[4] and visions before midnight.

[OBSERVATIONS ON GRAFTING.[1]]

[MS. SLOAN. 1848, fol. 44—48 ; 1882, fol. 136, [137 ; AND ADDITIONAL MSS. NO. 5233, fol. 58.]

IN the doctrine of all insitions, those are esteemed most successful which are practised under these rules :—

That there be some consent or similitude of parts and nature between the plants conjoined.

[4] *the ivory gate.*] The poets suppose two gates of sleep, the one of horn, from which true dreams proceed ; the other of ivory, which sends forth false dreams.

[1] *Observations, &c.*] "*Generation of plants,*" was the title given by Dr. Ayscough to this paper : which, in all probability, was written for and addressed to Evelyn.

That insition be made between trees not of very different barks; nor very differing fruits or forms of fructification; nor of widely different ages.

That the scions or buds be taken from the south or east part of the tree.

That a rectitude and due position be observed; not to insert the south part of the scions unto the northern side of the stock, but according to the position of the scions upon his first matrix.

Now, though these rules be considerable in the usual and practised course of insitions, yet were it but [reasonable for searching spirits to urge the operations of nature by conjoining plants of very different natures in parts, barks, lateness, and precocities, nor to rest in the experiments of hortensial plants in whom we chiefly intend the exaltation or variety of their fruit and flowers, but in all sorts of shrubs and trees applicable unto physic or mechanical uses, whereby we might alter their tempers, moderate or promote their virtues, exchange their softness, hardness, and colour, and so render them considerable beyond their known and trite employments.

To which intent curiosity may take some rule or hint from these or the like following, according to the various ways of propagation :—[2]

Colutea upon anagris—arbor judæ upon anagris—cassia poetica upon cytisus—cytisus upon periclymenum rectum—woodbine upon jasmine—cystus upon rosemary—rosemary upon ivy—sage or rosemary upon cystus—myrtle upon gall or rhus myrtifolia—whortle-berry upon gall, heath, or myrtle—coccygeia upon alaternus—mezereon upon an almond—gooseberry and currants upon mezereon, barberry, or blackthorn—barberry upon a currant tree—bramble upon gooseberry or raspberry—yellow rose upon sweetbrier—phyllerea upon broom—broom upon furze—anonis lutea upon furze—holly upon box—bay upon holly—holly upon pyracantha—

---

[2] *propagation.*] A brief memorandum occurs here in the original, in these words :— "*To insert the Catalogue,*" evidently showing that the author intended the list of his proposed experiments to be here introduced. Having met with such a Catalogue (in *MS. Sloan.* 1843, fol. 44—48) I have not hesitated to transplant it hither as the one intended. Several of the names are so illegible that it is impossible not to fear they may be incorrectly given.

a fig upon chesnut—a fig upon mulberry—peach upon mulberry—mulberry upon buckthorn—walnut upon chesnut —savin upon juniper—vine upon oleaster, rosemary, ivy— an arbutus upon a fig—a peach upon a fig—white poplar upon black poplar—asp upon white poplar—wych elm upon common elm—hazel upon elm—sycamore upon wych elm— cinnamon rose upon hipberry—a whitethorn upon a black- thorn—hipberry upon a sloe, or skeye, or bullace—apricot upon a mulberry—arbutus upon a mulberry—cherry upon a peach—oak upon a chesnut—katherine peach upon a quince —a warden upon a quince—a chesnut upon a beech—a beech upon a chesnut—an hornbeam upon a beech—a maple upon an hornbeam—a sycamore upon a maple—a medlar upon a service tree—a sumack upon a quince or medlar—an hawthorn upon a service tree—a quicken tree upon an ash —an ash upon an asp—an oak upon an ilex—a poplar upon an elm—a black cherry tree upon a tilea or lime tree—tilea upon beech—alder upon birch or poplar—a filbert upon an almond —an almond upon a willow—a nux vesicaria upon an almond or pistachio—a cerasus avium upon a nux vesicaria—a cor- nelian[3] upon a cherry tree—a cherry tree upon a cornelian —an hazel upon a willow or sallow—a lilac upon a sage tree —a syringa upon lilac or tree-mallow—a rose elder upon syringa—a water elder upon rose elder—buckthorn upon elder—frangula upon buckthorn — hirga sanguinea upon privet—phyllerea upon vitex—vitex upon evonymus—evony- mus upon viburnum—ruscus upon pyracantha—paleurus upon hawthorn—tamarisk upon birch—erica upon tamarisk —polemonium upon genista hispanica—genista hispanica upon colutea.

Nor are we to rest in the frustrated success of some single experiments, but to proceed in attempts in the most un- likely unto iterated and certain conclusions, and to pursue the way of ablactation or inarching. Whereby we might determine whether, according to the ancients, no fir, pine, or picea, would admit of any incision upon them; whether yew will hold society with none; whether walnut, mulberry, and cornel cannot be propagated by insition, or the fig and quince admit almost of any, with many others of doubtful truths in the propagations.

[3] *cornelian.*]   Cornel-tree.

' And while we seek for varieties in stocks and scions, we are not to omit the ready practice of the scion upon its own tree. Whereby, having a sufficient number of good plants, we may improve their fruits without translative conjunction, that is, by insition of the scion upon his own mother, whereby an handsome variety or melioration seldom faileth—we might be still advanced by iterated insitions in proper boughs and positions. Insition is also made not only with scions and buds, but seeds, by inserting them in cabbage stalks, turnips, onions, &c., and also in ligneous plants.

Within a mile of this city of Norwich, an oak groweth upon the head of a pollard willow, taller than the stock, and about half a foot in diameter, probably by some acorn falling or fastening upon it. I could show you a branch of the same willow which shoots forth near the stock which beareth both willow and oak twigs and leaves upon it. In a meadow I use in Norwich, beset with willows and sallows, I have observed these plants to grow upon their heads ; bylders,[4] currants, gooseberries, *cynocrambe*, or dog's mercury, barberries, bittersweet, elder, hawthorn.

MS. SLOAN. 1869, fol. 12—60, 62—118, COLLATED WITH 1874 and 1885.]

[*Hints and Extracts ; to his Son, Dr. Edward Browne.*]

SEVERAL hints which may be serviceable unto you and not ungrateful unto others I present you in this paper ; they are not trite or vulgar, and very few of them anywhere to be met with. I set them not down in order, but as memory, fancy, or occasional observation produced them ; whereof you may take the pains to single out such as shall conduce unto your purpose.

That Elias was a type of our Saviour, and that the mocking and railing of the children had reference unto the derision and reviling of our Saviour by the Jews, we shall not deny, but whether their calling of him bald pate, crying,

---

[4] *bylders.*] Qu. bilberry ?

ascende calve, had any relation unto Mount Calvary, we shall not be ready to affirm.

That Charles the Fifth was crowned upon the day of his nativity carrieth no remarkable consideration, but that he also took King Francis prisoner upon that day, was a concurrence of accidents which must make that day observable.

Antipater, that died on his birth-day, had an anniversary fever all his life upon the day of his nativity, needed not an astrological revolution of his nativity to know the day of his death.

Who will not commend the wit of astrology?—Venus born out of the sea hath her exaltation in Pisces.

Whosoever understandeth the fructifying quality of water will quickly apprehend the congruity of that invention which made the cornucopia to be filled with flowers by the naiades. or water nymphs.

Who can but wonder that Fuchsius should doubt the purging quality of manna, or derive *aloe sucotina* from *succus citrinus*, which every novice now knows to be from Socotara, an island from whence 'tis brought?

Take heed of confidence and too bold an opinion of your work: even the famous Phidias so erred in that notable statua of Jupiter made in a sitting posture, yet so that if he had risen up he had borne up the top of the temple.

Transcriptional erratas, ignorance in some particulars, expedition, inadvertency, make not only moles but wens in learned works, which notwithstanding being judged by their better parts admit not of reasonable disparagement. I will not say that Cicero was slightly versed in Homer, because in his books *De Gloria* he ascribeth those verses unto Ajax which were delivered by Hector. In the account of Hercules, Plautus mistakes nativity for conception. Pliny, who was well seen in Homer, denieth the art of picture in the Trojan war, and whereas it is plainly said, *Iliad* Σ, 483, that Vulcan engraved in the arms of Achilles the earth and stars of heaven. And though I have no great opinion of Machiavell's learning, yet am I unwilling to say he was but a weak historian, because he commonly exemplified in Cæsar Borgia and the petty princes of Italy; or that he had but a slight knowledge in Roman story, because he was mistaken in placing Commodus after the emperor Severus.

Wonderful without doubt and of excellent signification are the mysteries, allegories, and figures of Holy Scripture, had we a true intelligence of them, but whether they signified any such thing as Gamaliel, Rampegnoli, Venetus, and others, do put upon them, is a great obscurity and Urim and Thummim unto me.

That the first time the Creator is called the Lord, in holy Scripture, was twenty-eight times after he was called God, seems an excellent propriety in Scripture; which gave him the relative name after the visible frame and accomplishment of the creation, but the essential denomination and best agreeable unto him before all time or ere the world began.

' Whether there be any numerical mystery in the omission of the benediction of the second day, because it was the first recess from unity and beginning of imperfection: and according to which mystery three angels appeared unto Abraham to bring him happy tidings, but two at the destruction of Sodom.

Whether Tubal Cain, the inventor of smith's work, be therefore joined with Jubal, the father of musicians, because musical consonances were first discovered from the stroke of hammers upon anvils, the diversities of their weights discovering the proportion of their sounds, as is also reported from the observation of Pythagoras, is not readily to be believed.

The symbolical mysteries of Scripture sacrifices, cleansings, feasts, and expiations, is tolerably made out by Rabbins and ritual commentators, but many things are obscure, and the Jews themselves will say that Solomon understood not the mystery of the red cow. Even in the Pagan lustration of the people of Rome, at the *palilia*, why they made use of the ashes of a calf taken out of the belly of the dam, the blood of an horse, and bean straw, hath not yet found a convincing or probable conjecture.

Certainly most things are known as many are seen, that is, by parallaxes, and in some difference from their true and proper beings; the superficial regard of things being of different aspect from their central natures; and therefore following the common view, and living by the obvious track of sense, we are insensibly imposed upon by consuetude, and only wise or happy by coestimation; the received apprehensions of true or good having widely confounded the substantial and inward verity thereof, which now only subsisting in the theory and acknowledgment of some few wise or good men, are looked upon as antiquated paradoxes or sullen theorems of the old world: whereas indeed truth, which is said not to seek corners, lies in the centre of things; the area and exterous part being only overspread with legionary vanities of error, or stuffed with the meteors and imperfect mixtures of truth.

Discoveries are welcome at all hands; yet he that found out the line of the middle motion of the planets, holds an higher mansion in my thoughts than he that discovered the Indies, and Ptolemy, that saw no further than the feet of the centaur, than he that hath beheld the snake by the southern pole.   The rational discovery of things transcends their simple detections, whose inventions are often casual and secondary unto intention.

Cupid is said to be blind; affection should not be too sharp-sighted, and love not to be made by magnifying glasses; if things were seen as they are, the beauty of bodies would be much abridged; and therefore the wisdom of God hath drawn the pictures and outsides of things softly and amiably unto the natural edge of our eyes, not able to discover those unlovely asperities which make oystershells in good faces, and hedgehogs even in Venus' moles.

When God commanded Abraham to look up to heaven and number the stars thereof, that he extraordinarily enlarged his sight to behold the host of heaven, and the innumerable heap of stars which telescopes now show unto us, some men might be persuaded to believe. Who can think that when 'tis said that the blood of Abel cried unto heaven, Abel fell a bleeding at the sight of Cain, according to the observation of men slain to bleed at the presence of the murderer?

The learned Gaspar Schottus dedicates his Thaumaturgus Mathematicus unto his tutelary or guardian angel; in which epistle he useth these words: *cui, post Deum conditorem*

Deique magnam matrem Mariam, omnia debeo. Now,[1] though
we must not lose God in good angels, and because they are
always supposed about us, hold lesser memory of him in our
prayers, addresses, and consideration of his presence, care,
and protection over us, yet they which do assert them have
both antiquity and Scripture to confirm them; but whether
the angel that wrestled with Jacob were Esau's good angel;
whether our Saviour had one deputed him, or whether that
was his good angel which appeared and strengthened him
before his passion; whether antichrist shall have any;
whether all men have one, some more, and therefore there
must be more angels than ever were men together; whether
angels assist successively and distinctly, or whether but once
and singly to one person, and so there must be a greater
number of them than ever of men or shall be; whether we
are under the care of our mother's good angel in the womb,
or whether that spirit undertakes us when the stars are
thought to concern us, that is, at our nativity, men have a
liberty and latitude to opinion.

Aristotle, who seems to have borrowed many things from
Hippocrates, in the most favourable acceptation, makes mention but once of him, and that by the bye, and without
reference unto his doctrine. Virgil so much beholding unto
Homer hath not his name in his works; and Pliny, that
seems to borrow many authors out of Dioscorides, hath taken
no notice of him. Men are still content to plume themselves
with others' feathers. Fear of discovery, not single ingenuity, makes quotations rather than transcriptions; of which,
notwithstanding, the plagiarism of many holds little consideration, whereof, though great authors may complain,
small ones cannot but take notice. Mr. Philips, in his
Villare Cantianum, transcribes half a side of my *Hydrotaphia,*
or *Urn Burial,* without mention of the author.[2]

Many things are casually or favourably superadded unto
the best authors, and the lines of many made to contain that
advantageous sense which they never intended. It was
handsomely said, and probably intended by Virgil, when on
every word of that verse he laid a significant emphasis, *una*

---

[1] *The learned Gaspar Schottus, &c.*] This passage is from a duplicate
of the present paragraph in *MS. Sloan.* 1874.

[2] *Mr. Philips, &c.*] This paragraph has a mark of erasure in the original.

dolo divum si fæmina capta duorum ; and 'tis not unlikely that
in that other, consisting altogether of slow and heaving
spondees, he intended to humour the massive and heaving
strokes of the gigantic forgers, *illi inter sese magna vi
brachia tollunt ;* but in that which admitteth so numerous
a transposition of words, as almost to equal the ancient
number of the noted stars, I cannot believe he had any such
scope or intention, much less any numerical magic in another,
as to be a certain rule in that numeration practised in the
handsome trick of singling Christians and Turks, which is
due unto later invention ; or that Homer any otherwise than
casually began the first and last verse of his Iliad with the
same letter.

Some plants have been thought to have been proper unto
peculiar countries, and yet upon better discovery the same
have been found in distant countries and in all community
of parts.

Jul. Scalig. in *Questionibus Familiaribus ;—*
    Extra fortunam est quicquid donatur amicis.

Many things are casually or favourably superadded unto
the best authors, and sometimes conceits and expressions
common unto them with others, and that not by imitation
but coincidence, and concurrence of imagination upon harmony of production.   Scaliger observes how one Italian poet
fell upon the verse of another, and one that understood not
metre, or had ever read Martial, fell upon one of his verses.
Thus it is not strange that Homer should Hebraise, and that
many sentences in human authors seem to have their original
in Scripture.   In a piece of mine, published long ago,[3] the
learned annotator hath paralleled many passages with others
of Montaigne's Essays, whereas, to deal clearly, when I
penned that piece, I had never read three leaves of that
author, and scarce any more ever since.

Truth and falsehood hang almost equilibriously in some
assertions, and a few grains of truth which bear down the
balance.

To begin our discourses like Trismegistus of old, with
"verum certe verum atque verissimum est," would sound
arrogantly unto new ears, in this strict enquiry of things ;

[3] *in a piece of mine.*] Viz. *Religio Medici ;* see vol. ii. page 326, where
this passage has been introduced in a note.

wherein, for the most part, *probably and perhaps*, will hardly serve the turn, or serve to mollify the spirits of positive contradictors.

If Carden saith a parrot is a beautiful bird, Scaliger will set his wits on work to prove it a deformed animal.

Few men expected to find so grave a philosopher of Polemo, who spent the first part of his life in all exorbitant vices. Who could imagine that Diogenes in his younger days should be a falsifier of money, who in the aftercourse of his life was so great a contemner of metal, as to laugh at all that loved it ? But men are not the same in all divisions of their ages: time, experience, contemplation, and philosophy, make in many well-rooted minds a translation before death, and men to vary from themselves as well as other persons. Whereof old philosophy made many noble examples, to the infamy of later times: wherein men merely live by the line of their inclinations: so that without any astral prediction, the first day gives the last, "primusque dies dedit extremum."—*Seneca.* Men are as they were ; and according as evil dispositions run into worse habits, being bad in the first race, prove rather worse in the last.

We consider not sufficiently the good of evils, nor fairly compare the mercy of providence, in things that are afflictive at first hand. The famous Andreas D'Oria, invited to a feast by Aloisio Fieschi, with intent to despatch him, fell opportunely into a fit of the gout, and so escaped that mischief. When Cato intended to kill himself, with a blow which he gave his servant that would not bring him his sword, his hand so swelled that he had much ado to effect it, whereby any but a resolved stoic might have taken a hint of consideration, and that some merciful genius would have contrived his preservation.

The virtues, parts, and excellences both of men and nations are allowable by aggregation, and must be considered by concervation as well as single merit. The Romans made much of their conquests by the conquered ; and the valour of all nations, whose acts went under their names, made up the glory of Rome. So the poets that writ in Latin built up the credit of Latium, and passed for Roman wits ; whereas if Carthage deducted Terence, Egypt Claudian, if Seneca,

Lucan, Martial, Statius, were restored unto Spain, if Marseilles should call home Petronius, it would much abridge the glory of pure Italian fancy; and even in Italy itself, if the Cisalpine Gauls should take away their share, if Verona and Mantua should challenge Catullus and Virgil, and if in other parts out of Campagna di Roma, the Venusine Apulians should pull away their Horace, the Umbrians their Plautus, the Aquinatians Juvenal, Volaterrani Persius, and the Pelignians of Abruzzo their Ovid, the rest of Rome or Latium would make no large volume.

Where 'tis said in the book of Wisdom that the earth is unto God but as a sand, and as a drop of morning dew, therein may be implied the earth and water or the whole terraqueous globe; but when 'tis delivered in the Apocalypse that the angel set his right foot upon the sea and his left upon the earth, what farther hidden sense there is in that distinction may farther be considered.

Of the seven wise men of Greece 'twas observed by Plutarch, that only Thales was well versed in natural things, the rest obtained that name for their wisdom and knowledge in state affairs.

Whether the ancients were better architects than their successors many discourses have passed. That they were not only good builders, but expedite and skilful demolishers, appears by the famous palace of Publicola, which they p e down and rased to the ground by his order in one daull d

Whether great ear'd persons have short necks, long feet, and loose bellies?

Whether in voracious persons and gourmands the distance between the navel and the sternon be greater than from the sternon unto the neck?

Since there be two major remedies in physic, bleeding and purging, which thereof deserves the pre-eminency; since in the general purging cures more diseases: since the whole nation of the Chinese use no phlebotomy, and many other nations sparingly, but all some kind of purgative evacuation: and since besides in man there are so few hints for bleeding from any natural attempt in horses, cows, dogs, birds, and other creatures.

Whether it be safe for obtaining a bass or deep voice to make frequent use of vitriol, and whether it hath such an effect?

To observe whether the juice of the fruit of *ficus Indica*, taken inwardly, will cause the urine to have a red and bloody colour, as is delivered by some and commonly received in parts of Italy where it plentifully groweth; and whether the juice of the prickly fig from America will not do the like?

That if a woman with child looks upon a dead body, the child will be pale complexioned.

Why little lap-dogs have a hole in their heads, and often other little holes out of the place of the sutures?

Why a pig's eyes drop out in roasting rather than other animals'?

Why a pig held up by the tail leaves squeaking?

Why a low signed horse is commonly a stumbler?

What is the use of dew claws in dogs?

Whether that will hold, which I have sometimes observed, that lice combed out of the head upon a paper, will turn and move towards the body of the party, and so as often as the paper is turned about?

What kind of motion swimming is, and to which to be referred; whether not compounded of a kind of salition, and volation, the one performed by the hands, the other by the legs and feet? What kind of motion sliding is; whether it imitateth not the *motus projectorum* upon a plane, wherein the *corpus motum* is not separated *a motore*?

Whether the name of a *palatium*, or palace, began first to be used for princes' houses in the time of Augustus, when he dwelt in *Monte Palatino*, as Dion delivereth, or whether the word is not to be found in authors before his time?

Whether the heads of all mummies have the mouth open, and why?

Why solipeds, or whole hoofed animals, arise with their fore legs first, bisulcous with their hinder?

Whether Noah might not be the first man that compassed the globe? Since, if the flood covered the whole earth, and no lands appeared to hinder the current, he must be carried with the wind and current according to the sun, and so in the space of the deluge, might near make the tour of the globe. And since, if there were no continent of America, and all that tract a sea, a ship setting out from Africa without other help, would at last fall upon some part of India or China.

Whether that of David, " convertentur ad vesperam et famem patientur ut canes," may be prophetically applied to the late conversion of the wild Americans, as it is delivered in *Gloriosus Franciscus Redivivus*, or the *Chronicles of the Acts of the Franciscans*, lib. iii.

Diogenes, the cynick, being asked what was the best remedy against a blow, answered a helmet. This answer he gave, not from any experience of his own, who scarce wore any covering on his head; yet he that would see how well a helmet becometh a cynick, may behold it in that draught of Diogenes, prefixed to his life, in the new edition of the *Epitome of Plutarch's Lives*, in English; wherein, in the additional lives, he is set forth, soldier-like, with a helmet and a battle-axe.

Aristotle, lib. animal.

Whether till after forty days, children, though they cry, weep not; or, as Scaliger expresseth it, "vagiunt sed oculis siccis."

Whether they laugh not upon tickling?

Why though some children have been heard to cry in the womb, yet so few cry at their birth, though their heads be out of the womb?

Whether the feeding on carp be so apt to bring on fits of the gout, as Julius Alexandrinus affirmeth?

Cardanus, to try the alteration of the air, exposeth a sponge, which groweth dark when the air is inclined to moisture. Another way I have made more exact trial; by putting a dry piece of sponge into one balance of a gold scale, so equally poised, with weights in the other balance, that it will hang without inclining either way. For then upon alteration of the air to moisture, the scale with the sponge will fall, and when the air grows hot and dry will rise again. The like may be done by *favago marina*, found commonly on the sea shore. The change of the weather I have also observed by hanging up a dry *aplyssalus marinus*, which grows moist and dry according to the air; as also *phasganium marinum*, sea laces, and others.

To observe that insect which a countryman showed Baricellus, found in the flowers of *Eryngium cichoreum*, which readily cure warts ; *est coloris Thalassini cum maculis rubris, et assimulatur proportione corporis cantharidi, licet parvulum sit. Acceperat ea rusticus, et singula in singulis verrucis digitis expressit unde exibat liquor.*

To make trial of this ; whether live crawfish put into spirits of wine will presently turn red, as though they had been boiled, and taken out walk about in that colour.

'Tis a ludicrous experiment in Baricellus ; to rub napkins and handkerchiefs with powder of vitriol for such as sweat or have used to wipe their faces ; for so they become black and sullied. Whether shirts thus used may not do something against itch and lice. Whether shirts washed or well rubbed in quicksilver would not be good to that end.

Whether a true emerald feels colder in the mouth than another.

Since these few observations please you, for your farther discourse and consideration, I would not omit to send you a larger list, scatteringly observed out of good authors, relating unto medical enquiry, and whereof you may single out one daily to discourse upon it ; which may be a daily recreation unto you, and employ your evening hours, where your affairs afford you the conversation of studious and learned friends.

Plut. in vita Cleomenis.

It chanced that Cleomenes marching thither, being very

hot, drank cold water, and fell on such a bleeding withal
that his voice was taken from him and he almost stifled.

Hippotus pricked Cleomenes in the heel, to see if he were
yet alive; whether this were not a good way of trial upon
so sensible a part?

Ammianus Marcellinus in vita Joviani.

He was found dead in his bed. It is said he could not
endure the smell of his bedchamber newly plastered with
mortar made of lime, or that he came to his end occasioned
by an huge fire kindled of coals, others that he crammed his
belly so full that he died of a surfeit. Whether all these
causes be not allowable?

Plut. in vita Julii Cæsaris.

There fell a pestilent disease among them, which came by
ill meats which hunger drove them to eat; but after he had
taken the city of Gomphes, in Thessalie, he met not only
with plenty of victuals, but strangely did rid them of that
disease: for the soldiers meeting with plenty of wine, drank
hard, and making merry, drank away the infection of the
pestilence: in so much that drinking drunk they overcame
their disease and made their bodies new again. The
soldiers were driven to take sea weeds, called algæ, and
washing away the brackishness thereof with sea water,
putting to it a little herb, called dogstooth, to cast it to their
horses to eat.

That America was peopled of old not from one, but several nations, seems probable from learned discourses concerning their originals: and whether the Tyrians and Carthaginians had not a share therein may be well considered:
and if the periplus of Hanno or his navigation about Africa
be warily perpended, it may fortify that conjecture; for he
passed the straits of Hercules with a great fleet and many
thousand persons of both sexes; founded divers towns, and
placed colonies in several parts of that shore; and sailed in
tolerable account as far about as that place now called Cabo
de Tres Puntas.

To these there is little question but the Carthaginians
sometimes repaired, and held communication with them.
The colonies also being a people of civility could not but

continue the use of navigation ; so that either the Carthaginians in their after researches might be carried away by the trade-winds between the tropics, or finding therein no difficult navigation might adventure upon such a voyage; and also their colonies left on so convenient a shore might casually, if not purposely, make the same adventure.

The Chinese also could hardly avoid, at least might easily have, a part in their originals. For the east winds being very rare, and the west almost constantly blowing from their shore, being once at sea they were easily carried to the back part of America.

If there were ever such a great continent in the western ocean, as was hinted of old by Plato, and the learned Kircherus considers might by subterraneous eruptions be partly swallowed up and overthrown, and partly leave the islands yet remaining in the ocean, it is not impossible or improbable that from great antiquity some might be carried from thence upon the American coast, or some way be peopled from those parts.

While Attahualpa, king of Peru, and Montezuma, king of Mexico, might owe their originals unto Asia or Africa.

Since the Indian inhabitants are found, at least conceived, to have peopled the southern continent, whether these, after debating over *terra incognita*, might not pass or be carried over into Magellanica or the south of America, may also be enquired, and some might not come in at this door.

If any plantations of civil nations were ever made from civil nations, how it comes to pass that letters and writing was unknown unto all the parts of America.

Why no wonder is likewise made how the Islas de los Ladrones, or islands of thieves, were peopled, since they are so far removed from any neighbour continent.

Aristot. lib. viii. cap. 22, *de hist. Animalium.*

How to make out that of Aristotle that all creatures bit by a mad dog became mad, excepting man: since by unhappy experience so many men have been mischieved thereby ; or whether it holdeth not better at second than at first hand, so that if a dog bite a horse, and that horse a man, the evil proves less considerable, as we seem to have observed in many. Whether St. Bellin's priests cure any after the hydrophobia ; whether hellebore, tin, garlick, treacle, and *pulvis palmarii* be the prime remedies against this poison ; and why the use of *alyssum galeni* is not more in request ; and how the cornel and service tree become such mischievous promoters of that venom ; and how far this venom takes place in Ireland, where they have no venomous creature, and not long ago very few quartan agues.

Whether that passage of *Deut.* xxviii. *verse* 68, " classibus reducet in Ægyptum," be not sufficiently made out by the record of Josephus, when Titus, after the taking of Jerusalem, sent all or most under seventeen years of age into Egypt.

If the prophet Jonah were contemporary unto Jeroboam and Osias, as good commentators determine, it is in vain to think he was the woman of Sareptha's son.

Whether, when he intended from Joppa unto Tarsis, he was bound for Tarsis in Cilicia, Tartessus in Bætica, of Spain, or Tarsis by which sometimes Carthage is called, it is not of moment to decide. 'Tis plain that they were strangers of the ship, since every one called upon his God, and since they demanded from whence he was ; which, although they did not by an interpreter, yet if they were of the colonies of the Phœnicians, either of Tartessus or Carthage, their language having no small affinity with the Hebrew, they might have been understood.

The story of Jonah might afford the hint unto that of Andromeda, and the sea monster that should have devoured her ; the scene being laid at Joppa by the fabulists : as also unto the fable of Hercules out of Lycophron, three nights in the whale's belly, that is of Hercules Phœnicius.

Some nations of the Scythians affected only or chiefly to make use of mares in their wars, because they do not stop in their course to stale like horses. Quære.

Plutarch.—To render their iron money unserviceable to other uses, the Lacedæmonians quenched it in vinegar. This way might make it brittle, but withal very apt to rust. Inquire farther of their drinking cup named *cothon*.

Whether that rigid commonwealth were not more strict in the rule and order, than measure, of their diet, or how their provision cometh short of a regular and collegian diet, when every one brought monthly into the hall one bushel of meal, eight gallons of wine, five pounds of cheese, and two pounds and half of figs, beside money for sudden and fresh diet.

What to judge of that law that permitted them not to have lights to guide them home from the common hall in the night, that so they might be emboldened to walk and shift in the dark.

Though many things in that state promoted temperance, fortitude, and prudence; yet were there many also culpable to high degrees; as justifying theft, adultery, and murder: while they encouraged men to steal, and the grand crime thereof was to be taken in the action: while they admit of others to lie with their wives, and had not the education of their own children: while they made no scruple to butcher their slaves in great numbers: and while they had apothetes or places to make away with their children which seemed weak or not so strongly shapen as to promise lusty men: and therefore well needed that Pagan fallacy that these ways were confirmed and ratified by the oracle of Delphos.

It was the custom of their midwives not to wash their children with water but with wine and water, whereby, if they were weak, they extenuated and much pined. Which whether a reasonable test of constitutions may be doubted.

Cato Utican being to convey a great treasure from Cyprus unto Rome, he made divers little chests, and put into every one two talents and five hundred drachms, and tied unto each a long rope with a large piece of cork, that if the ship should miscarry, the corks might show where the chests laid at the bottom of the sea. A good piece of providence, and done like Cato. Whether not still to be practised, if the make of our ships, with deck upon deck, would admit of it.

How the ancients made the north part of Britain to bend so unseasonably eastward, according to the old map, agreeable unto Ptolemy? Or how Pliny could so widely mistake as to place the Isle of Wight between Ireland and England, if it be not mistaken for the Isle of Man or Anglesea.

Julius Cæsar being hard put to it near Alexandria, leaped into the sea, and, laying some books on his head, made shift to swim a good way with one hand. Sertorius being wounded in a battle with the Cimbrians, with his corslet and target swam over the river Rhosne. He that hath seen that river may doubt which was the harder exploit.

Upon the memorable overthrow of the Cimbrians, not far from Verona, by Marius and Catullus, the contention arose whose soldiers were most effective to the victory. For that decision Catullus conducted the ambassadors of Parma, then in the camp, to view the bodies of the dead, where they might behold the pila, or Roman javelots, in their bodies, which Plutarch saith had Catullus's name upon them. Whether this were not extraordinary, for we read not of such a constant custom to set their leader's names upon them.

St. Vincent, whose name the noble cathedral of Lisbon beareth, was a courageous and undaunted martyr in the persecution of Dioclesianus and Maximianus. Attacked at Evora, by Dacianus the Roman governor, and afterwards racked and tortured to death at Abyla, the Moors dispersed his bones at St. Vincent's, a place upon the *Promontorium Sacrum* of Ptolemy, now called the Cape of St. Vincent, the most western headland of Europe. Upon my print of St. Vincent these few lines may be inscribed:—

> Extorque, si potes, fidem,
> Tormenta, carcer, ungulæ,
> Stridensque flammis lamina,
> Atque ipsa pœnarum ultima,
> Mors, Christianis ludus est.
> *Prudentius in hymno St. Vincentii.*

Though in point of devotion and piety, physicians do meet with common obloquy, yet in the Roman calendar we find no less than twenty-nine saints and martyrs of that profession, in a small piece expressly described by Bzovius (in his *Nomenclatura sanctorum professione medicorum*). A clear and naked history of holy men, of all times and nations, is a work yet to be wished. Many persons there have been, of high devotion and piety, which have no name in the received canon of saints; and many now only live in the names of towns, wills, tradition, or fragments of local records. Wherein Cornwall seems to exceed any place of the same circuit, if we take an account of those obscure and probably Irish saints to be found in Carew's survey of that country, affording names unto the churches and towns thereof; which clearly to historify might prove a successless attempt. Even in France, many places bear the names of saints, which are not commonly understood. St. Malo, is Maclovius; Disier, Desiderius; St. Arigle, St. Agricola; St. Omer, St. Audomarus. Many more there are, as St. Chamas, St. Urier, St. Loo, Saincte Menehoud, St. Saulye, St. Trouve, St. Riquier, St. Papoul, St. Oaen; and divers others which may employ your enquiry.

The punishment of such as fled from the battle, whom they called at Sparta *trepidantes,* was this. They can bear no office in the commonwealth; it is a shame and reproach to give them any wives, and also to marry any of theirs; whosoever meeteth them may lawfully strike them, and they must abide it, not giving them any word again; they are compelled to wear poor tattered cloth gowns, patched with cloth of divers colours; and worst of all, to shave one side of their beards and the other not. Whether the severity of this law of Lacedæmon, and which sometimes they durst not put in execution, were ingenious, rational, and commodious, or to be drawn into example?

Plut. in vita Crassi.

Hyrodes the king fell into a disease that became a dropsy after he had lost his son Pacorus. Phraates, his second son, thinking to set his father forwards, gave him drink of the juice of *aconitum.* The dropsy received the poison, and one drove the other out of Hyrodes' body, and set him on foot again.

Turkish History, in the Life of Morah, p. 1483.

Count Mansfield died: the news whereof coming to duke John Ernestus, already weakened with a fever fourteen days, he fell into an apoplexy. His body was opened, and not one drop of blood found, but his heart withered to the smallness of a nut.

, *Olearius.*

In the travels of Olearius, and in his description of Persia, he delivers that the Persians commonly cure the sting of a scorpion by applying a piece of copper upon the wound; and that himself, being stung in the throat by a scorpion, was cured by the application of oil of scorpions, and taking treacle inwardly; but that for some years after he was troubled with a pricking in that part, when the sun was in Scorpius.

The princess of Coreski, taken prisoner by the Tartars, received a precious stone of rare virtue, which applied unto the eyes of the brother of the Tartar, whose prisoner she was, in a short time recovered his sight. Whether any such virtue probable or possible by that means? *Turk. Hist. in the Life of Achmet.*

[*On Coagulation.*]

So many coagulations there are in nature; and though we content ourselves with one in the running of milk, yet many will perform the same.

The maws or stomachs of other animals, as of pigeons.

The inner coat of the gizzard of wild ducks and teal, not the pike, or maw of a pike, which seems of strong digestion.

Several seeds may do it, the best the seeds of carthamus, not too much dried.

Many others not, as not the seed of pæony. Myrobalans powdered do it.

The milk of spurge doth it actively; the milk of fig; that of lettuce; succory; tragopogon; apocinon. Whether salerdine?

Whereby whey and cheese might be made more medical; milk of lettuce and sowthistle will not hold the colour, but grow black and gummy, yet strongly coagulate milk.

The opium and scammony.

The inward skin of the gizzard of turkeys will actively coagulate; so will the crop; the chylus or half digested matter in the crop did the like, and strongly. That in the gizzard was too dry.

The milk of a woman full of the jaundice, that nursed a child, infected the same; yet the milk was blue and a laudable colour, and would not be coagulated by runnet, nor after long stirring did manifest any colour or febrical tincture.

To try and observe the several sorts of coagulations or runnets; whether any will turn all kinds of milk, or whether they be appropriate. That of a hare we find will turn that of the cow. To observe further whether it will coagulate that of a mare or ass, or woman, and how the coagulum stands in multifidous animals; as in whelps and kittens, and also in swine and bats. The runnet of cows is strong, for it coagulates the milk of herbs. The milk in whelps' maws did the milk of cows, but the runnet of cows, as we have tried in several women's milk, will not coagulate the same. The runnet of rabbit coagulates well the milk of a cow. Neither that nor calf's runnet did make a good coagulum of mare's milk, leaving only a gross thickness therein, without serous separation.

Of the several sorts of milk and lacical animals; of the several sorts of coagulums; of all kinds of mineral coagulation.

> Of tin with aquafortis
> of . . . . . . antimony
> of soap
> of the coagulum of blood
> . . . . of milk

How far the coagulating principle operateth in generation is evident from eggs which will never incrassate without it; from the incrassation upon incubiture, when heat diffuseth the coagulum, from the *chalaza* or gelatine, which sometime . . . . three nodes, the head, heart, and liver.

What runnet the Scythians used to separate mare's milk is uncertain; cow's runnet we have not found to do it, but the same we have effected by the maws of turkeys. Whether the buttons of figs or the milk of spurge which are strong coagulators? Quære.

Coagulum in the first digestion, in the second or blood, whether not also in the last digestion or stomach, of every particular part, when the coagulate parts become fine and next to flesh, and the rest into cambium and gluten?

Whether the first mass were but a coagulation, whereby the water and earth lay awhile together, and the watery or serous part was separated from the sole and continuating substance, the . . . . . . separated by coagulation, and the inner part flowing about them?

The blood of man and pig, falling upon vinegar, would not coagulate, but lie thin and turn of the colour of musca-dell. Bled upon aquavitæ, it did coagulate, though weaker, and maintained its colour. Upon vinegar, it keeps long without corruption, and becometh blackish. Bled upon a solution of saltpetre in water, it coagulates not, keeps long and shoots into nitrous branched particles, which separated, it lasteth long and contracteth the smell of storax liquida, and the glass or urinal being inclined, it strokes long figures ...... conjoined by right lines.

White dung of hens and geese coagulates milk.

Mare's milk very serous, not equally running with coagulum [of] fig, except some cow's milk be added; perhaps the Scythians used a mixture of goat's milk. Spirits of salt poured upon mare's milk, makes a curdling which in a little space totally dissolved into serum.

Woman's milk will not coagulate with common runnet: try whether the milk of nurses that are concerned may be run.

Mrs. King's milk, Octob. 23 (1650), would not run, but only curdled in small roundels like pins' heads, as vinegar will curdle milk.

The semichylus or half-digested humour of young lobsters, in a cod's stomach, did it very well.

The entrails of soles coagulated milk, so also the stomach of sandlings. The stomach of a tench would not, nor of a rat, nor of a whiting or gudgeon; and that of smelts did it in winter; the maw of a cod did it well; the appendages about the maw indifferently also of smelts.

Milk of different nature according to the different times of gestation, which is to be observed to know the differences of milk in several seasons, it being so commonly ordered, that cows come in the spring, so that milk grows thick about Christmas.

The *verum coagulum* seems seated in the inner skin of the gizzard, for the outward and carnous part would not do it. The maw of a bittern did it well. The mutings also of a bittern and a kestrell. The inward skin in the maws of partridges, or the substance contained therein, not yet fully digested.

Sow's milk run very well with runnet and skin of green figs; even ripe do it well.

Runnet beat up with the whites of eggs, seems to perform

nothing, nor will it well incorporate, without so much heat as will harden the egg.

The peculiar coagulum of stomachs to make stones, as bezoar.

Milk of poppy runs milk.

The stomachs of turkeys dry and powdered doth it well; so also the dry and chaffy substance in the gizzard after some months, but the carnous substance not.

The buttons of figs, which prove figs the next year, doth it very well, either green or dried; salt alone will do it if plentiful; whether saltpetre, salt upon saltpetre or sal-gemmæ; vide.

The curdled milk in the stomach of a pig coagulates cow's milk. Adding salt cleanly, runnet may be made out of milk put into the maw of a turkey. As also a pig will do it very well.

The appendages below the lower orifice of the stomach will coagulate milk when the substance will not do it; as tried in cods, these are filled with a little thick humour, very remarkable in salmon, wherein they are of exceeding largeness.

Buttermilk, or churn milk, will not be turned with runnet, but being warm will run itself, as will also milk in the summer.

The milk of mares is very serous, and will not run with the cow's runnet; in the summer we made it run with turkey's gizzard, and fig's buttons; the same in October we could not effect, neither with turkey, figs, cow's, nor pig's runnet; whether it be so serous that the caseous parts cannot hold together the other, may be doubted; although, if unto an ounce of cow's milk you add an ounce of water, it will notwithstanding coagulate in the caseous part, leaving the whey asunder. And if you mix equal parts of mare's and cow's milk, the runnet will take place.

The skin of a peacock's gizzard very well.

As also the dried milk of spurge and lettuce, above a year old; the chylus of animals; the chylus of plants; the stomach of an horse, and chylus contained in it, did very well coagulate.

Beef taken out of the paunch of a kestrel four hours after, turned very strongly.

A clean and neat seeming runnet may be made in the crop of a turkey, and milk and salt put therein will coagulate and grow hard like runnet; but surely the same must be old to be effectual, for after a month upon trial, we could not find it to run cow's milk.

The strawy substances in the stomach of a pig, turned milk well in October, also the fresh white dung of a goose did very well, that best which is whitest probably.

The inward skin of a duckling, six days old, as also the hard and chaffy substances in the same, did it very well.

Spirits of salt and aquafortis, gently poured on milk, will strongly coagulate; but in a woman's milk, we find it not effectual, which would not coagulate upon a large quantity, nor would salt in gross body effect it, nor the other common coagulums.

Try whether the milk of children vomited will do it.

The dung of chickens in some degree.

The shells and half digested fragments in a lobster's stomach that had nearly cut the skin did it.

How butchers make sheep's blood to hold from concretion; whether by agitation when it is fresh, and so dispersing the fibres which are thought to make the concretion? Unto such, a great quantity of runnet added could make no concretion.

Eggs seem to contain within themselves their own coagulum, evidenced upon incubation, which makes incrassation of parts before very fluid.

Rotten eggs will not be made hard by incubation, or decoction, as being destitute of that spirit: or having the same vitiated. They will sooner be made hard if put in before the water boileth.

They will be made hard in oil, but not so easily in vinegar, which by the attenuating quality keeps them longer from concretion; for infused in vinegar they lose the shell, and grow big and much heavier than before.

Salt seems to be the principal agent in this coagulation, for bay salt will run milk alone if strongly mixed, and so it will, though mixed with some vinegar. Vinegar alone will curdle it, not run it.

In the ovary, or second cell of the matrix, the white comes upon the yolk, and in the later and lower part, the shell is made or manifested. Try if the same parts will give any coagulation unto milk. Whether will the ovary best?

The whites of eggs drenched in saltpetre will shoot forth a long and hairy saltpetre, and the egg become of a hard substance; even in the whole egg there seems a great nitrosity, for it is very cold, and especially that which is without a shell (as some are laid by fat hens,) or such as are found in the egg poke or lowest part of the matrix, if an hen be killed a day or two before she layeth.

Several hens produce eggs commonly of the same form, some round, some long, neither strictly distinguishing the sex.

The proper uses of the shell; for the defence of the chicken in generation, promotion of heat upon incubation, and protection therein lest it be broken by the hen, either upon incubation or treading with her claws upon them, as also to keep and restrain the chicken until due time, when the hen often breaks the shell.

Difference between the sperm of frogs and eggs.

Spawn, though long boiled, would not grow thick or coagulate.

In the eggs of skates or thornbacks, upon long decoction the yolk coagulates, not the greatest part of the white.

If in spawn of frogs the little black specks will concrete, though not the other.

The white part of the mutings of birds dried run milk, not leaving any ill savour. Try in that of cormorants, hens, turkeys, geese, kestrels.

The chylus in the stomach of a young hen strongly coagulated, the stomach also itself though washed.

The white and cretaceous mutings of a bittern made a sudden coagulation, the like hath the dung of ducks and hens.

The coagulate stomach of kittens would not convert women's milk, nor cows', though in good quantity; which after coagulated by addition of calf's runnet.

The chylus in a young rabbit run cow's and bitch's milk, 1653.

The seeds of the silver or milk thistle run milk also.

Mucilaginous concretions are made by liquid infusions and decoctions, imbibing the gum and tenacious parts, until they fix and determine their fluidity.

2 B 2

As is observable in gums, hartshorn, and seeds, especially lentous natures, as quince psyllium, mallows, &c. when these tenacious parts are forced out by ignition, they afford no farther concretion, as in burnt hartshorn, wherein there are lost most of the separable parts, and so little of salt as makes the preparation questionable, if given with the same intentions with the other.

Wherein it is presumable the water may also imbibe some part of the volatile salt, as is manifested sometimes when it is exposed to congelation, and standeth long in pewter dishes ; some part fastening upon the crown or upper circle, and also discolouring the pewter.

But whether the mucilages or jellies do answer our expectation of their quantities while we think we have a decoction made of two ounces and a half which affordeth a jelly of almost a pint ; the horns again after they were dried wanted not a drachm, the jelly dried left little but a small gummy substance.

Half an ounce of *ichthyocolla* or isinglass, will fix above a pint of water ; and in half a pint of jelly of hartshorn there is not above two drachms.

Much hartshorn is therefore lost in the usual decoction of hartshorn in shavings or raspings, where the greatest part is cast away.

For the same may be performed from the solid horn sawed into pieces of two or three ounces or less, and the same pieces will serve for many jellies.

The calcination of hartshorn by vapour of water is a neat invention, but whether very much of the virtue be not impaired, while the vapour insinuating into the horn hath carried away the tenacious parts and made it butter, and hath also dissolved those parts which make the jelly ; which may be tried if a decoction be made of the water from whence the vapour proceedeth, and especially if the calcination hath been made in vessels not perspirable.

[*On Congelation.*]

NATURAL bodies do variously discover themselves by congelation.

Bodies do best and [most] readily congelate which are aqueous, or water itself.

Of milk the wheyish part, in eggs we observe the white, will totally freeze, the yolk, with the same degree of cold, grow thick and clammy like gum of trees, but the sperm or tread hold its former body, the white growing stiff that is nearest it.

The spirits of things do not freeze : if they be plentiful, they keep their bodies from congelation ; as spirits of wine, *aqua vitæ*, nor is it easy to freeze such, when French wine cannot resist it. But congelation seems to destroy or separate the spirits, for beer or wine are dead and flat after freezing, and in glasses ofttimes the most flying salts will settle themselves above the surface of the water.

Waters freezing do carry a vegetable crust foliated surface upon them, representing the leaves of plants, and this they do best which carry some salt or vegetable seminals in them. Rain water which containeth seminal atoms, elevated by exhalations, making the earth fruitful where it falleth. Snow water will also do, as containing these seeds, and salt nitrous coagulum, whereby it was formerly concreted. The lyes or lixivium of herbs will do it well, but the juices of herbs or waters wherein these essential salts have been dissolved, far better, as we have tried in that of scurvy grass, chalie, nettles. Jellies of flesh will do the like, as we have tried in that of cow's and calf's foot, wherein, though the surface be obscured, yet will there be several glaciations intermixed, and so excellently foliated, that they will leave their impression or figure in the next part of the jelly which remaineth uncongealed, and being beheld in a magnifying glass, either in the day or night against a candle, affordeth one of the most curious spectacles in nature, nor will these little conglaciated plates so easily dissolve as common ice, as carrying perhaps a greater portion of carnel nitre in them.

But, what is remarkable most of congelations, simple or compounded, they seem to carry in their surface a leaf of one figure, which somewhat representeth the leaf of a fern or brake,* from a middle and long rib spreading forth jagged leaves ; so a lixivium of nettles, wormwood, wild cucumber, scurvy grass, will shoot in the same shapes ; a solution of salt or sugar will do the like and also a decoction of hartshorn, and the salt distilled of the blood of a deer and dissolved in water, carried the same shape upon calcination ; but the shootings in the jellies of flesh carry smaller branches and like twigs without that exact distinction of leaves.

But the exact and exquisite figurations, and such as are produced above the surface of the liquor, in the side of glasses by exhalation from the liquor compounded with, is best discoverable in urinals and long bellied glasses, and often happeneth over urines, where the figures are very distinct arising from a root, and most commonly resembling coralline mosses of the sea, and sometimes larger plants, whereof some do rise in so strong a body, as to hold their shapes many months, and some we have kept two or three years entire.

Water and oil behave differently from congelation ; a glassful of water frozen swells above the brim, oil congelated subsideth.

Congelation is a rare experiment ; is made by a mixture of salt and snow strongly agitated in a pewter pot, which will freeze water that's poured about it. But an easier way there is, by only mixing salt and snow together in a basin, and placing therein a cup of water, for when the snow doth thaw and the congealing spirits fly away, they freeze the neighbour bodies which are congealable ; and, if the vessel wherein the snow melteth stand in water, it freezeth the water about it, which is excellently discerned by mixing snow and salt in an urinal, and placing it in water.

This way liquors will suddenly freeze which a long time resist the diffused causes in the air, as may be experienced in wine, and urine, and excellently serveth for all figurations ; this way will in a short time freeze rich sack, and

* ¶There is some *regent* salt which carrieth them into the form of brake or long rib jagged plant.

crust *aqua vitæ* about the side of the cup or glass, if weak and with a light addition of water.

A small quantity of *aqua vitæ*, mingled with water, is not able to resist this way of congelation; but therein the ice will not be so hard and compact, and hollow spaces will be left at the surface.

That the sea was salt from the beginning, when that principle was cast into the whole mass of this globe, and not occasioned by those ways the ancients dreamt of, seems almost beyond doubt: wherein . . . . salt was so tenderly sprinkled as not to make that part inhabitable, and therefore, however some seas near the tropic where the same is strongest be conceived so to contain more salt, the seas with us do hardly make good five in the hundred.

It is no easy effect to condense water and make it take up a lesser space than in its fluid body; congealed into ice it seems to lose nothing, but rather acquireth a greater space and swelleth higher, as is manifestible in water frozen in eaures[1] and glasses.

This way eggs will suddenly freeze through their whole bodies.

Eyes will freeze through all the humours and become in short time like stones. By this way upon . . . . only the watery humour will congelate under the cornea, and show like a cataract or *albugo*, the iris also loses its colour, and this way the humours may be taken out distinctly; the hardest to freeze is the crystalline, yet laid upon snow and salt it groweth hard and dim, as though it had been boiled.

Whether such a congealing spirit be not the raiser of cataracts, *gutta serena*, apoplexies, catalepsies, and the like may be inquired.

In the congelation of snow there is much space required, and dissolved it will not occupy half the space it possessed before, for it is congealed in a vaporous body and in some rarefaction from its original of water.

Mineral water or quicksilver . . . . by taking off the fluidity, takes up a greater space than before, although allowance be made for the body that forceth it.

---

[1] *eaures.*] This may be *pannes* in MS. but I am inclined rather to think he meant ewers—spelt, according to French derivation, *eaures.*

Salt and snow pursue their operations most actively, while it freezeth: and in coldest weather dissolve sooner, for when it begins to thaw, the operation is troublesome; the snow loseth his tenacity, grows hard and brittle, and salt thrown upon it makes it harder for a little space, and is longer in dissolving it. Salt answereth awhile to send back the parting spirit upon itself, and mixing with it while it holdeth fast, makes a little congelation.

Lime unslaked mixed with snow would dissolve it; not freeze water set into it.

Snow dissolved, without salt, would not freeze water set in it. Herein we may also sometimes observe the very motion and stroke of the coagulum; for when the snow and salt are aptly conjoined, and the liquor to be congealed be put in a flat thin cup of silver, if it chance to dissolve at that time, in any quantity, it will instantly run curdled whey; the spirit separated will make a curdled cloud at the bottom or side of the cup, and fix that part first; for, contrary unto common congelation, if the cup standeth upon snow, and that at the bottom thaweth it, the liquor first freezeth at the bottom, and while the liquor in the flat cup freezeth within the basin, the outside of the basin will be thick frosted, and if it stands will adhere unto the table.

It is observable in this way of congelation, that the liquor freezeth last in the middle of the surface, as being furthest from the action of the snow and flying spirit; nor is this only effected by snow and salt, but by snow and saltpetre or alum; but the quickest congelation [is] by snow and salt, the other mixture remaining longer without dissolution: and therefore, on some earth snow lieth longest, and seldom long near the sea-side; and if two vessels be filled, the one with snow alone, the other with a mixture of salt, the salt snow will dissolve in half the time, and ice in the like manner.

This way it is possible to observe the rudiments and progress of congelation; it beginning first with *striæ*, and having shoots like the filamental shoots of pure nitre, and the interstitial water becomes after conjoined.

The same is also effected by ice powdered or broken like sugar between dry bodies, and mixed with salt; and is also performable without mixture of salt bodies, by snow alone, as it falleth to solution, and the congelating spirit separateth; so water in a very thin glass set in a porringer of snow, and set upon salt will freeze, the salt being able to dissolve it through the pewter. And, therefore, catarrhs and colds are taken and increased upon thaws; the leaves of trees withered and blasted where snow dissolves upon them; and something more than mere water fixed, because it spoileth leather, and alters the colour thereof to walk long in snow, especially when it melteth; and this congelative spirit, that penetrateth glass and metal, is probably the same which is felt so penetrating and cutting in winds, and according to frequent relations, hath left whole bodies of men rigid and stiff, even to petrification, in regions near the pole; and may assign some reason of that strange effect on our men, some that were left in Greenland, when they touched iron it seemed to stick to the fingers like pitch, the same being mollified and made in the same temper as it is, by the acid spirits of sulphur, if a red hot iron be thrust into a roll thereof.

In the congealing of tinctures, as . . . . . and saffron, if we narrowly observe it, there still remaineth whiteness, and the tincture seemeth to lie distant and less congealed. Starch, a strong congelation may be made, wherein the atoms of the powder may be distinguished, and sensibly observed to cast their colour upon parts, which they do not corporally attain.

To freeze roughly, or make ice with elevated superficies, the water must be exposed warm, and the liquor thick, the better as in jellies, while the exhalation elevating the surface, is held in and frozen in its passage.

Oil put upon snow, in an open mouth glass, and sharp at the bottom, makes a curdling which lasts a long time, and gives a mixed taste of snow and oil, pleasant unto the palate, and excellent against burning.

Snow upon a thaw freezeth itself, while the spirits of some parts dissolved, flying out, do fix the neighbour parts unto them.

Snow closely pressed, dissolves into about half its measure; lying loose, and as it falleth, dissolving, takes up little more than a fifth part.

Snow upon a thaw needeth no addition, and ice at that time will freeze, the pot being melted in it.

Salt maketh snow to melt; so may you bore a hole through

ice with salt laid thereon, with armoniac. Sugar will also
do the like, but in a slower manner; the like dully with
pepper.

To make ice crack, throw salt upon it.

Ice splits star-wise.

In the making of ice with snow and salt, we find little
variety in practice, and the reasons drawn peculiar upon the
salt; but this we have observed to be effected by other bodies,
of no probability to produce such an effect, as without salt
to effect it in a pot of snow, with ginger, pepper, liquorice, sugar, chalk, white lead, wheat-flour, sulphur, husk of
almonds, charcoal.

Water that is easily rarified will hardly or not at all admit
of pressure, or be made to take up a lesser space than its
natural body, and as it stands in its natural consistence.

In snow it takes up a very much larger space than in water;
even in ice, which takes off the fluidity, and is a kind of fixation, it will not be contained in the same circumference as
before in its fluid body, a glass filled with water and frozen
in salt and snow, will manifestl rise above the brim. Eggs
frozen, the shell will crack, andyopen largely, and there will
be found no hollow space at the top or blunter part which
comes first out upon exclusion of the hen, and yet it will
remain of the same weight upon exact ponderation. Ice is
spongy and porous, as may be observed upon breaking, and
in glasses wherein it is frozen, and seems not to be so close
and continued as in its liquid form. Beside there are many
bubbles ofttimes in it, which though condensed, are not of
the congelable parts, and take up a room in the congelation;
which may be air mixed with the water, or the spirits thereof,
which will not freeze, but separating from the pure water,
set themselves in little cells apart, which upon the liquation
make the spaws and froth which remaineth after, in standing vessels thawed, which makes all things frozen lose their
quickness; the spirits chased into several conservations,
flying away upon liquefaction, and not returning to an intrinsical and close mixture with their bodies again; and
therefore an apple frozen, and thawed in warm water, the
spirits are called out, and giving a sudden exhalation, the
same never tastes well after; whereas, put into cold water,
they are kept in, and while they raise themselves, through

the mass again, and are not carried out by a warm thaw: and this way are noses and cheeks preserved in cold regions, by a sudden application of snow unto them.

The same assertion is verified in metallical water, or quick-silver, which is closer in its own body than by any fixation; for either mortified or fixed, it takes up a much larger space than in its fluid body.

Quære how oil;—and whether metal, silver, and gold, liquefied, takes not up lesser room than when it is cold and congealed again: but these having attained their natural consistence and closeness, seem to take up a larger space when they are forced from it, and therefore seem to shrink as in moulds; and then in their cruding before solution to stretch and dilate themselves; as is observable in iron pierced, which smoothly admitting a nail when it is cold, will not so easily admit it being red hot.

Why the snow lies not long near the sea-side; by reason it is dissolved by salt exhalation of the sea, or from the like in the earth near the sea, which partaketh of that temper.

Why it is so cold upon a thaw; by reason of the exhaling of those freezing parts which lie quiet in the snow before.

Why snow makes a fruitful year, and is good for corn; because it keeps in the terreous evaporatives, concentrates the heat in seeds and plants, destroys mice and the principles of putrefaction in the earth, which breedeth vermin.

Why it changeth the colour of leather, making black shoes russet, which water doth not; by reason of the admixture of nitrous and saline parts, which drink in the copperas parts which make the deep colour.

The common experiment of freezing is made by salt and snow; where salt dissolving the snow sends out the con-gealing spirit thereof, which actively is able to fix the fluid element about it.

But the same effect will follow from other conjunctions, from vitriol, nitre, alum; and what is remarkable, from bodies which promise no such effect, as we have tried in pepper, ginger, chalk, white lead, charcoal-powder, liquorice.

And from ice itself stirred and beaten in a pint pot.

[*On Bubbles.*]

THAT the last circumference of the universe is but the bubble of the chaos and pellicle arising from the grosser foundation of the first matter, containing all the higher and diaphanous bodies under it, is no affirmation of mine; but that bubbles on watery or fluid bodies are but the thin gumbs of air, or a diaphanous texture of water arising about the air, and holding it awhile from eruption. They are most lasting and large in viscous humidities, wherein the surface will be best extended without dissolving the continuity, as in bladders blown out of soap. Wine and spirituous bodies make bubbles, but not long lasting, the spirit bearing through and dissolving the investiture. Aqua-fortis upon concussion makes few, and soon vanishing, the acrimonious effluvia suddenly rending them: some gross and windy wines make many and lasting, which may be taken away by vinegar or juice of lemon. And therefore the greatest bubbles are made in viscous decoctions, as in the manufacture of soap and sugar, wherein there is nothing more remarkable than that experiment, wherein not many grains of butter cast upon a copper of boiling sugar, presently strikes down the ebullition and makes a subsidence of the bubbling liquor.

Boiling is literally nothing but bubbling; any liquor attenuated by decoction sends forth evaporous and attenuated parts, which elevate the surface of the liquor into bubbles; even in fermentations and putrefactions wherein attenuation of parts are made, bubbles are raised without fire.

Glass is made by way of bubble, upon the blowing of the artificer.

Blisters are bubbles in leaves, wherein the exhalation is kept in by the thickness of the leaf, and in the skin, when the [membrane] thereof holds in the attenuated or attracted humour under it.

Fire blisters even dead flesh, forcibly attenuating the water in the skin and under it; and cantharides and crowfoot raise blisters by a potential fire and armoniac salt in them, attenuating the humour in the skin and under, which stretches and dilateth the parts, prohibiting its evolution.

Bubbles are white, because they consist of diaphanous humour or air fermented; and air under ice a thicker *tergunt* makes a grosser and stronger white, but in icterical and jaundiced urine the bubbles are yellow, according to the tincture diffused through the water, which investeth the airy contènts of its bubbles. Even man is a bubble, if we take his consideration in his rudiments, and consider the *vesicula* or *bulla pulsans*, wherein begins the rudiment of life.

Froth or spume is but a coagulation or conglobation of bubbles, and gross skins are but the coats of bubbles subsiding, or at least bodies which are fat and subphureous, keeping the surface, are apt to make them, and therefore are not without the active parts, as is observable in the spume of iron and steel.

Pitch and resinous bodies have also their bubbles, but they rise highest at the first, whilst the aqueous parts are attenuated, do copiously and crowdingly fly up, do elevate the viscous parts which largely dilate before their division, for that being spirit these bubbles are less, and if water be thrown upon it recover their force again; as is also discernible in the ebullition of soap, till the aqueous parts be spent, and the salt of the lixivium and oil and tallow entirely mixed.

The bubbles of oil will not last, the air pierceth, opening or perspiring their thin coats; water under oil makes not bubbles into the oil, but at the side or bottom.

Water and oil do best concur to the making of bubbles, air or exhalation included in a watery coat, or air in an oily habit, as in oil boiled wherein there are some watery parts or vaporous attenuations that are invested in their eruption.

Fire makes none, for that is too subtle to be contained and too fluid and moving to be contained; not affecting a circle but a pyramidal ascension, which destroys inclusion; the nearest resemblance thereof is in water thrown upon strong oil, wherein the water suddenly rising seemeth to carry up a strong bubble about it.

Quicksilver seems to have bubbles, being shaken together, but they are but small spherical bodies like drops of water, which hold in some bodies, to avoid discontinuation.

[*On Vegetation, &c.*]

To manifest how lasting the seminal principles of bodies
are, how long they will lie incorrupted in the earth, or
how the earth that hath been once impregnated therewith,
may retain the power thereof, unto opportunity of actuation,
or visible production,—a remarkable garden where many
plants had been, being digged up, and turned a fruitless
ground, after ten years being digged up, many of the plants
returned which had laid obscure; the plants were blattaria,
stramonium, hyoscyamus flore albo, &c.; and little less have
we observed that some plants will maintain their seminality
out of the earth, as we have tried in one of the least of
seeds, that is of marjorum.

How little snails or perriwinkles rely upon the water, and
how duck-weed is bred, some light may be received from this
experiment. In April we took out of the water little herbs
of crow-foot and the like whereon hung long cods of jelly;
this put in water, and so into an urinal exposed unto the sun,
many young perriwinkles were bred sticking to the side of
the glass, some aselli, or sows, which fled from the water, and
much duck-weed grew over, which, cleared once or twice,
now hath grown again.

That water is the principle of all things, some conceive;
that all things are convertible into water, others probably
argue; that many things which seem of earthly principles
were made out of water the Scripture testifieth, in the genealogy of the fowls of the air; most insects owe their original
thereto, most being made of dews, froths, or water; even
rain water, which seemeth simple, contains the seminals of
animals. This we observed, that rain water in cisterns,
growing green, there ariseth out of it red maggots, swimming
in a labouring and contortile motion, which after leaving a
. . . . case behind them, turn into gnats and ascend above
the water.

When the red worm tends to transformation, it seems to
acquire a new case, and continues most at the surface of the
water; two motions are observable, the one of the red worm
by a strong and laborious contortion, the other, a little before
it comes to a gnat, and that is by jaculation or sudden spring,

which if it use not, it ariseth to the surface, and soon after ariseth into a gnat.

Little red worms and less than threads are found in great numbers in ditches and muddy places, where the water is almost forsaken; whereof having taken a large number included in a glass, they would stir and move continually in fair weather like eels, pulling some part of their bodies above the mud, and upon the least touch of the glass would all disappear and contract into the mud. They lived that remaining part of summer, and after a hard winter showed themselves again in the succeeding summer. Therein I observed two things, the exquisite sense and vivacity of these imperfect animals, which extended unto two years.

All solid bodies are rendered liquid before they are qualified for nutriment; and the solidest bodies seem to be sustained by the thin bodies of waters, as is very remarkable in trees, especially oak, and birch, and sycamore, wherein the nutriment ascendeth in a mere body of water, as by wounding them at the spring is very discernible.

Thus we also observe that plants will be nourished long in rain water, as is very observable in mint, basil, and other plants, which being cropped, will shoot out roots, which will augment them by mere attraction of watery nutriment.

Whether the quantities of plants may not this way be sensibly altered deserves experiment; whether the liquor impregnated with colours may not communicate the same upon necessity of this single aliment; whether smells may not be impressed; whether when it purges corrected, and purgative qualities imbibed.

If others answer, mint and basil, though they sprout largely, yet they will hardly afford flowers, much less seed;—senecio, or groundswell, seems best to promise it.

Groundswell, put into water in December, lived, was frozen in January, sent forth flowers in the end of February, flowered and vanished in the beginning of May.

Bulbous roots, once shot, will flower there, and no wonder therein, for some will flower being hung up, having a sufficient stock of moisture for flowers that are precocious.

Plants will not only grow in the summer, but also in the winter if they be such as then continue green, as scurvy grass and groundswell. They will hold best which are put into the water with their roots, otherwise they will either not shoot them forth in the winter, or be long about it; as we tried in scurvy grass. Rue stood almost three months, without putting any roots forth, fresh and verdant; spurge stood 'well with the root, as chamomile, and featherfew, and parsley. Mint and scordium, put in about July, stood and grew all summer, shot plentiful roots, from whence came fresh sprouts out of the glass when the other decayed, and some now stand under water, Feb. 17. Mint grew up in several branches in April, and now groweth, June 28. Mint, set in water in May, grew up, and seemed to die, but sprouted again about October, stood all winter, and grew up in many branches the next spring.

Rue, set in October, without shooting any roots, grew about two inches in the winter, shot forth above forty roots in the spring, and grew much all the summer, flowered July and August.

Scurvy grass grew all winter, flowered in the spring, but seeded not, other put in in February, near to flower, shot roots, flowered and seeded in May, and shot new leaves under water.

Try how they will thrive in aqua vitæ, wine, vinegar, oil, salt water.

Many were put in, none grew or thrived, but suddenly decayed in aqua vitæ, wine, vinegar, salt water; oil draweth not at all, and so it dieth.

Mint would not grow in water and sugar, nor in strong rose water, but, unto two ounces of water adding but two or three spoonfuls, it thrived and acquired a richer smell. Seeds of plants which seed in the water of glasses, prove fruitful, as tried in those of scurvy and spurge, which now grow at the spring, being sowed about September before.

Asarum which had stood about two years in water, and twice cast the leaves; of these the leaves given maintained their vomitive quality.

How little, beside water alone, will support or maintain the growth of plants, beside the experiment of Helmont we have seen in some which have lived six years in glasses; and asarum which grew two years in water and lived; cast the leaves, maintained its vomiting quality.

Fertile seeds sink, but when they germinate they rise up

and come up to the top of the water, for then the seed fer-
ments and swells, and breaks the closure or covering.

The seed of an almond or plum, at first when it is hollow
and windy swimmeth, afterwards sinketh, yet take out the
nib and it sinketh.

In bay leaves commonly used at funerals, we unknowingly
hold in our hands a singular emblem of the resurrection ; for
the leaves that seem dead and dry, will revive into a perfect
green, if their root be not withered; as is observable in bay
trees after hard winters, in many leaves half, in some almost
wholly withered, wherein though the alimental and aqueous
juice be exhausted, the radical and balsamical humour remaining, though in a slender quantity, is able to refresh itself
again ; the like we have observed in dead and withered furze.

[*On Tobacco.*]

ALTHOUGH of ordinary use in physic, the anatomy of tobacco is not discovered, nor hath Hoffmanus in his work of
thirty years relieved us. That which comes fermented and
dyed unto us affords no distinct account, in regard it is infected with a decoction or lixivium, which is diverse according to different places, and some ascend no higher than
urine. Adulterations proceed further, adding euphorbium
or pepper, and some do innocently temper it with gum of
guaiacum.

The herb simply in itself and green or dried, is but flat,
nor will it hold fire well upon ordinary exsiccation. Other
plants are taken in the pipe, but they want quickness and
hold not fire, only prick and draw . . . . . . by their fuligo,
which all smoke will do ; and probably other herbs might be
made quick and fire well, if prepared the ·same way, that
is by fermentation, for in that alteration the body is opened,
the fixed parts attenuated by the spirit, the oily parts diffused and the salt raised from the earthly bed wherein it
naturally lieth obscure and heavy.

It containeth three eminent qualities, sudorific, narcotic,
and purgative ; from the subtle spirits and flying salt, sweat
seems to proceed, for the ashes will not do it. The narcotic
depends on the *humor impurus ;* for the vapour thereof contains it, and the burnt part loseth it, as in opium. Poppy
seeds dried are ineffectual, and the green heads work most

powerfully; the same is observable in the *mandichoca* root, which being a strong poison, is harmless being dried. The purgative quality lieth in the middle principle, which goes not away by a gentle heat; for the water purgeth not, the smoke but very doubtfully, and seldom in clysters of the smoke of three or four pipefuls, nor in the salt thereof, neither incineration, but in the middle principles of the nitrous salt, and such parts as are to be extracted by tincture, infusion, or decoction, whose actives remain in the menstruum, and therefore that which is decocted, and after dried, grows faint in the purgative quality, if it returneth.

Of tobacco there is the male and female; the male the best. Yellow rhubarb is often taken for the true plant.

Tobacco may be made or cured without a *caldo*, and will ferment and grow brown long laid together, and hung up will grow brown. To advance the same the caldo may be added before the rolling up, for then it will have a quicker taste and sweeter smell.

The leaves first ripe make the best when they grow gummy and brittle; they must be often cleared of the sprouts that grow upon the same stem and the *baschros* left out.

To make the best tobacco, these to be taken, and of the male; and a good caldo used, and kept awhile, till time digest remaining crudities.

[*On the Ivy.*]

CONCERNING ivy these remarkable:—The leaves less indented, scarce angular toward' the top; like many herbs which laciniate at the lower leaves, little at the upper.

It beareth twice a year, spring and .... It groweth not readily about every tree; most about oak, ash, elm, thorn; less about wich hazel; hardly observed about firs, pine, yew.

Whether it will not delight about trees that are perpetually green may be inquired. It seldom ariseth about holly or not to great bigness; the perpetual leafing prevents the arise or hindering the growth or twisting.

Whether there be not also a dissimilitude in their motions, not one enduring the approximation of the other.

That they follow the sun in their windings is hard to make out upon impartial observation; hops do it more clearly, which nothing turning are commonly directed that way by the husbandman.

Inquire how it ariseth from the primary root.

Try whether ivy will bear when cut from the root; whether it may have sufficient stock remaining for once, or whether it may not attract somewhat by the *cerni*.

[*On the Fig Tree.*]

CONCERNING the fig tree, some things are remarkable from its proper nature; that it is a tree of plentiful sap and milk diffused throughout, which will drop from the trunk and branches if seasonably cut at the spring.

That it is the general plant for admission of insition, engrafting; and though miseltoe seldom or never groweth thereon, yet it becomes a fit stock for most plants.

That it was the coagulum or runnet of the ancients, wherewith they turned their milk and made cheese, as is remarkable from Aristotle *de Animal.* and illustrates that passage in Homer and Euripides, and might frustrate all the use of other herbs and hath its name from thence and which we find so great effect; and might therefore be medically used in the place of coagulum, which having that virtue may serve for dissolution of blood coagulated.

That they have fruits without any flower, as jessamine flowers without fruit or seeds; that these are the forerunners of fruit the year following, and stay in buttons all the winter, making figs the year after.

Of this two parables, remarkable in the Scripture.

Cursed for barrenness, as being less tolerable in that tree than any, which is the stock of all other trees, and therefore more considerable that nothing grew upon it, on which all other trees will grow, and in this consideration probably the *phallus* or *virile neuter* and the image of Priapus the god of fertility and semblance of fecundation was formed out of a fig tree. And whether in the Hebrew notation there be any natural fertility implied, whilst we find it from a word that signifieth twins and plural generations, may admit of consideration.

That our first parents covered their secret parts with fig-leaves, which tree was after sacred unto Priapus, I shall not deduce upon genteel imagination.

DOMESTIC CORRESPONDENCE.

THE earliest specimens of Sir Thomas Browne's family correspondence, which have been discovered, are his letters to his younger son Thomas, while in France; of which the following, preserved in No. 391 of the Rawlinson Collection of MSS., at the Bodleian Library, Oxford, seem to have been transcripts by Mrs. Elizabeth Lyttelton, his daughter. The series is entitled, *Letters of my Father's which he writ to my Brother Thomas when he went into France, at 14 years of age;* 1660. I have not thought proper to alter the spelling of these letters; but would observe that its faultiness must not be charged on Sir Thomas. He wrote so illegibly (as those are well aware who have been fated to decypher his hieroglyphics) that his orthography was left at the mercy of the copyist, who, in the present case, seems not to have been remarkably skilled in that accomplishment.

Dr. Browne to his son Thomas.—Decr. 22, Norwich, [1660.]

HONEST TOM,—I hope by God's assistance you have been some weeks in Bourdeaux. I was yesterday at Yarmouth where I spoke with your uncle Charles Mileham who told me Mr. Dade would accommodate you with what moneys were fitting for defray of your charges in any kind, and therefore would not have mee at present send you any bill to receive any particular summ, but however when I hear from you I will take care for such a bill to be sent to Mr. Dade to whom in the mean time present my true respects and service and be sure to be observant of what he shall advise you; be as good a husband as possible and enter not upon any cours of superfluous expences; be not dejected and malencholy because you can yet have litle comfort in conversation, and all things will seem strange unto you.

Remember the camells back and be not troubled for any thing that other ways would trouble your patience here, be courteous and civil to all, put on a decent boldness and avoid *pudor rusticus*, not much known in France. Hold firm to the Protestant religion and be diligent in going to church when you have any litle knowledge of the language. God will accept of your desires to serve him in his publick worship tho you cannot make it out to your desires ; be constant not negligent in your dayly private prayers, and habituate your heart in your tender days unto the fear and reverence of God. It were good you had a map of France that you might not be unacquainted with the several parts, and to resort unto upon occasion for your information ; view and understand all notable buildings and places in Bourdeaux or near it, and take a draught thereof, as also the ruind Amphitheatre, but these at your leisure. There is I think a book in french calld *Les Monuments* or *les Antiquites de Bourdeaux*, enquire of the same ; read some books of french and latin, for I would by no means you should loose your latin but rather gain more.

Ned comes not home this Xtmas[1]. I shall God willing remember your new years gift. Give me an account of your voyage by sea as perticuler as you can, for I doubt you had a rough passage ; be temperate in dyet and wary to over heat yourself; remember to *compremere et non extendere labra.* To God's providence I commit you. I have sent a little box by this ship.—Vostre tres chere Pere,

THO: BROWNE.

Dr. Browne to his son Thomas.—Jan. 31, *Norwich*, [1660-1.]

HONEST TOM,—I was glad to receive your letter, where you gave a good account of your voyage ; take notice of all things remarkable, which will be pleasant unto you hereafter ; if you goe to Saintes you may better learn the languadge and I think there is a Protestant church ; be as good an husband as you can ; to write and cast account will be necesarie ; for either singing painting or dancing if you

---

[1] From Cambridge where he then was, at Trinity College.

learn let it be but for a while; painting will be most usefull if you learn to draw landskips or buildings, the other takes up much time and your own private practise will sufficiently advantage you. I would be glad you had a good handsome garb of your body, which you will observe in most there, and may quickly learn if you cast of *pudor rusticus*, and take up a commendable boldness without which you will never be fit for anything nor able to show the good parts which God has given you. I would think it very happy if you had more Latin, and therefore advantage yourself that way if possible; one way beside learning from others will be to read the scripture or chapters thereof dayly in french and Latin and to look often upon the grammars in both languages. Since you went, there was a little box with 4 knives and a pair of gloves, &c. in it which I hope you received. Commend my humble service and respects to Mr. Dade and when you send unto him acknowledge your obligations to him, and how industrious you will be in all returns of gratitude which shall ever fall within your power. Sir Joseph Pain[2] writes often to Mr. Dade. Some riseings there have been in London of the Anabaptists, fift Monarchie men and others, but soon suppresd and 13 executed. Upon the King's letter 5 of our Aldermen were put out which had got in in the usurpers time in other mens places, Andrews, Allen, Davie, Ashwell, &c. Yesterday was an humiliation and fast kept to divert the judgments of God upon us and our posteritie for the abominable murther of King Charles the first and is by act of Parliment to be kept yearly on that day for ever. Ned is at Cambridge. Nancy still in London. God's mercifull providence guide and protect you. —Your ever loveing father,   THOMAS BROWNE.

Dr. Browne to his son Thomas.—March 10, *stylo. vet.* [1660-1.]

HONEST TOM,—I presume you are by this time at Xaintes. If you live with an apothecairie you may get some good by observing the drugs and practise which will be noe burden and may somewhat help you in latin; I would be at some reasonable charge if any young man would assist you and

[2] Of Norwich.

teach you french and latin dayly as they are to be found commonly; you are not only to learn to understand and speak french but to write it which must be dun by practise and observation because they write and speak differently, and in what you write in English, observe the points and date your letters. Write whether you like the place and how language goes down with you, be not fearfull but adventure to speak what you can for you are known a stranger and they will bear with you, put on a desent bold-ness and learn a good garb of body, be carefull you loose not such books or papers wherein you take notes or draughts. Let nothing discontent or disturb you, trust in God to return you safe to us; by this time you may attempt to hear the Protestant preachers; live soberly and temperately, the heat of that place will otherwise mischief you and keep within in the heat of the day. Mr. Bendish is or was Mr. Johnson's prentice of Yarmouth, lives at Rochelle. I will get Mr. Johnson to write unto him about you; my respects and service to Mr. Dade. I received a letter about 3 weeks agoe from you. The Amphitheatre of Bourdeaux was built by the emperor Gallienus whose coyns you have seen, there is one also at Perigeaux in Perigort a neighbour pro-vince; you live upon the river Charante within the compass of the old English possessions which was from the Pyrenean hills unto the river La Charante, to the mouth whereof Cognac wines are brought down, which we drink in summer. Frequent civill company. God bless thee.—Vostre tres chere pere, T. BROWNE.

Dr. Browne to his son Thomas.—Aprill 22, Norwich, [1661.]

HONEST TOM,—I hope by this time thou art got some-what beyond *plaist il,* and *ouy Monsieur,* and durst ask a question and give an answer in french, and therefore now I hope you goe to the Protestant Church to which you must not be backward, for tho there church order and discipline be different from ours, yet they agree with us in doctrine and the main of religion. Endeavour to write french; that will teach you to understand it well, you should have signi-fied the apoticary's name with whom you dwell, in such a

place you may see the drugs and remember them all your
life. I received your letter and like your description of the
place, both the Romans and English have lived there; the
name of Santonna now Xaintes is in the geographie of
Ptolemie who lived under Antoninus, as also Porto Santonicus
where Rochelle stands, and Promontorium Santonicum where
now Bloys. My coyns are encreased since you went I had
60 coynes of King Stephen found in a grave before Christmas, 60 Roman silver coyns I bought a month agoe, and Sir
Robert Paston will send me his box of Saxon and Roman
coyns next week, which are about thirtie, so that I would
not buy any there except some few choice ones which I
have not already; but you doe very well to see all such
things, some likely have collections which they will in
courtesie show, as also urns and lachrimatories: any friend
will help you to a sight thereof, for they are not nice in
such things. I should be content you should see Rochelle,
and the Isle of Rhee salt works are not far from you, for the
sommer will be too hot to travail and I would have you
wary to expose yourself then to heats, but to keep quiet and
in shades.   Write some times to Mr. Dade civil letters with
my service. I send at this time by Rochelle whither the
ships will be passing from Yarmouth for salt. Point your
letters hereafter, I mean the ends of sentences. Christ
church[3] is in a good condition much frequented, and they
have a sweet organ; on Tuesday ·next is the Coronation
day when Mr. Bradford preacheth; it will be observed with
great solemnity especially at London: a new Parliament on
the 8th of May and there is a very good choice almost in all
places. Cory the Recorder, and Mr. Jay, 2 Royallists gained
it here against all opposition that could possibly bee made;
the voyces in this number, Jaye 1070, Corie 1001, Barnham
562, Church 436. My Lord Richardson and Sir Ralph
Hare caryed it in the county without opposition. Lent was
observed this year which made Yarmouth and fishermen
rejoyce. The militia is settled in good hands through all
England, besides volunteer troops of hors, in this citty
Collonell Sir Joseph Pain, Lieutenant Coll. Jay, Major
Bendish, Captain Wiss, Brigs, Scottow, 2 volunteer troops
in the country under Mr. Knivet and Sir Horace Townsend,

[3] Norwich Cathedral.

who is made a lord. Good boy doe not trouble thyself to send us any thing, either wine or bacon. I would have sent money by exchange, but Charles Mileham would not have me send any certain sum, but what you spend shall be made good by him. I wish some person would direct you awhile for the true pronunciation and writeing of french, by noe means forget to encrease your Latin, be patient civil and debonair unto all, be temperate and stir litle in the hot season : by the books sent you may understand most that has pasd since your departure, and you may now read the french Gazets which come out weekly. Yesterday the Dean preached and red the Liturgie or Common prayer, and had a comunion at Yarmouth as haveing a right to doe so some times, both at St Marys the great church at Lynn and St Nicholas church at Yarmouth as he is Dean. It is thought by degrees most will come to conformitie. There are great preparitions against to-morrow the Coronation day, the County hors came hither to joyn the Regiment of foot of this citty, a feast at the new hall, generall contributions for a feast for the poor, which they say will be in the market place, long and solemn service at Christ Church beginning at 8 a Clock and with a sermon ending at twelve. Masts of ships and long stageing poles already set up for becon bonfires, speeches and a little play by the strollers in the market-place an other by young Cityzens at Timber Hill on a stage, Cromwell hangd and burnt every where, whose head is now upon Westminster hall, together with Ireton and Bradshows. Have the love and fear of God ever before thine eyes ; God confirm your faith in Christ and that you may live accordingly, Je vous recommende a Dieu. If you meet with any pretty insects of an[y] kind keep them in a box, if you can send *les Antiquites de Bourdeaux* by any ship, it may come safe.

(*No Signature.*)

Dr. Browne to his son Thomas.—Norwich, June 24, [1661.]

HONEST TOM,—I received yours dated in May, God continue thy health, no ships yet going for Rochelle or Boardeaux, I cannot send an other box, I hope you have received the last, be as good an husband as possible; when the next ship goeith you shall have such things from your mother as are desired. Practise to write french and turn latin into french, be bold and adventrous now to speak; and direct yourself by grammar especially for the moods and tenses, now you have leisure observe the manner of the french courts, their pleading if there be any court in Xaintes. We wanted you at the Guild (where neither was Ned); Mr. Osborn Mayor: and we were engaged in hanging our house, which was dun to purpose. Ned is at Cambridge, Nancy we expect in July about the assises. By this time the ships are gon to convey hither[4] Donna Cathara, infanta of Portugall the kings sister who is to be our queen; the English are unwilling to part with Dunkirk and Jamaica and have about 6000 souldiers in Dunkirk, so that we doubt how the Spaniards will take it; you may find such news in the french Gazzets if they come to your town. A parliment is now setting and a convocation of the Clergie made up of all the bishops, deans, archdeacons, and a minister chosen out of every county by the clergie thereof; the Bishops are voted to set again in the house of Peers or Lords, the house of Commons received the Sacrament by the book of Common Prayers or liturgie in Westminster church. In Norwich the Court of Aldermen and Common Councell have made a law to resort to the Cathedrall every Sunday, and to be not only at sermon but at prayers, which they observe; these small things I write that you might not be totally ignorant how affairs goe at home. Thy writeing is much mended, but you still forget to make points. I have paid the bill drawn by Mr. Dade upon Charles. Pray present my true respects to him. Remember what is never to be forgot, to serve and honour God. I should be very glad you would get a handsome garb and gate. Your mother and all send their good wishes. I rest your ever loveing father,

THO. BROWNE.

[4] The king had recently, in his opening speech to the Parliament, May 8, 1661, adverted to his treaty of marriage with the Infanta of Portugal, and intimated his intention of sending his fleet to bring her over. He also spoke of the cession of Dunkirk and Jamaica—as objects likely to be contended for by Spain, in the event of the marriage taking place.

Dr. Browne to his son Thomas.—Norwich, Nov. 1, [1661.]

HONEST TOM,—I hope by this time you have received the box and books sent by the french ship which came to Yarmouth and returned to Rochelle. I should be glad to hear of your health for I know the country where you are is very sickly, as ours is heer. God of his mercy preserve you and return you safe. Except you desire to return by sea, I would be at the charge of your return by Paris in the spring, observe the manner of trade, how they make wine and vinegar, by that we call the rape, which is the husks and stalks of the grape, and how they prepare it for that use. Commend me kindly to Mr. Dade and Mr. Bendish. Read books which are in french and Latin, for so you may retain and increase your knowledge in Latin: some times draw and limn and practise perspective. We hear the Protestants in France are but hardly used, noe doubt the king will be carefull to keep them low haveing had experience of their strength. However serve God faythfully and be constant to your religion. The Parliment adjourned last August sets again on the 20th of November, when they will publish a strict act for uniformitie in the Church. Our bishop Dr. Reynolds my loveing friend hath been in Norwich these 3 months; he preacheth often and comes constantly to Christ church on Sunday mornings at the beginning of prayers, about which time the aldermen also come, he sitteth in his seat against the pulpit, handsomely built up and in his episcopall vestments, and pronounceth the Blessing or the Peace of God, &c. at the end: where there is commonly a very numerous congregation and an excellent sermon by some preacher of the Combination, appointed out of Norfolk and Suffolk, the one for winter the other for sommer. The bishops set again in the house of Lords and our bishop is goeing thither. My Lord Townsend is made ld. lieutenant of Norfolk and hath the power of all the militia, which hath trained by regiments in severall parts of the country. Sir Joseph Pain our Collonell trayned our regiment of the citty last week. Be temperate and sober in the whole course of your life, keep noe bad or uncivill company, be courteous and humble in your conversation, still shunning *pudor rusticus,* which undoes good natures, and practise an handsome garb and civil boldness which he that learneth not in France travaileth in vain.   God's blessing be upon you.   I rest your ever loveing father,

Tho. Browne.

Corn is very dear ; the best wheat 4 or 5 and forty shillings the comb, which is 4 bushells.   The king of Portugal resigns up Tangere, a town on Africk side in Barbarie in the midle of the streights mouth, whether my Ld. of Peterborough is goeing with a regiment of foot and 2 troops of hors to take possession.   All Parliment money must be brought in to the mint and coyned with the king's stamp and is not to pas corrant beyond December the first.   You may stay your stomack with litle pastys some times in cold mornings, for I doubt sea larks will be too dear a collation and drawe too much wine down; be warie for Rochelle was a place of too much good fellowship and a very drinking town, as I observed when I was there, more than other parts of France.

Dr. Browne to his son Thomas.—Jan. 4, [1661-2.]

Honest Tom,—I have not written unto you since November because I thought you had been removed from Rochelle, but now understanding you are still there, I send this by land with my good wishes and prayers unto God to bless you, and direct you in all your ways.   So order affairs that when you remove, you may be accomodated with money when you come to Paris.   There is a book cald *les Antiquites de Paris* which will direct you in many things, what to look after, that litle time you stay there, beside you may see many good new buildings, since you have been at Rochelle you might have seen the Isle of Rhe, and salt works if you had any opertunety.   Serve God and honour him with a true sincere heart, your old friend Mr Bradford preacheth to-morrow at Xt church, as being his turn in the Combination, on the 30 of this month an humiliation is to be kept annually for ever by act of Parliament, in order to the expiation of God's judgments upon the nation for the horrid murther of King Charles the first, acted upon that day.   I sent a box

unto you by a ship that went to Rochelle in the beginning
of November. , Your mother and all send their good wishes.
I rest your loveing father, T. B.

God bless thee. You may. learn handsom songs and
aires not by book but by the ear as you shall hear them
sung.

Just as were closing up the box I now send you I received
your letter and box, where by I see you are mindfull of us
and are not idle. You may surely stay safely in Rochelle
being strangers, but if you find good convenience I am as
willing you should be any where elce, for where ere you are
it will be best to move to Paris in the beginning of March,
and there is noe citty considerable near Rochelle but Nantes,
where you will be upon the Loir, on which many good cittys
stand. Be guided herein by advice of friends. God bless
you. By this time I hope you have received the former box
I sent about a month agoe. I wish you had acquaintance
with some Protestant in Nantes if you goe thither or might
be recommended, for there are English also. Your ever
loving father, T. B.

No apology, it is hoped, need be offered for printing
the following journal. It affords us a pleasant glimpse of
the amusements of Norwich, at a time when it was the residence of a nobleman of the highest rank, who appears to
have associated without reserve with its leading families, and
to have made it his study to promote the gaieties of the place.
Mr. Edward Browne's own participation in those gaieties is
placed in most amusing contrast with his more professional
occupations. His morning dissections and prescriptions,
relieved by his evening parties,—the interest he evinces in
the marvellous powders of Dr. de Veau,—his faith in a
magical cure for the jaundice,—and not least, the gravity of
which he tells of "a serpent vomited by a woman," which
"she had unfortunately burnt" before he arrived to see
it;—all these afford abundant evidence, that, "though on
pleasure bent," he was keen in his pursuit of knowledge,
though too ready to believe all he heard, and much more than
he saw.

[MS. SLOAN. NO. 1906.]

JANUARY 1 [1663-4]. I was at Mr. Howard's,[3] brother to the duke of Norfolk, who kept his Christmas this year at the duke's palace in Norwich, so magnificently as the like hath scarce been seen. They had dancing every night, and gave entertainments to all that would come; hee built up a roome on purpose to dance in, very large, and hung with the bravest hangings I ever saw; his candlesticks, snuffers, tongues, fireshovels, and andirons, were silver; a banquet was given every night after dancing; and three coaches were employed to fetch ladies every afternoon, the greatest of which would holde fourteen persons, and coste five hundred pound, without the harnasse, which cost six score more. I have seen of his pictures which are admirable; hee hath prints and draughts done by most of the great masters' own hands. Stones and jewells, as onyxs, sardonyxes, jacinths, jaspers, amethists, &c. more and better than any prince in Europe. Ringes and seals, all manner of stones and limmings beyond compare. These things were most of them collected by the old earl of Arundel,[4] who employed his agents in most places to buy him up rarities, but especially in Greece and Italy, where hee might probably meet with things of the greatest antiquity and curiosity.

This Mr. Howard hath lately bought a piece of ground of Mr. Mingay, in Norwich, by the water side in Cunsford, which hee intends for a place of walking and recreation, having made already walkes round and crosse it, forty foot in bredth; if the quadrangle left be spacious enough hee intends the first of them for a bowling green, the third for a wildernesse, and the forth for a garden.[5] These and the like noble things he performeth, and yet hath paid 100,000 pounds af his ancestors debts.

[3] Henry, afterwards created Lord Howard of Castle Rising, subsequently Earl of Norwich and Earl Marshal of England, became, on the death of his brother Thomas, sixth Duke of Norfolk. He was the second son of Henry-Frederic, and grandson of Thomas the celebrated Earl of Arundel, whose magnificent collection of marbles he afterwards, at the suggestion of Evelyn, presented to the University of Oxford. At the same time he presented his grandfather's library, valued at 10,000*l.* to the Royal Society.

[4] Mr. Howard's grandfather.

[5] Which was long afterwards called "My Lord's Gardens."

January 2. I cut up a bull's heart and took out the bone, &c.

January 3. I heard Mr. Johnson preach at Christchurch, and Mr. Tenison at St. Luke's chappell, and took notice that the sun rose in an eliptical or oval figure, not round, the diameter was parallel to the horizon.

January 4. I went to dinner to Mr. Briggs, where there was some discourse of Drabitius'[6] prophesy. I went to Mr. Howard's dancing at night; our greatest beautys were Mdm. Elizabeth Cradock, Eliz. Houghton, Ms. Philpot, Ms. Yallop; afterwards to the banquet, and so home.—*Sic transit gloria mundi!*

January 5. Tuesday, I dined with Mr. Howard, where wee dranke out of pure golde, and had the music all the while, with the like, answerable to the grandeur of [so] noble a person : this night I danc'd with him too.

January 6. I din'd at my aunt Bendish's, and made an end at Chrismas, at the duke's place, with dancing at night and a great banquet. His gates were opend, and such a number of people flock'd in, that all the beere they could set out in the streets could not divert the stream of the multitudes, till very late at night.

January 7. I opened a dog.

January 8. I received a letter from Sr. Horden, wherein hee wrote word of Mr. Craven's play, which was to bee acted immediately after the Epiphany.

January 9. Mr. Osborne sent my father a calf, whereof I observed the knee joynt, and the neat articulation of the put bone which was here very perfect. I dissected another bull's heart ; I took of the *os scutiforme annulare* and *aritænoide* of a bullock. This day Monsieur Buttet, which playes most admirably on the flagellet, bagpipe, and sea trumpet, a long three square instrument having but one string, came to see mee.

January 10. Mr. Bradford preached at Christchurch.

January 11. This day being Mr. Henry Howard's birthday, wee danc'd at Mr. Howard's till 2 of the clock in the morning.

[6] A Moravian Protestant minister, who declared himself inspired in 1638, and uttered various prophecies, which were printed in 1654. He was at length arrested, tried, condemned, and beheaded at Presburg, in 1671.

January 12. Cutting up a turkey's heart.

A munkey hath 36 teeth ; 24 *molares*, 4 *canini*, and 8 *incisores*.

January 13. This day I met Mr. Howard at my uncle Bendish's, where he taught me to play at l'hombre, a Spanish game at cards.

January 14. A munkey hath fourteen ribs on each side, and hath clavicles.

Radzivil in his third epistle[7] relates strange storys of diving in the river Nile.

There are one million of soelgers to guard the great wall of China, which extends from east to west three hundred leagues: author, *Belli Tartarici Martin Martinius.*

January 15. Wee gat a boare's bladder.

I took out the bones of the *carpum* in a munkey's forefoot, which were in number ten.

January 16. Wee had to dinner a weed fish, very like to an haddock. I went to Mr. Dye's, where I saw my lady Ogle and her daughter Ms Anne, an handsome young woman: afterwards, with Mr. Alston, I went to see Mr. Howard's garden in Cunsford. At night I read two letters which my father had formerly received from Island, from Theodorus Jonas, minister of Hitterdale, which were to be sent to Gresham Colledge.

January 17. I waited upon my lady Ogle, Ms Windham, and Ms An. Ogle, to Christchurch; Mr. Scambler of Heigham preached: in the afternoon I heard Mr. Tofts at St. Michael's of Must Paul.[8] The weather is extraordinarily warme for this season of the year, our January is just like April.

January 18. I saw Cornwall's collection of cuts, where I met with some masters which I had not seen before, as Quellinus, Hans Sebalde, Beham, Petrus Isaacs, Breemburg, Blocklandt, A. Diepenbeck.

January 20. Tonambaus would sweeten a whole pond with sugar and cause it to bee drunk drye.

January 21. I shew'd Dr. de Veau about the town; I sup'd with him at the duke's palace, where he shewed a

[7] Nicol. Christ. Radzivili Hierosolymitana Peregrinatio, iv. Epistolis comprehenнa; fol. Brunsbergæ, 1601. Id. fol. Antwerp. 1614.

[8] St. Michael *ad Placita,* or at Plea ; see *Blomfield.*

powder against agues, which was to bee given in white wine, to the quantity of 3 grains. He related to mee many things concerning the duke of Norfolke that lives at Padua, *non compos mentis,*[9] and of his travailes in France and Italy.

January 22. This morning I went to Lowe's, the butcher, here I saw a sheep cut up. Wee eat excellent hung beefe for our breakefast, and Mr. Davie gave to mee and Mr. Gardner a bottle of sack aud Renish wine after it. I heard Dr. de Veau play excellently on the gitterre, and Mr. Shadwel on the lute. Mr. Gibbs gave mee a Muscovian rat's skin, the tayle smells very like muske; the servants to the late Russian embassadors, which were here last winter, 1662, brought over a great number of them, and sold them for shillings a piece to people about the streets in London. This day two fishermen brought a mola to shore; wee have one of them, catch'd a great while agoe, in our house.

January 23. Don Francisco de Melo came from London with Mr. Philip Howard,[1] the queen's confessour, to visit his honour Mr. Henry Howard; I met them at Ms Deyes, the next day in Madam Windham's chamber.

I boyled the right forefoot of a munkey, and took out all the bones, which I keep by mee.

In a putbone the unfortunate casts are outward, the fortunate inward.

January 24. Mr. Wharton preached in the morning, at Christchurch, and in the afternoon at St. Peters. This day it snowed and was somewhat colde, but for a longe while before wee have scarce had any winter weather.

January 26. I went to Norris his garden, where I saw *Aconitum hyemale* in flower, which is yellow. I saw a little childe in an ague upon which Dr. de Veau was to try his febrifuge powder, but the ague being but moderate and in

---

[9] Thomas, fifth Duke of Norfolk; eldest son of Henry-Frederic, Earl of Arundel. He was attacked with a distemper of the brain, while at Padua with his grandfather, the celebrated Earl of Arundel: and died on the continent, in 1677. He had been, in 1664, restored to all the titles of his ancestor who was beheaded in 1572.

[1] Third grandson of the great Earl of Arundel. While on the continent with his brothers and his grandfather, he was induced by a Dominican to turn Catholic and to join that order: he became Lord Almoner to Charles the Second's Queen, and subsequently received a cardinal's cap from Clement X.

the declension, it was thought too mean a disease to try the strength and efficacy of his so extolled powder.

January 27. My cousin Barker came from London.

January 28. I went to the butchers to see oxen killd; one oxe had his omentum growing to his side or *peritonæum* all along by the spleen, I saw the *ductus virtsungianus* out of the pancreas into the duodenum. I saw the water distilled. At night wee had a dancing at Mr. Houghton's, with Mr. Henry Howard, his brother Mr. Edward, and Don Francisco de Melo, wee had sixe very handsome women, Ms. El. Houghton, Ms. El. Cradock, Ms. Philpot, Ms. Bullock, Ms. Shadwell and Ms. Tom Brooke; wee staid at it till almost four in the morning.

January 29. I cut up an hare wherein I could find no omentum. At night I saw a great pike opened. A munkey hath six *vertebræ lumborum*.

January 30. Mr. Gill preached at Christ church in the morning. A magical cure for the jaundise;—Burne wood under a leaden vessel fill'd with water, take the ashes of that wood, and boyle it with the patient's urine, then lay nine long heaps of the boyld ashes upon a board in a ranke, and upon every heap lay nine spears of crocus, it hath greater effects then is credible to any one that shall barely read this receipt without experiencing.

January 31. Mr. Kinge preached at Christ church in the morninge and Mr. Seaman at St. George's in the afternoon.

February 1. I tooke notice that the *Nantuates* were not rightly placed in *Horneus* map for Cæsar's Commentaries. I boyled the head and foot of an hare to save the bones.

February 2. I saw a cockfighting at the Whitehorse in St. Stephens.

February 3. I saw Helleboraster in flower. I cut up a hare which had one young one in the left corner of the uterus. I cut up a hedgehog, with a pretty large omentum.

February 5. I went to see a serpente that a woman living in St. Gregories church yard in Norwich vomited up, but shee had burnt it before I came.

February 6. Mr. Clarke exhaled for us water taken out of a salt springe in a medow betwixt this and Yarmouth; there remained gray salt, but in a small quantity in proportion to the water.

February 8. I saw a polypus which was taken out of Mr. Townsend's nose; it was of a soft fleshy substance, with divers glandules in it, it was about three inches longe. Mr. Croppe extracted it.

February 9. The Bishop's son of Skalhault in Islande was here this afternoon, of whom I enquired many things concerninge his country.

February 10. I dissected a badger.

February 13. Wee drew valentines and danced this night at Mr. Howards. Hee was gat by Ms. Liddy Houghton and my sister Betty by him.

February 16. I went to visit Mr. Edward Ward, an old man in a feaver, where Ms. Anne Ward· gave me my first fee, 10 shillings.

February 22. I set forward for my journey to London, baited at Thetford, and reached Cambridge this night, 46 miles of; where I was entertained by my good friends, Mr. Nûrse, Mr. Craven, Mr. Bridge, &c.

February 23. I proceeded in my journey to London, as farre as Hodsdun, 27 miles more ; where I lodged this night with some of my countrey men.

February 24. This morning I rode the last seventen mile to London, where, setting my horse at the George, I visited Mr. Nat. Scottow, Dr. Windate, Ms. Howell, and laide this night at my cosin Barker's in Clarkenwell.

February 25. I went to hear an anatomy lecture at Chirurgeons hall, and ordered my businesse so as to see the dissection on preparing of body by the chirurgeons, as well as to hear the discourse of the parts by Dr. Tearne,[2] who reads this time ; this is the third humane body I ever saw dissected at Chirurgeon's hall.

February 25. This morning Dr. Tearne made a speech in latine and afterwards read *de Cuticula*. I din'd at Dr. Windates, and in the afternoon heard the second lecture, wherein these parts following were insisted upon ; *Ventriculus cum orificiis suis, intestina, mesenterium*, which I having before the lecture well observed in the anatomizing roome, did receive the greatest satisfaction from the lecture. This night I walk'd into St. James his Parke, where I saw

[2] Dr. Christopher Tearne, of Leyden, M.D. originally of Cambridge, Fellow of the College of Physicians. He died in 1673.

many strange creatures, as divers sorts of outlandish deer, Guiny sheep, a white raven, a great parot, a storke, which, having broke its owne leg, had a wooden leg set on, which it doth use very dexterously. Here are very stately walkes set with lime trees on both sides, and a fine Pallmall.

February 26. I heard the third lecture, in which these parts following were taken notice of; *glandulæ renales, renes, vesica, arteria et vena præparantes, testiculi, penis.*

I went to the signe of the Queen's armes in St. Martins, where in the celler, being arched and close, the roof is all covered with a slimy substance formed into the figures of grapes or bunches of grapes, which, although sometimes wiped of, will encrease againe by the steame or vapour of the wine from the vessels ; a pretty rarity and worth the observation. I brought some of these grapes away with mee. In this cellar, not long since, one pulling down a partition of boardes founde the body of a dead man with his leg in a payre of stocks, the body afterwards stirred fell into ashes. I met with Mr. Hollingworth and Mr. Udal, who promised, if it pleaseth God to continue our healths, to meet mee at Paris the first of November next or else to forfeit forty shillings.

February 28. It being Sunday, I went to the Queen Mother's chappel, which is a stately one, well painted and adorned with a large golde crucifixe, a most admirable paynted crucifix, tapers, lamps, and the like. I noted some at confession, in little wooden apartments, and having satisfied my curiositie in observing the manner of their worship, I left this chappell of Sommerset house, and passing through a crowde of Irish beggars, I went to the Savoy church, where the liturgye of England is read in French. In the afternoon I read a sermon to Madam Fairfax, my dear sister Cottrell, and Nansy; and afterwards waited upon Madam Cottrell home to her house in St. James his parke, which is handsomely built upon a piece of grounde, which the kinge gave to Sr. Charles.[3]

February 29. I was at the chymists to inquire for *spiritus*

[3] Sir Charles Cottrell, master of the ceremonies to King Charles II. married Sir Thomas Browne's daughter. He translated Cassandra, and was one of the translators of Davila's History of the Civil Wars of France.

urinæ, spiritus cornu, sal cornu cervi et cinnaberis anti-monii.

I carried some Islande stones to one Royall, a stone cutter living over against the spur, at the upper end of Woodstreet. I eat for my dinner a Woodstreet cake, which cakes are famous for being well made.

March 1. I went to see Dr. Dee living in Crouchet Friers, but hee was not within. I was at Mr. King's, living in little Britain, an ingenious chirurgeon, who shewed mee parts of many things that hee had dissected, as a liver of a man excarnated, a spleen excarnated, a man's *vena porta*, the *chorion* and *amnion* of a woman, the uterus and all parts belonging to it, the coats in the third stomach of an ox neatly separated. I being desirous to see the inside of a man's stomacke hee cut up one for mee which hee had by him, the gutts opened and dried, the cæcum part of the *colon* and *ilium* dried, so as there was plainly to see the manner of the iliums insertion into the colon of a man, and the valve; and many other parts, which hee kept dryed in a large paper booke. This afternoon I went to see a collection of rarities of one Forges, or Hobarte, by St. Paules, among which were many things which I never saw before, as a sea-elephantes head, a Lazy of Brazil, an Indian Serpente, &c. I went to Arundell house where I saw a great number of old Roman and Græcian statuas, many as big again as the life, and divers Greek inscriptions upon stones in the garden. I viewed these statuas till the approching night began to obscure them, beinge extreamly taken with the noblenesse of that ancient worke, and grieving at the bad usage some of them had met with in our last distractions. From hence by water to Sr. Charles Cotrels, where taking leave of my dear sister, I returned to my cousin Barkers in Clarkenwell.

. March 2. I went to Mr. Foxe's chamber in Arundell house, where I saw a great many pretty pictures and things cast in brasse, some limmings, divers pretious stones, and one diamonde valued at eleven hundred pound; and, having received letters from him to carry to his honour Mr. Henry Howarde at Norwich, I tooke horse at the George in Lumbard street, and gat to Chelmsford this night, travelling 25 miles through that pleasant county of Essex.

March the 3d. I rose very early, and set forward on my journy by four of the clock, so as betwixt eight and nine I got to Colchester; a very large, but a stragling towne, the heart of the towne standing upon an hill, but it shoots out long streets into the valleys, on all hands. From hence to Ipswich, where I dined. A very great and clean neat towne, standing advantagiously upon a river so as ships come up to the towne. There are about 12 churches in it, and it gives place in bignesse to nere a towne in England. From hence this afternoon I rode to Thwait, through the Pye roade, a very deep uneven roade; so, having roade about 45 miles this day, I thought it best to ride no further, although it were not yet night, and I might easily have reached Scole. The man of the house seemed to bee a very honest fellow, and gave as kinde entertainment as his house was capable of. Hee had a daughter which was not fifteen, and yet as tal as most women. I observed that to one in the jaundice hee gave the green ends of goose dunge steep'd in beere, and then strayned and sweetned, a country remedy.

March the 4. Having roade about two mile, I came to the white horse; a horse carv'd in wood, upon a wooden structure, like a sighne post, an old woman and a gardener one standing behind and another before the horse; underneath hanges a globe, out of which comes four hands, which directs passengers in the crosse roads (which meet iust in these places) one standes towards Norwich, the contrary towards Ipswich, one to Bury and the other to Framlingham. About three mile further I came to Scoale, where is very handsome inne, and the noblest signe post in England, about and upon which are carved a great many stories, as of Charon and Cerberus, of Actæon and Diana, and many other, the sighne it self is the white harte, which hangs downe carved in a stately wreath. Fifteen mile more to Norwich, whether I gat about eleven of the clocke; and in the afternoon waited upon Mr. Howard, and delivered him his letters, and to little Mr. Fox (heir to Mr. Fox of London), who dances a jig incomparably.

March 5. I dissected a shoveler.

March 9. I went to Norris his garden where I saw black Hellebore in flower, which is white; the white Hellebore is not yet come up.

I drank some birch tree liquor, which now runneth.

March 10. I saw Mr. Howards closet, in which are a great number of delicate limmings, but one pretty large one, of our blessed lady with our Saviour in her armes, more than extraordinary. There are two heads in agate pretty large, a great many things cut and turnd in ivory, delicate china dishes, divers things cut in fine stones, a pearle in the fashion [of] a lion very large, and child's head and thigh bone very neat; divers things in gold and delicate workmanship, worthy so noble a person's closet.

March 11. I had a great deal of discourse with one Mr. Flatman a chirurgion that had lived in the gold country in Guiny, about that country, the inhabitants, their manners, our plantation at Cormontine, and the trafficke with the natives: as also about Lisbone, Barbadoes, and Jamaica, where hee had likewise been.

March 12. I dissected a frog, whose skin doth not stick close to the *membrana carnosa*, but is easily flead.

March 13. Mr. Flatman told mee the Portuguez used this way to the Jews or those that are in the inquisition, to make them dye in the Christian religion of the Church of Rome;—they put a cord about their neck the end of which is put through the hole of a great post so as they on other side may streitn or slack the rope, choke or save them again as they please which they doe till with the extremity of the paine they professe what they will have them, and then immediately strangle them.

March 17. I received a letter from Mr. Rand, wherein hee sent mee the inscription of the columne to bee set up at Rome upon the Corsican's expulsion.

March 18. I received a letter from my worthy friend Mr. Isaac Craven, who, being sent by the society of Trinity College in Cambridge, of which he is fellow, to compliment the Marquisse of Newcastle and the Marchionesse for their workes presented to our library, was pleas'd to write me a short relation of his journy through Stamford, Grantham, Newark, Southwell, (where is a pretty minster,) and Mansfield, to Wellbeck the Marquisse his house; where hee saw many pictures of Vandike, and a fine cabinet, but above all his fine stable and brave horses for the great saddle, of which the Marquisse (as his noble booke horsmanshippe

will testify) hath no small number nor ill managed, and is
without compare the best horsman living, taking delight
dayly, although hee bee now threscore and eleven years old,
to see his horses practice.

March 22. I gave 5 shillings in earnest for my coach-hire
to London, 20s. in all he is to have.

March 27. I tooke leave of my friends; my cousin
Dorothy Witherly gave me ten shillings, my aunt Bendish
gave me a ringe.

March 28. I set out towards London; Mr. Arrowsmith
and my brother accompanied mee as far as Attleborough;
this night wee layd at Barton mills; I had the kings
chamber for my lodging, where Charles the first once layd:
upon the wall, between the door and the chimney, there is
written with the kings owne hande *Caualleiro Honrado*.

March 29. We bayted at Chesterford, and lodged at
Bishop Stafford at the George, this day I had much discourse with Mr. Bedingfield, about his travailes in Flanders,
Artois, Brabant, &c. wee had to our suppers pike and
crafish.

March 30. By two of the clock in the afternoon wee gat
to London, where Mr. Uvedal and Mr. Rand met mee at
the Green Dragon, I waited upon Mr. Howells family, delivered a letter to my cousin Betty Cradock, and laid in
Clerkenwell.

March 31. I measured the pell mell in St. James Parke,
which is above twelve hundred paces longe. I went to
Morgan's Garden at Westminster; St. Pauls church is 43 of
my paces broad, Westminster Abbey is 33, Christchurch at
Norwich 28, Christchurch at Canterbury is 30.

April the 1. I took money for my journey, at a gold-
smith's in Lumbardstreet, ten pound; most of it in gold and
French coyne.

April 2. I took leave of my friends in London. My
cousin Garway, my cousin Cradock, Mr. Uvedale, and Mr.
Hollingworth, accompanied mee this night to Gravesend;
wee had a pleasant passage downe the river of Thames,
sometimes sayling, sometimes rowing, close by many hundred
brave ships which trade to most parts of the known world.
About 1 in the morning my friends left mee, and I went to
bed at the blew Anchor to refresh mee against the morrow.

April 3. I rode from Gravesend through Rochester to Sittenborne. Rochester hath a pretty cathedral church, in which is a neat quire; and a bridge over the Medway inferior to few; it is extreamly high and long, the water runs under it with such a force at lowe water, that all the river is covered with a white foame. From Sittenburne I took a fresh horse, and rode fiften miles further to Canterbury, through a pleasant countrey, having the sight of the river most part of the way on my left hand; the cherry grounds on both, in great numbers, in which the trees are planted equi-distantly and orderly. I went to Christchurch, the cathedral church at Canterbury, which is an extreame neat church, very long, 30 paces broad. I saw in it the Black Prince's tombe; the painted glasse, most of which is of a fine blew colour, is excellent: the front is neat, having two steeples on each side, the tower of the crosse isles is handsome. There is an extreame bigge steeple at the east end begun, but finished no higher than the church. Under the quire is another church, which is made use of by the Walloons. There is a double crosse in this church. In Canterbury are fiften parishes. Hence I roade to Dover, and had a sight of the land in France three miles before I came to my journey's end. This night I lay'd at Mr. Carlisle's, the clarke of the passage, at the Kingshead.

April 4. I walked to the seaside, where I found very large sea girdles, some seastarres, many lympits, and divers hearbs. In the afternoon I saw Dover castle, a very large one, and situated upon an high rock, with many fine roomes in it. They shew mee the horn which was blown at the building of the castle, which is made of brasse. I saw likewise a very longe gun called Basiliscus, 23 foot 8 inches long, which was very neatly carved. Captain John Stroade is Mr. of the castle.

April 5. I went to sea to see them catch lobsters, sea spiders, wilkes, Spanish crabs, crabwilkes, or *Bernardi eremitæ*, &c. Wee gat our passe portes, and

April 6. Betimes in the morning, wee set sayle for Calais in the packet boat; wee gave five shillings a piece for our passage, and having a fair winde, wee gat in four houres time into Calais roade, from whence a shallop fetch'd us to shoare. At our entryng of the port wee payd threepence a piece

for our heads ; they searched my portmantle at the gate and
the custom house, for which I was to pay 5 sols. After that
agreed with the messenger for 40 livres to Paris. I dined at
Monsieur la Force his house, at the sighne of the Dragon,
and so walked out to see the towne. I was not sick at all in
coming over from Dover to Calais, upon the sea, but yet
could hardly forbear spuing at the first sight of the French
women : they are most of them of such a tawny, sapy, base
complection, and have such vgly faces, which they here set
out with a dresse would fright the divell. They have a short
blew coat, which hath a vast thick round rugge, in the place
of the cape, which they either weare about their necks or pull
over their heads, after such a manner as tis hard to guesse
which is most deformed, their visages or their habits. This
afternoon I went to the church which is a fair one, dedicated
to our Blessed Lady ; the large marble altar is noble, many
chappells as to St. Peter, and others, are well adorned ;
in an oval chappell, behinde the altar, I saw the priests
instruct the common people, and the young folkes of the
towne, in matters of religion, and learne them to say their
prayers. I went to a convent of Cordeliers, where Père
Barnatie, whose right name is Dungan, an Irishman, was
very civill to us, and shew all about the convent, and had
much discours with us about England, and other countries.
Wee saw a monastery of nuns ; their altar in their chappell
was covered with very rich lace. The Port Royall is a very
stately building. I agreed with the messenger for forty
livres to Paris, and

April 7. Wee set forward about 2 of the clock in the
afternoon, and got to Boulogne 7 leagues, where I saw the
Port. The buildings here, as at Calais, are of stone, and
the street evenly paved, but there are very few shops.

April 8. Wee dined at Monstreuil. There they search
my portmantle again, and I, not knowing I was to take a
passe at Calais, was put to some inconvenience, and had
like to lose my stockins, which were in my portmantle ; but
that one that travayled along with mee could speake both
English and French, who perswaded [them] I was no
merchant, and with fair words I got of. This night I layd
at Bernay.

April 19. Wee dined at Abbeville, a great towne, built

much after the English fashion, with wooden houses. I saw St. Voluhran's church, which hath a most stately front with two steeples in it, and a great deal of neat carving both in the stone and in the wood [of] the gates. I layd this night at Pois, a small towne.

April 20. I got to Beauvais, time enough (if I had listed) to heare masse; however, I went to see St. Pierre's church, which is an extream high one, and very stately. The North and South ends are most noble, the church paved with marble, checquered with stone: there is no building westward, beyond the cross isle, which makes the church but short; but if there were a body answerable to the rest, I think it might compare with most churches in Christendome. This night I layd at Tilierre. This day was the first day in which I saw vineyards, pilgrims, or was sprinkled with holy water.

Wee roade this day divers times beteewn rowes of apple trees a great waye; they are likewise set here orderly as the cherrytrees in Kent. Most of the country betwixt Calais and Paris is open, and sewen with corn, so as wee had fine prospects upon the top of every hill.

April 11, *St. v.* 21, *stylo novo.* Wee bayted at Beaumont, where after dinner each of us gave a messenger *trente solz*, for his care of us in our journey.

This after noon wee rode through St. Dinnis, where there is a noted church, in which are a great manye stately tombes of the Kings of France and other nobles. About four of the clock wee entered Paris, just by *Maison des Enfans Trouvés*, so through Fauxbourg St. Denis, and other places to the sighne of Ville de Soissons, dans rüe de la Vererie, where the messenger lodges. This night I walked about to see Pont Neuf, upon which standes a noble copper statua of Henry the fourth, the statuas of our Saviour, and the Samaritan woman, by a delicat fountain, made in the shape of a huge cockle-shell, which allwayes runs over. I went to Monsieur Michel de Clere, who lives in Rüe de Chevalier de Guet, and tooke an hundred liures of him, I went and hired a chamber in Rüe St. Zacharie˒ for 7 liures *par mois*, and so, *je vous souhaitte le bon soir.*

The following unfortunately is the only letter, which has been met with, from Sir Thomas to his son Edward during his Tour in France and Italy. The letter to which it is a reply is wanting.

Dr. Browne to his Son Edward.

DEARE SONNE EDWARD,—I recaived yours of Sep. 23. I am glad you have seene more cutt for the stone, and of different sex and ages; if opportunitie seemeth, you shall doe well to see some more, which will make you well experienced in that great operation, and almost able to performe it yourself upon necessitie, and where none could do it. Take good notice of their instruments, and at least make such a draught thereof, and especially of the dilator and director, that you may hereafter well remember it, and have one made by it. Other operations you may perhaps see, now the sumer is over; as also chymistrie and anatomie, The sicknesse[1] being great still, fewe I presume will hasten over. Present my services and thancks unto Dr. Patin. I hope Dr. Wren is still in Paris.[2] I should be glad the waters of Bourbon might benefitt Sir Samuel:[3] and those of Vic Mr. Trumbull. God bee praysed that you recovered from the small pox, which may now so embolden you, as to take of, at least abate, the sollicitude and fears which others have. Mr. Briot[4] may at his pleasure attempt at translation, for though divers short passages bee altered or added, and one [or] two chapters also added, yet there is litle to be expunged or totally left out; and therefore may beginne without finding inconvenience: in my next I will send you some litle directions for a chapter or two to be left out, and

[1] The plague which was so fatal in England.
[2] Afterwards Sir Christopher Wren.
[3] Sir Samuel Tuke.
[4] Briot. Peter Briot translated a number of English Works into French—a History of Ireland; an Account of the natural productions of England, Scotland, and Wales; Lord's History of the Banians; Ricault's History of the Ottoman Empire. He appears from the present letter, to have had some intention of translating Pseudodoxia Epidemica, but probably abandoned it : for the only French translation I have seen bears the date of 1738, and is from the seventh edition, viz. that of 1672.

a coppy of the third and fourth editions,[5] which are all one, as soone as pleaseth God to open an opportunitie.   Whatever your gazette sayth, that the Indian fleet,[6] is come in without seeing any of our ships, wee are sure wee have two of their best in England, beside other shipps, making up in all the number of thirtie ; and what shipps ether of warre or merchands came home unto them were such as wee could not meet or not watch, having got the start of us : it holds still that the prisoners amount to about three thousand.   Wee here also that a caper[7] of twentie gunnes was taken not far from Cromer, last Saturday, by a frigat, after two howers fight.   God blesse you ; I rest your loving father,

THOMAS BROWNE.

September 22, styl. v. [1665.]

The sicknesse which God so long withheld from us, is now in Norwich.   I intend to send your sisters to Claxton, and if it encreaseth, to remove three or four miles of; where I may bee serviceable upon occasion to my friends in other diseases.   Paris is a place which hath been least infested with that disease of such populous places in Europe.   Write mee word what seale is that you use.

Here we take our leave of the elder son till towards the autumn of 1668, when we shall again find him indulging his roaming propensities in fresh adventures.   The following are the only letters which have been preserved from Sir Thomas to the younger son Thomas during his short and brilliant career in the service of his country.   He entered the English navy in the close of 1664, just when the nation was rushing,

[5] The third, fol. 1658, but published with Religio Medici, Hydriotaphia, and Garden of Cyrus, in 1659 : the fourth, 4to. 1658, with the two latter pieces only.

[6] The Dutch East India fleet, of which the greater part reached their own ports in safety, in consequence of the failure of an attack on them in August, 1665, by an English squadron, under Sir Thomas Tyddiman, at Bergen in Norway, where they had taken refuge.   Lord Sandwich soon afterwards captured some of the larger Indiamen, and a number of others.   Sir Thomas Browne's younger son, Thomas, distinguished himself on board the Foresight, at Bergen.

[7] A privateer, or private ship.

with the utmost enthusiasm, into the Dutch war, and when Charles II., to gratify the public eagerness, as well as to further his own views, was making every possible exertion to equip and man a fleet capable of meeting the powerful navy of Holland, assisted, as it was expected to be, by that of France. The moment was auspicious for our young adventurer; who appears to have obtained his commission without delay, and made his first voyage up the Mediterranean on board the *Foresight*, commanded by Captain Brookes, the brother of Sir Robert Brookes,[8] an intimate friend of his father's. He returned in time to join the grand English fleet under the command of James, Duke of York, assisted by Prince Rupert and the Earl of Sandwich; and was present, on the third of June, 1665, at the first great action, off Lowestoft, with the Dutch, under Opdam, which terminated in the total defeat of the enemy, who lost four admirals, seven thousand men, and eighteen ships. Browne had the good fortune soon afterwards to distinguish himself in the unsuccessful attempt made, by Lord Sandwich and Sir Thomas Tyddiman, to seize the two rich Dutch East India fleets which had taken shelter in the neutral Danish harbour of Bergen, on the coast of Norway;[9] and was engaged in the subsequent capture of a portion of those fleets, in September. In the winter of the same year he made his second voyage up the Mediterranean, with Sir Jeremy Smith, during which period Louis XIV. declared war against the English, and fitted out a fleet to assist the States General. Browne, on his return from the Streights, took a share in all the actions of 1666. In the unexpected and unequal conflict between the entire Dutch fleet, under De Ruyter and Van Tromp, and one division of the English fleet, under the Duke of Albermarle, during the unfortunate absence of Prince Rupert with the other divison in quest of the French fleet under the Duke of Beaufort, his ships was in the duke's division. In that furious engagement, and during the subsequent four days' fight in July, after the junction of Prince Rupert, he acquired, as will be seen, a character for the most able con-

[8] Lord of the Manor of Wanstead, and M.P. for Aldboro', Suffolk.
[9] See "Sir Gilbert Talbot's Narrative of the Earl of Sandwich's Attempt upon Bergen in 1665;" *from MS. Harl.* 6859. *Archæologia*, xxii. 33.

duct, and the most undaunted bravery. · He was present, in
the following month, at the destruction of the town of Bran-
daris, with a hundred and fifty Dutch merchantmen and
some line of battleships; and, in the close of the year, was
again sent as convoy to the Mediterranean, on board the
Marie Rose, in the fleet under Admiral Kempthorne. From
thence he returned to Portsmouth in about May, 1667. And
here, unfortunately, all traces of him are lost.—The most
diligent inquiries have not hitherto enabled me to discover
the sequel of his history: a solitary allusion, in a letter
written many years after, adverts to him in terms which
prove that he had been long dead. But how and when he
died, I have, to my great mortification, not as yet been able
to ascertain. His career was brief and splendid; but of
its close we know nothing. Enough appears, however, to
prove, beyond all doubt, that he possessed a character and
talents of no ordinary calibre; which, had he not been early
cut off, would have secured to him, in the profession he had
chosen, a distinction not inferior to that which his amiable
father attained through the more quiet paths of philosophy
and science.

Dr. Browne to his son Thomas.

Tom,—I presume you are in London, where you may
satisfie yourself in the buisinesse; do nothing rashly, but as
you find just grounds for your advantage, wch will hardly
bee at the best deservings, without good and faythfull friends;
no sudden advantage for rawe though dangerous services.
There is another and more safe way, whereby Capt. Brookes
and others come in credit, by going about 2 yeares before
they were capable of places; [with] which I am not well
acquainted. God and good friends advise you. Bee sober
and complacent. If you cood quit periwigs it would bee better,
and more for your credit. If Mr. Rand live in London informe him of Ned. Hee would teach you Latin quickly, by
rule and speech. God blesse you.—Your loving father,

TH. BROWNE.

If you are not in hast for the present, it would bee of advantage to learne of Mr. Goulding or others, the practicall
mathematicks and use of instruments.

Ned sent you a print of Domenic Ottoman, one of Hibraim the Grand Signor's sonnes, the brother of Mahomet, now raigning. Hee was taken at sea by a shippe of Malta, 1652, at 18 yeares of age ; now a Christian and a dominican friar; your brother saw him at Turin. It is a very good and serious face ; on the back side he sent more French verses concerning the pope and king of France, and that one Chairo[1] of Milan is now the famous paynter. ¿You may see hee went through many of those townes I mentioned, and the passing of Mont Cenis.

Dr. Browne to his son Thomas.

Honest Tom,—God blesse thee, and protect thee, and mercifully lead you through the wayes of his providence. I am much greived you have such a cold, sharpe, and hard, introduction, wch addes newe feares unto mee for your health, whereof pray bee carefull, and as good an husband as possible, wch will gayne you credit, and make you better trusted in all affayres. I am sorry you went unprovided with bookes, without which you cannot well spend time in those great shipps. If you have a globe you may easily learne the starres as also by bookes. Waggoner[2] you will not be without, wch will teach the particular coasts, depths of roades, and how the land riseth upon several poynts of the compasse. Blundevill[3] or Moxon[4] will teach you severall things. I see the litle comet[5] or blazing starre every cleare evening, the last time I observed it about 42 degrees of hight, about 7 o'clock, in the constellation of Cetus, or the whale, in the head thereof; it moveth west and northerly, so that it moveth towards Pisces or Linum Sep-

[1] The name is not to be decyphered in the original *hieroglyphics*, and is not explained by our copy of the letter referred to.
[2] Wagenar, L. Jans. E. Speculum Nauticum ; translated into English by Ant. Ashley, 1588.
[3] Thomas Blundeville, of Newton Flotman, in Norfolk. Referring probably to his "Theorique of the Planets," or "Exercises in Arithmetic, Cosmography, Astronomy," &c.
[4] Joseph Moxon, F.R.S. Concerning the Use of Globes, fol. 1659.
[5] Mentioned by Mr. Edward Browne, in his letter, Rome, Jan. 2, 1664-5.

tentrionale pisces. Ten degrees is the utmost extent of the
tayle. Anno 1580, there was a comet seen in the same
place, and a dimme one like this discribed by Mæstlinus.[6]
That wch I saw in 1618 began in Libra, and moved northward, ending about the tayle of Ursa Major; it was farre
brighter than this, and the tayle extended 40 degrees, lasted
litle above a moneth. This now seen hath lasted above a
moneth already, so that I beleeve from the motion that it
began in Eridanus or Fluvius. If they have quadrants,
crosse-staffes, and other instruments, learn the practicall use
thereof; the names of all parts and roupes about the shippe,
what proportion the masts must hold to the length and
depth of a shippe, and also the sayles. I hope you receaved
my letters from Nancy, after you were gone, wherein was a
playne electuary agaynst the scurvie.

Mr. Curteen stayed butt one night, pray salute him sometimes, my humble service to Captaine Brooke, whom I take
the boldnesse to salute, upon the title of my long acquaintance with his worthy brother Sr. Robert and his lady. God
blese you.—Your loving father,   THO. BROWNE.

Norwich, January 1, [1664-5.]

Forget not French and Latin. No such defence agaynst
extreme cold, as a woollen or flannell wascoat next the skinne.

Dr. Browne to his son Thomas.—1667.

I receaved yours, and would not deferre to send vnto you
before you sayled, which I hope will come vnto you; for in
this wind, neither can Rear-admirall Kempthorne come to
you, nor you beginne your voyage. I am glad you like Lucan so well. I wish more military men could read him ; in
this passage you mention, there are noble straynes ; and such
as may well affect generous minds. Butt I hope you are
more taken with the verses then the subject, and rather embrace the expression then the example. And this I the
rather hint unto you, because the like, though in another
waye, is sometimes practised in the king's shipps, when, in
desperate cases they blowe up the same.[7] For though I

---

[6] Michael Mæstlinus, a celebrated German astronomer, published
several treatises on Comets.

[7] In the action of the 3rd of June, 1666, Albemarle, the Commander

know you are sober and consideratiue, yet knowing you also
to be of great resolution ; and having also heard from ocular
testimonies with what vndaunted and persevering courage
you have demeaned yourself in great difficulties ; and
knowing your captaine to bee a stout and resolute man ;
and with all the cordiall friendshippe that is between you ;
I cannot omitt my earnest prayers vnto God to deliver you
from such a temptation. Hee that goes to warre must pa-
tiently submit vnto the various accidents thereof. To bee
made prisoner by an vnequall and overruling power, after a
due resistance, is no disparagement ; butt upon a carelesse
surprizall or faynt opposition ; and you have so good a memorie that you cannot forgett many examples thereof, even
of the worthiest commanders in your beloved Plutark. God
hath given you a stout, butt a generous and mercifull heart
withall ; and in all your life you could never behold any
person in miserie butt with compassion and relief ; which
hath been notable in you from a child : so have you layd up
a good foundation for God's mercy ; and, if such a disaster
should happen, Hee will, without doubt, mercifully remember you. Howcuer, let God that brought you in the world
in his owne goode time, lead you through it ; and in his
owne season bring you out of it ; and without such wayes
as are displeasing vnto him. When you are at Cales, see if
you can get a box of the Jesuits' powder at easier rate, and
bring it in the bark, not in powder. I am glad you haue
receaued the bill of exchange for Cales ; if you should find
occasion to make vse thereof. Enquire farther at Tangier
of the minerall water you told mee, which was neere the
towne, and whereof many made use. Take notice of such
plants as you meet with, either upon the Spanish or African
coast ; and if you knowe them not, putt some leaves into a
booke, though carelessely, and not with that neatenesse as in
your booke at Norwich. Enquire after any one who hath
been at Fez ; and learne what you can of the present state
of that place, which hath been so famous in the description
of Leo and others. The mercifull prouidence of God go
with you. *Impellant animæ lintea Thraciæ.*—Your louing
father,   THOMAS BROWNE.

in-chief, confessed his intention rather to blow up his ship, and perish
gloriously, than yield to the enemy.

Mr. Thomas Browne to his Father.—May, 1667.

Sir,—I receaved not your letter at Cales before wee were readie to returne; and therefore sent no answere, in hope I should bee in England before that could come vnto your hand: and, God be' thanked, I am now riding in Portland Road, and, if the wind favour, hope to bee to-morrowe at Portsmouth, from whence this is to come vnto you. The last I writ vuto you was from Plimmouth, from whence wee sayled the 21st of Februarie, with Rere-admirall Kempthorne, and about fiftie marchand shippes. The order, and manner of the sayling of our men of warre in this expedition, I have set downe in a sheet of paper, as ordered by our admirall. The 28th wee had the length of the North Cape; and were ordered to convoy in all the marchand shippes in our fleet which were bound for Lisbone. So the first of March wee stood into Cascales Road, and saw our convoy safe up the river;[8] and being to make hast after our fleet, that night wee got almost Cape Spichel or Picher; the next day Cape St. Vincent; and the sixth day wee arriued at Tangier; two dayes before the admirall. There wee stayed four dayes, then wayghed, and went for Cales; where wee stayed about a fortnight, to bring away such shippes as were readie for our convoy. I found Mr. Knights ashoare at Porto Sta. Maria; of whom I tooke up an hundred and fiftie six peeces of eight; which I haue now aboard in sherry sack; and which I hope will turn to good account. I have also six jarres of tent, each containing about three gallons; which I intend to present vnto my friends; and a roll of excellent tobacco, as they tell mee who have taken of it; very noble sweet waters, and orange flower butter, which may prove welcome presents to some friends. I stayed three dayes at Porto Sta. Maria, which is a large towne belonging to the Duke of Medina, wherein are two very fine churches; the one of St. Victor, the other of St. Anna; severall also of the king's galleys are layd up in this river, which cometh from the citty of Xeres, commonly called Sherrez. From hence I passed over to Cales, where I stayd some dayes: a very strong and well peopled place, with severall fayre

---

[8] Tagus.

churches, of one whereof I tooke a draught; butt the streets
are narrow and ill paved, hauing little or no fresh water
butt what is brought from other places; from whence also
they have their hearbes, fruits, meal, and other necessaries;
standing itself on a meere sand, it little differs from the
figure of it in Brawne's Book of Citties. From hence wee
sayled with our convoy of marchands, which came in timely
enough for us, and hauing made the South Cape were agayne
ordered to go into Lisbone with the Revenge, who had sprung
a leake. Wee stayd one day, and left the Revenge, to bring
away the marchantmen in the river. I was not sorry I stayd
no longer; hauing been twice there before, and hauing taken
a full view and observation of that place and all considerable
places, forts, castles, and the famous conuent of Belim, in
my first voyage in the Foresight with Captain Brooke, when,
for a fortnight, wee dailie visited the court, attending the
commands and dispatches of the Conde Melhor, the favorite,
and minister of state, who sent divers letters and juells to
our queen. Wee have had much fowl weather, and contrarie
winds since wee parted from Lisbone, till within these six
dayes. Wee had putt into Plimmouth this morning, butt it
blowing hard last night, wee overshot the port, being up
with the Steart Poynt by break of day; and this evening
wee are come to an anchor.

Mr. Thomas Browne to his Father.—May, [1667 ?]

HONORD SIR,—I am newlie come into Portsmouth, and
have alreadie disposed of my adventure from Cales. Wee
came in with full expectation that wee should have found
our fleet readie for this summer's action; butt, to the great
grief of ourselves, and all honest publick spirited souldiers
and seamen, wee find all contrairie to our desires; and that
our great and most considerable shipps shall not be employed
this summer. And in the meane time wee vnderstand, for
certaine, the Duch are coming out with a good fleet. I
confess as yet I vnderstand not this counsell at land; but I
dare confidently say, wee shall sadly repent of it. The
Duch would never have given us this advantage; and I
beleeve they will not neglect to make vse of it now wee

haue giuen it them. Sir Thomas Allen hath a squadron of shippes at Plimmouth of the third and fourth rate, butt not able to oppose a fleet. Some shipps are heere, together with the Souereign, which is vnprouided. Wee heare of none in the riuer of Thames; nor how the fort at Sheerenesse is fortified or manned. I am sure it was butt in meane case when I was at it in January. To treat for peace thus vnprovided, without a cessation of armes, or acts of hostilitie, is not pleasing vnto us; butt wee are readie to embrace a peace which should bee made with our swords in our hands. We stayed butt four dayes at Tangier, this voyage: of the towne I tooke a draught before, which I have sett downe in my Journall of my voyadge with Sir Jeremie Smith, which I sent vnto you; and I can say litle more of it than what I said there, only, the mole goeth well forward, they hauing the assistance of some Italians acquainted with that kind of work: tis a very great attempt, the sea being deepe, and as they aduance will bee deeper, and then they will come from a rocky to a sandy bottome, where the stones will sinck deeper, and the work take time to settle. When it is compleat it will be a notable peece, and scarce to be matched. I should thinck that in some places it were as easie to build an amphitheatre. I was curious to obserue the whole manner and way of making of it; and spent some time in obseruing, discoursing, and questioning about it; and haue set downe the way of it. I walked agayne about the line on the land side, and viewed the forts, redoubts, and workes, which make it very strong. When I first saw it with Captain Brookes, I thought it a poore and contemptible place; butt since I perceave, there are diuers new buildings, and the towne is fuller, and hath diuers nations in it, and they haue notably thriued by this warre, and like to driue a trade. Of that great masse of building, like stony stares, by the sea side, at the bottome of the towne, which is sett downe grossely in the mappe of Tangier, in Braun's Book of Citties, I could learn no more then that the Moors, in old time, kept their market upon them, butt who built them is vncertain, though they seeme of good antiquitie. Of the city of Fez men heere knowe as litle of it as though it were much farther of. I beleeve it is much altered since Leo Africanus described it, by reason of the continuall warres : and I doubt is not so noble a place now as Vincent Leblanc, a much later trauayler, made ɩ it. I spoke with a Jew, who informed me much of severall parts of Barbarie ; and told mee that some of their nation had been at Fez, and were then but at Arzilla. I obliged him much by two English knifes ; and he promised mee that hee would gett an account.sett downe by them, which he would putt into French, and I should haue it whenever I came again, or sent for it ; hee intending to abide in Tangier. Three Spaniards which were imprisoned by the Moors about Azamore, by contriuing a wooden key to open the prison doore, made their escape and came to Tangier.

Tangier is situated to the westward of the bay, upon the bending of a hill, from whence to the sea-side is a very great descent ; it is almost four-square, the best street in it is that which runneth from Port Catherine down to the Key Gate, and is called the Market ; the other streets somewhat narrow and crooked ; the mole will be of great vse for the securitie of shippes, the road being too open. I take this to bee an ancient citty, as the old castle and stayres to the seaward though now much ruined do testifie ; yet not that Tingis from whence Mauritania Tingitana had its name ; and which is so often mentioned in ancient histories ; as, namely, by Plutarch, in the life of Sertorius, where it is set downe that hee.passed over from Spayne and tooke Tingis, and finding a tomb reported to bee that of Antæus, he broake it open, and found therein bones of an exceeding length : which must surely bee understood of that which is now called Old Tangier, situated a little more eastward in the bay ; where I haue seen a great ruinous building and] a broken bridg ouer the river, with ruins which shewe it to haue been a more ancient habitation then this of our Tangier.

Letter from Sir Thomas Browne to his Son,. a Lieutenant of his Majesty's ship the Marie Rose, at Portsmouth.
[*May or June*, 1667.]

DEAR SONNE—I am very glad you are returned from the strayghts mouth once more in health and safetie. God continue his mercifull providence over you. I hope you maintaine a thankful heart and daylie bless him for your great deliverancès in so many fights and dangers of the sea, whereto you have been exposed upon several seas, and in all seasons. of the yeare. When you first under tooke this service, you cannot butt remember that I caused you to read the description of all the sea fights of note, in Plutark, the Turkish history, and others; and withall gave you the description of fortitude left by Aristotle, " Fortitudinis est inconcussum δύσπληκτον a mertis metu et constantem in malis et intrepidum ad pericula· esse, et malle honestè mori quam turpiter servari et victoriæ causam ·præstare.. Præte- rea autem fortitudinis est laborare et tolerare. Accedit autem fortitudini audacia et animi præstantia et fiducia, et confidentia, ad hæc industria et tolerantia." That which I then proposed for your example, I now send you for your commendation. For, to· give you your due, in the whole cours of this warre, both in fights and other sea affairs, hazards and perills, you have very well fullfilled this charac- ter in yourself. And· although you bee not forward in com- mending yourself, yett others have not been backward to do it for you, and have so. earnestly expressed your courage, valour, and resolution; your sober, studious, and observing cours of life;. your generous and obliging disposition, and the notable knowledge you have obtayned in military and all kind of sea affayres, that it affoordeth no small comfort unto mee. And I would by no meanes omitt to declare the same unto yourself, that you may not want that encourage- ment which you so well deserve. They that do well need not commend themselves; others will be· readie enough to do it for them. And because you may understand how well I have heard of you, I would not omitt to communicate this unto you. Mr. Scudamore, your sober and learned chaplaine, in your voyage with Sir Jeremie Smith, gives you no small commendations for a sober, studious, courageous, and diligent person; that he had not met with any of the fleet like you, so . civill,. observing, and diligent ·to your charge, with the reputation and love of all the shippe; and that without doubt you would make· a famous ·man, and a reputation to your country. Captain Fenne, a meere rough seaman, sayd that if hee were too choose, he would have your company before any he knewe. Mr. W. B. of Lynn, a stout volunteer in the Dreadnought, sayd in my hearing, that you were a deserving person, and of as good a reputation as any young man in the fleet. Another who was with you at Schellinck's, highly commended your sobrietie, carefullnesse, undaunted and lasting courage through all the cours of the warr; that you had acquired no small knowledge in navigation, as well as the military part. That you understood every thing that belonged unto a shippe; and had been so strict and criticall an observer of the shipps in the fleet, that you could name any shippe sayling at some distance; and by some private mark and observation which you had made, would hardly mistake one, if seventie shippes should sayle at a reasonable distance by you. You are much obliged to Sir Thomas Allen, who upon all occasions speakes highly of you;[1] and is to be held to the fleet by encouragement and preferment: for I would not have him leave the sea, which otherwise probably he might, having parts to make himself considerable by divers other wayes. Mr. I. told mee you were compleatly constituted to do your country service, honour, and reputation, as being exceeding faythfull, valiant, diligent, generous, vigilant, observing, very knowing, and a scholar. How you behaved yourself in the Foresight, at the hard service at Bergen, in Norway, captain Brookes, the commander, expressed unto many before his death, not long after, in Suffolk; and particularly unto my lord of Sandwich, then admiral, which thoughe you would not tell me yourself, yet I was informed from a person of no ordinary qualitie, C. Harland, who when you came aboard the admiral after the taking of the East India shippes heard my lord of Sandwich, to speak thus unto you. "Sir, you are a person whom I am glad to see, and must be better acquainted with you, upon the account which captain Brooke gaue mee of you. I must encourage such persons and give them their due, which will stand so firmly and courageously unto it upon extremities wherein true valour is best discovered. Hee told me you were the only man that stuck closely and boldly to him unto the last, and that after so many of his men and his lieutenant was slayne, he could not have well known what to have done without you." Butt

[1] There is evidently some omission here, either in the original or the copy; the following sentence appears to be Sir Thomas Allen's remark, the beginning of which is apparently wanting.

beside these I must not fayle to tell you how well I like it, that you are not only Marti but Mercurio, and very much pleased to find how good a student you have been at sea, and particularly with what success you have read divers bookes there, especially Homer and Juvenal with Lubines notes. Being much surprised to find you so perfect therein that you had them in a manner without booke, and could proceed in any verse I named unto you. I am glad you can overcome Lucan. The other bookes which I sent, are, I perceive, not hard unto you, and having such industrie adjoined unto your apprehension and memorie, you are like to proceed [not only] a noble navigator, butt a great schollar, which will be much to your honour and my satisfaction and content. I am much pleased to find that you take the draughts of remarkable things where ere you go; for that may bee very usefull, and will fasten themselves the better in your memorie. You are mightily improved in your violin, butt I would by no meanes have you practise upon the trumpet, for many reasons. Your fencing in the shippe may bee against the scurvie, butt that knowledge is of little advantage in actions of the sea.

The absence of any correspondence between Sir Thomas and his son Edward from 1665 to 1668, favours the supposition that the latter resided at Norwich during the greater portion of that period. He was incorporated of Merton College, Oxford, in June, 1666, and took his degree, Doctor of Physick, July 4th, 1667. In August, 1668, he went over to Holland, but probably intending only a short excursion. He remained abroad, however, for nearly a year and a half, extending his travels from place to place, far beyond his original plan, and in direct opposition to his father's urgent and reiterated requests. His letters to his father are so voluminous, that it was absolutely necessary to omit the far greater portion. This is the less to be regretted, as the substance of them has been published in his Travels, fol. 1685.

Dr. Edward Browne to his Father.

SIR,—I stayed 4 dayes at Rotterdam, where Mr. Panser was very obliging. Great shipps come up to their howses

through most of the graefts or cutts out of the Maes, which
I obserue as yet no where els.   From Rotterdam I passed
by Ouerschee to Delft.   In an howse of this towne, I saw
the marks in a wall which a bullet made at prince William,
who was thereby murthered.   From Delft I went to the
Hague.   I saw the princes court, the piazza by it full of
green trees, the princes grandmothers howse, the cours where
the coaches meet, and many fine howses in the towne, the
pell mall, the wood, the park, and went downe to Scheuelin,
where our king tooke shipping at his return to England.
From thence I went to Leyden, and one day I made an excursion to Alphen, with Mr. Thompson of Lynne; heere wee
dyned at a country mans howse.   In this place they make
much oyle for soape, make great store of tyles, and build
boates.   On Monday I came back to Leyden by Goukerk,
where is the oldest hows in Holland.   In Leyden I tooke
notice of that antiquitie called Hengist his castle, or the
Berg.   In the anatomy schooles, are a very great number of
sceletons, the 2 leggs of an elephant, the sceleton of a whale
taken out of another whale, and what not; diuers sceletons
of men and woemen, some with muscle, one with the whole
flesh and skinne; but I haue since seen farr neater curiosities of this kind at Amsterdam, performed by Dr. Reus.
From Leyden I came to Harlem, where, being alone, I fell
in company with the gouernor of Maynhems sonne, who is
a captaine heere, and now going agaynst the duke of Lor-
raine, in seruice of the Electour Palatine.   From hence in
3 hours I passed to Amsterdam, where I haue seen so many
curiosities, and am so highly satisfied, that I thinck I cannot
see better; butt many tell mee Antwerp surpasseth it, which
I hope to see suddenly.   In the howse where I lodge, there
lyes also one Mr. Vernon, an Englishman, who hath trauelled
these 6 yeares, speakes excellent Latin, Spanish, Italian,
high Duch, and French; hath been almost in all parts of
Christendom, beside Barbarie, with him I haue seen many
things.   I heare your booke of Vulgar Errors is translated
into low Duch, and now in the presse.

EDWARD BROWNE.

Amsterdam, Sept. 14, 1668.

Dr. Edward Browne to his Father.

SIR,—My last I wrote to you from Middleburg, since which time I have been at Brussells, and am returned unto Antwerp. In Brussells, there are 3 hundred howses infected, so I made litle stay there. I wayted, upon Mrs. Waldegraue, a nunne, in the English Colledge, who presents her duty to my lady, my sisters, and spake very worthily of yourself, in remembrance of the great good. you had done her father Sir Henry. . . . .

From Terueer I went to Middleburg, where Mr. Hill, the minister, was exceeding obliging. I dined at his house ; hee gave. mee a booke, and when I went to Vlussing, accompanied mee to the boat, and sent his kinsman with mee ; hee told mee that the same man who translated your Religio Medici hath translated your Vulgar Errors into low Duch. At Brussells they cannot dissemble their joy that Castle Rodrigo[1] hath left them, and stuck not to say upon his departing on Michaelmas day, that their patron, St. Michael, had now overcome and cast out the diuell. I pray direct a letter to mee, at Frankfort, my letter of credit being for that place, upon Monsr. Pierre de Neufille.—Your obedient sonne,   EDWARD BROWNE.

Antwerp, Octob. 1, styl. nouo, 1668.

Dr. Browne to his son Edward.

DEARE SONNE,—I have receaued seuerall letters from you, the last dated Sept. 14, from Amsterdam, by Mr. Pecket, and am sorry I cannot write so often to you, not knowing wheither to direct, but I would not omitt to aduenture this unto you in Mr. Johnsons couert to Mr. Houenaer. The mony you tooke up is payd, and though you have a letter of credit for a great summe, yet I conceaue and hope you will take up butt a part, for the yeare is spent and I would not have you make wide excursions. I receaued some prints by Mr. Dearesly which I like. Captain Cox is not yet re-

[1] The Marquess of Castel Rodrigo, the Spanish governor of the Low Countries.

turned. I like it well that you take notice of so many particularities. Enquire also after the policie and gouernment
of places. Wearie not nor tire thyself, butt endeauour to
preserue thy health by sparing thyself from labour and obseruing a good dyet. I am glad you haue met with a person
who speakes so many languadges; you may practise your
Latin and Italian with him, little troubling your head with
the languadge of the Netherlands. I am glad you haue seen
the best of Holland. What way you tooke from Utreckt I
am uncertaine; but probably, toward Antwerp, which were
very well worth the seeing, if the contagion and disorder of
souldiers in those parts will permitt. But before this can
probably come to your hand, you may have seen that place.
Buy no bookes but what are small and portable, if any: for
by London we can send for such bookes as those parts afford.
Nancy writ mee word that shee receaued a letter from you.
Your mother, Betty, and sisters, pray for you, wishing your
returne, which God prosper. Many friends enquire after
you: but no letters have come for you, since the last I sent
to Yarmouth, they understanding you are abroad. When
you were at Amsterdam, I wished you had enquired after
Dr. Heluetius, who writ Vitulus aureus, and saw proiection
made, and had pieces of gold to shew of it. Hold up thy
spirits and bee not deiected that you receaued no more
letters, for if we were assured of their deliuery we would
write weekely. God blesse you and protect you. I am,
your euer loueing father,   THO. BROWNE.

Sept. 22, *Norwich*, 1668.

I wish you would bring ouer some of the red marking
stone for drawinge, if any very good. One told mee hee
read in the French gazette, that the Duch had discovered
the north-east passage to China round about Tartarie. I do
not care whether you go into Zealand, but if you should,.
Flushing and Middleburgh are only worth the seeing.

If you have opportunitie, you may obserue how the Duch
make defences agaynst sea inundations. Obserue the seuerall
fish and fowle in markets and their names. Wee haue not
heard a long time of Lewis de Bills, his practise of preseruing
bodyes, &c. What esteeme haue they of Van Helmont, in
Brabant, his own country? Since I wrote this, I receiued

yours this morning, from Dort, and am exceedingly glad
to see how God hath blessed you, and that you haue had
aduantages beyond expectation. Your accounts are very good
of all things. God blesse you. Madam Burwell is at present with mee. Hee and shee send their seruice. We are
on the declination of the assises which last 2 dayes. The
contagion may hinder you from going into Flanders, butt
Brabant, I thinck, is not much vnder it. Mr. Johnson is
with mee at this hower, and I hast to send this by his letter
to Mr. Houenaer. The mercifull protection of God bee
with you. Mr. Johnson, Hawkins, Whitefoote, Robins, &c.
salute you.

Dr. Edward Browne to his Father.—Wien in Austrich,
Novemb. 29, styl. nouo.

Sir,—I wrote to you from Passaw. Since when it hath
pleased God to continue his blessings in my health and
a prosperous passage to Vienna. The farther I go the
more my desires are enlarged, and I desire now to see Pres-
bourg, Leopoldin, the strong fortification which the emperour
hath built in lieu of Newheusel, as also Rab, Comorra, Buda,
and Chremnitz, where the gold mines are, and other places:
butt I haue trespassed too farre alreadie upon your goodnesse, and intend to looke no farther. Here is at present a
Tartarian ambassadour, desiring a league offensiue and de-
fensiue with the emperour, his name Cha Gagi Aga, Cha
signifieth master, Gagi somewhat like proselyte, and Aga
signifieth king. They haue brought diuers horses with them
of high esteem here, but not the least beautifull. Some of
the Tartars haue syluer rings, with the same signature as
the Turkish seales. They take much tobacco in very long
pipes; their tobacco is not in rowles butt in leaues and drye.
Heere is a fayre in the citty, where yesterday I mett the
Tartars, who were strangely delighted with it, and very much
with the babies and figures in gingerbread. The emperour
presented the Cham of Tartarie with a siluer bason and
ewer, and a fine wach of curious work; sent also presents to
the 4 brothers of the great Cham, to the chamarine his wife,

and to his sisters ; yet after all this kindnesse they are jealous heere, as hauing newes out of Hungarie, that Sieben-bergen is to bee putt into the hands of the Tartars. The varietie of habits in this place is very remarkable, as of Hun-garians, Transyluanians, Grecians, Croatians, Austrians, &c. In the riuer there is kept a tame pellican, which heere they call a lettelgantz or spoon goose. I saw a comedie in the Jesuit's colledge, the emperour and empresse present. In the emperours chappell is very good musick, vocall and instru-mentall, performed by Italians, whereof some are eunuchs. I saw the emperour at chappell on Wednesday, hee hath a very remarkable aspect, and the Austrian lipp extraordi-narily. Count Cachowitz is Maistre del Hostell. Mon-tecuculi, the generall, is a leane tall man. On St. Nicholas day I sawe the emperours mother and his 2 sisters, as they lighted out of their coach to enter into the monasterie of St. Nicholas, his sisters are very beautifull sweet ladyes. The empresse hath a very good looke butt somewhat sad at present, perhaps too sollicitous about her deliuerie. I would willingly leaue this place in order to my returne the first weeke in February, or sooner if I haue the happinesse to heare from you.

Dr. Browne to his son Edward.—*Dec.* 2, *Norwich,* 1668.

DEAR SONNE,—Vpon the receit of your letter from Passau upon the Danube, dated Nou. 1, styl. vet. I got our louing friend Mr. Couldham to send this vnto Venice, to Mr. Hayles, in whose hands it may lye till you ether call or send for it. I am sorry you are to make that long round agayne, and once more be inclosed within the Alpes : butt if it hath pleasd God to bring you safe to Venice out of Germanie, and through so bad a winter passage, with your thankfull acknowledgments vuto God, make the best vse you can of such places for your improuement and knowledg the time you linger there ; and whereuer you go, in your returne, bee neuer without some institution or the like of physick, whereof you may dalie or often read, and so con-tinue to study the method and doctrine of physick, which intention[1] upon varietie of objects of other subjects may

[1] Intentness.

make you forget. Wearie not nor wast your spirits too much in pursuing after varietie of objects, which I knowe you cannot butt do with earnestnesse, for thereby you shall, by God's blessing, conserue your health, whereof I am very sollicitous. Make what conuenient hast you can homewards and neerer England, according as the passages and season will permitt. To returne by sea is thought by all no fitt or good way for you: 'tis very hazardous in many respects, nothinge considerable to bee learned, and of litle credit. In places take notice of the gouerment of them, and the eminent persons. Burden not yourself with superfluous luggage, and if you buy any thing lett it bee of easie portage. Keepe yourself still temperate, which virtue may conserue your parts. You are in your trauayl able to direct your self; God also direct and preserue you. I do not know that you shall want accommodation for mony, butt Mr. Couldham hath been so courteous as to write to Mr. Hayles, in case of necessitie, to accommodate you; whereof I hope you will make vse butt vpon good occasion, and moderately. Informe your self concerning the state of Candia, and enquire whether there bee any relation made thereof, so far as it hath yet proceeded. Padua, I presume, you will take notice of agayne: butt seriously I would not haue you make excursions remote and chargeable. Consider how neerely it concerneth you to bee in your country improuing your time to what you intend, and what most concerneth you. Of all your letters sent out of Germanie, that only wch you sent from Bingen miscarried. I wish you had met with Heylin, or some short description and diuision of those countryes as you trauayled, and if you haue not, do it yet; for that may produce a rationall knowledge of them, confirmed by sence, and giue you a distinct apprehension of Germanic, wch to most proues the most intricate of any in Europe. Your mother prayes for you and sends her blessing, and would bee happy to see you. Shee is in health, as your sister B. and Moll Franc liuely and cheerily, butt leane, and another sharpe feuer [may] yet soone take her away. Beside limning, Bet practiseth washing in black and colours, and doth very well. All is quiet enough, butt the countryman complaines, and rents are still badly payd, corne and inward commodities being at lowe coste. It hath yet been an open winter, no snowe, fewe and small frosts, much rayne and wind, wch hath made catarrhs, coughs, and rheumatismes . . . . affectinge the most common diseases among us. The parliament is adiourned to the 1 of March. Mr. England of Yarmouth was prickt for knight of the shiere, but got of, and Sr George Viner, a Londoner, prickt in his place. The Bishop and Mr. Hawkins haue been some moneths in Norwich: he enquireth of you. I receiued your things in Capt. Coxe's ship, the Concord. The description of Amsterd. Mr. Primerose brought mee. My lady Maydston was well satisfied with your letter. Mr. Skippon is to marry Mr. Brewster's daughter, of Wrentham by Southwold, as I heard credibly. It were well you could obserue any thinge in order to the Royall Societie. These things I put together, though the whole letter may bee vnsertaine to come to you. Your letter from Passau not assuring your determination: but before you can receaue this, I hope to receaue one from Vienna, which may tell more of your resolution, and whether you intended to returne by Prague or Venice. The mercifull protection of God go with you, guide and direct and blesse you, and giue you euer a gratefull heart vnto him.—Your louing father,   THOMAS BROWNE.

Dr. Browne to his son Edward.—Decemb. 15, *styl. vet.* 1668, *Norwich.*

DEARE SONNE,—I receaved yours from Vienna, dated Decemb. 6, when I came home this evening: and would not deferre to write to Mr. Johnson this night, to Yarmouth. 16 days ago I writ to Venice, according to the desire of your former letter, wch Mr. Couldham, your friend, enclosed to Mr. Hayles; and writ unto him, that, if you were necesitated for mony, you might be conveniently accommodated, wch I did out of abundant caution; becaus you expressed no desire thereof, and I thought you had still gone on upon the credit from Mr. Hovenaer, whch might have been continued from place to place. None of your letters have miscarried, butt onely one from Bingen; pray bee moderate as possible in what summes you take up, and especially not to take up much at a time, butt after the rate which you have yet done., If you had declared your intention for Vienna, wee had not fayled to have sent, some way or other, that you might have receaved ours at your first coming thither. You have travayled far this winter, wch hath yet proved very favorable. I would have you spare your self as much as you could conveniently, and afford some rest unto your spirits, for I see you have observed much and been earnest therein. My prayers you have daylie for you, and want not assistance to my utmost abilitie. Wch way you intend to take in your returne, I know not. I should bee glad if you covld escape a journey to Venice, but rather thither then any further eastward, ether to Poland, Hungarie, or Turkie; which both myself and all your friends do heartily wish you would not so much as thinck of. Your letter is very obscure at the end, that I would not forbid you any thing that might happen in the meane time for your advantage, wherein I pray consider yourself seriously, and lett your thoughts and determinations bee very well grounded. From Constantinople, or Turkey, I am most averse, for many reasons, wee all wish you in England, or neerer it. I doubt not butt that you will ever have a gratefull heart unto God, who hath thus farre protected you. If you had gone to Venice, wee were very solicitous how you would have returned, and all were against going (by sea) as not only inconvenient, butt dangerous and uselesse unto you, and of no great credit. Have alwayes some physick treatise to reade often, least this varietie of obiects unsettle the notions of it. Vienna is an universitie, and some things probably may be learned in knowledge and chymistrie; it were fitt to take a good account of the emperor's court, &c. being upon the place. My L. Maydstone was glad of your letter. Sr Daniel Harvey[1] is by this time in Turkey, and my lord, probably upon coming away, as they heare. Pray bee mindfull to order your speech distinctly and leasurably, and not after that precipitous way of France. Your mother sends her blessing, sisters their love, and wishes for you; the mercifull and gratious protection of the Almightie bee with you.

[1] He married the sister of Ralph, Duke of Montague, was knighted, made Ranger of Richmond Park, and afterwards Ambassador to Constantinople.

This letter will bee somewhat long a coming to you; when you go from Vienna, leave order with Mr. Beck, how to send to you; for probably I may send one not many dayes after this.—Your ever loving father,   THO. BROWNE.

Dr. Browne to his son Edward.—Norwich, Dec. 21, 1668.

DEAR SONNE,—The same day whereon I receaved yours, Decemb. 6, I sent unto Mr. Johnson, Decemb. xv, to write to Mr. Hovenaer, to accommodate you with a letter of credit or exchange, at Vienna, and inclosed a letter of myne to bee sent by Mr. Hovenaer. Mr. Johnson hath writ me word, that hee wrote the next day, and that, if the letter doth not unfortunately miscarrie, you shall, God willing, heare of it. Hee sayth hee also writ to Mr. Dreenstein, at Venice, and also one to Monsr. Morelli, I thinck, at Venice, in your behalf, and to accommodate you, if need required; and this I suppose hee did, because you writ before that you intended for Venice. Mr. Couldham also sent a letter of myne to you, in one of his, to Mr. Hayles, to keep it while you called or sent for it, and whereby he desired Mr. Hayles to accommodate you, if need required; wch letter is, by this time of my writing, at Venice. Now all this is done out of my abundant care and caution for you, butt I hope you will heare from Mr. Hovenaer at Vienna; for I should bee glad you might decline Venice, and so, after a bad journey, bee shut up agayne within the Alpes. Vienna is at a great distance, and there is litle communication between it and London, so that it is not so easie to send unto you as to receave from you, and I beleeve postage is to bee twice payd, after it goes from London, before it will come to Vienna, butt where I yet knowe not, butt have taken the best care I can at London. Direct no letters immediately to Norwich, for you mention one lately sent so directed wch I received not; one I receaved from Mr. Panser, who sent it from Rotterdam. Before you leave the place you may write something of it, and of the emperour's court. Which way you will returne I cannot advise, only am very unwilling you should go farther. If you come southerly, by Ausberg, Ulme, &c. to Strasburg, you gett at last unto the Rhyne, butt after an hilly and long passage, and not a great roade; if you go by Prague, and so, through part of Saxonie and Turingia, by Erfurt, it is a long way also, butt perhaps more travayled from Vienna; and if you were in Turingia [you] might find convenience for Cologne, eschewing the countries, townes, and provinces, on or toward the Baltick, lesse worth the seeing of any, and the coldest.   God direct, guide, and protect you, and returne you safe unto all the longing desires of your friends, who heartily wish you were at a more tolerable distance. All yours, except one from Bingen and another directed lately to Norwich, have come to my hand.   Take notice of the various animals, of places, beasts, fowles, and fishes; what the Danube affordeth, what depth, if conveniency offers; of mines, minerall workes, &c.   They say spelter or zink is made in Germanie;. from thence also pompholyx, tutia, mysi, sori, zaffera, &c.   You are to bee commended for observing so well alreadie; I wish you could take notice of something for the information of the Soc. Reg. to learn speciall medicines and preparations : butt, as I still saye, try not thy spirits too farre, but give due rest unto them; I doubt not butt you will be warie of the vice of the country.   Beat not thy head too much about the languadge; you will learne enough to proceed ......if you shall thinck fitt.   Wee lately read the seidge of Vienna by Solyman, when it was much weaker than at present; now the bullwark of Xtendom. I should be sorry you should want money at this distance; I hoped you had once taken up more, by your credit at Franckfort, upon Mr. Neufville.   Tis generally sayd that Mr. Howard goes embassadour to Morrocco unto Taffelsur; who hath driven Guiland into Argier, whether hee is fled; taken Benboker, and killed the king of Morrocco, and is crowned king of Morrocco and Fez.   Mr. Mayow, your friend, hath putt out a booke, *De Respiratione et Rachitide;* some endemical and proper diseases there may bee in those parts where you are also.   Your mother, sisters, and many friends recommend, praying and wishing for you.   The mercifull protection and blessing of God bee with you.— Your loving father,   THOMAS BROWNE.

I shall bee very happy to heare you have receaved this; and of your resolutions toward your country : beleeve it, no excursion into Pol. Hung. or Turkey addes advantage or re-putation unto a schollar.

Dr. Browne to his son Edward.—Norwich, Dec. 23, 1668.

DEARE SONNE,—I wrote unto you eight dayes ago, which Mr. Johnson, of Yarmouth, sent inclosed to Mr. Hovenaer, of Amsterdam, to bee sent unto you, with a bill of credit from him to Vienna; which I hope you have receaved. I sent one to Venice, three weekes ago, inclosed in Mr. Couldham's letter to Mr. Hayles, whereby you might bee accommodated if you fayled elswhere. Hee sayth one Mr. Hobson keepes the howse, though Mr. Hayles bee consul; butt I beleeve the letter is in Mr. Hayles' hand, if hee left it not with Mr. Hobson; butt you need not retard your journey for the letter only, which will take some time to recover, and there is nothing peculiar in it or private. Yesterday I receaved another from you, which I thought had miscarried, of an elder date, November 24; wherein I understood what accommodation there was for travayl to Prag, Magdeburg, and other good townes, to Hamburch; which, though a great place, is a good way from Amsterdam; and to come from Hamburch by sea, in winter, is very discouraging, from rough seas and benumbing weather. Spare thyself what you can, and preserve your health, which is precious unto us all. I am very glad you are in an howse where you are so kindlye vsed; if Mr. Beck hath any friend in England, wee will endeavour to expresse no ordinarie kindnesse unto him. That I wrote two dayes agoe, I sent to London to your sister, to get Mr. Skoltowe to send it, in some marchand's letter, or deliver to the post, paying the postages part of the way; butt this I send to London, to bee delivered to the forraine post, paying what they require; which I putt to the adventure, though perhaps you may haye left that place before this may come unto you. You mention travayling from some places, in three dayes and three nights; but I think travayling by night, in those parts and in winter, very uncomfortable and hazardous unto health. God send you still happy rencountres and good company. It were good to have an *Itinerarium Germanicum.* Heylin accounts twenty-one universities in Germany, whereof Vienna one (butt I doubt chiefly for divinitie), Coln, Mentz, Heydelberg, Franckford, Leipsick, Jena, Wittenberg in Saxonic, Prag, which is thought the greatest citty in Germanie, made out of four citties, like Passaw out of three.   Studie the mappe of Germanie, and have the chorographie thereof distinctly in your head, with the politicall divisions and governments, which are therein more numerous then in Italie; the lesser owing some acknowledgment to the greater, beside free cities.   Just now I heare that Mr. Johnson will write agayne, this night, to Mr. Hovenaer.   Dresden is accounted one of the remarkablest places of Germanie; where the duke's court.   Magdeburg is I beleeve rebuilt, since burnt by Tilly, in the Suedish warres.   Brunswick sayd to bee bigger then Nuremberg.   Take the best account you can of Vienna as to all concernes; for tis hard to find any peculiar account of it.   Bohemia is a round large country, about two hundred miles diameter, containing many mines, mineralls, and stones.   Bohemia granates, and other stones, you may take notice of, if you passe that way; in the country, and at Prag, and at Vienna, such stones may bee seen probably.   I have heard that among the emperour's rarities several conversions there are of basser metall into gold.   Take notice of the great and many cellars in Vienna.   Learne the most authentic account how the half moone was set upon St. Stephen's; which, in Brawne's Booke of Citties, seemes a very noble one.   If you can fix any probable place where a letter may meet you, I will endeavour to find out a way to send a letter.   Wee have had no winter till this day, and not now like to hold, so that we fear a back winter.   A Yarmouth man just now tells mee that about ninety vessells, great and small, went out this yeare to other parts, with red herrings.   The king is sending the order of the garter to the young King of Sarden, by my lord of Carleisle.   Dr. Merrett's comment upon *Neri de Arte Vitriaria* is new come out in Latin.   His *Pinax Rerum Britanicarum* not yet published; I send to him agayne next weeke.   Mr. Mayoc, of All Souls, his booke *De Respiratione et Rachitide*, newly come out; also Mr. Boyle's continuation of new experiments concerning the spring and weight of the ayre, English, 4to.   I keepe the sheets of the Transactions as they come out, monethly.   Our forrein letters do not despayre of Candy.   Sir Thomas Allen hath renewed and confirmed the peace with Argiers.   Sure you have gazettes at Vienna.   Tangier in a good con-

dition. The parliament adjourned to the first of March.
Mr. Hawkins, White, Rob. Bend. &c. recommend, wishing
a good returne. God's blessing bee with you.— Your loving
father, THOMAS BROWNE.

Dr. Edward Browne to his Father.—Vienna, April 28, 1669.

MOST HONOURED FATHER,—I wrote to you the last post.
Most of my letter was concerning dampes in mines; which
account may be, by it selfe, if you thinke fit, sir, communicated to Mr. Oldenburg; if not, at my returne, which I
hope in God will be in a few months, with the rest of my
observations. I have now taken up three hundred florins in
preparation to goe into Turkey this next weeke; but, if it
please God, I hope to be at Vienna again by that time that
I can have an answer to this. I hope, sir, you will forgive
me this excursion, and helpe me to returne to you by giving
me credit again upon the same marchants as formerly, the
same way, by Mr. Johnson, for the heirs of Mr. Fuchs:
Mr. Triangle particularly, at Vienna; for he tells me that
my credit is limited so as I have had all, which I knew not.
Since my returne out of Hungary, I have had, since my
coming abroad, 700 reichs-tallers: but I hope, with God's
blessing, a small summe more will helpe me to come safe
home. I shall continue to write still; and shall have many
occasions; and it will make me happy at my returne to hear
from you, sir, and from any of my friends. My duty to my
most dear mother, and love to my dear sisters.—Your most
obedient sonne, EDWARD BROWNE.

Dr. Edward Browne to his sister Betty.—Venetia, July 5,
st. nov. 1669.

DEAR SISTER BETTY,—Though I make many journeys,
yet I am confident that your pen and pencill are greater
travellers. How many fine plaines do they passe over, and
how many hills, woods, seas doe they designe? You have
a fine way of not onley seeing but making a world; and
whilst you set still, how many miles doth your hand travell!
I am onely unfortunate in this, that I can never meete you
in any of your voyages. If you had drawne your lines more

towards Austria, I should have been a greater emperour, in
my owne conceit; but I hope you denied me that favour
upon no other account then that I should make the more
haste to you, who know not how to live without something
of you.   If so your intention is good, but, like yourselfe,
too severe to your loving brother,   EDWARD BROWNE.

Dr. Edward Browne to his Father.—Prague, Nov. 9, 1669.

MOST HONOURED FATHER,—I wrote to you the last of
October, just before my leaving Vienna.   I am since (thanks
be to God) safely arrived here.   My greatest joye would
be to receive a letter from you, sir; but I know not how
to propose any probable way of accomplishing it, unlesse
sir, that you would be pleased to write to Hamburg.   Sir
Nevel Catlin, I beleeve, hath a brother there, a merchant,
Mr. James Catlin, formerly my school-fellow; a letter sent
to him for me would come to my handes, if that it pleaseth
God to give me safe journey thither.   Gottenberg, or Cottenberg, is eight Bohemian miles from Prague.   They have
worked here seven hundred years; there are about thirty
mines.   I went down into that which was first digged, but
was afterwards left for a long time; but now they dig there
again.   It is called the Cotna, auff der Cotten, upon the
Cotten or Coate hill.   A monke walking over this hill founde
a silver tree sticking to his coate, which was the occasion
that they afterwards built these mines, and the place retaines
this name of Cottenberg.   I have read that the princesse
and great sorceress of Bohemia, Libussa, did foretell many
thinges concerning these mines; but in such matters I
beleeve little; knowing how confident men are in such
superstitious accounts.   In the mines at Brunswick is
reported to be a spirit; and another at the tin mine at
Slackenwald, in this kingdome, in the shape of a monke,
which strikes the miners, singeth, playeth on the bagpipe,
and many such tricks.   But I doubt, if I should go thither,
I should finde them as vain as Montparions drumme; but
the winter, and my great desire to return home speedily,
will not permit me to goe so farre out of the way.   From
Gottenberg by Colline and Bohemian Broda, to Prague;
where, I thanke God, I am very well, after such tiresome

voyages as I have made; and when I looke back upon all the dangers from which it hath pleased God to deliver me, I can not but with some assurance also hope that his infinite goodness will also bring me backe into my owne country and blesse me there with the continuance of my dear father's life, health, and prosperity. I have divers thinges to write to you, sir, concerning Turkhia; but I will not trouble you, sir, too much at once. I know, sir, that you cannot but reasonably be offended with my long stay abroad; especially in countryes of small literature; but I hope that your displeasure will not continue, and that you will adde this to the rest of your great goodnesse and indulgence to me, to pardon my rashnesse, and the expense I have put you to. My duty to my most dear mother, and love to my sisters and friends. I am uncertaine which way I shall take. Travelling is not certain here, as in France. If it were not for my portmantle, I would buy a horse, and come streight into the Low Countreys.—Your most obedient sonne,

ED. BROWNE.

Dr. E. Browne, after his travels, settled in London. From the directions of his father's letters, we gather that he changed his residence several times before 1673. In that year he was tempted to another short visit to the continent, which is described in his travels, fol. 1686, at p. 180. July 29, 1675, he was elected a fellow of the College of Physicians, and lectured in that and several succeeding years.[1] He was first chosen censor in 1678. From 1675, throughout the whole of his father's life, he resided in Salisbury-court, Fleet-street. During the long period of his

[1] The following communications from Dr. Edward Browne appeared in the Philosophical Transactions :—

Of two parhelias, or mock suns, seen in Hungary, Jan. 30, 1668 : vol. iv. p. 953, published May 10, 1669.

On the damps in the mines of Hungary : iv. 965, June 21, 1669.

Relation of the quicksilver mines of Friuli.—Account of the Zirchnitzer sea in Carniola : iv. 1080, Dec. 13, 1669.

Account of the copper mine of Hern Grund, in Hungary, as also of the stone quarries and Talc rocks in Hungary : v. 1042, May 23, 1670.

On the mines, minerals, baths, &c., in Hungary : v. 1189, April 25, 1670.

Queries and answers concerning the Zirchnitz sea : ix. 194, Dec. 14, 1674.

practice in London he was in constant correspondence with his father; from whom it is quite evident he derived much of the materials of his lectures, and great assistance in all his engagements, both literary and professional. He appeared to have had considerable practice among the higher ranks, both in London and in the country. He attended the celebrated earl of Rochester in his dying illness, at Woodstock park. Some of Sir Thomas's letters have been omitted, and several are considerably abridged, especially those which are strictly professional, and such as contain passages for his son's lectures.

Sir Thomas Browne to his son Edward.—June 21, [1675.]

DEAR SONNE,—Some occasion of this letter is, to rectifie a mistake in the paper of yours, which I sent yesterday, by Mr. Miller, Mr. Tho. Peck's brother in-lawe, who dwells not farre from you and by whom I returned the first of your lectures; in that I putt in a paper, with the draught of the kidney, and heart of a vitulus marinus or seale, which Betty drewe out fresh, from one I had in blewe paper before. The mistake was this; that I sett it downe the kidney of a dolphin, for it is the kidney of a vitulus marinus, and is not much unlike that of a dolphin, in the numerous divisions; butt it may serve to showe in discowrsing of the kidney. The passage you mentioned out of Bartholomeus Georgevitz, is not to bee omitted for it comes in very well; it is a prettie little booke, and you having seen something of Turkie, I wish you would read it over, for it may bee often useful unto you.—Your loving father,   THOMAS BROWNE.

A litle shippe, with 6 small gunnes, came up from Yarmouth to Carrowe Abbey, this night, and hath taken a great deale of mony by selling wine and the like; a strange number of people resorting unto it, taking twelve pence for every shott[2] at healths.

---

[2] The King in Hamlet, may illustrate this passage:—he says,
  "This gentle and unforced accord of Hamlet
  Sits smiling to my heart; in grace whereof
  No jocund health that Denmark drinks to-day,
  But the great cannon to the clouds shall tell."
                              Hamlet, Act I. *Sc.* 2.

Sir Thomas Browne to his son Edward.—Feb. 25, [1676?]

DEAR SONNE,—My neibour, Mr. Bickerdik, going towards
London to-morrowe, I would not deny him a letter; and I
have sent by him Lucretius his six bookes *De Rerum Natura,* because you lately sent me a quotation out of that author, that you might have one by you to find out quotations,
which shall considerably offer themselves at any time.
Otherwise I do not much recommend the reading or study-
ing of it, there being divers impieties in it, and 'tis no credit
to be punctually versed in it; it containeth the Epicurean
naturall philosophie.   Mr. Tenison, I told you, had written
a good poem, "*contra huius sæculi Lucretianos,*" illustrating
God's wisdome and providence from anatome, and the
rubrick, and use of parts, in a manuscript dedicated to mee
and Dr. Lawson,[1] in Latin, after Lucretius his style.[2]   With
it goes along a very litle Tullies offices, which was either
yours or your brothers; 'tis as remarkable for the litle sise
as the good matter contained in it, and the authentick and
classicall Latin.   I hope you do not forgett to carry a Greeke
testament allwayes to church, you have also the Greeke or
septuagent translation of the other parts of scripture; in
reading those bookes, a man learnes two good things together,
and profiteth doubly, in the language and the subject.   You
may at the beginning of Lucretius, read his life, prefixed by
Petrus Crinitus, a learned philologer or humanist, and that
he proved mad and dyed by a philtrum or pocula, given him
by his wife Lucillea.   Mr. Tho. Peck and his good wife are
dead; shee died in childbed some 8 or 9 moneths past; he
left this life about a moneth ago.   Hee found obstacles that
he could not come to Skickford,[3] without compounding with
the widdowe in possession for a thousand pound, though his
father, Mr. James Peck, parted with his owne share upon
tolerable termes unto Mr. Thomas.   Hee lived in Norwich,
was growne very fatt, and dranck much.   Theye saye hee

[1] Dr. Lawson was brother-in-law to Archbishop Tenison, each having
married a daughter of Doctor R. Love, Master of Corpus Christi College,
Cambridge.

[2] This MS. was never published.

[3] Qu. Spixworth?

dranck dayly a quart bottle of clarett before dinner, one at
dinner,. and. one at night.   If any company came to him,
which was seldome, hee might exceed that quantitie : however, he made an end of that proportion by himself; he died
suddenly, none being with him.   His daughter finding him
indisposed, asked whether shee should send unto mee, hee
putt it of, and soon after was found dead.   Hee had litle or
no money in his howse ; his father James sent ten pounds
for his buryall, which served the turne.   Surely if he had
lived a little longer, hee would have utterly spoyled his
brayne, and been lost unto all conversation.   Happy is the
temperate man.   God send all my friends that virtue.   God
blesse my daughter Fairfax, my daughter Browne, and the
little ones.—Your loving father,   THOMAS· BROWNE.

Sir Thomas Browne to his son Edward.—June 14,. [1676.]

DEAR SONNE,—I am sorry to heare Mr. Bishop is so
much his owne foe ; surely his brayne is not right.   Probably
you may heare agayne of him, before hee returnes into his
country ; hee seemed to be fayre conditiond when hee was
in these parts, though very hypochondriacall sometimes.
Mr. Hombartston, whenever his brayne is distempered,
resolves upon a journey to London, and there showes himself, acts his part, and returnes home better composed, as
hee did the last time ; hee would not bee persuaded to bleed
agayne before hee went.   If the dolphin were to be shewed
for money in Norwich, litle would bee gott ; if they showed
it in London, they are like to take out the viscera, and
salt the fish, and then the dissection will be inconsiderable.
You may remember the dolphin opened when the king was
heere, and Dr. Clark was at my howse, when you tooke a
draught of severall parts very well ; wch Dr. Clark had sent
unto him.   Bartholinus hath the anatomie of one, in his
centuries.   You may observe therein the odde muscle
whereby it spouts out water, the odde larynx, like a goose
head, the flattish heart, the lungs, the *renes racemosi*, the
multiple stomach, &c.   When wee washed that fish a kind
of cuticle came of in severall places on the sides and back.
Your mother hath mast[4] to dresse and cooke the flesh, so as

⁴ Sic MS.

to make an excellent savory dish of it ; and the king being
at Newmarket, I sent collars thereof to his table, which
were very well liked of. —Your loving father,

Tho. Browne.

Sir Thomas Browne to his son Edward.—March 7, [1676-7.]

Dear Sonne,—Ever since Friday night last, untill Tuesday, wee have had such boysterous cutting and freezing
winds, that the weather hath been allmost intollerable, and
much hurt done, both at sea and land ; chimneys blowne
downe, and tiles, and one man killed by a wall blowne downe
in Norwich ; the wind east and somewhat northerly.   Such
a cutting season there was, in March, many years ago, at
the time of assizes in March ; when so many gentlemen
dyed after, and among them your old friend Mr. Earle.   So
that if they had the like weather in Flanders, the French
must have a very hard time at the seiges of Valenciennes
and St. Omar,[5] which most men write St. Omer, forgetting
that St. Omar hath its name from St. Andomarus.   So,
many townes' names derived from saints are observed ;
St. Mallowes is St. Mallovius ; St. Didier St. Desiderius.
I have heard that St. Omar was a place famous for good
onyons, and furnished many parts therewith ; some were
usually brought into England, and some transplanted,
which were cryed about London, and by a mistake called
St. Thomas onyons.   I mett with my old friend Dr. Pere-
grine Short, and his sonne, Dr. Thomas Short.   Dr. Thomas
told mee of severall dissections, given them notice of by
Dr. Short of London, and specially of a boare, whereof you
writt unto mee.   And I told him you would shewe a newe
way of dissecting the brayne at these lectures ; hee sayd
none could performe that dissection butt Mr. Hobbes, and
that it was thought the best way for the dissection of the
brayne of man, butt for sheep, &c. Dr. Willis his way was
best.   In *Bartholini, centuria 4ta, historia trigesima, titulo
Anatome Gulonis,*[6] I find something peculiar in the gutts of

---

[5] Taken by the French in the spring of 1677.

[6] The Wolverene or Glutton ; *Mustela Gulo,* Lin.   The story here
mentioned was first related by Olaus Magnus, and has been repeated by
Gesner, Topsell, &c. Gmelin and Buffon, and later naturalists, regard it
as a mere fable.

a gulo. This is a devouring ravenous quadruped, frequent about the bignesse of a dogge, which filleth itself with any caryon, and then, when it can eat no more, compresseth itself between two trees standing neere together, and so squeezeth out, through the gutts, what it hath devoured, and then filleth itself agayne. This was thought very strange, considering the division of the gutts, their complications, foulds, and cæcum; till Petrus Pavius or Pau, a famous professor of Leyden, dissected a gulo; for thereby hee found that this voracious animal had no such divisions in the gutts as are to be found in other quadrupeds; butt one gutt, *undique sibi simile*, nor any way changing figure, which is the cause that this animal, by compression of the abdomen, can squeese out what is receaved, as having no cæcum, and all the gutts being as it were one *intestinum rectum* . . . . . God blesse you all, and endowe you with prudence, sobrietie, and frugality and providence.—Your loving father,

THOMAS BROWNE.

Sir Thomas Browne to his son Edward.—Nov. 23, [1677.]

DEAR SONNE,—I received your's yesterday; and therein how the societie had received a letter from that great astronomer, Hevelius, of Dantzick; with an account of an eclipse, and a new starre in Cygnus;[7] but what new starre, or when appearing, I knowe not; for there was a new starre in that constellation long agoe, and writ of by many. If it bee now to bee seen it is worth the looking after. I have not had the Transactions for divers moneths; but some that have had them tell me there is account of some kind of spectacles without glasses, and made by a kind of little trunk or case to admitt the species with advantage. I have read of the same in the Transactions about a yeare ago;[8] but now I hear such instruments are made and sold in London; and some tell mee they have had them heere. Enquire after them, and where they are made, and send a payre, as I remember there is no great art in the making thereof. I am

[7] Hevelius's letter on Lunar Eclipses was published in the Trans. for Jan. 1676; vol. xi. 590 : and his letter on the New Stars, Jan. 2, 1677; vol. xii. 853.
[8] Phil. Trans. vol. xi. 691.

glad to heare that Isaac Vossius is living, and in England.
You send some of his notes and observations upon the geographie of Mela; in that particular of Mount Hæmus and
possibility of seeing the Euxine and Adriatick sea from the
top thereof. In that piece he promiseth a mappe of Old
Greece. I wish I knew whether he had yett founde any
such mappe or tract publick. I presume hee came over with
the Prince of Aurange;[9] and it were no hard matter to bee
in his company at his owne or the prince's lodgings. You
may tell him you have been in some parts of Greece, as
Macedonia and Thessalie; and ask his opinion of the mappe
of Laurenbergius, of Greece, which placeth the Pharsalian
Fields on the north of the river Peneus; whereas at Larissa
all accounted it to the south, and about three dayes journey
from thence; and may signifie how unsatisfactory you find
the mappe either of [Ortelius] or others, in placing the
towns through which you passed in Macedonia, as also in
[Servia], omitting divers, and transplacing others. He will
bee glad to discours of such, and of Olympus, which is not
so well sett downe. I doubt not but that hee speaketh
French and Italian, if not English, besides Latin. 'Tis a
credit to knowe such persons; and therefore devise some
way to salute him. I perceave you are not so well satisfied
with London as you thought to have been; and am therefore
sorry that you have obliged yourself to that place by taking
a chamber for so long, or else to bee at a fruitless charge of
the lodgings; but I would not have you discontented. If
either your health or second thoughts incline you to live
heere, wee shall bee willing; where you may see and observe
practice, and practise also, as opportunity will by degrees
permitt; and a great deale of money may bee saved which
might serve you hereafter, and your sisters. However, in
the meane time, make the best use you can of London.—I
rest your loving father,   THOMAS BROWNE.

Sir Thomas Browne to his son Edward.—Jan. 5, [1677-8.]

DEAR SONNE,—There is one Vansleb, who hath writt a description of Egypt: hee writt in 1672 or 3, and it is newly

[9] This was not the case. The Prince of Orange came over Oct. 10,
1677. Vossius resided in England from 1670 till 1682, when he died.

translated into English in 8vo. Hee seemes to have been employed to collect antiquities, butt especially manuscripts, for the King of France; for hee sayth hee sent divers to his library, to which purpose hee learnt the Arabick tongue, and writes much of his historie out of the Arabick writers, who writt long since the Greeks; and gives many particulars not mentioned by them, though many are fabulous and superstitious. Hee travelled not only into Lower Egypt, butt into the Upper, above or southward of Grand Cayro, and setts downe many monasteries, and the noble ruins of many, hardly to be mett with in other writers. Hee went into divers caves of the mummies, and in one hee sayth hee found many sorts of birds, embalmed, and included in potts, one whereof hee sent into France. Hee also sayth, that he found empty eggs, whole and unbroaken, butt light and without any thing in them. Hee speakes of the hieroglyphicall cave in Upper Egypt, the walls whereof full of hieroglyphycall and other old writing, butt much defaced, with divers others, and also a noble column of Antoninus, &c. Of the great pyramids hee sayth, that the north side is larger then that of east or west. Tom, God be thanked, is well, so I hope you are all. God blesse you all.—Your loving father,   THO. BROWNE.

Sir Thomas Browne to his son Edward.—May 8, [1678.]

DEAR SONNE,—I receeved the print of Stonehenge, of the singing at the hospitall, and chorus, by Mr. Richardson, an honest taylor in the close. That of Stonehenge is good, according to the south and west prospect; [the] chorus I have not yet perused. 'Tis rare to find a heart without a pericardium. Columbus observed it in one body, and Bartholinus also in an hydropicall person; vide. lib. *Centuriar Historia* xx. In the same chapter he writes, *de septo cordis pervio* in the same person, communicated to him by Dr. Brodleck, professor of Tubinge, in the Duke of Wertemberg's dominions.

I perceave my lady F. bled, and hath had newe prescriptions; I hope they may be beneficial unto her.

Considering the bitter quality of the *cerumen*, or earwax lining the eare, a man might thinck that horse-leaches would have litle delight to insinuate themselves into the eare;

butt thereof there have been some examples, and Severinus
found out a good remedie for it, in a person of Naples,
who had one gott into his care; for to that purpose hee
moystend the outward part of the care; whereupon the leach
came out to suck the blood. You may mention it in the
discourse about the eare. See *Bartholini, centuria* 4*ta.*

Men are much in doubt yet concerning the warre; and
the proceedings of the Duch seem butt odde. God direct
our English counsells for the best.

Tom is much delighted to thinck of the guild; the inaior,
Mr. Davey, of Alderhollands, intending to live in Surrey
howse, in St. Stephen's, at that time; and there to make
his entertaines; so that hee contrives what pictures to
lend, and what other things to pleasure some of that parish,
and his schoolmaster, who lives in that parish. God blesse
my daughter Browne and you all.—Your loving father,

THO. BROWNE.

Sir Thomas Browne to his son Edward.—Feb. 14, [1678-9.]

DEAR SONNE,—You make often mention of a censors[1]
daye, which I suppose is some day sett out for the censor
to convene upon the colledge affayres; and when, perhaps,
you may have a dinner. If there bee a lecture at the colledge after this sessions it will bee expected that the physitians of the colledge should be there, especially at the
opening of the theatre. And, therefore, when you intend at the same time to have a private preparing body at
Chirurgeon's hall, you may have a diversion, and not be able
to bee at the colledge, except you can contrive the buise-
nesse better then I apprehend as yet. Being arrived so
high as censor, it will concerne you to putt on some gravity,
and render yourself as considerable as you can, in conversation in all respects. 'Tis probable there will bee a great
number at the lecture the first time, the place being capacious; butt, being read in Latin, very many will not bee
earnest to come hereafter, and the place being so large, there
are like to bee more spectators than auditors. Your lecture
at Chirurgeon's hall will, I perceive, bee somewhat late this

[1] Dr. E. Browne was elected censor of the College of Physicians,
Sept. 30, 1678.

yeare; so that you may bee forcèd to dissecte the brayne
the first day in the afternoon, or the next morning. I writt
unto you by my last to read Mr. Duncan's way of dissecting
the brayne, mentioned in the Transactions of the R. S. last
August.[2]   Wee heare Sir Jos. Williamson is out of his
secretarie's place, and my Lord Sunderland putt in, whose
acquaintance you might well have continued.   Sir Joseph is
like to be chosen burgesse for Thetford, as hee was before,
and Sir William Coventrie, the other secretarie of the counsell, will be for Yarmouth.   Sir Joseph, I beleeve, found his
secretarie's place to bee of some danger, for hee could not
well refuse to signe what the higher powers would command;
and if it were agaynst any lawe, the parliament would question him as they did the last session.   I am sorry to find
that my Lord Sterling and L. Dunblayne would have been
chosen at Abingdon if the designe had succeeded; for
thereby 'tis knowne that my lord treasorer strikes in.   On
Monday next is the election for burgesses of Norwich; on
the same day for knights of the shyre for Suffolk. My Lord
Huntingdon, a worthy honest yong gentleman, Sir Lyonell
Talmach his sonne, of Suffolk, standeth.   Duke Lauderdale
maryed his mother.   Hee lost it the last time, because,
though the gentry were much for him, yet the people feared
hee would prove a meere courtier.   Sir Samuel Bernardiston
also stands, who was knight of the shyre last time, and some
others.   The election is commonly at Ipswich, where the
seamen and watermen are very rude and boysterous, and
take in with the country party, as they call it.   Tom
would have his grandmother, his avnt Betty, and Franck,
valentines; butt hee conditioned with them that they should
give him nothing of any kind thatt hee had ever had or seen
before.   God send my daughter Fayrfax a good time.   God
blesse you all.—Your loving father,   THO. BROWNE.

Sir Thomas Browne to his son Edward.—Feb. 24, [1678-9.]

· DEAR SONNE,—Since you take in the *unques* in this lecture, I presume you have read and considered what Dr.

·[2] See Phil. Trans. xii. 1013.—Explications novelle et Mechanique des
Actions Animales, où il est traité des fonctions de l'ame, &c.   Par M.
Duncan, D. en Med. in 12mo. à Paris, 1678.

Glesson sayd thereof, in his last work ; and also anatomically describe them. Riolanus hath a small peculiar tract, "*De Unguibus*," in his Encheiridion. Hippocrates was therefore so curious as to prescribe the rule in cutting the nayles, that is not longer or shorter then the topps of the fingers. Vide Hippocrates *De officina med.* That barbers of old used to cutt men's nayles is to be gathered from Martial, lib. 3, epigram. 74. You may do well to cast an eye on Martial sometimes *cum notis variorum.* There is much witt, and good expressions therein, and the notes containe much good learning; the conceit and expression will make them the better remembered. God blesse you all.—Your loving father, THOMAS BROWNE.

Sir Thomas Browne to his son Edward.—March 1, [1678-9.]

DEARE SONNE,—Though the *cerumen* bee not sett downe in your catalogue *de partibus internis,* yet I conceive you mention it in your discourse, because it is in *meatu auditorio,* and the place from its melleous consistence and colour called *alveare.* I sett down this following, because it may bee brought in after the description of the eare, or when you speake of deafenesse. " Riolanus observeth that a man deaf from a bad conformation of the organs· of the care, picking his eare too decpc, unawares peirced the tympane membrane, and moved or broake the litle bones, and afterward came to· heare ; and, thereupon, proposeth the question, whether such a practise might not bee attempted, which I confesse I should bee uery warie to encourage; and I doubt fewe have attempted that course, which hee also proposeth, agaynst the *tinnitus* and noyse in the cares : that is to perforate the *mastoides,* and so to afford a vent and passage unto the tremultuating spirits and winds. Rolfinckius sayth, that from violent causes the little bones in the care may be dislocated, and so deafnesse followe. Bone-setters would be much to sceke on this cure; but the only waye is, by a' strong retention and holding of the breath, which may probably reduce them into their proper place; which if it fayleth, incurable surditie ensueth. And, therefore, although wee seeme to knowe and bee well acquinted with the naturall structure and parts of the eare, in sound bodyes, and such as have had no impediment in hearing, yett, because wee do not enquire, at least butt rarely, into that organ in dead men who have been notoriously deaf, wee may bee sometimes to seeke, in the particular causes of deafnesse; and therefore very reasonable it is, that wee should more often embrace or seeke out such opportunities. For hereby wee might behold the tympane too thick or double in some, the chord or bones not rightly ordered, the *fenestri* or windowes, *cochlea* or *labyrinthus* ill-conformed in others; with other particular causes, which might induce a deafnesse from nativity." You may adde some other, as defects in the auditory nerves.

I presume my cosen Barker is come to London, my humble service unto him. I find Mr. Gay in the catalogue of the elected. Though the common letters, which come from London, come not to Norwich till Tuesday morning, yet the newes letters of coffie howses come to us on Monday, by noone, as being brought on purpose from Beckles, where the Yarmouth post leaveth them. Wee heare by them, that the king approveth not the speaker; and have the king and chancellor's speeches. I presume there was a good appearance at the new theatre, especially of such who understand Latin. God send my daughter Fairfax a good delivery. God blesse my daughter Browne, and you all.—Your loving father,

THOMAS BROWNE.

Sir Thomas Browne to his son Edward.—April 2, [1679.]

DEARE SONNE,—You did well to observe Ginseng. All exotick rarities, and especially of the east, the East India trade having encreased, are brought in England, and the best profitt made thereof. Of this plant Kircherus writeth in his *China illustrata,* pag. 178, cap. "*De Exoticis Chinæ plantis.*" I perceive you are litle acquainted with our Norfolk affayres; and knowe not the late differences. Sir John Hobart complayne of some illegal proceedings in the election, and petiond the howse about it; and delivered my Lord Yarmouth my Lord Lieutenant's letter, which hee is sayd to have writt in the behalf of Sir Christopher Calthorp and Sir Neville Catelyn, which was construed as a thrating letter, and sett the howse in such a heat, that they had like

to have been presently dismissed the howse.   But the
farther examination is appoynted about a fortnight hence,
and many thinck there will bee a newe election.   What will
bee the issue wee knowe not, yett wee heare Sir Christ.
Calthorp fell sick last weeke, of the small pox.   I think hee
lodgeth in Westminster.   If the election bee made agayne,
'tis sayd parties will stand agayne.   Mr. Verdon, keeping no
rule and travelling about, hath his ague agayne, and notwithstanding intends to go to Thetford assises, on Thursday.
I dought these election businesses, and the charge that may
go along with it, doth something discompose his mind.   I
perceive you are yet at some uncertainte of a publick
lecture, butt bee provided, for 'tis very likely they will have
one.   An old acquaintance, Mr. Shadwell, was with me at
Norwich; hee speaketh well of you, butt wisheth you were
not over modest in this world, where that virtue is litle esteemed.   I am afraid that unseasonable qualitie makes you
decline the friendshippe of my Lord B. of London, which
others would thinck themselves happy in.   Some say that
Mrs. Harmin is much better, butt a weeke ago they sayd
shee was in a consumption, and sum decline in it.   It was
expected every post that the parliament would be dissolved
or prorogued, which cannot now bee so expected, because a
proclamation is published for a fast.[3]   My service to my
cosen Barker, cosen Hobbes, and cosens Cradock.   I read
a sermon of Dr. Tillotson, preched at the Yorkshire
[Feast], December 3, which hee dedicates to the twelve
stewards of the company.   Wee have not seen Dolfiney
yett.   Tom remembers his duty and love to his sister.   God
blesse you.

Sir Thomas Browne to his son Edward.—April 25, [1679.]

DEAR SONNE,—Most of our gentlemen and wittnesses concerning the election, are ether returned or return to morrow.
The day of election, for a new choyce of the knights for
Norfolk will be on Monday come sevenight.   Sir John Hobart, Sir Christopher Calthorpe, and Sir Neville Catelyn
stand agayne, and they [say] also Mr. Windham of Fel-

[3] Parliament was prorogued May 27, and afterwards dissolved.

brigge.[4]   There is like to bee very great endeavouring for the places, which will still keep open divisions which were too wide before, and make it a countrey of Guelphs and Ghibellines.   I am sorry to find my Lord of Aylesbury left out of the list of the privie counsell, hee beeing so worthy and able a person, and so well qualified for the publick good. Tom presents his duty; my love and blessing unto you all.— Your loving father,   THO. BROWNE.

Sir Thomas Browne to his son Edward.—April 28, [1679.]

DEAR SONNE,—A Norwich man in London, sent a letter hither to a friend to this effect, that being at a coffie howse, hee sawe Mr. Rob. Bendish, in a high distraction, breaking windowes, and doing outrageous things, so that they were fayne to laye hold of him; what became of him afterwards hee sayth nothing.   This came to his father's eare, who is much troubled at it, butt can do very litle for him, having been at great charges for him before.   Now if you heare of any such distraction, or what is become of him, you may give a touch therof in any of your letters, butt I would not urge you to bee buisine therein; but I heare my brother Bendish hath allreadie writt to a friend to informe him of the truth thereof, which is like to bee done before you can say any thing in a letter from London.   These are the sad ends of many dissolute and governless persons, who, if they bee of a sheepish temper, runne into melancholy or futaity, and if [they] prove haughtie and obstinate into a maniacal madnesse.   I am glad you left Madame Cropley better, you had the opportunity to see the shipps and forts upon the river. I am glad there is so strong a shippe built at Wolleige, and a large shippe a second rate, I wish we had half a dozen of them.   The bill against popery is intended to be very. severe,[5] but the howse of Lords will moderate it: and whether the king will allowe of it, it is yet uncertaine, or

---

. [4] The house had after long delays, decided on the 21st of April, that none of the candidates were duly elected, and fresh writs were accordingly issued on the 22d.   But before the new members had time to take their seats, parliament was dissolved; so that in point of fact the county of Norfolk was not represented in that Parliament.

[5] A bill for the more speedy conviction of Popish recusants was brought in and read a first time March 27.

what execution there will bee of it, may yet bee as doubtfull.
The deferring of the trial of our election may' much incom-
mode the gentlemen who who went up for witnesses, and also
encrease the charge, and how matters will bee determined wee
are butt uncertaine.   Monday is the day appoynted, but
whether it will not be putt off to a farther day wee are in
doubt.[6] Litle Tom comes loaded from the fayre this day,
and wishes his sister had some of them.   God blesse you
all.   I rest your loving father,   THOMAS BROWNE.
    Take notice of the sea horse skinne.

Sir Thomas Browne to his son Edward.—May **7**, [1679.]

DEAR SONNE,—It is not well contriued by the chirurgeons that you are at such vncertainties about your lectures,
and it will bee very inconuenient to beginne the lectures on
Saturday, by reason of Sunday interuening, and the hard
keeping of the body in this warme and moyst wether.   Butt
I remember you read so once before, butt with some incon-
ueniency.   Our election was the last Monday.   The competitors were the former elected Sir Christopher Calthorp
and Sir Neuille Catelyn, and Sir John Hobart and Mr.
Windham.   I neuer obserued so great a number of people
who came to giue their voyces ; but all was ciuilly carryed
at the hill, and I do not heare of any rude or vnhandsome
caryadge, the competitors hauing the weeke before sett
downe rules and agreed upon articles for their regular and
quiet proceeding.   They came not down from the hill vntill
eleven o'clocke at night.   Sir John Hobart and Sir Neuille
Catelyn caryed it, and were caryed on chayres about the
market place after eleuen o'clock, with trumpets and torches,
candles being lighted at windowes, and the markett place
·full of people.   Dr. Brady was with mee that day, who
presents his seruice and speakes well of you, and sayth hee

---

    [6] On the 21st April, the house had summoned Mr. Verdun, under-
sheriff of Norfolk, "to answer his miscarriages and ill practices in elect-
ing of knights of the shire for Norfolk." The said examination was repeatedly postponed, 'till the new election had taken place, and John Jay,
the high sheriff, having refused to make a return, was ordered, on the
12th of May, to be taken into custody. On the 24th, Sir T. Hare's
petition against Sir J. Hobart's return was presented, and on the 27th,
parliament was adjourned, so that neither of the elections was ever
settled.

was your constant auditor, and sayth yours are very good lectures, and proper to the intention, as being very good and profitable, which they haue rarely been formerly. Hee came with Sir Thomas Hare, of Stowe, Sir Ralph Hare's sonne, and not long of age. Sir Thomas was of Caius Colledge, and brought, they · say, four ‡hundred for Sir Neuille and Sir Christopher,⁷ and Dr. Brady brought eighteen or nineteen from Cambridge, schollars, who were freeholders in Norfolk. These were the number of the voyces.

Sir John Hobart - - - 3417
Sir Neuille Catelyn - - 3310
Sir Christopher Calthorp - 3174
Mr. Windham - - - - 2898

I do not remember such a great poll. I could not butt obserue the great number of horses which were in the towne, and conceiue there might haue been five or six thousand which in time of need might serue for dragoone horses; beside a great number of coach horses, and very good sadle horses of the better sort. Wine wee had none butt sack and Rhenish, except some made prouision thereof before hand, butt there was a strange consumption of beere and bread and cakes, abundance of people slept in the markett place, and laye like flocks of sheep in and about the crosse. My wife sent the receit for orenge cakes, and they are comfortable to the stomack, especially in winter, but they must be eaten moderately, for otherwise they may heartburne, as I haue sometimes found, especially riding upon them. Tom presents his duty. God blesse you all.—Your louing father,   THO. BROWNE.

Sir Thomas Browne to his son Edward, May 29, [1679.]

DEAR SONNE,—Mr. Alderman Wisse went this day to London, with his wife, whose brother, Mr. Utting, keeps the Green Dragon, at Bishopsgate. By him I sent a letter, and a small box, and therein an East India drugge called *sebets* or *zebets* or *cussum sebets*.⁸ It was brought from the East

---

⁷ Sir Thomas Hare and others petitioned the House, but unsuccessfully, against the return of Sir John Hobart.

⁸ Probably salep, the roots of orchis, which renders water very thick and gelatinous, and is imported threaded on strings not unlike one of

Indies by order from Mr. Tho. Peirce, who liveth near Norwich, 1663, who gave mee some divers yeares agoe. Hee sayth that there was considerable quantitie brought into England; butt not being a good commodity, it was sent back agayne; butt he reserved a box full, whereof these I send were a part, hee sayth they in those countries thicken broath with it, and it serveth to make gellies. I never tried it nor knowe whether it bee wholsome, for they looke a little like Ahouai Theveti, or Indian morris bells, in Gerard or Johnson's herball, which are sayd to bee poysonous. I send them unto you because you being acquainted with many of the East India Company, you may enquire about it and satisfie yourself as well as you can, for perhaps few knowe it, and 'tis good to know all kinds of druggs and simples. In the list of commodities brought over from the East Indies, 1678, I find among the druggs tincal and toothanage,[9] set downe thus; 105,920 toothanage, 49,610 tincal. Enquire also what these are, and may gett a sample of them.

Mr. John Jaye, our high sheriffe, was sent for by the Howse of Commons, for not sending the writts or writings, certifying those who were elected in good time; butt hee fell sick, before the pursuivant came in Norwich, of a fever, and so the pursuivant was fayne to returne this daye or yesterday, with a certificate of his inability to take such a journey, and a promise that when hee shall bee able, hee will bee ready to come up, if they thinck fitt, butt Sir John Hobart and Sir Neville Catelyn are now admitted into the howse, and probably hee will hear no more of it. I do not yet heare that Mr. Verdon and Dr. Hylliard are discharged.[1] Mrs. Verdon went to London, to have her sonne touched; if you see her, remember my service. She was very earnest to have her litle sonne touched, being very hard to admit of medicines.—Your loving father,   THOMAS BROWNE.

My service to Mr. Deane and his lady, and to Mr.

the figures here referred to. It has never been much used in England. —*Note by Mr. Gray.*

[9] Tutenage, called in this country zinc.—*Gray.*

[1] They were summoned to the house on the subject of the Norfolk election.

Dobbins, when you see him; my cosens Cradock, cosens Hobbs, and all our friends. . Write your letters at the best advantage, and not when the post is ready to go. Wee heare a noyse of the poysoners in France,[2] butt do not well apprehend it, wee, who imitate the French in their worse qualities, may not unlikely follow them in that.

Sir Thomas Browne to his son Edward.—June 28, [1679 ?]

DEAR SONNE,—I heard that some shipps passed by Yarmouth, with souldiers in them for Scotland, six or seven dayes past, and the coffie and common news letters tell us something of the rebellion in Scotland, butt I think very imperfectly. A litle more time will better informe us of that buisinesse; and they are like to bee more effectually dealt with and brought to reason, by the English forces, when there shall bee a sufficient number of them in Scotland; for the rebells hope, and others doubt, whether those of their nation will fight heartily agaynst them; for tis sayd there are more discontented in Scotland than those in armes. So that this may bee a coal not so soon quenched; though it was begun by the lowest sects, yet the Scots are very tenacious of the Protestant religion, and have entertained feares and jealousies of dessignes to introduce the Roman, from their observation of the affayres in England: and are not like to bee quieted long, without a parliament. And if that should bee broake of to their discontent, they would bee contriving agayne, and the English parliaments would bee butt cold in suppressing them. When the duke of Monmouth giveth a further account, wee may see farther into the buisinesse. When the wether proves cold and fitt for dissections if you have opportunity, take notice of a beare: tis commonly sayd that a beare hath no breast bone, and that hee cannot well runne

---

[2] This seems to refer to the Marchioness of Brinvilliers, who was beheaded, and her body burned to ashes, 17 July, 1676, for poisoning her father, two brothers, and divers other persons, in conjunction with one Sainte-Croix. This affair making a great noise, and the public mind being apprehensive of the practice of poisoning being common, a court was established at Paris, in 1679, under the name of La Chambre ardente for the trial of these offenders; but it is said that this was only a political manœuvre to throw an odium on the enemies of the court.— *Gray.*

downe a hill, his heart will so come up toward his throat.
Examine therefore the pectorall parts, and endeavour to find
out the ground of such an opinion at opportunity. I
once dissected a beare which dyed in Norwich, and I have
the lower jaw and teeth ; tis a strong animal, hath notable
sinewes and teeth.

This day one came to showe mee a booke and to sell it ;
it was a *hortus hyemalis*, in a booke, made at Padua, butt I
had seen it above thirtie years ago, and it containes not
many plants. You had a very good one or two if you have
not parted with them. Love and blessing to my daughter
Browne and you all.—Your loving father,

                                        THOMAS BROWNE.

_____

Sir Thomas Browne to his son Edward.—July 4, [1679.]

DEAR SONNE,—I have not heard a long time any thing
concerning, or from the R. S. That which you mention of
Monsier Papin[3] would bee farther enquired into and the
way of it, may-bee, how it is performed, for it may bee
usefull. There was one Papin, a Frenchman, who wrote
De pulvere sympathetico about 20 years ago.[4] You say the
bones are softened without any liquor, that is, as I understand, without beeing infused or boyled in any liquor, and
therefore I suspect it must bee effected by humid exhalation
or vapour, by being suspended or placed in the vapour, so
that it may act upon the body to bee mollified. According
to such a kind of way as in that which is called, the philosophicall calcination of hartshorne, made by the steeme of
water, which makes the hartshorne white and soft, and easily
pulverisable ; and it is to bee had at some apothecaries
and chymists ; and whether a fish boyled in the steeme
of water will not have the bones soft, I have not tried.
Whether hee useth playne water or any other, mixed or

[3] Papin exhibited to the Royal Society, on the 22d May, 1679, bones
softened by a new method. He afterwards published a work on the
subject : "The New Digester ; or the Engine for the softening of bones,
by Denys Papin, F.R.S." 4to. Lond. 1681. Evelyn (in his Diary, by
Bray, vol. i. 542) has given an amusing account of a most philosophical
supper of flesh and fish, cooked in M. Papin's digesters.

[4] Nicholas Papin, father of the preceding, who wrote "La Poudre
de Sympathie defendue contre les objections de M. Cattier." 8vo.
Paris. 1651.

compounded, any spirituous steeme, we are yet to learne.
The steeme of common water is very piercing and active,
the steemes in baths likewise, and also the fume of sulphur.
You have seen a sweating tubbe of myne whereof the
figure is in Loselius "*De Podagra*," a booke in duodecimo;
wherein the steeme of the water doth all, as in some the
steeme of *aqua vitæ*. Write agayne of Papin's farther experiments. My service to Dr. Grewe. The large egge
with another lesser within it was a swann's egge which I
sent divers yeares past unto the Royal Societie. I had
before met with an egge within an egge, as in hennes egges
and turkey's egges. I kept any I found in that kind, in a
box inscribed *ovula in ovis*. At last I met with a swan's
egge of that kind, which I presented unto the R. Societie,
having never before nor since mett with another from a
swanne. Tom presents his duty. Love and blessing to my
daughter Browne. Wee can hardly avoyd troubling
her, from the importunity of friends, to buy things in
London. Little Susan, I believe is returned out of the
country. Wee cannot have a bill from Mr. Briggs before
Monday, when, God willing, it will be sent. Yesterday was
a fayre butt windy day, a fire beginning at a dyer's howse
in Dearham, a markett towne, the greatest part of the towne
was burnt downe.

Sir Thomas Browne to his son Edward.—July 7, [1679.]

DEAR SONNE,—Perhaps by this time you have inquired
farther into the art of softening of bones. Consider that
hydrargyr softeneth *nodes* and takes of *exostoses :* and as I
remember Riolan saw the bones of a dead body cereous or
somewhat soft like wax, which hee thinkes was a body infected with the lues, butt I know not whether mercureall
meanes had been used. Quicksylver brings gold into a soft
and pappy substance, by an *homalgama*. Bones were soft
at first and solids have been fluid; butt probably the artist
only sheweth the experiment or *quod sit*, affording litle
light how to effect the same. Tis not improbable that the
kinge will knowe it, and so that it may in time become a
common culinary practise. I am not so well contented that
you should bee putt to read lectures at this time of the

yeare, butt if they will insist upon it, it cannot well be hindred. The bill is enclosed.—Your loving father,

THOMAS BROWNE.

Sir Thomas Browne to his son Edward.—Octob. 6, [1679.]

DEAR SONNE,—Wee heare that his majestie was to leave Newmarket on last Saturday,[5] being desired to come to London by the privie counsell. Upon what occasion wee know not, but most men are well contented that hee should not staye at Newmarket, so long as it was given out that he intended; for the country is still sickly, the wether uncertaine, and it rayneth allmost daylie; so that the cheif diversions are within doores, by cockfiting and playes. The players being so numerous that they have sent out a colonie to Bury of whom a lady, who was there at a play gave me a very tragicall and lamentable description. That honest heartie gentleman Mr. Cotterell, was on Saturday at my howse, who told mee you were with his children, who were very ill; when you see his lady present my service unto her, hee came with my lady Adams. There was also Mr. Colt who belongeth to prince Rupert, who sayd hee sawe you lately, I thinck with Dr. Needham, also madame Prujeane, who maryd Sir Francis Prujeane's grandson, and liveth at Hornechurch, in Essex, ten miles from London; and others. Wee newly heare that Sir Robert Clayton[6] is chosen L. maior. I heare that hee and Mr. Morris have been noted scriveners, and gott great estates; and so Mr. Browne may have the neerer acquaintance with them. Some scriveners in London gett great estates, butt when they dye many have lost great summes by them, they having purchased estates with other mens money, and so ordering the matter that others cannot recover their money. This was observable in the rich scrivener, Mr. Child, butt it may be good to have friends who have acquaintance with my L. maior. This day beginneth St. Fayths fayre, the greatest

⁵ Evelyn (Memoirs, vol. i. 512) mentions the king as then newly returned from Newmarket, Oct. 23rd, 1679.

⁶ This prince of citizens, as Evelyn calls him, had served the office of sheriff in 1672, was chosen mayor, Oct. 1679, and represented the city in the parliaments of 1678, 79, 89, 95, 1700, 1701, and 1705, in which year he died.

in these parts; and Tom should have had a sight thereof, butt that it hath proved so very raynie wether. In your travells you say St. Veit or St. Fayth, perhaps Veit may signifie fayth in High Duch, butt St. Fayths day in the almanach, when our fayr is kept, was *sancta fides*, a holy virgin of Agen, in France, unto whom many churches were dedicated; as St. Fayth under St. Pauls, and others. I do not at present remember any churches wch bear the name of Sanctus Vitus or St. Veit in these parts. I wish wee were now at peace with the Algerines; they are now too well provided to be forced by us, and there will bee great number of captives to be redeemed, and what care can bee taken for it is doubtfull, considering all things. God give you health and grace to serve him all your dayes. Loue and blessing to my daughter Browne, and litle Susan, and you all. I beleeve your troublesome office of censor is growing now towards an end.—Your loving father,

THOMAS BROWNE.

Sir Thomas Browne to his son Edward.—Novemb. 7, [1679.]

DEAR SONNE,—I am glad at last to understand that you returned about twelve dayes agoe from Cobham hall, and that my L. O. Bryan is come to London; her brother the duke of Richmond was a good natured brisk man, and was at my howse twice, when hee came to Norwich. It is sayd also that shee is a fine courteous lady. Sir Joseph hath also the repute of [a] worthy and highly civill gentleman, and is not probably without a good study of bookes : being now president of the R. S. and having been a student of Queen's Colledge, in Oxford and as a benefactor hath rebuilt a part of that old colledge. I find by your description, that Cobham hall is a very notable place, and few to compare with it; so that, in your long staye, you might have somewhat within or without to divert you. The many excellent pictures must needs bee recreative; the howse also in St. James's square is a noble one and not many exceed it. Butt I am exceedingly sorry for the death of that worthy honest gentleman, Dr. Jaspar Needhame,[2] and the colledge will have a great losse of him. Have a speciall care of your

---

[7] He died Oct. 3, 1679, aged 57.—*Evelyn's Memoirs,* i. 512.

owne health; under the providence and blessing of God,
there is nothing more like to conserve you, and enable you
to go about, and wach, and to mind your patients, then temperance and a sober life. And 'tis not unlikely that some
of the Drs. patients may fall to your share. Bee kind to
Mr. Austin Briggs and his wife, daughter to old Mr. Cock
the miller, a good woeman, and a lover of Tom, and our
kind neibours both of them, although Mr. Briggs owne
brother in London, Dr. Briggs, may do much for them.
All the noyse hoere is of the new plot, sett up to make
nothing or littell of the former which I perceave no contrivance can effect. I am sorry Mr. Gadbury is in trouble,
upon erecting of schemes and calculating nativities, and as I
remember, it is high treason to calculate the nativitie of the
king, especially when procured by ill designers. Service to
Madame Burwell, my lady Pettus, Sir Will. Adams, and
his worthy lady who went towards London yesterday, and
shee intends to call at your howse very soone. Remember
me to my coseus Cradock, cosens Hobbes, Mr. Nathan
Skoltowe, when you see him, and all our friends. To my.
sonne Fairfax, my daughter Fairfax, Betty, Frank, Tom,
and Sukey. My daughter Fairfax and litle one, I believe is
not in London. God blesse you all and be loving and kind
together.—Your loving father, THOMAS BROWNE.

Sir Thomas Browne to his son Edward.—Nov. 24, [1679.]

DEAR SONNE,—The feverish and aguish distempers, which
beganne to be common in August, are now very much
abated, and few fall sick thereof: only there are very great
numbers of quartans; 'tis also a coughing time. Extraordinarie sickly seasons woorrie physitians, and robb them of
their health as well as their quiet; have therefore a great
care of your health, and order your affayres to the best
preservation thereof which may bee by temperance, and
sobrietie, and a good competence of sleepe. Take heed that
tobacco gayne not to much upon you, for the great incomo-
dities that may ensue, and the bewiching qualitie of it, which
drawes a man to take more and more the longer hee hath
taken it; as also the *ructus nidorosus,* or like burnt hard
eggs, and the hart burning after much taking at a time, and

also the impayring of the memorie, &c. I am glad you like a playne dyet; affect but ordinarie sawces. I thanck you both for the *psoe*,[8] which I desire to see, butt I beleeve it may render the blood more apt to ferment, and bee distemperd, and unquiet, and our owne sawces are best agreeable unto our bodyes. There is a book in a middle folio, lately published by Paul Ricaut, esqr. of the lives of Morat or Amurat the fourth, of Ibrahim, and of Mahomet the fourth, present emperour. In this are delivered the taking of New-hewsell, the battail at St. Goddard, the fights between count Souches and the visier of Buda, actions of Nicholas Serini, his burning the bridge of Esseck, the Grand Signors being at Larissa, the seidge of Candia, &c., and things acted in late times, which might not bee unpleasant unto yourself when you have time to cast your eye upon that booke. I am glad you did not read at Chirurgeon's hall, last yeare, because thereby you are provided for this. I am sorry for the death of your neibour, honest Dr. Needham. I doubt hee thought himself still a yong man, and so took the paynes of a yong man, and so acted beyond the shere of abillity of body: *sed quosdam "nimia congesta pecunia cura strangulat:"* Juvenal. God blesse you, my daughter Browne and you all. Present our service and thancks to Mr. Boone and Mrs. Boone, my cosens Hobbes, my cosen Cradock, Madame Burwell, Mrs. Dey, and all friends.   THOMAS BROWNE.

Sir Thomas Browne to his son Edward.—Nov. 28, [1679.]

DEAR SONNE,—I receaved yours. I am glad to heare wee have so many shipps launched and hope there may bee more before the spring. God send faythfull, valiant, and sober commanders, well experienced and carefull; above all, if places bee sould or given by favor only, such virtues will concerne butt contingently. The French are a sober, diligent, and active nation, and the Dutch, though a drincking nation, yet managed their warre [more] carefully and advantageously then the English, who thought it. sufficient to. fight upon any termes, and carry too many gentlemen and great persons to be killed upon the deck, and so encreaseth, the number of the slayne and blott their uictories. Pray

---

[8] Probably "soy."—*Gray.*

represent my service to sir John Hinton when you see him, 'tis a long time agoe since I had the honour to knowe him beyond sea. Mr. Norborne maryed sir Edm. Bacon's daughter, who was [a] very good lady, and dyed last summer, and I thinck hee was a member of the last parliament. Performe your businesse with the best ease you can, yet giving every one sufficient content. I beleeve my lady O. Bryan is by this time in better health and safetie ; though hypochond and splenitick persons are not long from complayning, yet they may bee good patients and may bee borne withall, especially if they bee good natured. A bill is inclosed; *espargnez nous autant que vous pourres, car je suis age, et aye beaucop d'anxieté et peene de sustenir ma famille.* God send my L. Bruce well in France and well to returne, surely travelling with so many attendants it must bee a great charge unto him. Dr. Briggs wrote a letter to mee concerning the *bronchocele* of his sister who was touched. Your mother and sisters remember to you, and Tom presents his duty. God blesse you all.—Your loving father,
                                                    THOMAS BROWNE.

Sir Thomas Browne to his son Edward.—Dec. 9, [1679.]

DEAR SONNE,—Wee are all glad to understand that the bill of mortallety decreased so much the last weeke; for people were fearefull that there might bee somewhat pestilentiai in the disease. The sentences of Cateline's conspiracy were, I beleeve, much taken notice of, and were very apposite to our present affaires. Wee understand the king hath issued out a proclamation for all papists or so reputed to depart from London ten miles ; which makes men conceive that the parliament will sitt at the prefixed time. I sawe the last transactions, or philosophicall collections of the R. S.[9] Here are some things remarkable, as Lewenhoecks finding such a vast number of litle animals in the melt of a cod, or the liquor which runnes from it ; as also in a pike or . . . . ; and computeth that they much exceed the number of men upon the whole earth at one time ; though hee computes that there may bee thirteen thousand millions

    [9] See "Hooke's Philosophical Collections," published in 1679, &c. in which will be found all the subjects of which notice is here taken.

of men upon the whole earth, which is very many. It may bee worth your reading, as also that of the vast inundation which was last yeare in Gascoigne, by the iruption of the waters out of the Pyrenean mountaines; as also of a flying man, and a shippe to sayle in the ayre, wherin here are some ingeneous discourses; likewise the damps in coale mines, and Lorenzini, a Florentine, concerning the torpedo; beside some other astronomicall observations. God blesse you all. Your mother and sisters send their respects, and Tom his duty.—Your loving father,   Tho. Browne.

Sir Thomas Browne to his son Edward.—Dec. 15, [1679.]

Dear Sonne,—Some thinck that great age superannuates persons from the vse of physicall meanes, or that at a hundred yeares of age 'tis either a folly or a shame to vse meanes to liue longer, and yet I haue knowne many send to mee for their seuerall troubles at a hundred yeares of age, and this day a poore woeman being a hundred and three yeares and a weeke old sent to mee to giue her some ease of the colick. The *macrobii* and long liuers which I haue knowne heere haue been of the meaner and poorer sort of people. Tho. Parrot was butt a meane or rather poore man. Your brother Thomas gaue two pence a weeke to John More, a scauenger, who dyed in the hundred and second yeare of his life : and 'twas taken the more notice of that the father of Sir John Shawe, who marryed my Lady Killmorey, and liueth in London, I say that his father, who had been a vintner, liued a hundred and two yeares, or neere it, and dyed about a yeare agoe. God send us to number our dayes and fitt ourselues for a better world. Times looke troublesomely; butt you haue an honest and peaceable profession which may employ you, and discretion to guide your words and actions. God blesse my daughter Browne and yourself.—Your loving father,   Thomas Browne.

Sir Thomas Browne to his son Edward.—Dec. 22, [1679.]

Dear Sonne,—You sett downe a plentifull list of good medicines. Lambs'-wooll[1] in water is also very good where men's stomacks will beare it. I remember Captain Bacon,

---

[1] Ale mixed with sugar, nutmeg and the pulp of roasted apples.

Sir Edm. Bacon's father of Redgrave, a talle bigge man, had once such an excruceating *dysuria acrimonia et ardor urinæ* that hee was beyond all patience; it being at that time of yeare when peaches were in season, I wished him to eat six or seven peaches, butt before the morning hee eat twenty-five, and found extraordinary relief, and his payne ceased. Have a care of your self this cold weather, wee are all in snowe, and 'tis now a proper time to freez eggs or the galls of animals with salt and snowe: as also how blood of animals freez, and how marrow in a small bone, and whether it will freez through the bone, the bone being covered with snowe and salt, with the like. I am fayne to keep my self warme by a fire side this cold weather. Tom presents his duty, and all their love unto my daughter, yourself, and all friends.— I rest your loving father,   THOMAS BROWNE.

Your sister Betty hath read unto mee Mr. Ricaut's historic of the three last Turkish emperours, Morat or Amurah the Fourth, Ibrahim, and Mahomet the Fourth, and is a very good historic, and a good addition unto Knolls his Turkish historie, which will then make one of the best histories that wee have in English.

Sir Thomas Browne to his son Edward, Jan. 19, [1679-80.]

DEARE SONNE,—Since I last writt unto you I have found out a way how you shall receave Ricaut's historie without sending it by the carts. I have desired Mr. George Rose, a bookseller in this towne, to write last Friday unto his correspondent, Mr. Clavell, stationer in London, at the Peacock, in St. Paul's churchyard, that you may have one of those bookes of him upon demand upon Mr. Rose's account, for I pay him heere in Norwich, at the rate which hee selleth the book here, and as soone as hee understands from Mr. Clavell that you have receaved it I paye him heere. I would not have you borrowe it because you may have it allwayes by you; the life of Mahomet the Fourth is larger than all the rest, and you having seen the grand signor now raygning, you may do well to knowe as much of his historie as you can. I wonder whether Galeazzi Gualdi doth write

still or not, if hee bee living;[2] there hath of late yeares
been a copious subject for him,   Mr. Ricaut hath also writt
of the present state of the Greek and Armenian churches,
by his majesties command.   I have read Sir George Ent's
booke[3] lately printed, in answer to Dr. Thruston;[4] 'tis pleasant to read, and very rationall done by two very good pens,
which may give a great deale of creditt unto the English,
there being very few bookes, or none, so elegantly writt ;
Dr. Thruston is very full of paradoxes in physick, and a
witty man also.   Heere was so much sider made this last
autumne, that there will not bee half so much French wine
spent heere as in other yeares, nor probably hereafter, for
there is so much planting of apple trees and fruits, that
they will become so cheap that there will bee litle profit
thereby ; the last was a strange plentiful yeare of fruit, and
my wife tells me shee bought above twentie quinces for a
penny ; the long southerly wind makes trees budde too
soone, and the corne to growe too forward, and wee are
afrayd of back winters, wch causeth diseases.   Love and
blessing to my daughter Browne and you all.—Your loving
father,   THOMAS BROWNE.

Sir Thomas Browne to his son Edward, July 7, [1680.]

  DEARE SONNE,—Wee vnderstood this weeke, by some of
our common news letters,[5] thas Sir Arthur Ingram was cutt
of the stone, and that the operation was performed in three

---

  [2] Count Galeasso Gualdo, an Italian historian, who died 1678. His
historical works, which related principally to the period in which he
lived, were numerous and extensive, and several of them were translated into English.
  [3] Antidiatribe ; seu Animadversiones in Malachiæ Thrustoni, M.D.
Diatribam de Respirationis usu primario. Auctore Georgia Entio, Eq.
Aur. M.D. et Col. Lond. Soc. 1679.
  [4] Malachi Thruston, M.D., De Respirationis usu, 12mo. Lug. Bat.
1671.
  [5] In the Monthly Review of "*The Ellis Correspondence,*" 2 vols. 8vo.
occurs the following passage :—"The greater part of this Correspondence is supposed to be formed of the letters which were written by a
description of persons not now in existence, and who are termed in one
of the extracts, the gentlemen who write the *news letters.* The necessity
of public journals which were not then invented, being thus provided
for by persons appointed to give information to those who required it
on public matters."—*Monthly Review, March* 1829, *p.* 359.

minutes.[6] Pray God hee may do well after it. Hee and his lady, about four yeares agoe, were at Norwich, and at my howse, and they were at Mr. Long's howse about a fortnight. I conceiue that in some part of the next weeke you must bee thinking agayne of your visitt at Woodstock.[7] And because you must be then in a park, I will sett downe some particulars " De Cervis " out of Aristotle and Scaliger, whereof you may enquire and informe yourself.[8] That their gutts are so tender, that they will breake upon a blowe, though their side be not broaken. There is a dayntie bitt accounted by many, called the inspinne, which may be the *intestinum rectum*, wch is very fatt, and, being broyled or fryed, is much desired by some. I haue seen it at some gentlemen's tables, butt my stomack went against it; you may enquire of it if you know it not: I think the gutt is turned side outward to make it. It is a particular bitt, and I know no other animal wherein the rectum is cooked up. Wee heare that the grand signor, Mahomet the Fourth, is dead, wch may alter the affayrs of those parts, and restore the seat of the empyre to Constantinople from Adrianople. Wee heare of the great penitence and retractation of my Lord Rochester,[9] and hereupon hee hath many good wishes and prayers from good men, both for his recouery here and happy state hereafter: you may write a few lines and certifie the truth thereof; for my cosen Witherley, who liveth with J Witherley, writt something of it to her mother in Norwich. Captain Scoltown acknowledgeth your great kindness to his wife. Sure they must haue some physitian at Tunbridge to aduise them upon all occasions. I was acquainted with Dr. Amerst while hee liued. God blesse you all.—Your loving father, THOMAS BROWNE.

Wee haue litle or none of *viscus quercinus,* or miselto of the oake, in this country; butt I beleeve they may have in the woods and parks of Oxfordshyre. And about this time the crevises[1] haue the stones or litle concretions on their

[6] The operator, Francis Collot, drew up an account of the operation, which is preserved in the British Museum, MS. Sloan. 1865.

[7] Woodstock Park, the seat of Lord Rochester, whom Dr. Edward Browne was now attending in his last illness.

[8] The quotation is omitted.

[9] Lord Rochester's letter to Bishop Burnet, June 25, 1680.

[1] Crevise, or Cray-fish, or Craw-fish ; from the French *écrévisse.*

head vender the shell or crusta, and there are plenty of crevises in those riuers.   God blesse my daughter Browne, litle
Sukey, and Ned, and be mercifull vnto us all, and keepe our
hearts firme vnto him.   Tom holds well, God be thancked.
Mr. Whitefoot is at the commencement.   I wish my Lord
Bruce may haue got good by his journey. Mr. Deane Astley,
who is now with mee, presents his seruice.

Sir Thomas Browne to his son Edward—Aug. 22, [1680.]

DEAR SONNE,—I was very glad to receaue your last letter.
God hath heard our prayers, and I hope will blesse you still.
If the profitts of the next yeare come not up to this, I would
not haue you discouraged; for the profitts of no practise
are equal or regular: and you haue had some extraordinary
patients this yeare, which, perhaps, some yeares will not
afford.   Now is your time to be frugall and lay up.   I
thought myself rich enough till my children grew up.   Be
carefull of your self, and temperate, that you may bee able
to go through your practise; for to attayne to the getting of a
thousand pounds a yeare requires no small labour of body
and mind, and is a life not much lesse paynfull and laborious
then that wch the meaner sort of people go through.   When
you putt out your money, bee well assured of the assurance;
and bee wise therein from what your father hath suffered.
It is laudable to dwell handsomely; butt be not too forward
to build or sett forth another mans howse, or so to fill it
that it may increase the fuell, if God should please to send
fire.   The mercifull God direct you in all.   Excesse in ap-
parell and chargeable dresses are got into the country,
especially among woeman; men go decently and playn
enough.   The last assizes there was a concourse of woeman
at that they call my lords garden in Cunsford, and so richly
dressed that some stranger sayd there was scarce the like to
bee seen at Hide Park, which makes charity cold.   Wee
now heare that this parliament shall sitt the 21 of October,
which will make London very full in Michaelmas terme.
Wee heare of two oestriges wch are brought from Tangier.
I sawe one in the latter end of king James his dayes, at
Greenwich when I was a schoolboy.   King Charles the first
had a cassaware, or emeu, whose fine green channelled

egge I haue, and you haue seen it.   I doubt these will not
bee showne at Bartholomew fayre, where every one may see
them for his money.   I haue read all or most of Dr. Loves
booke[2], which is a pretty booke, and giues a good account
of the lowe countrey practise in that disease, and hath some
other obseruables.   I knewe one Mr. Christopher Loue,
sonne vnto the Dr. Loue, warden of Winchester colledge,
who was an actiue man agaynst the king in the late warres,
and got a great estate ; butt I think hee was fayne to fly upon
the kings restauration.   The chirurgions haue made choyce
of new officers ; tis probable they may agree, and so you
may read the next lent.   The king comes to Newmarkett
the next moneth.   A Yarmouth man told mee that hee sawe
Dr. Knights at the Bath ; perhaps hee will not bee at Newmarkett.   I beleeve you neuer sawe Madame Baxter. Since
Mr. Cottrell and his lady and child are with Sir W. Adams
they speake often of you, and all go to London at Michaelmas.   Mrs. Dey is at my howse, butt returnes with Madame
Burwell.   Mr. Parsons his sermon[3] is like to sell well.
God blesse my daughter Browne and you all.—Your loving
father,   THOMAS BROWNE.

Sir Thomas Browne to his son Edward.—Oct. 15, 80.[4] .

DEARE SONNE,—I thinck you are in the right, when you
say that physitians coaches in London are more for state
then for businesse : there being so many wayes whereby
they may 'bee assisted, and at lesser charge and care in
London.   The Thames and hackney coaches, being no small
help, beside the great number of coaches kept by private
gentlemen, in and about London.   When I read Gages
travells in America, many yeares ago, I was much surprised
to find that there were twentie thousand coaches in Mexico,
perhaps there may be now in London half that number.
When Queen Elizabeth came to Norwich, 1578, she came on
horseback from Ipswich, by the high road to Norwich, in
the summer time ; but shee had a coach or two, in her

---

[2] Morley, Charles Love, M.D.   De Morbc Epidemico, annorum
1678-9, 8vo. London, 1680.

[3] Probably on the death of Lord Rochester.

[4] The date, thus abridged, is original.   The present letter was published, but not correctly, in *Retrospective Review,* vol. i. 162.

trayne. She rid through Norwich, unto the bishop's palace,
where she stayed a weeke, and went sometimes a hunting
on horseback, and up to Mushold hill often, to see wrestling
and shooting, &c.   When I was a youth, many great persons
travelled with 3 horses, but now there is a new face of
things.   I doubt there will bee scarce cortex enough to bee
to suffise the nation.   God bless you all.—Your loving
father,   THOMAS BROWNE.

Sir Thomas Browne to his son Edward.   Nouemb. j, [1680.]

DEAR SONNE,—Mr. alderman Briggs, my neighbour, who
is our burges, went to London last Thursday, and in another
coach Mr. Alderman Man and others; between Barton
Mills and Thetford, both the coaches were robbed by 3 high-
waymen; but not much money was lost, passengers vsually
trauelling with litle money about them, but the coachman
lost fifteen pounds which he caryed to buye a horse.
Captaine Briggs, my neibour, would haue made some resistance but they presently tooke awaye his sword which hee
used to weare in the parliament: his man also was gone out
of sight, and none of the trauellers would joyne with him to
make resistance.

Just now while I am writing, a poore woeman of a hundred
and fiue yeares old next Christmasse, seems to bee vnder the
common distemper.   Shee dwells in one of the towers of the
wall, and we vse to be charitable vnto her, and your sisters
give her often some relief. Joh. More, who was one hundred
and 2 yeares old, to whome your brother Thomas gaue something weekely all the while hee was abroad, dyed of these
autumnall distempers, as did also the old man beyond Scoale
Inne, who wayted on the Earle of Leicester, when Queen Eliz.
came to Norwich, and who told mee many things thereof. God
blesse you all.—Your loving father,   THOMAS BROWNE.

Sir Thomas Browne to his son Edward.—Nov. xi, [1680.]

DEARE SONNE.—I writt to you lately, of the poore woeman,
of a hundred and five yeares old, laking one moneth; shee hath
had this continuall autumnal tertian fever, and there is good
hopes of her recovery, for she can now rise and sett up out of
her bed, and desires a litle wine, which shee could [not] endure

in her distemper. Your sisters sawe her yesterday, who use
to give her money; shee sees so well, that shee kuewe them
at a distance, and her hearing is good. Formerly they gave
not the cortex to quartanarians, before they had been ill a
considerable time, butt I think it should be good to give it at
the beginning, before their bloods are corrupted by the length
of the disease. Write whether they do not give it early in
London.—Your loving father,   THO. BROWNE.

Sir Thomas Browne to his son Edward.—Dec. 27, [1680?]

DEAR SONNE,—Wee are all very sorry for the losse of
the litle one;[5] God give us still grace to resigne our wills
unto his, and patience in all what hee hath layd out for us.
God send you wisedome and providence, to make a
prudent use of the moneys you have from mee, beside what
you gett and otherwise. Least repentence come to late
upon you, consider that accidental charges may bee alwayes
coming upon you, and the folly of depending or hoping to
much upon time turnes yet to come; since yeares will
creepe on, and impotent age accuse you for not thincking
early upon it. The christening and buryalls of my children
have cost mee above 2 hundred pounds, and their education
more; beside your owne, which hath been more chargeable,
then all the rest putt together; and therefore consider well
that you are not likely to playe in this world, or in old age,
and bee wise while you are able to gett, and save somewhat
agaynst a bad winter, and uncertaintie of times. God blesse
you all.—Your loving father,   THO. BROWNE.

Sir Thomas Browne to his son Edward.—Jan. 5, [1680-1.]

DEAR SONNE,—My daughter Browne writt mee word,
that you went last Thursday, to Ampthill, to my L. Bruce
his sonne, which hath made us very sollicitous concerning
you, because you tooke such a journey, when you had
wached with the duke of Richmond the night before, as also
because it was exceeding bad travelling, and worse then it
hath been all this winter, and exceeding cold. I hope you
are returned and in health, and that the yong lord is better.
I beleeve it may bee expected that, upon your returne, you

[5] Probably "little Ned."

should visit the duke, you being so suddenly called from him. Mr. Thomas Wood, of Braken, enquired of you, and gives you thancks for your kindnesse to his daughter Mrs. Betty, who was with you the last summer, and gott much good by Tunbridg waters. His old father died the last weeke, and left him a fayre estate in lands, beside good summes of money, which may paye the debts which the oversparing hand of his father made him contract, by borroweng and takeng up of money. I beleeve hee is fiftie-four yeares old, at least.. Sir William Cooke, of Broome, is 85 or 6 yeares old, and likely to live; so that that honest and worthy gentleman, his sonne, captain Cooke, is like to stay yett awhile before hee cometh to the estate. Mr. Thomas Holland, who liveth at Bury, cannot bee so litle as fiftie, and Sir John Holland, who is his father, like to live some yeares. These are the old heyres which the country lookes upon, and wonder at their fathers, who are not like at last to encrease their goods by sparing, since a considerable part must bee dispersed into the hands of creditors. Heere is a printed speech, supposed to be my L. Shaftsburies, it is cacht up and read by many : there are many passages in it litle to the honour and reputation of the king.[6] Though the commons howse bee free, and the howse of lords also, for what they say within their walls, yet [it] is much that their speeches should be printed and sent about. Tom, God be thanked, is well. God blesse my daughter Brown and little Susan.—Your loving father,

THOMAS BROWNE.

Sir Thomas Browne to his son Edward.—Feb. 1, [1680-1.]

DEARE SONNE,—Wee have been exceeding solicitous for Mrs. Jane Allington, and the great sorrowe my good Lady Adams was like to haue if she should dye. And therefore you did very well to giue us that wellcome notice that shee was well agayne. I took notice this weeke of the notable voyce of a hound aboue all other doggs; and therefore at your opportunity you may examine the vocal organs of a hound; there may be something considerable, perhaps,

---

[6] A speech lately made by a noble peer of the realm. London, printed for F. S. at the Elephant and Castle in the Royal Exchange, in Cornhill, 1681.—2 pp. sm. folio *in Bib. Mus. Brit.*

beside the rest, from the frame of his mouth and slabbing lipps. I haue not seen Sir W. Adams since hee came into Norfolk. I beleeve hee hath been buisie about the election for knights of the shyre. Butt iust as I am writing Sir William Adams comes to me, and deliuered your letter and token to Tom, who was very glad, and presents his duty and thanks to his father and mother, and loue to his sister. Four stood, Sir J. Hobart, Sir Peter Gleane, Sir Jacob Astley, and Sir Thomas Hare. It was a hard canuas: Sir John caryed it by a hundred voyces, wanting two or three. Sir Peter by sixteen or seventeen, which hee had more then Sir Jacob. Sir Thomas Hare had the fewest, yet not many lesse then Sir Jacob. Sir Peter had like to haue lost it, by the great and tempestuous wind wch was on last Sunday night, and held the greatest part of Monday, which was the election day. The Yarmouth men came to Norwich, either by boat or horse, the day before, to the number of three hundred, for Sir John and Sir Peter; butt there were three boates which were to come on Sunday night, with fishermen, for Sir John and Sir Peter, butt the wind was so high and contrarie that they were fayne to returne. Only sixteen or seventeen of them were so re-solute that they went on shoare and came on foot, which made Sir Peter to haue the second voyce. Sir Henry Hobart was chosen one of the burgesses for Lynne, and Alderman Taylor the other, who was burgesse the last par-liament. Sir Joseph Williamson and Mr. William Harbord were chosen agayne. Mr. Hoast and Sir Robert Steward for [Rysing] as before. Ours are like to be chosen agayne, as also the knights of the shyre for Suffolk. God blesse you all. I shall, God willing, soone write agayne.—Your loving father, THOMAS BROWNE.
My serue to my lady Adams.

Sir Thomas Browne to his son Edward.—Feb. 28, [1680-1.]

DEAR SONNE,—A great part of our newes hath been, of late, made out [of] severall elections, and the circumstances of them. Sir James Johnson and Mr. England are burgesses for Yarmouth. Sir James is a sober and understanding person, very civill, and your kind acquaintance. Sir Robert

Kemp and Sir Philip Skippon are chosen for Dunwich as before, the towne having sent unto them desiring them to accept of the place. So wee have butt two newe parliament men for Norfolk. Sir James Johnson for Yarmouth, and Sir Henry Hobart for Lynne. And for ought I perceave there is no considerable number of new men chosen in other parts. I find in the newes letters that Mr. Whittle, the kings chirurgeon, is dead, and that your neibour Mr. Moullins, is sworne in his place; butt which of the Moullins I knowe not, perhaps Mr. Peirce may bee in Scotland with the duke. I am sorry to find that the King of England is fayne to reduce his howsehold expences to twelve thousand pounds p. annum, especially hee having a farre greater revenue then any of his predecessors. God keepe all honest men from penury and want; men can bee honest no longer then they can give every one his due : *in fundo parsimonia* seldome recovers or restores a man. This rule is to be earned by all, *vtere divitiis tanquam moriturus, et idem tanquam victurus parcito divitiis.* So may bee avoyded sordid avarice and improvident prodigallity ; so shall not a man deprive himself of God's blessings, nor throwe away God's mercies ; so may hee bee able to do good and not suffer the worst of evils. Two earthern bottles floatting upon the sea, with this motto, " *si collidimur frangimur,*" is applycable unto any two concernes whose interest is united, and is to conserve one another ; which makes mee sorry for this dissention between the king and the people, that is, the major part of them, as the elections declare. God send a happy conclusion, and bee reconciled unto us, and give us grace to forsake our sinnes, the *boutefeux* and incendiaries of all. God blesse you all.—Your loving father,   THOMAS BROWNE.

---

*Sir Thomas Browne to his daughter Mrs. Lyttleton—
Sept.* 15, [1681.]

DEARE BETTY,—Tho it were noe wonder this very tempestious and stormy winter, yet I am sorry you had such an uncomfortable sight as to behold a ship cast away so neer you; this is noe strange tho unwelcom sight at Yarmouth, Cromer, Winterton, and sea towns : tho you could not saue them, I hope they were the better for your prayers, both

those that perishd and those that scapd. Some wear away
in calmes, some are caried away in storms : we come into
the world one way, there are many gates to goe out of it.
God giue us grace to fit and prepare our selues for that
necessity, and to be ready to leaue all when and how so ever
he shall call. The prayers of health are most like to be
acceptable ; sickness may choak our devotions,. and we are
accepted rather by our life then our death : we have a rule
how to lead the one, the other is uncertain, and may come
in a moment. God I hope will spare you to serve him long,
who didst begin early to serve him. There died thirty-six
last week in Norwich. The small pox very common ; and
we must refer it to Gods mercy when he pleaseth to abate
or cease it ; for the last run of the small pox lasted much
longer then this has yet dun. Your brother Thomas went
once from Yarmouth in the evening, and arrived at the Isle
of White the next day at one o'clock in the afternoon, but
it was with such a wind, that he was never so sick at sea as
at that time. I came once from Dublin to Chester at
Michaelmas, and was so tossed that nothing but milk and
possets would go down with me for two or three days after.
Your self is not impatient, you will haue noe cause to be
sad : giue no way unto melancholy, which is purely sadnes
without a reasonable cause. You shall never want our
dayly prayers, and also our frequent letters. God bless you
both—I rest your loving father,   THOMAS BROWNE.

: *Sir Thomas Browne to his son Edward.—Jan.* 9, [1681-2.]

DEAR SONNE,—I presume you are carefull of your health,
and not only to regayne butt to conserve it. Long health is
apt to begett security, and God mercifully interposeth some
admonitions and rubbs to make us consider ourselves, and
to carry a warie hand in our affayres of all kinds. The
merciful providence of God go ever with you, and continue
to blesse you. Mr. Carpenter, who brought the letters, is
secretary of Jersey, and when or whether hee goes back to
Guernzey, I beleeve is uncertaine : for, to obtaine conveniency of passage, the Jersey men come commonly to
Guernzey. I thinck you did well not to hazard your
selfe at that time by such a journey as to Lewys, whereof

part is a very bad waye. I remember, when I was very
yong, and I thinck butt in coates, my mother carryed mee to
my grandfather Garawayes howse in Lewys. I retaine only
in my mind the idea of some roomes of the howse and of the
church.. Our maior was sent for by ' a letter to appeare
before the king and counsell the weeke before Xmas; some
chief brewers of Norwich and excisemen had accused him for
putting downe some alehouses, and denying to license
others, and hindring the kings profitt. Butt when hee had
shewen that he did butt what the law required of him, that
there were still an unreasonable number of ale-houses, and
that they were a great occasion of debaucherie and povertie
in the towne, so that the rates of the poore have been encreased eight hundred pounds more then formerly, hee was
dismissed with commendations. His maiestie soone per-
ceaved the excisemen and brewers made a cloake of his
interest for their owne, and would not have his subjects de-
bauched and impoverished upon his account. Wee have
had much cyder given us this winter, and now at Christmas it
is apt to gripe many, and so hard that they drinck it with a
little sugar. That which was sent you from Guernsey may
probably bee good, but having been upon the sea tis likely
it may be hard. My wife and others, except myself, drinck
a little at meales; and Tom calls for the bottomes of the
glasses, where tis sweetest, and cares little for the rest. It
helps to make good syllibubs in the summer. A great part
of our newes is of the king of Fez and Morocco's embassadour, with his presents of lyons and oestridges.[7] I remember an embassadour who, in King Charles the First's time,
came from the king of Morocco to help him to besiedge
Sally, then revolted from him; hee besiedged it by land, and
the English with eight shipps by sea, and so the town was
taken. Hee brought with him many gallant horses, for a
present with strong tayles and very long maines, and pictures thereof were taken; and there is one still in this
towne; and, at a gentleman's. howse in the country the
picture of the Moorish embassadour on horseback, as hee
rid through London at his entry, as bigge as the life, which
cost fiftie pounds, and is a noble peece, about as bigge as

---

[7] Evelyn i, 537, 8.

Titian's[8] Charles the First on horseback, in the hall of the Duke's place. I am glad my cosen Cradock is come of so well. Tis like my L. S. will sett still, and content to have escaped such a danger. Love and blessing to you, my daughter Browne, and you all, as also from my wife; love from Franck, duty from Tom.—Your loving father,

THOMAS BROWNE.

I doubt all my letters sent [to] Guernsey within these two moneths lye still at Southampton; the wind having continued southerly and westerly at this time of yeare beyond observation, to the great detriment of many marchauds.

Sir Thomas Browne to his son Edward.—Feb. 15, [1681-2.]

DEAR SONNE,—I receaved yours by the last post, which you writt after eleven o'clock at night, and made a shift to send it the same night. You did well to observe the eclipse, for it was a totall one, and remarkable. By this time probably you have conferred with knowing persons about it, your doubts were rationall, and also your thoughts of the Apogæum, and how the shadowe of which should bee so faynt as not to obscure the moone more, whereas some times it hath been observed, "*Lunam eclipsatum interdum penitus in cœlo evanuisse.*" Butt I doubt not butt something will be sayd hereof at the R. S. or elsewhere, from whence they will receave accounts, and also from Mr. Flamsted. The wind hath been these 3 dayes at south west agayne, so that wee may expect letters from Guernsey. Wee heare the Duches of Portsmouth goeth for France, some time in March. I doubt the English will not like the setting up a colledge of physitians in Scotland,[9] nor their endeavouring to sett up an East India and straight company.[1] They hope

[8] This is an error; Titian died in 1576. It was Vandyck to whom Charles I. repeatedly sat.

[9] 29th Nov. 1681, the king, by his letters patent, incorporated certain physicians in Edinburgh and their successors, into a body politick, by the title of the President and Royal College of Physicians, at Edinburgh.

[1] 29th Oct. 1681, Charles II. granted a charter to "the Company of Merchants of the city of Edinburgh." It was confirmed June 15, 1693, till which time the trade of Edinburgh seems to have been confined to Norway, the Baltick, and England.

to do anything, by the favor and encouragement of the
duke. If they sett up a colledge and breed many physitians,
wee shall be sure to have a great part of them in England.

Mr. Clarke tells me that he sawe 2 ostridges in London,
in Cromwell's time. Though you sawe an ostridge in the
Duke of Florance his garden, yett I do not perceave you
sawe any one among the curiosities and rarities of any of
the princes of Germany. Perhaps the king will send some
of his to the King of France, the Prince of Orange, &c. the
losse of the Netherlands hath been very great, butt I hope
not so great as is related. God blesse you all.—Your loving
father,   THOMAS BROWNE.

Sir Thomas Browne to his son Edward.[2]—June 16, [1682.]

DEAR SONNE,—I have sent the 4 sheets you sent mee, by
captaine Lulmans eldest sonne, who went this morning
towards London, in the 2 dayes coach, and a paper within
them. I am glad you have putt an end to that labour,
though I am not sorry that you undertooke it. Wee are
glad to understand, by my daughter Browne's letter, that
my daughter Fairfax is delivered of a sonne. The blessing
of God bee with them both, and send them health. The
vessel of sider sent you from Guernzey was rackt, it came
not out of Normandie butt from Guernzey, though it was
not of my sonne and daughters making. They might
have made much, there being plenty of apples, butt they
made butt 2 or 3 hoggesheads themselves for their own use.
Your sister tells mee that they have plentie of large
oysters, like Burnham oysters, about Guernzey, and all
those rocky seas to St. Mallowes, and have a peculiar way of
disposing and selling of them, that they are not decayed or
flatt before they bee eaten. They bring them into the haven
in vessells that may containe vast quantities, and when they
come at a competent distance from the peere head, they
anker and cast all the oysters overboard into the sea; and
when the tide goeth away, and the ground bare, the people
come to buy them, and the owners stand on drye ground
and sell them. When the tide comes in, the buyers retire,
and come agayne at the next ebbe, and buye them agayne,

[2] Retrospective Review, vol. i, p. 162.

and so every ebbe till they bee all sould. So the oysters are kept lively, and well tasted, being so often under the salt sea water, and if they had a vessell of a hundred tunne full they might sell them while they were good, being thus ordered allthough it should take sometime to sell them all. This seems a good contrivance, and such as I have not heard of in England. Wee hope Captain Cotton is got by this time to Guernzey, though the winds have been often crosse to gett from the Downes thither, it hath been in the north these 3 dayes, and it was yesterday so cold that we could have endured a fire. Captain Cotton intended to call at Southampton, if possible, for divers letters and despaches, which had been retarded by the lasting south-west wind, which I doubt hee could not performe. My daughter hath heard twice from Guernsey, since shee came to Norwich, and once from Lychfield, from Mrs. Katherine Litelton, her 'husband's sister, a singular good woeman. I heare Mrs. Suckling is well at her brother's in Suffolk, butt shee dares not yet adventure to Norwich, with her children, for feare of the small pox. The warlike provisions of the emperour and empyre, &c. hath the countenance of a warre, butt the summer is farre advanced. Wee heare the Duchesse' of Portsmouth hath found much benefitt by the waters, and is returning into England. The peace with Argier gives some life unto the Yarmouth men, and no small content unto all.

Dr. Edward Browne to his Father.—Oct. 3, 1682.

MOST HONOURED FATHER,—The salary of the hospitall is so ordered that it comes to twenty shillings a weeke : for the patients within the house, the physitian receives quarterly nine pounds and a noble, and for the out patients at Easter, fiften pounds, which comes to fifty-two poundes and a noble in a year; for which hee cannot write less then six thousand præscriptions. We want a good chalybeat electuary, that doth not purge, for ours doth sometimes. I know not who invented it, and it is not well compounded, yet it doth much good; it is this,—

R. Rad. Raphani rustic. ʒiij.	Limaturæ Chalȳbis ʒij.
Cort. Ligni Sassafras ʒiij.	Conserv. Cochleariæ hortensis ʒj.
Rad. jalappæ,	Theriacæ Diatessar. ʒvj.
Rad. Mechoacan. ā ʒss.	Conserv. Marrubij
Trium Santal. ā ℈ij.	Conserv. Absynt. vulgaris ā ʒss.
Rassuræ Eboris ʒss.	Oxymel. scyllit q. s. m. f. Electuar.
Crem. Tartari ʒj.	

I thinke to have this made ready, but if you please to adde or alter it, it shall not be made up till I hear from you, sir.

R. Conserv. Absynt. vulgaris ʒij.	Limaturæ Chalyb. ʒiij.
Conserv. Rosar. Rubrar. ʒxij.	Syr. de Quinq. Rad. q. s. m. f. Elec-
Zinzib. condit. ʒiiij.	tuar.
Cort. Winter. ʒj.	

And so it may be a standing medicine, as well as the other. They make use of pills in old coughs and diseases on the lungs, which they call *pilulæ nigræ*, which are these,

R. Rad. Enulæ	Sacchari Cadi ā lib. j.
Rad. Irid. florent.	Picis liquidæ q. s. m. f. Massa.
Sem. Anisi	

but I præscribe more of a strong *diacodium* they make. Pray, sir, write me word how you make your *syrupus de scordio*, for it is not knowne in London. Pray, sir, thinke of some good effectual cheape medicines for the hospitall; it will be a piece of charity, which will be beneficiall to the poore, hundred of years after we are all dead and gone. The purging electuary, which is divided into boluses of half an ounce, or six dragmes, as it is ordered, is thus,

R. Electuarii lenitivi ʒxij.	Syr. Rosar. solutivi q. s. m. f. Elec-
Cremor. Tartar. ʒiij ʒvj.	tuarium.
Jalap. Pulv. ʒijss.	

We make much use of *caryocostinum* and jalep powdered, which are also often taken in four ounces of the purging decoction, which is made of senna, rhubarb, polypody, sweet fennell seeds, and ginger. Their scurvy grass drinke is good; they allow three barrells every weeke of it, to every barrell they put a pound of horse raddish, four handfulls of common wormwood, fifteen handfulls of scurvy grasse, garden scurvy grasse, fifteen handfulls of brokelime, and fifteen handfulls of water cresses, to a barrell of good ale; which the poor people like very well.

St. Thomas Hospitall is larger than ours, and holds forty or fifty persons more; we have divers of the king's soldiers in the hospitall. My wife sent downe the last weeke, a pastborde box, by the waggons, with candlesticks for Mrs. Pooly, and chocolate for my lady Pettus. My duty to my most dear mother, and love to my sister, and Tomy.—Your most obedient sonne,   EDWARD BROWNE.

MISCELLANEOUS CORRESPONDENCE.

Dr. Browne to Dr. Henry Power.   [1647 ?][1]

Εκ Βιβλίου κυβερνῆτα [i. e. statesman from the book] is grown
into a proverb; and no less ridiculous are they who think out of
book to become physicians. I shall therefore mention such as
tend less to ostentation than use, for the directing a novice to
observation and experience without which you cannot expect to
be other than ἐκ βιβλίου κυβερνήτης. Galen and Hippocrates must
be had as fathers and fountains of the faculty. And, indeed,
Hippocrates's *Aphorisms* should be conned for the frequent use
which may be made of them. Lay your foundation in anatomy,
wherein αυτοψία must be your *fidus Achates.* The help that
books can afford you may expect, besides what is delivered
sparsim from Galen and Hippocrates, Vesalius, Spigelius, and
Bartholinus. And be sure you make yourself master of Dr.
Harvey's piece *De Circul. Sang.;* which discovery I prefer to
that of Columbus. The knowledge of plants, animals, and
minerals, (whence are fetched the *Materia Medicamentorum*)
may be your πάρεργον; and, so far as concerns physic, is attain-
able in gardens, fields, apothecaries' and druggists' shops. Read
Theophrastus, Dioscorides, Matthiolus, Dodonæus, and our
English herbalists: Spigelius's *Isagoge in rem herbariam* will
be of use. Wecker's *Antidotarium speciale,* Renodæus for composition and preparation of medicaments. See what apothecaries
do. Read Morelli *Formulas medicas,* Bauderoni *Pharmacopæa,*
Pharmacopæa Augustana. See chymical operations in hospitals,
private houses. Read Fallopius, Aquapendente, Paræus, Vigo,
&c. Be not a stranger to the useful part of chymistry. See
what chymistators do in their officines. Begin with *Tirocinium*
Chymicum, Crollius, Hartmannus, and so by degrees march on.

---

[1] From a reference in Mr. Smith's letter, p. 360, there seems little
doubt that the present (which appears to have been communicated to
the world by Dr. Richard Middleton Massey, F.R.S.) was addressed to
Dr. Henry Power, of New-Hall, near Ealand, Yorkshire; author of
Experimental Philosophy, in Three Books, containing new Experiments,
Microscopical Mercurial, and Magnetical, 4to. 1664.

Materia Medicamentorum, surgery and chymistry, may be your diversions and recreations; physic is your business. Having, therefore, gained perfection in anatomy, betake yourself to Sennertus's *Institutions*, which read with care and dilligence two or three times over, and assure yourself that when you are a perfect master of these institutes you will seldom meet with any point in physic to which you will not be able to speak like a man. This done, see how institutes are applicable to practice, by reading upon diseases in Sennertus, Fernelius, Mercatus, Hollerius, Riverius, in particular treatises, in counsels, and consultations, all which are of singular benefit. But in reading upon diseases satisfy yourself not so much with the remedies set down (although I would not have these altogether neglected) as with the true understanding the nature of the disease, its causes, and proper indications for cure. For by this knowledge, and that of the instruments you are to work by, the *Materia Medicamentorum*, you will often conquer with ease those difficulties, through which books will not be able to bring you; *secretum medicorum est judicium*. Thus have I briefly pointed out the way which, closely pursued, will lead to the highest pitch of the art you aim at. Although I mention but few books (which, well digested, will be *instar omnium*) yet it is not my intent to confine you. If at one view you would see who hath written, and upon what diseases, by way of counsel and observation, look upon Moronus's *Directorium Medico-practicum*. You may look upon all, but dwell upon few. I need not tell you the great use of the Greek tongue in physic; without it nothing can be done to perfection. The words of art you may learn from Gorreus's *Definitiones Medicæ.* This and many good wishes,—From your loving friend,   THOMAS BROWNE.

Dr Henry Power to Dr. Browne.—Ch. Coll. Camb. 15th Sept.
1648.

RIGHT WORSHIPFULL,—I cannot but returne you infinite thankes for your excessive paynes in doubling of your last letter to mee, both pages whereof were so exceeding satisfactory to my requests, as that I know not wheather of them may more justly challenge a larger returne of thankes from mee. For the forepage I have traced your commands, and simpled in the woods, meadows, and fields, instead of gardens, which being obvious and in every countrey, I may easyly hereafter bee made a garden herbalist by any shee empirick. I have both Gerard with Johnson's addition, and Parkinson; the former has the cleerer cutt, and outvies the other in an accurate description of a plant; the latter is the better methodist, and has bedded his plants in a better ranke and order. I compared, also, Dodonæus with them, who does very well for a short and curt herbalist: yet I shall embrace Gerard above all, because you pleased to honour him with your approbation. For the back side of your letter, I am extreamely satisfied in your resolves of my quære, I confesse I run into too deepe a beliefe and too strong a conceipt of chymistry, (yet not beyond what some of those artists affirme) of the reproduction of the same plant by ordinary way of vegetation, for (say they) if the salt be taken and transferred to another countrey and there sowed, the plant thereof shall sprout out even from common earth. But it will be satisfaction enough, to the greatest of my desires, to behold the leafes thereof shaddowed in glaciation, of which experiment I hope I shall have the happynesse to be ocularly evinced at some opportunity by you.

Sir, I have a great desire to shift my residence a while, and to live a moneth or two in Norwich by you: where I may have the happynesse of your neighbourhood. Here are such fewe helpes here, that I feare I shall make but a lingering progresse unlesse I have your personall discourse to further and prick forwards my slow endeavours. But I shall determine of nothing till I see you here, in which journey I could wish (were it not to the disadvantage of your affaires) you would prevent our expectations. Sir, I have now by the frequency of living and dead dissections of doggs, run through the whole body of anatomy, insisting upon Spigelius, Bartholinus, Fernelius, Columbus, Veslingius, but especially Harvey's circulation, and the two incomparable authors Des-Cartes and Regius, which, indeed were the only two that answered my doubts and quæres in that art. I have likewise made some little proficiency in herbary, and by going out three or four miles once a weeke have brought home with mee two or three hundred hearbs. I have likewise run through Heurnius, which I very well allow of for a peripateticall author; hee is something curt *De urina*, which I conceive to bee a very necessary piece in physick now the circulation is discovered; for since the urine is channelled all along with the blood, through almost all the parenchymata of the body, before it come to the kidneys to bee strained and separated, it must needes carry a tincture of any disaffected or diseased part through which it passes. For Sennertus I cannot yet procure him, but 'tis sayd hee is comming out in a new letter, and then I question not but I shall have him. Mr. Smith presents his humble respects to you, and shall bee extreame glad to give you a deserved welcome to Cambridge, who may doe it, perchance, more nobly yet not more heartyly then will—Your most obliged friend and servant,

HENRY POWER.

Sir, my father Foxcroft and mother in their last to Cambridge forgott not to tender their best respacts to you, which I have requited in the like returne of yours to them (according to your request) this last journey.

––––––––

Mr. Merryweather to Dr. Browne.[2]*—Cambridge, Magd. College, Octob.* 1, 1649.

HONOURED SIR,—To know and be acquainted with you, though no otherwise than by your ingenious and learned writings, which now a good part of Christendom is, were no contemptible degree of happiness: the fool-hardy enterprize of translating your book might seem to give me some small title to a further pretence; but it is my great unhappiness, that as small as this is, I have forfeited it already upon several scores. I undertook a design, which I knew I could not manage without certain disadvantage and injury to the author; and after, though I saw the issue no happier than I expected, yet I could not be content to conceal or burn it, but must needs obtrude to the large world, in beggarly and disfigured habit, that which you sent out in so quaint and polisht a dress. Besides, I might have acquainted you with it sooner, presented you with a copy, begged pardon sooner for these miscarriages, which now I may justly fear is too late. The truth of it is, sir, I have some real pleas and justifications for most of these crimes; and have, with impatience, waited for some opportunity to have represented them by word of mouth, rather than writing; which I hoped to have had the happiness to have done when I was lately at Norwich, as my honoured friend, Mr. Preston, of Beeston, will assure you, whom I desired, after we found not you in the town, being unwilling to continue this incivility any longer, to present you with a copy at his first opportunity, which I question not but by this time you have received. Thus much, sir, at the least I had done sooner, if I had not been hindered by a constant unwelcome rumour, all the time I was abroad in the Low Countries and France (which was the space of some years after the impression,) that you had left this life: upon what ground the report was raised I know not, but that it was so, many then with me, and some of them not unknown to your self, can witness. When I came at Paris, the next year after, I found it printed again, in which edition both the epistles were let out, and a preface, by some papist, put in their place, in which making use of, and wresting some passages in your

[2] Mr. Merryweather returning from his travels in France and Holland, Anno 1649, went to Norwich, to acquaint the Doctor with the different sentiments entertained abroad of the Religio Medici; but he being at that time from home, Mr. Merryweather left a book with a friend, to be presented him the first opportunity, and shortly after writ the following letter from Cambridge.

book, he endeavour'd to shew, that nothing but custom and education kept you from their church. Since my return home, I see Hackius, the Leyden printer, hath made a new impression, which furnished me afresh with some copies, and whereof that which I left with Mr. Preston is one, as is easily observable by the difference of the pages, and the omission of the errata, which were noted in the first, though the title page be the same in both. These frequent impressions shew the worth of the book, which still finds reception and esteem abroad, notwithstanding all that diminution and loss which it suffers by the translation; which I am the willinger to observe, because it found some demurr in the first impression at Leyden; and upon this occasion, one Haye, a book-merchant there, to whom I first offered it, carried it to Salmasius for his approbation, who in state, first laid it by for very nigh a quarter of a year, and then at last told him, that there were indeed in it many things well said, but that it contained also many exorbitant conceptions in religion, and would probably find but frowning entertainment, especially amongst the ministers, which deterred him from undertaking the printing. After I showed it to two more, de Vogel and Christian, both printers; but they, upon advice, returned it also; from these I went to Hackius, who, upon two days deliberation, undertook it. Worthy sir, you see how obstinately bent I was to divulge my own shame and impudence at your expence; yet seeing this confidence was built upon nothing else but the innate and essential worth of the book, which I perswaded myself would bear it up from all adventitious disadvantages, and seeing I have gained rather than failed in the issue and success of my hopes, as it something qualifies the scruples, which the conscience of my own rashness had in cold blood afterward raised, so I hope it will conduce to the easier obtaining pardon and indulgence from you for the miscarriages in it. This, I am sure, I may with a clear mind protest, and profess, that nothing so much moved me to the enterprize as a high and due esteem of the book, and my zeal to the author's merit, of whom I shall be ever ambitious to show my self an admirer, and in all things to give some testimony that I am, honoured sir, your most affectionate, and most devoted servant,   JOHN MERRYWEATHER.

Dr. Browne to John Evelyn, Esq.—Norwich, Jan. 21, 1657-8.

WORTHY SIR,—In obedience unto the commands of my noble friend, Mr. Paston, and the respects I owe unto soe worthy a person as yourself, I have presumed to present these enclosed lines unto you, which I beseech you to accept as hints and proposalls, not any directions unto your judicious thoughts. I have

not taken the chapters in the order printed, butt sett downe
hints upon a few, as memorie prompted and my present diversions would permit; readie to bee your servant further, if your
noble worke bee not alreadie compleated beyond admission of
additionalls : esteeming it no small honour to hold any communication with a person of your merit, unto whom I shall
industriously endeavour to expresse myself.—Sir, your much
honouring friend and servant,   THOMAS BROWNE.

———

John Evelyn, Esq. to Dr. Browne.—Co. Garden, Lond. 28 Jan.
[1657-8.]

HONOURED SIR,—By the mediation of that noble person,
Mr. Paston, and an extraordinary humanity of your owne, I find
I haue made acquisition of such a subsidiary, as nothing but his
greate favour to me, and your communicable nature could haue
procur'd me. It is now, therefore, that I dare promise myselfe
successe in my attempt; and it is certaine that I will very justly
owne your favours with all due acknowledgements, as the most
obliging of all my correspondents. I perceive you haue seene
the *proplasma* and delineation of my designe,[3] which, to avoyde
the infinite copying for some of my curious friends, I was con-
strain'd to print; but it cannot be imagined that I should haue
travell'd over so large a province (though but a garden) as yet,
who set out not many moneths since, and can make it but my
diversions at best, who haue so many other impediments besieg-
ing me, publique and personall, whereoff the long sicknesse of
my *unicus*, my only sonn, now five moneths afflicted with a
double quartan, and but five yeares old, is not one of the least ;
so that there is not danger your additionalls and favours to your
servant should be prevented by the perfection of my worke, or
if it were, that I should be so injurious to my owne fame or
your civility, as not to beginn all anew, that I might take in
such auxiliaries as you send me, and which I must esteeme as
my best and most effectuall forces. Sir, I returne you a thousand acknowledgements for the papers which you transmitted
me, and I will render you this account of my present vnder-
taking. The truth is, that which imported me to discourse on

———

[3] A projected work bearing the title, *Elysium Britannicum*, the plan
of which is given in Upcott's *Miscellaneous Writings of J. Evelyn, Esq.*
This work was intended to comprise forty distinct subjects, or chapters,
disposed in three books. One of the chapters was " *Of the coronary
garden, &c.*," to which Sir Thomas Browne's tract, " *Of garlands, and
coronary or garland plants,*" was intended as a contribution. The work
however, was never completed ; though parts of it remain among the
MSS. at Wotton. One chapter only, " Of Sallets," was published in
1699, under the title, " *Acetaria ; a Discourse of Sallets.*"

this subject after this sorte, was the many defects which I encounter'd in bookes and in gardens, wherein neither words nor cost had bin wanting, but judgement very much; and though I cannot boast of my science in this kind, as both vnbecoming my yeares and my small experience, yet I esteem'd it pardonable at least, if in doing my endeauour to rectifie some mistakes, and advancing so vsefull and innocent a divertisement, I made some essay, and cast in my symbole with the rest. To this designe, if forraine observation may conduce, I might likewise hope to refine upon some particulars, especially concerning the ornaments of gardens, which I shall endeavor so to handle, as that they may become usefull and practicable, as well as magnificent, and that persons of all conditions and faculties, which delight in gardens, may therein encounter something for their owne advantage. The modell, which I perceive you haue seene, will aboundantly testifie my abhorrency of those painted and formal projections of our cockney gardens and plotts, which appeare like gardens of past-board and marchpane, and smell more of paynt then of flowers and verdure : our drift is a noble, princely, and universal Elysium, capable of all the amœnities that can naturally be introduced into gardens of pleasure, and such as may stand in competition with all the august designes and stories of this nature, either of antient or moderne tymes; yet so as to become vsefull and significant to the least pretences and faculties. We will endeauour to shew how the aire and genious of gardens operat vpon humane spirits towards virtue and sanctitie, I meane in a remote, preparatory and instrumentall working. How caues, grotts, mounts, and irregular ornaments of gardens do contribute to contemplatiue and philosophicall enthusiasme; how *elysium, antrum, nemus, paradysus, hortus, lucus,* &c., signifie all of them *rem sacram et divinam;* for these expedients do influence the soule and spirits of man, and prepare them for converse with good angells; besides which, they contribute to the lesse abstracted pleasures, phylosophy naturall and longevitie: and I would have not onely the elogies and effigie of the antient and famous garden heroes, but a society of the *paradisi cultores,* persons of antient simplicity, Paradisean and Hortulan saints, to be a society of learned and ingenuous men, such as Dr. Browne, by whome we might hope to redeeme the tyme that has bin lost, in pursuing *Vulgar Errours,* and still propagating them, as so many bold men do yet presume to do. Were it to be hoped, *inter hos armorum strepitus,* and in so generall a catalysis of integrity, interruption of peace and propriety, the hortulane pleasure, these innocent, pure, and vsefull diversions might enjoy the least encouragement, whilst brutish and ambitious persons seeke themselues in the ruines of our miserable yet dearest country, *quis talia fando*—?—But, sir, I will not importune you with these matters, nor shall they be able to make me to desist from my designe, so long as you reanimate my languishings, and pardon my imperfections. I greately thanke you for your discourses, and the acoustic diagramme, &c. I shall be a faithfull reporter of your favours to me. In my philosophico-medicall garden you can impart to me extraordinary assistances, as likewise in my coronary chapter, and that of transmutations c. i. lib. 3. Norwich is a place, I understand, which is very much addicted to the flowry part; and what indeede may I not promise myselfe from your ingenuity, science, and candor? And now to shew you how farr I am aduanced in my worke, though I haue drawne it in loose sheetes, almost euery chapter rudely, yet I cannot say to haue finished anything tollerably farther than chapter xi. lib. 2, and those which are so completed are yet so written that I can at pleasure inserte whatsoeuver shall come to hand to obelize, correct, improve, and adorne it. That chapt. of the history of gardens being the 7th of the last booke, is in a manner finished by itselfe, and, if it be not ouer tedious, I thinke it will extreamely gratifie the reader : for I do comprehend them as vniversally as the chapter will beare it, and yet am as particular in the descriptions as is possible, because I not onely pretend them for pompous and ostentatiue examples, but would render them usefull to our trauellers which shall goe abroad, and where I haue obscrued so many particularities as, happly, others descend not to. If you permitt me to transcribe you an imperfect summ of the heads, it is to let you see how farr we correspond (as by your excellent papers I collect) and to engage your assistance in suppliing my omissions ; you will pardon the defects in the synchronismes, because they are not yet exactly marshalled, and of my desultory scribbling.

CHAP. VII. LIB. III.

Paradise, Elysian fields, Hesperides, Horti Adonidis, Alcinoi, Semyramis, Salomon's. The pensile gardens in Babylon, of Nabucodonosor, of Cyrus, the gardens of Panchaia, the Sabean in Arabia Felix. The Egyptian gardens out of Athenæus, the Villa Laura neere Alexandria, the gardens of Adominus, the garden at Samos, Democritus's garden, Epicurus's at Athens, *hortorum ille magister*, as Pliny calls him. That of Nysa described by Diodorus Siculus ; Masinissa's, Lysander's, the garden of Laërtes, father of Ulysses, ex Homero. Theophrastus's, Mithridates' gardens : Alexandrus's garden at Sydon, Hieron's Nautilus gardens out of Athenæus ; the Indian king's garden out of Ælian ; and many others, which are in my scattered adversaria, not yet inserted into this chapter.

Amongst the ancient Romans.—Numa's garden, Tarquin's, Scipio Africanus's, Antoninus Pius's, Dioclesian's, Mæcenas's, Martial's gardens ;

the Tarentine garden, Cicero's garden at Tusculum, Formia, Cuma ; the
Laurentine garden of Pliny junior, Cato, at Sabinus, Ælius Spartianus's
garden, the elder Gordian's, Horti Cassipedis, Drusi, Dolabella's garden,
Galienus's, Seneca's, Nero's, the Horti Lamiani, Agrippina's, the Esquiline, Pompey's, Luculla's most costly gardens, &c.

More moderne and ̨at present.—Clement the 8th's garden; the Medicean,
Mathæos garden, Cardinal Pio's ; Farnesian, Lodovisian, Burghesean,
Aldobrandino's, Barberini's, the Belvedere, Montalta's, Bossius's, Jus-
tiniane's, the Quirinal gardens, Cornelius's, Mazarini's, &c.

In other parts of Italy.—Ulmarini's at Vacenza, Count Giusti's at
Verona, Mondragone, Frescati, D'Este's at Tivoli. The gardens of the
Palazzo de Pitti in Florence ; Poggio, Imperiale, Pratoline, Hieronymo
del Negro's pensile garden in Genoa, principe d'Oria's garden, the Mar-
quesi Devico's at Naples, the old gardens at Baiæ, Fred. Duke of
Urbine's garden, the gardens at Pisa, at Padoa, at Capraroula, at St.
Michael in Bosco, in Bolognia ;. the gardens about Lago di Como, Sig-
nior Sfondrati's, &c.

In Spaine.—The incomparable garden of Aranxues, Garicius's garden
at Toledo, &c.

In France.—Duke of Orleans at Paris, Luxemburg, Thuilleries,
Palais Cardinal, Bellevue, Morines, Jard. Royal, &c.

In other parts of France.—The gardens of Froment, of Fontaine
Beleau, of the Chasteau de Fresnes, Ruel, Richelieu, Couranat, Cauigny,
Hubert, Depont in Champagne, the most sumptuous Rincy, Nanteuile,
Maisons, Medon, Dampien, St. Germain en Lay, Rosny, St. Cloe, Lian-
court in Picardy, Isslings at Essonne, Pidaux in Poictiers. At Anet,
Valeri, Folembourg, Villiers, Gaillon, Montpellier, Beugensor, of Mons.
Piereskius. In Loraine, at Nancy, the Jesuites at Liege, and many
others.

In Flanders.—The gardens of the Hofft in Bruxelles, Oroenendael's
neere it, Risewick in Holland. The court at the Hague, the garden at
Leyden, Pretor Hundius's garden at Amsterdam.

In Germany.—The Emperor's garden at Vienna, at Salisburgh ; the
medicinall at Heidelburg, Caterus's at Basil, Camerarius's garden of
Horimburg, Scholtzius's at Vratislauia, at Bonne neere Collen, the
elector's there : Christina's garden in Sweden made lately by Mollet ;
the garden at Cracovia, Warsovia, Grogning. The elector's garden at
Heidelburg, Tico Brache's rare gardens at Vraneburge, the garden at
Copenhagen. Tho. Duke of Holstein's garden, &c.

In Turkey, the East, and other parts.—The grand Signor's in the Ser-
raglio, the garden at Tunis, and old Carthage ; the garden at Cairo, at
Fez, the pensal garden at Pequin in China, also at Timplan and Poras-
sen ; St. Thomas's garden in the island neere M. Hecla, perpetually
verdant. In Persia, the garden at Ispahan ; the garden of Tzurbugh ;
the Chan's garden in Schamachie neere the Caspian sea, of Ardebil, and
the citty of Cassuin or Arsacia ; the garden lately made at Suratt in the
East Indies by the great Mogoll's daughter, &c.

In America—Montezuma's floating garden, and others in Mexico.
The King of Azcapuzulco's, the garden of Cusco ; the garden in Nova
Hispania. Count Maurice's rare garden at Boavesta in Brasile.

In England.—Wilton, Dodington, Spensherst, Sion, Hatfield, Lord
Brook's, Oxford, Kirby, Howard's, Durden's, my elder brother George
Evelyn's in Surry, far surpassing any else in England, it may be my
owne poore garden may for its kind, perpetually greene, not be vnworthy
mentioning.

The gardens mentioned in Scripture, &c.

Miraculous and extraordinary gardens found upon huge fishes' backs
men over growne with flowers, &c.

Romantique and poeticall gardens out of Sydney, Spencer, Achilles
Statius, Homer, Poliphele, &c.   All these I have already described,
some briefly, some at large according to their dignity and merite.

But this paper, and my reverence to your great patience,
mindes me of a conclusion.—Worthy sir, I am your most
humble and most obliged servant,   J. EUELYN.

Sir, I beg the fauour of you when you see Mr. Paston to
make my seruice acceptable, and to let him knowe how greately
I thinke my selfe obliged to him for this civillity.

I make bold to send you another paper of the chapters,
because I have there added another chapter concerning Hortulan
entertainments ; and I intend another for wonderfull plants, &c.

If you thinke me worthy of the continuance of these fauours
to your servant, your letters will infallibly find me by this
addresse :—" For Mr. Iohn Euelyn, at the Hauk and Feasant
on Ludgate Hill, London."

Dr. Browne to John Evelyn, Esq.[4]

WORTHY SIR,—Some weekes past I made bold to send you a
letter with an enclosed paper concerning garlands and coronarie
plants, which I hope you have received, having directed it unto
the Hawke and Pheasant, on Ludgate-hill.   If you think fit to
make use of such a catalogue as I sent therewith, I could add
unto it.   However for *Moly flore luteo,* you may please to put
in *Moly Hondianum novum.*   I now present unto you a small
paper which should have been attended with a catalogue of
plants, wherein experiments might bee attempted by insition
and wayes of propagation ; but probably you may be provided
in that kind.   Yet I have not met with any of that nature and
particulars, this extending beyond garden plants unto all wild
trees among us.   This, if you please, you may command within
very few dayes, or any thing in the power of, sir, your honoring
friend and servant,   THOMAS BROWNE.

I pray my humble service unto Sir Robert Paston when you
see him, which you may now at pleasure, he being of the House,
and an highly deserving and loyall member of it.

---

⁴ Indorsed by Evelyn " Dr. Browne from Norwich."

The gardens upon great fishes I would not tearme miraculous gardens, but rather extraordinarie and anomalous gardens, or the like.

Mr. Dugdale to Dr. Browne.—Blyth-hall, near Colhill, in Warwickshire, 4th Oct. 1658.

HONOURED SIR,—By your letter, dated 27th September (which came to my hands about two days since) I see how much I am obliged to you for your readinesse to take into consideration those things which I desired by the note sent to Mr. Watts; so that I could not omitt, but by this first opportunity, to returne you my hearty thanks for the favour. I resolve, God willing, to be in London about the beginning of the next terme, and by Mr. Watts (my kind friend) will send you some of the bones of that fishe which my note mentioneth.

Certainly, sir, the gaining Marshland, in Norfolk, and Holland, in Lincolnshire, was a worke very antient, as by many circumstances may be gathered; and therefore considering the industry and skill of the Romans, I conceive it most like to have been performed by them. Mr. Cambden, in his Britannia, speaking of the Romans in Britaine, hath an observation out of Tacitus in the life of Agricola; which Dr. Holland (who translated Cambden) delivers thus: viz. that the Romans wore out and consumed the bodies and hands of the Britans, in clearing of woods, and paving of fens. But the words of Tacitus are, *paludibus emuniendis*, of which I desire your opinion; I meane, whether the word *emuniendis* do not meane walling or banking.

Sir, I account my selfe much happy to be thus far known to you as I am, and that you are pleased to thinke me worthy to converse with you in this manner, which I shall make bold still to do upon any good occasion, till I be more happy by a personall knowledge of you, as I hope in good time I may, resting your very humble servant and honourer,   WM. DUGDALE.

Mr. Dugdale to Dr. Browne.—From my chamber, at the Herauld's Office in London, 9th Nov. 1658.

HONOURED SIR,—Yours of October 27th, with that learned discourse inclosed, came safe to my hands the last weeke, for which I return you my most hearty thanks, being highly satisfyed therewith. Since the receipt thereof, I have spoke with Mr. Jonas Moore (the chiefe surveyor of this great worke of drayning in Cambridgeshire and the counties adjacent) who tells me that the causey I formerly mentioned is sixty foote broad in all places where they have cutt through it, and about eighteen inches thickness of gravell, lying upon the moore, and now in many places three foote deepe under a new accession of moore.

It seemes I mistook when I signifyed to you that Mr. Ashmole had some Romane coynes, which were found in the fens; for he now tells me that he hath nothing as yet, but that urne which Jonas Moore gave him; but my Lord St. John had divers, as he tells me, which are lost, or mislayed.

Jonas Moore now tells me, that very lately, in digging a piece of ground which lyes within the precincts of Soham (about three or four miles from Ely), the diggers found seven or eight urnes, which by carelessnesse were broken in pieces, but no coyne in or near them. The ground is about six acres, and in the nature of an island in the fenne, but no raysed heap of earth to cover them, as he tells me. I resolve to intreat Mr. Chichley (my very good friend), who is owner thereof, to cause some further digging there; for they are of opinion that there are many more of that kind; and then I shall be able to satisfy you better, and what is found in them. Sir Thomas Cotton is not as yet come up to London, otherwise I would have sent you some of those bones of the fishe, which I will be sure to do so soon as he comes.

Mr. Ashmole presents his service to you, with great thanks for your kinde offer, desiring a note of what manuscripts you have that may be for his purpose, whereupon he will let you know whether he wants them or not; for he hath others than what he hath formerly made use of. I hope I shall obtain so much favour of the adventurers, as to procure one of those large heaps of earth to be cut through, to the end that we may see whether any urnes or other things of note are covered therewith.

Sir, this favour which you are pleased to afford me, thus to trouble you with these things, I highly value, and shall rest at your commands wherein I may serve you,

WILLIAM DUGDALE.

Dr. Brown to Mr. Dugdale.—Norwich, Nov. 10th, 1658.

SIR,—Your observation is singular, and querie very ingenious, concerning the expression of Tacitus in the life of Agricola, upon the complaint of the Britans, that the Romans consumed and wore out their bodyes and hands, *sylvis et paludibus emuniendis,* that is, whether thereby walling or bancking the fennes is not to bee understood according to the signification of the word *emunire.*

This, indeed, is the common and received signification, as probably derived from the old word *mœnire,* that is, *mœnibus cingere,* to wall, fence, or fortifie by enclosure, according to the same acception in warlike munitions and entrenchments.

But in this expression strictly to make out the language of the author, a sense is to be found agreeable unto woods as well as fennes and marshes ; the word *emuniendis* relating unto both, which will butt harshly be expressed by any one word in our language, and might cause such different and subexpositive translations.

And this may be made out from the large signification of the word *munire*, which is sometimes taken not only to wall, fence, or enclose, butt also to laye open, and render fitt for passage. Soe is that of Livie expounded by learned men, when, in the passage of Hannibal over the Alpes, he sayth, *rupem muniendam curavit*, that is, he opened a passage through the rock ; and least the word should bee thought rather to be read *minuendam*, a fewe lines after, the word is used agayne ; *et quies muniendo fessis hominibus triduo data.*

And upon the same subject the like expressions are to bee founde in the Latin translation of Polybius, sett forth by Casaubon, *labore improbo in ipso principitio viam munivit.* And for the gettinge downe of his caryages and elephants from the hills covered with ice and snowe, it is afterwards sayd, *Numidus ad viam muniendam per vices admovet vixque tertio demum die elephantos trajecit,* which cannot well be understood by raysing any banks and walls, butt by removing the snowe, planing the wayes, and making it passable for them.

Which exposition is received by Godelevæus upon Livie, and also the learned Turnebus, *Adversariorum*, lib. xiii. " Interpretor autem munire, per rupem viam aperire eamque in ea munire et tanquam struere, eam cædere et opere laboreque militari complanare, et æquare iter aut deorsum deprimere et declive reddere quodam anfractu molli. Itaque qui aggerem jaciunt, fossas aperiunt, vias muniunt, militiæ munitores vocantur."

And therefore when Dr. Holland translated this passage in Cambden out of Tacitus, by cleering of woods and paving the fennes, hee may be made out by this acception of *munire*, extending unto fennes and woods, and comprehending all pyoners work about them. As likewise Sir Henry Savile, when hee rendreth it by paving of bogges and woods ; and as *viam munire* is also taken in Livie, that is, *lapidibus sternere.*

And your owne acception may also bee admitted, of walling and banking the fennes, which the word will also well beare in relation to *paludibus*, beside the other signification of causies, wayes, and passages, common unto woods and fennes ; nor only the clearing of woods and making of passages, butt all kind of pyoning and slavish labour might bee understood in this speech of Galgacus which with stripes and indignities was imposed upon the Britans in workes about woods, bogges, and fennes ; and soe comprehend the laborious aggers, banks, and workes of secure-

ment against floods and inundations, wherein they were imployed by the Romans, a careful and provident people, omitting
noe waye to secure or improve their dominions and lands, lost
by carelesse ignorance in the disadvantages of sea and waters,
and which they were first to effect, before they could well
establish their causies over the marshes.

And so the translation in two words may be tolerably made
by one. By clearing the woods and fennes, that is, the woods
by making them passible, by rendering them open and lesse fit
for retreat or concealment of the Britans ; and by clearing
the fennes either for passage or improvement, and soe comprehending cawsing, paving, drayning, trenching, fencing, and embanking agaynst thieves or sea-floods.—I remain, sir, yours, &c.

THOMAS BROWNE.

Mr. Dugdale to Dr. Browne.—London, 17th Nov. 1658.

HONOURED SIR,—Yours of the 10th instant came safe to my
hands, with that learned discourse inclosed, concerning the word
emunire, wherein I perceive your sense is the same with my
good friends Mr. Bishe and Mr. Junius (with both whome I have
also consulted about it). I have herewithall sent you one of
the bones of that fish, which was taken up by Sir Robert
Cotton, in digging a pond at the skirt of Conington Downe,
desiring your opinion thereof and of what magnitude you think
it was.

Mr. Ashmole presents his best service and thanks to you, for
your kinde intention to send him a list of those books you have,
which may be for his use.

That which you were told of my writing any thing of Norfolke was a meere story ; for I never had any such thing in my
thoughts, nor can I expect a life to accomplish it, if I should ;
or any encouragement considerable to the chardge and paynes
of such an undertaking. This I mean as to the county, and not
my Fenne History, which will extend thereinto. And as for
Mr. Bishe, who is a greate admirer and honourer of you, and
desires me to present his hearty service and thanks to you for
that mention you have made of him in your learned discourse
of Urnes. He says he hath no such purpose at all, nor ever
had ; but that his brother-in-law Mr. Godard (the recorder of
Lynne) intends something of that towne, but whether or when
to make it publique he knows not.

And now, sir, that you have been pleas'd to give me leave to
be thus bold with you in interrupting your better studies, I
shall crave leave to make a request or two more to you. First,
that you will let me know where in Leland you finde that expression concerning such buriall of the Saxons, as you mention

in your former discourse concerning those raysed heaps of earth, which you lately sent me; for all that I have seene extant of his in manuscript, is those volumes of his *Collectanea* and *Itineraryes*, now in the Bodleyan Library at Oxford, of which I have exact copies in the country.

The next is, to entreat you to speake with one Mr. Haward (heir and executor to Mr. Haward lately deceased, who was an executor to Mr. Selden) who now lives in Norwich, as I am told, and was a sheriffe of that city the last yeare: and to desire a letter from him to Sir John Trevor, speedily to joyne with Justice Hales and the rest of Mr. Selden's executors, in opening the library in White Friars', for the sight of a manuscript of Landaffe, which may be usefull to mee in those additions I intend to the second volume of the Monasticon, now in the presse; for Sir John Trevor tells me, that he cannot without expresse order from him, do it: the rest of the executors of Mr. Selden being very desirous to pleasure me therein. If you can get such a letter from him for Sir John Trevor, I pray you enclose it to me, and I will deliver it, for their are 3 keys besides.

And lastly, if at your leisure, through your vast reading, you can point me out what authors do speake of those improvements which have been made by banking and drayning in Italy, France, or any part of the Netherlands, you will do me a very high favour.

From Strabo and Herodotus I have what they say of Ægypt, and so likewise what is sayd by Natalis Comes of Acarnania: but take your owne time for it, if at all you can attend it, whereby you will more oblige your most humble servant and honourer,   WILLIAM DUGDALE.

Dr. Browne to Mr. Dugdale.[5] *Norwich, Dec. 6, 1658.*

WORTHY SIR,—I make noe doubt you have receaued Mr. Howard's letter unto Sir John Trevor. Hee will be readie to doe you any seruice in that kind. I am glad your second booke of the Monasticon is at last in the presse. Here is in this citty a conuent of Black Friers, which is more entire than any in these parts of England. Mr. King took the draught[6] of it when he was in Norwich, and Sir Thomas Pettus, Baronet, desired to have his name sett vnto it. I conceive it were not fitt in so generall a tract to omit it, though little can be sayd of it, only

[5] Not in Hamper's Correspondence of Dugdale.—This letter bears the indorse in Dugdale's hand-writing—" Dec. 6, 1658, Dr. Browne's letter (not yet answered)."

[6] Qre : to ask the Docter whether ever he saw this draught.—*MS. marginal Note by Dugdale in the Original.*

coniectur'd that it was founded by Sir John of Orpingham, or
Erpingham, whose coat is all about the church and *six-corner'd
steeple*. I receaued the bone of the fish, and shall giue you some
account of it when I have compared it with another bone which
is not by mee. As for *Lelandus*, his works are soe rare, that
few private hands are masters of them, though hee left not a
fewe; and therefore, that quotation of myne was at second hand.
You may find it in Mr. Inego Jones' description of *Stonehenge*,
page 27; having litle doubt of the truth of his quotation, because
in that place hee hath the Latine and English, with a particular
commendation of the author and the tract quoted in the margin,
and in the same author, quoted p. 16, the page is also mentioned;
butt the title is short and obscure, and therefore I omitted it.
Leylande Assert. Art. which being compared with the subject of
page 25, may perhaps bee *De Assertione Arthuri*, which is not
mentioned in the catalogue of his many workes,[7] except it bee
some head or chapter in his *Antiq. Britannicis* or *de Viris
illustribus*. I am much satisfied in the truth thereof, because
Camden hath expressions of the like sense in diuers places; and,
as I think in Northamptonshire, and probably from Lelandus:
for Lambert in his perambulation of Kent, speakes but some
times of Lalandus, and then quoteth not his words, though it is
probable hee was much beholden unto him having left a worke
of his subject *Itinerarium Cantii*.

Sir, having some leasure last weeke, which is uncertaine with
mee, I intended this day to send you some answer to your last
querie of banking and draining by some instances and examples in the four parts of the earth, and some short account of
the cawsie, butt diuersions into the country will make me defer
it until Friday next, soe that you may receive it on Mondaye.—
Sir, I rest your very well-wishing friend and servant,

THOMAS BROWNE.

Mr. Dugdale to Dr. Browne.—London, 24 *Feb.* 1658.

HONOURED SIR,—Being now (through God's goodnesse) so wel
recovered from my late sicknesse, as that I do looke upon my
bookes and papers againe, though I have not as yet adventured
abroad, in respect of the cold, I do againe salute you, giving you
great thanks for your continued mindfulnesse of me, as appears
by that excellent note which I yester a   received from you,
touching the drayning made of late dyŷars by the Duke of
Holstein, it being so pertinent to my business. My thanks
for what you sent me from your learned observations touching

[7] Assertio Inclytiss. Arturi, &c. 4to. 1540, 1544. Translated by R.
Robinson, 4to. 1582. Published by Hearne, 8vo. Oxford, 1715.

the banking and drayning in other forreign parts, I desired my good friend Mr. Ashmole to present to you, when I was not able to write my self; which I presume he did do.

And being thus emboldened by these your favours, I shall here acquaint you with my conceipt touching this spacious tract in forme of a sinus or bay, which we call the great levell of the fenns, extending from Linne, beyond Waynflete in Lincolnshire, in length; and in breadth, into some parts of the counties of Norfolk, Suffolk, Cambridge, Northampton, Huntington, and Lincoln, intreating your opinion therein. That it was at first firme land, the sea having no recourse into it, I am induced to believe, when I consider the multitude of trees, viz. firre, oake, and of other kindes, that are found in those draynes and diggings which have of late years been made there; nay, some with their rootes standing in the ground below the moore, having been cut off about two foote above the ground, as I guesse; which I my selfe saw at Thorney, they having been dig'd up in that fen. And Mr. Godard (the recorder of Linne) assures me, that lately in Marshland, about a mile off Magdalene bridge, at 17 foot deepe (upon occasion of letting down of a sluce), were found below the silt (for of that nature is all Marshland and Holland) in the very firme earth, furr-bushes as they grew, not rotted; and nut-trees with nuts not perisht; neither of which kind of bushes or trees are now growing upon that silthy soil of Marshland, though it be fruitfull and rich for other vegetables. The like firr-trees and other timber is found in great abundance in Hatfield level, in the Isle of Axholme, where I am assured from ocular testimony, that they find the rootes of many firr-trees as they stand in the soyle, where they grew, below the moore, with the bodyes of the trees lying by them, not cut off with an axe or such like thing, but burnt, the coall appearing upon the ends where they were so burnt asunder: therefore when, or on what occasion it was that the sea flowed over all this, as appears by that silt at the skirt of Conington Downe, wherein the bones of that fish were found whereof you have one, is a thing that I know not what to say to, desiring your opinion thereof.

I shall now tell you how I do conclude that it became a fen, by the stagnation of the fresh waters; which is thus, viz. that the sea having its passage upon the ebbs and flows thereof, along by the coast of Norfolke to the coast of Lincolnshire, did in time, by reason of its muddinesse, leave a shelfe or silt, betwixt those two points of land, viz. Rising in Norfolke, and the country about Spilsby in Lincolnshire, which shelfe increasing in height and length so much, as that the ordinary tides did not overflow it, was by that check of those fluxes, in time, so much augmented in breadth, that the Romans finding it considerable for the fertility of the soyle (being a people of great ingenuity and industry) made the first sea-banks for its preservation from the spring tides, which might otherwise overflow it. And now, sir, by this settling of the silt the soyle of Marshland and Holland had their first beginning; by the like excesse of silt brought into the mouths of these rivers which had their out-falls at Linne, Wisbiche, and Boston, where the fresh waters so stop'd, as that the ordinary land-floods being not of force enough to grinde it out (as the term is) all the levell behind became overflowed; and as an ordinary pond gathered mud, so did this do moore which in time hath increased to such a thicknesse that since the Podike was made to keep up the fresh water from drowning of Marshland on the other side, and the bank called South Ea Bank, for the preservation of Holland from the like inundation, the levell of the fen is become 4 foot higher than the levell of Marshland, as Mr. Vermuden assures me, upon view and observation thereof. And this, under correction of your better judgment, whereunto I shall much submit, do I take to be the originall occasion of Marshland and Holland, and likewise of the fens.

But that which puzles me most is the sea coming up to Conington Downe; as I have sayd therefore, perhaps by your great reading and philosophicall learning you may shew me some probable occasion thereof. That the sea hath upon those coasts of England, towards the North-west, much altered its course as to the height of its fluxes and refluxes, is most apparent from those vast banks nere Wisbiche, which you shall observe to be about 10 foot in height from the now levell earth, which levell is now no lesse in full height than 10 foot, as I am assured, from the ordinary levell of the sea, as it rises at the present.

I shall be able to shew about what time it was that the passage at Wisbiche was so silted up, as that the outfall of the great river Ouse, which was there, became altered, and was diverted to Linne, where before that time the river was not so large; it being in King Henry III.'s time, as my testimonyes from records do manifest. And I finde in King Edward III.'s time, that upon the river Humber the tides flowed 4 foot higher than before they did, as the commission for raysing the banks upon the sides of that streame, as also of the great causey betwixt Anlaby and Hull, doth testify.

Having now sufficiently wearied you, I am sure, for which I heartily desire your pardon, I shall leave you to your own time for considering of these things, and vouchsafing your opinion therein, resting your most humble servant and honourer,

WILLIAM DUGDALE.

Mr. Dugdale to Dr. Browne.—London, 29 Nov. 1659.

HONOURED SIR,—Yours of the 17th instant came to my hands about 4 days since, with those inclosed judicious and learned observations, for which I returne you my hearty thanks.

Since I wrote to you for your opinion touching the various course of the sea, I met with some notable instances of that kinde in a late author, viz. Olivarius Uredius, in his history of Flanders; which he manifesteth to be occasioned from earthquakes.

I have a great desire that you should see my copy, before I put it to the presse. It is now in the hands of the late chief justice St. John, who desired the perusall of it. In Easter term I resolve (God willing) to be again in London; for I am now going into Warwickshire; and then if you be not here, I will endeavour to contrive some safe way for conveying my papers to you: resting your most obliged servant and honourer,

WILLIAM DUGDALE.

Mr. Dugdale to Dr. Browne.[3]*—From the Herald's Office, in London, 5th April,* 1662.

HONOURED SIR,—Having at length accomplisht that worke, whereunto you have been pleased to favour me with so considerable assistance, and whereof, in page 175, I have made some brief mention, I here present you with a copye thereof. Some other things I have in hand of my owne, which (God sparing me life and health) will ere long be ready for the presse. But at present, at the desire of my lord chancelour, and some other eminent persons, I am taken up much with the ordering of Sir Henry Spelman's works for the presse, viz. that part of his Glossary long since printed, with corrections and additions, as he left it under his own hand; and the other part of it to the end of the alphabet: and of his second volum of the Councells, which will reach from the Norman Conquest to the abolishing of the pope's supremacy here. There are many things, which I shall from my own collections add to these workes, from records of great credit; for without such authorities I will not presume to meddle. If in any old manuscripts, which have or may come to your view, you can contribute to these works, I know it will be very acceptable. Sir, if your occasions should bring you to London, I should thinke myself happy to wayt on you.—Resting ever your most obliged servant and honourer,

WILLIAM DUGDALE.

[3] This letter is not in Hamper's Correspondence of Dugdale.

[*The letters between Sir Thomas Browne and Dr. Merritt relate chiefly to the Natural History of Norfolk.*]

Dr. Browne to Dr. Merritt.—July 13, 1668.

MOST HONORED SIR,—I take the boldness to salute you as a person of singular worth and learning, and whom I very much respect and honour. I presented my service to you by my son some months past; and had thought before this time to have done it by him again. But the time of his return to London being yet uncertain, I would not defer those at present unto you. I should be very glad to serve you by any observations of mine against the second edition of your Pinax, which I cannot sufficiently commend. I have observed and taken notice of many animals in these parts, whereof three years ago a learned gentleman of this country desired me to give him some account, which, while I was doing, the gentleman, my good friend, died. I shall only at this time present and name some few unto you, which I found not in your catalogue. A *Trachurus*, which yearly cometh before or in the head of the herrings, called therefore a horse. *Stella marina testacea*, which I have often found upon the sea-shore. An *Astacus marinus pediculi marini facie*, which is sometimes taken with the lobsters at Cromer, in Norfolk. A *Pungitius marinus*, whereof I have known many taken among weeds by fishers, who drag by the sea-shore on this coast. A *Scarabæus Capricornus odoratus*, which I take to be mentioned by Moufetus, fol. 150. "I have taken some abroad; one in my cellar, which I now send;" he saith, "*Nucem moschatam et cinnamomum vere spirat.*" To me it smelt like roses, santalum, and ambergris. I have thrice met with *Mergus maximus Farensis Clusii;* and have a draught thereof. They were taken about the time of herring-fishing at Yarmouth. One was taken upon the shore, not able to fly away, about ten years ago. I sent one to Dr. Scarborough. Twice I met with a *Skua Hoyeri*, the draught whereof I also have. One was shot in a marsh, which I gave unto a gentleman, which I can send you. Another was killed feeding upon a dead horse near a marsh ground. Perusing your catalogue of plants, upon *Acorus verus*, I find these words :—"found by Dr. Brown neer Lynn:" —wherein probably there may be some mistake; for I cannot affirm, nor I doubt any other, that it is found thereabout. About 25 years ago, I gave an account of this plant unto Mr. Goodyeere, and more lately to Dr. How, unto whom I sent some notes, and a box full of the fresh *juli*. This elegant plant groweth very plentifully, and leaveth its julus yearly by the banks of Norwich river, chiefly about Claxton and Surlingham; and also between Norwich and Hellsden-bridge; so that I have known Heigham church, in the suburbs of Norwich, strewed all over with it. It has been transplanted, and set on the sides of marsh ponds in several places of the country, where it thrives and beareth the julus yearly.

Sesamoides salamanticum magnum;—why you omit *Sesamoides salamantium parvum?* This groweth not far from Thetford and Brandon, and plentiful in neighbour places, where I found it, and have it in my *hortus hyemalis*, answering the description in Gerard.

Urtica romana, which groweth with button seed bags, is not in the catalogue. I have found it to grow wild at Golston by Yarmouth, and transplanted it to other places.

Dr. Browne to Dr. Merritt.—Aug. 18, 1668.

HONORED SIR,—I received your courteous letter, and am sorry some diversions have so long delayed this my second unto you. You are very exact in the account of the *fungi.* I have met with two, which I have not found in any author; of which I have sent you a rude draught inclosed. The first, an elegant *fungus ligneus,* found in a hollow sallow. I have one of them by me, but, without a very good opportunity, dare not send it, fearing it should be broken. Unto some it seemed to resemble some noble or princely ornament of the head, and so might be called *fungus regius ;* unto others, a turret, top of a cupola, or lantern of a building; and so might be named *fungus pterygoides, pinnacularis,* or *lanterniformis.* You may name it as you please. The second, *fungus ligneus teres antliarum,* or *fungus ligularis longissimus,* consisting or made of many woody strings, about the bigness of round points or laces; some above half a yard long, shooting in a bushy form from the trees, which serve under ground for pumps. I have observed divers, especially in Norwich, where wells are sunk deep for pumps.

The *fungus phalloides* I found not far from Norwich, large and very fetid, answering the description of Hadrianus Junius. I have a part of one dried still by me.

Fungus rotundus major I have found about ten inches in diameter, and [have] half a one dried by me.

Another small paper contains the side draughts of *fibulæ marinæ pellucidæ,* or sea buttons, a kind of squalder; and referring to *urtica marina,* which I have observed in great numbers by Yarmouth, after a flood and easterly winds. They resemble the pure crystal buttons, chamfered or welted on the sides, with two small holes at the ends. They cannot be sent; for the included water, or thin jelly, soon runneth from them.

Urtica marina minor Johnstoni, I have often found on this coast. *Physsalus* I have found also. I have one dried, but it hath lost its shape and colour.

Galei and *caniculæ* are often found. I have a fish hanging up in my yard, of two yards long, taken among the herrings at Yarmouth, which is the *canis carcharius alius Johnstoni*, table vi. fig. 6.

Lupus marinus, you mention, upon a handsome experiment, but I find it not in the catalogue. This *lupus marinus* or *lycostomus*, is often taken by our seamen which fish for cod. I have had divers brought me. They hang up in many houses in Yarmouth.

Trutta marina is taken with us. A better dish than the river trout, but of the same bigness.

Loligo sepia, a cuttle; page 191 of your Pinax. I conceive, worthy sir, it were best to put them in two distinct lines, as distinct species of the molles.

The *loligo, calamare*, or *sleve*, I have also found cast upon the sea-shore; and some have been brought me by fishermen, of about twenty pounds weight.

Among the fishes of our Norwich river, we scarce reckon salmon,[9] yet some are yearly taken; but all taken in the river or on the coast have the end of the lower jaw very much hooked, which enters a great way into the upper jaw, like a socket. You may find the same, though not in figure, if you please to read Johnston's folio, 101. I am not satisfied with the conceit of some authors, that there is a difference of male and female; for all ours are thus formed. The fish is thicker than ordinary salmon, and very much and more largely spotted. Whether not rather *Boccard gallorus*, or *Anchorago Scaligeri*. I have both draughts, and the head of one dried; either of which you may command. *Scyllarus*, or *cancellus in turbine*, it is probable you have. Have you *cancellus in nerite*, a small testaceous found upon this coast? Have you *mullus ruber asper?*—*Piscis octangularis Bivormii?*—*Vermes marini*, larger than earth-worms, digged out of the sea-sand, about two feet deep, and at an ebb water, for bait?[1] They are discovered by a little hole or sinking of the sand at the top about them.

Have you that handsome coloured jay, answering the description of *garrulus argentoratensis*, and may be called the

[9] In June, 1827, I knew of two salmon-trout in our Overstrand mackarel nets.—*G.*

[1] Bait for codling.—*G.*

parrot-jay? I have one that was killed upon a tree about five years ago.[2]

Have you a May chit, a small dark grey bird, about the bigness of a stint, which cometh about May, and stayeth but a month; a bird of exceeding fatness, and accounted a dainty dish? They are plentifully taken in Marshland, and about Wisbeech.

Have you a *caprimulgus*, or dorhawk;[3] a bird as a pigeon, with a wide throat bill, as little as a titmouse, white feathers in the tail, and paned like a hawk?

Succinum rarò occurrit, p. 219 of yours. Not so rarely on the coast of Norfolk.[4] It is usually found in small pieces; sometimes in pieces of a pound weight. I have one by me, fat and tare, of ten ounces weight; yet more often I have found it in handsome pieces of twelve ounces in weight.

Dr. Browne to Dr. Merritt.—Sept. 13, [1668.]

SIR,—I received your courteous letter; and with all respects I now again salute you.

The *mola piscis* is almost yearly taken on our coast. This last year one was taken of about two hundred pounds weight. Divers of them I have opened; and have found many lice sticking close unto their gills, whereof I send you some.

In your Pinax I find *onocrotalus*, or pelican; whether you mean those at St. James's, or others brought over, or such as have been taken or killed here, I know not. I have one hung up in my house, which was shot in a fen ten miles off, about four years ago; and because it was so rare, some conjectured it might be one of those which belonged unto the king, and flew away.

Ciconia[5], *rarò huc advolat*. I have seen two in a watery marsh eight miles off; another shot, whose case is yet to be seen.

Vitulus marinus. In tractibus borealibus et Scotia. No rarity upon the coast of Norfolk.[6] At low water I have known them taken asleep under the cliffs. Divers have been brought to me. Our seal is different from the Mediterranean seal; as having a rounder head, a shorter and stronger body.

---

[2] The Garrulous Roller.

[3] Not uncommon; I had a young one brought me a few years ago.—*G.*

[4] It is becoming scarce at Cromer. The fat amber most commonly occurs.—*G.*

[5] The Stork.

[6] Very rarely seen at Cromer. I think they are met with on sandbanks near Hunstanton.—*G.*

Rana piscatrix.[7] I have often known taken on our coast; and some very large.

Xiphias or *gladius piscis*, or sword-fish, we have in our seas. I have the head of one which was taken not long ago entangled in the herring-nets. The sword about two feet in length.

Among the whales you may very well put in the *spermacetus*, or that remarkably peculiar whale which so aboundeth in spermaceti. About twelve years ago we had one cast up on our shore near Wells, which I described in a peculiar chapter in the last edition of my " Pseudodoxia Epidemica ; and another was divers years before cast up at Hunstanton ; both whose heads are yet to be seen.

Ophidion, or, at least, *ophidion nostras*, commonly called a sting-fish, having a small prickly fin running all along the back, and another a good way on the belly, with little black spots at the bottom of the back fin. If the fishermen's hands be touched or scratched with this venemous fish, they grow painful and swell. The figure hereof I send you in colours. They are common about Cromer. See Schoneveldeus, " *De Ophidia*."

Piscis octogonius, or *octangularis*, answering the description of Cataphractus Schonevelde ; only his is described with the fins spread ; and when it was fresh taken, and a large one. However, this may be *nostras*, I send you one ; but I have seen much larger which fisherman have brought me.

Physsalus. I send one which hath been long opened and shrunk, and lost the colour. When I took it upon the sea-shore, it was full and plump, answering the figure and description of Rondeletius. There is also a like figure at the end of Muffetus. I have kept them alive ; but observed no motion, except of contraction and dilatation. When it is fresh, the prickles or bristles are of a brisk green and amethist colour. Some call it a sea-mouse.[8]

Our mullet is white and *imberbis ;* but we have also a *mullus barbatus ruber miniaceus*, or *cinnaberinus ;* somewhat rough, and but dry meat. There is of them major and minor, resembling the figures in Johnstonus, tab. xvii., Rotbart.

Of the *acus marinus*, or needle fishes, I have observed three sorts. The *acus Aristotelis*, called here an addercock ; *acus major*, or garfish, with a green verdigrease back-bone ; the other, *saurus acui similis*. *Acus sauroides*, or *sauriformis*, as it may be called, much answering the description of *saurus Rondeletii*. In the hinder part much resembling a mackerell. Opening one, I found not the back-bone green. Johnstonus writes nearest to

[7] Frog-fish.

[8] I have seen a sea-mouse taken out of a cod-fish, but they are not common at Cromer.—*G.*

it, in his *Acus Minor*. I send you the head of one dried, but the bill is broken. I have the whole draught in picture. This kind is much more near than the other, which are common, and is a rounder fish.

Vermes marini are large worms found two feet deep in the sea-sands, and are digged out at the ebb for bait.

The *avicula Maialis*, or May chit, is a little dark grey bird, somewhat bigger than a stint, which cometh in May, or the latter end of April, and stayeth about a month. A marsh bird, the legs and feet black, without heel; the bill black, about three quarters of an inch long. They grow very fat, and are accounted a dainty dish.

A dorhawk, a bird not full so big as a pigeon, somewhat of a woodcock colour, and paned somewhat like a hawk, with a bill not much bigger than that of a titmouse, and a very wide throat; known by the name of a dorhawk, or preyer upon beetles, as though it were some kind of *accipiter muscarius*. In brief, this *accipiter cantharophagus*, or dorhawk, is *avis rostratula gutturosa, quasi coaxans, scarabæis vescens, sub vesperam volans, ovum speciosissimum excludens.* I have had many of them, and am sorry I have not one to send you. I spoke to a friend to shoot one, but I doubt they are gone over.

Of the *upupas*, divers have been brought me; and some I have observed in these parts, as I travelled about.

The *aquila Gesneri* [9] I sent alive to Dr. Scarburg, who told me it was kept in the colledge. It was brought me out of Ireland. I kept it two years in my house. I am sorry I have only one feather of it to send you.

A shoeing-horn, or barker, from the figure of the bill and barking note; a long-made bird, of white and blackish colour; fin-footed; a marsh-bird; and not rare some times of the year in Marshland. It may upon view be called *recurvirostra nostras,* or *avoseta;* much resembling the *avosetæ* species in Johnstonus, tab. 5. I send you the head in picture.

Four curlews I have kept in large cages. They have a pretty shrill note; not hard to be got in some parts of Norfolk.

Have you the *scorpius marinus Schoneveldei*?

Have you put in the *musca tuliparum muscata*?

That bird which I said much answered the description of *garrulus argentoratensis*,[1] I send you. It was shot on a tree ten miles off, four years ago. It may well be called the parrot jay, or *garrulus psittacoides speciosus*. The colours are much faded. If you have it before, I should be content to have it again; otherwise you may please to keep it.

---

[9] The Golden Eagle.   [1] The Garrulous Roller.

Garrulus Bohemicus[2] probably you have. A pretty, handsome bird, with the fine cinnabrian tips of the wings. Some which I have seen have the tail tipt with yellow, which is not in their description.

I have also sent you *urtica mas*, which I lately gathered at Golston, by Yarmouth, where I found it to grow also twenty-five years ago. Of the *stella marina testacea*, which I sent you, I do not find the figure in any book.

I send you a few flies, which, some unhealthful years, come about the first part of September. I have observed them so numerous upon plashes in the marshes and marish[3] ditches, that, in a small compass, it were no hard matter to gather a peck of them. I brought some, what my box would hold; but the greatest part are scattered, lost, or given away. For memory's sake, I wrote on my box *muscæ palustres autumnales*. Worthy Sir, I shall be ever ready to serve you, who am, Sir, your humble servant,   THOMAS BROWNE.

Dr. Browne to Dr. Merritt.—December 29, [1668.]

SIR,—I am very joyful that you have recovered your health, whereof I heartily wish the continuation for your own and the public good. And I humbly thank you for the courteous present of your book. With much delight and satisfaction I had read the same not once in English. I must needs acknowledge your comment more acceptable to me than the text, which I am sure is a hard, obscure piece without it, though I have not been a stranger unto the vitriary art, both in England and abroad. I perceive you have proceeded far in your Pinax. These few at present I am bold to propose, and hint unto you; intending, God willing, to salute you again. A paragraph might probably be annexed unto Quercus. Though we have not all the exotic oaks, nor their excretions, yet these, and probably more supercrescencies, productions, or excretions, may be observed in England.

Viscum — polypodium — juli — pilulæ — gemmæ foraminatæ foliorum — excrementum fungosum verticibus scatens — excrementum lanatum—capitula squamosa jacceæ æmula—nodi—melleus liquor—tubera radicum vermibus scatentia—muscus—lichen —fungus—varæ quercinæ.

Capillaris marina sparsa, fucus capillaris marinus sparsus; sive, capillitius marinus; or sea-perriwig. Strings of this are often found on the sea-shore. But this is the full figure, I have seen three times as large.

---

[2] The Waxen Chatterer.   [3] Marshy.

I send you also a little elegant sea-plant, which I pulled from a greater bush thereof, which I have, resembling the backbone of a fish. *Fucus marinus vertebratus pisciculi spinum referens, ichthyorachius;* or what you think fit.

And though perhaps it be not worth the taking notice of *formicæ arenariæ marinæ,* or at least *muscus formicarius marinus:* yet I observe great numbers by the sea-shore, and at Yarmouth, an open sandy coast, in a sunny day, many large and winged ones, may be observed upon, and rising out of the wet sands, when the tide falls away.

Notonecton, an insect that swimmeth on its back, and mentioned b Muffetus, may be observed with us.

I send you a white reed-chock by name. Some kind of *funco,* or little sort thereof. I have had another very white when fresh.

Also the draught of a sea-fowl, called a sheerwater, billed like a cormorant, fiery, and snapping like it upon any touch. I kept twenty of them alive five weeks, cramming them with fish, refusing of themselves to feed on anything; and wearied with cramming them, they lived seventeen days without food. They often fly about fishing ships when they clean their fish, and throw away the offal. So that it may be referred to the *lari,* as *larus niger gutture albido rostro adunco.*

Gossander.—*Videtur esse puphini species.* Worthy sir, that which we call a gossander, and is no rare fowl among us, is a large well-coloured and marked diving fowl, most answering the merganser. It may be like the puffin in fatness and rankness; but no fowl is, I think, like the puffin, differenced from all others by a peculiar kind of bill.

Burganders, not so rare as Turn[4] makes them, common in Norfolk, so abounding in vast and spacious warrens.

If you have not yet put in *larus minor,* or stern,[5] it would not be omitted, so common about broad waters and plashes not far from the sea.

Have you a yarwhelp, barker, or latrator, a marshbird about the bigness of a godwitt?

Have you *dentalia,* which are small univalve *testacea,* whereof sometimes we find some on the sea-shore?

Have you put in *nerites,* another little *testaceum,* which we have?

Have you an *apiaster,* a small bird called a bee-bird?

Have you *morinellus marinus,* or the sea dotterell, better coloured than the other, and somewhat less?

[4] This name is very illegible in the original.
[5] Probably *sterna hirundo* and *minuta.* See Sir Thomas's paper "On the Birds, &c. of Norfolk."

I send you a draught of two small birds; the bigger called a chipper, or *betulæ carptor;* cropping the first sproutings of the birch trees, and comes early in the spring. The other a very small bird, less than the *certhya*, or eye-creeper, called a whin-bird.

I send you the draught of a fish taken sometimes in our seas. Pray compare it with *draco minor Johnstoni.* This draught was taken from the fish dried, and so the prickly fins less discernable.

There is a very small kind of smelt; but in shape and smell like the other, taken in good plenty about Lynn, and called prims.

Though *scombri* or mackerell be a common fish, yet our seas afford sometimes, strange large ones, as I have heard from fishermen and others; and this year, 1668, one was taken at Leostoffe, an ell long by measure, and presented to a gentleman, a friend of mine.

Musca tuliparum moschata is a small bee-like fly, of an excellent fragrant odour, which I have often found at the bottom of the flowers of tulips.

In the little box I send a piece of *vesicaria* or *seminaria marina* cut off from a good full one, found on the sea-shore.

We have also an ejectment of the sea, very common, which is *funago*, whereof some very large.

I thank you for communicating the account of thunder and lightning; some strange effects thereof I have found here; but this last year we had little or no thunder or lightning.

Dr. Browne to Dr. Merritt.[6]*—Norwich, Febr.* 6, [1668-9.]

HONOURED SIR,—I am sorry I have had diversions of such necessity, as to hinder my more sudden salute since I received your last. I thank you for the sight of the spermaceti, and such kind of effects from lightning and thunder I have known, and about four yeares ago about this towne, when I with many others saw fire-balls fly, and go off when they met with resistance, and one carried away the tiles and boards of a leucomb window of my own howse, being higher than the neighbour howses, and breaking agaynst it with a report like a good canon. I set down that occurrence in this citty and country, and have it somewhere amongst my papers, and fragments of a woeman's hat that was shiver'd into pieces of the bignesse of a groat. I have still by me too, a litle of the spermaceti of our whale, as also the oyle and balsam which I made with the oyle and sper-

---

[6] Published (erroneously) as a letter to Mr. Dugdale.

maceti.   Our whale was worth 500lib. my apothecarie got about
fiftie pounds in one sale of a quantitie of sperm.

I made enumeration of the excretions of the oake, which
might be observed in England, because I conceived they would
be most observable if you set them downe together, not
minding whether there were any addition: by *excrementum
fungosum vermiculis scatens* I only meant an usual excretion,
soft and fungous at first, and pale, and sometimes cover'd in
part with a fresh red, growing close unto the sprouts; it is full
of maggots in litle woodden cells, which afterwards turne into
litle reddish brown or bay flies.   Of the *tubera indica vermiculis
scatentia* I send you a peece, they are as big as good tennis-balls
and ligneous.

The litle elegant *fucus* may come in as a difference of the
abies, being somewhat like it, as also unto the 4 *corallium* in
Gerhard, of the sprouts, whereof I could never find any
sprouts, wings, or leaves as in the *abies*, whether fallen off I
know not, though I call'd it *ichthyorndius* or *pisciculi spinam
referens*, yet pray do you call it how you please.   I send you now
the figure of a *quercus mar.* or *alga*, which I found by the sea-
shore, differing from the common as being denticulated, and in
one place there seems to be the beginning of some flower-pod or
seed-vessell.

A draught of the *morinellus marinus,* or sea dotterel,[7] I now
send you; the bill should not have been so black, and the leggs
more red, and a greater eye of dark red in the feathers or wing
and back: it is less and differently colour'd from the common
dotterell, which cometh to us about March and September: these
sea-dotterels are often shot near the sea.

A yare-whelp or barker,[8] a marsh-bird, the bill two inches
long, the legges about that length, the bird of a brown or russet
colour.

That which is knowne by the name of a bee-bird,[9] is a litle
dark gray bird; I hope to get one for you.

That which I call'd *betulæ carptor,* and should rather have
call'd it *alni carptor,* whereof I sent a rude draught; it feeds
upon alderbuds, nucaments, or seeds, which grow plentifully
here; they fly in little flocks.

That call'd by some a whin-bird,[1] is a kind of ox-eye, but the

[7] The ring plover or sea lark, plentiful near Blakeney; *charadrius
hiaticula.*—G.

[8] Names of two distinct species, the *godwit* or *yarwhelp, scolopax
ægocephala,* and the *spotted redshank* or *barker, S. Totanus.* The description agrees with neither.

[9] Probably the *beam-bird,* or flycatcher; *Muscicapa Grisola.*—G.

[1] Possibly the golden-crested wren, *Motacilla Regulus.*

shining yellow spot on the back of the head, is scarce to bee well imitated by a pensill.

I confesse for such litle birds I am much unsatisfy'd on the names given to many by countrymen, and uncertaine what to give them myself, or to what *classis* of authors cleerly to reduce them. Surely there are many found among us which are not described; and therefore such which you cannot well reduce, may (if at all) be set down after the exacter nomination of small birds as yet of uncertain class or knowledge.

I present you with a draught of a water-fowl, not common, and none of our fowlers can name it, the bill could not bee exactly expressed by a coale or black chalk, whereby the little incurvitie at the upper end of the upper bill, and small recurvitie of the lower is not discerned; the wings are very short, and it is finne-footed; the bill is strong and sharp, if you name it not I am uncertain what to call it, pray consider this *anatula* or *mergulus melanoleucus rostro acuto*.

I send you also the heads of *mustela*,[2] or *mergus mustelaris mas. et fæmina*, called a wesel, from some resemblance in the head, especially of the female, which is brown or russet, not black and white, like the male, and from their preying quality upon small fish. I have found small eelcs, small perches, and small muscles in their stomachs. Have you a sea-phaysant, so commonly called from the resemblance of an hen-phaisant in the head and eyes, and spotted marks on the wings and back, and with a small bluish flat bill, tayle longer than other ducks, longe winges, crossing over the tayle like those of a long winged hawke.[3]

Have you taken notice of a breed of *porci solidi pedes?* I first observed them above twenty yeares ago, and they are still among us.

Our *nerites* or *neritæ* are litle ones.

I queried whether you had *dentalia*, becaus probably you might have met with them in England; I never found any on our shoare, butt one brought me a few small ones, with smooth small shells, from the shoare. I shall inquire farther after them.

Urtica marina minor, Johnst. tab. xviii. I have found more then once by the sea-side.

The hobby and the merlin would not bee omitted among hawks; the first comming to us in the spring, the other about autumn. Beside the ospray,[4] we have a larger kind of eagle, call'd an *eruh*.[5] I have had many of them.

---

[2] This must be the smew, *mergus albellus :* which comes on the coast of Norfolk in hard winters.—*G.*

[3] The pin-tailed duck.—*G.*

[4] Several ospreys have been taken near Cromer.—*G.*

[5] *Erne ?*—The white-tailed or cinereous eagle ; *falco albicilla.*

Worthy deare sir, if I can do anything farther which may be serviceable unto you, you shall ever readily command my endeavours ; who am, sir, your humble and very respectfull servant,

THOMAS BROWNE.

Dr. Browne to Dr. Merritt, Feb. 12, 1668-9.

WORTHY SIR,—Though I writ unto you last Monday, yet having omitted some few things which I thought to have mentioned, I am bold to give you this trouble so soone agayne. Have you putt in a sea fish called a bleak, a fish like a herring, often taken with us and eat, but a more lanck and thinne and drye fish ?

The wild swan or elk would not bee omitted, being common in hard winters and differenced from our river swans, by the *aspera arteria*. *Fulica* and *cotta Anglorum* are different birds though good resemblance between them, so some doubt may bee made whether it bee to bee named a coot, except you set it downe *Fulica nostras* and *cotta Anglorum*. I pray consider whether that water-bird whose draught I sent in the last box, and thought it might bee named *anatula* or *mergulus melanoleucos, &c.*, may not bee some *gallinula*, it hath some resemblance with *gallina hypoleucos* of Johnst. tab. 32, butt myne hath shorter wings by much, and the bill not so long and slender, and shorter legs and lesser, and so may either be called *gallina aquatica hypoleucos nostras*, or *hypoleucos anatula*, or *mergulus nostras*.

Tis much there should bee no *icon* of *rallas* or *ralla aquatica;* I have a draught of some, and they are found among us.

THOMAS BROWNE.

The *vescaria* I sent is like that you mention, if not the same, the common *funago* resembleth the husk of peas, this of barley when the flower is mouldred away.

Sir Robert Paston to Dr. Browne.—Oxnead, April the 5*th,* 1669.

HONORED SIR,—On Saturday night last, going into my laboratorie, I found som of the *adrop* (that had beene run foure or five times in the open ayre, and euerie time itts ætheriall attracted spiritts drawne of from itt) congealed to an hard candied substance, the which I ordered my man to grind in a marble to attenuate itts parts, and make itt more fitt for attraction, and comming in in the operation, I chid my servant for grinding itt where white lead had before beene ground, for I found it from itts fuscye red color, looke licke white lead ground with

oyle, butt more lustrous, and he to convince that the stone was cleane, ground som of the same before my face 'on a tile,' with another muller, which came to the same color 'and viscositye. I must confess that gave me a transport to find the ayre had worked such an effect. Uppon about half a pound of this I cohobated[5] som of itts ætheriall spiritt, which itt nottwithstanding tinged red, and I am now drawing itt of againe, for I think I had better have exposed itt in itts consistence to the open ayre againe, though I find itt hard to run into anye thin-substance; yett perhapps the viscous matter may be more pretious, and by often grinding, exposing, and distilling, itt may att last goe a white and spiss water, such an one 'as' philosophers looke after, or att least be fitt to receiue, and be acuated[6] with, the ......and saline parts of the ætheriall spiritt, when that operation comes in hand if itt affords us anye that way. I haue given Mr. Henshaw an accompt of this, which I beleeve will please' him, and I desire your advice in the point how to proceed upon't, for certainlye if these matters have anye truth in them, wee are upon the brink of a menstruum to dissolve mettalls in generall. The keys are not yett fitted to your table, butt I hope will be by Thursday; my service to your ladye, and excuse this relation with that generous condescention that allowes you to consider even the lowest thinges.—Sir, I am, your humble servant,
                                        ROBERT PASTON.[7]

The Earl of Yarmouth to Sir Thomas Browne.—Septembr. the 10th, 1674.

HONORED SIR,—The great ciuility of your letter is an obligation I haue som time layne under, adiourning my returne on purpose that I might haue som thinge to discourse. My friend, Mr. Henshaw (who is lately returned from his employmt. of envoye extraordinary in Denmark), and has brought over with him many curiositys; the principle of which lyes in the Unicornes horne, in which he has as much as he prises att foure or five hundred pounds, beeing three very long hornes of the fish called puach and seuerall peeces; many rarityes of amber; great store of *succinum*[8] beeing found about those shores, and a very large peece he gave mee, which was found in the earth many miles from the sea; he has one piece in which a drop either of water or quicksilver is included, which turnes round as the amber is moved, and severall with insects in them. He confesseth he had licke to have beene cheated by a merchant with a piece that had somwhat included in itt, which he found to bee rosin,

[5] Distilled again.
[7] Created Earl of Yarmouth, Jan. 1673.
[6] 'Acidified.
[8] Amber.

and wee have a way to counterfeitt itt very handsomely, which
he has taught mee, and, if wee had a workman to help us,
might doe many pretty thinges of that nature. He has seuerall
peeces of the mineralls of Dronthem ; he has brought over a vegetable called the *alga saccharifica,* which, when he putt itt in the
box, had nothing on the leaves, and in bringing has attracted a
matter in tast and feeling licke sugar. He tells mee the former
King of Denmark was curious in all manner of rarities, and has
one of the best collections of that kind in the world, as allsoe a
most famous library of choyse collected bookes, butt this king's
delights are in horses, and the discipline of an army, of which he
has thirty thousand brauely equipped, which Mr. Henshaw saw
encamped att the rendevous att Colding, in Juteland ; allsoe a
potent navy ready to assist those that will pay the most for them.
The king, att his comming away, gave him considerable presents
to the value of betweene five and six hundred pounds, and has
written such a character of him that I feare may invite him
thither agayne, if our king has any occasion to send one. He
was there acquainted with the principle physitian, one Bouchius,
a great louer of chymistry, butt I thinke nott much experienced
in itt, who assumed that leafe gold by continuall grinding for
som fourteen dayes, and then putt into a retort *in nudo igne*
yields some dropps of a blood red licquor, and the same gold
exposed to the ayre, and ground againe, doth *toties quoties* yield
the same ; this is now under the experiment of a physitian in
this towne, to whome I gave the process to undertake the tryall,
and shall bee able shortly to give you an accompt of itt. I have
little leysure and less convenience to try anything heere, yett my
owne salt will sett mee on work, having now arrived to this that
I can with foure drachmes of itt dissolve a drachme of leafe gold
into an high tincture, which by all the art I have is nott sepe-
rable from the menstruum which stands fluid, and is both before
and after the solution of the gold as sweet almost as sugar,
soe farr is itt from any corrosive nature. I am gooing to seale
up two glasses, one of the menstruum with gold dissolved in
itt, and another of the menstruum *per se,* and to putt them
in an athanor, to see if they will putrify, or what alteration
will happen. I have att Oxned seene this salt change as blacke
as inke, I must, att the lowest, have an excelent *aurum potabile,*
and if the signes wee are to judge by in Sendivogius' description
bee true, I have the key which answers to what he says, that if
a man have that which will dissolve gold as warme water doth
ice, you have that out of which gold was first made in the earth.
My solution is perfectly agreeable to itt ; dissolves itt without
hissing, bubble, or noyse, and doth itt *in frigido :* that which
encourages mee is that I shall make my lump with spiritt of

wine, which I could never by under twelve shillings a quart, and
now heere is one, which Prince Rupert recommended mee to,
that sells it for eighteene pence the quart, and will fire gun-
powder after itts burnt away in a spoone, and answers all the
tryalls of the highest rectified spiritt of wine. I shewed some of
itt to Dr. Rugeby, who thinkes itt must com from molosses,
butt whatever itt comes from, there itt is in all qualities, bearing the highest tryalls of spiritt of wine. Sir, I pray take my
thankes for your kind remembrance of mee, and if you can
recommend mee to any author that can further enlighten my understanding, pray doe. My wife ioynes with mee in the present-
ments of our services to your lady and yourself. I begg your
pardon for tiring you with soe many words to soe little purpose,
and am, Sir, your most humble servant,   YARMOUTH.

Sir Thomas Browne to Elias Ashmole.—Norwich, Oct. viij,
1674.

HONORD SIR,—I give you late butt heartie thancks for the
noble present of your most excellent booke; which, by the care
of my sonne, I received from you. I deferred this my due
acknowledgment in hope to have found out something more of
Dr. John Dee, butt I can yett only present this paper unto you
written by the hand of his sonne, Dr. Arthur Dee, my old
acquaintance, containing the scheme of his nativity, erected by
his father, Dr. John Dee, as the title sheweth; butt the iudg-
ment upon it was writt by one Franciscus Murrerus, before
Dr. Arthur returned from Russia into England, which Murrerus
was an astrologer of some account at Mosko. Sir, I take it for
a great honour to have this libertie of communication with a person of your eminent merit, and shall industriously serve you
upon all opportunities, who am, worthy good sir, your servant
most respectfully and humbly,   THOMAS BROWNE.

From Dr. How[1] to Dr. Browne.

SIR, MY CHOISEST, ETC.—I received your rare present, and
shall answere your summons for yourselfe, or friends, with any
faire florall returnes, pacquet of seeds, or if this place may any
wayes instrumentaly present mee yours I shall putt on such
affected employments. For the dresse of our garden, that you
may know the modell, this rough title may acquaint you: *Bota-
notrophium Westmonasteriense, tentaminibus noviter exploratis
hortensibus, medicinalibus, tingentibus, imprægnatum.* The

[1] William How, of St. John's Coll. Oxon. a captain of horse in K.
Charles I.'s army, afterwards a physician in London; first in Lawrence
Lane, then in Milk Street, a noted herbalist of his time. He published
"Phytologia Britannica," &c. Lond. 1650: and died in 1656.

style to this discourse will appeare Roman; nor shall I present
you with a catalogue of nude names, a mode taken upp to prevent further scrutinyes, in which designes the most experienced
botanists find too much anxiety; the younger student meetes
with nothing but confusion.   Therefore to each recited plant
you shall have the originall author annexed, and paged, that
with small labor they may peruse the plant; but to nondescribed
species who refuse limitts, wee shall present them delineated in
theire names.   The method wee intend in paging authors may
bee discerned in this instance: *Pimpinella moschata, sive Agri-
moniæ folio, quorundam Agrimonoides.   Fab. Columnæ minus
cognit. stirp.* pag. 145; after wee have thus circumscribed the
plant wee shall adde our experiments; to this *hortensiall* (wherein acquirements *de novo* are onely to bee inserted); to that, *medicinall*, if never formerly approved in physicke, or applyed to
such particular disturbances; to those, *tinctoriall*, if by theire
iuyces, or decoctions any such qualityes may be perceived.   For
the knowledge of our garden series whereby you say something
might bee annexed, wee almost equaly boast what our clyme
may produce, so that however you may appropriate your diges-
tions, wee easily may render them classicall; though I must be
compelled to confesse you haue enrich't mee with the *Pimpinella*.   The *Carduus Hisp. siue Carduus aculeatus, Math. edent.
Bauh.* pag. 496, I further want: yett our little instructed farme
numbers aboue 2200 species, submitting to no European culture;
which fabricke might be compleated with any of your mature
explorate additions! since our designes shall acknowledge those
inuentions with affixed titles!   Wee are emboldened from your
" Common Errors," pag. 103;—" Swarmes of others there are,
some whereof our future endeauors may discouer:" and being
rauished with those learned enquiryes, pardon this pressing discourse, therefore vented, *possit ut ad monitum facere tuum.*
Pag. 102;—" That *Ros solis* which rotteth sheep hath any such
cordiall vertue upon us, wee have reason to doubt."   If the salu-
brious operation in decoctions upon tabid bodyes might purchase
credentialls, troopes of physitians might appeare combatants:
nor the rotting of sheepe in cur apprehensions any wayes op-
pugnes his alexipharmacy in man: *Pinguiculam oviaricum gre-
gem omnes villatici uno ore necare asserunt.   Matronæ graves
Cambro-Britannicæ ex pinguicula parant syrupum, uti rosa-
ceum ad evacuandos pueros: ruricolæ mulieres boreales ex pulte
avenacea, aut alio jusculo addita pinguicula pueros purgant,
evacuare phlegma verisimile.*   " That cats haue such delight in
the herbe *nepeta*, called therefore *cataria*, our experience cannot
discouer."   I haue numbred about 2 rootes of *nep.* in my garden
16 cats, who never destroied those plants, but have totally de-

spoyled the neighbouring births in that bedd to a yard's distance, rendring the place hard, and smooth like a walke with theire frequent treddings : but of this *una litura potest.* I find many of my lord Bacon's experiments concerning phytologie in his 6 and 7 centuries, very crude. If you may commend any of these heads to Dr. Short for his enlargments, it must proue a fauor which cannot more obleidge, yours most obseruant,

Milk Streete, Sept. 20, 55.   WILL. HOW.

[*Interesting extract from a very long letter addressed to Dr. Browne by M. Escaliot.*]

Surat, Jan. 26, 1663-4.

ON Tuesday, the fifth of January, about ten in the morning, a sudden alarme was brought to our house from the towne with news that Seua-Gee Raya, or principal governor, (for such assume not the name of kings to them selues, but yet endeuor to bee as absolute each in his prouince as his sword can make him,) was coming downe with an army of an vncertaine number upon Surat, to pillage the citty, which news strook no small consternation into the minds of a weake and effeminate people, in soe much that on all hands there was nothing to be seene but people flying for their lives, and lamenting the loss of their estates, the richer sort, whose stocke of money was large enough to purchase that favor at the hands of the gouernor of the castle, made that their sanctuary, and abandoned their dwellings to a merciless foe, wich they might well enoughe haue defended with the rest of the towne had thay had the heartes of men. The same day a post comes in, and tells them that the army was come within tenne course or English miles, and made all hast forward, wich put the cowardly and vnfaithful govenor of the towne to send a seruant to Sevagee to treat of some conditions of ransome. But Sevagee retaines the messenger and marches forwards with all speed, and that night lodged his camp about 5 miles English from the city, and the governor perceueing well that this messenger returned not againe, and that Sevagee did not intend to treat at that distance, he craues admission into the castle and obtaineth it, and soe deserted his towne.

The city of Surat is the only port on this side India, wich belongs to the Mogol, and stands upon a river commodious enough to admitt vessells of 1000 tun, seven milles up, at wich distance from the sea, there stands a reasonable strong castle well manned, and haueing great store of good guns mounted for the securing of the riuer at a conuenient distance, on the north east and south sides of this castle is the citty of Surrat built of a large extent and very popelus. Rich in marchandise, as being

the mart for the great empire of the Mogol, but ill contriued into
narrow lanes and without any forme. And for buildings consists
partly of brick, soe the houses of the richer sort partly of wood,
the maine posts of wich sort only are timber, the rest is built of
bambooes (as they call them) or caines, such as those youe make
your angles at Norwich, but very large, and these being tyed
togather with the cords made of coconutt rinde, and being
dawbed ouer, with dirt, are the walls of the whole house and
floors of the upper story of their houses.   Now the number of
the poore exceedingly surmounting the number of those of some
quality, these bamboo houses are increased vnmeasurably, soe
that in the greater part of the towne scarce two or three brick
houses are to bee seen in a street, and in some part of the towne
not one for many streets togather; those houses wich are built of
bricke are vsually built strong, their walls of two or two and a
half feet thicke, and the roofes of them flat and couered with a
plaster like plaster of Paris, wich makes most comodous places
to take the euening aire in the hotter seasons; the whole town
is unfortified ether by art or nature, its situation is upon a larg
plaine of many miles extent and their care hath been so little to
secure it by art, that they have only made against the cheefe
auenues of the towne, some weake and ill built gatts and for the
rest in some parts a dry ditch, easily passable by a footman,
wanting a wall or other defence on the innerside, the rest is left
soe open that scarce any signe of a dich is perceiuable; the
people of the towne are either the marchants, and those of all
nations almost, as English, Dutch, Portugalls, Turkes, Arabs,
Armenians, Persians, Jews, Indians, of seueral sorts, but principally Banians, or els Moores the conquerors of the country
Hindues, or the ancient inhabitants or Persees, whoe are people
fled out of Persia ages agoe, and here and some miles up the
country settled in great numbers. The Banian is one who thinks
it the greatest wickedness to kill any creature whatsoever that
hath life, least possibly they might bee the death of their father
or relation, and the Persee doth supperstitiously adore the fire
as his God, and thinks it an vnpordonable sin to throw watter
upon it, soe that if a house bee fired or their clothes upon their
backs burning thay will if thay can hinder any man from quenching it.   The Moores ar troubled with none of these superstitions
but yet through the unworthy couetuousness of the gouernour
of the towne thay had noe body to head them, nor none vnto
whome to joyne themselves, and soe fled away for company,
whereas if there had been 500 men trayned, and in a readyness,
as by order from the king there ever should, whose pay the
gouernour puts into his own pocket, the number to defend the
citty would haue amounted to some thousands. This was the
condition of the citty at the tyme of its inuasion.

The inuader Seva Gee is as I haue said by extraction a Rayar
or a gouernour of a small country on the coast southward of
Basiue, and was formerly a tributary to the King of Vijapore,
but being of an aspiring and ambitious minde, subtile and withall
a soldier, hee rebells against the king, and partly by fraude,
partly by force, partly by corrup oftion the kings gouernours of
the kings castles, seaseth many of them into his hands. And
withall parte of a country for wich the King of Vijapore paid
tribute to the Mogul. His insolencys were soe many, and his
success soe great, that the King of Vijapore thought it high
tyme to endeavor his suppression, or els all would be lost. Hee
raises his armies, but is worsted soe euery where by the rebbell,
that he is forced to conditions to release homage to Sevagee of
those lands wich hee held of him, and for the rest Sevagee was
to make good his possession against the Mogol as well as hee
could, after some tyme of forbearance. The Mogol demands his
tribute from him of Vijapore, whoe returns answer that hee had
not possession of the tributary lands, but that they were de-
taynced from him by his rebbell who was grown too strong for
him. Upon this the Mogol makes warr both vpon the King of
Vijapore and Seuagee, but as yet without any considerable suc-
cesss ; many attempts have been made, but still frusterated either
by the cuning, or valour, or money of Seuagee : but now of late
Kuttup Chawn, an Umbraw, who passed by Surrat since I
arriued with 5000 men, and 14 elephants, and had 9000 men
more marched another way towards their randevouz, as wee hear
hath taken from him a strong castle, and some impression into
his country, to deuest wich ware it is probable he took this
resoluetion for inuation of this country of Guzurat. His person
is described by them whoe haue seen him to bee of meane stature,
lower somewhat then I am erect, and of an excellent proportion.
Actual in exercise, and when euer hee speaks seemes to smile a
quicke and peercing eye, and whiter then any of his people.
Hee is distrustfull, seacret, subtile, cruell, perfidious, insulting
over whomsoever he getts into his power. Absolute in his commands, and in his punishments more then severe, death or dis-
membering being the punishment of every offence, if necessity
require, venterous and desperate in execution of his resolues as
may appeare by this following instance. The King Vijapore
sends down his vnckell a most accomplished soldier, with 14000
men into Sevagee's country : the knowne vallor and experience
of the man made Seuagee conclude that his best way was to
assassinate him in his owne armye by a sudden surprise. This
conduct of this . attempt, how dangerous soever, would haue
been vndertaken by many of his men of whose conduct hee might
haue assured himselfe, but it seemes he would haue the action

wholly his own, hee therefore with 400 as desperate as himselfe
enters the army vndiscovered, comes to the generalls tent, falls
in upon them, kills the guard, the generalls sonne, wounds the
father, whoe hardly escaped, seiseth on his daughter and carries
her away prisoner, and forceth his way backe through the whole
army, and returns safe without any considerable loss, and afterward in dispight of all the King of Vijapore could do, hee tooke
Rajapore, a great port, plundered it, and seised our English
marchants, Mr. Rivington, Mr. Taylor, and digged vp the
English house for treasure, and kept the marchants in prison
about 8 months.

Wedensday, the 6th Janu: about eleven in the morning,
Sevagee arriued neere a great garden, without the towne about
a quarter of a mile, and whilst hee was busied in pitching his
tents, sent his horsmen into the outward streets of the towne, to
fire the houses, soe that in less then halfe an houer wee might
behold from the tops of our house two great pilliers of smoke,
the certaine signes of a great dissolation, and soe they continued
burning that day and night, Thursday, Friday, and Saturday;
still new fires raised, and every day neerer and neerer approaching our quarter of the towne, that the terror was great, I know
youe will easily belieue, and upon his first beginning of his
firing, the remainder of the people fled as thicke as possible, so
that on Thursday the streets were almost empty, wich at other
tymes are exceeding thicke with people, and we the English in
our house, the Duch in theirs, and some few marchants of Turkey and Armenia, neighbours to our English house, possessed of
a seraw, or p ace of reception for strangers, were left by the
gouernor and his people, to make what shift we could to secure
ourselves from the enemys: this might the English and Duch
have done, leaving the towne, and gooing over the riuer to
Swalley to our shipps, which were then riding in Swalley hole,
but it was thought more like Englishmen to make ourselves ready
to defend our liues and goods to the uttermost, than by a flight
to leaue mony, goods, house, to merciless people, and were confirmed in a resolution, that the Duch alsoe determined the same,
though there was no possibility of relieuing one another, the
Duch house beeing on the other side of towne almost an English
mile asunder.

In order, therefore, to our better defence, the president, St.
George Oxinden, a most worthy, discreet, courageous person,
sent advice to our ships at Swalley of our condition, with his
desires to the captains to spare him out of their ships what men
they could, and wee in the meane tyme endeavoured to fitt our
house soe well as wee could, sending out for what quantity of
prouision of victualls, watter and pouder we could gett, of wich

wee gott a competent store. Tow brass guns we procured that day from a marchant in towne, of about three hundred weight a piece, and with old ship carriages, mounted them, and made ports in our great gate for them, to play out of, to scoure a shorte passage to our house; that afternoone we sent aboard a ship in the riuer for guns, and had tow of about six hundred a piece, sent up in next morning, with shott conuenient; some are sett to melt lead and make bullets, others with chezels to cutt lead into slugs, no hand idle, but all imployed to strengthen every place, as tyme would give leaue to the best advantage. On Weddensday men arriued to the number of forty odd, and bring with them tow brass guns more, our four smaller guns are then carried vp to the tope of the house, and three of them planted to scoure two greet streets, the four was bent vpon a rich churles house (Stogee Said Beeg of whom more by and by) because it was equally of hight and being posesed by the enemy might haue beene dangerous to our house; captaines are appointed and every man quartered and order taken for relieuing one another vpon necessity; a fresh recrute of men coming of about twenty more, wee than began to consider what houses neere vs might bee most prejudiciall; and on one side wee tooke possession of pagod, or Banian idol temple, which was just vnder our house, wich hauing taken wee were much more secured on that quarter; on the other a Morish Mesecte where seuerall people were harboured, and had windowes into our outward yard, was thought good to bee cleared and shutt vpp, wich accordingly done by a party, all the people sent to seeke some other place to harbour in. Things being thus reasonably well prepared, newes is brought vs that Mr. Anthony Smith, a servant of the companyes, one whoe hath been cheife in severall factoryes, was taken prisoner by Seuagee soulderiers as he came ashore neere the Duch house, and was comeing to the English,—an vnfortunate accedent wich made vs all much concerned, knowing Seuagee cruelty, and indeed gaue him ouer as quite lost: hee obtaines leaue some few houers after to send a note to the president, wherin hee aquants him with his condittion, that hee being brought before Savagee hee was asked what hee was and such like questions, and att last by Sevagee told that he was not come to doe any personall hurte to the English or other marchants, but only to revenge him selfe of Oroin Zeb (the great Mogol), because hee had invaded his counttry, had killd some of his relations, and that hee would only have the English and Duch give him some treasure and hee would not medle with their houses, else hee would doe them all mischeefe possible. Mr. Smith desired him to send a guard with him to the English house least hee should finde any mollestation from his men, but hee answers as yet hee must not goe

away, but comands him to bee carried to the rest of the mar
chants, where, when hee came, hee found the embassador from
the great king of Ethiopia vnto Oram Zeb prisoner, and pinioned
with a great number Banians and others in the same condition :
hauing set there some tyme, about halfe an hower, hee is seised
vpon by a cupple of black rogges, and pinioned in that extremety
that hee hath brought away the marke in his armes with him ;
this what hee writt and part of what he related when wee gott
him againe.   The president by the messenger one of Sevagee
men, as we imagined, returned answer that hee wounderd at
him, that professing peace hee should detaine an English man
prissoner, and that if he would send him home, and not to suffer
his people to come so neere his house as to give cause of suspi-
tion, hee would hurt none of his men, other wayes hee was vpon
his owne defence upon these tearmes ; wee were all Wedensday
and vntil Thursday about tow at afternoon, when perceiueing
tops of lances on the other side of a neighbour house, and haueing called to the men to depart and not come so neere vs, but
thay not stirring and intending as wee concluded to sett fier to
the house, on the quarter whereby our house would have been
in most eminent danger of being fiered alsoe, the president
comanded twenty men vnder the comand of Mr. Garrard Aungier, brother to my lord Aungier, to sally forth vpon them, and
another party of about soe many more to make good their re-
treate, they did soe, and when they facd them, judgd them to
bee about twenty-five horsmen well mounted, they discharged
at them and wounded one man and one horse, the rest fac'd about
and fled but made a shift to carry off their wounded man, but
the horse fell, haueing gone a little way ; what became of the
wounded man we cannot tell, but Mr. Smith saw him brought
into the armey upon mens shoulders and shewed there to
Sevagee ; two of our men were hurt, one shott slightly into the
legg with an arrow, the other rashly parting from the rest and
runing on before was cutt deep ouer the shoulder, but thanks
to God in a faire way of recovery.

On Wedensday afternoone a party of the enemy came downe
to Hogee Said Begs house, hee then in the castle, one of a pro-
digous estate, and brake open the vndefended doores, and ther
continued all that night long and till next day, that we sallyed
out vpon their men on the other quarter of our house, they appeared by two or three at a tyme vpon the tope of his house,
to spye what preparations wee made, but as yet had no order to
fier vpon them, we heard them all night long beating and breaking open chests and doores, with great maules, but were not
much concerned for him, for had the wretch had soe much heart
as to have stood vpon his guard, the 20 part of what they tooke,

from him, would have hiered soe many men as would haue
secured all the rest ; when they heard that we wear abroad in
the streets they imediatly in hast deserted the house, and that
as it afterwards appeared, in such hast as to leave tow baggs of
mony dropt downe behind them, yet with intention as they told
the people they mett (such poore wretches as had nothing to
loose and knew not whether to flye) to returne next day [to] fier
the house, but that was prevented. On Friday morning, the
president sent vnto the castle to Hogee Said Beg to know whether he would permitt him to take possession of and secure a
great company of warehouses of his adjoyneing to our house,
and wich would bee of great consequence to preserve both his
goods and our house, hee testified his willingness, and immediately from the tope of our house by help of a ladder we entred
it, and haueing found the enemie, haueing beene all Wedensday
afternoon and night till past Thursday noone plundering the
great house, had likewise entered and begun to plunder his first
warehouse, but were scard and that little hurt was done, they
had time to carry nothing that is yet knowne of, and only broken
open certaine vessells of quickesilver, which there lay spilt about
the warehouse in great quantetye ; wee locked it vp and put a
guard in the roome next the street, wich through help of a belcoone secured by thicke planks tyed to the belcoone pillers, soe
close on to another as no more space was left but for a muskett
to play out, was so secured as no approach could bee made againe
to the doore of his great house or any passage to the warehouse,
but what must come vnder dainger of our shott.   In the afternoone on Friday, Sevagee sends Mr. Smith as his messenger to
our house with propositions and threats, haueing first made him
oblige himselfe to returne, and with all obliging himselfe when he
did returne, that hee would doe him noe hurt, what soeuer
mesage hee should bring, his message was to send him 3 lacks of
rupees ; (every lack is 100,000, and every rupee is worth 2s. 3d.)
or elss let his men freely to doe their pleasure to Hogee Said
Begs house, if not threatening to come and force vs, and vowed
to kill euery person in the house, and to dig vp the houses foundation.   To this it was answered by the messenger that came with
Mr. Smith, that as for his two propositions he desired tyme to mak
answer to them till the morrow, they being of soe great moment,
and as for Mr. Smith that hee would and did keep him by force,
and hee should not returne till than, when if hee could consent to
either proposition hee would send him.   Mr. Smith being thus
returned to vs, youe may bee sure each man was inquisitive to
know news ; whoe told vs for their number, they did giue themselues out to bee 10,000, and they were now at least a very
considerable armey, since the coming of two rayers with their

men whose names hee knew'not: that their horse were very good, and soe indeed, those wich we saw were: that when hee came away, hee could not guess by the mony heaped vp in tow great heapes before Sevagee his tent, than that he had plundered 20 or 25 lack of rup. that the day when hee came away in the morning, there was brought in neere vpon 300 porters laden each with tow baggs of rupees, and some hee guessed to bee gold, that thay brought in 28 sere of large pearle, with many other jewels, great diamonds, rubies, and emeralds (40 sere make 37 pound weight) and these with an increedable quantety of mony, they found at the house of the reputed richest marchant in the world, his name is Verge Vora, his estate haueing beene esteemed to bee 80 lack of rup.

That they were still every hower, while hee was there, bringing in loods of mony from his house; his desire of mony is soe great, that he spares noe barbours cruelty to extort confessions from his prisoners, whip them most cruely, threatens death, and often executeth it, [if] they doe not produce soe much as hee thinks they may, or desires they should, at least cutts of one hand, some tymes both; a very great many there were, who hearing of his coming went forth to him, thinking to fare the better, but found there fault to there cost; as one whoe come to our house for cure, hee went forth to meete him and told him he was come from about Agra with cloth, and had brought 40 oxen loaded with it, and that hee came to present him with it all, or elss what part hee should please to command. Sevagee asked him if he had no mony, hee answered that he had not as yet sold any cloth since hee came to towne, and that he had no mony: the villaine made his right hand to bee cutt of imediately, and than bid him begone, he had noe need of his cloth; the poore old man returns, findes his cloth burnt, and himselfe destetute of other harbor, comes to the English house where hee is dresed and fed.

· But to proceed, Mr. Smith farther tells vs, that on Thursday their came a young fellow with some condition from the govenor, wich pleased Sevagee not at all, soe that hee asked the fellow whether his marster, being now by him cooped up in his chamber, thought him a woman to accept such conditions. The fellow imediately returns, "and we are not women; I have somewhat more to say to youe;" drawes his dagger, and runs full at Sevagee breast; a fellow that stood by with a sword redy drawne, strikes betwcen him and Sevagee, and strikes his hand almost of, soe that [it] hung but by a pece of flesh; the fellow haueing made his thrust at Sevagee with all his might, did not stop, but ran his bloody stumpp against Sevagee breast, and with force both Sevagee and hee fell together, the blood being seen upon Sevagee the noise run through the camp that hee was killed, and the crye went, kill the prisoners, where upon some were miserably hacked ; but Sevagee hauing quitted himselfe, and hee that stood by hauing clouen the fellows scull, comand was given to stay the execution, and to bring the prisoners before him, wich was imediately done, and Sevagee according as it came in his minde caused them to cut of this mans head, that mans right hand, both the hands of a third. It comes to Mr. Smith turne, and his right hand being comanded to bee cutt of, hee cryed out in Indostan to Sevagee, rather to cutt of his head, vnto wich end his hatt was taken of, but Sevagee stopt execution and soe praised be God hee escaped.

There were than about four heads and 24 hands cutt of after that Mr. Smith was come away, and retayned by the president, and they heard the answer hee sends the embassador of Ethiopea, whome hee had sett free upon delivery of 12 horses and some other things, sent by his king to Oron Zeb, to tell the English that hee did intend to visitt vs, and to raise the house and kill every man of vs.

The president resolutly answers that we were redy for him and resolued not to stire, but let him come when hee pleased, and since hee had as hee saide resolued to come, hee bid him come one pore, that is about the tyme of a watch, sooner than hee intended. With this answer the ambassador went his way, and wee heard no farther from him any more but in the terrible noise of the fier and the hideous smoke wich wee saw, but by Gods mercy came not soe neere vs as to take hold of vs, ever blessed be his name. Thursday and Friday nights were the most terrible nights for fier: on Friday after hee had ransaked and dug vp Vege Voras house, hee fiered it and a great vast number more towards the Dutch house, a fier soe great as turnd the night into day; as before the smoke in the day tyme had almost turnd day into night; rising soe thicke as it darkened the sun like a great cloud. On Sunday morning about 10 a clocke as thay tell vs hee went his way. And that night lay six courss of, and next day at noone was passed over Brooch river, there is a credable information that he hath shipt his treasure to carry into his own country, and Sr George Oxenden hath sent a fregate to see if hee can light of them, wich God grant. We kept our watch still till Tuesday.

I had forgote to writte you the manner of their cutting of mens hands, which was thuss ; the person to suffer is pinioned as streight as possibly they can, and then when the nod is giuen, a soldier come with a whitle or blunt knife and throws the poore patient downe vpon his face, than draws his hand backwards and setts his knee upon the prisoners backe, and begins to hacke and cutt on one side and other about the wrest, in the meane tyme the poore man roareth exceedingly, kicking and bitting the

ground for very anguish, when the villiane perceiues the bone
to bee laid bare on all sides, hee setteth the wrest to his knee
and giues it a snap and proceeds till he hath hacked the hand
quite of, which done thay force him to rise, and make him run
soe long till through paine and loss of blood he falls downe, they
then vnpinion him and the blood stops.

Dr. E. Browne to his Father.—September 7, 1671.

Most Honoured Father,— Sir, I have formerly sent you
word of Captain Narborough's voyage in the Sweepstakes to
Baldavia in the South Sea; and having since been in his company, and seen Mr. Thomas Wood's mappes of the southern
parts of America, and of Tierra del Fuego, and enquired after
many things in their voyage, I will set downe as much as I can
in this sheet of paper, least that you should not meete with any
other account; seing divers of those who understande most of
the voyage are seeking out further employe, and Mr. Woode, who
giveth me the greatest satisfaction in everything, thinks still
upon greater actions, and hath already offered his service to the
East-India Company to goe for Japan. The Sweepstakes was
long upon the Atlantick ocean, before they made the coast of
America, almost five moneths; the Pinke, which went with them,
being but a slow sayler. The day before they saw lande, they
left the Pinke, with order for her to stay at such and such places,
and afterwards to come in to the Streights of Magellan, and there
remain till they met; but the Pinke, being once out of sight,
shifted her course, and with eighteen men in her, bore away for
Barbados, and so into England, reporting the Sweepstakes to be
lost. The rest continued their voyage, and the next day, discovering America belowe the river of Plate, they hasted away to
Port Desire, and there put in. At the mouth of this port is one
of the best sea-markes in the world—a vast rock, in the shape of
a tower. They went up here to Le Maire's Islande, and
found a leaden boxe, with an account of his voyage so farre
in it. They went also to Drake's Islande, where Sr Francis
Drake executed one of his officers, and went up and downe the
country; but saw no inhabitants, although they were sensible that
the country was not without people; for they had divers things
stolen from them, and at their return thither, they founde a
modell of their owne shippe, of the bignesse of an ordinary boate,
built by the Indians out of peeces of boards and broken oares
which the English had left there. Mr. Woode founde two mussell
shells here tyed together with peeces of guts and divers peeces
and kernels of gold in them, some of which I have seen, they lost
or left upon the sande I suppose by some American. At their
coming hither they saw divers graves, and some of them very

long, which they tooke at first to be the sepulchres of the Patago-
nian gyants, written of by Magellan and others, and pictured in
mappes with arrowes thrust downe their throates; but, opening
their tombes, which are heapes of stones thrown over them,
they founde none to exceed our stature, and the people which
they saw all along that coast are rather lowe; and Captain
Narborough affirmes, that he never sawe an American in the
southern parts so high as himself. They opened many tombes,
as they say, out of curiosity; I know not whether they might
not also have hopes of finding treasure buried with them, for
certainly there is much gold in some of those countryes, and
the Indians in other places seeing a gold ring on the captain's
finger, would pointe to the hills and to the·ring, intimating
from whence that metal came; but as to the tombes, they at
last discovered the reason of their great length, and founde that
it was their way to bury one at the foot of another, the head of
one touching the feet of the other, perhaps man and wife, for
they have brought home a man and a woman's skull taken out
of one grave laiing in that posture, so that they have hereby
discovered that the race of the gyants are much diminished in
their stature. From Port Desire they sayled to Port Julian,
another faire port; they stayed also here sometime; but this,
of all things which they relate, seemeth most strange, that,
going up the country, they discovered a lake of salt, or rather
a field of granulated·salt, of some miles over; some of which
they separated from the rest near the border. At their return
thither, three days after, there was no salt at all left, except
what they had separated at some distance from the other,
neither had it rained from the time they first sawe it to the time
they cam thither again and found none; the salt had been above
the earth about a foot deepe, and Mr. Woode, pacing and examining the grounde whereon it had layne, founde a deep hole
or well in the middle. I can imagine no other way to solve
this, then by comparing it to the Lake of Zirknitz, where the
water springs out from under the grounde and retires againe, or
rather like to a tide's well, which often ebbes and flowes, and
so might springe out of the grounde, dissolve the salt, and
carry it with itselfe into the earth again by large passages.
The quantity of salt was great which afterwards disappeared;
for to use their own expression, there was more salt than
would serve all the shippes in the world. From hence they
sayled to the streights of Magellan, where they spent five or
six weekes giving names to the islandes, capes, inlets, bayes,
harbours, and remarkable places, most of their acquaintance
sharing in their discovery, and the Duke of Yorke's servants
names are given to many places; amongst whome Mr. Henry

Savill, whom I formerly travelled with in Italy, gives his name to the southermost part which they saw off Tierra del.Fuego.

At the coming into the streights, they pass a double narrow, and afterwards it is larger and full of islands. The country is mountainous on each side and the hills covered with snowe all the year long; so that they sayle as in a deepe vally. The sea in the middle is so deepe as they could finde no bottome—six hundred fathomes would doe nothing; but near the shoars they found anchorage, which they exactly marked. There are many rivers and inlets into these streights, but they wanted their Pinke much to discover more, and they thinke Tierre del Fuego to be many islandes. They saw many fires there; from hence it had its name. They are not the flames of burning mountaines, but the inhabitants make fires, and also burne the grass and weeds, as in Hungary, where I have seen the country on fire for a great way together. Most of these islandes are full of seales of a larger size than oures, many of which they killed, no otherwise than by knocking them on the head, and salted them up. They tooke also a great number of penguins, which served the seamen in the voyage. About the middle of the streights they touched at a place on the north shoare, called Port Famine, where there was formerly a plantation of Spaniards, but they were starved to death. Near to this place, further on, they discovered a country full of provisions, and have therefore named it Cape Plenty. The inhabitants of the streights goe all naked, men, women, and children: some few onely wearing a circle of net about their heades, like our shoemakers, although the country be cold in 53 and 54 degrees of southern latitude. Their colour is much the same with the other Americans, and differs little from them that live under the line; they goe all with bowes and arrowes, and many of them conversed freely with the English, came on boarde, and went a shoare, eat and dranke with them, without taking any great notice of any thinge. They would eat the meat and anoint themselves all over with the fat and grease; they painte themselves rudely, and when they came to the English, sometimes in sight of them, rather then want that ornament they woulde daube up one eye or one side of their face with clay or dirt. The whole country on this side from the river of Plate to Cape Plenty in the streights, or thereabouts, is one great plaine, the same with Pampas, where no trees growe, and the captain compared it to New Market heath. The other side it is all hilly, and the rivers runne downe so impetuously into the South sea, that they may see them runne a long way into the ocean, and have fresh water out of great rivers at the sea side. Beyond the streights

they sailed up to Castro, an island where the Spaniards live,
there being none of them now upon all the coast of America,
between that place and the river of Plate; from Castro they
went to Baldavia, but I have not room to write what passed
there.—Your m. o. son, E. B.

Sir Thomas Browne to Mr. Elias Ashmole.

I was very well acquainted with Dr. Arthur Dee, and at one time
or other hee hath given me some account of the whole course of
his life: hee gave mee a catalogue of what his father Dr. John
Dee had writt, and what hee intended to write, butt I think I
have seen the same in some of his printed bookes, and that
catalogue hee gave me in writing I cannot yet find. I never
heard him say one word of the booke of spirits, sett out by
Dr. Casaubone, which if hee had knowne I make no doubt butt
hee would have spoake of it unto mee, for he was very inquisitive
after any manuscripts of his father's, and desirous to print as
many as hee could possibly obtaine; and therefore, understanding that Sir William Boswell, the English resident in Holland,
had found out many of them, which he kept in a trunck in his
howse in Holland, to my knowledge hee sent divers letters unto
Sir William, humbly desiring him that hee would not lock them
up from the world, butt suffer him to print at least some thereof.
Sir William answered some of his letters, acknowledging that
hee had some of his father's works not yet published, and that
they were safe from being lost, and that hee was readie to showe
them unto him, butt that hee had an intention to print some of
them himself. Dr. Arthur Dee continued his solicitation, butt
Sr. William dying I could never heare more of those manuscripts
in his hand. I have heard the Dr. saye that hee lived in Bohemia with his father, both at Prague and other parts of Bohemia.
That Prince or Count Rosenberg was their great patron, who
delighted much in alchymie; I have often heard him affirme,
and sometimes with oaths, that hee had seen projection made
and transmutation of pewter dishes and flaggons into sylver,
which the goldsmiths at Prague bought of them. And that
Count Rosenberg playd at quaits with silver quaits made by projection as before; that this transmutation was made by a powder
they had, which was found in some old place, and a booke lying
by it containing nothing butt hieroglyphicks, which booke his
father bestowed much time upon; but I could not heare that he
could make it out. Hee sayd also that Kelly delt not justly by
his father, and that he went away with the greatest part of the
powder and was afterwards imprisoned by the Emperor in a
castle, from whence attempting an escape downe the wall, hee

fell and broake his legge and was imprisoned agayne. That his father, Dr. John Dee, presented Queen ·Elizabeth with a little of the powder, who having made triall thereof attempted to get Kelly out of prison, and sent some to that purpose, who giving opium in drinck unto the keepers, layd them so faste asleepe that Kelly found opportunity to attempt an escape, and there were horses readie to carry him away; butt·the buisinesse un-happily succeeded as is before declared. 'Hee sayd that his father was in good credit with the Emperour Rodolphus, I thinck, and that hee gave him some addition unto his coat of armes, by a mathematicall figure added, which I thincke may bee seen at Mr. Rowland Dee's howse, who had the picture[1] and coat of armes of Dr. John Dee, which Dr. Arthur Dee left at Mr. To-ley's when hee dyed. Dr. Arthur Dee was a yong man when he saw this projection made in Bohemia, butt hee was so inflamed therewith, that hee fell early upon that studie and read not much all his life but bookes of that subject, and two years before his death contracted with one Hunniades, or·Hans Hanyar, in London, to be his operator. This Hans Hanyar having lived long in London and growing in years, resolved to returne into Hungarie; he went first to Amsterdam where hee was to remain ten weeks, till Dr. Arthur came unto him.· The Dr. to my know-ledge was serious in this buisinesse, and had·provided all in readinesse to goe; but suddenly hee heard that Hans Hanyar was dead.

If hereafter any thing farther occurreth to my memorie I shall advertize. ' *(No Signature.)*

From Sir Thomas Browne to Mr. John Aubrey.

WORTHY GOOD SR.—I receaved your courteous letter and therein Mr. Woods his request. Dr. Thomas Lushington was borne at Canterbury, was chaplaine unto Dr. Corbet, bishop of Norwich, and afterward unto Prince Charles, now our king, in his minority; was rector of Burnham, in Norfolk, and dyed and was buryed at Sittingbourne, in Kent.

'Hee writt a Logick, after a new·method, in Latin. A com-ment upon·the Hebrews English, both printed·at London.

Hee writt also a Latin Treatise of the Passions, according to ·Aristotle and ·Thomas Aquinas. And also upon the Theologie of Proclus,[2] butt they never were published as I could heare, and I knowe not whether any one hath the coppies.

I was borne at St. Michaels Cheap in London, went to schoole at Winchester' Colledge, then went to Oxford, spent some yeares

[1] His portrait is preserved in the Ashmolean Museum—*W. H. B.*
[2] Probably *MS. Sloan.* 1838.—*Catalogue of Browne's MSS.* No. 1, 4to.

in forreign parts, was admitted to bee a *Socius Honorarius* of the College of Physitians in London, knighted September, 1671, when the King, Queen, and Court came to Norwich; writt *ReligioMedici* in English, which was since translated into Latin, French, Italian, High and Low Dutch.

Pseudodoxia Epidemica; or Enquiries into Common and Vulgar Errors, translated into Dutch, four or five years ago.

Hydriotaphia, or Urne Buriall.

Hortus Cyri, or de Quincunce.

Have some *Miscellaneous Tracts* which may be published.

I can give you little or no account of any writers of Pembroke Colledge, and I believe Mr. Woods may better informe himself upon the place. Dr. Stamp, who was I think chaplaine to the Queen of Bohemia, and preached sometimes at Stepney, published somewhat, but I remember not the title. There was one Dr. Dowdswell, a learned man, lately prebend of Worcester, butt whether hee published any thing I knowe [not]; as also Dr. Bludworth, a divine, and Dr. William Child, now one of the Masters of Chancerie.

Some accept against an expression they sometimes use at Oxford in bookes printed at the theatre,—*Ex Typographia Sheldoniana*, and think better of *Ex Typographio* or *Typographeio*, or *Typis Sheldonianis.*

Sr. your friends who persuade you to print your *Templa Druidum, &c.* do butt what is fitt and reasonable. I shall observe your desires as to observation of such things as you require. My wife and daughters present their respects and service. I rest, Sr. your affectionate freind and servant,

Norwich, March 14, 1672-3.   THO. BROWNE.

From Sir Thomas Browne to Mr. John Aubrey.

WORTHY SIR,—I was not unmindful of Mr. Wood's desires; butt the deane, in whose hands the records are, being of late much out of the towne, occasiond this delay: I now send you inclosed what is to be found. You will find Mr. Robert Talbot named in the first of Edward the sixth; butt when hee dyed as to the yeare is uncertaine, for after this I send, the church hath no register untill the 7th yeare of Queene Elizabeth, after which there is a good account of the prebends; but Mr. Talbot's name not to bee found among them, so that hee dyed before that time.

Bishop Corbet never had any epitaph I could here of, though there are many that can remember his death, and some the place where hee was buried; and though there have been many bishops buryed in this church, yett there are butt

3 that have epitaphs, viz. Bishop Parkhurst, B. Overall, and B. Montague; the rest have fayre tombs, but no inscriptions. A clark of the church told mee, that in the late times above an hundred brasse inscriptions were stolne out of the church, and, therefore, to prevent *all oblivion of the rest, I tooke* the best account I could of them at the king's returne, from an understanding singingman of 91 *years* old, and sett them downe in a booke, which otherwise would chance in a short time been forgotten; the churchmen little minding such things. Bishop Herbert, the founder of that church in William Rufus his time, was borne in Oxford, and so probably had his education there. I do not find that he writt any thing; butt hee was a famous man, and great builder of churches; as this cathedrall, St. Margaret's at Lynne a fayre church, St. Nicolas at Yarmouth, an handsome church at Elmeham in Norfolk, and St. Leonards chappell upon the hill by Norwich. In the 3rd or 4th of our Bishops there was also one John of Oxenford. For Broadgate Hall, I was of it butt about a yeare before it was made Pembroke Colledge. Bishop Bonner was of that house, and Camden, as old Dr. Clayton told mee, and *Noticia Oxoniæ* mentions. Dr. Budden, also a civilian, was principall not very long before my time, and Dr. Clayton remembered him. Hee hath left some things in writing, but perhaps hee was first of Magdalen colledge, having writ the life of William of Waynfleet.

I am glad you have been so observant as to take notice of the Roman castrum in those parts you mention.

There hath been a Roman castrum by Castor neere Yarmouth, but plowed up and now nothing or litle discernible thereof; butt I have had many Roman coynes found thereabout: that castle you mention there is an old remainder of Sr. John Fallstafs house. There is also a Roman Castrum 3 miles from Norwich, at Castor, anciently Venta Icenorum, containing about 30 akers of gro n , where there are still playne marks of the 4 portæ, and I have had many coynes from thence, and some other antiquities. There is also a castrum at Brancaster by Burnham in Norfolk, containing 8 akers of ground; butt the rampier of that is almost digged downe. I hope you proceed in your observations concerning the Druids stones. I pray my humble service and good wishes unto that worthy gentleman Mr. Wood. I rest, Sr. your very respectfull freind and humble servant.

THO. BROWNE.

GENERAL INDEX.

THE END.

PRINTED BY COX (BROTHERS) AND WYMAN, GREAT QUEEN STREET.

Lightning Source UK Ltd.
Milton Keynes UK
UKHW021950211118
332759UK00015B/1064/P